The
Great
Seamen of Elizabeth I

The Real Francis Bacon
I was James the Second's Queen
King James the Third of England
Nell Gwyn

The
Great
Seamen of Elizabeth I

BRYAN BEVAN

Illustrated

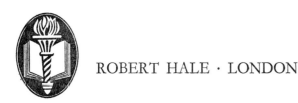

ROBERT HALE · LONDON

© Bryan Bevan 1971
First Published in Great Britain 1971

ISBN 0 7091 2015 X

Robert Hale & Company
63 Old Brompton Road
London S.W.7

PRINTED IN GREAT BRITAIN
BY EBENEZER BAYLIS AND SON LIMITED
THE TRINITY PRESS, WORCESTER, AND LONDON

Contents

Illustrations

Acknowledgments

To my publishers for so helpfully suggesting the subject of this book and for their cooperation at all times.

To my wife for taking me to visit the haunts of the First Elizabethan pirates in Cornwall, and for her encouragement.

To my friend Sir Charles Petrie for kindly lending me a book published in Spain, which contains letters of Count Gondomar, referring to Sir Walter Ralegh's last Guiana Voyage.

To Professor Claveria, former Director of the Spanish Institute in London, for his help and encouragement.

To the Directors of the Archives of the Indies, Casa Lonja, Seville for allowing me access to their invaluable archives.

To Commander and Mrs. W. R. Gilbert of Compton Castle for showing us their home, and for their helpfulness.

To the Librarians of the Devon County Library, Exeter, for their kindly interest and help.

To my brother-in-law, Mr. Philip Rashleigh of Menabilly, for allowing me to study his family papers.

To Mr. Hull, Archivist of the County Record Office, Truro, for his assistance.

To the London Library for their trouble and care.

Chronological Table of Important Dates

1532   Birth of John Hawkins.
1533   Birth of Queen Elizabeth I.
1536   Birth of Charles, Lord Howard of Effingham.
1539   Birth of Humphrey Gilbert.
1541   Birth of Francis Drake (most probably).
1542   Birth of Sir Richard Grenville.
1543   Birth of John Davis (uncertain).
1552   Birth of Richard Hakluyt the younger.
1554   (*circa*) Birth of Walter Ralegh.
1555   Birth of Thomas Cavendish or Candish (uncertain).
1558   Accession of Queen Elizabeth I.
1558   Birth of George Clifford, Third Earl of Cumberland.
1562   Jean Ribauld, French explorer, founds first colonies in Florida.
1562/3   John Hawkins' first slave-trading voyage.
1564/5   John Hawkins' second slave-trading voyage.
1567/8   John Hawkins' third voyage.
1567   Birth of Robert Devereux, Second Earl of Essex.
1571   Inquisition begun in Mexico.
1576   Martin Frobisher's first voyage in search of the Northwest Passage.
1577   Martin Frobisher's second voyage.
1578   Martin Frobisher's third voyage.

1577/80   Francis Drake's famous voyage circumnavigating the world.

1578   Humphrey Gilbert's first voyage.

1578   John Hawkins appointed Treasurer of the Navy.

1583   Sir Humphrey Gilbert's last voyage to colonize Newfoundland.

1584   Philip Amadas and Arthur Barlow make early voyage of discovery to Virginia.

1585   Sir Francis Drake's West Indian voyage.

1585   John Davis' North-west Passage expedition.

1585   Sir Richard Grenville's voyage to Virginia to plant a colony.

1586/98   The twelve privateering voyages of George Clifford, Earl of Cumberland.

1586/88   Voyage of Thomas Cavendish to South Seas, circumnavigating the world.

1587   John White's expedition to Virginia.

1587   Sir Francis Drake's Cadiz expedition.

1587   John Davis' expedition to Greenland and northern latitudes.

1588   The Spanish Armada.

1590   Death of Sir Francis Walsingham.

1591   Last fight of the *Revenge*.

1591   Death of Sir Richard Grenville.

1591/92   Expedition of Thomas Cavendish, jointly with John Davis, to the South Seas and Philippines.

1592   Death of Cavendish at sea.

1594   Richard Hawkins' expedition to the South Seas.

1594   Death of Sir Martin Frobisher at Plymouth.

1595   Sir Walter Ralegh's first Guiana expedition.

1595   Last joint expedition of Sir John Hawkins and Sir Francis Drake to San Juan de Puerto Rico.

1595   Death of Sir John Hawkins at sea.

1596   Death of Sir Francis Drake at sea.

1596   Second Cadiz expedition.

1596   Expedition of Laurence Keymis to Guiana.

1597   The Islands Voyage.
1598   Death of King Philip II of Spain.
1601   Execution of Robert Devereux, Second Earl of Essex.
1603   Death of Queen Elizabeth I.
1603   James I ascends the throne.
1603   Sir Walter Ralegh imprisoned in the Tower.
1605   Death of John Davis.
1606/11   Captain Christopher Newport's expeditions to Virginia.
1607   Ralegh Gilbert colonizes Maine.
1607/11   Voyages of Henry Hudson.
1609   Robert Harcourt's expedition to Virginia.
1616   Death of Richard Hakluyt the younger.
1617   Sir Walter Ralegh's last Guiana voyage.
1618   Sir Walter Ralegh's execution.

CHAPTER I

The Elizabethan Age

The first Elizabethan era is aptly described as the heroic age, and its glory and splendour is partly owing to the enterprise, fortitude and magnificent powers of endurance of its navigators. We are not only concerned with the valiant seamen-pirates, such as Sir Francis Drake, Sir John Hawkins, and Sir Richard Grenville of the *Revenge*, but also with the privateers and countless humble seamen whose exploits are recorded in the immortal epics of the younger Richard Hakluyt*.

Yet the English were late in embarking on voyages of exploration. Richard Hakluyt the younger, when serving as chaplain to the English ambassador, Sir Edward Stafford, at the embassy in Paris, had cause to lament that the English were sometimes criticized for "their sluggish security and continuall neglect of the like attempts."[1] The great age of discovery for the Spanish explorers and navigators such as Hernando Cortés,† who conquered Mexico, and the Conquistador Francisco Pizarro, who annexed Peru, was mainly in the early part of the sixteenth century. Earlier, during the fifteenth century, that lonely visionary and genius Prince Henry the Navigator, living at Sagres, organized the voyages of discovery of the Portuguese mariners down

---

* A cousin of the elder Richard Hakluyt, who was a lawyer of the Middle Temple.
† In 1519 Cortés sailed from Cuba on his famous voyage into the Gulf of Mexico.

the west coast of Africa, leading to the ultimate triumph of Vasco da Gama's rounding of the Cape. It was on 1st January 1502, ten years after Christopher Columbus first landed in America that the Portuguese explorer, Gonçalo Coelho*, sailed into the harbour of Rio. The famous voyages of discovery of Christopher Columbus—the Iberian explorer, a son of a Genoese wool comber—to the West Indies and to the American coastline, took place from 1492 onwards.

It was not until the middle of Elizabeth's reign in the 1570s that the Elizabethan navigators, stimulated by the challenge and menace of Spanish sea power and domination in the Indies and Latin America, gradually made England a great maritime nation. Naturally there had been earlier explorers. Typical of these was a Derbyshire man, Sir Hugh Willoughby, who in 1553—the last year of the reign of Edward VI—embarked on an ill-fated voyage of discovery in search of the North-east Passage. Hakluyt described the scene on a June afternoon as the ships sailed out of Deptford, and saluted the young king, who was in his palace of Greenwich. It was a fine sight, for the courtiers ran to join the excited crowds lining the banks, or craned their necks from palace windows. Under the patronage of Edward, Willoughby's fleet consisted of three ships, the *Bona Esperanza*, the *Edward Bonaventure* and the *Good Confidence*. Hakluyt as a patriot proudly wrote: "It cannot be denied, but as in all former ages, they (the seamen) have been men full of activity, stirrers abroad and searchers of the remote parts of the world." The moving spirit during the short reign of Edward VI for expansion overseas was the ambitious John Dudley, Duke of Northumberland,[2] father of Elizabeth I's favourite Robert, later Earl of Leicester.

The dogged and consummate achievement of the Elizabethan mariners and explorers was to forge the beginnings of the British Empire. We think of the Elizabethan era as spacious, but this is really a fallacy. An American scholar, Professor Parks,†

* He believed that he was at the mouth of a great river, so he named the place Rio de Janeiro.

† *Richard Hakluyt and the English Voyages* by George Bruner Parks, introduction by James A. Williamson.

visualized the age as narrow and needy. An intellectual period when men were groping for light, bent on the fascinating study of man and nature as well as of books. Much has been written about the swashbuckling zest of the adventurers, but they were also influenced by other motives. A typical Elizabethan explorer was partly a patriot, but in his nature were other subtle motives, ambition, jealousy of his rivals, cupidity, a lust for gold, religious zeal, and a growing hatred of Spain. The truth is that patriotic Englishmen, such as the intrepid explorer John Davis, Sir John Hawkins and Sir Francis Walsingham—a remarkable patron of the Elizabethan seamen—well aware of the desperate plight of their country, dedicated their lives to preserve it. Sir John Hawkins is, perhaps, chiefly remembered for his slave-trading activities in the West Indies, but as treasurer to the Navy Office he performed magnificent services in preparing the fleet which subsequently defeated the Spanish Armada in 1588. This was despite the intrigues of rivals, who incessantly accused him of corruption. Some of the Elizabethans invested their fortunes in maritime adventures, only to be ruined. One of these was the merchant-patriot, Michael Lok, who, after making some fortunate investments in European trade, later staked every penny on the Arctic voyage to Cathay. He was later declared bankrupt, imprisoned, and died in exile. Walsingham, a chronic invalid, devoted his life to Elizabeth's service, though she never personally liked him. He was an extremely able, conscientious minister, but he died in debt in 1590. Sir Humphrey Gilbert, who on the whole has been underrated, was a man of undoubted patriotism. He once wrote to his elder brother John: "He is not worthy to live at all that for fear or danger of death shunneth his country's danger or his own honour." The Elizabethans aimed high; Sir Philip Sidney, for example, so admired by his contemporaries. He wrote in *The Arcadia*: "He who aims at the Sun knows well that he can never hit the mark: Yet sure he is he shall shoot higher than he who aims at a bush." As Professor Rowse has written: "the final achievement of the Elizabethan Age, its vast enduring monument

2

. . . is the English expansion overseas, the fact that North America is inhabited by English-speaking stock".[3]

The Elizabethan Age was certainly a revolutionary one, though the Queen herself had an instinctive dislike of revolution. Though it was an acquisitive age, vulgar in its ostentation, cruel, superstitious, and violent, it was at the same time the most stimulating era in our history, when men were stirred by original thoughts. Its noblest minds, such as Sir Philip Sidney, aspired to higher spiritual wisdom. The Elizabethan navigators, too, despite many faults, possessed the qualities which make for greatness. They were inspired by a queen who happened to be a genius; they possessed a sense of purpose, enthusiasm and faith in themselves and in their country, and they were sincerely religious. The piratical impulse was strong in them. Sir Francis Drake and John Davis, for instance, were conscious of their destiny, and had a sublime belief in the rightness of their cause. Davis was a man of integrity, an author as well as an experienced navigator. There is a mystical element in his writings:

> There is no doubt that we of England [he wrote] are this saved people, by the eternal and infallible presence of the Lord predestinated to be sent into these Gentiles in the sea, to those Isles and famous Kingdoms, there to preach the peace of the Lord: for are not we only set upon Mount Zion, to give light to all the rest of the world? Have we not the true handmaid of the Lord to rule us, unto whom the eternal majesty of God hath revealed his Truth and Supreme power of Excellency? It is only we, therefore, that must be these shining messengers of the Lord, and none but we.[4]

It is curious that the navigators should sometimes think of themselves as missionaries. Their steadfast protestantism was certainly a powerful element in inspiring the voyages of discovery.

Elizabeth I succeeded her half-sister Mary as queen when she was twenty-five, and throughout the forty-five years of her reign she was the inspiration not only of her brave seamen, but of her people. James Anthony Froude in his noble tribute to the Elizabethan mariners, is seldom fair to the Queen their mistress.

He accuses her of niggardliness, refers to "her numbing hand" and her reluctance to make preparations or to order supplies before the Spanish Armada sailed. Despite her faults of character, her vanity, her irresolution, her tendency to procrastinate, her feline cruelty, she was naturally merciful. She was also a highly trained genius and a brilliant linguist. According to a Venetian diplomat, Giovanni Carlo Scaramelli, she possessed nine languages so thoroughly that each appeared to be her native tongue.[5] She not only spoke perfect Latin, but French, Spanish, and Italian extremely well. An amusing story is related about her that when in her sixty-fourth year she encountered the Polish Ambassador, who angered her by making disdainful references to her in a speech, she turned on him with an angry torrent of Latin, which must have astounded him. She told her courtiers with some vehemence, though not without humour, "God's death [her favourite oath], my Lords! I have been enforced this day to scour up my old Latin for this varlet; it had lain rusting long enough."

Elizabeth really loved her people and had an instinctive understanding of them. She was shrewd enough to be very accessible. Bishop Goodman, when a boy in 1588—the year of the Armada—was together with some companions when they were informed: "The Queen is gone to Council, and if you will see the Queen you must come quickly." The excited boys ran to Whitehall, where they were admitted to the courtyard, illuminated by torches. After an hour's wait the Queen came out "in great state". The boys exclaimed with fervour: "God save your Majesty! God save your Majesty!" Then the Queen said in her shrill voice, "God bless you all, my good people!" Bishop Goodman relates that "we cried again, 'God save your Majesty!' The Queen then replied, 'You may well have a greater prince, but you shall never have a more loving prince'." It is evident that this experience wrought a powerful impression on the boys, "for shows and pageants are ever best seen by torchlight, that all the way long we did nothing but talk what an admirable Queen she was, and how we would adventure our lives to do her service". Elizabeth had dedicated her life to her country, and passionately loved England.

She was a consummate actress, an exhibitionist, and a highly gifted, subtle woman of the Renaissance. On one occasion during the visit of the ugly, pocked-marked Duc D'Alençon* to England (1581) when negotiations were begun for a possible marriage between the Queen and D'Alençon, the Duc's secretary, Pierre Clausse Seigneur de Marchaumont was entertained by the Queen to a sumptuous banquet on board Drake's ship the *Golden Hind*† at Deptford, "finer then ever had been seen in England since the time of King Henry". Whether by accident or design, Elizabeth's purple and gold garter slipped down and was trailing as she entered the ship. With a gallant gesture Marchaumont stopped and picked it up and would have liked to have kept it for his master, but the Queen insisted that she had nothing else with which to keep her stocking up and promised to give it to him when she returned to the palace. Much to the delight of Marchaumont, who gave an account of the incident to D'Alençon, she later sent him the garter. It is curious to record that the expenses of the French prince's visit were mainly paid for out of the Spanish booty brought back by Sir Francis Drake in the *Golden Hind*.[6]

William Camden, the contemporary historian, bestows high praise on Queen Elizabeth. He refers to her as the "all glorious, all vertuous, incomparible and matchless patterne of Princes, the glory, honour and mirror of womankind, the admiration of our age". He relates that strangers named her Majesty the Queen of the Sea, the North-Star, the restorer of the naval glory. The pearls, which she wore so lavishly, were given to her as an appropriate present to the Queen of the Sea. It is probable that he eulogized Elizabeth too much "for preparing a fleete, the best furnished with all sorts of instruments of navigation and warre, that ever Great Britain saw".[7] In reality Sir John Hawkins

---

* Young brother of Henri III of France.
† This famous ship lay in a dry berth at Deptford for many years. Fragments of her timber were later used to make a chair, which is now in the Bodleian Library.

deserved most of the credit. It was owing to the endeavours of Hawkins rather than the Queen that the wages of the mariners were increased during her reign. Where Camden praised her, another contemporary naval authority Sir William Monson accused her of niggardliness.

The Queen was deeply interested in naval matters, liked to christen ships whenever possible, encouraged colonization overseas, particularly in Newfoundland and Virginia, and was certainly a shrewd investor in the enterprises of Sir Francis Drake, Sir Martin Frobisher and others. She could outswear any of her sea captains. A year after she ascended the throne, we find her in early July 1559 sailing in her state barge from Greenwich to Woolwich, so as to name a new ship the *Elizabeth Jonas*. Greenwich Palace where she had been born on 7th September 1533, was her favourite palace. 'After a goodly banquet there was great shooting of guns and casting of fire about made for pleasure." The Queen always delighted in fireworks. In christening this ship the *Elizabeth Jonas* the Queen was showing her gratitude for her deliverance from the fury of her enemies during her early, difficult life. She had been miraculously preserved in a similar way as the prophet Jonas who had been delivered from the belly of the whale. Elizabeth was superstitious as were many of her contemporaries. She insisted on renaming a fine galleon called the *Repentance*, built by the Treasurer of the Navy, Sir John Hawkins because she considered the *Dainty* a more fortunate name. Sir Richard Hawkins in that fine work *The Observations* tells us:

The *Repentance* being put in perfection, and riding at Deptford, the Queenes Majestie passing by to her Pallace of Greenwich, commanded her bargemen to row round about her, and viewing her from post to sterne, disliked nothing but her name, and said that shee would christen her anew, and that thenceforth shee should be called the *Dainty*; which name she brooked as well for her proportion and grace, as for the many happie voyages she made in her Majestie's services.[8]

Sir Richard Hawkins was the commander of the *Dainty* during her famous voyage to the South Seas in 1593, which he graphically describes in his writings. It is, perhaps, unfortunate that Sir Richard Grenville's ship the *Revenge* was not renamed, since Richard Hawkins considered her the unluckiest ship in the Queen Majesty's navy.

Elizabeth was greatly interested in Martin Frobisher's first voyage in search of the North-west Passage. According to Christopher Hall, master of the *Gabriel*, who wrote an account of the voyage, "on the 8th of June 1576 about twelve of the clocke we wayed at Deptford, and set saile all three of us and bare downe by the Court, where we shotte off our ordinance and made the best show we could." Her Majesty was at her Palace of Greenwich, and as was her wont, watched the departure of the expedition from a window "with shaking her hand at us out of the window". She later sent one of her gentlemen aboard Frobisher's ship to tell him that she approved of their activities and gave them hearty thanks. She commanded Frobisher to come next day to the Court to take his leave of her. The Queen later invested £1,000 in Frobisher's second voyage. In 1585 when Sir Richard Grenville, Sir Walter Ralegh's cousin, commanded the First Virginia Voyage, the Queen contributed a ship of her own, the flagship the *Tiger*, which was of 180 tons.

She certainly inspired Drake in his determination to make a circumnavigation of the world. According to his own account, the Queen told him in an interview: "Drake! So it is that I would gladly be revenged on the Kynge of Spayne for dyvers iniuries that I have receyved."* She further sought his advice how this was to be done. Lord Burghley, Elizabeth's cautious Chief Minister, opposed this voyage, which must have exasperated the celebrated navigator. On landing at Plymouth Sound, Drake's first question was: "Is the Queen still alive?" He realized that without her support he would be compelled to face powerful enemies.

---

* *New Light on Drake 1577-1580* by Zelia Nuttell (Printed for the Hakluyt Society).

It is curious that the Queen tried to dissuade Sir Humphrey Gilbert from embarking on his last ill-fated voyage in 1583, but her subtle female instinct bade her that Gilbert was a man "noted of not good hap by sea". All her life Elizabeth dabbled in astrology, and the occult and metaphysical strongly appealed to her, though her contemporary Queen Catherine of Medici, who incidentally had a high opinion of Elizabeth's astuteness, was much more superstitious. Elizabeth's interest in astrology was no doubt fostered by Dr. John Dee. She consulted Dee on many occasions, sending Lord Robert Dudley to him privately to ask him to select a propitious date for her coronation. The wise old seer chose Sunday 15th January 1559, and it certainly turned out well.

Although Elizabeth liked to describe herself as "mere English", to me she seems to display traits of her Welsh ancestry in her imaginative sense, her histrionic ability, and in the suspicious aspects of her character, so marked towards the end of her reign. She inherited her father Henry VIII's interest in the navy, but in some aspects of her complex character she rather resembled her Welsh grandfather Henry VII, a wary, prudent king, who was an extremely able financial administrator. As Francis Bacon described him, "He was a prince, sad, serious, and full of thoughts and memorials of his own land, especially touching persons." Both had been schooled in dissimulation and had learnt to distrust others from an early age. Her passion for solvency and her strain of avarice are reminiscent of Henry VII. On the other hand Henry VIII resembled his maternal grandfather—the sensual extrovert Edward IV. The Queen certainly respected the memory of her grandfather. When talking to her scholarly Keeper of the Records in the Tower, William Lambarde, on one occasion she asked him the meaning of praestita. Lambarde explained to her that it signified moneys lent by her progenitors to their subjects upon bond for repayment. Whereupon Elizabeth replied: "So did my good grandfather King Henry VII, sparing to dissipate his treasure or lands."

Henry VII also may be described as a patron of at least several of the navigators, for he was financially interested in the voyage of John Cabot—a Venetian, who first discovered the mainland of Newfoundland. The King granted letters patents to John Cabot and his three sons, Lewis, Sebastian and Sancius "for the discoverie of new and unknown lands".[9] In 1497—the thirteenth year of the reign of Henry VII—John Cabot and his son Sebastian sailed from Bristol, and on 24th June about five o'clock in the morning discovered a land which they called Prima Vista, because they had first seen it from the sea. The island of St. John derived its name because it was discovered upon the day of John the Baptist. John Cabot brought home three savages, whom he had captured, and presented them to Henry VII in the Palace of Westminster. "These were clothed in beasts skins, and did eate raw flesh, and spake such speech that no man could understand them, and in their demeanour like to bruit beastes."[10] Robert Fabian's Chronicle mentions that he encountered two of these men at Westminster Palace when they were dressed like Englishmen, but he never heard them utter one word. The boy King Edward VI subsequently granted Sebastian Cabot an annuity of one hundred and thirty-six pounds thirteen shillings and fourpence per annum and made him grand Pilot of England. International piracy was certainly an acute problem during Henry VII's reign, because of the dangers of reprisals leading to full-scale war. On one occasion the King summoned the Mayor of Exeter and two or three of his brethren to Westminster to discuss the misdeeds "of divers evil disposed personnes our soubgiettes [subjects] now lieing upon the seas as common pirates".[11]

Everybody played their part in encouraging the intrepid Elizabethan seamen and in promoting their voyages. It was no single group which inspired these adventurers. No statesman was more indefatigable than that stern, puritanical statesman Sir Francis Walsingham, the patron of Sir Humphrey Gilbert and his brother Adrian and of that great navigator John Davis, born at Sandridge on the banks of the Dart in Devon. Then there were Sir Christopher Hatton, patron of Sir Francis Drake, out of compliment for whom the famous navigator changed the name of his ship the *Pelican* to the *Golden Hind* because it was Hatton's crest. Others of the expansionist school were Robert Dudley Earl of Leicester*—the lover of the Queen, a patron of the valiant seamen and of writers, who has been underrated by historians. He was one of those who advocated the cause of Francis Drake, against the advice of the more cautious statesmen represented by Lord Burghley. The handsome, sinister Leicester was the patron of his nephew Philip Sidney and of the young Robert Devereux Earl of Essex, his step-son. Sir Edward Dyer, too, a courtier and a poet, whose family hailed from Somerset, played a notable part, being an early patron of the younger Richard Hakluyt. Then there was that renowned nobleman George Clifford, third Earl of Cumberland, an elegant courtier and great privateer. The Queen had a special affection for him, despite his roving instincts. That visionary Welshman, Dr. John Dee, a mathematician and astrologer, was the friend and confidant of the Gilberts, and of John Davis the Arctic explorer. He was deeply interested in navigation, and certainly stimulated interest in the seamen's voyages. The Queen, who chose wisely those she wished to serve her, appreciated the advice of the brilliant man, and he enjoyed her favour, and even occasionally her generosity. Nothing is accidental in the inspiring story of the creation of the British Empire overseas. All is part of a pattern, a mighty fabric, and the Elizabethan seamen's achievements are all the more memorable considering the enormous odds and obstacles against them. No man was more influential in the Age of Discovery than Sir Walter Ralegh, a man of many parts, who was misunderstood in his own time, only to be amply compensated by the fulsome tributes of later historians. A strange genius, whether viewed as a writer or a navigator, who held advanced ideas about colonization. That haughty, arrogant man—at least in the eyes of his contemporaries—could be gentle enough with the Indians when he explored that tantalizing country of Guiana in South America and told them about the Queen, thousands of miles away.

* Leicester's illegitimate son by Lady Douglas Sheffield, Sir Robert Dudley was to become a celebrated navigator.

The great writers of that age, such as Shakespeare, Marlowe, Philip Sidney, Richard Hakluyt, Francis Bacon, Edmund Spenser and John Donne, who accompanied Essex to Cadiz when a young man, were undoubtedly influenced by the Age of Discovery. Marlow makes the dying Tamburlaine declare:

> Give me a map, then let me see how much
> Is left for me to conquer all the world,
> That these, my boys, may finish all my wants.

Nor must we forget the generosity and magnificent part played by the Elizabethan merchants, such as William Sanderson and Sir Thomas Smythe, who risked their capital in maritime adventures and commercial enterprises. These were real patriots, and men of vision and imagination. It was owing to their endeavours that Anthony Jenkinson was sent to Russia and, later, Thomas Roe to the Court of the Great Mogul at Agra.

In the days of the first Elizabeth, those citizens who lived in a sea-port such as Plymouth or Southampton, or in a river-port, like London, were brought into daily touch with ships and seamen. The river was then London's main thoroughfare, and people were used to sailors in every district of that city. The Queen in her splendid state barge might often be seen travelling from Greenwich Palace or from Hampton Court to Whitehall for some ceremonial occasion. It was at Deptford on 4th April 1581 that Queen Elizabeth went on board the *Golden Hind*, the first ship to sail round the world. There she knighted its captain, Francis Drake. On one later occasion Drake presented the Queen's Majesty with a fan of red and white feathers, with a gold handle inlaid with half-moons of mother-of-pearl and diamonds. The fan had recently been introduced at Elizabeth's Court from Italy, and was usually worn by ladies hanging from the point of the stomacher. Many of the courtiers wishing to please her presented her with fans, so that the Queen at one time owned twenty-seven. Sometime after Drake's return from his voyage of circumnavigation of the world, Bernardino de Mendoza, the Spanish diplomat, reported to Philip II that the corsair had presented the Queen with a crown set with five emeralds, three of which were "almost as long as a finger". The two round ones were valued at 20,000 crowns, "coming as they do from Peru".*

For the ordinary citizen innumerable wherries for hire were in constant demand at all the public stairs. The cry of the watermen needing custom was a familiar one. "Eastward Ho!" or "Westward Ho!" they shouted, and their language was sometimes extremely coarse.[12] Although they were licensed to charge fixed fares, their demands were often extortionate. According to John Taylor, the water-poet, there were no fewer than 40,000 watermen who plied their craft between Windsor Bridge and Gravesend. Taylor was born at Gloucester in 1580, so that he had only attained 23 years at the end of Elizabeth's reign. According to his own account, he had made prior to 1603 sixteen voyages in the Queen's ships. However, his career as a Thames waterman belongs rather to the reign of James I. I may be forgiven for referring to his verses, for they are both amusing and intriguing. Stowe relates that Execution Dock, just below Wapping Old Stairs, was the customary place of execution for hanging of pirates and sea rovers, "at the low water marke, there to remaine, till three tides had overflowed there." Taylor wrote:

> We thus our voyage bravely did begin
> Down by St. Katherine's, where the Priest fell in,
> By Wapping, where as hang'd drowned Pirate dye; . . .[13]

The London watermen were as skilful as gondoliers and were proud of the prowess with which they manoeuvred through London Bridge, then the glory of London. Once during an expedition when he landed at Cromer Towne, John Taylor and his party were mistaken for pirates.

> For why, some women and some children there
> That saw us land were all possest with fears:
> And much amazed, ran crying up and doune
> Some said that we were pirats, some said theeves,
> And what the women says, the men beleeves!

An incident is related in the summer of 1579, which reveals

* 9th January 1581.

Queen Elizabeth's lion-hearted courage. It so happened that she was in her private barge on the Thames, travelling between Deptford and Greenwich, attended by the Lord Admiral Edward Clinton Earl of Lincoln, the French Ambassador,* and by her favourite Sir Christopher Hatton. Suddenly a shot rang out, which struck one of the rowers within 6 feet of Her Majesty. The poor fellow was gravely wounded. Not for one moment did the Queen lose her regality. "Good fellow," she said to him, whilst giving him her scarf, "be of good cheer, you shall want for nothing." When somebody suggested that this was an attempt to murder her or the French Ambassador, the Queen vehemently declared, "She could believe nothing of her people which parents would not believe of their children."[14] Small wonder that most of her subjects were inspired by her courage.

The Elizabethan age was a quarrelsome one. George Clifford, third Earl of Cumberland, quarrelled with one of his sea captains William Monson, who subsequently became a naval authority. Richard Grenville, too, was implicated as a young man in a fatal brawl near St. Clement Dane's when he killed a man. Indeed it was customary for young courtiers to go armed in the streets. When Mercutio taunts his friend Benvolio for being quarrelsome, he might be describing an Elizabethan nobleman such as Henry Wriothsley, Earl of Southampton, or any Elizabethan adventurer. He tells him: "Thou art like one of these fellows that when he enters the confines of a tavern claps me his sword upon the table, and says, 'God send me no more need of thee!' . . . Thou! why, thou wilt quarrel with a man that hath a hair more or a hair less in his head than thou hast."

In the eyes of Elizabeth's mighty antagonist, Philip II of Spain, brooding in the gloomy Escurial, the sea captains, such as Drake and Hawkins, were pirates or corsairs. To Lope de Vega, the famous Spanish poet, who sailed in the Spanish Armada (1588), because he had been disappointed in a love affair, "Drake was Satan himself, the incarnation of the Genius of Evil, the archenemy of the Church of God."[15] Lope de Vega's epic poem *The*

* Jehan de Simier.

Dragontea describes the corsair as the dragon, the ancient serpent of the Apocalypse. It is fascinating to read the published letters of the Spanish ambassadors at Elizabeth's Court, informing the Spanish king about their activities. The wily, courteous Guzman de Silva, for instance, while diplomatic relations between England and Spain were not broken, wished to entice John Hawkins during the 1560s into the service of the King of Spain. The correspondence of Guzman de Silva and a later Spanish Ambassador, Bernardino de Mendoza, graphically describe the piratical activities of Thomas Cobham, brother of the Lord Warden of the Cinque Ports, and those of Sir Thomas Stucley. To Mendoza, Drake was "the master thief of the unknown world". A study of the Venetian State Papers also reveals that that great seafaring people, who produced Marco Polo, had a healthy respect for the Elizabethan seamen. A Venetian Ambassador wrote: "He enjoyed the reputation of being above all western nations expert and active in all naval operations, and great sea-dogs." By 1603, which marked the end of Elizabeth's reign, the English were reputed to be good seamen and better pirates.

It is customary to think of the first Elizabethan era as dead, but the spirit of that glorious age is very much alive for those who seek for it. It is alive in the Elizabethan houses, such as Hardwick Hall in Derbyshire, completed by that notorious termagant Bess of Hardwick in 1597; and in that intimate Tudor house of the Sidneys, Penshurst Place, where Sir Philip Sidney first saw the light in 1554. As we walk along New Street, that fascinating ancient street adjoining Plymouth's Barbican, we glow with a strange excitement as we imagine the Elizabethan sea captains striding down to the harbour to embark on their voyages. There at Sutton harbour the ships were being built. There, too, on Plymouth Hoe, where Drake's statue stands so proudly, he was playing bowls with other sea captains when the Spanish Armada was sighted.* No county is richer in memories of the seamen

---

* The game of bowls does not rest on contemporary evidence, but has been traced as early as 1624, according to Dr. J. A. Williamson, when survivors of the Armada were still alive.

than Devon. Buckland Abbey near Yelverton, was the home of Sir Richard Grenville of the *Revenge*, a Cornishman. We can imagine the fiery adventurer cogitating over his projects for overseas exploration in the great hall, which he largely created. It is unlikely that Grenville would have sold Buckland Abbey to two intermediaries (Christopher Harris and John Hele) had he known that they were acting for Francis Drake—his rival, who first came to live at Buckland Abbey in the autumn of 1581. In Saltash across the border in Cornwall lived in a little cottage on a hill the lass Mary Newman, who Drake wooed for his first wife. They were married in the church of St. Budeaux nearby in 1569, and Lady Drake, as she later became, was sometime Mayoress of Plymouth. Then there is Compton Castle, a fine example of a fortified manor house, the home of Sir Humphrey Gilbert, who colonized Newfoundland, and of his younger son, Ralegh, who colonized Maine in America. This historic place is still lived in by Commander and Mrs. Walter Ralegh Gilbert,* descendants of Sir Humphrey. Nearby in glorious wooded country above the River Dart is Greenway House, the birthplace of Humphrey Gilbert. There in that house, which looks down on Dittisham across the river, Walter Ralegh would sometimes stay with his half-brother during his boyhood. Tradition says that Ralegh planted the first potato ever grown in England at Greenway. As he sat musing by the anchor stone in the stream near Dittisham he would, perhaps, be already haunted by his dreams of voyages to America. It is likely that the Gilberts worshipped at the ancient church of St. George's in Dittisham with its lovely fifteenth-century stone wineglass pulpit.

Ralegh was actually born at Hayes Barton, a farmhouse, near East Budleigh in Devon. For a pilgrim, a memorable place to visit, because the birthplace of this Elizabethan should be more widely known. When one wanders in East Budleigh's lanes, listening to the music of the brooks, one can imagine the pensive boy† fishing the sluggish streams near his home. Hayes Barton, a

---

* The ancient castle has been beautifully restored.

† Most people are familiar with the picture by Sir John Millais, painted at

place especially dear to Ralegh's heart, was never owned by Ralegh's father. There is an original letter* in the Royal Albert Museum at Exeter, which clearly shows that Ralegh constantly hankered to buy Hayes "a farm sometyme in my father's possession". Here is part of the letter:

Mr. Duke,

    I wrote to Mr. Prideux to move you for the purchase of hayes a farme sometyme in my father's possession, I will most willingly give you whatsoever in your conscience you shall deem it worthe, and if you shall att any tyme have occasion to use mee, you shall find me a thankfull friend to you and youres. ... I am resolved if I cannot intreat you to build att colliton but for the natural disposition I have to that place being borne in that house I had rather seat myself there than anywhere else . . .

He signs the letter, "your very willing frinde W. Ralegh". Mr. Duke, however, refused to sell Hayes Farm to Ralegh.

John Davis, the Arctic explorer, was also a Devon man, born at Sandridge near Stoke Gabriel—there is romance in the very name. He married a girl named Faith Fulford from Bozoms Hele† in the parish of Dittisham at the medieval church of Stoke Gabriel.‡ The ancient yews in the churchyard were there long before Davis came here. He sailed from Dartmouth on many of his voyages. When we visit Dartmouth Castle, built by Edward IV and the ancient St. Petrox Church, which adjoins it, we think of the dauntless navigator craning for a last look of the mainland, while the waves beat against the rocks below the castle ramparts.

Budleigh Salterton, called "The Boyhood of Ralegh". It shows Ralegh and another boy eagerly listening to an old mariner, while he relates stories of some distant magical land.

    * Letter written in 1584. A copy is in the room where Ralegh was born at Hayes Barton Farm.

    † Now known as Bozomzeal.

    ‡ On 29th September 1582, according to the church registers now in the City Library Archives, Exeter.

Notes

CHAPTER I

1   Richard Hakluyt, *Voyages*, Vol. 1, p. 2. Epistle dedicated to Sir
     Francis Walsingham.
2   A. L. Rowse, *The Expansion of Elizabethan England*, p. 159.
3   *The England of Elizabeth*, p. 29.
4   "The English Voyages of the Sixteenth Century" in Hakluyt's
     Principal Navigations (Hakluyt Society 1905 XII, p. 32. n 1).
     Also:
     J. E. Neale, *The Age of Catherine de Medici* and "Essays in Eliza-
     bethan History".
5   C.S.P. Venetian, 7th April 1603.
6   *Shakespeare's England*, Vol. 1, p. 93.
7   *Diary of Henry Machyn*, Camden Society, p. 203, edited by J. G.
     Nichols.
8   Sir Richard Hawkins, *The Observations of Sir Richard Hawkins*,
     edited from the text of 1622 by James A. Williamson (1933), p. 9.
9   Richard Hakluyt, *Voyages* (Everyman Edition), Vol. V, p. 83.
10   *Ibid.* Vol. V, p. 91.
11   City Library, Exeter.
12   *Shakespeare's England*, Vol. I.
13   John Taylor's poem, "A Discovery by Sea from London to Salis-
     bury".
14   Sir Harris Nicholas, *Memoirs of the Life and Times of Sir Christopher
     Hatton Vice Chamberlain and Lord Chancellor to Queen Elizabeth,
     1540–1591*, p. 119.
15   James Anthony Froude, *English Seamen in the Sixteenth Century*
     (1901).

CHAPTER II

The Seamen

Most people rightly think of Henry VIII in his later career as a gross sensualist and cruel tyrant, but they fail to recognize the value of his work in building the Tudor navy. As has already been said, Elizabeth inherited her interest in the navy and seamen from her father. Henry when he first came to the throne in 1509 was an attractive personality, gay, brilliant, musical, and ambitious. To Erasmus he seemed the glory of the new age that was unfolding. Henry with his histrionic instincts liked to play the part of an amateur pilot. When he launched a vessel he would wear a rich vest and breeches of cloth of gold, and a scarlet hose, with a gold chain and whistle.[1] The King in fact had an expert knowledge of ships. His most famous ship, the 1,000-ton *The Great Harry* or *Henri grace à Dieu*, built in 1514, together with the three small barques also constructed, cost him £8,708 5s. 3d. On the *Great Harry* there were 349 soldiers, 301 mariners and 50 gunners. In the *Ark Royal*, the flagship in which Elizabeth's Lord Admiral Charles Lord Howard of Effingham served during the Armada in 1588, there were far fewer soldiers—125 altogether and 300 mariners. During his reign Henry had the foresight to add eighty-five sea-going vessels to the navy, thus enabling him to hold the balance of power between the Emperor Charles V and Francis 1 of France. He was intelligent enough to realize the

3   33

important part gunpowder would play in wars. During the early years of his reign, Henry repaired his dockyards, built new ships on improved models, and imported Italians to cast him new types of cannon.[2] The Tudor king constituted an Admiralty Department.

The Navy Board which Henry inaugurated at Deptford in 1546—at the end of his reign—consisted of a Treasurer, Comptroller, Surveyor and Clerk of Ships, and lasted in that form until 1832. This was later of inestimable value to Elizabeth I, for it enabled her to send fleets to sea with a speed and efficiency which was to astonish Philip II. Since he considered Portsmouth too vulnerable, Henry founded two new royal dockyards at Deptford and Woolwich in the estuary of the Thames.[3] The letters of Sir Edward Howard, Henry VIII's Lord Admiral, are strongly reminiscent of Lord Howard of Effingham's later letters to Elizabeth I. Sir Edward Howard wrote on one occasion: "Sir, for God's Sake haste your council to send me down our victuals, for, if we shall lie long, the common voice will run that we lie and keep in the Downs, and do no good but spend money and victuals, and so the noise will run to our shames."[4] He thought the *Mary Rose* "the noblest ship of sail at this hour that I trow be in Christendom".

If Henry VIII took only a minor interest in exploration overseas, he certainly was a patron of several of his seamen. The jovial king was on friendly terms with several of his sea captains, whom he had met at Portsmouth and Southampton. Old William Hawkins of Plymouth, father of a more famous son, Sir John,* was much esteemed by the Tudor king for "his wisedome, valure, experience, and skill in sea causes".[5] William Hawkins undertook three long and celebrated voyages during 1530 and 1532 to the coast of Brazil, which was very rare in those times. He first traded for ivory, elephants' teeth and other commodities on the coast of Guinea, and when he reached Brazil he behaved with such discretion and wisdom that during his second expedition the

---

* Later Treasurer of Queen Elizabeth I's navy.

Brazilian chief agreed to accompany Hawkins on his return to England, provided that Martin Cockeram, a sailor from Plymouth should remain in Brazil as hostage. The Brazilian chief was an object of interest and curiosity to Henry VIII and his Court when he was presented to the King at Whitehall. "For in his cheekes were holes made according to their savage manner, and therein small bones were planted, standing an inch out from the said holes, which in his own countrey was reputed for a great braverie. He had also another hole in his nether lip, wherein was set a precious stone about the bignes of a pease."[6] Later he died at sea on his way home to his country. It was feared that the natives would take reprisals against Martin Cockeram, but they were evidently satisfied that every care had been taken of their chief. Cockeram was brought home in a Brazilian ship and apparently survived in Plymouth to an old age, according to the later testimony of Sir John Hawkins.

Henry was also patron to Robert Thorne, another Plymouth man, who went on a voyage to search for the North-west Passage, an enterprise which was later to obsess the Elizabethan navigators such as Martin Frobisher. Robert Thorne's expedition proved abortive. He was a London merchant, who lived a long time in Seville, and Richard Hakluyt the younger relates that he wrote to Henry VIII imploring him to take an interest in discoveries in the Indies and other countries.

Queen Elizabeth has been accused by Froude and other historians of parsimony after she ascended the throne in 1558, but so far as the navy is concerned she spent a great deal of money on her ships, such as the medium-sized galleon the *Foresight*. John Hawkins alleged that the Queen had paid as much as £9,000 for timber and plank, and complained that the nation had not received £4,000 value from the transaction. The real culprits were the dishonest sea-captains, pursers, cooks and master-gunners. For instance, Elizabeth has been blamed for her niggardliness in supplying her navy with powder and ammunition during the Armada, when it was later discovered that the dishonest master-gunner of the *Ark Royal*, Hamon, had stored forty barrels away in his house, according to the evidence of a neighbour named Charlton, "which was to 'Her Majesty in that fighte greate hindrance".[7]

On Elizabeth's accession the whole merchant navy of England engaged in lawful commerce amounted to about 50,000 tons. It was obvious to Sir William Cecil, the Queen's Chief Minister, that time was needed to restore the navy. Elizabeth constantly encouraged the privateers, because it suited her convenience, though she was ready to disown them, if necessary. The distinction between privateering and piracy was really a legal one.[8] The privateers possessed a definite commission from a recognized authority to take action against a designated enemy, while the pirate was acting independently and had no such authority. The word pirate is derived from the Latin *pirare*, to rob or to plunder. Such notorious Elizabethan pirates were Robert Hicks, John Callis or Challice, and Thomas Cobham. Sir Francis Drake's famous West Indies expedition of 1585 was a semi-official undertaking[9] not a privateering expedition, because the great seaman on this occasion was acting on her instructions as her admiral. Her investment on this occasion was about £20,000, and she supplied two ships out of the twenty-five engaged in the expedition. On the other hand the 1589 voyage of George Clifford, third Earl of Cumberland, is a classic example of a privateering undertaking, though the Queen encouraged Cumberland to undertake it and lent him her ship the *Victory* as his flagship. Elizabeth took some of the more notorious privateers into her service. Ned Horsey, for instance—who had been a Channel rover during the reign of her half-sister Mary I—was created Sir Edward and Governor of the Isle of Wight. He then proceeded to allow the island to become a base for Dutch, English and French pirates. Strangways, whom the Spaniards feared, was killed at Rouen, while the valiant Champernoune fell later at Coligny's side at Moncontour.

Nobody worked harder for the Elizabethan seamen than Sir John Hawkins, a Plymouth man, who may be described as the true founder of the Elizabethan navy. In 1509, at the beginning of the reign of Henry VIII, a seaman's pay was 5s. per month. As a reward for faithful service, it was raised to 6s. 8d. at the end of the reign. Since, however, the shilling was shortly afterwards devalued, it brought the seamen little benefit. In 1578 Hawkins became Treasurer of the Navy, and it was owing to his advocacy of the seamen's claims that their pay was raised to 10s. per month in 1585—three years before the Spanish Armada sailed. Both Sir John Hawkins and his son Sir Richard were deeply interested in the seamen's health. Hawkins hoped that by raising his pay, "Her Majesty's ships would be furnished with able men, such as can shift for themselves, keep themselves clean from vermin or noisomeness, which bredeth sickness or mortality." Hawkins also inaugurated an almshouse for ten poor mariners at Chatham. In 1590, together with Charles Lord Howard of Effingham, greatest of Lord Admirals, and Sir Francis Drake, he founded the Chatham Chest, a contributory fund for which every seaman was obliged to pay 6d. a month out of his wages. The Chatham Chest is a familiar sight today to visitors to the National Maritime Museum at Greenwich. The fund was eventually merged with that of the Royal Hospital at Greenwich.

Sir John Hawkins gave some salutary instructions to the seamen. "Serve God daily," he ordered them, "love one another, preserve your victuals; beware of fire, and keep good company."* If these commands were not obeyed too often, it was not the fault of the Treasurer of the Navy. Miles Phillips, a seaman serving under Hawkins, relates that in Sir John's flagship every morning and evening the boatswain took a book in English, like those which the clergy had in England, and went to the mainmast, where all the sailors, soldiers and the captain knelt on the deck— and all attended under pain of twenty-four hours in irons. All being on their knees, the said boatswain recited the Lord's Prayer and the Creed, word for word, and then made the same prayers, which are made in England.† Willoughby and Chancellor provided these regulations: "That no blaspheming of God or

---

* Keep station in a fleet.
† *Hawkins of Plymouth* by James A. Williamson, p. 71.

detestable swearing be used in any ship, nor communication of ribaldry, filthy tales, or ungodly talk be suffered, neither carding, dicing, tabling, nor other devilish games to be frequented."[10] Small wonder, if the Elizabethan seamen, particularly those engaged in long voyages, did not frequently disregard these pious instructions. Brutal, though possibly effective, penalties were enforced for habitual swearers and blasphemers. A marlin spike was "clapt into their mouths, and tied behind their heads, and then to stand a whole hour, till their mouths be very bloody; an excellent cure for swearers".[11]

Sir Richard Hawkins, who was a religious man, relates in his *Observations* during his voyage to the South Seas (1593) that he attempted to banish swearing from his own ship the *Dainty*, and the two other ships. After giving thanks to the Almighty on one occasion when the *Dainty* was on fire, and in real danger of being destroyed, Sir Richard ruled that in every ship there should be a ferula, or palmer, given to the first seaman who was "taken with an oath". To discharge his offence, it was necessary to find another swearer or blasphemer. The first offender was then entitled to give him a *palmada* or stroke on the palm, and hand over to him the instrument of punishment. The seaman who had it in his possession at the time of evening or morning prayer was to receive the punishment of three *palmadas* from the Captain. Sir Richard Hawkins, who was by no means a strict disciplinarian added: "in vices custom is the principal sustenance; and for their reformation it is little available to give good counsel or make good laws and ordinances, except they be executed".[12]

It must not be imagined that the Elizabethan seaman was always eager to serve in the Queen's ships, for the contrary was often the case. A powerful inducement was sometimes the opportunity to indulge in pillage. A naval authority and contemporary, N. Boteler, wrote: "as for the business of pillage ... there is nothing that more bewitcheth them, nor anything wherein they promise themselves so loudly, nor delight in more manly". The term pillage actually referred to anything loose on deck which was not part of the ship or cargo, and it was legitimate for a seaman to take possession of these objects. To 'break bulk' or plunder the cargo, however, was an offence. The finest minds of the age became increasingly concerned about the frequent abuses indulged in by seamen. For instance Sir Richard Hawkins wrote:

> No less worthie of refermation are the generall abuses of marriners and souldiers who robbe all they can, under the colour of pillage, and after make ordinance, cables, sayles, anchors, and all above Deckes, to belong unto them of right, whether they goe by thirdes or wages; ... every gallant that can arme out a shippe taketh upon him the name and office of a Captaine, not knowing what to command nor what to execute. Such Commanders for the most part consort and joyne unto themselves disorderly persons, Pyrates, and Ruffians, under the title of valour and experience. ... Yea I have seene the Common sort of Mariners, under the name of Pillage, maintaine and justifie their robberies most insolently before the Queenes Maiesties Commissioners, with arrogant and unseemly termes.[13]

Pillaging was clearly made the pretext for various crimes at sea. Sir William Monson refers to the many abuses. Master-gunners were often appointed because they had bought their positions, rather than owing to their own merits. In Elizabethan times seamen were divided into various categories.

The mariners were the able-bodied seamen, while the sailors (a word just coming into use towards the end of the century) were elderly men employed for responsible but less active tasks. Ordinary seamen were known as younkers. The grommets were an intermediate rating, and there were also boys known to Shakespeare as ship-boys.[14]

How did the seaman fare with regard to his food and drink? He was allowed per day a gallon of beer and a pound of biscuit. On four days of the week he was supposed to get two pounds of beef, or sometimes pork and pease. On the remaining three days he was allowed fish, two ounces of butter and a quarter of a pound of cheese. These might be considered adequate rations, but in practice the system did not work well. Very often the victuallers on shore, who supplied the provisions, were dishonest as were the pursers on board the ships. John Lyly, in his play *Gallathea*, acted before the Queen at Greenwich on New Year's Day at night by the children of Paul's London,* has amusing allusions to the life of a seaman. Robin, one of the characters, says: "Sea? Nay, I will never saile more. I brooke not their diet. Their bread is so hard, that one must carie a whetstone in his mouth to grinde his teeth: the meat so salt, that one would think after dinner his tongue had been pow'red ten daies!"

Early in Elizabeth's reign Edward Baeshe—an honest man— was appointed Surveyor of Victuals. It was the custom for Baeshe to be paid 4½d. for each seaman in harbour and 5d. when at sea. Very often when the seamen were on active service they were put on short allowance, so as to preserve their food. For instance the Lord Admiral, Howard of Effingham, informed the Lords of the Council on 22nd June 1588 that they had been compelled to resort to 'scantyings' for reasons of economy. "I protest before God," he wrote, "we have been more careful of her Majesty's charges than of our own lives." 'Scantyings' is a technical expression meaning that the seamen were put on short allowance, or six men to a mess instead of four. During the Cadiz voyage of Sir Francis Drake in 1587, the seamen mutinied, mainly on the grounds of the execrable quality of their food. They begged their captain

> to weigh of us like men, and let us not be spoiled for want of food, for our allowance is so small we are not able to live any longer on it. . . . For what is a piece of beef of half a pound among four men to dinner, or half a dried stock fish for four days in the week, and nothing else to help withal—yea, we have help, a little beveridge worse than pump water. We were pressed by her Majesty to have her allowance, and not to be thus dealt withal; you make no men of us, but beasts.[15]

Small wonder if disease was rife among the seamen.

The system of manning the navy was similar to that when an army was required. It was known as 'pressing' or 'taking-up'.

* 1592.

Although it was subject to abuses, it worked on the whole fairly well. It was a kind of conscription enforced on all seamen, a system of compulsory naval service. 'Pressing' certainly had nothing akin to the press gangs of the eighteenth century. Instructions were issued by the Admiralty to local officers, commanding them to summon all seamen before them and to serve as many of them as were required with a notice to proceed by a certain day to the H.Q.s of the fleet, usually Gillingham. Each of the seamen were then supplied with money for the journey known as 'coat and conduct money'.[16]

During the celebrated islands voyage of Robert Devereux, Earl of Essex—Queen Elizabeth's favourite—this system of 'pressing' failed to be effective, for Essex complained about the poor quality of seamen employed. Sir William Monson was present in the *Rainbow* on this voyage. Essex wrote to the Lords of the Privy Council: "None are discharged but men utterly insufficient and unserviceable taken up by the pressmasters, in mariners clothes, but shall not know any one rope in the ship." He again referred to his grievance: "We are at our wit's end to find her Majesty's fleet thus weakly and wretchedly manned as it is. We did from Weymouth advertise your Lordships, My Lord Admiral (Howard of Effingham), and Mr. Secretary (Sir Robert Cecil) of the monstrous abuse in the pressmasters that sent the men which brought us hither." Some of the men had never even been to sea, while the experienced mariners "for 20s. a-piece let go". When Essex tried to obtain a further supply of seamen from Dorsetshire "there appeared not a man, but either were underhand, discharged by the pressmasters, or made a jest of the press".[17] Press warrants were issued by the Privy Council, on the authority of the Queen's Commission, and directed to the vice-admirals, lieutenants, and justices of the peace of the maritime counties. It was really the mayors and constables who selected the men to go on these voyages, and unfortunately some of them were open to bribery and corruption. During times of great national emergency such as the threat of the Spanish Armada it was naturally easier to get men to enroll.

All the same the English seamen were for the most part very skilled. They seem to have handled their ships with considerable ability under the difficult conditions prevailing in that age. Six years after Elizabeth ascended the throne in 1564 proposals were made to nominate a pilot-major to ensure a knowledge of seamanship in navigation. Despite the advantages of a School of Cosmography and Navigation at Seville, under the supervision of the pilot-major of Spain, it cannot be maintained that the Spanish seamen were nearly as skilled or experienced as the English.

Elizabeth's appointment of Charles Lord Howard of Effingham as Lord Admiral was a wise one, for he had at heart the comfort and well-being of the seaman. Among the manuscripts in the British Museum is a letter in Howard's handwriting to Lord Burghley, in which he refers to two poor knaves that came from Westchester (Chester) "that stryved for a place to hang up their netting for to lie in, and the one of them had a piece of candle in his hand, and in striving the candle fell down where there lay some oakum. It might have bred some mischief, but it was quickly put out. It was in the *Elizabeth Bonaventure*, but I hope to make them a warning to others to beware."[18] Howard was very proud of his seamen. On 28th May 1588 he wrote to Lord Burghley from Plymouth: "My good Lord, there is here the gallantest company of captains, soldiers and mariners that I think was ever seen in England. It was a pity that they should lack meat, when they are so desirous to spend their lives in her Majesty's service." The crucial problem in the age of the first Elizabeth was the supply of provisions and to attempt to prevent them from becoming rancid. Howard was always the seaman's friend. He wrote to Burghley on 22nd December 1587, suggesting that they should be paid one month's wages in advance, "because their long journeys out of all places of this realm, and this bad season makes them unprovided of apparel and such necessaries". It was hardly surprising that the seamen were reluctant to join the Queen's ships.

The ships were invariably overcrowded, while the standard of hygiene was very low. The seamen's food was often contaminated, since it was almost impossible to preserve it in a wholesome condition. Nothing was known about antiseptics, consequently a major operation often proved fatal. Another reason deterring them was the knowledge that longer voyages into tropical regions brought them into contact with a variety of diseases, such as bubonic plague carried by rats, and scurvy, a very common disease during the later sixteenth century. During Drake's 1585 expedition to the West Indies 300 seamen died of malaria caught in the woods of the Cape Verde Islands. Sir Richard Hawkins, a conscientious, enlightened navigator, who shared his father's interest in the health of his seamen, relates that 10,000 men died of scurvy during Elizabeth's reign. His opinion was that sour oranges and lemons were the best cure for it. He was also convinced that Dr. Steven's water was an efficacious remedy for this complaint, as was oil of vitry, if a seaman were to take two drops of it mingled in a draught of water, with a little sugar. "I wish", wrote Hawkins, "some learned man would write of it, for it is the plague of the sea and the spoil of mariners." It was not realized in the days of the first Elizabeth that scurvy was caused by dietary deficiency owing to lack of vitamin C. The symptoms were very unpleasant because pimples appeared on the gums of the seamen, their teeth began to fall out, and enormous, ugly blotches appeared on their skin. Sir John Hawkins always insisted on the importance of cleanliness. He was in advance of his age, because many of his contemporaries were convinced that sickness was a visitation of God, which it was useless and even impious to fight against. Sir Richard Hawkins wrote: "It is a common calamitie amongst the ordinary sort of mariners, to spend their thrift on the shore, and to bring to sea no more cloaths than they have backes; for the bodie of man is not refreshed with anything more, then with shifting cleane cloaths, a great preservation of health in hott countries."

Sir Richard Hawkins strongly criticized the system of imprests, whereby a seaman sometimes received advances of pay for his services. He wished to abolish it. Experience taught him that when they returned from their voyages they "come more beggarly home, then when they went forth, having received and spent their portion before they embarked. In such a way they were forced to thieve, or to incur debts."

Hammocks were first used in Elizabeth's navy during 1597 towards the end of her reign. A warrant then authorized payment for 300 bolts of canvas "to make hanging cabines or beddes ... for the better preservation of the seaman's health". During his voyage to the South Seas in 1594 Sir Richard Hawkins alludes to the *hummaccas* (beds) used by the Indians in Brazil or the West Indies. Hammocks are quaintly referred to in late Elizabethan inventories as "Brazil beds".

A classic example of the difficulties of undertaking an important privateering expedition is given by Sir Richard Hawkins[19] when he was at Plymouth during 1593.

> And so I began to gather my company on board, [he wrote] which occupied my good friends and the Justices of the town two days, and forced us to search all lodgings, taverns and alehouses. For some would ever be taking their leave and never depart; some drink themselves so drunk that except they were carried aboard, they of themselves would not be able to go one step; others knowing the necessity of the time feigned themselves sick; others to be indebted to their hosts and forced me to ransom them; one his chest, another his sword; another his shorts; another his card and instruments for sea; and others, to benefit themselves of the imprest [money] given them, absented themselves; making a lewd living in deceiving all whose money they could lay hold of; which is scandal too rife among our seamen.

Thomas Cavendish the great navigator, who hailed from Suffolk, told Hawkins that such men had been seen swaggering boldly about the streets, having robbed him of £1,500. Monson, however, considered that others should share the blame for the seaman's reluctance to serve on these voyages. He wrote, "the seaman's usage hath been so ill that it was no marvel they show unwillingness to serve the Queen. For if they arrive sick from any voyage, such is the charity of the people ashore that they shall sooner die than find pity unless they bring money with them."[20]

Captain Nathaniel Boteler in the first of *Six Dialogues* gives an interesting description of the duties of naval officers in the days of the first Elizabeth. Starting with the swabber upwards, he mentions that his office is to see the ship kept neat and clean, and that as well in the great cabin, as everywhere else betwixt the decks.[21] Shakespeare mentions the swabber in Act II of *The Tempest*:

> The master, the swabber, the boatswain and I,
>   The gunner and his mate,
> Lov'd Mall, Meg, and Marian and Margery,
>   But none of us cared for Kate. . . .

A man taken in a lie was usually employed by the swabber on the dirtiest work of the ship, but the job only lasted for a week. The quartermaster's post was to rummage in the hold upon every occasion, and to supervise the steward in delivery of food to the cook, and in his pumping and drawing of the beer. Another duty of the quartermaster was to steer the ship. The purser was the accountant officer, and, as we have seen, he sometimes embezzled funds entrusted to his care.

The cockswain's task was to look after the shallop or barge*. It was customary for him to carry a whistle, so that he could encourage the rowers. The other officers who had whistles were the master and the boatswain. Those familiar with *The Tempest* will remember that the boatswain cried lustily: "Heigh, my hearts! Cheerly, my hearts! yare, yare! Take in the topsail. Tend to the masters whistle. Blow, till thou burst thy wind, if room enough!"† The boatswain's main responsibilities were to take charge of all ropes, rigging, cables and flags. Among his duties was superintending the long-boat, and also the supervision of punishments to the seamen, such as 'keel-raking', sometimes known as keel-hauling, and ducking at the yard-arm. The boatswain used his rod pretty vigorously on the ship's boys, and this

---

* Newly referred to as barge in 1634 during the reign of Charles I.
† Act I, Sc. 1.

chastisement was usually administered on a Monday morning. Some of the seamen were superstitious enough to believe that they would not encounter a fair wind until the ship's boys had been brought to the chest to be whipped. We have already mentioned the master-gunner, an important officer on any ship. It was the custom for the master-gunner and his mates to eat and sleep in the gun-room.

The master was the navigating officer of the ship, and his main task was to be expert in using astrolabe, back-staff, cross-staff, quadrant and other navigating instruments. He was in charge of the sailing of the ship and indeed often the most important officer under the captain. We know that William Eston was master during the first voyage from Dartmouth of John Davis in June 1585, to discover the North-west Passage. When the captain and the master encountered foggy weather during this voyage "being in distrust how the tyde might set them, they caused the *Mooneshine* to hoyse out her boate and to sound".[22] When William Eston shot a porpoise, known as a Darlie head, John Jane wrote that "it did eat as sweete as any mutton", no doubt welcome variety for the seamen used to their monotonous diet.

Nathaniel Boteler relates that "A lieutenant's place at sea is as on the shore; for in the Captain's absence he is to command in Chief". Many of the ships involved in the fight against the Spanish Armada (1588) carried lieutenants. After that period they were not used on ships for many years until towards the end of James I's reign (1625). The lieutenant's office was really a school for commanders. A sea-captain in the first Elizabethan age had to be a man of considerable skill and experience.[23]

The supply of seamen's clothing was usually a private speculation. In 1586 Roger Langford, a paymaster of the navy, provided men with canvas caps, shirts and shoes, but he unfortunately lost £40 on the speculation. Six years earlier the Government sent over clothes for the seamen on the Irish Station, but the money had to be deducted from their wages.[24]

It must not be imagined that nothing was done on a seaman's behalf, if he were maimed. It is true, however, that no naval hospitals or hospital ships existed in Elizabethan England. Those seamen put ashore after the Spanish Armada had to be paid out of Charles Lord Howard of Effingham's pocket, or given a licence to beg. A typical example was the licence granted by Howard to a maimed seaman called William Browne, to beg for a year in all churches. 'A canoneer', named Thomas Benson, a Cornishman, who was injured during the bitter fighting on the *Revenge*, was ordered by the Privy Council to be pensioned from the fund for wounded soldiers, provided his story was proved to be true.[25]

In 1591 six months' pay was given to widows of men killed in the *Revenge*, while two years later Sir John Hawkins as Treasurer of the Navy was ordered to pay 2s. a week for twenty weeks to twenty injured seamen. William Storey having lost a leg, received £1 13s. 4d. in compensation. A master mariner called Robert Miller was given £200 out of forfeited goods in consideration of his services and losses at sea. Among the *State Papers* is a letter sent to the Mayor of Bristol during 1595, which reminds him that a hospital for seamen once existed in Bristol.[26] A need clearly arose for the re-establishment of a new hospital, since a great number of mariners had been maimed in the Queen's service. He was instructed to provide one by means of a levy on the Newfoundland fishing vessels, a lucrative venture.

It was not until two years before the end of Elizabeth's reign (1603) that the Poor Law of 1601 established the responsibility of every parish for providing pensions for disabled mariners. It was decreed that the sum should not amount to more than £10 for a mariner or £20 for an officer.[27]

The annual harbour pay was a little lower than sea pay. For instance in 1589 a master received £26 1s. 8d., a boatswain £10 17s. 3d., a purser £8 13s. 9d., a cook £7 12s. 1d., a carpenter £10 8s 7d., a gunner £9 15s. 6d. and a mariner £6 10s. 0d.[28]

Few surgeons were employed on the Elizabethan ships, and the standard of medical knowledge was very rudimentary. One of the most distinguished was William Clowes, who served Lord Howard of Effingham in a personal capacity on his flagship the *Ark Royal*. He is mainly known for his book on military surgery. It was customary for the Company of Barber-Surgeons to provide one of their number, but in practice this service was much abused. Unfortunately the College of Physicians disdained to co-operate with the Company of Barber-Surgeons. Although a merchant captain was convinced as early as 1573 that malaria was caused by a mosquito's bites, no doctor was willing to make use of the seaman's experience until the end of the nineteenth century.[29]

Few historians have given much thought to the musicians, who accompanied the explorers on their long and arduous voyages. Edward Haie, who was Captain of the *Golden Hind* during Sir Humphrey's last ill-fated expedition to Newfoundland (1583) and wrote a superb account of it for Hakluyt, mentions that it included about 260 men. These were shipwrights, masons, carpenters, and also mineral men and refiners. The object of carrying musicians was not only to encourage and sustain the morale of the seamen, but also to attract the natives. As Edward Haie relates: "Besides, for solace of our people and allurement of the savages, we were provided of musike in good variety: not omitting the least toyes, as Morris dancers, Hobby horses, and Maylike conceits to delight the savage people, whom we intended to winne by all faire meanes possible."[30]

Similarly, when John Davis, a very experienced navigator sailed from Dartmouth with two ships—the *Sunshine* of London and the *Moonshyne* of Dartmouth—in search of the North-west Passage in 1585, there were four musicians. John Jane tells in his account of this voyage written for Hakluyt that their names were James Cole, Francis Ridley, John Russell and Robert Cornish. When the explorers had crossed the Atlantic and made contact with the Eskimos in what is now known as Davis Strait, "the people of the country, having spied us, made a lamentable noise, as we thought, with great outcries and skreechings: we hearing them thought it had beene the howling of wolves".[31] When a party of seamen landed from the ships they brought their musicians, who played to the Eskimos, while they themselves danced.

Queen Elizabeth I, the Armada Portrait by George Gower. This was
painted shortly after the defeat of the Armada

Sir Francis Walsingham, 1530?–1590

This made such a favourable impression on the natives, that they were more than willing to barter for their clothes, which were made of sealskins and birds' skins. The narrator tells us that the seamen during this expedition complained of their short allowance. It was found necessary to make new arrangements, so that "every messe being five to a messe should have foure pound of bread a day, twelve nine quarts of beere, six Newland fishes; and the flesh dayes a gill of pease more: so we restrained them from their butter and cheese".

Sir Francis Drake, like Nelson, was much beloved by his seamen, but he would never brook any insubordination or disobedience from his subordinates. When William Burrough, who was Drake's vice-admiral on the Cadiz voyage of 1587, quarrelled with his commander, Drake wanted to have him court martialled. He had Burrough sent home in the *Golden Lion*. Burrough later complained of his treatment to Lord Burghley. Drake could be ruthless enough to those who intrigued against his authority. When the mysterious, Italianate Thomas Doughty indulged in disloyal acts amounting to mutiny during Drake's circumnavigation of the world, he had no hesitation in ordering his execution. Drake's democratic ideas were in advance of his age. He had no great use for the gentlemen who accompanied his voyage of circumnavigation, nor was he willing to give them special privileges to distinguish them from the professional seamen. He told them roundly: "Here is such a controversy between the sailors and the gentlemen, and such stomaching between the gentlemen and the sailors, that it doth even make me mad to hear it. But, my masters, I must have it left for I must have the gentlemen to haul and draw with the mariners and the mariners with the gentlemen." Drake is today perhaps more admired than any of the other celebrated navigators. Stow described him as being of low stature, with grey eyes, of strong limb, round-headed, brown-hair, full-bearded, and he was of a cheerful countenance. He resembled Nelson in many ways. Both loved the dramatic gesture, and Drake was fond of ostentation and avaricious of fame. Most people like a little judicious flattery, and Drake

4

certainly preferred lots of it. This man of genius had a hot, quick temper, and he was capable of violence; but many found his charm irresistible. As already mentioned, Drake was strict with his men. He could not stomach them indulging in strong language on board his ships, nor would he give them license to gamble with cards or dice, or to visit brothels. This strange, ardent man could be gentle enough in his dealings with the native Indians and Negroes of the Caribbean and America, and in this trait he resembled Ralegh. He possessed some skill in treating the Indian natives, and it was his habit to administer "lotions, plasters and ointments according to the state of their griefs". Drake had a passionate conviction of the rightness of the protestant religion and this sentiment was of enormous importance in his life.

To my mind the fortitude and endurance of the humble seamen captured by the Spaniards at San Juan de Ulua in Mexico* (1568), is no less wonderful than the superb courage of Sir Francis Drake, of Sir Richard Grenville and of George Clifford, third Earl of Cumberland. How inspiring is the story of Job Hortop, that powder-maker, who came from Bourne in Lincolnshire, and who was appointed one of the gunners in the Queen's ship the *Jesus of Lubeck*. This seaman survived the excruciating tortures practised by the Spanish Inquisition, to return to England after twenty-three years. Less fortunate than Hortop was that enterprising mariner Robert Barrett of Saltash, master of the *Jesus*, who was also captured by the Spaniards in Mexico during Hawkins' third voyage. He was later burnt to death in Seville market-place, which lay near the Renaissance palace of the Contratácion House. Another Cornishman, whose name deserves to be remembered, was Edward Rawes of Fowey, who had been employed by the English government on intelligence work—but at his own risk— to observe the movements of the Spanish fleet. He was captured and died in prison. In 1580 by way of compensation his widow was granted the privilege of exporting a hundred quarters of corn[32] from Devon to Cornwall, probably without having to

---

* During the third voyage of Sir John Hawkins.

pay compensation. When we read about the bestiality of the Spanish Inquisitors, it is as well to remember that cruelty is not the prerogative of, nor confined to one nation. Many Spaniards indeed shuddered at the horrors of the Inquisition. In our own history we are mindful of the Smithfield fires during the Marian persecutions, and of the reign of terror which descended on England in 1679 when many innocent Catholic lives were sacrificed to the whims of an unscrupulous blackguard, Titus Oates. In more recent times the monstrous cruelty of the Nazis in their concentration camps and gas chambers, where thousands of people were exterminated. One day a film should be made recording the story of Hawkins' third voyage to the West Indies when Job Hortop, Robert Barrett, Miles Phillips and other seamen were forced to endure the rigours and tortures of the Spanish Inquisitors. Their stories will be described more fully in a later chapter.

Notes

CHAPTER II

1 State Papers Venetian, October 1515.
2 J. A. Froude, *English Seamen in the Sixteenth Century*, p. 12.
3 John Bowle, *Henry VIII*, p. 67.
4 *Ibid*.
5 Richard Hakluyt, *Voyages*, Vol. VIII, p. 13.
6 *Ibid*, p. 14.
7 A. L. Rowse, *The Expansion of Elizabethan England*. Oppenheim, p. 146.
8 Kenneth R. Andrews, *Elizabethan Privateering* (1964).
9 *Ibid*.
10 Christopher Lloyd, *The British Seaman 1200–1860*, (1965).
11 Orders to be used in King's or Queen's Majesties Ships or Navy being upon the Seas in Fashion of War (1568). Christopher Lloyd, *The British Seaman*.
12 Sir Richard Hawkins *Observations* (1904 edition), pp. 35–41. Also: Robert Southey, *English Seamen*.
13 Sir Richard Hawkins, *Observations*, p. 110.
14 *Shakespeare's England*, Vol. I, pp. 116 and 167.
15 Christopher Lloyd, *The British Seamen 1200–1860*. Oppenheim, p. 384.
16 Julian Corbett, *Drake and the Tudor Navy*, p. 382.
17 Monson, *Tracts*, Vol. 2.
18 B.M. *Harleian MSS*, Caeaer Collection 6994, f. 102.
19 Sir Richard Hawkins, *Observations*, ed. James A. Williamson (1933).
20 Monson II, p. 244.

21 *Shakespeare's England*, Vol. I, p. 165.

22 John Jane's account, Richard Hakluyt *The English Voyages*, Vol. V., p. 283.

23 *Shakespeare's England*, Vol. I.

24 Acts of the Privy Council, 14th August 1580.

25 *Maritime History of Cornwall*, Vol. I.
    Acts of Privy Council, 11th January 1595–6.

26 C.S.P.D., 5th October 1595.

27 43 Eliz. C.3. Also: Christopher Lloyd, *The British Seaman 1200–1860*.

28 B.M. Harleian MSS 442, 173.

29 Christopher Lloyd, *The British Seaman 1200–1860*.

30 Richard Hakluyt, *Voyages* (Everyman Edition), Vol. VI, p. 12.

31 *Ibid.* Vol. V, p. 285.

32 Acts of Privy Council, 26th May 1580.
    See also John Keast, *The Story of Fowey* (1950).

CHAPTER III

The Pirates

We suspect that Queen Elizabeth retained a sneaking affection for pirates, although she was later forced to take measures to crush or to severely limit their activities. Surely she sometimes remembered that handsome rake, Thomas Lord Seymour, the Lord Admiral, who had tried to seduce her.* When complaints were made to her of the piratical activities of her seamen on the Irish seas, she may have recalled that Tom Seymour during the brief reign of her half-brother Edward VI in 1548, had been accused among other offences of dealings with pirates. He was charged with the offence of having endeavoured to get into his own possession "the strong and dangerous Isles of Scilly". The Queen and her Privy Council were naturally anxious to stamp out piracy, but there were difficulties. There were few ships available for policing the seas, so it was essential to depend on the efforts of the vice-admirals and Commissioners in Piracy appointed to each coastal county. At the beginning of her reign there were 400 recognized pirates. As we have seen, well-known families in the West of England such as Champernounes, Killigrews, and Careys began their careers as Channel rovers. Piracy was rife, and nobody was immune. In 1573 the Earl of Worcester, whilst

* When she was Princess Elizabeth.

employed on a diplomatic mission when he travelled to France as the bearer of a christening present from Elizabeth to the infant daughter of Charles IX, was attacked on the high seas between Dover and Boulogne. Eleven or twelve of the nobleman's attendants were killed. Southampton, parts of the Lincolnshire coast, Studland Bay in Dorset, Dartmouth, the Helford river, and Padstow in Cornwall, swarmed with pirates. The two most celebrated sea-robbers in Elizabethan days were Robert Hicks of Saltash in Cornwall, and John Callice (or Challis), born at Tintern in Monmouthshire, fellow-rogues in villainy—and more of them anon.

Martin Frobisher was certainly a great seaman, and we are apt to consider this intrepid Yorkshireman—who was born near Doncaster, though his family originally came from Denbigh in Wales—as a highly respectable personality. Thomas Fuller in his *The Worthies of Devon* mentions that the learned Mr. Carpenter in his geography includes him amongst the famous men of Devonshire, ("but why should Devonshire, which hath a flock of worthies of her own, take a lamb from another country")! The truth is that throughout his life Frobisher was a rough diamond, certainly no lamb, fierce, quarrelsome, unruly and jealous of Drake. It was fortunate for him that he later acquired an influential patron in Ambrose Dudley, Earl of Warwick, brother of the Earl of Leicester, who possessed the Queen's ear. During his early career Frobisher was engaged in various murky, discreditable acts of piracy, which involved him in considerable trouble. The historian, James A. Williamson, during his researches on Frobisher, unearthed new material which reveals that the seaman was engaged in several piratical incidents.[1] We first hear of Frobisher as a boy travelling to the Gold Coast in 1553 with Thomas Wyndham, as a member of the crew. He was one of the forty survivors of the 140 members of the expedition who had sailed. A year later he sailed with John Lok. After having been captured by negroes, he was handed over to the Portuguese, who imprisoned him at Elmina. After his release we find him employed by English traders in Morocco, who sold firearms to the Moors and Hebrew bibles to the Jews. These activities were a suitable training for Frobisher's piratical ventures.

Early during Elizabeth's reign the Huguenot wars of religion prevailed in France. The Queen's policy and that of her ministers was to take the part of the Huguenots by assisting them with a small army, transported to Havre, referred to in contemporary writings as "New Haven". The English were loath to leave Havre, since they hoped to use it as a means of extorting the restitution of Calais, recently lost by Queen Mary I. Its defence proved, however, unsuccessful, for the majority of the garrison died of plague. At this period the seas abounded with merchant-men aided by masses of privateers attempting to reap a rich reward by swooping upon French commerce. Among the privateers was a wealthy ship-owner, a Norfolk squire named John Appleyard of Wymondham, who equipped three ships by the Queen's command "to serve at New Haven at the beginning of the business there".[2] To justify his own part in these proceedings Appleyard posed as a single-minded patriot, but we know too little about his character to be able to form an estimate whether his opinion of himself was the truth. We know, however, that he appointed Martin Frobisher to command the largest of the ships named the *Anne Appleyard*, which he later regretted. Frobisher was now, in 1563, aged about 27. There is a certain amount of material about his piratical activities among the High Court of Admiralty papers in the Record Office.

Much to the Norfolk squire's rage and consternation, reports about Frobisher's alleged illicit activities on the *Anne Appleyard* began to filter through to him, namely that "he had committed great robberies and spoils at the seas". It was complained that the Yorkshireman had captured three Flemish (neutral) merchantmen trading between Antwerp and Spain. There were stolen goods consisting of "certain hangings of leather, richly made", which amounted to a great sum. These valuables had been landed at St. Ives in Cornwall. Appleyard later found six among Frobisher's seamen who were willing to give evidence against their captain, provided they were allowed to retain their own booty. During his investigations Appleyard discovered that the principal receiver of the stolen goods was a certain Richard Erizey, who possessed a cellar full of stolen property. He was forced to blab that there were some objects of small value left by Frobisher at his house, but that he understood that they had been deposited in settlement of a debt. Another receiver was named Thomas Mallett. It was alleged that Martin Frobisher had given Mallett's wife silks and other valuables, "being of the spoil of the said bulks". When Appleyard succeeded in obtaining the local officer of the Admiralty's permission to make a search of Mallett's house he found nothing. No doubt Frobisher had a prearranged understanding with his accomplice that he would divulge nothing incriminating.

I have no desire to over-emphasize Frobisher's part in these shady proceedings, for his name is an honoured one among the illustrious seamen who made our country great. Yet he is the only one among the famous sea-captains who has been proved guilty of naked piracy in home waters.[3] His own defence when accused of these offences in the High Court of Admiralty was far from convincing, if not absurd. He glibly maintained that he had been attacked by two strange vessels, which "had spoiled and beaten him very sore". He seemed embarrassed when he was asked the nationality of these ships, and vaguely replied that he did not know, but was certain that they were not English. He gave evidence that his adversaries had left him neither compass, running-glass nor candles, so that he despaired of making port. To account for the articles found on the *Anne Appleyard*, Frobisher told an unconvincing story that the pirates on the other ships had pressed upon him, six bales of soap, one pipe and a half of oil, one hogshead of acqua vitae, two pieces of grograin silk, and other articles. Unfortunately we have no record of the verdict of the High Court of Admiralty. Frobisher, however, was in Launceston Gaol for a time during 1564.

He was also in his early career involved in a further piracy case together with Thomas Cobham, a well-known Elizabethan pirate, whose brother was highly connected. His enemy, John

Appleyard, once again accused Frobisher. Together with Richard Erizey he was joint owner of a privateering vessel named the *Bark Frobisher*, which had been engaged on a cruise under the command of Maxwell the Scott—a notorious sea-robber—during the early 1560s. England and Spain still enjoyed at that period peaceful relations, and the Queen was not anxious to incense Philip II. The chief witness for what occurred was James Shelyn, its quartermaster, who affirmed that the *Bark Frobisher* was sailing together with another ship commanded by Thomas Cobham when they encountered four Spanish ships, all neutrals. After a bitter and prolonged fight Cobham and Maxwell boarded the largest Spanish vessel and seized her. They then made for the Irish coast and later for St. Ives, where they divided the booty at Erizey's house. Cobham was notorious for his depredations on Spanish shipping. On one occasion he murdered a Spanish friar. Guzman de Silva, the Ambassador of Spain, complained to Queen Elizabeth, who became so indignant that she talked of hanging Cobham. But he was a younger brother of Lord Cobham, Lord Warden of the Cinque Ports, and his life was spared.

The Acts of the Privy Council in the 1570s abound with cases of piracy. During 1576 Sir Richard Grenville was accused of this offence, but it was proved to be only a prize case of enemy's goods in a neutral ship.[4]

The vice-admirals were often suspected of illicit practices, particularly in their relations with pirates. In 1563 a general order was made that they should only act in conjunction with the commissioners for the suppression of piracy, so as to avoid any appearance of connivance. In 1570, one of the vice-admirals for Cornwall, named William Lower, ignored an order of the Privy Council to restore certain goods taken by John Mitchell of Truro, which they "impute unto him dealing with the said Mitchell". Six years later Lower was obliged to appear again before the Council for illegally detaining cargoes. In 1579, however, when he had ceased to be vice-admiral, he was fined for various transactions with pirates. Another vice-admiral named John Arundel was accused of various dealings with a pirate who sailed a Scotch ship from Torbay to the Helford river in Cornwall and sold the cargo to Arundel and to others. The Helford river was a favourite haunt of pirates, and was often referred to as 'Stealford River'.

Sir John Killigrew of a well-known Cornish family was a jovial old rascal, nearly always in chronic debt. During 1588—Armada year—he was both Vice-Admiral for Cornwall and Governor of Pendennis Castle, with its magnificent and commanding view of Falmouth. In November 1588 we find Killigrew marching about the country with an armed retinue. Consequently, the sheriff was ordered to levy a sufficient force to capture him and to storm Pendennis Castle. Killigrew had been making a nuisance of himself for years. After having been accused of 'outrages, disorders and riots' the Council requested the Lord Admiral Charles Lord Howard of Effingham to remove Killigrew from office. At least he was fortunate in having powerful connections at Court, for his relation, William Killigrew, was groom of the chamber at Queen Elizabeth's court.

The records reveal that the Cornish vice-admirals were less trustworthy than those in any other county. It is hardly surprising that piracy flourished here. In 1580 a commission was issued to inquire into the conduct of one of the vice-admirals, by whose negligence or connivance a pirate named Husson and most of his crew had escaped from Falmouth.[5] Many subordinate officials were also continually suspected of complicity and corruption. One of the vice-admirals named Edward Seymour had to appear before the Council if he could not, or would not, produce a subordinate, who had brought goods from pirates in the Helford river.

Early in 1565 Sir John Chichester and Sir Peter Carew were sent on a special mission to Devon and Cornwall to inquire into acts of piracy. Not only was it found difficult to capture the pirates, but when they were caught, it was certainly a problem to obtain their conviction, for Elizabethan juries were notoriously sympathetic to them. The pirates usually had agents, receivers of stolen goods, informers and partners, to be found in every class of Elizabethan society. Typical of these was Thomas Maynarde of Plymouth, who confessed that he had been an intermediary.[6] Maynarde, however, received a light sentence, since he was merely sentenced to restore to the owner the value of the forty bags of wood he had sold on behalf of the pirate. During the Huguenot wars with France they were sometimes given the choice of enrolling so as to fight at Havre. For instance, during the winter of 1562–3, twenty-one from various Devon prisons welcomed the opportunity of going there, despite the plague then prevalent in the French town.

From 1577 onwards the English government had to adopt more severe measures to repress piracy.[7] New regulations were provided whereby the aiders and abettors ashore of the sea-robbers were to be prosecuted and fined. It was intended that the penalties enforced should be a compensation for the victims. To encourage those enterprising spirits willing to risk their lives in capturing them, commissions were granted to private persons to set out ships for this purpose.[8] The takers of pirates were recompensed with a proportion of the goods found on board. In those days Dartmouth—that lovely Devon town—was a favourite haunt for marauders. Its records reveal that John Plomleigh, its mayor, was fined £100 for dealings with pirates. Thomas Ridgeway was fined as much as £150 for similar offences.[9] The career of Sir Humphrey Gilbert comprises a number of piratical incidents. It was reported in 1579 that disorderly crews under his command were haunting Torbay and had pillaged a Spanish vessel in Dartmouth. Sir John Gilbert, Humphrey's elder brother at Compton Castle, was compelled to compensate the Spanish owner.

Few people have heard today of John Callice (or Challice), an Elizabethan pirate born at Tintern in Monmouthshire. In his own times he was an object of terror on the High Seas. It is uncertain whether Callice was of English or Welsh parentage, but it is likely that he had Welsh blood. According to his own account, he left home at the age of 12 and, arriving in London, was reared by Alderman William Bond as a merchant.[10] William Bond was a haberdasher by profession and alderman of Candlewick Ward. A man of some means, he owned Crosby Place and died in 1576. Callice had a spell as a mariner, and later gained further experience by "trading upon merchants' voyages from the River of Thames". About 1571 he became a sea-rover, sailing with William Wynter the younger and others to serve Her Majesty in various ships, and continued in that service, mainly at Belle Isle and Rochelle, about a year. About 1574 he was gaining some notoriety for acts of piracy. When serving as captain under Sir John Barkeley, he forcibly boarded a ship called the *Grace of God*, owned by Acerbo Velutelli, and after carrying her into Cardiff, sold the cargo.[11] He was captain and master of a flyboat humorously named 'The Coste me Noughte', and a warrant for Callice's arrest was issued 12th April 1574. During that summer he was reported to be indulging in piratical actions off Holy Island, including the taking of a valuable prize from a ship named the *Salvatore*, which possessed a lading of corn, flax and "clapbordes". Again, together with Simon Fernandez, a Portuguese, and John Sallman of Cardiff, a mariner, on the *Oliphante*, he was sailing off the Azores at the end of 1574, when he boarded a Portuguese ship of 60 tons. When he reached Penarth, he sold the cargo of sugar and Brazil wood, valued at £1,200. Although he was indicted for this offence and acknowledged his guilt, he seems to have escaped punishment. During the summer of 1575 we find Callice associating with pirates in Brixham, Devon. Some of the prizes and loot were handed over to a dishonest official named Gilbert Peppitt, Sergeant of the Admiralty. He later faced sixteen charges of receiving. William Hawkins, head of the family shipping business in Plymouth, incurred the censure of the authorities several times over the activities of his ships—on one occasion together with Sir Richard Grenville, when they were criticized for misdemeanours in the *Castle of Comfort*, which they jointly owned.[12]

The Privy Council in 1576 considered that Callice was such a menace that letters of commission for his apprehension were handed over to the Admiralty representatives in the West. On

17th November John Crofts left Hampton Court charged with a special mission to arrest the pirate. Reaching Wales two weeks later, he discovered that Callice was in Penarth, trying to dispose of several valuable prizes he had obtained in the *Red Lyon*. It was fortunate for Callice that he had many useful friends in Wales only too willing to shield him from trouble. The Privy Council at the beginning of 1576 sent a severe letter to Sir John Perrot, Vice-Admiral of South Wales, informing him that Callice "arriving latelie at Milford, was lodged and housed in Hereford West [Haverford], and being there knowen was suffered to escape, and their lordships do not a letill marvell of such as are justices in those parts".[13] Perhaps they also suspected the activities of Sir John Perrot, who was not averse to sharing the booty with the pirates, although he was fond of swearing that he would cut their throats and gain £2,000 by clearing the seas.[14] Most people in Wales had dealings with the pirates, including the uncle of Robert Devereux, Earl of Essex, who lived at Lamphey in Pembrokeshire. Robert Hicks, the Cornish pirate from Saltash, although he had fewer friends in Wales than Callice, recompensed his Welsh helpers in kind: a barrel of rye "for keeping one of his company which was hurt aboard him"; three pecks of rye for some delicious Milford oysters.[15]

During 1577 Robert Hicks joined forces with John Callice, and they even became attached to each other. On Easter Monday, when they were at Yarmouth Road, Callice and his fellow-pirate attacked two Scottish barks. One of them was named the *Swallow of Leith*; it was on a voyage to France with freight worth £922. Hicks was Captain of the *Golden Lion*. On 10th May between the Isles of Scilly and Ushant he captured a ship called the *Jonas* (Jonathan), which was sailing for Lisbon with a cargo of corn and clapboards. After giving some of the booty to a receiver, Hicks took her to Cork and from thence to Milford.

Much material about Callice and Hicks exists in the Record Office. There is no need to be sentimental, but I must admit to a sneaking affection for Robert Hicks. No pirate who is loyal to his comrades can be described as wholly nefarious. On one occasion when Hicks was at Milford with a prize of corn he wrote Callice that he wished his friend were with him aboard the *Neptune*, vowing that he would not withold any groat or groatsworth of his. "Brother Callys," he quaintly told him ". . . . Yf all I have of myen owne to my shert maye stand you in steade you maye as fare command yt as mye brother borne." Callice had been arrested, and during June 1577 had been brought from the Tower to the custody of the Admiralty Marshal at Southwark. From there he wrote to the Secretary of State, Sir Francis Walsingham, interceding with him for his life. He wrote Walsingham: "These are from the bottom of my harte to advise yor honour that I do bewayle and lament my former wofull and wicked lief Wherefore I beseche the livinge God for his sonn Jesus Christe his sake to forgive me my manyfold offences against his Divine M^{atie} and the Queenes highness cravinge herewith Her M^{aites} most gracious mercy." If his life was granted to him, he was willing to reveal the favourite haunts of other pirates. Callice, who possibly was more craven by nature than Hicks, wrote a second undated letter to Walsingham, informing him that another pirate, Solivan Beere of Berehaven, with the help of Frenchmen, was planning a treasonable landing in Ireland and had suggested engaging him as a pilot. Callice, however, had powerful friends, and he eventually obtained his freedom by means of James Douglas, Earl of Morton, who interceded on his behalf with Queen Elizabeth I. By patent writ the Queen graciously agreed to pardon him for all offences committed by sea and land.[16]

During 1577 Robert Hicks was also causing the Privy Council much trouble. There is a letter directed to Sir John Arundel, Sir John Killigrew, and Richard Grenefield (Grenville) and others commissioning them to inquire into an act of piracy, which had recently occurred. The ship concerned was "Our Lady of Aransusie, laden with iron, and, taken upon the Coast of Galizia [Galicia] by one Captain Hix of Saltashe, whereby they are authorized to make searche within the haven of Helforde and other places there abouts". Grenville was commanded to see that onc of the pirates associated in this affair named Hammond was closely guarded when travelling through Cornwall; for it was suspected that some attempt might be made to rescue him "within that shire".

Robert Hicks and John Callice, together with ten other pirates, made a brutal attack on a Danish ship named the *Golden Lyon*, owned by John Petersen, a subject of the King of Denmark. For this wanton act three sea-robbers named Bleryn, Milles and Bagg were hanged at Wapping during July 1577. The King of Denmark complained to the Queen that restitution of property must be made to John Petersen and to others. Hicks was eventually captured by George Winter and brought to London for examination by the Judge of the Admiralty. He was to be especially questioned as to "who were the receivers of suche goods and merchandizes as was taken by him and Callice in the *Golden Lyon* from John Petersen subjects to the King of Denmark".[17] Hicks was sent to Ireland, where he remained for some time in the custody of the Lord President of Munster.

There is a letter from Ambrose Dudley, Earl of Warwick; his brother, the Earl of Leicester, and Mr. Secretary Walsingham, ordering the Lord Deputy of Ireland to have "Robert Hix" conveyed from Ireland to England.[18] Henry Killigrew was ordered to pay John Petersen of "Elsenuns in Denmark" £50 "out of the fynes of suche as have dealt with matters of piracy, in respects of spoiles committed upon hym by Hix and Callice".[19] Hicks was later hanged during March 1578.

Among the receivers of goods, including hogsheads of wine, pillaged from Hicks' ships, were members of well-known Cornish families such as Walter and John Rashleigh. The latter gained renown because he owned a ship named the *Francis of Foy*. Rashleigh's ship sailed with Frobisher upon his third voyage to Meta Incognita[20], that undiscovered territory lying to the west of Greenland and reputed to be rich in mineral resources. During the voyage the *Francis* was in deadly peril, when surrounded by ice and a dense fog which suddenly descended upon the seamen. John Rashleigh the younger succeeded to his father's property when the elder Rashleigh died in 1582. He was a wild seaman who

(*left*) Sir Christopher
Hatton, 1540–1591,
patron of Sir Francis
Drake

(*right*) Sir John
Hawkins, *Herwologia
Anglica*, 1620

(above left) Sir Martin Frobisher, painted by Cornelius Ketel. (above right) Ambrose Dudley, Earl of Warwick, patron of Sir Martin Frobisher. Engraving by George Vertue

sailed with Drake on the *Francis* on his voyage to the West
Indies in 1585. During this voyage the captain of this ship, whose
name was Moon, lost his life. We shall encounter John Rashleigh
again during 1588, when the Spanish Armada was off the coasts of
Britain.

It is curious that John Callice, the Monmouthshire pirate,
escaped execution, for during 1580 we find him still operating in
the North Seas. In May a commission was issued to Thomas
Williams, Vice-Admiral of the Counties of Pembroke, Carmarthen
and Cardigan, to arrest Callice and two other pirates named
Thomas Clarke and Isaac Tooley. Two years later Callice's
chequered career assumed a new and more respectable guise
when he served as lieutenant under Captain William Fenner in
the galleon *Fenner*, a privateer commissioned to make prizes of
Spanish and Portuguese vessels.[21] With characteristic restlessness
we next hear of him fighting with the Turks of the Barbary
States. During the winter of 1585–6 one of Sir Francis
Walsingham's intelligence agents, an Irishman named Nicholas
Skiddle of Cork, wrote to his master that one Captain John
Challis had arrived in Cork out of Barbary; he gave out that he had
aboard his ship twelve barrels of gold; "he is gone back again to
sea and whither God knoweth".[22] Callice met his end in Barbary.

Another Elizabethan pirate was Captain John Piers of Padstow.
He has been described as "a tall slender man, having long black
hair on his head hanging almost down to his shoulders, his
visage being a pale sickly colour and somewhat more hair in the
upper part of his beard towards his ears than on his chin, being of
the age of twenty-eight or thirty years".* His career in the official
papers begins in 1552, though he may have had dealings with
Lord Thomas Seymour in 1549 or earlier. As already mentioned
it was a superstitious age, and many people attributed Piers'
success to his mother being a witch. He caused the Mayor of Rye
considerable trepidation during 1581, because, with his own
small bark of 35 tons and another one of 18 tons, he managed to

---

* *Dorset Elizabethans at Home and Abroad*, by Rachel Lloyd.

5

blockade the harbour, so that, according to the mayor, "None can go forth or come in." During October 1581 he was captured by chance in Studland Bay in Dorset, a favourite haunt of pirates. His captor was Thomas Walsh, himself a sea-robber.

The Privy Council wrote to Francis Earl of Bedford, informing him "that there is latelye apprehended at Stutland in the Countie of Dorsett one John Piers, a verie notorious pirate borne in Cornwall, who hathe an olde mother dwelling at Padstowe, noted to be a witch, to whom by reporte the said Piers hathe conveyed all such goodes and spoiles as he hathe wyckedlie getten at the Seas".[23] The Acts of the Privy Council reveal that pirates were sometimes hanged at Studland Bay when gibbets were erected in the surrounding districts.

Bedford appointed Sir Richard Grenville and his cousins George Grenville and Thomas Roscanock as commissioners to inquire into the matter. During this trial it was made clear that Anne Piers, the pirate's mother, had been a receiver of various stolen goods, including a great coverlet or rug which she had carried from the sea shore at twelve o'clock one night and left in a barn at Padstow. One can imagine the scene in this lonely, lovely Cornish harbour. The old woman sitting patiently on a mow of corn, with the soft lapping of the water, and the stealthy approach of two men "bringing a great rug fardled up upon a staff between them".[24] Another witness gave evidence that her husband coming from Bristol was aboard Piers' ship at Lundy, and "had of him a parrot, a little firkin of soap and two calivers".[25] The vice-admiral apparently received the parrot. Grenville and his fellow justices inquired diligently into the matter whether or not the wretched old woman Anne Piers was a witch. They inquired "of some of the better sort and of most credit of the town of Padstowe and of the said parish . . . whether they know or ever heard that Anne Piers of Padstow did practise witchcraft or had the name to be a witch". The answer in the negative spared her from a dreadful fate. Piers was taken to Dorchester Gaol, from whence he succeeded in escaping owing to the corruption of his keepers. He was recaptured and later executed on

Studland beach, having been brought there together with other prisoners from Corfe Castle in waggons.

Parts of the Lincolnshire coast were swarming with pirates. During 1577 there is a letter to the Mayor of Boston from the Privy Council directing him that "Certen pirattes which have committed sundrye pyracies at Yngolmels Haven otherwise called *Theefes Creeke*, to be by him staied in that towne." There are appreciative letters to Sir Edward Stradling, and others, commissioners for piracies within the County of Glamorgan, commending them for their diligence and care in Her Majesty's service in apprehending the pirate Clarke, "who appeared within the streame of Severne over againste Pennarth Head".

Another case of New Year's Day 1582 reported in the Acts of the Privy Council[26] concerned that genial old scoundrel Sir John Killigrew, who was not unlike Sir John Falstaff. A Spanish ship the *Marie of San Sebastian*, 140 tons burden, was driven owing to stormy seas down the Channel into Falmouth harbour. A few days later the ship was boarded by a gang of men, who were actually Sir John's servants. After seeking for booty, they carried the Spanish ship out to sea. When appealed to, the Privy Council soon discovered that the plot had originated with Mary, Sir John's wife. Sir Richard Grenville and Edmund Tremayne were two of the justices who were appointed to inquire into this case. Sir John's son, also named John, also got into serious trouble with the authorities. In 1595, towards the end of Elizabeth's reign, Killigrew was accused of warning Elliott, a pirate operating in the Helford river of the approach of one of Her Majesty's ships, HMS *Crane*; of supplying him with provisions, and of being handsomely recompensed for his services. This Elliot may be described as a traitor, for he soon afterwards entered the Spanish Service.[27] Consequently he differed from some of the Elizabethan pirates, who, despite their acts of violence and brutality, still possessed a kind of loyalty to England and would not have betrayed their country. It was even suggested that John Killigrew, because of his dealings and friendship with Elliott, had promised to deliver Pendennis Castle into the hands of the Spanish. The English spies operating in Spain were warned concerning Killigrew's disloyalty.

It is useless to be sentimental about pirates: and yet who knows by what strange twist of character they have embarked on their hazardous and lawless career? In some of them the half-patriot was merely latent, while others were influenced by their insatiable lust for gold. Patriotism and piracy were often hard to distinguish. For example, during July 1557 two Scottish ships were seized by Walter Ralegh* and two other Devon men. The Privy Council were much incensed and were about to take proceedings against them when news arrived that the Scots were over the border. Walter Ralegh and his companions immediately became heroes, instead of being branded as malefactors.

Sir Thomas Stucley,† that unstable, disreputable cousin of Sir John Hawkins, was a colourful personality, but he proved disloyal to his queen. King Philip II of Spain, moreover, was at one time complaining of the piratical activities of Captain Tomás Estuclây: how, for instance, he had broken into a Spanish port in Galicia and robbed a Portuguese merchant of more than 15,000 ducats' worth of merchandise. William Camden had a very poor opinion of Stucley, and we cannot quarrel with it. He calls him a

> riotous prodigall, and vaine-glorious fellow, who after he had consumed all his estate, retired into Ireland. . . . After belching up most unworthy reproaches of his Princess, who had done him many favours, slipped over into Italie to Pope Pius the Fifth, and by his flattering tongue insinuated beyond all credit into the favour of this pernicious old man, who breathed out the ruine of Queene Elizabeth, making great brags, and promising that with three thousand Italians, he would drive all the English out of Ireland, and burne the English fleet.[28]

At one time he enjoyed the Queen's favour and she granted him her licence to sail "with God's help" from this her Grace's

---

* Father of the celebrated Sir Walter Ralegh 1552–1618.
† 1525–1578.

Realm of England, to the country called Terra Florida, "for the further discovery of those parts thereof that as yet be unknown". Queen Elizabeth had jokingly asked Stucley "whether he would remember her when he was seated in his new kingdom". "I will write to you," said lusty Tom, with a touch of insolence in his voice. "In what language?" asked the Queen. "In the style of Princes, as one to another—to our dear Sister!"[29] The arrogance and the conceit of the man may have amused the Queen on this occasion, but later she had cause to dislike and distrust him. Stucley was a swashbuckler, a typical Elizabethan in his restlessness and acquisitive sense, and a man so insinuating and persuasive that he could have charmed the very birds from the trees. Yet Tom Stucley was a traitor, and his heroic death on the sands of Barbary does not exculpate him from this stigma. Richard Hakluyt gave a short account of Stucley's last voyage into Barbary (1578), when he absurdly referred to himself as the Marquis of Ireland.

Notes

CHAPTER III

1   James A. Williamson, *Piracy and Honest Trade: An Elizabethan Contrast* (Blackwood, 1930).
2   *Ibid.*
3   James A. Williamson, *The Age of Drake*, p. 44.
4   *A History of Cornwall. Maritime History*, Vol. I.
5   *Ibid.*
6   Acts of the Privy Council, 7th December 1564.
7   Acts of the Privy Council, 11th July 1577.
8   Add. MSS. 34150, fol. 61, 64.
9   Add. MSS. 12505, fol. 333.
10 C. L'Estrange Ewen, *The Golden Chalice* (1939).
11 *Ibid.*
12 H. C. A. Exams. 22.
13 Acts of the Privy Council, 12th January 1576.
14 See also C. L'Estrange Ewen, *The Golden Chalice.*
15 A. L. Rowse, *The Expansion of Elizabethan England.*
16 Acts of the Privy Council 1577–78, Vol. X.
17 *Ibid.* Vol. X.
18 *Ibid.* Vol. X, p. 70.
19 *Ibid.* Vol. X, p. 146.
20 A. L. Rowse, *Tudor Cornwall;* also John Keast, *The Story of Fowey* (1950).
21 C. L'Estrange Ewen, *The Golden Chalice.*
22 S. P. Ireland 1586–1588, p. 71.
23 Acts of the Privy Council, October 1581. Vol. XII, p. 228.
24 Acts of the Privy Council.

25 A. L. Rowse, *Sir Richard Grenville of the Revenge*.
26 Acts of the Privy Council, Vol. XIII, p. 315, 356.
27 *Maritime History of Cornwall*, Vol. I.
28 *Camden Annales* (1625) p. 257.
29 John Izon, *Sir Thomas Stucley* 1525–1578.

CHAPTER IV

Patrons of the Seamen

No man during the Elizabethan age did more to stimulate
exploration and voyages of discovery overseas than Sir Francis
Walsingham,* that stern, fanatical statesman, the enemy of Mary
Queen of Scots, whom he referred to on one occasion as "that
devilish woman" when writing to the Earl of Leicester fifteen
years before her death. Camden wrote of Walsingham: "He was a
person exceeding wise and industrious . . . a strong and resolute
maintainer of the purer religion [Protestantism], a diligent
searcher out of hidden secrets, and one who knew excellently well
how to win men's affections to him, and to make use of them
for his own purposes." Thomas Fuller relates[1] that Francis
Walsingham was born in Kent, and that his family had long
flourished at Chislehurst. He thought that they originally derived
their name from Walsingham in Norfolk. He was educated at
Kings College, Cambridge, and later gave Philip II of Spain the
Bible from Kings College Library as a present. Maybe he wanted
to convert him. No doubt Walsingham's long residence abroad,
particularly as ambassador in Paris during the Massacre of St.
Bartholemew gave him that deep insight into and experience of
foreign affairs and knowledge of men, which was later to stand
him in good stead as Secretary of State. A man of culture and

* 1530?–1590.

learning, he was the father-in-law and intimate friend of Sir Philip Sidney, and was described by Edmund Spencer as the great Maecenas of his age.[2]

Richard Hakluyt the younger relates, when dedicating the first edition of his *Voyages* to Walsingham in 1589, the powerful impression made on him by a visit to his cousin the elder Richard Hakluyt in the Middle Temple. His cousin had shown him some books of cosmography and ancient maps, eagerly devoured by the young man. Reaching for the Bible the older man had turned to Psalm 107.* "They which go downe to the sea in ships, and occupy by the great waters, they see the works of the Lord, and His wonders in the deepe ..." "which words of the Prophet together with my cousin's discourse (things of high and rare delight to my young nature), tooke in me so deepe an impression, that I constantly resolved, if ever I were preferred to the University ... I would by God's assistance prosecute that knowledge and kinde of literature, the doores whereof (after a sort) were so happily opened to me." In such a way Hakluyt received his inspiration to embark on his great life's work.

We certainly discover in Walsingham's introvert and reserved character two elements from which spring the foundations of the British Empire, religious zest for the Protestant cause and commercial enterprise.[3] Yet, unlike Sir Humphrey Gilbert or Sir Walter Ralegh, the fiery puritan had no vision of Empire. He was mainly attracted to overseas discoveries as a means of wealth, like most of his contemporaries. The Gilberts, Drake, John Davis and Frobisher all owed much to the support and encouragement of Walsingham. The motives of the Secretary of State in fostering their ambitions were partly due to his implacable hatred of Spain, fostered by his puritanism, and partly owing to a fondness for investing in speculative ventures, very characteristic of the Tudor Age. Yet Walsingham can hardly be described as a sympathetic personality. His portrait in the National Portrait Gallery is that of an astute, determined statesman, who had

* Verses 23 and 24.

probed the defects of character of his fellow-men. In his persecution of the Roman Catholics he seems to us at once cold and remorseless, even admitting that such an attitude was essential in the dangerous times in which he lived. In his encouragement of maritime trade the Secretary of State deserved high honour, and a study of the correspondence of the leading navigators of the age makes it clear that his considerable part in promoting maritime exploration was far more marked than Lord Burghley's.

In 1562 Walsingham became a member of the Muscovy Company, and thus began his long connexion with English trade overseas.[4] He was also later intimately associated with the affairs of the Levant Company, which was mainly begun owing to the efforts of two London merchants, Sir Edward Osborne and Richard Staper. When Secretary of State, Walsingham made a small investment of £25 in Martin Frobisher's first expedition in search of the North-west Passage (1576). His contribution was probably only a gesture to please Ambrose Dudley, Earl of Warwick,* Frobisher's chief patron, who certainly used his influence in securing the goodwill of the Queen and in persuading some of the other courtiers to invest in the enterprise. Actually Lord Burghley invested £50, while Warwick and his brother Robert Dudley, Earl of Leicester, subscribed the same amount. It is also recorded that Thomas Radcliffe, Earl of Sussex, Leicester's enemy, contributed £50; while Philip Sidney, Walsingham's son-in-law, invested £25. The Queen, with her customary shrewdness, did not invest at all. Though he did not achieve a great deal on this voyage, Frobisher certainly added to geographical knowledge. He sailed round the southern point of Greenland, along the coast, and crossed over to Baffin Island. A member of the navigator's crew had found a piece of an unknown black ore or pyrites on one of the northern islands, and this was brought home to be examined by an Italian alchemist, Baptiste Agnello, because it was supposed that it contained gold. Walsingham had no high expectations. He regarded it merely "as an

---

* 1528?–1590, 4th son of John Dudley, Duke of Northumberland.

Alchemist matter. Such as divers others had been brought to her Majesty."

Yet there was no lack of subscribers for Frobisher's second voyage. The Queen invested £500, and lent her ship, the *Aid*,[5] while the prudent Lord Burghley subscribed £100, and Walsingham rather over £200. Frobisher sailed in the *Aid* on Whit Sunday 1577, and several other small ships comprised the expedition, including the *Gabriel*, whose captain was Mr. Fenton, "a gentleman of the Earl of Warwick's". It is recorded in Hakluyt's *Voyages* by Master Dionise Settle that two seamen were lost in the course of this voyage, one owing to "God's visitation, and the other homeward cast over borde with a surge of the sea". Frobisher returned to England in September with some 200 tons of the black ore. Walsingham made a much larger investment of £475 in the Yorkshire navigator's third voyage when he penetrated into Hudson Bay and mistakenly imagined that he had found the Passage. The Queen now subscribed as much as £1,350, while Edward de Vere, Earl of Oxford, Burghley's son-in-law, invested the large sum of £2,000. Financially the expedition proved a disaster, for the Queen and Oxford lost a great deal of money.

Michael Lok, who had promoted this enterprise, was ruined by it, and sent to prison.[6] Lok, a business man who had lived in Flanders and Spain, related that he had helped Frobisher in all sorts of ways. He had lent him all his books, charts, maps and instruments. After quarrelling with Frobisher, Lok complained to Walsingham: "I have made my house his home, and my purse his purse at his need and my credit his credit to my power when he was utterly destitute both of money, and of credit and of friends."[7] In the early days Frobisher had lodged in Fleet Street, to be nearer to Lok, at Widow Hancock's house in Mark Lane. After his return from his second voyage, Captain Frobisher, now lacking the money he was wont to have at Lok's hands, flung into a terrible rage, "lyke a made best [mad beast]".[8] Lok accused him of false slanders and making shameful reports about him. The truth was that Frobisher was a boastful man and capable of violent behaviour. Before his third voyage Frobisher "grew into such a monstrous mind, that a whole Kingdom could not contain it; but already by discovery of a new world, he was become another Columbus". If Lok not unnaturally felt aggrieved, Frobisher's wife Dame Isabel was even more bitter. She wrote to Sir Francis Walsingham between 1576–1578: "I am the most miserable poor woman in the world, whereas my former husband Thomas Rigget a very wealthy man had left me with ample portions for myself and all my children, my present husband (Captain Frobisher) has spent everything and put us to the wide world to shift." She was starving in a small room at Hampstead. She begged Sir Francis to recover a debt of £4 due to her husband. Amidst all her recriminations we do not hear Frobisher's side of the story, harassed as he must have been by debts and anxieties connected with his voyages.

Sir Francis Walsingham was recognized in the Privy Council as one of the chief advocates of a policy hostile to Spain. Others of the expansionist school were the Earl of Leicester and Sir Christopher Hatton. Consequently in 1577 when Francis Drake was planning his famous expedition to circumnavigate the world, Walsingham gave him all his support, and Leicester and Hatton, who were Drake's patrons, used their endeavours to forward this enterprise. It is uncertain how much money Walsingham invested, but he was a member of a syndicate, including the Queen, Leicester and Hatton. Elizabeth had a large financial stake in Drake's voyage. As is well known, the voyage proved an enormous success, and those who had had the foresight to back it were certainly richly rewarded. Francis Drake brought back with him £500,000, though most of this money no doubt was paid into the royal treasury.

One of Walsingham's qualities was courage, and he certainly needed it in his relations with the Queen, his royal mistress. On one occasion on 20th August 1581 he wrote to Sir Christopher Hatton from Paris: "I hear that I stand in so hard terms with Her Majesty as I fear any persuasion I can use in furtherance of Sir Francis Drake's voyage will rather hurt than help."[9] Elizabeth was at least astute enough to retain Walsingham in his position as

Secretary of State though she rather disliked him.* He was too frank to be a good courtier.

Walsingham's greatest service in aiding maritime exploration overseas was, perhaps, to use his influence in securing from the Queen for Sir Humphrey Gilbert the charter granted him in 1578 to discover and colonize "remote heathen and barbarous lands not actually possessed of any Christian prince". He also persuaded the Queen—though this may not have presented much difficulty—in granting her licence for Gilbert to sail on his first voyage. Humphrey Gilbert was grateful to Walsingham for his services on his behalf, for he wrote him in November 1578: "My principal care is to satisfy you above all others because your Honour was the only means of my licence. . . . As you have been alway the pillar unto whom I leant, so I hope you will always remain."

Before Sir Humphrey Gilbert's last famous voyage to colonize Newfoundland, we find Walsingham writing† to Master Thomas Alworth, a merchant and mayor of Bristol, requesting him to supply the adventurers with "some further supply of shipping then yet he hath. Your good inclination to the westerne discoverie I cannot but much commend," he tells him. To achieve his purpose, Walsingham sent Richard Hakluyt and Thomas Steventon with a special message to Aldworth.[10] The reply of this merchant is characteristic of the helpfulness of business men towards western discovery. Thomas Aldworth assured the Secretary of State that the Bristol merchants were willing to offer the sum of 1,000 marks, "and a ship of three-score, and a barke of 40 tunne, to bee left in the countrey under the direction and government of your sonne in law Mr. Carlile, of whom we have heard much good".

Walsingham was far-seeing enough to visualise the importance of trade with the Far East. At the end of 1580 he was instrumental in sending Drake back to the Spice Islands with a fleet of merchantmen. His project for an English East India Company

----

* She nicknamed Walsingham 'her Moor', because he was the real founder of the British Secret Service.

† 11th March 1582.

anticipated by twenty years the formal inauguration of English trade with the Far East.[11]

John Dee, whose influence on the Elizabethan seamen was so beneficial, was extremely proud of his Welsh ancestry. His father Rowland Dee had held the minor office of Gentleman Server to Henry VIII, and he was in fact the Chief carver at the King's table and manager of the royal kitchen.[12] It was Robert Dudley, Earl of Leicester, who first brought Dee to the Queen's notice. He was a man of many parts, a brilliant mathematician, geographer, and expert in matters of navigation, the Queen's valued astrologer and a fine scholar. The curious thing is that he was born under the sign of Cancer, and those interested in astrological lore are aware that natives of this sign are always attracted to the sea. Indeed Dee played a fascinating role in Elizabethan history acting as adviser in navigation to Frobisher and his mariners, and he was the friend of Humphrey and Adrian Gilbert, and of John Davis. In a sense he was a real inspiration to the latter, one of the great seamen of that age, and he was the principal organizer of the company, which sent the navigator to discover Davis Strait in 1585. He was consulted as to Queen Elizabeth's title in 1577 to Greenland, Eastotiland (Labrador) and Friseland (the Canadian lands farther north). One of his other activities was to act as geographical adviser to the Russian Company in its North-east Passage expedition (1580). Once again it is necessary to stress that Dee was a Welshman, and he visualized his country as a greater Britain, not as England at all. John Dee was far in advance of his time, being an ardent propagandist for imperialism. Indeed he invented the phrase 'the British Empire'. He was in favour of a powerful navy, and urged that it should serve as the world's police force, "a Petty Navy Royall of three score tall ships or more, but in no case fewer".[13] He was an original thinker in advocating that in his 'Petty Navy Royall' all pirates should be summoned home and given the opportunity to serve in the new fleet. A man of insight and imagination, he understood that their piratical activities owed much to their sense of frustration and impotence.

Aubrey gives a lively description of Dee. "Hee had a very faire cleare rosie complexion; a long beard as white as milke; he was tall and slender; a very handsome man. . . . He wore a gowne like an artist's gowne, with hanging sleeves, and a slitt; a mighty good man he was."

The private diary of Dr. John Dee[14] reveals the intimate relations he enjoyed with Sir Humphrey Gilbert and his half-brother Adrian, and with John Davis. Here are typical entries: "On September 10th (1580) Sir Humphrey Gilbert granted me my request to him, made by letter, for the royalties of discovery, all the North above the parallel of the 50 degree of latitude, in the presence of Stoner, Sir John Gilbert (his brother), his servant or reteiner." Dee's house was at Mortlake on the river, and the Queen sometimes visited him there. On 17th September he writes:

The Queene's Majestie cam from Rychemonde in her coach, the higher way of Mortlak felde, and when she cam right against the church she turned down towards my house. . . . She beckend her hand for me, I cam to her coach side, she very speedily pulled off her glove and gave me her hand to kiss; and to be short asked me to resort to her Court, and to give her to wete when I came there.

The Queen indeed treated Dee with considerable kindness, and not without generosity. On one occasion she came to his door on horseback attended by her Court. There she was gracious enough to tell him "that the Lord Treasurer Burghley [who had formerly been no friend of his] had gretly commended my doings for her Title, which he had to examyn". All sorts of people consulted Dee, including that jovial old scapegrace Sir John Killigrew, who was in difficulties for compounding with a Spaniard, who had been robbed. For "devising the way of protestation to save him harmless". Dee was to be rewarded with a gift of fish during Lent, and as Killigrew was a chronic debtor this form of expressing his appreciation would cost him little. Again, on 23rd January 1582: "The Right Honourable Mr. Secretary Walsingham cam to my house, where by good lok he found Adrian Gilbert, and so talk was begunne of North-West Straights of discovery." And on 6th March 1583: "I, and Mr. Adrian Gilbert, and John Davis, did mete with Mr. Alderman Barnes, Mr. Tomson, Mr. Yong and Mr. Hudson, about the N.W. Voyage." On 16th April 1590 there is the melancholy entry: "Good Sir Francis Walsingham died at night hora undecima." Another celebrated visitor to Dee's house at Mortlake was Thomas Cavendish, the celebrated navigator, who "sayled round about the world", and came together with his uncle Richard to see Dee. John Davis and Adrian Gilbert visited Mortlake to warn him against the dishonest, hypocritical and devilish dealings of a woman named Emery, "an errant strumpet", as the seer refers to her. If this Renaissance scholar had not later travelled overseas to Bohemia and other countries, it is certain that he would have been closely concerned with the project to colonize Virginia during 1585. As it is he sailed with Frobisher in the *Gabriel* in 1576. According to Hakluyt, Dee invested £25 in this voyage. During this voyage Frobisher ventured near the ice-bound shores of Hudson Bay, though he almost certainly did not see the straits later discovered by Henry Hudson. There is a tradition that Dee visited St. Helena in his early life, but the *Dictionary of National Biography* is probably incorrect when it maintains that Dee travelled there.[15] It is known that Thomas Cavendish during 1588 was the first English seaman to have reached St. Helena,* a small island in the South Atlantic.

An early patron of Richard Hakluyt the younger was Sir Edward Dyer, a poet and a courtier. Indeed Hakluyt seems to have had an affectionate regard for him, and his allusion to him in his writings is warmer than to anybody else. Dyer was the son of a country gentleman in Somerset, and he entered the service of the Earl of Leicester as a confidential secretary where he became acquainted with Leicester's nephew, Sir Philip Sidney.[16] The acquaintance between the two young men ripened into an intimate friendship. We know that Sidney bequeathed his books

---

* St. Helena discovered by the Portuguese Admiral, João da Nova Castella (1502).

to Dyer and Fulke Greville* in his will. Dyer was also an early patron of Martin Frobisher and helped to organize the funds for Frobisher's first voyage. He also became a patron of a Bristol merchant John Frampton, who fell foul of the Spanish Inquisition and later became a minor writer and translator of important works. Whilst he was buying wines in Malaga the Spanish Inquisitors searched Frampton's ship and discovered a harmless pre-Reformation book, published in English. He was arrested in the early 1560s and taken to the headquarters of the Inquisition, the Castle of Triana at Seville. After having been questioned about his religious beliefs, he was tortured and later released from imprisonment. He was ordered never to leave Spanish territory and to wear for life the San Benito, the dress worn by the convicts under the Inquisition. Frampton later succeeded in escaping from Spain to England, and spent much of the remainder of his life translating into English Spanish works which clearly revealed to his fellow-countrymen the wealth monopolized by Spain in the New World across the seas. Among Frampton's works was *Joyfull Newes out of the newe founde World*, a translation of a Spanish work about the natural products of America. He dedicated this book to the poet Dyer with these words: "I founde no man that I know in that respect more worthy of the same than your worshippe, nor yet any man, to whom so many schollers, so many travellers, and so manye men of valor, suppressed or hindered with povvertie, or distressed by lacke of friends in Courte are so muche bounde to as to you."[17]

Frampton continued to dedicate books to Dyer, and among his other works is *The most famous travels of Marcus Paulus* (the first English version of Marco Polo). His real importance is that he was responsible for much of the propaganda of Elizabethan imperialism. So was Thomas Nicholas, a merchant living at Teneriffe in the Canary Islands, who was arrested for alleged heresy in 1560 on the evidence of prostitutes and thieves. After escaping from prison, Nicholas managed to reach England where

* Lord Brooke.

6

he devoted himself to translations of Spanish works, such as *History of the Conquest of the West Indies, now called New Spain,* and *The Discovery and Conquest of Peru.* Their writings certainly stimulated the minds of the Elizabethans and influenced them in their ambitious projects to expand overseas.

Now let us turn to Sir Christopher Hatton, that tall handsome man who has never been taken very seriously, because he happened to be an extremely graceful dancer and a special favourite of Queen Elizabeth. She created him Lord Chancellor.* Few people realize that Hatton was the chief patron of Sir Francis Drake at Court, and, as already mentioned, Drake during his circumnavigation of the world acknowledged his indebtness to Hatton by changing the name of his famous ship the *Pelican* on entering the Magellan Straits to the *Golden Hind,* because Sir Christopher's crest was 'a hind trippant Or'. Hatton was far from being a nonentity. He was patron of explorers, such as Sir Ralph Lane, his cousin, who accompanied Sir Richard Grenville on his voyage to Virginia in 1585, and subsequently became its first Governor.[18] Sir Edward Dyer introduced Dee to Hatton, and the learned scholar later dedicated to Sir Christopher the first volume of his work on the British Empire, entitled *General and Rare Memorials pertaining to the perfect art of Navigation.* Hatton was not only a principal shareholder in Drake's voyage round the world, but a speculator in Frobisher's voyage to discover the North-west Passage. Hatton's representative on these voyages was a sea-captain called Captain George Best, who sailed in the *Anne Francis.* He wrote a long treatise showing how the whole world is habitable. Best was one of the captains responsible for discovering quantities of black ore, and he christened one of the islands where he found it Best's Blessing. He was an industrious, humorous man and he named after Sir Christopher Hatton the place still known as Hatton Headland on Resolution Island, south of Frobisher Bay. Hakluyt relates:[19] "the eleventh of August the Captaine of the Anne Francis [Best] taking the Master of the

---

* He retained this post until his death in 1591.

shippe with him, went up to the toppe of Hattons Hedland, which is the highest land of all the streights to the ende to descry the situation of the countrey underneath." When Edward Fenton sailed to the East Indies and Cathay in April 1582, Hatton invested £250, and Leicester—always a generous speculator in these enterprises—invested over £2,000.

William Camden praises Hatton. He refers to his "modest sweetness of condition ... his pious nature, he was a great reliever of the poor, of singular bounty and munificence to students and learned men".

Thomas Doughty—that mysterious, Machiavellian personality —boasted that he introduced Francis Drake to Hatton at Court. This may be true, but is far from certain. We know that Drake had Queen Elizabeth's permission for the voyage round the world and that he constantly later said that he held a commission from her. In an interview with the great Devon seaman, she specially warned him that he should keep the matter dark from the Lord Treasurer Lord Burghley. At that period (1577) the statesman still hankered for peace, and with his cautious instincts he had a temperamental dislike of such piratical enterprises. It is certain that Burghley suspected that Drake intended to raid Spanish ships and the Spanish dominions on the west coast of South America. It is more than possible therefore that Burghley used Thomas Doughty as a kind of secret agent on this voyage, and that he had Burghley's instructions to thwart Drake. There is in the British Museum in the hand of Drake's chaplain, Francis Fletcher, a detailed account of Drake's circumnavigation of the world.[20]

Drake's fleet consisted of the *Pelican*, in which he sailed as admiral. A sea-captain named John Winter, a nephew of Admiral Sir William Winter, served as Drake's vice-admiral in the *Elizabeth*, while Captain John Thomas, a friend of Sir Christopher Hatton, commanded the *Marigold*, a bark of 30 tons. John Chester was Captain of a fly-boat named the *Swan*, while a pinnace the *Benedict* was commanded by Thomas Moone. Drake was partial to splendour, the dramatic touch, and to the sound of trumpets and other musical instruments. Whilst on board the *Pelican*, he dined to the music of John Brewer his trumpeter, who had been employed by Sir Christopher Hatton. Thomas Doughty and his brother John were among the gentlemen volunteers on this voyage. Captain Thomas behaved with conspicuous bravery when the *Marigold* was menaced by fog and storm, and he went ashore to save Drake, who was in a small boat, engrossed in a survey off the coast of Patagonia.

It is ironical, when we consider the later events which transpired, that the mariners while they were at Port St. Julian, discovered by Ferdinand Magellan, found a gibbet where it was supposed the explorer had hung some of his mutinous crew. It was soon apparent that Thomas Doughty was taking the opportunity to intrigue against Drake, and stirring up discontent, even rebellion, among members of the crew. Hakluyt's account relates: "Our generall began to enquire diligently of the actions of Mr. Thomas Doughtie, and found them not to be such as he looked for, but tending rather to contention or mutinie, or some other disorder, whereby (without redresse) the successe of the voyage might greatly have been hazarded."

As already mentioned the Elizabethan was a superstitious age. Men believed in witchcraft and satanic powers. Drake himself believed that the terrible storms had been caused by some mysterious agency. Could it be that this friend Thomas Doughty, whom he had trusted, in reality was possessed of an evil spirit, and powers of witchcraft? There were not wanting enemies of Doughty, including Drake's own trumpeter, John Brewer, ready to warn his master that Doughty was opposed to the expedition and that he had been coarsely familiar with him.

He resolved to bring Doughty to trial, and during the proceedings it was proved that he had attempted to incite the seamen to mutiny. He rather rashly admitted that the Lord Treasurer Mylord Burghley had been cognizant of Drake's projects from the beginning and possessed a 'plot' of Drake's route.

"No, that he hath not," quoth Master Drake.

"He had it from me," parried Master Doughty.[21]

Though this affair even today remains mysterious and controversial, it is manifest that Drake considered himself betrayed. He was always a strict disciplinarian, and it seemed essential, if the voyage was to be a success, for Thomas Doughty to die. It is possible to accuse Drake of harshness, but it is difficult to understand what other course was open to him. Doughty expressed a wish to receive the Holy Communion, and after Drake and Doughty had dined together they both knelt before Mr. Fletcher in true Elizabethan fashion, receiving it from his hands. Then the executioner asked Doughty's forgiveness for the act he was about to do. A blinding flash, and Master Drake with a gesture held up the gory head to exclaim in the presence of the awed mariners: "Lo, this is the end of traitors."

When Drake and his company arrived at Valparaiso, a ship containing eight Spaniards and three negroes mistook them for fellow-countrymen. Beating their drums, they prepared a botija (jar) of wine of Chili to drink their healths. Their illusions were rudely shattered when Thomas Moone struck one of the Spaniards, crying at the same time, "Abaxo, Perro."* Another man was so amazed to see "persons of that quality" in those seas, that he crossed and blessed himself, while another swam ashore to the town of Santiago to warn the inhabitants of their arrival.

Aspects of Drake's famous circumnavigation of the globe will be discussed later in this work. The voyage is a marvellous epoch in English nautical history. Not only had Drake been the first Englishman to navigate the Pacific and Indian Oceans, but he had also visited the valuable islands used by the Portuguese. Its importance, too, lies in Drake's realization of the dream of Columbus to sail to the East by way of the West. After he had made a successful raid on Nombre de Dios, during 1573, he had climbed a rugged ridge, on which was a giant tree which could be climbed by steps. In an emotional mood the great-hearted seaman immediately prayed God "to give him life and leave to sail once in an English ship upon that sea". Calling to him one

---

* "Go down, dog."

of his captains, John Oxenham, a Plymouth man, he acquainted him with his resolution. John Oxenham impulsively made a hearty vow by God's grace to follow him. It was the error of this rash, but gallant, seaman to try and anticipate Drake, during 1575. After landing on a part of the isthmus, he launched a pinnace on a river flowing into the Pacific. Here he captured two Peruvian ships laden with silver and gold, only to be pursued by the Spaniards, who arrested him and after taking him to Lima hung him as a pirate.[22] Perhaps when he later proudly sailed in the Pacific Ocean Drake ruefully recalled the fate of John Oxenham.

Sir Philip Sidney, one of the greatest of the Elizabethans, a poet of genius, had all the restlessness of a man of action, though his intimate friend and mentor the scholar Hugo Languet once wrote him: "By nature and inclination you are formed for gentleness and soldiers cannot be kept to their duty without severity." Sidney with his idealistic longing to found a new world overseas, tried to join Martin Frobisher's expedition in 1577, and his enthusiasm may have been enhanced by his investment of £50 in this voyage. Languet wrote him in November doing his utmost to discourage his young friend.

And now I fear England will be tempted by the thirst for gold, and rush forth in a body to the islands which Frobisher has lately dis-covered and how much English blood do you suppose must be spilt in order that you may keep possession of them? ... Beware, I entreat you, lest the cursed hunger after gold which the poet speaks of creeps over that spirit of yours, into which nothing has hitherto been admitted but the love of goodness and the desire of earning the good will of all men. ... If these islands have fixed themselves deeply in your thoughts, turn them out before they overcome you.'[23]

Languet need not have worried that there existed the slightest danger that Sidney's spirit would be corrupted by the lust for gold.

Later during 1585 Philip Sidney restlessly again planned to join the expedition of Sir Francis Drake to the West Indies in 1585. He wished to serve as general of the land forces, while

Sir Francis Walsingham's other son-in-law, Christopher Carleill, was to have another military appointment. With Fulke Greville as companion Sidney hastened to Plymouth to join Drake. That night as the two friends lay in their hard beds in their cabin, with the fluttering candles waxing uneasily in their sockets, Greville described the displeasure which appeared in the gallant mariner Sir Francis Drake's face when he heard of their arrival, "as if our coming were both beyond his expectation and desire". In fact Drake had at once written an urgent letter to the Queen, informing her of Sidney's arrival, and Elizabeth now commanded Sir Philip to return to Court. Drake with his instinctive knowledge of human nature knew that Sidney would not be suited for this sort of appointment. Yet he was keenly interested in American colonization, and Richard Hakluyt made a dedication to him in his first collection of *Voyages*, published in 1582.

Henry Carey, Lord Hunsdon,* a maternal cousin of Queen Elizabeth, whom she was attached to (she called him 'my Harry'), was the patron of Thomas Cavendish (Candish). There is a letter from this great navigator, who hailed from Trimley in Suffolk, relating to his famous voyage round the world and written to Hunsdon.[24] Cavendish informed his patron:

> It hath pleased the Almighty to suffer mee to circompasse the whole globe of the world, entring in at the Streight of Magellan, and returning by the Cape de Buena Esperanza. . . . I navigated alongst the Coast of Chili, Peru, and Nueva Espanna, where I made great spoiles: I burnt and sunke 19 sailes of ships small and great. . . . I sailed along the Ilands of the Malucos, where among some of the heathen people I was well intreated, where our countrey men may have trade as freely as the Portugals, if they will themselves. From thence I passed by the Cape of Buena Esperanza, and found out by the way homeward the island of S. Helena where the Portugals use to relieve themselves.

There is the customary fulsome tribute to the Queen. "All which

* Lord Chamberlain at Elizabeth's Court. He had done her some service during the Northern Rebellion (1570).

services with my selfe I humbly prostrate at her Majesties feet, desiring the Almighty long to continue her reigne among us."[25] In his play *Rosalynde** (1590), dedicated to Lord Hunsdon, Thomas Lodge a sailor, mentions that during a voyage to Terceira (Azores) and the Canaries "to beguile the time with labour, I writ this book: rough, as hatched in the storms of the ocean, and feathered in the surges of many perilous seas".† Later, Lodge embarked on Cavendish's terrible last voyage to the South Seas, the Philippines, and the coast of China. They sailed from Plymouth on 26th August 1591. He wrote *A Margarite of America* whilst his ship ploughed her lonely way through the Straits of Magellan. Thomas Fuller wrote of Cavendish: "Pity, so illustrious a life should have so obscure a death."

It was customary for the navigators to name landmarks in honour of their patrons. For instance, during Frobisher's second voyage he named a harbour and an island‡ after Anne, Countess of Warwick, third wife of his patron and an intimate friend of the Queen. Thomas Ellis relates in his account of Martin Frobisher's third voyage that the mariners built a little house in the Countess of Warwick's island. They furnished it "with many kinds of trifles, as Pinnes, Points, Laces, Glasses, Kombes, Babes on horseback and on foote, with innumerable other such fansies and Toyes".

To my mind George Clifford, third Earl of Cumberland, an Elizabethan aristocrat and a great buccaneer, is one of the most attractive of the celebrated seamen. The Queen herself may be described as Cumberland's patron, for she lent him ships for some of his voyages, although she refused to loan him money on one occasion. According to Lady Anne Clifford, who greatly admired her father, he always shared the privations of the meanest (most humble) seamen. He was never too proud to mend his own main mast, to reef in a sail, nor to divide his share of food and drink with others. Like Charles Lord Howard of Effingham, he was a

---

* The original of Shakespeare's *As You Like It*.
† *William Shakespeare* by A. L. Rowse, p. 304.
‡ Warwicks Anne Island and Sound.

thoughtful and considerate commander of the seamen in his care. It must be admitted that the handsome Cumberland, for whom the Queen had a particular affection, was very extravagant. Lady Anne Clifford tells us that her father had "an extream love for horse races, tiltings, Bowling matches and Shooting, and that such expensive sports did contribute more to the wasting of his estate". His portrait by Nicholas Hilliard reveals a handsome face full of character, and Cumberland wears a glove mounted with jewels in his cap, for he was the Queen's Champion. It is related that the Queen had dropped her glove on one occasion, and we suspect that it was done on purpose. He was born in 1558, when Elizabeth ascended the throne, and was to survive his royal mistress three years.

In 1591 the Queen wrote Cumberland a letter, which reveals her ironical humour. Cumberland was on one of his privateering voyages, and Her Majesty was a partner, for she had lent him one of her ships, the *Garland*. Elizabeth wrote him:

Right Trusty and well-beloved Cousin, we greet you well. It may seem strange to you that we should once vouchsafe to trouble our thoughts with any care for any person of roguish condition, being always disposed rather to command others to chasten men of that profession. But such is our pleasure at this time . . . as we are well content to take occasion by our letters to express our great desire to hear of your well-doing . . . hoping well of good success in the action now you have in hand. . . . Provided always you do not requite this our good meaning with betraying our extraordinary care of you to our Knight Marshal here, who may by this our partiality to you abroad grow bold hereafter in favouring them at home whom we would not have him suffer to pass uncorrected for divers their misdemeanours. And so do we for this time (with this aforesaid caution) make an end, assuring you of our most princely care for your safety and daily wishes of your safe return, whereof we shall be right glad as any friend you have. Dated at our Court of Bishop's Waltham, whither we are returned from our progress where we have spent some part of this summer in viewing our fortifications at Portsmouth and other of our principal towns along the sea coast.

The letter has the superscription: "Your Very Loving Sovereign, Elizabeth R." No Queen was more hard-working than Elizabeth, and in her insistence in inspecting the vital sea fortifications she resembled Charles II, who thought nothing of rising at 5 a.m. to go to Chatham for the same purpose.

Elizabeth's strength as a queen rests in the vital fact that she never married. That she sometimes longed to experience the emotions of a normal woman, we can have little doubt. Especially during the early days of her reign when she was in love with "her sweet Robin", Lord Robert Dudley, and was wont to stroke his neck on halcyon summer days. Perhaps she submitted herself to Dudley as her lover for a while, aware in her inmost being that she could never satisfy the needs of a normal woman, such as childbearing and domesticity. Her doting behaviour with the unattractive Duc D'Alençon, merely signified the frustration of a sexually dissatisfied woman. That she inspired her renowned seamen was partly owing to her unmarried state, for they vied with one another by means of their discoveries to obtain her favour. Her reply to Robert Dudley, Earl of Leicester, father of an illegitimate famous seaman,* on one occasion inferred that she resented being ruled by any man. "God's death, my Lord," she told him, "I have wisht you well, but my favour is not so lockt up for you, that others shall not partake thereof." As Sir Robert Naunton relates, she preferred to rule by factions.

* Sir Robert Dudley.

Notes

CHAPTER IV

1 *The Worthies of England,* p. 75.
2 Conyers Reed, *Sir Francis Walsingham.*
3 Katherine Garvin ed., *The Great Tudors.*
   Conyers Reed, *Sir Francis Walsingham.*
4 *Mr. Secretary Walsingham and the Policy of Queen Elizabeth,* Vol. II.
5 *Calendar of State Papers. Colonial East Indies,* p. 11.
6 A. L. Rowse, *The Expansion of Elizabethan England.*
7 *Calendar of State Papers. Colonial Service, E. Indies,* p. 51.
8 *Ibid.*
9 Sir Harry Nicolas, *Memoirs of Sir Christopher Hatton. The Life and Times of Sir Christopher Hatton.*
10 *Hakluyt's Voyages* (Everyman Edition), Vol. 6, p. 79.
11 Conyers Reed, *Mr. Secretary Walsingham and the Policy of Queen Elizabeth,* Vol. II.
12 Richard Deacon, *John Dee* (1968).
13 *Ibid.*
14 From the original manuscripts in the Ashmolean Museum, Oxford. Edited by James Orchard Halliwell.
15 Dee's latest biographer, Richard Deacon, refutes it.
16 John Buxton, *Sir Philip Sidney and the English Renaissance* (1954).
17 *Ibid.*
18 Eric St. John Brooks, *Sir Christopher Hatton.*
19 Richard Hakluyt, *Voyages* (Everyman Edition), Vol. V, p.261.
20 MS. 61.
21 Eric St. John Brooks, *Sir Christopher Hatton.*

22   Account by Lopez Vaz, Richard Hakluyt, *Voyages* (Everyman Edition), Vol. VII, pp. 64, 65, 66.

23   C. Henry Warner, *Sir Philip Sidney*.

24   Richard Hakluyt, *Voyages* (Everyman Edition), Vol. VIII, p. 278.

25   *Ibid.* Vol. VIII, p. 278. Account by John Jane, a friend of John Davis.

CHAPTER V

Philip II of Spain and John Hawkins

If Philip II of Spain had been alive today, he would have found a happy niche for himself as a civil servant. He had the mind of a bureaucrat, for he was hardworking, methodical, precise, and gave too much attention to detail. The Venetian ambassador Michael Soriano described him: "He is small in stature, but he is so well made, so well proportioned and dresses with such good taste and chooses his clothes so cleverly that one could not imagine anything more perfect." His constitution was so delicate that he was compelled to live with regularity. Though his appetite was substantial, he had no taste for fish or fruit, "nor anything which might engender ill humour". He had known a fleeting happiness during his third marriage to Elizabeth of Valois,* but in later life he became morbid and morose.

Though he ruled a mighty empire, he preferred to live in his sombre palace of the Escorial near Madrid, begun in 1563 by Juan Bautista de Toleda and finished twenty years later by Juan de

---

* Philip's four wives were: (1) Maria of Portugal;
                              (2) Queen Mary I of England;
                              (3) Elizabeth de Valois;
                              (4) Queen Ann, mother of Philip III.

Herrera, a pupil of Michelangelo. Built to honour God and St. Lawrence, Philip called his palace 'San Lorenzo el Real'. To build the Escorial, Philip, who had a taste for art, ordered that silver chalices and golden candelabra should be brought from Milan, then a part of his empire, tapestries from the Spanish Netherlands, a marvellous variety of woods from the New World; marble from the Sierra Nevada (California), steel from Toledo, and the works of Titian and Tintoretto from Venice.[2]

There he sat working in his austere study, brooding on the perfidy of "his sister the English Queen", swamped by an avalanche of papers daily arriving from the Spanish dominions of Naples, Milan, Mexico and Peru, and other places. From London his suave, able Ambassador Guzman de Silva would report to him about the suspected voyages of John Hawkins of Plymouth, and the piratical activities of the evil Thomas Cobham. The Kings' habit was to cover the margins of the reports in his small spidery handwriting. When he wished to remember a particular point he would write "*ojo*"—attention. When Guzman de Silva wrote the King about Hawkins' intended voyage to Guinea, Philip wrote in the margin of the despatch, "advise the Council of the Indies of this and also of that which is contained in some other letters on the same subject".

He was sensual and introspective but cold by temperament and rarely showed any passion. Augustine Nani, the Venetian Ambassador in Spain, has recorded that the King on one occasion towards the end of his life[3] betrayed a great deal of emotion when referring to Elizabeth of England. Seizing a candelabra he declared vehemently that he would pawn even that in order to be avenged on the Queen, and that he was resolved to accomplish this. Perhaps this cold, passionless man had gradually learnt to hate Elizabeth. Once he had planned a political marriage with her, now he seldom thought of her without feeling vindictive. Francesco Soranzo, Venetian Ambassador in Spain, who wrote a penetrating character study of Philip II after his death in 1598, refers to him: "He was a Prince who fought with gold rather than with steel, by his brain rather than by his arms. . . . He was one of the richest Princes the world has ever seen, yet he has left the revenues of the Kingdom and of the Crown burdened with about a million of debts. . . ."

During the 1560s Elizabeth and Philip were anxious so far as possible to maintain amicable diplomatic relations. Guzman de Silva, a resourceful diplomat and the Spanish King's representative in London during that period, reported an interview with Queen Elizabeth when she had come in her state barge from Greenwich to Westminster during July 1564. On the 24th Guzman de Silva begged the Queen to inquire what voyages were to be undertaken by Captain John Hawkins of Plymouth "and to make him give assurance that he would not plunder Your Majesty's subjects". The Queen's reply was extremely gracious, but it is doubtful whether she would commit herself in any way. Actually John Hawkins on his second voyage sailed from Plymouth on 18th October to the coast of Guinea and to the Indies. His fleet included the *Jesus of Lubeck*, the *Tiger*, a bark of 50 tons, and the *Swallow*. John Sparke[4] relates that an unfortunate accident occurred, at the cutting of the foresail, when one of the officers was killed. During this expedition Hawkins managed to induce the Spanish officials to trade with him, for the law excluding foreign vessels from trading with Spanish colonists in the Indies was not strictly enforced. Guzman de Silva during the autumn of 1565 reported to King Philip that John Hawkins had returned to Plymouth. During his stay on the island of Santo Domingo he had traded with the Spaniards, and had brought over to England over 50,000 ducats in gold, pearls, hides and sugar as the payment for the slaves he had sold. Guzman de Silva was in favour of trying to prevent such expeditions in future. One day during October (1565) the Spanish Ambassador encountered Hawkins at the palace when the sea captain told him that he had commerce in various parts of the Indies and that the Spanish Governors had given him permission to do so. Hawkins agreed to show de Silva their certificates.

To gain more information the wily de Silva asked Hawkins to dine with him. He formed a favourable opinion, and reported to the Spanish King: "Hawkins is considered a good sailor, and he appears to be a clever man."[5] Even as early as 1566 it would appear that de Silva was plotting to entice Hawkins into the service of the King of Spain. Perhaps de Silva was aware that the mariner would occasionally refer to "his old master, the King of Spain", signifying that he had done some service as a pilot for Philip, whilst in England eleven years before. Little did he know the man. "He is not satisfied with things here," he told Philip II, "and I will tell him he is not a fit man for this country, but would be much better off if he went and served Your Majesty, where he would find plenty to do as other Englishmen have done."[6] Again he urged in his letters that the best policy was to get Hawkins out of the country. By doing so the sea captain could not teach others, "for they have good ships and are greedy folk, with more freedom than is good for them". It is almost certain that Hawkins was acting as a sort of unofficial intelligence agent for the Queen and Sir William Cecil, but it must be remembered that England and Spain were still officially at peace. Cecil confidentially told de Silva that he had no liking for the slave-trading ventures of Hawkins, and was unwilling to invest in them. By the early summer of 1566 de Silva suspected that Hawkins was in reality fitting out another expedition to the Indies, and not for the purpose of "serving Your Majesty", as he wrote the King of Spain. Hawkins indeed caused Philip II deep offence. He warned Sir Thomas Chaloner the English Ambassador, who was half-Spanish, that if such expeditions were repeated, mischief would come of it.

To Philip, the actions of Hawkins, Grenville and Drake, and the other seamen, amounted to piracy. He wrote to his Ambassador in London on 12th August 1566: "You will use every effort with the Queen and Council to stop the robberies which English pirates are constantly committing on our subjects, which should not be committed, since between me and the Queen such perfect peace and concord exist, and it is not right that the violence and insolence of subjects should cast any shadow thereupon."[7] Queen Elizabeth in her interviews with de Silva showed her customary resourcefulness and cleverness. She said that she was aware that some of her Privy Council had a financial interest in Hawkins' voyages, but they did not intend him to go to any place forbidden by King Philip. Nor had his intention been to do so. He had been forced, however, by contrary winds to these places where he traded with the licence and permission of the governors. Until she had been satisfied on this point she had refused to see him. Sir William Cecil* asked de Silva to furnish the English government with a memorandum of the places where it was forbidden to trade without King Philip's licence. His answer did not apparently satisfy the Ambassador, for he told Cecil that if these people, meaning the seamen, were not prevented from going to the prohibited places, he would be obliged to make a formal protest to the Council on the King of Spain's behalf. For the time being Philip seems to have been satisfied, for he instructed de Silva at the end of 1566 to thank the Queen for complying with his request, and the Ambassador made a special journey to Nonsuch† in Surrey—a favourite palace of Elizabeth's—for this purpose.

There is an interesting allusion to John Hawkins' third slave-trading voyage in 1567. The Spanish Ambassador refers to the Queen's ship the *Jesus de Lobie*, (almost certainly the *Jesus of Lubeck*, which formed part of the expedition). "The robberies at sea still continue," wrote de Silva, "as do also the efforts to find a remedy for this ancient grievance."

In February 1564 Thomas Cobham—a wild, lawless man for whom it is difficult to feel any sympathy—with two ships hailing from Newcastle, committed an act of piracy on a Spanish ship belonging to a Señor Martin Saeuz de Chaves. This Spanish ship was on its way from Flanders to Spain, with a cargo valued at 80,000 ducats. It also contained forty convicts being sent for hard labour in Philip of Spain's galleys. Luis Roman, in making his petition to Queen Elizabeth for redress stated: "They attacked the ship with artillery, as if they were mortal enemies, and killed

---

* Cecil was not raised to the peerage as Lord Burghley until spring 1571.
† Elizabeth was frequently there in the last ten years of her reign.

7

a brother of the owner." Guzman de Silva told the King of Spain that Thomas Cobham had been lodged in the Tower. When the Spanish Ambassador in an interview with Elizabeth, referred to the large number of pirates who still infested the seas, the Queen parried (she was an artist at this), saying that she believed many of the pirates were Scotsmen, who spoke English to avoid discovery. The Ambassador took the opportunity to press on the Queen the importance of punishing Thomas Cobham. He had powerful connections at Court, who were trying hard to get the pirate released. During July, Cobham, when tried for these offences, was partly acquitted by a jury of twelve men. Evidently it was clear to the Judge of the Admiralty that the jury were prejudiced, for he did not submit the whole case to them. The Spanish Ambassador took good care to keep the Queen well informed about the proceedings, for she peremptorily ordered her Privy Council to charge the members of the jury with giving a false judgement. They were later fined £20 each, also to six months' imprisonment and "to be put in the pillory with papers stuck on them like a cuirass".

In a retrial of his case Cobham was found guilty. His sentence in its refined cruelty sounds medieval, and after all the Elizabethans could be bestial enough. After being taken back to the Tower he was ordered to be stripped entirely naked, his head shaved, and the soles of his feet beaten. His back was to rest on a sharp stone, while a piece of artillery was to be placed on his stomach inflicting terrible pain on the wretch, though not heavy enough to cause death. His nourishment during his torment was to be 3 grams weight of barley and the filthiest water in the prison. One can conjecture that nobody could survive these tortures long. It was fortunate for Cobham that he had influential relations and that he in fact did not have to submit to this punishment after all. There were, however, many people without influential friends, who were subjected to this barbarous and degrading torture.

Thomas Cobham's brother, Lord Cobham, Lord Warden of the Cinque Ports, had no sympathy for his crimes, for he was pro-

Spanish. His wife Lady Cobham came stealthily to see de Silva, accompanied by other relations, though she feared the Queen's anger lest she should discover her visit. Most of the Cobham family were pro-Spanish, but their main anxiety was to prevent this disgrace to their house. They pleaded with the Ambassador to intercede with the Queen to suspend the execution of the sentence for some time until they had written to King Philip himself to beg him to use his influence to have the sentence waived. The Ambassador expressed every sympathy with Lady Cobham, but assured her that he was prevented from complying with her requests. Thomas Radcliffe, Earl of Sussex, a nobleman of forthright honesty, later spoke to de Silva on Thomas Cobham's behalf, informing him that he was a near kinsman of his own and of many of the highest people in the land. De Silva wrote his sovereign: "This Cobham is a bad man and a great heretic as I am assured, but I do not think they will carry out the sentence."[8] The suave and courteous de Silva had been an excellent appointment as Spanish Ambassador in London, but Philip II, possibly determined to adopt a more aggressive policy against England, sent during May 1568 as his successor Guerau de Spes, a haughty, indiscreet firebrand, and Catalan knight, who hated Cecil and lacked all de Silva's subtlety. All the same Hawkins had been clever enough during 1566 to deceive de Silva as to his feigned intentions to serve the King of Spain. This great navigator from Plymouth was the first to challenge the Spanish hegemony on the high seas, and to demonstrate in no uncertain fashion that the English outmatched the Spaniards.[9] Philip blundered in sending Guerau de Spes as his envoy to England.

There is an interesting letter from Antonio de Gueras, a Spanish merchant in London, revealing that Thomas Cobham, together with thirty other gentlemen of high position, was involved in the Duke of Norfolk's conspiracy concerning the Queen of Scots in May 1572.

Guerau de Spes' letters to his master during January 1569 sometimes refer to Courtney and Hawkins, who had captured three Flemish sloops and a Spanish ship carrying valuable cargoes and brought them to the port of Plymouth and elsewhere on the Devon coast.

It would be difficult to find two characters more different than Philip II and his great antagonist Francis Drake. At least both Drake and the Spanish king had one thing in common, a passionate conviction that God was on their side.[10] Philip II* was about six years older than Elizabeth I, and fourteen years older than Drake, who was born about 1541 at Crowndale near Tavistock in Devon, the son of a tenant farmer who was an ardent lay preacher and who went to live in Kent with his large family. His god-father was Francis Russell, afterwards Earl of Bedford, who gave him his name Francis.[11] Drake's father Edmund was appointed chaplain to the naval dockyard at Chatham near Gillingham. The early influences in the life of the Devon seaman were very marked. Drake was as ardent a Protestant as Philip II was a devoted papist. One of Drake's shipmates, Morgan Tillert, later testified during the Inquisition in Mexico that Drake during his early manhood had done his utmost to convert his companions.[12] This Welshman sometimes known as Michael Morgan later confessed that he had become a heretic by the persuasion of his shipmate Francis Drake. Drake learnt seamanship from his experiences in the coasting trade from an old skipper, who seems to have been attached to him, for he bequeathed him his boat. Two of Drake's qualities were his flashes of opportunism amounting to genius and his marked egotism throughout his life. Philip was slow in coming to a decision, mystical and devious, while Drake was an extrovert, and his mind worked rapidly, sparkling with inspiration. It is a defect in Philip's character that, profoundly mystical as he was, he was incapable of understanding the great works of El Greco, a contemporary then working at Toledo. The austere Escorial situated near Madrid on the southwestern slopes of the Guadarrama has nothing in common with Buckland Abbey, the later Rennaisance home of Sir Francis Drake, to some extent the work of Sir Richard Grenville. To visit the

* Born at Valladolid, 1527.

two places is to glimpse for a horrifying moment the gulf which existed between the minds of the Elizabethan navigators and of the lonely Spanish king, a brooding fatalist ruling over his mighty empire.

Guerau de Spes was succeeded as Spanish Ambassador in London by Don Bernardino de Mendoza, who often refers to "Drake the pirate" in his letter to his master. He warned Philip on 20th September 1577: "As they carry on their evil plans with great calculation, there is a suspicion that Drake the pirate is to go to Scotland with some little vessels and enter into a convenient port, for the purpose of getting possession of the prince of Scotland* for a large sum of money; where upon he will bring him hither convoyed by the ships that are there."[13]

Six months later at the end of March 1578 when Drake was engaged in his circumnavigation of the world, Mendoza informed King Philip: "I have also heard that six weeks before Christmas, Captain Drake with four or five ships left here for Nombre de Dios and the land of Camarones (Cameroons) which voyage he made before with Captain Hawkins very successfully, and fought with Pero Menendez. These ships were fitted out here on the pretence that they were going to Alexandria for Currants." In September 1579 there arrived a courier from Seville with the disastrous intelligence that Drake the Corsair had passed through the Straits of Magellan and had stolen in the Southern Sea gold and silver, worth 200,000 ducats, belonging to His Majesty, and 400,000 ducats, the property of Spanish merchants. Relations between England and Spain were now extremely bad, and Mendoza strongly protested to Queen Elizabeth about the prizes taken by English pirates from the King of Spain's subjects. "I only get to know of the cases through Englishmen, as the owners themselves do not reveal their losses," Mendoza told Philip II.

After Drake's return from his voyage round the world, Mendoza pressed for frequent audiences with Queen Elizabeth to protest against the robbery of Spanish treasures and for the

* James VI, who was to become James I of England in 1603.

Queen to punish Drake. On one occasion, on 20th October 1581, he came over by boat to Richmond Palace to demand that the Queen should restore the Spanish treasure. Elizabeth was suffering from a pain in her hip and remained seated in her couch, rather than coming forward a few paces from her dais to greet the Ambassador, which was her usual custom. After commiserating with Elizabeth concerning her ailment, the Ambassador came to his real business. The Queen's shrill voice resounded throughout the audience chamber, so that Mendoza stung to the quick, possibly, used stronger expressions than he had intended. "Madame," he was unwise enough to warn her, "if you will not listen to words, we must try cannon, and see if you can hear that." The Queen's quiet, relentless purpose was more to be feared than her terrible, hysterical Tudor rages. She told Mendoza that if he spoke like that, she would put him in a place from which he could not speak at all.[14] The Ambassador, now fearful for his own safety, hastily murmured some suitable compliment. "Nobody can gainsay so beautiful a lady." Mendoza reported that the vain Queen actually smiled, and seemed to soften, but she was only playing a part and was not really deceived. Whatever she may have been in her earlier life, she was not vain as an elderly woman. On one occasion in 1596 when a Venetian diplomat, Francesco Grandenigo had an audience of Her Majesty, she told him slightly pathetically: "My brother the King of France (Henri IV) writes to me that I am to show you the most beautiful things in this kingdom, and the first thing you have seen is the ugliest, myself."[15] But that was fourteen years later. Now Mendoza heard her say *sotto voce* as she managed to rise and go over to a window recess: "Would to God that each had his own and all were content." So, Mendoza fumed and threatened, and referred to Sir Francis Drake as "the master-thief of the unknown world", but could accomplish little.

When that indomitable Elizabethan, Sir Philip Sidney, was mortally wounded at Zutphen in 1587 and died shortly afterwards at Arnheim, Mendoza was magnanimous enough to regret it. He wrote that howsoever he was glad King Philip his master had lost in a private gentleman a dangerous enemy to his Estate, yet he could not but lament to see Christendom deprived of so rare a light in these cloudy times and bewail poor widow England that, having been many years in breeding one eminent spirit, was in a moment bereaved of him by the hands of a villain.[16] And Mendoza hated all heretics.

After Elizabeth had created Drake a knight on board the *Golden Hind*, she wrote a letter of importance to Philip of Spain, which is tantamount to Britain's first declaration of freedom of the seas. "The use of the sea and air", she asserted, "is common to all, and neither Nature, nor use nor custom permit any possession thereof." As for Philip, a brooding resentment against 'El Draco', the impetuous, bearded seaman, obsessed his secret thoughts, like a cancer, and he offered a reward of £40,000 for his capture, dead or alive.

Bernardino de Mendoza continued to report to Philip concerning the discoveries of the English navigators. In the early spring of 1578* he mentions the second voyage of Martin Frobisher. "The land they discovered, they say, is near the country called Labrador, which joins Newfoundland where the Biscay men go in search of whales. This may well be believed, as they say the natives they saw are much like the savages found there, and dressed in the same way with the skins of seals." Eighteen months later he told his master that Humphrey Gilbert[17] ('Ongi' as Mendoza refers to him) had landed in Galicia in Spain where he had sacked the hermitage. Later Mendoza was especially interested in the colonizing voyages of 'Ongi' Gilbert when it was proposed that two spendthrift Catholic gentlemen, Sir George Peckham and Sir Thomas Gerrard, should be given permission to settle in Florida. More of this later. It is more than possible that Martin Frobisher during the middle 1570s may have intrigued to serve Spain, for a Spanish correspondent, Antonio de Guaras, reported that the navigator had decided to go to Flanders to offer his services to His Excellency the Governor of the Spanish Netherlands: "He is

* 31st March.

the best seaman and the bravest in this country," wrote Guaras, "and his great name and valour will be already known in Flanders." Drake would hardly have agreed with this.

The Spanish authorities usually refer to Drake as "the English Corsair" in their accounts of his daring depredations on the cities of Cartagena, Santo Domingo, and elsewhere in the Caribbean during his voyage of 1585–86. It is fascinating to study the accounts of the raids on the Spanish cities from their point of view, and Miss Irene Wright, who has done much diligent research among the original archives of the Indies at Seville, has published a book on this subject.[18] It is clear that the fiery Devon seaman was an object of terror to the Spanish people dwelling in these islands, courageous though they often were, and the importance of Drake's voyages during these years prior to the invasion of the Armada will be discussed in a later chapter. This expedition was to mark in the eyes of Francis Drake's contemporaries a further stage in the duel or deadly conflict between the seaman and his antagonist, Philip II of Spain.

Notes

CHAPTER V

1 Fox-Bourne, *English Seamen under the Tudors*, Vol. 2, p. 152.
2 Lacey Baldwin Smith, *The Elizabethan Epic*.
3 23rd July 1596. 473. *Calendar of State Papers*, Venetian.
4 E. J. Payne ed., *Voyages of Elizabethan Seamen*, p. 9.
5 *Spanish State Papers* Domestic.
6 *Ibid.*
7 *Ibid.*
8 *Ibid.*
9 Conyers Read, *Mr. Secretary Cecil and Queen Elizabeth*.
10 Ernle Bradford, *Francis Drake*.
11 Purchas, IV, 1179.
12 James A. Williamson, *The Age of Drake*, p. 72. The Trial of
   Michael Morgan alias Morgan Tillert copied by O. R. G. Conway.
13 20th September 1577. B.M. *Add. MSS.* 26,056b.
14 Elizabeth Jenkinson, *Elizabeth the Great*.
15 *Calendar of State Papers*, Venetian MSS. Vol. IV, 505.
16 C. H. Warren, *Sir Philip Sidney*, p. 226.
17 *State Papers*, Spanish.
18 Irene A. Wright, *Further English Voyages to Spanish America 1583–1594*.

CHAPTER VI

Sufferings of the Mariners

The narrators in the immortal epics of Richard Hakluyt's voyages are often simple seamen, but one is struck by the vividness and sincerity of their writings. They even attain grandeur on occasions, as it were by accident. Such are the accounts of John Hortop or Hartop, a Lincolnshire seaman (already mentioned), who served during the third voyage of John Hawkins in 1567, and who had the ill-fortune to be captured by the Spaniards at San Juan de Ulua in Mexico. Remembering his sufferings after thirty-two years and the cruelties practised by the Inquisition when men were flogged and burnt alive, Hortop begins his narrative: "Not untruely nor without cause said Job the faithful servant of God (whom the Sacred Scriptures tell us, to have dwelt in the land of Hus) that man being borne of a woman, living a short time, is replenished with many miseries: which some know by reading of histories, many by the view of other calamities, and I by experience in myself."[1] In the first edition of Hakluyt's *Voyages*, there is a lively account of the adventures of David Ingram, another mariner, who took part in this expedition. Unfortunately Hakluyt later had reason to suspect the veracity of Ingram's tales, and the story was not included in later editions.

Then there is the narrative of Miles Phillips, even more vivid and arresting, who also served during Hawkins' third voyage.

When captured he was a boy of only fourteen. After his arrest he was taken with some other seamen to Mexico, where he experienced kindness and courtesy from the Spaniards and also gross cruelty.

And so travailled on our way towards Mexico till we came to a toune within forty leagues of Mexico, named Mestitlan, where is a house of blacke friers. ... The friers sent us meat from the house ready dressed and the friers, and the men and women used us very courteously, and gave us some shirts and other such things as we lacked. ... The next morning we departed from there with our two Spaniards and Indian guard: of these two Spaniards the one was an aged man, who all the way did very courteously intreate us, and would carefully go before to provide for us both meat and things necessary to the uttermost of his power; the other was a young man who all the way travelled with us, and never departed from us, who was a very cruel caitive, and he caried a javeline in his hand, and sometimes, when as our men with very feebleness and faintnesse were not able to goe so fast as he required them, he would take his javelin in both his hands, and strike them with the same betweene the necke and the shoulders so violently, that he would strike them downe; then would he cry, and say, Marchad, marchad Ingleses perros, Luterianos enemigos de Dios: which is as much to say in English, as March, march on you English dogges, Lutherans, enemies to God.

We can almost hear the anguished cries of the wretched seamen and the frenzied curses of the young Spaniard as he lashed them with his whip. More cruelties have been perpetrated in the name of religion than anything else. It is difficult for us to imagine, but in that age of intolerance men sometimes even supposed that they were obeying God's will in inflicting the horrors of the Inquisition on the heretics. Such was Philip II of Spain, a typical Spaniard, who at least when in England as the consort of Mary I had urged moderation in religious matters on his fanatical wife and her ministers.[2]

Francis Fletcher described a storm at sea in this manner: "The seas were rolled up from the depths as if it had been a scroll of parchment."[9] And William Strachey's graphic description:

"The Sea swelled above the clouds and gave battle to Heaven. It could not be said to raine; the waters like whole rivers did flood in the ayre."[4] And again his powerful description with its suggestion of terror of a storm shrouding Bermuda in its strange eerie light when the fleet of Sir Thomas Gates and Sir George Somers in 1609 was wrecked upon its shores:

> the clouds gathering thick upon us and the winds, singing and whistling most unusually ... day turned into night, the blackness of the heaven ... the strange light that appeared upon the mainmast, shooting from shroud to shroud, all the pumps continually going and the ship having to be run ashore upon the island commonly called 'the Devils Islands', feared and avoided of all sea travellers alive, above any other place in the world.[5]

The sea expresses every emotion known to mankind. She is at once gentle, benignant, fickle, ever mutable, beautiful, remorseless, passionate and cruel. To the Elizabethan seamen battling with the elements, and haunted by superstitious fears, she was full of terror, like a siren mistress beckoning and enticing them to their own destruction. Small wonder if the seamen were not notoriously superstitious. William Strachey* relates that Sir George Somers whilst on the watch beheld an apparition of a little round light, like a faint star, trembling and streaming along with a sparkling blaze ... tempting to settle as it were upon any of the four shrouds.[6]

Hark to the groans and sufferings of the seamen during Lord Cumberland's third voyage, so vividly described by Edward Wright, who accompanied the expedition as engineer, master and mathematician. Wright later published in 1599 a work entitled *Certaine Errors in Navigation*. The sailors suffered excruciably from scarcity of water. At first each man drank only half a pint at a meal, then they were reduced to a quarter of a pint and finally as water became unobtainable, they were given three or four spoonsful of vinegar at their meals so scarce did water

---

* Somewhat doubtfully identified with a William Strachey of Saffron Waldron in Essex, who married in 1588 and was alive in 1620. William Strachey later became a colonist and writer on Virginia.

become that every effort was made to catch the rain. Wright himself was vigilant enough, waiting parched with thirst at a scupper hole with "dishes, pots, cannes and jarres", eager to drink the water, foul as it was, to slake his thirst.[7] Wright tells us that the Spanish prisoners—poor devils—"would crave of us, for the love of God, but so much water as they could hold in the hollow of their hand". The seamen even put bullets in their mouths to alleviate their thirst. There were constant cries for water, and men lay exhausted and emaciated until they finally died. Some were thrown overboard, "and more men were lost from this cause than had died in the whole expedition". At last one December day a mighty storm in the heavens raged, but the water caught in the ship was discovered to be so bitter and muddy, owing to the ship's dirt, that sugar was needed to "sweeten it withall". It is a pity, perhaps, to destroy the romantic illusions about the Elizabethan seamen possessed by many today.

When we read John Jane's account of Thomas Cavendish's last voyage in 1591, we are struck by his realism. Jane was a Cornishman, who relates that he only went on this voyage for the sake of his friend the navigator Captain John Davis, who commanded the *Desire*. Off Cape Froward (aptly named), near the Straits of Magellan, the mariners were forced to endure terrible storms and incessant snow. Many of the seamen died "with cursed famine, and miserable cold, not having wherewith to cover their bodies, nor to fill their bellies, but living by muskles, water and weeds of the sea, with a small reliefs of the ship's store in meale sometimes". Instead of giving any possible medical attention to the many sick men in the galleon, they were cast ignominiously and uncharitably ashore where they ended their lives in utter destitution; "Master Cavendish (Candish) all this while being abord the *Desire*", acording to the account of Jane who certainly had no liking for him.

Then there is the classic account of Edward Haie of Sir Humphrey Gilbert's last ill-fated colonizing voyage to Newfoundland, when Gilbert lost his life on the *Squirrel*, "sitting abaft with a booke in his hand". His famous last words have been often quoted by historians, but bear repetition. "We are as neere to heaven by sea as by land."[8] Haie relates that seamen, who had served all their lives on the ocean, had never witnessed more outrageous seas. When the mariners saw "an apparition of a little fire by night, known to them as Castor and Pollux", they gloomily predicted that it was a malevolent sign signifying further tempests.

It is true that the Elizabethan seaman was often both desperate and unscrupulous. Many of the crew were inexperienced boys, and the great majority were under thirty. As we have seen, disease was only too prevalent, and most people considered that illness was a visitation of God upon sinful men. Sir John Hawkins and his son, Sir Richard, were among the few commanders who strove by practical measures to improve the lot of the seamen.

Every schoolboy is familiar with the story of the last fight of the *Revenge*, and the death of Sir Richard Grenville (1591). As told by Sir Walter Ralegh—a masterly descriptive writer—it still excites us today as it inspired Sir Richard's contemporaries. In his account Ralegh wrote:

> All the powder of the *Revenge* to the last barrell was now spent, all her pikes broken, fortie of her best men slane, and the most part of the rest hurt. . . . Sir Richard commanded the master gunner, whom hee knew to be a most resolute man, to split and sinke the shippe; that thereby nothing might remaine of glory or victory to the Spaniards.[9]

The hazards of a seaman's life have been stressed, but there were calm, uneventful periods when commanders were compelled to use all their ingenuity to keep their men occupied. Sir Richard Hawkins, for instance, relates in his *Observations** that during his long voyage to Brazil in 1594 he organized sports on shore, such as the West Country sport of hurling,† in which the bachelors were the opponents of the married men. One day whilst on shore the seamen disturbed a large number of ursine seals (Sir Richard

* pp. 76–87.
† Hurling is still played today at St. Columb near Padstow on the north coast of Cornwall. Daniel Defoe in *A Tour Through Great Britain* described it as "a brutish and furious game".

calls them sea wolves) as they lazily lay sleeping. The men were actually climbing a hill when the seal sentinel with a shrill cry awakened his fellows. Hawkins humorously relates that when the sea wolves charged the seamen: "Not a man that withstood them escaped the overthrow, and after they had recovered the water, they did as it were, scorn us, defied us, and danced before us." At other times the seamen found diversion in collecting pearls in considerable quantities from mussles.[10] They were found to be a very refreshing drink. Sir Richard Hawkins' *Observations* abounds with curious scientific information.

The bitter experiences of John Hortop and Miles Phillips throw some light on the Spanish Inquisition's treatment of the Elizabethan seamen, and it is consequently fascinating to discuss their stories in detail. The object of John Hawkins' third voyage, which left Plymouth on the 2nd October 1567, was slave-trading, similar to that of the two previous voyages. Hortop relates that he had been pressed to go to the West Indies on Sir John Hawkins' third voyage; Sir John appointed him one of the gunners in Her Majesty's ship, the *Jesus of Lubeck*. Hawkins himself was captain and the ship soon proved herself a rotten, unseaworthy vessel. The *Jesus* was of 700 tons, one of the largest ships in the fleet, but she was rotten owing to prolonged neglect during the reigns of Edward VI and Mary I. She had been originally purchased by Henry VIII from the Hanseatic League in 1545. Robert Barrett of Saltash was Master of the *Jesus of Lubeck*, while John Hampton was Captain of the *Minion*, and John Garret Master; Thomas Bolton was Captain of The *William and John*, and Hawkins' young cousin Francis Drake, aged about 27, was on board the *Jesus* with his commander. Only later during the voyage was he appointed Captain of the *Judith*. Two other ships, the *Angel* and the *Swallow*, formed part of the expedition. Within 40 leagues of Cape Finisterre the mariners encountered fearful tempests, and lost some of their long boats "and a pinnesse [pinnace]* with some men".

---

* Warship's double-banked boat, usually eight-oared boat in Elizabethan days.

On 11th October, however, the wind changed, and, the weather being fair, Hawkins' fleet sailed for the island of Teneriffe in the Canaries. Arriving at Cape Verde on 18th November (according to John Hawkins' own account), they landed 150 men, with the purpose of obtaining some Negro slaves. Hortop relates that Hawkins, "Our generall", was the first that leapt on land, followed by a Captain Dudley and eight of the ship's company. Unfortunately Hawkins, Dudley and the rest were wounded by poisoned arrows. Hawkins indeed might well have lost his life, had it not been for a friendly Negro, who taught him to draw the poison out of his wound with "a clove of garlike". He himself relates: "I myself had one of the greatest wounds, yet, thanks be to God, escaped."[11] Hawkins, always deeply interested in medicine, relates that the remainder of the wounded men died strange, horrible deaths, with their mouths shut some ten days before they expired. At Sierra Leone, Hortop refers in his awe-struck way to "monstrous fishes called sharks, which will devoure men". Hortop was sent with others to capture two caravels, which were also trading with the Negroes. The rivers of Sierra Leone abounded with a queer kind of monster, a sea-horse, which possess enormous teeth, and short legs. Two seamen, who were rash enough to approach too near this beast, were instantly devoured. The Negroes on the shore had discovered a very successful method of dealing with these monsters, for when the sea-horses at night attempted to reach their cabins in the woods they felled a great tree. Vigilantly awaiting their coming, they had the satisfaction of seeing them held up by the logs, because of the shortness of their legs. They then became easy prey for the bows and arrows of the excited Negroes.

Hawkins left Sierra Leone at the beginning of February 1568, and reached Dominica—that beautiful island in the West Indies—in late March. There the mariners took in fresh water. Dominica was inhabited only by Caribs. At Margarita, an island lying off the coast of Venezuela, Hawkins was anxious to take in fresh victuals and wrote a diplomatic letter to the Governor.

Sir Francis Drake, painted by an unknown artist, 1541–1596

(*above*) *Golden Hind*, a modern watercolour reconstruction by G. Robinson.
(*left*) Elizabeth Sydenham, daughter and heiress of Sir George Sydenham, second wife of Sir Francis Drake. After Drake's death she married Sir William Courtney of Powderham. This portrait was painted *circa* 1585 by an unknown artist

Worshipful,

I have travelled in your island only to the intent to refresh my men with fresh victuals, which for my money or wares you shall sell me, meaning to stay only but 5 or 6 days here at the furthest. In the which time you may assure yourself, and so all others, that by me or any of mine there shall no damage be done to any man; the which also the Queen's Majesty of England, my mistress, at my departure out of England commanded me to have great care of, and to serve with my navy the King's Majesty of Spain, my old master* if in places where I came any of his stood in need.[12]

At Borburata, on the mainland of Venezuela, after Hawkins had received a polite refusal from the Governor Ponce de Leon that he might be granted a licence to trade, he nevertheless remained two months enjoying friendly relations with the Spaniards and selling them his merchandise. Although the Governor cited the King of Spain's imperative instructions that trade was forbidden, they were not always obeyed.

John Hortop—gunner on the *Jesus of Lubeck*—quaintly observes that in the neighbourhood of Placencia the mariners found "a monstrous venemous worm with two heads: his body was as bigge as a man's arm, and a yard long". The resourceful Master Robert Barrett cut this monster in half with his sword, making it "as blacke as if it were coloured with ynke". In the neighbourhood of Borburata were many man-eating tigers, cunning beasts, which leapt on their victims by stealth, if given the opportunity, and devoured them.

Off the western part of Cuba a series of misfortunes started to dog the mariners. Heavy storms struck the fleet. The *Jesus of Lubeck* was already severely damaged, with water pouring in below and rotten spars carried away aloft. Hawkins, however, was too honourable a seaman to abandon the *Jesus*, for she was Queen Elizabeth's investment in this enterprise. He therefore firstly sought on the coast of Florida for a haven in which to careen the

---

* It is curious that Hawkins should refer to Philip II as "my old master", but it is supposed that the navigator had done the King of Spain some service when he came to England in 1554.

ship,[13] but it was not possible to land because of the shallowness of the coast. Another storm, which lasted three days, now drove them towards the Mexican port of San Juan de Ulua, the harbour from whence silver from the Mexican mines was shipped to Spain. As Hawkins' fleet entered San Juan de Ulua, the Spanish officials supposed that it was their plate-fleet approaching and fired a salute to welcome them. Realizing their mistake after they had boarded Hawkins' ship, they escaped as soon as possible. Much to Hawkins' embarrassment, the treasure-fleet of Spain with the new Viceroy of Mexico, Don Martin Enriquez, on board, was hourly expected at San Juan de Ulua. Hawkins was in an awkward predicament. If he were to deny access to the Spanish fleet, that would be a hostile act amounting to war. He was well aware that he did not possess the Queen's authority for such an action—indeed, as he reveals in his account of the affair, he feared "the Queen Majesty's indignation in so weighty a matter". Hawkins therefore decided to make conditions. As he saw the Spanish flota or treasure-fleet approaching, he charged an envoy to demand strict terms from the Spaniards as to the price of their entry.

To Don Martin Enriquez, proud and arrogant, a grandee of Spain, doubtless impatient to land in his new dominions, John Hawkins was merely a Lutheran pirate. The insolence of this fellow was really intolerable. One of Hawkins' conditions was the exchange of hostages of rank in pledge of good faith. It was decided by the Viceroy's council that these terms must be accepted by the Spaniards until the flota was safely berthed in San Juan de Ulua. After which the corsairs could be attacked and chastised for their presumption. What transpired reveals that the Spaniards were guilty of gross treachery. Don Martin Enriquez sent Hawkins a very friendly letter, but at the same time planned to board the *Jesus of Lubeck* and the *Minion* with Spanish seamen and soldiers from Vera Cruz in Mexico. There the English corsairs would be treacherously attacked and killed. Hawkins, however, since he had noticed some suspicious movements in the Spanish vessels, decided to send Robert Barrett, master of the *Jesus*, who spoke fluent Spanish, to request an explanation from the Viceroy. According to Hawkins' account, the Viceroy then blew a trumpet, which was the arranged signal for a general massacre of the English seamen, who had gone ashore. Many were killed by the Spaniards, who had pretended to be their friends.

Hawkins now showed considerable skill in manoeuvring the *Jesus* into the centre of the haven, where a bitter fight broke out between the English and the Spanish seamen. It was a great satisfaction to Hawkins when the *Jesus* with her guns sank one and burnt another of the two Spanish ships-of-war, which had acted as escorts to their treasure-fleet. But the ancient *Jesus* was in a sorry state, and Hawkins was forced to command the *Minion* and Francis Drake, now Captain of the *Judith*, to take the seamen and goods out of the *Jesus*. The Spaniards now fired two of their own ships, and they were fast approaching the *Jesus*, "which bred among our men a marvellous fear",* so that some cried "Let us depart with the *Minion*", while others cried "Let us see whether the wind will carry the fire from us". The Spaniards captured the *Jesus*, and about 200 men managed to jump into the *Minion*, although there were scarcely enough victuals to feed them for a fortnight. The small ships *Angel* and *Swallow*, part of Hawkins' third expedition, were also lost. Hawkins relates: "So with the *Minion* only and the *Judith*, a small bark of fifty ton, we escaped; which bark the same night forsook us in our great misery." Drake's part in this affair has never been satisfactorily explained, though William Borough, who disliked him, accused him later of having deserted his commander at San Juan.† Hawkins was forced to disembark on a part of the Mexican shore one hundred men—among them the master of the *Jesus*, Robert Barrett, John Hortop and Miles Phillips, while with the other hundred he sailed for England. It must have been a hard choice for the seamen to decide whether they would prefer "to abide with a little pittance the mercy of God at sea",

---

* John Hawkins' own account.
† Neither Hortop nor Phillips corroborates this charge.

or whether they desired to yield themselves to the mercy of the Spaniards.

It was a miserable voyage home for the men who had stayed in the *Minion*. Many of them died from disease or famine, while the survivors—the number of fifteen—arrived in Mount's Bay in Cornwall in the third week of January 1569.

John Hortop's account, occasionally inaccurate, makes it clear that a mutiny had broken out among the seamen owing to lack of victuals; indeed, food was so scarce that they were driven to "eate hides, cats, rats, parrots, munkies and dogges". It was at this stage that Hortop and others stated that they would rather go on shore to shift for themselves among enemies, than to starve on board the *Minion*. Hawkins certainly cannot be accused of callous behaviour in abandoning the seamen under his command, for he gave them the choice whether they would stay on board or whether they would prefer to land. Hortop relates that Hawkins was greatly grieved to leave them behind him, and that he embraced them all. If God sent him safe home, he vowed that he would do his utmost to ensure that those seamen who survived should be brought back to England. Hawkins through many dark years never forgot his promise.

Hortop relates the adventures of the seamen, how members of an Indian tribe "willed us to give unto them some of our clothes and shirts, which we did", and how John Cornish, who spoke Spanish, was slain by an Indian boy's arrow. For seven days the men trudged wearily towards a town named Panuco, eating nothing but roots and guavas, a fruit which resembled figs. They were then taken prisoner by some Spaniards, who did not ill-treat them. Hortop constantly shows a very lively interest in the crabs and strange fruits in these parts of Mexico. He found running along the sands some white crabs which provided excellent nourishment, while he also relished the fruit known as avocottes to the Spaniards. He described them as resembling an egg, and the fruit was "as blacke as a cole, having a stone in it". Then the seamen were brought to the King's palace in Mexico. Outside the walls they were told to sit down, while a crowd of curious people, by no means hostile, plied them with questions. They were taken to a tanner's house, where two priests and two friars visited them. After some of them had said their prayers in Latin, the priests reported to the Viceroy that they were good Christians. Many of the sick seamen were even sent to hospitals, where some of them were cured and many died. It must be remembered that the Inquisition was not inaugurated in Mexico until January 1569. A year later Doctor Moya de Contreras was appointed Inquisitor-General for Mexico. The Viceroy wanted to hang the seamen, and actually ordered a new pair of gallows to be erected in the market-place, but he was overruled by some noblemen, who begged him to await instructions from King Philip II of Spain about what should be done to them. Meanwhile the Viceroy imprisoned in his palace Robert Barrett, the former master of the *Jesus of Lubeck*, an able and resourceful man, while Hortop and other seamen were sent to Tescuco, a town seven leagues from Mexico "to card wooll" and to perform other menial work among the Indian slaves.

Eventually, after many adventures, Robert Barrett, Hortop and others were shipped as prisoners to Seville in Spain. They were taken to the Contratación House, a Renaissance palace, which stood in Seville market-place, near the majestic Cathedral. From there Hortop, Robert Barrett, John Gilbert, John Emerie and Humphrey Roberts managed to escape, but were later recaptured and again imprisoned in the Contratación House. They were now put in the stocks. Their gaoler petitioned that these troublesome men should be transferred to the Castle of the Inquisition, which lay in Triana. After a year's further imprisonment, the seamen, haggard and emaciated, were brought out in a procession, each holding a candle in his hand and wearing the coat with St. Andrew's Cross on their backs. A high scaffold had been erected in the plaza de St. Francisco, the chief square of Seville. There the seamen were forced to wait for two hours on benches, to be gazed on by the crowd, some of whom murmured, "Burn those heretics", while others more kindly disposed seemed to pity them. Opposite the seamen were the Inquisition judges and the clergy, seated on their benches. After one of the priests had preached a sermon, an official named Bressinia called the names of Robert Barrett and John Gilbert. These seamen were brought before the judges, who sentenced them to be burnt in Seville market-place. Hortop and John Bone were sentenced to the awful punishment of being consigned to the galleys for ten years. The remainder, including Thomas Marks and Humphrey Roberts, received smaller sentences. Hortop tells us that he served altogether twelve years in the galleys, being chained with four others. His allowance was a daily one of 26 ounces of coarse black biscuit and water, just sufficient to keep the wretched man alive. For clothing Hortop wore during the entire year, two shirts, two pairs of breeches of very coarse material, and a red coat of coarse cloth, which could be very easily donned or taken off. He also sometimes wore "a gowne of haire with a fryer's hood". How the poor devils fared under the scorching Spanish sun is not difficult to imagine. Once a month a barber would shave his hair and beard. It is, perhaps, superfluous to add that Hortop and his companions were often flogged and were sometimes tormented by hunger and cold. After twelve years—and one wonders how he could have survived this treatment—he was transferred to the Inquisition prison in Seville. After a further term in captivity, he was forced to serve a Spaniard named Hernando de Soria, in a menial capacity. It was not until October 1590—twenty-two years after the fight at San Juan de Ulua—that John Hortop managed to escape from Spain in a fly-boat laden with Flemish merchandise,* such as wine and salt. It was fortunate for Hortop that he was rescued near St. Lucar by an English ship, the galleon *Dudley*. On 2nd December he landed at Portsmouth. An official there sent him with letters to a Privy Councillor, Thomas Radcliffe, Earl of Sussex, who ordered his secretary to examine the seaman, ascertain from him how long he had been away from England and to give him a detailed account of his adventures.

Miles Phillips' description of his experiences in Mexico and

---

* The Flemings were subjects of Philip II of Spain.

Spain is also of absorbing interest. On the whole he was a little more fortunate than Hortop, but he nevertheless endured terrible privations. Before the Inquisition came to Mexico the seamen were treated with kindness and courtesy by some people, including the Grey Friars. What impressed Phillips was the piety of the Spaniards. In a church in Mexico, which he calls "Our Ladyes Church", no horseman would go away without kneeling before an image of Nuestra Señora de Guadalupe in silver and gilt and praying that she would shield him from all evil.

Miles Phillips and his companions were ordered by the Viceroy, Don Martin Enriquez, to be taken to a house of correction and punishment for ill people at Tescuco—a town within eight leagues* of the capital. This place corresponded to Bridewell in Tudor London. These houses of correction were inhabited by depraved people, who trafficked in the sale of Indian slaves for periods of ten or twenty years. Soon, however, Miles Phillips and others were taken to a prison of Tescuco, where they were strictly confined and almost starved. At this critical juncture Phillips and the other seamen were fortunate enough to meet a man named Robert Sweeting. He was of mixed nationality, having an English father and a Spanish mother. Owing to Sweeting's help, they were able to obtain various victuals, such as mutton, hens and bread, from the Indians. After about two months' confinement in this prison, Phillips and the others managed to escape one dark night when the rain beat relentlessly on the wretched men. They were soon caught by the Spaniards, however, and brought before the arrogant Don Martin Enriquez. With awful gestures the Viceroy and judges threatened to hang the seamen for the serious offence of breaking King's prison. In the Governor's palace they once again encountered the English gentlemen used as hostages by John Hawkins at San Juan de Ulua, and Robert Barrett, too, imprisoned in Don Martin Enriquez's own house and soon to meet a terrible death in

* Twenty-four miles.

Seville. Here Miles Phillips was employed in odd jobs. He relates that nearly a hundred men were allowed a ration of two sheep a day, while everybody ate two loaves a day—but they were equivalent to halfpenny loaves.

For a time Phillips did not fare too badly as a slave or servant to a Spanish gentleman. It was the custom in Mexico for Spaniards to possess Indian or Negro slaves, and Phillips was later appointed as an overseer of the natives, who toiled in the silver mines of these Spanish grandees. Here Phillips was adequately recompensed for his work, and some of the seamen even became rich, being worth 3,000 or 4,000 pesos. This employment lasted for three or four years.

These relatively prosperous conditions did not last, for the dreaded Inquisition was flourishing in Mexico and Peru during 1571. Though it may have been popular among many of the Spaniards, it was feared and hated by some of them. The *Auto da Fé* or Act of Faith was a spectacular public ceremony, designed to appeal to the Spanish sense of the theatrical and also to impress the people with a detestation of heresy. The solemnity of the occasion seemed to represent the contemporary conception of the awe-inspiring drama of the Day of Judgement. In its inhumanity and cruelty the Spanish Inquisition has been exceeded by the Nazis under Adolf Hitler and by the Chinese Communists in our own times, but there is no need to minimize its horrors. It has been mentioned by one authority—Martin Hume—that Philip II, a typical Spaniard, was a perfect embodiment of the feeling of his country at this time, for the enormous majority of Spaniards exulted in the idea and were convinced that their nation, and particularly their sovereign, had been appointed to make common cause with God for the extirpation of his enemies. It is dangerous therefore to consider the Spanish Inquisition— terrible as it may appear to us—from the standpoint of 1970—400 years later.

In his account of his adventures, Phillips mentions that he was forced to wear the San Benito, or penitential garment. The San Benito, however, was not invented by the Spanish Inquisition.[14]

In 1486, almost a hundred years before the English sailors were arrested by the Spaniards in Mexico, an important *Auto da Fé* was held at Toledo in Spain. In the course of which 200 penitents, reconciled under the Edict of Grace, were ordered to wear in public for a year a San Benito. Two years later Torquemada gave instructions that the penitents should don for life a San Benito of black or grey cloth, 18 inches long and 9 inches wide, like a small tabard hanging on breast and back, with a red cross on the front and back of the dress.[15] The instructions of 1561 tell us that the abito penitencial (a penitential coat or garment) was made of yellow linen or cloth, with two red aspas (crosses). In 1574 the first *Auto da Fé* was held with magnificence and pomp in the city of Mexico. An imposing theatre had been built in the great market square close to the Cathedral. Two weeks before the events were to take place, the Spanish people crowded into the city from the surrounding villages to witness the *Auto da Fé*, curious and eager as they were to gaze on the wretched heretics. There were solemn processions through the streets to the market square by the Viceroy, the Senate, and no doubt numerous priests. It lasted from six in the morning till five in the evening. Some of the victims, including English seamen, were burnt to death, while two heretics, an Englishman and a Frenchman, were released. Others accused of polygamy and various sorceries were reconciled to the Roman Catholic Church.[16]

Miles Phillips and his companions were now imprisoned by the Inquisition after all their property had been seized. The only light in their dungeons was the flicker of a candle, and in this eerie, horrible place were confined together two men, who often could not see one another. Sometimes they were forced to go before one of the Inquisitors, who severely examined them as to their religious sentiments. They were ordered to repeat the Pater Noster, the Ave Maria and the Creed in Latin, which many of the seamen were unable to accomplish. Robert Sweeting, the man of mixed nationality, again stood their friend by acting as interpreter and assuring the Inquisitors that the men were word perfect in English, though their Latin might be very faulty. Then the dreaded questions in the stern, brusque, brutal voices of the Inquisitors: "Do you or do you not believe that the host of bread, and the wine in the chalice are the very true and perfect body and blood of our Saviour Christ?" Many of the seamen must have been sorely tempted to say "Yes", whatever religious opinions they held. Then after endless questioning, the fiendishly designed tortures, the rack, the admissions wrung from the men dripping in sweat in their deep agony, carefully stored away and used against them at their trials. Worst of all, perhaps, the anticipation that they might be borne to the Quemadero to be burnt alive at any time.

Phillips relates that the Spaniards erected a large scaffold in the middle of the market-place. About two weeks before the day appointed for the Inquisitors' judgement there was a solemn proclamation made throughout the city to the sound of a trumpet and the beating of attabalies.* It was announced that whoever should go to the market-place on such a day would hear the sentence of the holy Inquisition against the English heretics and Lutherans. The night before the judgement some officials came to the prison bringing with them San Benitos—coats made of yellow cotton and red crosses upon them both on the front and at the back. The seamen passed a restless night, because the officials were so busily engrossed marshalling them in an enormous yard "and placing and pointing us in what order we should go to the scaffold or place of judgement upon the morrow". The next morning each man was given for his breakfast a cup of wine and a slice of bread fried in honey. At 8 o'clock, dressed in their San Benitos, which were not usually worn within doors, the men marched with a rope about their necks, and holding in one hand a large, unlighted green wax candle. On either side of them went two Spaniards. The scaffold—a large hall—contained not only the Viceroy, the Chief Justices and others, but also about 300 White, Black and Grey Friars. "Then there was a solemne Oyes made, and silence commanded, and then presently beganne their severe and cruell judgement."[17]

* Phillips calls them a kind of drum.

Roger, the chief armourer on the *Jesus of Lubeck*, was sentenced to 300 lashes on horseback, and afterwards condemned to the galleys as a slave for ten years. One wonders how he could have survived such a savage sentence. John Gray and John Moon, of Looe in Cornwall, and others were sentenced to 200 lashes on horseback, and afterwards to be sent to the galleys for eight years. Miles Phillips was comparatively fortunate, for the Inquisitors sentenced him to serve in a monastery for five years, without any lashes. He was also to wear a San Benito or fool's coat, as he calls it. George Ribley of Gravesend, a seaman, was ordered to be burnt at the stake, but first strangled,*[18] while Peter Momfrie and Cornelius the Irishman, whose real name was John Martin of Cork, were ordered to be burnt to ashes. These men were soon escorted to the market-place, where the dreadful sentence was duly carried out.

On Good Friday 1575 Miles Phillips and his companions were brought into the courtyard of the Inquisitors' palace. Sixty men were ordered to mount on horseback and, naked from the waist upwards, they were taken though the principal streets of Mexico and cruelly flogged. To add to the horror, the people were encouraged to witness this spectacle, presumably partly to deter them from similar offences. Before this cavalcade went a couple of criers who exclaimed all the time: "Behold these English dogs, Luterianos enemigos, enemies to God." In conspicuous places were the Inquisitors, themselves mocking the wretched men with cruel jibes, and the Inquisitors' familiars to gain credit with their masters did likewise. Man's inhumanity to man. How we have cause to rue it throughout the centuries.

Meanwhile Miles Phillips, who had little reason to love the Spaniards, was appointed an overseer to Indian workmen in a monastery of the Black Friars. They were in the process of building a new church. Phillips was an adaptable man, and after learning Mexican Spanish very fluently he discovered that the Indians were a lovable kindly people, who mostly hated their

* This was the more merciful custom in use during the Inquisition in Mexico.

Spanish masters. It is probably true that many of the Spaniards and some of the priests from the monastic orders detested the Inquisition, though they greatly feared it. After five years the Chief Inquisitor ordered that the San Benito should be taken off the seaman and hung in the principal church with a notice prominently displayed: "An heretic Lutheran reconciled." Miles Phillips was now given comparative freedom to travel about the country, though he was well aware that his every action was spied upon. Meanwhile some of Phillips' companions had settled down in Mexico: David Alexander and Robert Cook who were in the service of one of the Inquisitors, married two Negro women; while Richard Williams had the sense to marry a rich widow with 4,000 pesos. Paul Horsewell, one of the men sentenced to serve in monastic orders, married the rich daughter of one that came in with Hernando Cortés. On one occasion Miles Phillips was summoned to the Inquisitors' presence and brusquely asked why he did not marry. Phillips replied that he was apprenticed to a silk-weaver for three years, to whom he had given 150 pesos to teach the trade. The Inquisitor then said in a stern voice: "I have information that you intend to run away. I charge you here upon pain of burning as an heretic relapsed, that you depart not this city, nor go near the port of San Juan de Ulua, or any other port." Phillips tactfully answered that he would obey these orders. He had no choice but to comply. Yet he constantly felt a longing to see England once again. On one occasion he was again arrested, but later after further adventures managed to escape to Poole Harbour in Dorset in February 1582 in a ship named the *Landret*.

One of the most bestial of the Chief Inquisitors in Mexico was Alonso de Peralta, who was appointed to his office in 1594. Under his jurisdiction there were frequent *Autos da Fé*. One of the victims named Luis de Caravajal, having noticed Peralta's sadistic face, later remarked that the mere sight of him "made his flesh creep".[19] Many prominent Englishmen suffered under the Inquisition, including John Drake, a cousin of Sir Francis. His ordeal was an appearance at an *Auto da Fé* as a penitent. Sir

Richard Hawkins was also imprisoned during the Inquisition at Lima in Peru.

There is the case of George Gaspar, an English Protestant, who was arrested by the Spanish Inquisition at Teneriffe in the Canary Islands about 1587 and accused of heresy.[20] A spy had reported that the man had been seen to turn his back on an image of the crucifixion during his prayers. To justify himself he declared that he addressed his prayers to God and not to images. He was later condemned to be burnt at the stake. In an attempt to avoid this awful fate, Gaspar plunged a knife, which he managed to conceal in his prison, into his stomach. Unfortunately the wretched man did not die from his self-inflicted wound, so the brutes of Inquisitors had him taken on a litter to the Quemadero, where he might still feel before death the exquisite refinement of the flames licking against his body. There is no doubt whatsoever that the hatred of Spain in the hearts of English seamen was fanned by the cruelty of the Spanish Inquisition.

John Hawkins never forgave the Spanish Viceroy for his treachery at San Juan de Ulua, but determined to do his utmost to procure the release of his seamen taken prisoner in Mexico. A gnawing, fierce detestation of Spain now smouldered in his heart. Hawkins was a great seaman and corsair, but he also had a flair for business and diplomacy, and whilst trading in the Canary Islands had established excellent relations with the Spanish authorities. Later in April 1571 Hawkins, a master of duplicity, sent Philip II a secret message at Madrid, alleging that he was tired of Elizabeth's fickle and tyrannical rule. He now wished to offer his services to the Spaniards, so that they could benefit from his maritime skill and his intimate acquaintance with English statecraft, provided that his old comrades the seamen should be released and that he would receive adequate financial recompense. Meanwhile Queen Elizabeth and Lord Burghley were kept fully informed by Hawkins of his secret intrigues with the Spanish King. Philip II, unlike his sister-in-law, was a poor judge of character, and, though he was cautious and distrustful by nature—which is hardly to be wondered at—he was as much a dissembler as the English Queen. One wonders whether Philip was really deceived by Hawkins' protestations, even if his ambassador Guzman de Silva had tried to persuade him some years before of the seaman's sincerity.

Notes

CHAPTER VI

1   Richard Hakluyt, *Voyages* (Everyman Edition), Vol. VI, p. 336.
2   Sir Charles Petrie, *Philip II of Spain*, p. 85.
3   Hakl. Soc. Pub., No. XVI, The World Encompassed.
4   *Shakespeare's England*, Vol. I, p. 175.
5   Purchas XIX.
6   *Samuel Purchas His Pilgrimes in Five Books* (1735), Chap. 6.
7   James A. Williamson, *George Clifford, Third Earl of Cumberland*.
8   Richard Hakluyt, *Voyages* (Everyman Edition), Vol. VI, p. 35.
9   *Ibid*, Vol. V, p. 7.
10 Robert Southey, *English Seamen*, p. 17.
11 John Payne ed., *Voyages of Elizabethan Seamen*.
12 James A. Williamson, *The Age of Drake*.
13 *Ibid.*
14 Henry Charles Lea, *A History of the Inquisition of Spain*, Vol. III.
15 *Ibid.*
16 *History of the Inquisition* abridged from the elaborate work of Philip Lumborch, p. 171.
17 Miles Phillips' narrative, Richard Hakluyt, *Voyages*, Vol. VI, p. 322.
18 A. L. Rowse, *The Expansion of Elizabethan England*.
19 Jean Plaidy, *The Spanish Inquisition*.
20 *Ibid.*

CHAPTER VII

Sir Humphrey Gilbert's Vision of Empire

Having lived in South Devon for the last year I go sometimes to Compton, that beautiful and historic village so associated with the Gilbert family. Looking down on the ancient Compton Castle with all its memories, the finest example of a fortified mediaeval manor house in the country, and surveying the wide sweep of rich Devon earth in the plough lands above the castle, I try to analyse "the great unrest" which impelled the navigators to embark on their voyages. What were the motives which drove those men so relentlessly, some of them to their own destruction?

James Anthony Froude in a fine passage has written:

The springs of great actions are always difficult to analyse—impossible to analyse perfectly—possible to analyse only very proximately; and the force by which a man throws out of himself a good action is invisible and mystical, like that which brings out the blossom and the fruit upon the tree. The motives which we find men urging for their enterprises seem often insufficient to have prompted them to so large a daring. They did what they did from the great unrest in them which made them do it, and what it was may be best measured by the results in the present England and America.

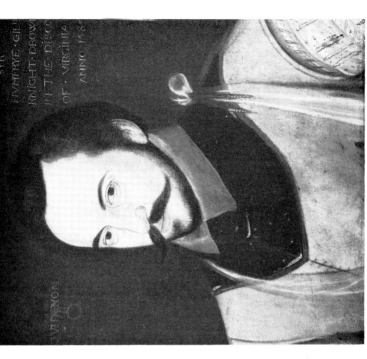

(*above left*) Richard Drake, cousin of Sir Francis Drake, whose business manager he was. He took charge of Spanish prisoners captured off Plymouth in 1588. Portrait by an unknown artist. (*above right*) Sir Humphrey Gilbert by an unknown artist. Gilbert colonized Newfoundland in 1583

George Clifford, 3rd Earl of Cumberland, 1558–1605. Miniature by
Nicholas Hilliard

Drake, Frobisher, Gilbert, Cavendish, Hawkins, Cumberland and Ralegh possessed very different characters, but they all had one thing in common, their restlessness. In the Elizabethan age, one of moral and intellectual upheaval, Humphrey Gilbert's "great unrest" and the originality of his mind are compelling. He has been correctly described as England's first Empire builder,[1] but his ideas have received far less attention and publicity than those of his half-brother Sir Walter Ralegh. Gilbert was the second son of Otho or Otes Gilbert of Greenway near Dittisham-on-the-Dart, where he was born. The Gilbert family seat was at Compton Castle. Humphrey Gilbert's mother was Katherine Champernoun, daughter of Sir Philip Champernoun of Modbury, Devon. After Otho Gilbert's death, his wife Katherine married Walter Ralegh, the father of a famous son.

John Hooker is the only authentic authority for Gilbert's youth. Humphrey was born in 1539, so he was thirteen years older than Walter Ralegh. Gilbert was educated at Oxford, and we know that in 1554 or 1555 he was a member of the young Princess Elizabeth's household. Aged about seventeen, he had originally been brought into her service by Katharine Ashley, Elizabeth's governess, who was related to Gilbert. In his portrait Humphrey is not unhandsome, with his brown beard, dark hair, sad, rather wistful expression and air of intellectuality. Like Richard Grenville, his cousin, Gilbert's early career was in the army. According to Dr. Williamson,[2] Gilbert first became interested in overseas expansion whilst on active service at Le Havre. There he became acquainted with Richard Eden, author of *A Treatise of the New India* and *The Decades of the New World*, and an intimate friend of the explorer Sebastian Cabot in his last years. Eden's purpose was to make known to the English seamen what the Spanish and Portuguese had already accomplished in the way of discovery. It is likely that Richard Eden stimulated the impressionable mind of the ardent Gilbert, and he would be further enlightened about the Spanish colonies in the West Indies and elsewhere by the sea captains who had ventured there. Humphrey Gilbert arrived home in England with two main objects: firstly to raid the Spanish West "in the manner of the Huguenots", secondly to open the North-west Passage to Cathay.[3]

For four years between 1566 and 1570 Gilbert served in Ireland as a soldier, and we are not really concerned with that part of his career. His experiences in Ireland, however, proved invaluable in broadening his concept of the purposes of colonization.[4] He was knighted about 1570, and a year later we find him elected a Member of Parliament for Plymouth. Gilbert became a member of the Muscovy Company by buying shares. He became acquainted with Anthony Jenkinson, celebrated for his highly successful travels in Russia and Persia, recorded in Hakluyt.

Gilbert's importance as an author exists in his work Discourse for *A Discovery for a New Passage to Cathay* (the North-west Passage), written early in 1566. This is a learned book, though its arguments are not always convincing. Gilbert petitioned the Queen about the North-west project during 1565.[5] "Pleaseth it Your Majestie. That whereas of longe tyme, there hath bin nothings saide or donne concerninge the discoveringe of a passage by the Northe, to go to Cataia and all other the east partes of the worlde." He beseeched the Queen that he might have the same privileges according to the articles following "and I nothinge doubting the good success doe meane God willinge to make tryall thereof, at myne owne costs and charges with the help of my freindes".

The Gilberts were neighbours and friends of John Davis, born at Sandridge on the River Dart, a great navigator of sterling honesty and integrity. He was one of the finest sea captains of the Elizabethan age, and the first to have discovered the Falkland Islands,* later to be visited by Sir Richard Hawkins. It is true that he lacked the brilliance of Sir Francis Drake and the violent temperament of Martin Frobisher, but he possessed remarkable scientific knowledge, being the inventor of the quadrant. Like Humphrey Gilbert, he was an author of two books, published in

---

* 14th August, 1592.

1594 and 1595. These are technical works called *The Seaman's Secrets* and *The World's Hydrographical Description*, which strongly advocated the continuance of the search for the North-west Passage. Davis was much admired by his contemporaries and nobody ever criticized his character except for Thomas Cavendish, who bitterly and falsely accused Davis of deserting him during his last ill-fated voyage. It is ironical that Davis should have been murdered by Japanese pirates (1605) in the Far East, since he is not known to have been involved in piratical activities in his early life. His voyages to the North-west are of importance, for they established the correct nature of the relation between Greenland and America. His magnificent courage at times when lesser men would have despaired was beyond praise.

Sir Humphrey Gilbert, too, was extremely brave, a man of noble ideals and bristling with original ideas. He had faults, too: a violent temper on occasions and a rash judgement and obstinacy which dismayed his contemporaries.

We have already discussed Walsingham's services in securing for Sir Humphrey the Letters Patents, granted by Queen Elizabeth (1578)* to discover and colonize "remote heathen and barbarous lands, countreys and territories, not actually possessed of any Christian prince".

The French Ambassador in London, Castelnau de Mauvissière refers to Gilbert's first expedition 1577–9 in a letter to Henri III of France.

> I shall learn what I can [he wrote] in order to give an account of it to Your Majesty and also of all other occurrences such as [the visits] of Sir Humphrey Gilbert, who comes to see me more often since he has learnt that I was aware of his plan. He sets out with a gallant company and three or four ships more than I had informed Your Majesty and, above all, he would not seek quarrels nor wars with the French if he went in that direction and if they should meet on such discoveries where there are enough for all.

It was in fact a French explorer, Jean Ribault, who founded the

* 11th June.

first colonies in Florida. After his return from his first Florida colony in 1562, Jean Ribault came to England[6]—not his first visit for he had known John Dudley, Duke of Northumberland, during the reign of Edward VI. Whilst in England, a project was formed for a joint Anglo-French expedition to sail under Ribault and the unstable Thomas Stukeley to carry on the French colony. North America was to a great degree unexplored. It is true that the French explorer, Jacques Cartier, had reached the St. Lawrence estuary, and, owing to Hakluyt's endeavours, his accounts of his two voyages had been translated into English.

These projects kindled sparks in Humphrey Gilbert's mind. His ideas were original, for in his *Discourse* he advocated an English settlement as a trading base half-way to Asia "about Sierra Nevada" (California). He was the first Englishman with the vision to realize the importance of colonization in America. Admirable as the whole scheme was, Gilbert's own beliefs were mistaken. He saw no reason why the malcontent members of the community, the dissolute and the idle should not make suitable or good colonists. He merely realized that England would be benefited if she were relieved of "those needy people who were daily consumed of the gallows". One must remember that in the mind of a typical Elizabethan were deep-rooted prejudices against colonization, and a natural reluctance to leave their native land. They were aware that heavy fines were imposed on absentees. Such obstacles demanded drastic solutions. In those early days, despite much religious persecution at home, it was not easy to attract suitable settlers.

Yet Francis Bacon—that far-seeing genius—clearly saw the dangers.

> It is a shamefull and unblessed thing, [he wrote] to take the scumme of people, and wicked condemned men, to be the people with whom you *Plant*: and not only so, but it spoileth the Plantation; For they will ever live like Rogues, and not fall to work, but be lazie, and doe mischief, and spend victuals and be quickly weary, and then certifie over to their country, to the discredit of the Plantation.[7]

His opinion was that the best types of colonists were gardeners, ploughmen, labourers, carpenters, apothecaries, surgeons and suchlike.

Humphrey Gilbert's first voyage (1578) to plant a colony on the coast of Florida was a failure. It was an imposing expedition consisting of ten ships fitted out with sufficient food for a year of voyaging.[8] There was no difficulty in obtaining funds for the expedition. Sir John Gilbert, Humphrey's elder brother, invested in the venture, and so did Adrian Gilbert—always interested in maritime adventure. Walter Ralegh, Humphrey's half-brother, then a young man of 26, was captain of *The Falcon*, a ship which belonged to Queen Elizabeth, and Carew Ralegh was captain of *The Hope of Greenway*.

The negative result of this expedition was unfortunate for Gilbert, for it gained him the reputation of being unlucky at sea. It is possible that Gilbert's object had been to pay for the voyage by various acts of piracy, but the undertaking had been badly mismanaged. Mendoza wrote Philip II that none of the seamen had been paid.

The last great undertaking of Gilbert's life was to plant a colony in Newfoundland. The only part of the coast familiar to English fishermen was the east and south-east portion of Newfoundland, where they used to catch cod on its outlying banks. By 1578 much of the knowledge gained about the interior of Newfoundland was owing to the industry of a Kentish gentleman named Anthony Parkhurst, who had accompanied John Hawkins on his second West Indian voyage and stayed on in Newfoundland. He later wrote two reports[9] about that territory, and Hakluyt gave him his support and encouragement. He addressed from Bristol to the elder Richard Hakluyt, the lawyer of the Middle Temple, a letter in which he described the climate, the country and the animals to be found there. Parkhurst was an enterprising traveller, and whilst in Africa and America "had found trees that bare oisters, which was strange to you, till I tolde you that their boughes hung in the water, on which both oisters and muskles did sticke fast, as their propertie is, to stakes and timber". Anthony Parkhurst found Newfoundland a temperate climate, and not so colde as foolish mariners doe saye. . . . The countrey is full of little small rivers all the yeere long proceeding from the mountaines, ingendred both of snow and raine. . . . aud plentie of Beares everywhere, so that you may kill of them as oft as you list; their flesh is as good as yong beefe, and hardly you may know the one from the other if it be poudred but two dayes. . . . There are sea guls, Murres, Duckes, wild GEESE, and many other kind of birdes store, too long to write, especially at one island named Penguin, where we may drive them on a planke into our shippe as many as shall lade them.

Gilbert was certainly familiar with Anthony Parkhurst's reports on Newfoundland, and they helped him when planning his own expedition (1583).

During July 1581 we find Sir Humphrey deeply depressed and forced to write to Sir Francis Walsingham that he was desperately in need of financial assistance. He had spent his own fortune and his wife's* on his colonization projects.

Sir, [he wrote] greate extremitie enforcethe me most humblie and earnestlie to crave your honors speedie furtherance of me for the small some of monye which remaynethe dewe for the service of her Majestie withe three shippes of mine in Ireland; a miserable thinge it is, that I poore man havinge served her Majestie in warres and peace, above seven and twentie years shoulde be nowe subjecte to daylye arestes, executions, and outlawries.

He was even forced to sell the clothes from the back of his wife who had brought him a good dowry.

In his vision of empire, Gilbert was far in advance of his age. He favoured a system of absolute monarchy, and when conceiving his ideal commonwealth, he advocated that the governor in organizing its defence should be assisted by thirteen councillors. The effect of the law-making powers granted by his patent was to make him almost absolute. The parishes, which were to be laid-out, were to centre round the church and parsonage. Gilbert wisely considered that no rentals should be paid to the colonists

---

* Gilbert married in 1570, Anne, daughter and heir of John Aucher.

until seven or ten years after the lands had been occupied, a policy certainly favoured by Sir Francis Bacon. He later wrote: "Planting of countries, is like planting of woods; For you must make account, to leese almost twenty yeares profit, and expect your recompense, in the end. For the principall thing, that hath beene the destruction of most plantations, hath beene the base, and hastie drawing of profit, in the first yeeres."[10] It is, perhaps, little known that many years later Bacon was a shareholder in Guy's Colony at Cupid's Cove, Newfoundland (1610).

Gilbert was a professed Protestant, though certainly not a bigoted one. When the first proclamation was made on North American soil, it was proposed that the public exercise of religion should be according to the Church of England. One wonders therefore whether the prominent Roman Catholic colonists and dissenters, who had been encouraged by Gilbert and Walsingham to settle in America, and promised freedom of worship, would have been entitled to it.

One of these was Sir George Peckham,* an intimate friend of Sir Humphrey's, and another was Sir Thomas Gerrard. The astute, far-sighted Sir Francis Walsingham, was anxious to help Gilbert undertake another voyage to America. Although a rigid puritan, he was not so bigoted as has been supposed. It so happened that he learnt through his secret agents that these two Catholics, Sir George Peckham and Sir Thomas Gerrard, were by no means averse to settling abroad. Might this not be an advantageous way of ridding England of trouble-makers and intriguers, who were probably disloyal subjects of the Queen at home? Don Bernardino de Mendoza, well-apprised as to what was happening, wrote to King Philip of Spain, that Walsingham had secretly proposed to two spendthrift Catholic gentlemen (i.e. Sir George Peckham and Sir Thomas Gerrard) who owned land "that if they helped Ongi Gilberto in his expedition, they would escape losing life and property". In consideration for this service the Queen on her part was willing to give them permission to

---

* Son of Edmund Peckham, Treasurer of the Mint through three reigns.

live in parts of Florida with freedom of conscience whilst still enjoying the use of their English properties.[11] Sir George Peckham and Sir Thomas Gerrard were in fact leaders of a group of Roman Catholics who were interested in the scheme to move overseas, provided they were permitted freedom to practise their religion. Mendoza, an arch meddler and intriguer, now took the opportunity to warn the papists through their priests that they would immediately have their throats cut if they went there, as Jean Ribault's men had already experienced.[12] In January 1584 Mendoza was expelled from England.

Gilbert's patent, which gave him the right to occupy any heathen lands not already in the possession of a European power was valid for only six years from June 1578. Four years later we find Gilbert anxious to persuade his friends to invest in a new voyage. For this purpose he sought to raise funds by allotting areas of his prospective possessions to sub-patentees, who included Dr. John Dee; Sir Philip Sidney, keenly interested in colonization; and Gilbert's friend, Sir George Peckham.[13] We know from John Dee's diary that during July 1582, Peckham came to visit him, "and promised me of his gift and of his patent 5000 akers of ye new conquest". This was to recompense the learned geographer for ascertaining the title to some lands overseas. Presumably Dee never obtained any financial benefit, despite the attractive prospects held out to him.

As already mentioned, the Queen—wisely, as matters later transpired—declined to invest in Gilbert's enterprise in 1583. Indeed we know from his letter to Walsingham that Elizabeth would have preferred Sir Humphrey to stay at home, considering him "as a man noted of not good happ by sea". Gilbert wrote Walsingham: "It hath pleased your Honour to let me understande that her Majestie of her especiall care had of my well doinge, and prosperous success hath wished my stay att home from the personall execution of my intended discovery as a man noted of not good hap by sea." Before Gilbert sailed, Elizabeth showed great interest in the expedition, and gave the rising favourite Sir Walter Ralegh a present, which he was to send

Gilbert. Ralegh, always a better courtier than his half-brother, for he excelled in flattery and excessive compliment, wrote to his half-brother from the Court at Richmond,

> I have sent you a token from Her Majesty an ancor guyded by a Lady as you see, and farther Her Highness willed me to send you worde that she wished you as great good hap in safty to your ship as if herself were ther in person desireing you to have care of yourself as of that which she tendereth of therefore for her sace [sake] you must provide for it[14].

Perhaps Ralegh had a curious presentiment of the death of his half-brother, for he ends his letter: "I commend you, to the will and protection of God, who sends us such life or death as He shall please, or hath appointed." He signs his letter: "Your trew brother, Rawley."

Among Gilbert's most eloquent admirers was the young Hungarian scholar Stephen Parmenius of Buda, who had recently arrived in England. Eventually he found his way to Oxford where he became acquainted with the younger Richard Hakluyt, who no doubt fanned the mind of the ardent young poet with enthusiasm for the New England to be founded in North America. Hakluyt introduced Parmenius to Gilbert, and the scholar showed so much enthusiasm to accompany the expedition that Gilbert readily agreed to it. No foreigner had been a greater admirer of England and her queen than this Hungarian, though his language is the artificial one of the Elizabethan Age. Stephen Parmenius refers to England:

> O! Anglia, happy island, famed for the blessings of peace and war, the glory of the wide world, now rich in resources and thickly peopled, having won renown by thy deeds, and reared thy head on high throughout the world, careful of thy destiny, lest some day thy wide spread dominions should fall by their own weights now mayst thou win new city walls for thy sons and extend thy rule far and wide.

He calls Elizabeth "Queen of the Sea". She from her lofty tower near the cool river looks forth, and even now on Father Thames she sees Gilbert's slanting sails gradually fade away in the distance.[15] Parmenius composed a poem in Latin, more than 300 lines long, and sent it to Gilbert.

The classic account of Gilbert's voyage of 1583 is by Edward Haie, captain of the *Golden Hind* (not Drake's ship). The expedition consisted of five main ships. These were the *Delight*, a vessel of 120 tons in which Gilbert sailed. William Winter was captain, and Richard Clarke, a seaman from Weymouth, was master of the *Delight*. Edward Haie was captain and owner of the *Golden Hind*, and William Cox of Limehouse went as master. Maurice Browne was captain of the small ship the *Swallow*, while William Andrewes was captain of the *Squirrel*, a ship of 10 tons. The largest ship of 200 tons was the bark *Raleigh*, which belonged to Sir Walter Ralegh. Her sea captain was a man named Butler, and Robert Davis of Bristol was her master. As already mentioned, there were 260 men aboard the various vessels, including shipwrights, carpenters, masons, refiners and musicians. Stephen Parmenius, highly delighted to be included in the expedition, was in the ill-fated *Delight*. It was fortunate for Richard Hakluyt that he did not join Gilbert's expedition, for earlier he had intended to do so, having a desire to see Newfoundland for himself.

Gilbert sailed from Plymouth on 11th June 1583, and from the first misfortune seemed to pursue him. Two days out from Plymouth an officer of the bark *Raleigh* signalled to "the generall" (Gilbert) as Haie refers to him, that Captain Butler and many of the crew were sick. Without warning the bark *Raleigh* now deserted and returned to Plymouth in a sorry state. It is also true that many of the mariners were Channel pirates, forced to embark on this enterprise as an alternative to standing their trial.

A marked fatalistic vein runs throughout Haie's narrative. This sea captain was a man of strong religious beliefs, and he considered that Sir Humphrey Gilbert, whose powerful personality he greatly admired, was a puppet in God's hands.[16]

After a perilous voyage of seven weeks, Gilbert sighted

Newfoundland on 30th July. A few days later on Monday 5th August, having arrived at the harbour of St. John, he formally took possession in the Queen's name of Newfoundland, which has the distinction of being the first and oldest dominion of the Crown overseas. Gilbert was a man of great dignity and nobility of mind, and the ceremony was an impressive occasion. Haie relates:[17]

> Munday following, the general had his tent set up, who being accompanied with his own followers, summoned the merchants and masters both English and strangers to be present at his taking possession of those countries . . . and 200 leagues every way, invested the Queenes Majestie with the title and dignity thereof, had delivered unto him (after the customs of England) a rod and a turf of the same soile, entering possession also for him, his heires and assignes for ever.

Gilbert proposed that three laws should be immediately enacted: firstly that the exercise of religion should be according to the rites of the Church of England, secondly the maintenance of Her Majesty Queen Elizabeth's right and possession of these territories. If anybody were to attempt anything prejudicial against the Queen's Majesty, or to dispute her rights, they would be guilty of high treason, and to be tried according to the law of England. Thirdly, if anybody was "to utter words sounding to the dishonour of the Queen, he would loose his eares" and have his ships and goods confiscated. "Not far from this place were the arms of England engraved in lead, and enfixed upon a pillar of wood."

It is evident during this voyage that insubordination, even mutiny, were rife among the seamen—especially in the *Swallow*—who committed various acts of piracies against fishermen on the coast. Many stole into the woods where they hoped to hide themselves until they could find transport to return to England. Others were suffering from diseases, and some had died. Gilbert, therefore anxious to get rid of the *Swallow*, decided to send her back to England with the sick and unfit.

On 20th August, together with the *Delight*, the *Golden Hind*, and the small *Squirrel*, Gilbert continued his voyage southwards towards Cape Breton. The Captain of the *Delight* was now Maurice Browne, who had been transferred from the *Swallow* with some of his men—"a vertuous, honest, and discreet gentleman", according to Haie, though he gave too much licence to the men under his command. Rather than embark again in the *Golden Hind*, Gilbert chose to sail in the *Squirrel*, a more wieldy ship.

When the mariners were within 15 leagues of the island of Sablon, Gilbert came near the *Delight* in his own small vessel, and consulted Clarke, the master, as to the best course. "Without question we must make west-south-west," advised Clarke. The wind was in the south and night was approaching. The sea captain feared that there were treacherous shoals near the shore. Gilbert's faults of character, his obstinacy, rashness and faulty judgement—for he always thought he knew best—were partly instrumental in leading to the destruction of others as well as to his own death. With a burst of temper he shouted at Clarke, "I command you to steer west-north-west." In vain Clarke tried to argue that such an order would mean that the *Delight* would be on the sands before daylight. Gilbert would brook no disobedience. "I command you in the Queen's name", he repeated, "to sail west-north-west." Clarke had no other course but to obey the general's order.

Haie's simple narrative has the inevitability of Greek tragedy. He describes the scene:

> The evening was faire and pleasant, yet not without token of storme to ensue, and most part of this wednesday night, like the swanne that singeth before her death, they in the *Admiral* or *Delight* continued in sounding of trumpets, with drummes and fifes; also winding the cornets, Haughtboys; and in the end of their jolitie, left with the battelles and ringing of dolefull knells.[18]

The next day, one of storm and dense mist, the *Delight* struck upon a shoal, and about one hundred people were drowned. It is evident that ill watch was kept on board the *Delight* the previous night, and that the carelessness of officers and men alike was partly responsible for the disaster. Amongst those drowned was Stephen Parmenius, who had intended to compose an ode in Latin to commemorate the expedition. Captain Maurice Brown also lost his life.

Meanwhile Gilbert, despite the vehement persuasion and entreaty of his friends, obstinately decided to remain on the *Squirrel*, though this ship, more truly described as a mere-cockboat of 10 tons, was already overloaded with guns and other material. Gilbert had a curious attachment to the *Squirrel*, which had as a mascot a red squirrel, the armorial crest of his family. It may well be that rumours had reached Sir Humphrey that the seamen were saying among themselves that he was afraid of the sea. At all costs he would remain in the *Squirrel* to share the perils of his men. During the homeward voyage Haie relates that experienced seamen testified they had never known more stormy seas.

There is the simple yet vivid description of Monday 9th September:

> In the afternoon, the frigate was neere cast away, oppressed by waves, yet at that time recovered: and giving foorth signes of joy, the generall [Gilbert] sitting abaft with a booke in his hand, cried out unto us in the *Hind* (so oft as we did approach within hearing) "we are as neere to heaven by sea as by land". Reiterating the same speech, well beseeming a souldier, resolute in Jesus Christ, as I can testifie he was.

So Gilbert, who had displayed magnificent courage, lost his life, while the pathetic survivors, including Captain Edward Haie in the *Golden Hind*, after incredible hazards, managed to put in at Falmouth* wreathed in such thick fog that the mariners were able to distinguish land with the greatest difficulty.

It may well be, as one of Sir Humphrey Gilbert's biographers[19] asserts, that his brother Adrian during his absence had been intriguing to supplant him. Adrian, a frequent visitor to Dr.

* 22nd September.

John Dee's house at Mortlake, was a Doctor of Medicine. Aubrey relates that he was a "great chymist and a man of excellent natural parts".[20] Mary Herbert, Countess of Pembroke, the beloved sister of Sir Philip Sidney certainly had a high opinion of Adrian Gilbert, for she maintained him at Wilton House as "her Laborator". Aubrey's gossip may be prejudiced. He relates that Adrian was "very sarcastic, and the greatest buffoon in the Nation; cared not for what he said to man or woman of what quality soever". Yet Adrian was an ardent promoter of geographical discovery, a minerologist and a mathematician of some repute.

It was left to Walter Ralegh, a man of genius, to carry on the noble projects which had formed in Gilbert's fertile mind. After Humphrey Gilbert's patent had expired, the Queen gave his half-brother a six-year patent for himself. In those early days Queen Elizabeth was greatly attracted to Ralegh, with his dark handsome good looks and charm of manner. He had not yet incurred her resentment by his secret marriage to her maid of honour Elizabeth Throckmorton.

If Sir Humphrey Gilbert's schemes were doomed to failure, he at least deserves to be honoured and remembered as our first builder of Empire, and as a man of imagination and vision.

Notes

CHAPTER VII

1 William Gilbert Gosling, *The Life of Sir Humphrey Gilbert, England's First Empire Builder* (1911).
2 James A. Williamson, *Age of Drake*.
3 *Ibid.*
4 A. L. Rowse, *The Expansion of Elizabethan England*.
5 B. M. *Add. MSS* 4159, f. 392.
6 D. B. Quinn, *Voyages and Colonising Enterprises of Sir Humphrey Gilbert*.
7 W. Aldis Wright, ed., *Bacon's Essays and Colours of Good and Evil*, p. 140.
8 J. H. Adamson and H. F. Folland, *The Shepherd of the Ocean*.
9 Printed in full in Prof. E. C. R. Taylor's *The Original Writings and Correspondence of the Time of Richard Hakluyt*.
10 W. Aldis Wright ed., *Bacon's Essays and Colours of Good and Evil*.
11 *Spanish Domestic Papers*, 11th July 1582.
12 Taylor II 27819.
13 James A. Williamson, *The Age of Drake*.
14 B.M. *Add. MSS* 4231, f. 85.
15 "Embarcation Ode to the Noble and Illustrious Humphrey Gilbert, Knight."
16 John Payne ed., *Voyages of the Elizabethan Seamen to America: Select Narratives from the Principal Navigations of Hakluyt*.
17 Richard Hakluyt, *Voyages* (Everyman Edition), Vol. 6, p. 18.
18 *Ibid*, Vol. VI.
19 William Gilbert Gosling, *The Life of Sir Humphrey Gilbert, England's First Empire Builder* (1911).
20 *Aubrey's Brief Lives*, edited by Oliver Lawson Dick.

CHAPTER VIII

Sir Walter Ralegh and America

John Aubrey relates that Ralegh spoke broad Devonshire to his dying day.[1] He also describes him as a tall, handsome and bold man. He was dark, with almost a Celtic darkness, although he came from an ancient Devon family. He had an exceedingly high forehead, and "a kind of pigge-eye", while his beard turned up naturally. Like Francis Bacon, he was a man of magnificent tastes, with an inclination to dress richly. He wore sometimes a white satin doublet, all embroidered with rich pearls, and a costly chain of great pearls was arrayed about his neck. The traditional story of Ralegh, Queen Elizabeth and the cloak seem to have some basis in fact, for Thomas Fuller[2] tells us that Captain Ralegh, having come out of Ireland to the English Court in good habit (his clothes being then a considerable part of his estate), one day encountered Queen Elizabeth, who was walking over "a plashy place". Ralegh, with a courtier's instincts, at once spread his elegant new cloak on the ground whereon the Queen trod gently.

Aubrey relates further picturesque details about Ralegh, for instance that he studied most in his sea voyages, when he always took with him a trunk of books and had nothing to divert him. He cannot be described as a great seaman, in the sense that Drake, Hawkins and Frobisher undoubtedly were, for Ralegh was an enigmatic personality, a man of many parts, a gifted writer with a superb imagination. None of his achievements were more remarkable than his constant obsession and indefatigable efforts to colonize in America. Yet Ralegh had many faults, despite his undoubted genius. He was a gross flatterer, even if we have to admit that it was essential to attempt to retain the favour of the Queen; he was proud, arrogant, passionate and capable at times of a violent temper, all qualities to be found among the Elizabethans. He sometimes distorted the truth.

From 1584, when he was a man of thirty, until his death on the scaffold during the reign of James I (1618), Ralegh used his feverish mind in furthering various schemes to gain the New World from Spain and make it part of an English Empire. Even from prison during 1609 he could write of the lovely land of Virginia: "I shall yet live to see it an English nation." No doubt James Anthony Froude also had Ralegh in mind when he wrote of the "great unrest" in the Elizabethan seamen—of that strange mystical vision which dominated their thoughts. "What it was, may be best measured by the results in the present England and America."

Ralegh's most recent biographers[3] opine that he probably first became interested in colonization projects in the New World during his early career as a soldier when he served in France under Admiral Coligny.

By 1584 tension between England and Spain was becoming acute. It was in April of that year that Ralegh sent two barks under the command of two sea captains, Philip Amadas of Plymouth and Arthur Barlow, to America, with Simon Fernandez as Portuguese pilot. The real purpose of the expedition was to reconnoitre a site for a colony in the southern section of the North American coast. In this project Ralegh had the enthusiastic support of Richard Hakluyt the elder, and his cousin Richard Hakluyt. This family originally came from the border county of Herefordshire. The younger Hakluyt wrote a work of considerable literary merit, *The Discourse of Western Planting*, while Amadas and Barlow were still at sea. His opinion was that North American colonization was a matter for the resources of the State rather

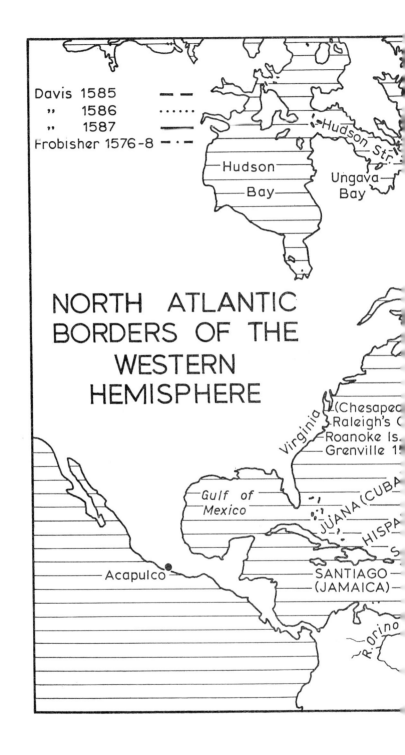

Davis 1585 — —
  " 1586 ......
  " 1587 ———
Frobisher 1576-8 — · —

Hudson Str.

Hudson
Bay

Ungava
Bay

NORTH ATLANTIC
BORDERS OF THE
WESTERN
HEMISPHERE

Virginia (Chesape
Raleigh's C
Roanoke Is.
Grenville 1

Gulf of
Mexico

JUANA (CUBA

HISPA

Acapulco

SANTIAGO
(JAMAICA)

R. Orino

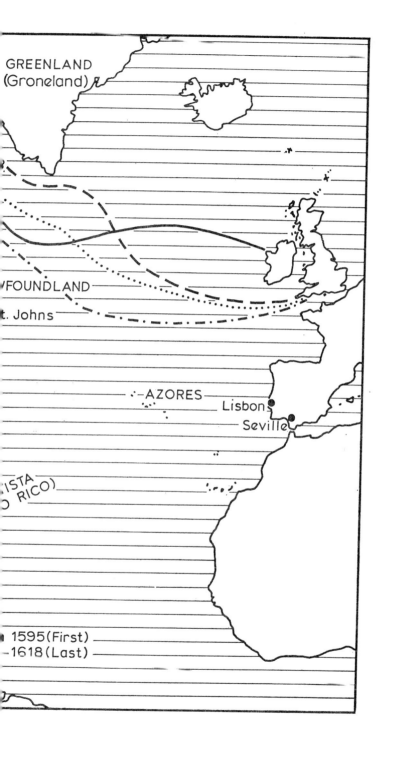

GREENLAND
(Groneland)

FOUNDLAND

t. Johns

AZORES
Lisbon
Seville

STA
RICO)

1595(First)
1618(Last)

than of private persons.[4] This would hardly have commended itself to the Queen's views, who often expected her buccaneers to finance their own voyages. Nevertheless, the Virginia voyages planned by Ralegh had her approval and backing. Walsingham also gave Ralegh his influential support.

Philip Amadas and Arthur Barlow sailed via the Canaries where they arrived on 10th May.[5] They then made for the West Indies, where "the ayre was found very unwholesome" for the seamen, many of whom became ill. However, sweet water and fresh victuals soon restored them to some semblance of health. The navigators sailed on to the low-lying coast of what is today North Carolina. At one stage of their travels they made landfall at Wocoken, an island which is part of a long sand reef off this coast. They considered it a suitable site for a settlement. One can sense their excitement, a kind of pristine wonder when treading on virgin soil and taking possession of some land in the name of Queen Elizabeth. Arthur Barlow wrote with rapture about the sandy coves and land so abounding with grapes, "as the very beating and surge of the sea overflowed them". Such moments of enchantment never cloy, for the pleasure given is in essence spiritual. To the tired, bruised spirits of the seamen, how resplendent it was to gaze on that promised land.

"This island had many goodly woodes full of deere, conies, hares, and fowle, even in the middest of summer in incredible abundance," wrote Barlow. "The woodes are not such as you finde in Bohemia, Moscovia or Hercynia, barren and fruitles, but the highest and reddest cedars of the world."

They made the acquaintance of the king whose name was Wingina. His kingdom was called Wingandacoa, "and now by her Majestie Virginia". The Indians of the mainland seemed to the mariners "most gentle, loving and faithful, void of all guile and treason, and such as live after the manner of the golden age". Amadas and Barlow brought back with them to England two lusty young Indians, Wanabese and Mantee.

Richard Hakluyt's important treatise, *The Discourse on Western Planting*, had been written "at the request and direction" of

Walter Ralegh. One of his chief aims was that England should become a self-supporting nation. It was maintained that silks, wine, olives and oil which now had to be imported, could be produced in America. Another object was a fierce attack on the Spanish Empire. It was known that most of the natives hated the Spaniards, consequently there should be no difficulty in persuading them to rise up against their Spanish oppressors. Ralegh indeed considered himself as the humane emancipator of the Indians.[6] Queen Elizabeth was always keenly interested in the colonizing projects concerning Virginia, and she helped her favourite in various financial ways through the farm of wines and giving him the licence to export clothes, and other privileges.

It is certain that Ralegh himself intended to lead the expedition. which was to plant the first English colony in America, but various reasons conspired to keep him in England. The Queen was also reluctant that Sir Walter should leave the Court, and he considered that his cousin Sir Richard Grenville would be a suitable person to command the expedition.

The character of this heroic Cornishman has been fully described by his biographer, Dr. A. L. Rowse.[7] "He was very typical of his age and class—that small class of captains and commanders by land and sea, which set the pace for the Elizabethan Age. Like them he was strenuous, hard-working, acquisitive, restless, devoted; more selfless than most, there was nothing of the egoist in him, as in so many of those others." Yet Grenville is not a particularly sympathetic, attractive personality; he was quarrelsome, capable of brutality and cruelty on occasions, even taking into consideration the standards of the age. "The great unrest" in him was as marked as in Humphrey Gilbert, in Walter Ralegh or in Francis Drake. Combined with these qualities was an element of unbalance, of over-strain. His subordinates were terrified of his violent temper and moods. Like Gilbert, his early career had been as a soldier, and he always considered himself as such.

In 1585 Grenville commanded a fleet consisting of seven ships: the *Tiger*, a ship lent by the Queen, a fly-boat called the *Roebuck*, built by Ralegh, the *Lyon*, a ship of 100 tons, the *Elizabeth*, of 50 tons, and a small bark the *Dorothy*. "There were also two small pinnesses."

An impressive number of people accompanied the expedition. There was Ralph Lane, the Queen's equerry, who quarrelled with Grenville, and who was to remain in Virginia one year to look after the colonists. There was Thomas Cavendish (Candish), who was later to circumnavigate the world. Another interesting personality was Thomas Hariot, the famous mathematician and a close friend of Sir Walter Ralegh. He later shared his imprisonment in the Tower. Hariot*—then a young man of twenty-five— went as scientific observer, and later wrote an interesting report about "the new found land of Virginia". The expedition also included a number of gentlemen, mostly from the West Country: John Arundell, Mr. Prideaux, Mr. Stukeley and John Rashleigh the younger. Another member was John White, distinguished artist and cartographer. The fleet sailed on 9th April from Plymouth, and five days later arrived at Lancerota and Forteventura in the Canaries. By 7th May Sir Richard Grenville had sighted the island of Dominica† in the West Indies.

During the voyage Grenville and his party stayed for some time on the northern coast of Hispaniola, where they found the Spanish governor and various gentlemen very courteous and agreeable. It is also interesting to relate that the English seamen and soldiers got on very well with their Spanish counterparts, although the latter were naturally at first mistrustful of the English. The Spaniards were invited to a sumptuous banquet, and they expressed their pleasure when the trumpets and other musical instruments sounded. As a return for this hospitality the Spaniards organized a kind of bull hunt in which Grenville's captains and gentlemen were mounted on horseback. One of the white bulls made for the sea, where he was slain by a seaman's musket. When we consider that 1585 was merely three years before the Armada and the growing political tension between

* Born in 1560.
† Discovered by Christopher Columbus (1493) on a Sunday.

England and Spain, such amicable scenes seem surprising. No doubt the vigilant, brooding Grenville was closely observing conditions in the Spanish Colonies.

Towards the end of June Grenville—accompanied by John Arundell, Mr. Stukeley, Ralph Lane, Thomas Cavendish, Thomas Hariot and John Rashleigh—landed on the American coast, firstly on the island of Wocokon. The colonists then moved to the island of Roanoke, where the explorer Amadas had spent some time during 1584. When one of the natives stole a silver cup, which was not restored, Grenville ordered that his village should be burnt to the ground. This was a harsh act, but we must judge it by contemporary Elizabethan standards, not by our own. There is no evidence that any of the natives lost their lives, for they had already fled to the woods. Would any of the great Elizabethan sea captains or commanders have acted differently? Sir Richard Hawkins, perhaps, a humane and just man; while Ralegh's treatment of the Indians was certainly enlightened. It must be remembered that the Indians on the mainland were frequently at war with those on the island of Roanoke.

Meanwhile Ralph Lane was writing to Ralegh, Sir Philip Sidney, and Walsingham complaining of Grenville's tyrannous and harsh behaviour to all the gentlemen on board. It would seem that the relations between Grenville and Lane grew even more strained both on board and on shore. At one time Grenville even considered bringing him to trial in the same way that Drake had tried Thomas Doughty. It was not easy for these Elizabethans, cooped up as they were in their small ships, to remain friendly. The petty jealousies, the constant wrangling, the clash of temperaments, all played their part in sowing discord among the leaders. Ralph Lane later supposed that Grenville had returned home with the express purpose of accusing Thomas Cavendish, Captain Clark, captain of the fly-boat, and others of various offences. Lane wrote to Sir Francis Walsingham

that it is not possible for men to behave themselves more faithfully and more industriously in our action. ... Contrarywise how Sir Richard Grenville, general, hath demeaned himself from the first day of his entry into government at Plymouth, until the day of his departure from hence over the bar in the Port Ferdinando, far otherwise than my hope of him, though very agreeable to the expectations and predictions of sundry wise and godly persons of his own country, that knew him better than myself.[8]

We do not know Grenville's side of the story, so it is difficult to form an opinion. It may well be that Lane's temperament clashed with Grenville's, and Lane certainly was only too ready to complain when things went wrong. If the relations between the two men were so strained, it is difficult to understand why Grenville appointed Lane Governor of Virginia for a year when he returned to England.

Greatly relieved that Grenville had left for England, Lane sat down to write to Richard Hakluyt the elder, of the Middle Temple, his impressions of Virginia.

We have discovered the maine to be the goodliest oyle under the cope of heaven, so abounding with sweete trees, that bring such sundry rich and pleasant gummes, grapes of such greatness, yet wilde, as France, Spaine, nor Italie have no greater, so many sorts of Apothecarie drugs, such severall kindes of flaxe, and one kind like silke, the same gathered of a grasse, as common there, as grasse is here.[9]

John White's delicate water-colour drawings of scenes of Ralegh's Virginia are in the British Museum. They depict the east coast of North America from Cape Lookout to Chesapeake Bay and inland to approximately longitude 77 degrees west. On the mainland between Chesapeake Bay and Albermarle Sound are shown the royal arms of Queen Elizabeth I, while those of Sir Walter Ralegh are revealed between Albermarle Sound and Pamlico River. Along the coastline we can distinguish the names of the Indian villages: Combec, Mashawatec, Skicóac, Chesepina, Sho, Titepano and others.

It cannot be pretended that Sir Ralph Lane was an outstanding personality. He was a conscientious, diligent man, not without imagination, but he was no diplomatist and he was unable to maintain friendly relations with the Indians. This was vital if the colonial venture was to succeed. Lane with his company of 107 men built a fort at the north end of Roanoke island, a convenient base for exploring the country. Lane travelled as far south as Secoton, an Indian village.* Lane wrote Sir Walter Ralegh that to the northward their farthest discovery was the country of the Chesapians, 130 miles distant from the island of Roanoak. "The passage to it was very shallow and most dangerous, by reason of the bred'th of the Sound, and the little succour that upon any flawe was there to be had."

The first attempt to create a colony in Virginia proved to some extent abortive, mainly because of the lack of experience of the English colonists. Among those who had remained with Lane in America for one year, was Thomas Hariot, the mathematician, a close friend of Sir Walter Ralegh. Thomas Hariot was indeed a highly successful colonist, for he took infinite trouble to learn the Indian language and attempted to establish harmonious relations with them. When he showed them such marvels as sea compasses, lodestones, a perspective glass (precursor of the telescope), the natives, very fearful, supposed that they were the works of gods rather than of men. Ralegh encouraged Hariot to write a detailed survey about Virginia. It can be found in Hakluyt's works.[10] Perhaps the most interesting part is Hariot's description of the people, with their primitive belief in many gods. He describes them as clothed with loose mantles made of deer skins, and aprons of the same material "round their middles". Their offensive weapons were mostly bows composed of witch-hazel, and arrows made of reeds. They also used wooden truncheons about a yard long. Naturally such a primitive people were very superstitious. Thomas Hariot relates that when their corn withered owing to a drought, the natives would approach the English settlers and fearfully inquire whether in any way they had offended them. Would not the Englishmen pray to their God of England that their crops might be preserved?

---

* The district now lies between the Pamlico and Neuse Rivers.

It is fascinating to compare these early descriptions of the natives of Virginia with those written by William Strachey, the colonist, who described the scenes at sea when the *Sea-Venture* was wrecked in the Bermudas during the great storm of July 1609. Strachey refers to the natives: "Their hair is black, grosse, long and thick; the men have no beardes; their noses are broad, flatt and full at the end, great bigg lippes, and wyde mouths yet nothing so unsightly as the Moores. . . . The women have handsome lymbes, slender arms and pretty hands, and when they sing they have a pleasant tange in their voices."

Sir Walter Ralegh maintained that he had spent as much as £40,000 of his own money on the Virginian colonial projects, though he probably exaggerated the amount. Despite the early setbacks and constant discouragement Ralegh did not despair. In 1587 he organized a new expedition to plant a colony in Virginia under the leadership of John White, the gifted artist, whom he appointed Governor. Twelve assistants were to serve under him. Ralegh gave the potential settlers a charter, and referred to White as the governor and his assistants of the City of Ralegh in Virginia. This expedition included about 150 men, but there were also women among them. They sailed from Plymouth on 8th May, and whilst in the West Indies many of the men and women became ill after eating a fruit which resembled green apples. They experienced a burning in their mouths and such an unpleasant swelling of their tongues that some of them could not speak.

When White reached Virginia in July 1587 he heard that fifteen men, who had been left at Roanoke by Sir Richard Grenville, had been killed by Indians. One of White's assistants named George Howe was unfortunate enough to stray from his company whilst catching crabs, and was slain by Indians as he waded in the water. White's daughter Eleanour married to Ananias Dare, one of his assistants, gave birth to a daughter in Roanoak, who was named Virginia, "the first Christian to be born in Virginia". Governor White eventually returned to England, so as to ensure that essential stores should be sent to the colonists, leaving about one hundred people to form a plantation in his absence. This further attempt to create a colony in Virginia was also doomed to failure. At home Ralegh, burdened as he was with official duties, promised to relieve the distress of the stricken colonists. He tried to organize a small fleet under Sir Richard Grenville, which was to transport "a good supply of shipping and men, with sufficiency of all things needful".[11] Unfortunately it was already 1588, and news that the Spanish Armada was about to sail had already reached England. Grenville as one of the leading sea captains could not be spared from his exacting duties at home. After incessant entreaties, White succeeded in obtaining from Ralegh and Grenville two small pinnaces, one of 30 tons named the *Brave*, the other called the *Roe*. White once again left England's shores, together with fifteen settlers and provisions intended for the relief of those already in Virginia. Instead of concentrating on their main object, however, the crews were tempted to cruise for prizes. The supplies never reached their destination. Some years later, in 1593, John White wrote to Richard Hakluyt the younger referring to his fifth voyage to Virginia, "which was no lesse unfortunately ended then frowardly begun, and as lucklesse to many, as sinister to my selfe". Ralegh constantly kept in contact with events in Virginia. In 1602 he sent out a bark under a Weymouth mariner named Samuel Mace to find John White's lost colony of 1587, but the seamen concerned, instead of obeying Ralegh's instructions, engaged in more profitable undertakings elsewhere.[12]

It was Sir Walter Ralegh who brought the new Indian weed, tobacco, into fashion in England, though Sir John Hawkins had originally introduced it twenty years before.* Ralegh became an ardent smoker. His friends were fascinated by the spectacle of Ralegh with his large silver-mounted pipe and wreaths of mysterious smoke issuing from his mouth. Thomas Hariot, with whom Ralegh had often discussed mathematics and astronomy, mentions tobacco in his *Briefe and True report of the new found land of Virginia.*

* Aubrey, however, relates that Ralegh was the first to bring tobacco to England.

There is an herbe which is sowed apart by itselfe, and is called by the inhabitants Uppowoc: in the West Indies it hath divers names, according to the severall places and countreys where it groweth and is used: the Spanyards generally call it Tobacco. The leaves thereof being dried and brought into powder, they use to take the fume and smoake thereof, by sucking it thorow pipes made of clay into their stomache and head; from whence it purgeth superfluous fleume and other gross humours. . . .

Aubrey could not resist relating a slightly malicious story about Hariot. Since Hariot could not believe the ancient story about the creation of the world, he was wont to murmur "*nihilo nihil fit*" (nothing comes of nothing). "But a *nihilum* killed him at last: for in the top of his nose came a little red speck (exceedingly small), which grew bigger and bigger, and at last killed him." Whilst he shared Ralegh's imprisonment during the reign of James I he was given an annuity of £200 per annum by Thomas Percy, Earl of Northumberland,* a fellow prisoner. One reason for James I's later hatred of Ralegh was the King's dislike of "the loathsome and devilish practice of tobacco-drinking".

Ralegh's importance as a founder of the British Empire was in reality the contribution he made to English colonial theory.[13] Together with his half-brother, Sir Humphrey Gilbert, he continually stressed both in speech and his writings the desirability of American colonization. The Spanish Empire to Ralegh was not so much to be robbed, but to be replaced by an English Empire. He certainly favoured a more enlightened and benevolent policy towards the South American Indians than most of his contemporaries. His concern for the native population was not altogether owing to altruistic reasons, but he hoped by just and humane treatment of the Indians they might be persuaded to rise against their Spanish oppressors. All the same Ralegh revealed a wholly admirable quality of tenderness in his dealings with the Indians.

Ralegh's downfall was owing to his roving eye, that he dearly

* The 'Wizard' Earl.

loved a wench. In his gossipy way John Aubrey relates an amusing story, which reveals at any rate one aspect of his character.

> He loved a wench well, [wrote Aubrey] and one time getting up one of the Mayds of Honour up against a tree in a wood ('twas his first Lady) who seemed at first boarding to be something fearfull of her Honour, and modest, she cryed, Sweet Sir Walter, what doe you me ask? Will you undoe me? Nay, Sweet Sir Walter! Sweet Sir Walter! Sir Walter! At last, as the danger and the pleasure at the same time grew higher, she cryed in the extasey, Swisser Swatter Swisser Swatter. She proved with child, and I doubt not that this Hero tooke care of them both, as also that the Product was more than an ordinary mortal.*

Unfortunately the lady concerned was Elizabeth, a daughter of Sir Nicholas Throckmorton, and a valued servant of the Queen's. She was one of Elizabeth's maids-of-honour, a lively, attractive girl, and Ralegh fell in love with her. Sir Walter secretly married her, not daring to tell the Queen his mistress. When Elizabeth discovered what had happened she was deeply resentful, for she could never really forgive any of her favourites for falling in love with other women. For a while Ralegh and Bess Throckmorton, now Lady Ralegh, languished in the Tower. For a courtier the worst punishment in Elizabethan England was to be banished from Court. Ralegh, however, was temporarily released from the Tower, so that he might go to Dartmouth to investigate the affair of the Portuguese ship *The Madre de Dios*. As chief employer of the privateer crews who had captured this ship, he was instructed to try to save some of its booty for the Queen. After discharging his duties, he was compelled to return to the Tower, but was later allowed by his royal mistress to retire to Sherborne, the resplendent mansion she had given him.

It was during these years—the early 1590s—that he became more and more obsessed with his dream of Guiana, a passion

---

* It is of deep interest that a will dated 1597 and signed by Ralegh has recently been discovered at Sherborne Castle in Dorset, Ralegh's home for fifteen years. The will proved that Ralegh had an illegitimate daughter by "one Alice Gould". He left a legacy to her and to Thomas Hariot and Laurence Keymis among others.

which was to become more insistent and urgent than his love of and interest in Virginia. Guiana was the name then given to the northern part of the Amazon and the whole of the Orinoco basins in South America. This part of the mainland was not yet effectively occupied by the Spaniards or Portuguese.[14] There is no doubt that Richard Hakluyt the younger stimulated Ralegh's growing interest in Guiana. In the *Discourse of Western Planting*, Hakluyt had written:

> All that part of America eastward from Cunana unto the river of St. Augustine in Brazil containeth in length along the sea side 2,100 miles. In which compass and tract there is neither Spaniard, Portuguese, nor any Christian man, but only the Caribs, Indians and Savages. In which places is great plenty of gold, pearl, and precious stones.

Ralegh's avid interest in the first Guiana venture was in reality a desperate attempt to regain the Queen's favour.

Ralegh learnt much about South America from one of his sea captains named Jacob Whiddon, "a man most honest and valiant,"[15] and a privateer in his service. In 1586 Whiddon had sailed with two ships, the *Serpent* and *Mary Spark*, to obtain prizes for Ralegh. During this voyage Whiddon managed to capture a Spanish official named Don Pedro Sarmiento de Gamboa, a man with an intimate knowledge of South America, particularly of the conquest of Peru. Ralegh became friendly with Don Pedro, and they sometimes discussed Guiana together. Ralegh was to write in 1596: "Many years since, I had knowledge by relation, of that mighty, rich and beautiful Empire of Guiana, and of that great and golden city, which Spaniards call El Dorado and the naturals Manoa."[16]

Ralegh was an active promoter of privateering, and another of his sea captains, George Popham,* whilst engaged on a voyage to Trinidad in the West Indies in 1595 obtained some valuable information about Guiana for Ralegh. A year earlier Ralegh again sent Jacob Whiddon to Trinidad to make a report about the

---

* A kinsman of Lord Chief Justice Popham.

situation there. Whiddon made the acquaintance of the Spanish Governor Don Antonio de Berrio, now an old man of seventy-four. During his stay, Whiddon lost eight of his men, who were lured to some woods by Indians on the pretext that they were to take part in a deer hunt, and treacherously slain by the Spaniards. Don Antonio de Berrio, an experienced soldier of Charles V, was a dogged explorer, who had already made three unsuccessful attempts to reach the rich empire of Guiana. During his second expedition, which lasted from 1585–88, Berrio had crossed the Orinoco from the west, and had tried to gain access into the mysterious highlands, but had failed. During his third expedition he had explored parts of the Caroni and found the Indians increasingly hostile to the Spanish.

Ralegh, desperately anxious to regain the Queen's lost favour, turned to poetry:

> To seek new worlds, for gold, for praise, for glory,
> To try desire, to try love severed far,
> When I was gone, she sent her memory
> More strong than were ten thousand ships of war.[17]

His wife Bess, smarting under the Queen's displeasure, wrote to the little hunchback Secretary of State, Sir Robert Cecil, with whom she maintained friendly relations, in February 1594: "I hope, for my sake, you will rather draw Sir Walter towards the east, then help him forward towards the sunset." She wanted her husband restored in favour at Court rather than he should sail on this hare-brained expedition. She was to prove a devoted wife.

Ralegh's fleet consisted of four ships, including one supplied by the Lord High Admiral, Lord Charles Howard of Effingham, called *Lion's Whelp*, commanded by Captain George Clifford. Captain Jacob Whiddon also accompanied Ralegh on this expedition. As was customary with him when at sea, Ralegh carried two trunk-loads of books in his cabin. Ralegh sailed on 6th February 1595, accompanied by several West Countrymen and relations, including John Grenville, Sir Richard Grenville's younger son, who was later killed, John Gilbert, eldest son of Sir Humphrey

Gilbert, and others. Richard Carew of Anthony relates that John Grenville was a valiant soldier, and "that the ocean became his bed of honour".* There were probably about 300 men composing this expedition, some of whom were soldiers and adventurers. While Ralegh, dark and pensive, restlessly roamed the deck, he delighted in watching the graceful dolphins leaping playfully out of the water. He arrived in Trinidad on 22nd March and anchored off Punto Gallo, now Icacos Point, in the south-west of the island.

A leading privateer who had landed in Trinidad before Ralegh was Sir Robert Dudley, bastard son of Robert Dudley, Earl of Leicester, by Lady Douglas Sheffield. Eager to explore the Guiana mainland, Dudley waited only a week for Ralegh's arrival, and when there was no sign of him, departed in order to pursue his privateering.

Ralegh was anxious to capture Don Antonio de Berrio, the Spanish Governor, who had behaved so treacherously to Captain Jacob Whiddon and his men the year before.

In his own account of the expedition dedicated to Lord Howard of Effingham, Ralegh relates that he wished to revenge himself on Berrio, but he actually treated the Spanish Governor after capturing him during a surprise attack on San Joseph† with magnanimity and considerable courtesy. It is evident that Ralegh wanted the old conquistador to supply him with as much information as possible about the highlands of Guiana. He wrote of him: "This Berrio is a gentleman well descended, and had long served the Spanish King in Millain, Naples, the Lowe Countries and elsewhere, very valiant and liberall, and a gentleman of great assuredness, and of a great heart: I used him according to his estate, and worth in all things I could, according to the small means I had." When Ralegh revealed to Berrio that he was resolved to explore Guiana, the Spaniard was "stricken with a great melancholy and sadness, and used all the arguments he could to

* Richard Carew of Anthony 1555–1620. *The Survey of Cornwall*, edited and with an introduction by F. E. Halliday.
† Now Port of Spain.

disuade him". He assured the gentlemen, who were present, that it would be labour lost. On the whole Ralegh and Berrio got on very well together. They feasted together on delicious little oysters, "very salt and well tasted". Ralegh gives a lively, brilliant picture of Trinidad, familiar to those who know and love that island even today. "From thence I rowed to another part, called by the naturals Piche,* and by the Spaniards Tierra de Brea." He relates that all their oysters grew upon boughs of trees, and not on the ground: "the like is commonly seene in other places of the West Indies and elsewhere".

Ralegh's great prose work *The Discoverie of the Large Rich and Bewtiful Empire of Guiana*[18] can be read with pleasure for its wonderful descriptive passages, delighting the ear as if it were music. For ascending the Orinoco River, Ralegh found his gallego extremely useful after her upper works had been removed and her hull re-equipped as a galley.[19] The trouble was that Ralegh's sophisticated life as a courtier and in prison had not prepared him for the hard life of an explorer. He relates that they were

al driven to lie in the raine and weather, in the open air, in the burning sunne, and upon the hard bords, and to dresse our meat, and to carry all maner of furniture in them, wherewith they were so pestered and unsavory, that what with victuals being most fish, with wette clothes of so many people thrust together, and the heat of the sunne, I will undertake there was never any prison in England, that could be found more unsavorie and lothsome, especially to my selfe, who had for many yeeres before beene dieted and cared for in a sort farre more differing.[20]

Ralegh was deeply sensitive to the beauties of nature, and he considered the scenery surrounding the River Orinoco the finest he had ever seen:

And whereas all that we had seen before was nothing but woods, prickles, bushes and thornes, heere we beheld plaines of twenty miles in length, the grasse short and greene, and in divers parts

* The Pitch Lake.

groves of trees by themselves, as if they had been by all the art and labour in the world so made of purpose; and stil as we rowed the Deere came downe feeding by the waters side, as if they had been used to a keepers call. Upon this river there were great store of fowle, and of many sorts and divers sorts of strange fishes, of marvellous bignes.

Unfortunately Ralegh lost one of his lusty negroes, who leaping out of the galley to swim, was immediately devoured by a "lagarto" (alligator). He relates:

When we ran to the tops of the first hills of the plains adjoining to the river, we beheld that wonderful breach of waters, which ran down Caroli (Caroni): and might from that mountain see the river how it ran in three parts, above twenty miles off, and there appeared some ten or twelve overfalls in sight, every one as high over the other as a church tower, which fell with that fury, that the rebound of waters made it seem as if it had been all covered over with a great shower of rain: and in some places we took it at the first for a smoke that had risen over some great towne.

It is tempting to succumb to Ralegh's superb imagery, but the real importance of his Guiana expedition was his success in dealing with the Indian tribes. This man, capable of such arrogance, with his hot, fiery temper, could be strangely gentle with the Indians. He possessed an intuitive understanding of their minds. He described one of the tribes, the Ewaipanoma: "They are reported to have their eyes in their shoulders and their mouths in the middle of their breasts, and that a long train of haire groweth backward between their shoulders." When Ralegh later related fantastic stories about them, there were plenty of his enemies in England to pour scorn at him, and ready to insinuate that this liar had all the time been skulking in Cornwall, and never been near the Orinoco River. Ralegh wrote with humility of the Indians: "they are for the most parte a people very faithfull, humble, patient, peaceable, simple, without subtility, malice, quarrels, strife, rancor, or desyer of revengement; as meeke as lambs, as harmless as children of ten or twelve yeares." He taught them about the Queen Elizabeth, "the great cicique [monarch] of the North". She was an enemy of the Castellani (Spaniards) and wished to deliver them, the Indians, from the tyranny and oppression of Spanish rule. This was Ralegh's policy to try to substitute in the Indian mind respect for the English, instead of rancour and fear of the Spaniards. They crowded round Ralegh as he told them in simple language of the great princess whom they now call Ezrabeta Cassipuna Aquere-mana. He gave special instructions to his men that they must not use force against the Indians, or molest their women, although his orders were sometimes disregarded. One cannot imagine Thomas Cavendish or Richard Grenville pursuing such humane conduct.

Ralegh's scientific curiosity is Elizabethan, for it reveals his interest in medicine. "There was nothing whereof I was more curious," he wrote, "than to finde out the true remedies of those poisoned arrows, for besides the mortalitie of the wound they make, the partie shot indureth the most insufferable torment in the world, and abideth a most uglie and lamentable death, sometimes dying starke mad."

As Margaret Irwin in her fine biography of Ralegh[21] so sensitively wrote, "The strange thunder of the waters" was to haunt Ralegh all his life. It haunted him, like a passion, never giving him rest until he returned to that mysterious and lovely country more than twenty years later. The story of his release from the Tower to embark on that last ill-starred expedition to Guiana and of his tragic death on the scaffold will be briefly told in a later chapter.

Notes

CHAPTER VIII

1 *Brief Lives*, p. 255.
2 *The History of the Worthies of England* (1663 edition), p. 262.
3 J. H. Adamson and H. F. Folland, *The Shepherd of the Ocean*.
4 Taylor ed., *Hakluyt's Voyages* II, 327 foll.
   A. L. Rowse, *Expansion of Elizabethan England*.
5 Richard Hakluyt, *Voyages* (Everyman Edition), Vol. VI, p. 121.
6 J. H. Adamson and H. F. Folland, *The Shepherd of the Ocean*.
7 A. L. Rowse, *Sir Richard Grenville of the Revenge*.
8 *Ibid.*
9 Richard Hakluyt, *Voyages* (Everyman Edition), Vol. VI, p. 140.
10 A briefe and true report of the New found land of Virginia; of the commodities there found, etc.
11 A. L. Rowse, *Sir Richard Grenville of the Revenge*.
    Account in First Edition of Hakluyt (1589).
12 A. L. Rowse, *The Expansion of Elizabethan England*, p. 225.
13 David B. Quinn, *Raleigh and the British Empire*.
14 *Ibid.*
15 Richard Hakluyt, *Voyages*, Vol VII, p. 282.
16 Ralegh's own account. Dedicated to Lord Howard of Effingham.
17 From "The Book of the Ocean Cynthia," Agatha Latham ed., *The Poems of Sir Walter Ralegh*.
18 Hakluyt Society.
19 David B. Quinn, *Raleigh and the British Empire*.
20 Richard Hakluyt, *Voyages* (Everyman Edition), Vol. VI, p. 286.
21 *That Great Lucifer*.

CHAPTER IX

Voyages of George Clifford, Third Earl of Cumberland

The Earl of Cumberland, a typical Elizabethan and a great buccaneer, made a dozen celebrated voyages during his life. Although he was really a privateer, he deserves an honoured place among the great seamen. When one considers his attractive qualities, his patriotism, that he was capable of statesmanship on occasions and that he had an intimate knowledge of seamanship, acquired by hard privations, one wonders why his life is not better known. His portrait by Nicholas Hilliard is that of a handsome man, chivalrous and romantic and one who would be favoured by women. Although he was about twenty-five years younger than the Queen, she certainly admired him for his dare-devil, adventurous spirit. She liked also to tickle his neck. Many sea captains and privateers sailed in Cumberland's expeditions: William Monson, Robert Withrington, Christopher Lister, James Langton, Nicholas Downton, John Watts, Christopher Colthurst and Henry Clifford among others. Gentlemen of rank and posi-tion were eager to volunteer in Cumberland's ships. He succeeded to the title—an ancient North Country one—in 1569 when he was barely eleven. It was one of the richest inheritances in the country. His daughter, Lady Anne Clifford, tells us that an extreme love for horse races, tiltings, bowling matches and shooting and all such expensive sports did contribute the more to the wasting of his estate.[1] His marriage to Lady Margaret Russell, daughter of his guardian the Earl of Bedford, was a splendid occasion at Court attended by the Queen. We know that Elizabeth approved of this match, and Lady Anne Clifford, whose diary of the Jacobean Court is of significant interest, relates that her mother was "cozen germain, twice removed" to her father. That Cumberland was deeply attached to his wife, "Sweet Meg", "good Megg",—as he quaintly calls her, at least for many years—is evident when we study his letters.[2] So greatly did Lady Anne Clifford (later Countess of Dorset) admire her father that she took infinite trouble to have accounts of his voyages collected *"out of the Relations, Observations and Journals of Severall credible and worthy Persons, actors and Commanders under the said Noble Earl in his severall Voyages and Expeditions"*. George Clifford, Earl of Cumberland, a famous privateer, possessed a generosity, a magnificence, all the more admirable when we consider the petty squabbles and jealousies rife among the seamen. He related that he had spent most of his fortune on his sea voyages. Towards the end of the Elizabethan era in 1600, he was to write: "I have spent in sea journeys, I protest, £100,000."[3]

Samuel Purchas, the vicar from Essex, who had never travelled more than 200 miles from his parish, was a diligent and remarkable editor of sea voyages. Though he lacked the younger Hakluyt's greatness and modesty, he wrote a remarkable work entitled *Purchas His Pilgrimes*, contayning a *History of the World, in Sea Voyages and Lande Travells* by Englishmen and others, published in 1625. Puchas was wont to take down from the lips of mariners the accounts of their travels.[4] All the same he borrowed much from Hakluyt, and he has been described by Professor Parks[5] as "the cringing, unctuous and indefatigable parson". Yet he tells us some lively details about Cumberland's voyages. He differed sharply from Richard Hakluyt the younger, who endured heart-breaking fatigue in his quest for information about the voyages. "What restless nights, what painful days, what heat, what cold I have endured," wrote that great man, "how many famous libraries I have researched into . . . what expenses I have not spared; and yet what fair opportunities of private gain, preferment and ease I have neglected."[6] Works which have really benefited mankind were gained the hard way.

The object of Clifford's first privateering venture in 1586 was mainly to free himself from the embarrassment of his overwhelming debts. Yet there were other motives, as there usually were with these Elizabethans; the desire for riches mingled with Cumberland's craving for honour and glory. One senses "the great unrest" in him, as with Drake, Frobisher and Grenville. Purchas relates that Cumberland's first voyage was begun from Gravesend, 26th June 1586. Cumberland did not sail himself on this voyage, and it was to prove an unlucky one. The *Red Dragon* as admiral, a ship of 260 tons with 130 men on board, was commanded by Captain Robert Withrington, while the *Bark Clifford*, a smaller vessel of 130 tons, had as its captain Christopher Lister. Included in the expedition were also the *Roe* and Sir Walter Ralegh's pinnace the *Dorothy*. During the voyage the mariners captured

a great foule monster whose head and backe were so harde that no sword could enter it, but being thrust in under the belly in divers places and much wounded he bowed a sword in his mouth as a man would do a girdle of leather about his hande and likewise the iron of a boare speare. He was in length about nine foote and had nothing in his belly but a certain quantities of small stones.[7]

John Sarracoll, a merchant, also wrote an account of this voyage for Hakluyt. Cumberland gave his captains orders that they were to sail for the Straits of Magellan and to take, if possible, £6,000 worth of prizes. As events transpired, however, the ships turned back before reaching the straits.[8] At Bahia in Brazil the seamen captured a few prizes which were of little value. By 1589 George Clifford's debts amounted to £6,800. Yet Queen Elizabeth had such a deep respect for Cumberland's qualities that she appointed him one of the Commissioners for the trial of Mary Queen of Scots.

During 1586 Cumberland wrote a very interesting letter to his wife, "My Sweet Meg", referring to Sir Francis Drake having taken one of the chief towns in all the Indies called Santo Domingo together with 300,000 ducats and much other wealth.[9] The letter is signed "Thine ever, George Cumberland". It was George Clifford, who on hearing news of the approach of the Armada during 1588, went on board the *Bonaventura* commanded by Captain George Raymond. So it was this nobleman who had the honour of bringing the news of the defeat to Gravelines. Samuel Purchas comments to "wanne that honour" "no sea can drowne, no age can weare out". My Lord Cumberland, together with Sir Robert Carey, rode to Tilbury Camp, where they found the Queen in the midst of her army. During the invasion of the Spanish Armada, Lord Cumberland owned the *Sampson*, which was involved in the fighting. Elizabeth always took a great interest in Cumberland's voyages and lent him one of her ships, the *Golden Lion*. From this vessel he wrote to his devoted wife, his "Sweet Meg": "God, I most humbly thank him, hath so mightily blessed me, that already I have taken a Dunkirk [ship] bound for Saint Lucar in Spain. I have sent Lister [captain] to see her unladen in Portsmouth."

Among those who served the Earl of Cumberland as a captain was William Monson, the celebrated naval historian, who is distinguished as being the first seaman to write any historical account of the warfare in which he played a part. He hailed from Lincolnshire, where his family had been country squires for several generations. Monson was born about 1567, so he was nine years younger than Cumberland. He seems to have been warmly attached to the Earl though he quarrelled with him. Whatever the reason for these bitter disputes may be, Monson was a querulous, difficult man. He ran away from home at an early age to go to sea. In early life he was a privateer, and as a seaman possessed marked ability. During the Armada campaign he served as a volunteer on board the Queen's pinnace *Charles*.[10] Two or three years later he became associated with the privateering voyages of the Earl of Cumberland. In 1591, during the fourth voyage, he was taken prisoner and incarcerated for a time in Lisbon Castle. He complains of "the cruel usage" of the Spaniards, though the English were just as capable of harshness against their enemies. Yet Monson's fellow-prisoners were treated with considerable courtesy by the Spaniards.

Rowland Whyte in a letter to Sir Robert Sidney* (9th February 1597–8) relates that Sir William Monson challenged My Lord of Cumberland to a duel "for having used some disgraceful words of him and his doings upon the Coast of Terceras[11] [Azores]". It would seem that the two friends were later reconciled. Towards the end of the Elizabethan era (1597), he became the flag-captain of Robert Devereux, Earl of Essex, and served in the *Rainbow*, described as the most rolling and laboursome ship in England, though exceptionally fast under sail. One of Cumberland's favourite captains was Christopher Lister, but Monson was probably jealous of him and accused him of errors of judgement and rashness during the Earl's third voyage to the Azores. Samuel Purchas, however, also alleges that Captain Lister was rash in various actions during this voyage. Edward Wright the mathematician and engineer, during Cumberland's third voyage in June 1589, wrote that Lister was "a man of great resolution".[12]

It has already been mentioned that Cumberland was a humane commander. For instance after he had captured Fayal in the Azores (Terceras), he gave strict orders that none of the churches, or religious houses on the island should be sacked. Unfortunately his commands were disobeyed by the soldiers and mariners, who searched the houses for chests of sweet wood, hangings and bedding. The booty which they managed to steal was of much value. The inhabitants were finally forced to pay a ransom of 2,000 ducats for the town, mostly in church plate. Samuel Purchas relates that Cumberland was severely wounded, "receiving three shot upon his target, and a fourth on the side not deepe, his head also broken with stones that the blood covered

* Younger brother of Sir Philip Sidney.

his face both it and his legs likewise burned with fire-balls".[13] Purchas praises the Earl for his dauntless courage and "noble charitie" when the men were deprived of water while sailing homeward, as related by Edward Wright. The other main narrative of Cumberland's third voyage is that of Linschoten, given by Richard Hakluyt in his seventh volume. This account may well be partly inaccurate. Whether or not the Earl burnt the castle at Fayal to the ground is at least uncertain. This authority accuses the Spaniards of cruelty, charging them as "bloody cruel and dishonest", but he evidently had a high opinion of Cumberland and his sea captains. His nobility in sharing the terrible privations of the seamen under his command during the return journey has already been alluded to.

The birth of his daughter, Lady Anne Clifford, is mentioned in a letter "to my sweet Megg" from Cumberland in early February, 1589.[14] During the following year the Earl was busy in London dealing with various matters, such as paying off the mariners. He was eager, however, to return to his ship and soon he was able to tell his wife: "I thank God I am with my ship and company lately arrived and, though we have tasted some extremities, yet myself was never better, nor I think never any lost fewer men."[15] He is glad to reassure his wife that the Queen had received him most kindly. Meanwhile he is making preparations for his fourth voyage.

Lady Anne Clifford alludes to this voyage:

> Though the miseries by sickness, death, famyne and many other misadventures happened in the preceding voyage, were sufficient to have moved his Lordshipp to have abjured for ever those maryne adventures, especiallie beinge neither his profession not yett urged by necessitie thereunto yett suche was his naturall inclynacon to pursue those courses in hope of honour and profitt in the end.

All the same his friends tried very hard to dissuade Cumberland from sailing on another voyage. During the fourth expedition he embarked on the Queen's ship, the *Garland*, a vessel of about 600 tons. There was a crew of about 300 on this ship. The *Garland*

had been built by Richard Chapman, one of the leading
Elizabethan shipwrights, and had cost about £3,200 to construct.
According to Lady Anne Clifford's narrative, other vessels
taking part in this voyage included the *Sampson*, commanded by
Captain John Morton; the *Golden Noble* of 260 tons by Captain
Edward Partridge; and a French ship named the *Allagata* of
80 tons. Lord Cumberland sailed in May 1591, and it was not
long before the mariners managed to capture a ship laden with
sugar. However, this was lost owing to an "irrecoverable leake".
It was during this voyage, as already mentioned, that Monson was
imprisoned in Lisbon Castle and remained in captivity until
July 1592.

While he was sailing near the coast of Spain, Cumberland
discovered that the *Garland* was (as Monson described it) "but
evil of sail". After much consultation the Earl decided to make
for English shores. Meanwhile he charged Captain William
Middleton in the *Discovery* or the *Moonshine* to warn Lord
Thomas Howard,* an experienced commander of seamen, and
Sir Richard Grenville of the *Revenge* that a Spanish fleet had sailed
and was close to the Azores. Lord Thomas most prudently
"weighed anchor", according to Monson, and drew his fleet
aside "to get the wind of the Spaniards". Grenville, however,
fought the Spaniards in an heroic action, which has been immor-
talized in poetry and prose. Monson charges Grenville with
rashness and that he turned his violent temper on those who
opposed his will. Cumberland's main service was to warn Lord
Thomas Howard, a favourite of Queen Elizabeth, of the danger,
and thus gain time for this commander to withdraw to safety
various ships, including the *Bonaventura*, the *Defiance*, the *Golden
Lion* and the *Nonpareil*, so that they could fight on further
occasions.

I have already mentioned the curious letter written by Queen
Elizabeth to her "right Trusty and well beloved cosyn" Cumberland on 9th September 1591. Longing to hold "his sweet Meg"

---

* Second son of Thomas, Fourth Duke of Norfolk.

in his arms again, Cumberland wrote to his wife from *The Garland*: "It hath pleased God, since I discharged Daniel Gerratt I have met with three hulks going into Lisbon, with great store of copper, bacon, ropes, corn, and merchant's goods, belonging to the enemy, which the wind being fair, I would not tarry to search, but have sent them home." Cumberland's tenderness of nature and kind heart are very manifest in these letters. "Sweet Meg," he conjures her, "so comfort thyself with pleasing thoughts that may find thee in such health and strength as I wish, and shall breed me more joy than anything in this world." And it is evident that she returned his love and eagerly awaited his return from the sea voyages.

Some of Cumberland's interesting correspondence is addressed to Sir Julius Caesar,[16] Judge of the Admiralty Court and includes references to his own ship with the intriguing name the *Malice Scourge*, which he had built.

His fifth voyage was of considerable importance, because the great carrack the *Madre de Dios* was captured then. Cumberland did not accompany this expedition himself, which he afterwards regretted. There is an interesting account in Hakluyt of the plans to capture the *Madre de Dios*; of the council held by the sea captains Nicholas Downton (who wrote an account of Cumberland's eighth voyage), Abraham Cocke, Captain Norton, Captain Christopher Newport,* and Sir Robert Crosse, who commanded the Queen's ship the *Foresight*. After a combined action by the various ships, the crew of the *Foresight* succeeded in boarding the *Madre de Dios*, supported by the fleet under the command of Sir John Burroughs in the *Roebuck*, a very humane commander. The carnage was terrible, and Hakluyt gives a vivid picture. "No man", he wrote, "could almost steppe but upon a dead carkasse or a bloody floore but specially about the helme where very many of them fell suddenly from stirring to dying." It is refreshing in this Elizabethan Age of cruelty and intolerance to read about the humanity of Sir John Burroughs, who treated the

---

* A great privateer associated with Newport, Virginia.

Spanish Captain Don Fernando de Mendoça with courtesy and kindness. Hakluyt describes Don Fernando as "a gentleman well stricken in years, well spoken, of comely personage, of good stature, but of hard fortune". The captured cargo included jewels of great value, spices, drugs, silks, nutmegs, carpets, and many other articles. After many adventures the *Madre de Dios* sailed into Dartmouth harbour, and the scene "looked like Bartholomew Fair",[17] according to an eye-witness. As might be expected, robbery and plunder were rife among the mob, and it was not until little Sir Robert Cecil was appointed Commissioner on behalf of the Queen that some order eventually emerged. As already mentioned, Sir Walter Ralegh was temporarily released from his imprisonment in the Tower to look into this affair. Ralegh wanted a commission set up to examine on oath the mariners as well as the citizens of Dartmouth as to what diamonds, rubies and other valuables had been pillaged. One of the duties of the joint Commissioners—Cecil, Ralegh and William Killigrew— was to pay the mariners their wages. Naturally, there were disputes as to the Queen's claim to these valuables and the share that Lord Cumberland was entitled to. There was much discontent among the crew that they had been bilked of their fair share of the goods.

Cumberland's eighth voyage, which occurred at the beginning of 1594, is a very interesting one, since the rich carack *Las Cinque Llagas** or *The Five Wounds* was then captured. There are various accounts of it. We have the description given by Captain Nicholas Downton in Hakluyt, the narrative of Samuel Purchas, and a fuller account in Robinson's Manuscripts, as mentioned by Dr. Williamson in his scholarly biography of Lord Cumberland. The Earl did not accompany this expedition, though he fitted out the expedition at his own expense. George Cave, a valiant sea captain, who was later killed, was Admiral of the Squadron. Captain William Anthony commanded the *Mayflower*, while Nicholas Downton was captain of Cumberland's ship the *Sampson*.

---

* Or *Cinco Chagas*.

Downton relates that he was wounded a little above the belly during the course of the action.

> The 13 of June we met with a mightie carack of the East Indies, called *Las Cinco Llagas*, or the Five Wounds. The *Mayflower* was in fight with her before night. I, in the *Sampson*, fetched her up in the evening, and as I commanded to give her the broad side, as we terme it, while I stood very heedfully prying to discover her strength: and where I might give counsel to boord her in the night.[18]

Downton relates that there was a fierce fire on the carack, and the lives of the seamen were in considerable jeopardy.

Robinson's narrative contains a graphic account of the sufferings of the Spanish seamen and grandees on the carack. We can imagine the gallants—both men and women—splendidly dressed, "yea and decked with rich chaynes of gold, jewelles, perles and pretious stones of great price stripping themselves of all this (with soe strange a strategeme seldome seene) all naked uppon a soddame desperatlie cast themselves into the seas". One man more desperate than the others ran upon the hatches and in a furious encounter with the Spanish captain of the carack reproached him bitterly, telling him how much he had to answer for before God in the casting away of so many Christian souls. The captain of the *Mayflower* named William Anthonie, and twenty other soldiers and seamen were killed during the action and thrown overboard. Robinson's narrative relates that the brave commander George Cave was wounded by a poisoned musket through both his legs. He was later brought back to London and buried in St. Gregorie's Church "near Paules church" in December 1594. A year later, one of Cumberland's captains, William Middleton, after returning from a voyage with Sir Francis Drake, died at Falmouth. Middleton was a Welshman, who had earlier carried the news of the approaching Spanish Armada to Howard of Effingham and Grenville in the Azores. He was talented as a poet and known to have made a translation of the psalms into Welsh.

According to a Venetian diplomat, the *Cinque Llagas* was the richest ship that had ever sailed from the East Indies. She was worth 2,000,000 ducats (over £3½ million sterling).

During 1594 Cumberland was unfortunate enough to incur the displeasure of his royal mistress, and it is evident that he resented her orders that all his ships entering harbours should be searched. It is almost certain that this right was not insisted upon.

Monson relates that Cumberland had a ship built, the *Malice Scourge*, named "because he tasted the envy of some that repined at his honourable achievement". She was 800 tons. This magnificent ship sailed in three of Cumberland's voyages and later performed excellent service for the East India Company. For instance, during the ninth voyage, Lord Cumberland wrote to Sir Julius Caesar, the helpful Judge of the Admiralty:

Mr. Cesar as I have heretofore bene in sundrye occasions beholden unto youe so nowe I shall agaen earnestly intreate youe in the behallffe of this bearer my servante who nowe is to goy to sea with me in this voyage a man very necessary for my service therein. And is nowe by processe out of the hyghe Courte of the Admyraltie called uppe for a matter comytted and done agaenst certayne Hamborough shippes eyghte years sence.

This letter was written aboard the *Malice Scourge*, near the Isle of Wight. It is signed "Your Lovying Frynd, George Cumberland".[19]

The Queen granted the Earl two special commissions under great Seal, the first of which gave him the right "to victual and arm for sea the Malescourge and such other ships and pinnaces . . . not exceeding 6", and commanding that "all prizes that shall be taken by you or by any person or persons appointed by you are to be brought into the most convenient haven without breaking bulk or making any distribution of shares until our further pleasure is known".[20] Elizabeth wanted to make sure that she would gain the bulk of the prizes from the *Malice Scourge*. From his ship Cumberland wrote an interesting letter to the Secretary of State, Sir Robert Cecil, mentioning that he had prepared his ships at no small charge to do Her Majesty service.[21] It is evident that Monson considered that he ought to have been appointed Vice-Admiral during Cumberland's ninth expedition, but he chose Captain James Langton instead. Monson again waxed indignant, and complained of the inconstant friendship "of my Lord of Cumberland". He later served under Robert Devereux, Earl of Essex, the Queen's rising favourite. Not much was accomplished during George Clifford's ninth voyage, except they attacked a large Spanish ship the *Saint Thomas*, "Vice Admirall of the King of Spain's fleet, but they lost her in the fog". However, they succeeded in capturing a caravel of 100 tons from St. Thomas with sugar, and also "three Dutch ships of the East Countries" containing various provisions for the King of Spain.

The twelfth voyage of Lord Cumberland's to Porto Rico in 1598 is of great importance, and it is timely to write about it. There is a curious allusion to it in a letter from Sir Robert Cecil to his rival Robert Devereux, Earl of Essex. "Lord Cumberland is a suitor to go a royal journey in October. The plot is very secret between Her Majesty and him; it is to be wished that his spirit which loves action be well cherished." Samuel Purchas gives two accounts of this voyage.[22] Cumberland himself sailed in his celebrated ship the *Malice Scourge*. Under him on the outward journey was Captain John Watts, while Captain James Langton took over the command on the homeward journey. The *Merchant Royal* was vice-admiral and commanded by the valiant Sir John Berkeley. Captain Robert Flicke was in charge of the *Ascension*, and Captain Henry Clifford commanded the *Sampson*. After Henry Clifford's death at Porto Rico, Christopher Colthurst took over his duty. There were 200 men on board the *Malice Scourge*, consequently all kinds of victuals were necessary for a fairly long voyage. Bread, meat, fish, pork, peas, oatmeal, cheese and candles for cabin use had to be provided. Every soldier or sailor was given a bottle of beer each day, while there was cider at a quart each day and wine at a pint per day. There were even six hogsheads of brandy, and we would like to know which of the sea captains consumed most.

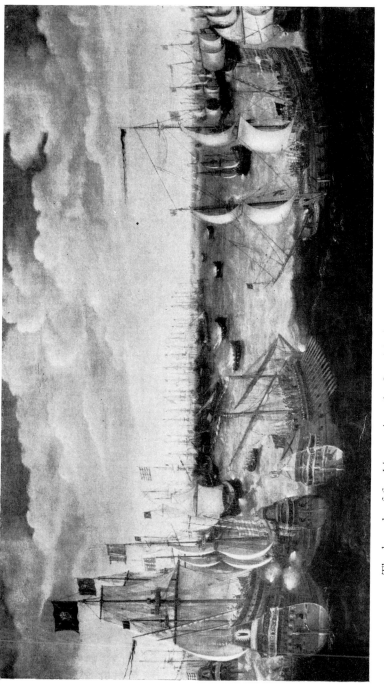

The launch of fireships against the Spanish Armada as painted by an unknown artist

(*above left*) John Rashleigh, 1554–1624, with his son Jonathan, who was let into the original picture at a later date. Painting by Hilliard and Vansomer. (*above right*) Lord Admiral Charles Howard of Effingham, Earl of Nottingham, 1536–1624. Painting by D. Mytens.

The account of Samuel Purchas includes Cumberland's own narrative of the twelfth voyage. The object of the expedition, although kept a secret, was to seize and to maintain the island of Porto Rico as a West Indian station—a possession of strategical importance for the interception of the Spanish lines of communication. Cumberland again reveals himself as a just, able and humane commander. His fleet arrived at Lancerota in the Canary Islands where he discovered

> in the Castle was not anything but some few peeces of ordnance dismounted. In the towne (whose houses were most beggarly) some little wine onely, which little was too much, for it distempered so many, that if there had been a strong enemie to have attempted, they should have found drunken resistence, the meaner sort being mostly overthrowne already, and the Commanders, some distempered with wine, some with pride of themselves, or scorne of others, for as there were very few of them but that fell to most disorderly outrage one with another.[23]

Sir John Berkeley, stricken by grief, warned the Earl that if he did not adopt severe measures to remedy this state of affairs, it would be the ruin of their voyage. The next day Cumberland went on shore to see his men trained, and took the opportunity of rebuking them for their faults. He was careful to read them his commission, so that they might know that he had the necessary authority to order punishments for every offence.[24]

It is evident that during this voyage Cumberland was in acute danger, and was nearly drowned. Purchas relates that

> by the stumbling of him that bore his Target he was overthrowne even to the danger of drowning for his armour so overburdened him that the Sergiant Major who possessed the doughty name of Hercules Foljambe*, that by chance was next had much adoe at the first and second time to get him from under the water: when he was up, he had received so much salt water that it drove him to so great extremity of present sickness that he was forced to lye downe in the very place in the cawsey till being somewhat recovered he was able

---

* He later appealed to King James I for a pension.

to be led to a place of some more safetie and care in which place
the bullets made him threatening musicke on every side.

These Elizabethans were valiant warriors.

Lord Cumberland was an excellent commander, for he was
stern, but just. One of his soldiers, who did violence to a Spanish
woman, was convicted by a court martial of the crime and condemned to die. He was hung in the market-place, where many
Spaniards saw him die. A seaman, who had desecrated various
objects in churches, was condemned to death but later pardoned.

Monson,* who was jealous of Cumberland and resented his
preference for other sea captains, is hardly fair when he implies
that the sole object of the Earl's twelfth voyage was plunder.
Indeed a close study of the expedition makes it certain that
Cumberland showed considerable statecraft.

His capture of Porto Rico was a brilliant naval action. When the
Spaniards sued for terms, requesting at the same time that they
might be translated into Spanish, Cumberland insisted on total
surrender. With arrogance he preferred to dictate his own
terms. Only one man was killed during the operation and three
wounded. Porto Rico was larger than Portsmouth, but not quite
the size of Oxford.[25] "The very key of the West Indies which
locketh and shutteth all the gold and silver in the Continent of
America and Brasilia." Unfortunately, it was necessary to
garrison Porto Rico with at least 500 men. It was July 1598, a
season when tropical diseases were very prevalent. Many of the
seamen and soldiers sickened with dysentery, no doubt aggravated
by the sudden changes in their food and drink. The impossibility
of preserving victuals in a wholesome condition always troubled
the Elizabethans. Two hundred men of Cumberland's crews died,
and over 400 lay desperately ill. Eventually it became imperative
that Porto Rico must be abandoned.

Before he was reluctantly forced to abandon Porto Rico,
Cumberland succeeded in obtaining a large booty of sugar,

---

* Sir William Monson later became a pensioner of Spain. Count Condamar, the
Spanish Ambassador in London, refers to him in 1616 as Socrates.

hides and other articles. After a conference with his sea captains it was decided that the *Malice Scourge* and the *Sampson* should leave at once, together with the *Elizabeth*, the *Guiana* and another vessel, while the remainder of the fleet should remain a little longer there under the command of the intrepid Sir John Berkeley, though gravely ill. When Cumberland's fleet was off the Azores, a mighty storm arose, so that the sea would "ship in waves into her of three or foure tunne of water".[26] We know that by the beginning of October the Earl was back in England.

It is curious that John Chamberlain in his correspondence with his friend Dudley Carleton underestimates the importance of this voyage. He fails to mention its strategic purpose as a military and naval action, and he omits to emphasize its immense psychological effect in undermining the prestige of Spain. "All they have done", he wrote, "is to take the town and Castle of Porto Rico; the Spaniards knowing of their coming, the property had been removed. All the Earl has brought (chiefly sugar and ginger) is worth but £15,000 or £16,000 not half the charge of the setting out besides the waste of shipping and loss of 600 men." In such a way are the motives of noble, high-minded men dimly understood and distorted by those incapable of appreciating them.

It is recorded that Lord Cumberland was the first among the celebrated seamen of the Elizabethan Age to refuse to have dealings with government contractors or suppliers of victuals after they had been found guilty of supplying bad food or drink. He took the trouble to ensure as far as possible that the seamen under his command were properly fed.[27] Like Drake and Ralegh he really loved England—a powerful motive which induced him to embark on his hazardous voyages as much as any religious sentiments or antagonism to Spain. He was resolved to weaken Spanish influence in the Indies. Although by birth an aristocrat, he was foremost in sharing the perils of his men, in mending his own main mast, or risking his own life on behalf of others. Seamen in any age are good judges of character, and those under his command loved and honoured their dare-devil earl.

The Elizabethan Age was not marked by fidelity or constancy

in marriage—at any rate among the courtiers. No doubt Lord Cumberland at home for brief respites at Court was occasionally tempted by the bright eyes of some voluptuous lady. All we know is, despite his great love for "his Sweet Meg", so transparent in his letters, that he was later unfaithful to her—which embittered their relations for a time. Despite his faults, including his frailty of nature, this tender-hearted man could write to his wife when he was gravely ill in his last letter.

> Sweet and dear Meg,
> Bear with, I pray thee, the short and innapt setting together of these my last lines, a token of true kindness, which I protest cometh out of an unfeigned heart of love to thee, for whose content, and to make satisfaction for the wrongs done to thee, I have, since I saw thee, more desired to return than for any other earthly cause.[28]

Lord Cumberland was only forty in 1598 during the voyage to Porto Rico. By that time most of his great contemporaries—the incomparable seamen—had died. Sir John Hawkins in the cabin of the *Garland*, at loggerheads with Sir Francis Drake, who died at sea in 1596 during their joint expedition. Sir Richard Grenville, too, had been killed in the epic fight of the *Revenge* some years earlier. Only Lord Charles Howard of Effingham, Sir Walter Ralegh, and John Davis, the intrepid sea captain, lived on into the uncongenial reign of James I: Lord Howard of Effingham, created Earl of Nottingham,* to play a distinguished part as a diplomat and statesman; Ralegh to languish in the Tower, tormented by the rancour of the feeble sovereign who had succeeded the great Elizabeth; and Davis, who had never indulged in piracy, to be killed in the land of Japan by pirates whilst the waves lapped those distant shores. Lord Cumberland, too, died in 1605, thus surviving by two years his royal mistress, who had sometimes chided or even reprimanded him for alleged misdemeanours. It is fitting that he should be buried in Skipton Parish Church, in the heart of the North Country, and his

---

* By Queen Elizabeth.

daughter, Lady Anne Clifford, had a magnificent monument erected to commemorate him. Not far away in Appleby church, lies "Sweet Meg", the devoted wife, to whose arms the gallant warrior had so longingly returned after his many voyages.

Notes

CHAPTER IX

1   James A. Williamson, *George, Third Earl of Cumberland.*
2   James A. Williamson quotes some of them in his biography.
3   James A. Williamson, *George, Third Earl of Cumberland.*
    Kenneth R. Andrews, *Elizabethan Privateering.*
4   George Sampson, *The Concise Cambridge History of English Literature,*
    (reprinted 1942), p. 186.
    Kenneth R. Andrews, *Elizabethan Privateering.*
5   Parks, p. 226.
6   Taylor, Vol. II, p. 433.
7   James A. Williamson, *George, Third Earl of Cumberland.*
8   Monson, *Tracts,* Vol. 2.
9   James A. Williamson, *George, Third Earl of Cumberland.*
10 *Ibid.*
11 Sidney Papers II, p. 93.
12 Richard Hakluyt, *Voyages* (Everyman Edition), Vol. IV, p. 355.
13 Purchas, *Pilgrimages,* Vol. IV.
14 James A. Williamson, *George, Third Earl of Cumberland 1558–1605,*
    p. 62.
15 *Ibid.*
16 B.M. *Add MSS. Caesar Papers.*
17 James A. Williamson, *George, Third Earl of Cumberland 1558–1605,*
    p. 89.
18 Richard Hakluyt, *Voyages* (Everyman Edition), Vol. V, pp. 70
    and 71.
19 B.M. *Add MSS. Caesar Papers.* 12506, fol. 95.
20 James A. Williamson, *George, Third Earl of Cumberland 1558–1605.*

21 *Ibid.*
22 Purchas, *Pilgrimages*, Vol. IV.
23 *Ibid*, Vol. IV, 1151.
24 *Ibid*, 1152.
25 James A. Williamson, *George, Third Earl of Cumberland 1558–1605*, p. 193.
26 *Ibid*, Rev. John Layfield's account.
27 *Ibid.*
28 The whole letter can be read in James A. Williamson, *George, Third Earl of Cumberland*, p. 270.

CHAPTER X

Sir Richard Grenville

Sir Richard Grenville is pre-eminent as the representative of the heroic, the glory and romance of the Elizabethan era. One can admire him for his virtues, yet it is difficult to like him. There was a harshness in his character, which repels rather than attracts. It is true, however, that he was as hard on himself as on his subordinates. From boyhood I have a picture of this Cornishman, in my mind, sitting and carousing with the Spanish captains. John Huighem van Linschoten relates in Hakluyt:

> He was of so hard a complexion that as he continued among the Spanish captains while they were at dinner or supper with him, he would carouse three or four glasses of wine, and in a taverne take the glasses between his teeth and crush them in pieces and swallow them downe, so that oftentimes the blood ran out of his mouth without any harme at all unto him: and this was told me by divers credible persons that many times stood and beheld him.[1]

One cannot expect an abnormal man to behave in a normal fashion. We have already briefly discussed Grenville's character when considering his Virginian voyage, and it is unnecessary to enlarge upon it.

Grenville was very conscious that he came of an ancient family, and he owned large estates in Devon and Cornwall. He would have looked down at Drake as of mere yeoman stock. Like Sir Humphrey Gilbert, he pursued the career of a soldier and in 1566 we find him serving in Hungary against the Turks. It is unlikely that Grenville fought during the great naval battle of Lepanto,[2] and Robert Southey is probably inaccurate when he writes that Grenville was present on board the Christian fleet during the fighting.[3]

Ralegh mentions that the father of "the late renowned Sir Richard Grenville (of the *Revenge*)" lost his life in the ill-fated *Mary Rose*, one of Henry VIII's ships.

From his portrait in the National Portrait Gallery, painted in 1571 when Richard Grenville was twenty-nine, he appears as a handsome young man with strange, hypnotic blue eyes, vigilant and serpent-like, ready to strike. His hair is fair, and his beard not very full. The whole impression is forceful, and Grenville was primarily a man of action, lacking the fancifulness and imagination of Sir Walter Ralegh and the vision of Sir Humphrey Gilbert. One senses in Sir Richard a fierce determination to dominate others. Such a man may have his admirers, though he arouses fear or repulsion in others. The Elizabethans were too individualistic not to feel resentment against a man apparently so sure of himself, prone to strange moods and violence when somebody dared to cross him.

Elizabeth—and once again we must emphasize her shrewdness —made use of Grenville, for his sense of duty was strong, but she can never have liked him. He was too honest to flatter her or caress her with his tongue like his cousin Sir Walter Ralegh, and he lacked the charm of Sir Francis Drake and the grace of Sir Christopher Hatton. Grenville married Mary St. Leger, the eldest daughter of Sir John St. Leger of Annery, near Bideford. It is almost certain that she was without personality, and perhaps hardly surprising since she was married to Grenville.

This heroic Cornishman was closely associated with the great South Sea Project, of the early 1570s, as his biographer reveals.[4] In the minds of these Elizabethans were forged the beginnings of the British Empire. It is impossible to discuss Grenville's project in detail, but it was directly related to the unknown Pacific continent. Some articles were presented to the Lord Admiral, Lord Clinton, which stated "The aptness and as it were a fatal convenience that since the Portugal hath attained one part of the new found world to the east, the Spaniard another to the west, the French the third to the north, now the fourth to the south is by God's providence left for England, to whom the others in times past have been first offered".[5] The scheme was sponsored by a group of West Country gentlemen led by Richard Grenville of Stowe in the County of Cornwall. Unfortunately so far as the seamen were concerned, an attempt was made during 1573 to improve the relations between England and Spain. For the time being this was achieved by the Convention of Bristol (1574). It was manifestly an unfavourable time for the Queen and the English Government to allow Grenville and his friends to organize an expedition, whose professed aim was to sail into the Southern Seas which the Spaniards considered their own monopoly. To reassure the Queen and Lord Burghley, the leaders of the expedition maintained:

> Our strength shall be such as we fear it not, besides that we mean to keep the ocean, and not to enter in or near any of their ports or places kept by their force. . . . In the places already subdued and inhabited by the Spaniard or Portugal we seek no possession or interest; but only if occasion be free, to traffic with them and their subjects which is as lawful and as much without injury as for the merchants in Portugal or Spain itself.

The Spaniards, however, regarded trading with their Indies or South American Empire as illegal or at least forbidden, though John Hawkins had certainly engaged in such activities. It was proposed that the Queen should have a share in this voyage.

The Spanish agent in London, probably Antonio de Guaras, wrote to the Governor of the Netherlands during May 1574:

> An English gentleman named Grenfield, a great pirate, and another called Champernoune, Vice-Admiral of the West, a co-father-in-law with Montgomeri, with others recently armed seven

ships four large and three small, with the advowed intention of going on a voyage of discovery to Labrador, but the real intention was to help Montgomeri in Normandy, which is very near the West Coast. . . . The fleet is very well fitted and found, and will carry 1,500 men, soldiers and sailors, 500 of them being gentlemen.[6]

Though de Guaras had grasped that an expedition was proposed, he had not divined its real nature.

The astute French Ambassador in London, La Mothe Fénelon, in his correspondence with Charles IX also refers to Grenville as "a great pirate". He reports that Grenville was preparing an expedition of seven ships with the object of discovering some passage towards the north.[7] La Mothe Fénelon also never guessed that the real destination of the proposed expedition was to the Pacific.

Diligent researchers, particularly Zelia Nuttall, discovered that John Oxenham, Drake's former sea captain, who was captured on the Pacific coast by the Spaniards after seizing two of their treasure-ships,* was forced to admit in his prison at Lima in Peru that Grenville had many conferences with him concerning his proposed South Seas voyage. Examined by the Inquisitors, Oxenham revealed that

an English gentleman named Richard Grenville, who lives at a distance of a league and a half from Plymouth [i.e. at Buckland Abbey], and is very rich, applied to the Queen for a licence to come to the Strait of Magellan and to pass to the South Sea, in order to search for land or some islands where to found settlements, because in England there are many inhabitants and but little land.

Ironically enough one wonders what Oxenham would say if he were alive today. It is tragic that this gallant sea captain, though no doubt a pirate in Spanish eyes, was forced to endure the ordeal of an *Auto da Fé*, and burnt at the stake.

It is now known that Francis Drake's great voyage (1577–80) was in origin a continuation of Grenville's projects for his

---

* During 1576.

Pacific expedition.[8] Drake was more fortunate than the Cornish-man, because by the end of 1575 it suited the subtle Queen Elizabeth to adopt a more aggressive policy against Spain. It must have been bitter gall for Grenville to hear later of the sensational success of Drake's voyage. Frustrated and full of ire, he retired to his mellow, lovely home, Buckland Abbey* near Yelverton, where he engrossed himself in the duties of a country gentleman and as Sheriff of Cornwall. With "the great unrest" which was part of his character, we can picture him, nervous and highly-strung, pacing the banqueting-hall, and thinking ruefully, not without secret contempt, of Francis Drake, sprung from yeoman stock, now taking all the limelight and the glory. We know that Grenville at first refused to serve under Drake during the massive preparations which were made to resist the Spanish Armada. The Government proposed to give Grenville the command of a squadron, so as to reinforce Drake, though well aware of the strained relations between the two men.

Bernadino de Mendoza wrote Philip II:

> It was proposed in the Council that Grenville, a gentleman who has always sailed with pirates, should command the Squadron, but it was objected that he would not serve under Drake, and it was necessary to send some person who would not raise questions but would obey Drake unreservedly, and it was therefore thought that Frobisher would be put into command.[9]

This is curious, because Frobisher was almost pathologically jealous of Drake, and it would be interesting to know why Mendoza considered that the tempestuous Frobisher would be more likely to co-operate with Drake than the Cornishman. Later Grenville was not too proud to serve under Drake, for he brought to Plymouth the galleon *Dudley* of 250 tons, the *Virgin God Save Her* of 200 tons and the *Tiger*. The *God Save Her* was commanded by John Grenville, Sir Richard's second son, who later sailed on Ralegh's Guiana voyage (1595). Sir Richard

* Another Grenville property was at Stowe, and they also owned a dower-house in Bideford.

Grenville performed selfless, devoted service during the Armada campaign, particularly in organizing the defences vital for resisting the invaders. Later Grenville served in Ireland, which he had known in his early life. He now once again became closely associated with plantation and colonization in Munster.

We come now to Grenville's heroic fight on the *Revenge*, in the Azores, familiar to every schoolboy. Sir Walter Ralegh's dramatic account provides brilliant reading, but it is somewhat biased.[10] Sir Richard Grenville and Sir Richard Hawkins were the only naval commanders during the reign of Queen Elizabeth I compelled to strike their flag to the Spaniards, though the reputation of the English for courage was greatly enhanced by both these men. The *Revenge*, launched at Deptford in 1577, was a fine ship of about 450 tons, a masterpiece of naval construction in Drake's opinion.[11] Sir William Monson, who strongly criticized Grenville for his tactics during the campaign, picturesquely described the *Revenge* as "low and snug in the water like a galliasse". "She was designed from the hour she was built, to receive some fatal blow," he wrote. She was a 34-gun ship, and possessed a secondary armament of twenty guns.

Besides Sir Walter Ralegh, the main English authorities were Monson's *Naval Tracts* and Sir Richard Hawkins' *Observations*, both written many years later. Then there is the account of the Dutchman, Van Linschoten, who lived in the Azores at this period. The best account, as mentioned by Dr. Rowse, is the *Spanish Relation*, a description by a Spanish officer actually present at the fight.

During the late summer of 1591, Lord Thomas Howard was sent to the Azores, with Sir Richard Grenville as his Vice-Admiral. Their fleet included six formidable fighting vessels of the Queen, three of the pinnace type, the bark *Raleigh* and some auxiliaries. The object of the expedition was to intercept the Spanish fleet from the West Indies. The Spanish commander was Don Alonzo de Bazan,* who was charged by Philip II to expel the

* Brother of the Marquess of Santa Cruz.

English from the Azores. He commanded an enormous fleet of fifty-five vessels, and as a precaution it was provided that the Spanish treasure should be shipped in some fast ships to follow later on. While Lord Thomas Howard sailed for the Azores, George Clifford, Earl of Cumberland, was privateering on the Spanish coast.

The English fleet were already at Flores and Corvo when Don Alonzo de Bazan with his Armada arrived at Terceira at the end of August. The Spanish ships were filled with soldiers as well as mariners. In some of them there were 800 soldiers and others 500. The English ships mainly contained mariners, except for a few servants of the commanders and several gentlemen volunteers.* Ralegh tells us that it was William Middleton, one of Cumberland's sea captains, "a very good sailor", who warned Lord Thomas Howard of the approach of the Spanish Armada. Let Ralegh take up the story:

> Many of our shippes companies were on shore in the Ilande, [he relates] some providing balast for their ships; others filling of water and refreshing themselves from the land with such things as they could either for money, or by force recover. By reason whereof our ships being all pestered and romaging, everything out of order, very light for want of balast, and that which was most to our disadvantage the one halfe part of the men of every shippe, sicke and utterly unserviceable.[12]

In the *Revenge*, for instance, there were as many as ninety sick men while in the *Bonaventura*, commanded by Captain Crosse, there were not sufficient seamen in good health to handle her main sail. The English fleet consisted of the Queen's six ships, the *Defiance*, the *Revenge*, the *Bonaventura*, the *Lion*, the *Foresight* and the *Crane*. According to Ralegh, the last two were small ships:

"The Spanish fleet," he wrote, "having shrouded their approach by reason of the island; were now so soone at hande, as our shippes had scarce time to way their anchors, but some of them were driven to let slippe their cables and set saile."

---

* According to Ralegh's account.

Sir Richard Hawkins pays Sir Richard this remarkable tribute: "Grenville was the last that remained," he wrote, "choosing rather to sacrifice his life, and to passe all danger whatsoever, than to fail in his obligation, by gathering together those who were ashore, though with the hazard of his ship and company."[13] Monson, however, praises the Lord Thomas for his wariness and caution in weighing anchor and giving the signal to the rest of his fleet to do likewise. Yet he accuses Grenville of stubbornness and rashness—charges which may be true. Monson alleges that Grenville was under the impression that the Spanish fleet came from the Indies, and was not "the Armada of which they were informed". When he was approached by his master and others to cut his main-sail so as to follow his Admiral (Lord Thomas Howard), Grenville utterly refused to move. Monson alleges that Sir Richard was so headstrong and rash that he violently turned on those who offered him this advice.[14] He uttered the dire threat that if any man laid hand upon the sail, he would have him hanged. Ralegh infers that Sir Richard had no other course but to resist the Spanish attack. Ralegh wrote of his cousin, "out of the greatnesse of his minde, he could not be persuaded". So, we possess these conflicting accounts of the heroic last fight of the *Revenge*.

The two most important galleons of the Spanish fleet were the great *San Phelipe* and the *San Barnabe*, the latter commanded by General Bertendona. While the Spaniards sailed in two squadrons into the Channel, they fired broadsides from their guns into the English ships. Both the *San Phelipe* and the *San Barnabe* tried to board Lord Thomas Howard's flagship the *Defiance*, but failed to achieve their purpose. The *San Phelipe*—an enormous ship—now grappled with the *Revenge*. Ralegh relates: "The great *San Philip* being in the winde of him, and coming towards him, becalmed his sailes in such sort, as the shippe could neither make way, nor feele the helme: so huge and high carsed was the Spanish ship, being of a thousand and five hundreth tuns." Amidst the confusion and the carnage it would seem that the *San Phelipe* boarded the *Revenge* with nine or ten soldiers, but was unable to maintain her ascendancy owing to a broken rope.[15] Bristling for a fight, General Bertendona rapidly came up to the *Revenge* in the *San Barnabe*. The Spanish ship lay on the larboard of the *Revenge*.

According to Ralegh's account, "the great *San Philip* having received the lower fire of the *Revenge*, discharged with crossebar-shot, shifted her selfe with all diligence from her sides utterly misliking her first entertainment".[16]

As night descended, the remainder of Lord Thomas Howard's squadron, save the *Revenge*, took the opportunity of hoisting their mainsails and taking to flight. The gallant little *Revenge*, denied any powerful support, was thus left on her own to resist the Spanish attack. Ralegh relates that early in the fight a small victualling ship named the *George Noble of London*, having been damaged by the Spanish gunfire, fell under the lee of the *Revenge*. When her captain offered his services to Grenville, he bade him to save himself and to leave him to his fortune[17]—the answer which one might expect from Sir Richard.

Dawn broke, and the *Revenge* still desperately resisted the Spanish Armada. By now Grenville's ship was severely damaged, unrigged and without her masts. Her condition was rapidly becoming desperate. Some of the Spanish ships, including the galleon *Ascension*, were so badly damaged by each other and by the *Revenge* that they sank.[18] As the epic struggle became ever more deadly, a small ship named the *Pilgrim*, commanded by Jacob Whiddon (Ralegh's sea captain) hove in sight. Ralegh relates that "she was hunted like a hare amongst many ravenous houndes, but escaped".

Sir Richard remained on the upper deck, grim, exposed, determined and obstinate, magnificent in his dauntless courage. Contemptuous of others as he had always been, he mockingly seemed to invite the musket shots of the Spaniards. Indeed as he stood there, he was wounded by one of these in the body. Then again gravely wounded in the head, and his chirurgeon killed beside him. Ralegh relates that Sir Richard

The *Ark Royal*, Lord Howard of Effingham's flagship during the Armada

An° · DNI · 1571 ·
ÆTATIS · SVÆ ·
29 ·

Sir Richard Grenville at the age of 29

finding himselfe in this distresse, and unable any longer to make resistance, having endured in this fifteene houres fight, the assault of fifteene severall Armadas ... (the *Revenge* not able to move one way or other, but as she was moved with the waves and billows of the sea) commanded the Master gunner, whom he knew to be a most resolute man to split and sinke the shippe: that thereby nothing might remaine of glory or victory to the Spaniards.

The master gunner stoutly supported Sir Richard, but he was opposed by the captain and the master. They implored Grenville to have a care of them, maintaining that the Spaniards would be only too ready to come to terms. Meanwhile the master went on board "the Spanish General", and discovered that the enemy were willing to agree that all their lives should be saved, and that they should be sent to England, provided a reasonable ransom was paid. Meanwhile the master gunner would have slain himself with a sword, but he was forcibly prevented from doing so and locked in his cabin.

The Spaniards are a brave nation, and Don Alonzo Bazan, the distinguished commander of the fleet, admired Sir Richard for his notable valour. He ordered that Grenville, who was dying, should be removed from the *Revenge*, to his own ship the *San Pablo*.* By this time the *Revenge* resembled a slaughter-house, being filled with the blood and bodies of the dead. Ralegh relates that "Sir Richard answered that he might do with his body what he list, for he esteemed it not; and as he was carried out of the ship hee swounded, and reviving againe desired the company to pray for him". The Spanish treated Grenville with all humanity, and did everything possible to save his life, although Don Alonzo Bazan may have been incensed by his stubborn resistance and consequently refused to visit him.

Linschoten reported the gist of Grenville's last words on board the *San Pablo*.

Feeling the hour of death be approach, he spake these words in Spanish, and said: Here die I Richard Grenville, with a joyful and

---

* The Dutchman Linschoten relates Grenville's last hours.

quiet mind, for that I have ended my life as a true soldier ought to do, that hath fought for his country, Queen, religion, and honour, whereby my soul most joyful departeth out of his body and shall always leave behind it an everlasting fame of a valiant and true soldier that hath done his duty, as he was bound to do. But the others of my company have done as traitors and dogs, for which they shall be reproached all their lives and leave a shameful name for ever.

These are moving words, and even now stir the human heart with admiration and pity. As Professor Rowse emphasizes,[19] the last sentence of bitter reproach for the perfidy of the members of Grenville's company, is characteristic of that strange, frenzied man. It would seem almost certain that the dying man was contemptuously referring to them, rather than to Lord Thomas Howard and the rest of the English fleet that had got away.

Ralegh wrote: "What became of his body, whether it were buried in the sea or on the land we know not: the comfort that remayneth to his friends is, that hee hath ended his life honourably in respect of the reputation wonne to his nation and countrey, and of the same to his posteritie, and that being dead, he hath not outlived his owne honour."[20]

Notes

CHAPTER X

1 Richard Hakluyt, *Voyages* (Everyman Edition), Vol. V, p. 38.
2 A. L. Rowse, *Sir Richard Grenville of the Revenge*, p. 64.
3 Robert Southey, *English Seamen*, p. 42.
4 A. L. Rowse, *Sir Richard Grenville of the Revenge*, p. 83 *et seq.*
5 *Spanish Papers, Domestic, Eliz.* 95, Nos. 63–4.
   A. L. Rowse, *Sir Richard Grenville of the Revenge.*
6 *Calendar State Papers Spanish*, 1568–79, 481.
7 A. L. Rowse, *Sir Richard Grenville of the Revenge*, p. 99.
8 *Ibid.*
9 *Calendar State Papers, Spanish*, 1587–1603, 93.
10 A report of the trueth of the fight about the Isles of Azores, the last of August 1591 betwixt the Revenge, one of her Majesties shippes and an Armada of the King of Spaine, Penned by the honourable Sir Walter Ralegh, Knight.
11 Julian Corbett, *Drake and the Tudor Navy*, Vol. I.
12 Richard Hakluyt, *Voyages* (Everyman Edition), Vol. V, p.3.
13 Sir Richard Hawkins, *Observations.*
14 Monson, p. 163.
   Robert Southey, *English Seamen*, p. 47.
15 A. L. Rowse, *Sir Richard Grenville of the Revenge.*
16 Richard Hakluyt, *Voyages* (Everyman Edition), Vol. V, p. 5.
17 *Ibid*, Vol. V, p. 5.
18 A. L. Rowse, *Sir Richard Grenville of the Revenge.*
19 *Ibid*, p. 315.
20 Richard Hakluyt, *Voyages*, Vol. V, p. 9.

CHAPTER XI

Drake Through Spanish Prisoners' Eyes

The Spanish were wont to say that Sir Francis possessed a magic mirror in which he could see fleets and armies moving hundreds of miles away. Drake was a genius with an uncanny insight into the mind of the enemy. His disciplined imagination—sometimes he gave free rein to it—and his superb confidence in himself enabled him to judge how the Spanish would react to certain circumstances. These powerful faculties gave him the zest to act with decision and speed.

None of the great mariners had a deeper vision of empire than Drake, with the possible exceptions of Sir Humphrey Gilbert and Sir Walter Ralegh. The principal object of Drake's circumnavigation of the world (1577) was discovery; and Lope de Vega, who served as a sailor during the invasion of the Spanish Armada, conceded this in his poem *La Dragontea*. Though he referred to the mariner as *"aquel Dragon de la Cruel Medea"*, he nevertheless could not conceal his admiration for him. He wrote:

> *Bien conocio la Regna tu gran pecho*
> *Que pudo hazer tremblar la mar profundo*
> *Quando te dio los tres navios solo*
> *Que vieron de un viaje los dos polos.**

* For translation see foot of facing page.

Drake's wonderful vision of empire during his voyage to circumnavigate the world was of "the New England", which he named "New Albion", a beautiful part of the Pacific Coast now known as California. The navigator laid the foundations of "the New England" in defiance of the Papal Bull, which had formerly divided the New World between Spain and Portugal, that courageous nation renowned for her intrepid and imaginative seamen. With his strongly developed religious instincts, Drake desired that the natives of "Nova Albion" should be benevolently treated, so that they might by preaching of the gospel be gradually persuaded to accept the protestant religion. With a sense of pride we can imagine that historic scene when Francis Drake, his chaplain Francis Fletcher, and the ship's company held the first Protestant service ever to be performed on a hill which commanded a magnificent panorama of the Golden Gate and the Bay of San Francisco on the Pacific coast of America.

Our traditional conception of Drake's character is somewhat altered when we study the absorbing accounts of the Spanish and Portuguese seamen and aristocrats, who were temporarily his prisoners. Historical students delving into the accounts of the captives of 'Captain Francis' are deeply indebted to the researches of that dedicated historian, Zelia Nuttall.[1] Descriptions of Drake's character and his activities during this voyage can be found among the archives of the Indies in the Casa Lonja in Seville, near the Gothic Cathedral.

During most of the sixteenth century the merchants of Seville were in the habit of conducting their business either in the Patio of Oranges or on the steps of the cathedral. If it was intensely cold or if the sun bore down too fiercely, they even moved to the cathedral itself. There was a constant babble and confusion, for the Spanish are a noisy people. It was owing to the Archbishop Sandoval y Rojas's endeavours that King Phillip II agreed that a

---

* Well did thy Queen know thy great valour,
Which might cause the depths of the sea to tremble,
When she gave thee the three vessels the only ones ever to sight,
In a single voyage, both poles.

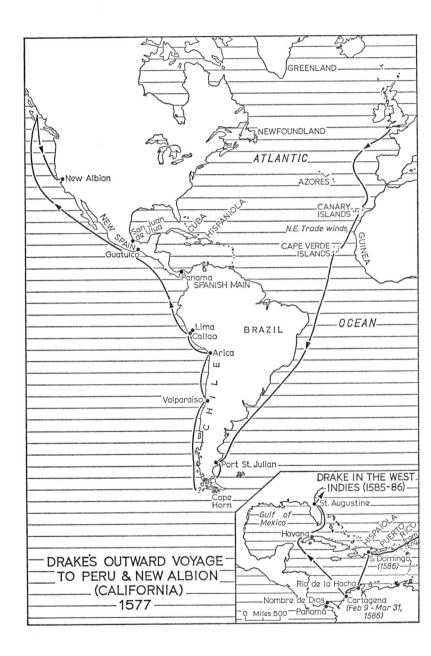

GREENLAND

NEWFOUNDLAND

ATLANTIC

New Albion

AZORES

CANARY ISLANDS

CUBA

HISPANIOLA

NEW SPAIN

San Juan de Ulua

N.E. Trade winds

CAPE VERDE ISLANDS

GUINEA

Guatulco

Panama

SPANISH MAIN

Lima
Callao

BRAZIL

OCEAN

Arica

C H I L E

Valparaiso

Port St. Julian

Cape Horn

DRAKE IN THE WEST INDIES (1585-86)

St. Augustine

Gulf of Mexico

Havana

HISPANIOLA

PUERTO RICO

from Eng.

S. Domingo (1586)

Rio de la Hacha

DRAKE'S OUTWARD VOYAGE TO PERU & NEW ALBION (CALIFORNIA) 1577

Nombre de Dios

Cartagena (Feb 9 - Mar 31, 1586)

Panama

0   Miles 500

more suitable place should be built for the merchants. In 1582 the Lonja of Seville was begun, and the architect was Juan de Herrera, who was mainly responsible for the building of Philip's great palace of the Escorial. Two centuries later King Charles III ordered that the Lonja should house the huge collection of Indies Archives. Today it possesses 38,000 papers and documents, including the diary of Colombus and the Mapa Mundi of Juan la Cosa.

These Spanish and Portuguese accounts clearly reveal new aspects of Drake's fascinating character and the magic of his personality, which impressed his prisoners, during 1577–80. They reveal hitherto unsuspected qualities in 'Captain Francis': his quaint satirical humour, and at times a religious tolerance remarkable for his age. It might be wondered how Drake of good yeoman stock could talk so intimately and with such ease with one of his prisoners, Don Francisco de Zarate, a Spanish aristocrat, until it is realized that Drake had considerable knowledge of Spanish. It is, perhaps, little known that in his youth Drake had been one of the twenty pages appointed to conduct to Spain Jane Dormer, who married the Duke of Feria.* Not only Spanish historians, but also mariners such as Juan Pascual, for a period one of his prisoners, testify to the fact that Drake could speak Spanish.

Nuño da Silva, the Portuguese pilot, who was captured by Francis Drake in the Cape Verde Islands, gives an intimate picture of the great navigator. Da Silva was a native of Lisbon and citizen of Oporto. From an early age he had been an ardent seaman, and when only eight years of age he had sailed to Brazil— as already mentioned, discovered by the Portuguese navigator Gonçalo Coelho† on 1st January 1502. Nuño da Silva acquired considerable experience sailing from Lisbon to Brazil. He was of low stature, not very grey-haired, and dark complexioned with a long beard.

---

* She was a favourite maid of honour to Mary I.

† The discovery of Brazil has been attributed to Gonçalo Coelho, but according to Robert Thorne it was discovered earlier.

This Portuguese pilot was later unfortunate enough to fall foul of the Spanish Inquisitors when he was compelled to make a sworn deposition concerning his experiences during 'Captain Francis's' voyage round the world.[2] His description of Drake is extremely interesting.

This Englishman [he testified] calls himself Francis Drake and is a man aged thirty-eight. He may be two years more or less. He is low in stature, thick-set and very robust. He has a fine countenance, is ruddy of complexion and has a fair beard. He has the mark of an arrow-wound in his right cheek, which is not apparent if one does not look with special care. In one leg he has the ball of an arquebuse that was shot at him in the Indies. He is a great mariner, the son and relative of seamen, and particularly of John Hawkins [Guillen Acquines in the Spanish documents], in whose company he was for a long time. He has with him a brother named Thomas Drake, who served as a sailor, like anyone of the crew. Thomas Drake is twenty-two years of age, has a fair complexion and a scanty beard, which is fair. He is low of stature, but is broad-shouldered and sturdy. He is a good seaman. Francis Drake took with him from England, all told 270 men . . . he had seated at his table, namely the captain, pilot, and doctor. He also read the psalms and preached. He also carried with him, from his country, a negro named Diego, who spoke Spanish and English, and who he had taken prisoner from a frigate in the North Sea, near Nombre de Dios, about seven or eight years previously.

If Drake was not in the habit, like Ralegh, of taking trunks laden with books in his cabin, he at least had a taste for literature. He carried with him on his voyage round the world three books on navigation, one of which was Magellan's *Discovery*. On one occasion a Spaniard peering over Drake's shoulder, noticed that he was engrossed in reading Foxe's *Book of Martyrs*. The Portuguese pilot's evidence reveals that Francis Drake was gifted as an artist. He would sometimes shut himself in his cabin, where he would draw and paint pictures of birds, trees and sea-lions. Nuño da Silva tells us that Francis Drake and his young cousin John, also a talented artist, were wont to spend hours in Drake's cabin painting pictures.

All Drake's Spanish prisoners maintained that he had the express orders of the Queen before embarking on this voyage. The Portuguese pilot revealed that after Drake had sailed half-way through the Strait of Magellan he ordered that the trunk of a tree, which was fifteen or twenty handbreadths wide, should be stored in the hold of the *Golden Hind* as ballast. He would take it to the Queen of England as a proof that he had passed the Strait of Magellan. He told da Silva and some Spanish prisoners that he was bound to return by the Strait "de Bacallaos"[3] (of stockfish). Later da Silva got into trouble with the Spanish Inquisitors when it was reported to them that he joined the other English Lutheran heretics in their services. It is evident that a Spanish mariner named Juan Pascual, a fellow-prisoner, gave evidence against him. The log-book of the Portuguese pilot is preserved in the Archives of the Indies in a *legajo*, or bundle, labelled "About explorations (or discoveries) of the Strait of Magellan".

An important Spanish prisoner of Drake's was Francisco de Zarate, a nobleman and cousin of the Duke of Medina-Sidonia. He was a member of the Noble Order of St. James's and wore its red enamelled cross, the emblem of military valour. Don Francisco's ship was captured by Drake on 4th April 1579 off the coast of Guatemala. Francisco de Zarate received much kindness and courtesy from Drake, and for at least six days engaged in conversation with him. Don Francisco divulged that Drake deprived him of few of his goods, and was courteous in doing so. When he helped himself to de Zarate's linen, Chinese porcelains and silks, he was apologetic, explaining that he needed them for his wife. This was his first wife Mary Newman, the Cornish sweetheart from Saltash whom he had married ten years before* at the Church of St. Budeaux near Plymouth. Greatly relieved at Drake's leniency, Don Francisco wrote to Don Martin Enriquez, Viceroy of Mexico: "I kissed his hands for that. He gave me in exchange for these trifles a falchion and a small brazier of silver."[4]

Don Martin Enriquez was the same Spaniard who had behaved

---

* 4th July 1569.

so treacherously to John Hawkins ten years before at San Juan de Ulua. In all fairness it must be stated that Don Martin was merciful and resourceful during the epidemic and plague and pest which raged during 1576 in New Spain (Mexico). Four years later he was appointed Viceroy of Peru by Philip II.

Francisco de Zarate gives a lively picture of Francisco Drac (as he refers to him). "He is a man of about thirty-five years of age, low of stature, with a fair beard [*barbirubio*], and is one of the greatest mariners that sails the seas, both as a navigator and as a commander." Don Francisco particularly mentions Drake's skill in the highest branch of the art of navigation, using the Spanish expression "*de altura*". Drake certainly never indulged in false modesty. Gaspar de Vargas, chief Alcalde of Guatulco (Mexico) wrote to Martin Enriquez: "Francis Drake is so boastful of himself as a mariner and man of learning that he told them that there was no one in the whole world, who understood the art of navigation better than he did." He arrogantly told the prisoners that it was fortunate for them that no soldier of his had been killed. If any of his men had been slaughtered, he would not have left a live man of those who might be there. He would have pillaged and destroyed Guatulco.[5] Gaspar de Vargas described Drake as "a man of medium height, with a red beard shading into white".

Francisco de Zarate wrote Don Martin Enriquez that he was convinced that Drake was commissioned by Queen Elizabeth. He had even shown him the commissions he had received from her. Sometimes in conversation he would refer a trifle sadly to Thomas Doughty, executed during this voyage. Although he spoke much good of this man, he could not act otherwise, because this was what the Queen's service demanded. The Spanish nobleman provides us with lively touches concerning Drake's tastes. He wrote the Viceroy of Mexico:

> Drake is served on silver dishes with gold borders and gilded garlands, in which are his arms. He carries all possible dainties and perfumed waters. He said that many of these had been given him by the Queen. He dines and sups to the music of viols. He

carries trained carpenters and artisans, so as to be able to careen the ship at any time. I understand that all the men he carries with him receive wages, because when our ship was sacked, no man dared take anything without his orders. He shows them great favour but punishes the least fault. Each one takes particular pains to keep his arquebus clean.

Don Francisco considered that Drake had no favourite.* Despite his severity, the Spaniard soon discovered that the General (Drake) was adored by his men.

The Spanish mariner, Juan Pascual, who was captured on Don Francisco's ship, in his deposition before the Inquisitors maintained that Drake's seamen were terrified of him. When the General paced the deck, they passed before him trembling with their hats in their hands, bowing to the ground. Pascual's evidence may, however, have been influenced by his fear of the Spanish Inquisitors.

If Drake was on the whole tolerant concerning religious matters in his behaviour to the Spanish prisoners, his seamen often conducted themselves differently. Whilst at sea, he noticed the boatswain of Drake's ship take a small sacred image that was on a table and begin to strike blows with it. Pascual remonstrated with the man, imploring him not to break it. The boatswain demanded: "What do you want it for?" Referring to the image, he said, "This is no good," and broke it instead into pieces against a beam of the ship. Juan Pascual was a native of Villanova in the Algarve (Portugal).

There is some evidence to show that the Spanish prisoners were treated with religious tolerance. A Spanish prisoner testified that he and others had been "allowed to tell their Christian beads as they were accustomed to do". Drake told them that if they did not wish to witness the daily "Lutheran ceremonies", they could retire to the prom or poop, or wherever they chose. When the Spanish Inquisitors later questioned Pascual as to whether Drake used force on the prisoners, he was obliged to admit that he had not seen Francis Drake do any harm to anybody. The

* *No tiene privado.*

Portuguese pilot, Nuno da Silva, for instance, had been permitted to eat at the General's table, and Drake often had friendly intercourse with him. We get glimpses of Drake at a religious service, as he knelt on a cushion in front of a table and chanted in a low voice, whilst all the other members of the crew responded. When Pascual was questioned whether he understood anything of what they prayed and preached, he answered that Francis Drake sometimes said: "By God's faith [a favourite oath] and if God wills, I will soon get out of this." Pascual stated on oath that Drake had a table brought out to the deck, without a cloth. He then took out a very large book and knelt down bareheaded and read from it in English. All the other Englishmen were also seated without their hats, and made responses. His evidence was damaging so far as Nuno da Silva was concerned, for he revealed that the Portuguese pilot took part in these services. Drake and his compatriots always ate meat during Lent, and his prisoners were compelled to eat biscuits and meat. They also drank wine.

Drake's references to Philip II are humorous, satirical, and ironical. He alluded to the Spanish King and himself as alternatively acting as each other's treasurer. The silver which he took from the King was for himself, while that taken from private individuals was for his Queen, his Sovereign lady.[6]

Francisco Gomez Rengifo, factor of the port of Guatulco, testified that Drake said to him— and his satirical sense of humour is very characteristic—

> You will be saying now this man is a devil, who robs by day and prays at night in public. This is what I do, but it is just as when King Philip gives a very large written paper to your Viceroy, Don Martin Enriquez, telling him what he is to do and how he is to govern, so the Queen, my Sovereign Lady, has ordered me to come to these parts. . . . I do regret to possess myself of anything that does not belong exclusively to King Philip or to Don Martin Enriquez, for it grieves me that their vassels should be paying for them. But I am not going to stop until I have collected the two millions that my cousin John Hawkins lost for certain at San Juan de Ulua.

All accounts show that Drake was fond of alluding to John Hawkins.

One cannot escape the impression that Drake's Spanish prisoners on the whole admired him. Pedro de Valdés when he eulogizes him seems immoderate. He said of Drake that "his felicity and valour were so great that Mars the God of War and Neptune the God of the Sea seemed to wait on all his enterprises", adding that his noble and generous courage had often been experienced by his enemies.

This forms a contrast to the terror aroused in the minds of Spanish civilians when they heard that Drake the corsair was about to pounce on their cities. They were wont to frighten their children into good behaviour by warning them that Drake would carry them off, if they were naughty.

Some of the most fascinating of the documents in the archives at Seville are the declarations by John Drake, made during 1587 under the examination of the Spanish Inquisitors. This talented boy was the son of Robert and Anna Drake, Francis Drake's uncle and aunt. Early in life he was left an orphan, and when aged ten went to live with his cousin Francis Drake, who was much older than him. He later served his distinguished cousin as a page, and also accompanied him to Ireland. At the age of fourteen or fifteen he sailed with Francis Drake in December 1577 on his famous voyage of circumnavigation in the *Pelican*. It was John (Juan) Drake, who earned the gold chain offered as a prize to the seaman who should first espy the treasure-ship named the *Cacafuego* (*Spitfire*). Francis Pretty, one of Drake's gentlemen-at-arms, relates in the Hakluyt account:[8] "It fortuned that John Drake going up into the top, descried her about three of the clock." The treasure-ship contained great riches, jewels, precious stones, and silver and gold. The capture took place at Cape de San Francisco, about 150 leagues south from Panama.

In the Spanish account of John Drake's first declaration it is stated that he was a nephew* of Captain Drake. This is incorrect

* *Sobrinho.*

for he was his first cousin. John Drake relates that there were not more than 160 soldiers and mariners on this voyage. He also corroborates the Spanish accounts that his cousin Francis was definitely commissioned by the Queen to embark on this voyage. There is a mysterious reference to Francis Drake being a native of Menguen, but there is no such place. It is known that he was born at Crowndale near Tavistock.* It is possible that John was trying to protect his cousin in thus giving a false name? There is also mention of Guillen Hawkins in the Spanish documents, probably William, nephew of John Hawkins. 'Captain Francis' was warmly attached to young John, for they spent many hours together in Drake's cabin, drawing and painting. Among the captains was John Thomas, who commanded the *Marigold*. Young Drake declared that an English seaman who tried to set fire to a ship was severely punished by his cousin. When they sailed along the coast towards Guatulco, they captured on their way a vessel bound for Lima, in which there travelled a gentleman named Don Francisco de Zarate. John Drake relates that his cousin took from Don Francisco's ship a Negress named Maria and the pilot named Juan Pascual. During their voyage they met with great storms, the sky all dark and full of mist. 'Captain Francis' gave the land that is situated in 48 degrees the name of New England (Nova Albion)† now known as California. It was only after two months and a half that they doubled the Cape of Good Hope‡, taking it in 36 degrees south. "This Cape is a most stately thing, and the fairest cape we saw in the whole circumference of the earth," wrote Francis Pretty. From Sierra Leone on the Coast of Guiana they sailed to Plymouth. John Drake was considered too young to accompany his cousin from Plymouth Castle to London together with one half of the silver and gold. He replied evasively to the Spanish Inquisitors when asked how much silver and gold was given to

* Tavistock has a fine statue of Drake by Boehm, a replica of which is on Plymouth Hoe.

† Partly because of the white banks and cliffs, which lay towards the sea, and partly because it might have some affinity with England: formerly known as New Albion.

‡ Discovered by the great Portuguese navigator, Bartholomew Diaz, in 1488.

the Queen and how much was retained by Drake. He probably did not know.

In June 1582 John Drake was captain of the *Francis*, a small ship belonging to his cousin, in Edward Fenton's ill-fated expedition.

Fenton's original intention had been to visit the Portuguese Stations on the Coast of India, but he now learnt that they had submitted to Philip II.[9] It was therefore decided to make for the Moluccas. William Hawkins (a nephew of John Hawkins) was second-in-command. Almost five years before he had been a circumnavigator in the *Golden Hind*. The failure of the voyage, largely due to the irresolution of Fenton, was not the fault either of John Drake or William Hawkins. Fenton indulged in bitter wrangling with the two mariners, who both protested against the abandonment of the expedition on the Coast of Brazil owing to scarcity of food. John Drake, who possessed the dare-devil spirit of his cousin, decided with his crew, consisting of seventeen men and a boy, to enter the River Plate, so as to obtain the provisions necessary for the continuance of the voyage. A Portuguese named Lopez Vaz gives an account in Hakluyt:[10] "Within five leagues of Seale Island, not farre from the place where the Earle of Cumberlands shippes did take in fresh water, shee [Drake's ship] was cast away upon a ledge of rockes." Fortunately, however, all lives were saved. The shipwrecked mariners, their clothing drenched, managed to get ashore on the South American mainland. After some fighting with the natives, Drake and his companions, who survived, were captured by the Indians One of them told the Spanish Commander, Captain Alonso de Vera y Aragon, who sent four horsemen to bring the prisoners to the town of Asuncion in Paraguay.

The Spanish captain at first treated Drake and the others with some consideration. Until it was discovered that John—now aged twenty—was the cousin of the dreaded 'Captain Francis'. Drake was destined never to see England again. He was now treated with increasing harshness, taken before Alonso de Vera and questioned whether he believed in the teachings of the Catholic

Church. So as to escape a worse fate, John Drake answered that he did, and the authorities ordered him "to hear mass", though the citizens demanded that he should not be allowed to do so because he had come with 'Captain Francis'.

John Drake and Richard Fairweather were imprisoned in a remote hermitage for more than a year, and were forbidden to hold any communication with anybody but the hermit, a native of Segovia named Juan de Espinosa, and another man named Juan de Rute.[11]

As already mentioned, John's account of his experiences during the circumnavigation voyage is among the important documents in Casa Lonja. So is his story of Edward Fenton's expedition almost five years later. There is an interesting allusion to William Hawkins (described as Guillen Acquines, in the Spanish documents). He at least managed to reach home. In June 1583 Fenton arrived in England, with William Hawkins a prisoner in irons. In later life Fenton managed to maintain friendly relations with John Hawkins, who nominated him to a seat on the Navy Board in 1589.[12]

During one of the sessions before the Spanish Inquisitors, John Drake was compelled to admit that he had been a Lutheran. Every attempt was made to convert him to Roman Catholicism. It is recorded that John made an appearance in the public *Auto da Fe* on 30th November 1589 when he was admitted to reconciliation with the Roman Catholic Church. As was customary in these cases, John was obliged to wear the yellow San Benito coat (the fool's coat, as Miles Phillips had once referred to it). He wore it for three years, after his incarceration in a monastery, having been sternly warned not to depart from the Indies under pain of incurring punishment as a relapsed heretic.

It would seem that Sir Francis Drake almost certainly believed that his cousin John was dead when he made his will in August 1595, for he omits to mention him, although he bequeathed much property to his brother Thomas.

It is, however, fascinating to add that many years later there is an official description of the *Auto da Fe* held in December

1650 in the Church of Santo Domingo at Cartagena, the capital of the Spanish Main. Among the penitents was a certain John Drake, who was ordered to make public penance. He was "absolved with a caution" and admitted to reconciliation with the Church of Rome. If alive in that year, John would have been an octogenarian, aged about eighty-seven. It is more than possible, however that the John Drake referred to could have been a son of Drake's cousin, born of a Spanish marriage. How curious it would be, if descendants of John Drake still existed in the West Indies or Latin America.*

It must not be imagined, despite Francis Drake's tolerance in dealing with the Spanish prisoners, that he did not possess a fiery, passionate temper. He hated injustice, and no Spaniard could defy him with impunity. An incident related in Hakluyt[13] reveals his character. During Drake's West Indian voyage (1585), he charged a negro boy, "with a flagge of white, signifying truce", to deliver a message to the Spaniards in one of the towns, which had fallen into his hands. Unfortunately one of their officers stung to madness cruelly "strooke the poore boy throw the body with one of their horsemens staves". Grievously wounded, he returned to the presence of his master, to die gasping at his feet. Deeply angry, 'the General', (as he is referred to by Thomas Cates) commanded that two friars who were his prisoners should be taken by the Provost Marshal to the same place where the boy was so brutally assaulted and hanged. He also gave orders that he would have two Spanish prisoners hanged every day, unless the Spanish officer who had done this deed, should be handed over to the English. It transpired that the Spanish themselves executed the offender while the mariners watched the grisly spectacle.

Drake's expedition to the West Indies in 1585, in which he captured two colonial capitals, San Domingo and Cartagena, was extremely successful. It is fascinating to study the story from Spanish sources. We are deeply indebted to the researches of

---

* We know that relations of Sir Francis Drake emigrated to Boston and to Hampton in New Hampshire during the seventeenth century.

Miss Irene Wright.[14] Here is a Spanish description of the conquest of Cartagena, the most important city of the Spanish Main. Pedro Fernández de Busto, governor of Cartagena, wrote to the Audencia at Panama:

> I do not know how to begin to tell your Lordship of my misfortune and the loss of Cartagena. I can only say that it must be God's chastisement of my sins and of those of others. Our Lord be praised for all. During the assault the *Francis of Foy* lost her captain, named Moon.
>
> On Wednesday, first day of Lent, Captain Francis's fleet appeared off the port of Cartagena at noon; and at sunset he occupied the harbour with twenty-three ships, not counting pinnaces. . . . That same night as soon as he had anchored from his boats the enemy landed 1000 men, pikes and harquebuses, in square formation. At two in the night the enemy arrived at the Caleta. It was the blackest night I have ever seen in my life. . . . The enemy is master of all . . . according to an Italian who deserted to us, the intention is there to await the fleet and armada which His Majesty (Philip II) may send. . . . This Corsair [Drake] is very confident that all the Negroes of Vallano who have come in from the bush will assist him . . . and for this purpose he has brought them many presents.

One almost feels sorry for the Spanish officials such as Don Pedro Vique y Monrique having to report to Philip II: "The Corsair came in on Ash Wednesday* and today, which is the last day of Lent he is in the harbour aboard his vessels with yards across. I do not know when he will leave. God confound him and grant your Majesty many years of life with increase of many kingdoms and lordships as this humble vassel desires."†

Vincenzo Gradenigo, Venetian Ambassador in Spain, related that he had heard from a Spanish witness that in San Domingo and throughout the Spanish isle (West Indies), Drake had behaved with such humanity to the Indians and Negroes that they all love him, and their houses were open to all English. Gradenigo described Drake: "He is thirty-seven years old, of mean birth,

* 12th March 1586.
† 8th April 1586.

but loaded with honours and riches by the Queen. He is of great courage as a captain, eager to please, severe in his justice, and so he is beloved by all."[15] There is an interesting character study of Drake as he seemed to the Spaniards at San Domingo: "a man of medium stature, blond, rather heavy than slender, merry, careful ... sharp, restless, well-spoken, inclined to liberality and to ambition, vainglorious, boastful, not very cruel."[16] Everywhere Drake aroused fear and a reluctant admiration in the minds of his enemies.

The judicial authorities humiliated an aborigine native of Santo Domingo named Juan Guillen, by condemning him to the Santo Domingo galleys. A Spanish seaman from Cartagena reported that Drake had captured that aborigine, and "that he was now in the corsair's company". Philip II's Treasurer at Havana reported to the King that the corsair had said that if he did not take Havana now, he would return with a larger fleet to take it. "Such is this corsair's daring," he added, "it may be presumed that he will act again unless your Majesty see to his chastisement."[17] The feeling was one of utter impotence when trying to take effective measures against this sea captain of genius.

Drake's audacious tactics during the expedition (1587) had the effect of delaying the sailing of the Spanish Armada. In his satirical way he now referred to "the singeing of the King of Spain's Beard". The Spanish preparations were very impressive: "the like preparation was never heard of nor known as the King of Spain hath and daily maketh to invade England,"[18] wrote Drake. Though his vice-admiral, William Borough, opposed Drake's intention to penetrate the harbour of Cadiz, despite the galley-squadron and the shore batteries defending it, the tactics proved a triumphant success. Borough argued that to act in such a way was a violation of the principles of command recognized since Henry VIII had created the Royal Navy. It was during this expedition that Drake ordered the arrest of Borough, who was confined to his ship the *Golden Lion*. Borough was distinguished as a navigator and hydrographer, but had little experience of warfare. Drake claimed that he had destroyed thirty-seven of Spain's most powerful vessels, including a large Biscayan ship of 1,200 tons, owned by the Marquis of Santa Cruz, a commander of vast experience. It was during this expedition that the rich carrack, *San Felipe*, was captured, much to the fury of Philip II. On 5th May Drake succeeded in capturing Sagres Castle in the Algarve, for Portugal was at this period under the domination of Spain. It is related that Drake with his own hands piled fagots against the gate of Sagres Castle and led his men in the storming of the citadel.[19] Drake wrote earnestly to Sir Francis Walsingham: "There must be a beginning of any good matter, but the continuing to the end, until it be thoroughly finished yields the true glory." Certainly the psychological effects of Drake's original strategy were of immense importance in undermining Spanish confidence when their Armada finally sailed. The effects in England were to influence the seamen to underestimate Spain's fighting power.

Notes

CHAPTER XI

1   Particularly her book *New Light on Drake*.
2   Legajo 266, Patronato E2, C. 5, L.2–21 No. 8 Casa Lonja, Seville.
3   Zelia Nuttall, *New Light on Drake*.
4   E. 2 C. 5, 22–21, No. 19 Patronato 266, Casa Lonja, Archives of the Indies.
5   Zelia Nuttall, *New Light on Drake*.
6   *Ibid*.
7   Legajo No. 266 Patronato E. 2 C. 5, 22–21 Archives of the Indies. Relacion del Captain Juan Drack (1587) Ingles.
8   E. J. Payne, *Voyages of Elizabethan Seamen*, p. 277.
9   James A. Williamson, *The Age of Drake*.
10 Richard Hakluyt, *Voyages* (Everyman Edition), p. 47.
11 Zelia Nuttall, *New Light on Drake*.
12 James A. Williamson, *The Age of Drake*, p. 216.
13 Richard Hakluyt, *Voyages* (Everyman Edition), Vol. VII, p. 90.
14 Miss Irene Wright, *Further English Voyages to Spanish America 1583, 1594* (Hakluyt Society).
15 *Calendar of State Papers*, Venetian.
16 *Further English Voyages to Spanish America 1581–1591*, p.155. A. L. Rowse, *The Expansion of Elizabethan England*.
17 A. de I., 542–4 (Archives of the Indies), Seville.
18 A. L. Rowse.
19 James A. Williamson, *The Age of Drake*.

CHAPTER XII

The Lord Admiral Howard of Effingham

The Spanish menace still remained acute for almost ten years after the defeat of the Armada, though it has been described as one of the decisive battles of the world. History teaches us that all great empires endure for a while, only to wither away or to perish. The event marked the imminent downfall of Spain and the rise of England as a great maritime power. It has been remarked that there exists no contemporary play which mentions Drake.[1] To the Elizabethans, the victory, though a decisive one, was a mighty episode in their relentless, cruel struggle with Spain. To us it seems the culmination of the warfare itself.

It was the Elizabethans' finest hour when a fiery glow of exaltation filled mens' hearts, illuminating the scene with a sombre beauty. It is during hours of peril that people reveal qualities of greatness, selflessness, and sacrifice, and we experienced it again under the dire menace of Nazi occupation of Europe during the Second World War.

By 1588 Charles Lord Howard of Effingham* had been Lord Admiral for three years. He was a man of fifty-two, a fervent Protestant, honourable, conscientious, and extremely tactful.

* 1536–1624.

THE
SPANISH
ARMADA

Orkney
Is.

Shetland
Is.

Bergen

Stavanger

*Drake &
Howard stopped
the chase*

Wrecks

Edinburgh

Firth of Forth

Dublin

Cork

JULY 27-8

Bristol

Scilly Is.

London

Amsterdam

Plymouth

July 19

Gravlines

Ushant

Paris

*Stormbound
until July 12*

Coruña

Bordeaux

Venice

Avignon

Genoa

POR-TUGAL

Lisbon
*Armada
sailed
May 20*

Madrid

Rome

Valencia

BALEARIC IS.

Seville

SARDINIA

Cadiz

Malaga

Algiers

0   Miles   400

His loyalty to the Queen cannot be questioned. A patent roll among the State Papers provides:

> Know ye that we, reposing special trust and confidence in the fidelity, prudence and zeal, experience, circumspection, industry and diligence of our beloved Councillor Charles Lord Howard Baron of Effingham, Knight of our illustrious Order of the Garter, High Admiral of England, Ireland, Wales, and of the dominions and islands thereof of the Town of Calais and the Marches of the same, of Normandy, Gascony and Aquitaine and Captain General of the Navy and mariners of our four kingdoms of England and Ireland—do by these presents, assign, make constitute, ordain, and depute the said Charles, to be our lieutenant-general, Commander-in-Chief, and Governor of an whole fleet and army at sea, now fitted forth against the Spaniards, and their allies, adherents or abettors, attempting or compassing any design against our kingdom, dominions and subjects.[2]

In his portrait apparently painted by Daniel Mytens in later life, Charles Howard with his aristocratic nose and trim beard gives an impression of honesty and candour.

Although he possessed no great experience of the sea, he was wise enough to defer to sea captains such as Sir Francis Drake, Sir John Hawkins and Captain Martin Frobisher. He valued their expert knowledge. He had a warm admiration for Sir John Hawkins and sprang to his defence. Owing to his support when he became Lord Admiral, the attacks of the carping critics on the Secretary of the Navy Board largely ceased. An attractive aspect of Charles Howard's character was his real love of and pride in the ships in which he sailed, particularly his flag-ship, the *Ark Royal* (Howard of Effingham called her *The Ark*). This fine ship of 600 tons, formerly known as the *Ark Ralegh*, was built by Richard Chapman for Sir Walter Ralegh, and launched on 22nd June 1587. However, before her launching she had been sold to the Queen for £5,000. During 1596 she again carried the flag of the Lord Admiral, Howard of Effingham, in the expedition to Cadiz.* He wrote to Lord Burghley: "I pray you tell Her Majesty

---

* In 1608 she was rebuilt and renamed the *Anne Royal*, presumably in honour of Queen Anne of Denmark, consort of James I.

for me that her money was well given for the *Ark Ralegh*, for I think her the odd [finest] ship in the world for all conditions.' He wrote Sir Francis Walsingham: "I protest it before God that were it not for Her Majesty's presence I had rather live in the company of these noble ships than in any other place. There is not one," he wrote with his customary enthusiasm, "but I durst, go to the Rio de La Plata in her." Lord Henry Seymour, who commanded the *Bonaventura*, proudly said that she could prove as strong a ship in twelve hours' fight with the Spaniards as she had in twelve hours on the shoal.

Far the most able and experienced of Philip II's admirals was Don Alvaro de Bazan, Marquis of Santa Cruz*, that dogged old Spanish grandee, who had been Captain General for the Ocean Seas. It was Santa Cruz who had crushed the naval power of the Turks in the Mediterranean at the Battle of Lepanto (1571). Overwhelmed with hard work and harassed by constant interference from Philip, he died on 19th February 1588. The King of Spain selected as his successor Don Alonso Perez de Guzmán el Bueno, Duke of Medina-Sidonia, who was Captain General of Andalusia. This Spanish aristocrat, who felt more at home among his orange groves at San Lucar than on a ship, had some military experience but absolutely none at sea. The Duke was modest and diffident about his own qualifications for assuming such a high command, not without justification. Yet he was a man of honour, and possessed some ability. He was of middle height, with a pensive, sensitive face and eyes, which have been described as "brooding rather than piercing".[3] He certainly did not lack intelligence.

One essential quality Medina-Sidonia lacked was the ability to inspire the seamen under his command. He wrote to Philip II's secretary:

My health is not equal to such a voyage, for I know by experience for the little I have been at sea that I am always sea-sick and always catch cold. My family is burdened with a debt of nine-hundred

* A Spanish historian Adolfo de Castro refers to him as a "*marino de gran valor esperencia*".

ducats, and I could not spend a real in the King's service. Since I have not had any experience either of the sea, or of war, I cannot feel that I ought to command so important an enterprise. . . . The Adelantado Major of Castile is much fitter for this post than I.[4]

Medina-Sidonia at least had the intelligence to write pessimistically to the Duke of Parma on 7th August 1588 that the Armada was so weighed down with cumbrous ships that it was difficult to proceed.[5]

It has frequently been remarked that the Armada was a religious crusade for the Spaniards, and that is true enough. It was intended to restore the ancient faith to England and to free the thousands of faithful Catholics, who had endured persecution from the heretics. Queen Elizabeth was denounced as "an incestuous bastard, begotten and born in sin of an infamous courtesan, Anne Boleyn". All the sailors and soldiers in the Spanish fleet were commanded to confess and hear mass before setting sail. No prostitutes were allowed on board and gambling and swearing were rigorously prohibited.[6] Lope de Vega, who was in Lisbon with the fleet, took the opportunity to visit a young mistress in the town. Medina-Sidonia, pious and conscientious, passed through the ranks of kneeling Spaniards, carrying to the Armada the sacred standard from the altar of the Cathedral at Lisbon. The blessing of Medina-Sidonia's standard was an imposing ceremonial act performed off Belem,[7] that lovely jewel of a Jeronymite church erected by King Manuel in honour of the Portuguese explorer Vasco da Gama's voyage to the East Indies.

William Camden[8] relates that the Spanish Armada consisted of 8,350 sailors, 19,290 soldiers, 130 ships and 2,080 galley slaves whose duty was to labour at the oars of the light galleys and the heavy galleasses. These were mainly Moorish and Turkish slaves. There were 2,630 great ordnance. A host of 600 monks, priests and chaplains embarked in the vessels.

Philip's strategic plan—and he was well aware of the risk of failure—was founded upon the illusion that his enormous ships, over-laden with men and ammunition to reinforce the Duke of Parma, could rendezvous with the Duke and escort his troops from

Flanders to England.[9] Parma warned the Spanish King "that it is going to be impossible for my ships ever to meet the Armada". Despite Parma's advice, Philip continued on his obstinate course.

Meanwhile preparations to resist the Spanish invader were being made in England. The great work of Sir John Hawkins in rebuilding the fleet when Treasurer of the Navy Board has already been stressed, and his part in defeating the Armada must not be underestimated. Hawkins preferred the smaller or middle-sized ships to the large ships such as the *Elizabeth Jonas*, the *Victory*, the *Triumph* and *White Bear*. Sir Walter Ralegh tells us the reason.

> We find by experience that the greatest ships are least serviceable, go very deep to the water and of marvellous charge . . . besides, they are less nimble, less manageable and very seldom employed. 'Grande navio, grande fatiga; saith the Spaniard, a ship of 600 tons will carry as good ordnance as a ship of 1200 tons and . . . the lesser will turn her broadside twice before the greater can wind once.[10]

Ralegh considered that six principles should be borne in mind in the building of ships. "She should be strong-built, swift, stout-sided, that she carry out her guns all weathers, that the hull and try well, which we call a good sea-ship and that she stay well when boarding and turning on a wind is required."[11] Drake chose for his flag-ship during the Spanish Armada campaign the *Revenge*, a medium-sized ship of 500 tons.[12] Nimble ships such as the *Defiance*, *Vanguard*, *Rainbow* and the *Revenge* proved easier to manoeuvre than the larger ships.

Hawkins' work was achieved, despite the opposition of his enemies, William Borough and Sir William Winter, who tried to poison Lord Burghley's mind against Hawkins by sly innuendoes and charges of corruption, accusing him of cunning and duplicity so as to maintain his pride and ambition, and for the better filling of his purse. Later during 1586 Hawkins and Borough were reconciled when Hawkins commanded a squadron at sea, and Borough served as his vice-admiral. The two most important master-shipwrights were Peter Pett and Matthew Baker, who was admired by John Davis. The lighter vessels were increasingly armed with culverin instead of cannon. These were easier to carry, had less recoil, and when in action possessed a longer range. William Hawkins wrote to his brother John from Plymouth in the spring of 1588, "The Ships sit aground so strongly, and are so staunch as if they were made of a whole tree."[13]

Hawkins had reason to be proud of his ships. He wrote to Lord Burghley on 17th July from Plymouth. "The four great ships, the *Triumph*, the *Victory*, the *Elizabeth Jonas*, the *Bear* one day had a leak, upon which there grew much ado . . . the leak was presently stopped of itself; and so the ship proceedeth with her fellows in good and royal estate, God be thanked."

When the Lord Admiral Charles Howard of Effingham arrived at Plymouth with the main body of the Queen's ships on 23rd May, Drake sailed forth to greet him with sixty sail. We can follow the campaign that frustrating summer in the official correspondence of the Lord Admiral. There is reflected his constant anxiety concerning victuals for the seamen and the maintenance of the navy. We find him writing to Burghley six weeks earlier from his house at Deptford: "I wrote to your Lordship before this long since of sundry extraordinary charges that were then grown in furnishing of the navy, which doth daily increase many ways; therefore I heartily pray your Lordship that they may be paid £2,000 out of the grant of £29,000."[14] One senses the heavy responsibilities of the man as he writes asking for six weeks wages to be paid to the seamen. The weather that summer was particularly stormy. We find Howard writing to Walsingham on 14th June: "The extremity of the weather in this place where it hath (held), hath caused me to continue here longer than I had meant." Meanwhile Drake, Hawkins and Frobisher were strongly urging Howard to take the offensive and to attack the Spaniards on their own coast.

Amidst the stress, and constant anxieties pressing on him, Howard does not lose his benevolence, nor his robust sense of humour.

Sir, [he writes] we have indured these three days, Wednesday, Thursday and Friday, an extreme continual storm. Myself and four or five of the greatest ships, have ridden it out in the Sound, because we had no room in Catwater for the lesser ships that were there. . . . Myself and my Company in these ships do continually tarry and lie aboard in all the storms, where we may compare that we have danced as lustily as the gallantest dancers in the Court.

He adds, no doubt deeply worried, "Sir, our victuals be not come yet unto us; and if this weather hold, I know not when they will come." From the *Ark* in Plymouth Sound he informed Walsingham that Sir Francis Drake, with a deep sense of duty, was co-operating most readily under his command: "Sir, I must not omit to let you know how lovingly and kindly Sir Francis Drake beareth himself, and also how dutifully to her Majesty's service, and unto me, being in the place I am in."* Five days later he is writing to Walsingham, begging the Queen not to spare expense so far as the fleet was concerned. By 22nd June his troubles were increased when thousands of seamen fell sick and were "fain to be discharged". When writing to the Council, Howard ends his letter: "From off board her Majesty's good ship the *Ark* your Lordship's Loving friend to command, C. Howard." Howard's Vice-Admiral, Lord Henry Seymour also wrote to Walsingham, deeply anxious about the shortage of food. "Sir:—I have strained my hand with hauling of a rope, whereby as yet I cannot write so much as I would."

We can imagine Howard in his cabin in the *Ark Royal* writing to the Queen to inform her that owing to the change of wind supplies of food had arrived. His pen scratches as the Lord Admiral boldly implores Queen Elizabeth: "For the love of Jesus Christ, Madam, awake thoroughly and see the villainous treasons about you, against your Majesty and your realm, and draw your forces round about you, like a mighty prince, to defend you. Madam, if you do so, there is no cause to fear." Howard was well aware that a Catholic fifth column in the kingdom were

* 14th June 1588.

prepared to rise against the Queen if the Spanish invasion succeeded.

On 17th July Howard, always ready to defend John Hawkins, wrote that he had heard there had been hard speeches in London against him "because the *Hope* came in to mend a leak which she had. It was such a leak," wrote the stout-hearted Lord Admiral, "that I durst have gone with it to Venice. But may they not be greatly ashamed that sundry times have [so] disabled her Majesty's ships which are the only ships of the World?" Then his mood of elation when he informs Walsingham on 21st July that a great number of Spanish ships had been descried off the Lizard. It was not merely Englishmen who were eager to enrol so as to take part in the struggle. A Genoese banker named Sir Horatio Palavicino wrote to Walsingham that he wished to join the Lord Admiral, in order to testify his loyalty to the Queen.

The Armada set sail early in July, but was driven back to Corunna by the gales. The Queen now gave her orders that the fleet might go and seek the Spaniards in their own ports, if it seemed best. Howard, Drake and Hawkins were not loath to be off to the Spanish coast, and some ninety armed ships spread their sails and left Plymouth Sound. The winds perversely changed and forced the English fleet to turn back to Plymouth. Once again the pressing problem of shortage of food supplies obtruded itself. The seamen were put on short allowance, six men being served four men's rations. Among the crews there was much sickness. Those stricken with fever were put ashore, while the Justices of the Peace in Devonshire and Cornwall made urgent appeals for fresh recruits.[15] It was rumoured in Plymouth that the great enterprise had been abandoned.

We are all familiar with the scene at Tilbury when Queen Elizabeth, mounted on a beautiful horse, white with dappled grey hindquarters, rode up and down the expectant ranks of her army, with the Earl of Leicester,* Lieutenant-General of the forces, walking at the horse's bridle. She dismounted and addressed them with words, which fire the imagination even today:

* Also Master of the Horse.

I know I have the body of a weak feeble woman but I have the heart and stomach of a king, and a King of England too, and think foul scorn that Parma or Spain, or any prince in Europe should dare to invade the borders of my realm, to which rather than any dishonour shall grow by me, I myself will take up arms; I myself will be your general, judge and rewarder of every one of your virtues in the field.

Men confided in one another that they would die for such a Queen.

On Friday 29th July, about 3 p.m. in the afternoon, Captain Thomas Fleming of the bark *Golden Hind*, who had been cruising in the Channel, arrived in Plymouth to report to Howard that he had descried a large number of Spanish ships near the Scilly Isles.[16] At nightfall on 31st July the English showed fine seamanship when the royal galleons and merchant ships sailed out of Plymouth Sound and anchored in the lee of Rame Head. Even the Spaniards paid tribute to their skill: "the enemy recovered the wind, their ships being very nimble and of such good steerage as they did with them whatever they desired."[17]

The opposing fleets faced each other, ready for the fight, the great Spanish galleons and the light, agile English vessels. The sacred banner of the Armada was unfurled in the clear morning air, while the Spanish, Portuguese and Italian seamen knelt on their decks, chanting their prayers "that Our Lord might give us victory over the enemies of His faith". Howard's reply was to send his pinnace, the *Disdain*, to deliver a personal challenge to the Duke of Medina-Sidonia, a medieval gesture. Among the Spaniards were many renowned seamen, especially their vice-admiral, Juan Martinez de Recalde, who commanded the rear-guard. Their ships had resounding names, such as the *San Juan*, *San Mateo*, *San Lorenzo*, *Nuestra Señora del Rosario*, *San Felipe* and the *San Martin*. Hawkins was proud of his cheeky, nimble ships, the green and white *Revenge*, the black and white *Bonaventura*, the brown *Lion* and the red *White Bear*.

No attempt will be made to give a detailed account of the fighting, since this has been done by Professor Garrett Mattingly.[18]

Several of the leading mariners including Lord Thomas Howard, Martin Frobisher and John Hawkins were knighted* by the Lord Admiral on board the *Ark Royal* during the action. Hawkins had richly earned the honour, not least because he had worked so hard to prepare such magnificent ships; and Frobisher was rewarded for his offensive action in the *Triumph*, largest of the English ships, which he commanded.

The most able of the Spanish admirals was undoubtedly Martinez de Recalde, who saw the necessity of securing a port as far west as possible. It is probable that Recalde had considered Berry Head and Hope's Nose, where three miles of perfect anchorage existed. If the Spaniards had landed there they might have had a bare chance of defeating the English fleet. It was Medina-Sidonia's error to refuse to consider this project, for he followed too closely the instructions of his Spanish king in the Escorial. Medina-Sidonia favoured a plan to seize the Isle of Wight.

It is strange how the Spaniards were pursued by ill fortune. They lost two of their ships by accident, rather than by enemy action. *The Nuestra Señora del Rosario*, one of their largest ships, containing a great store of arms and ammunition, collided with another Andalusian ship and lost its bowsprit. Later she also lost her foremast. On board the *Rosario* were 118 seamen and 300 soldiers. Drake's part in this affair was rather mysterious. During the fight he seems to have turned aside in the *Revenge* to pursue a minor enterprise of his own,[19] apparently to investigate some strange ships seen in the moonlight sailing westwards. Without giving Howard any notice of his intention, he ordered that the *Revenge*'s lantern, which was supposed to guide the whole fleet, should be extinguished. Drake had an uncanny instinct for sensing the exact spot in the vast ocean where he could discover specially valuable prizes. It was amazing luck for him to find that the crippled flagship *Nuestra Senora del Rosario* was within a cable's-length of the *Revenge*. In the captain's cabin there were

---

* The only decoration the Lord Admiral had power to bestow.

found 55,000 gold ducats. Escorting Drake's ship were the *Roebuck*, commanded by Captain Jacob Whiddon, a Plymouth privateer and two of Drake's pinnaces.

It cannot be pretended that Don Pedro de Valdés, who commanded the *Rosario*, made any show of resistance, though the plight of his ship was by no means desperate. At first Don Pedro had intended to bargain with the English commander, but hearing that it was Drake, he was willing to yield himself a prisoner, after receiving a promise of fair treatment. One wonders whether it would have been more honourable if Don Pedro had not submitted so easily to Sir Francis. The *Rosario*'s castles loomed so high over the English ships that she would have been extremely difficult to board. Perhaps Don Pedro had heard accounts of Drake's courteous treatment of Spanish prisoners during 1577–1580. For a short time the Spanish commander was Drake's guest on the *Revenge*, and then he was conducted to the *Ark Royal*, where he was presented to Lord Howard. Meanwhile Jacob Whiddon, one of Ralegh's captains, was ordered to escort the crippled *Rosario* into Torbay. Three hundred and ninety-seven prisoners of war from this galleon and other vessels were imprisoned for a while in the Spanish Barn, built in 1196, which adjoins the ancient Torre Abbey in Torquay. The Hakluyt account relates:

> The day following, which was the two and twentie of July, Sir Francis Drake espied Valdez his shippe, where unto hee sent foorth his pinnasse, and being advertised that Valdez himself was there and 450 persons with him, he sent him word that he should yeeld himself. . . . Upon which answere Valdez and his company understanding that they were fallen into the hands of fortunate Drake, being mooved with the renoun and celebritie of his name, with one consent yeelded themselves, and found him very favourable unto them.[20]

None of Drake's contemporaries seemed to blame him for this episode, except for Sir Martin Frobisher, who thought that Drake was trying to deprive him and others of their share of the booty on the *Rosario*. With much obscene language he swore: "Drake thinks to cozen us of our shares in the loot, but we will have them, or I will make him spend the best blood in his belly."

The *San Salvador*'s loss was owing to a fire, which set the ship ablaze. It was probably caused by the explosion of some barrels of gunpowder.

Howard's plan of loosing eight fire-ships at midnight on Sunday 28th July, and sending them blazing among the crowded Spanish vessels, proved very effective. Some of the ships were compelled to cut their cables and made off in the darkness, fouling themselves as they did so.

The decisive fighting, the battle of Gravelines occurred on Monday 29th July. The English gunnery proved especially deadly. According to the Spanish Relation:

> Don Alonso de Leyva and Juan Martinez de Recalde and the *capitana* (flag-ship) of Oquendo, and all the ships of the camp-masters, as well as Castillians and Portuguese ... sustained the assault of the enemy as stoutly as was possible, so as all these ships were very much spoiled and almost unable to make further resistance, and the greater part of them without shot for their ordnance.[21]

Some of the finest Spanish galleons were sunk, while the *San Mateo* and *San Felipe* were cast ashore on the coast of Zealand and brought into Flushing. The carnage among the soldiers and seamen was terrible. Eight of Spain's finest galleons had been lost, while the remainder of the Armada had sustained considerable damage. Many Spanish ships were destroyed off the coast of Ireland. Some of their noblemen were drowned, and "divers slaine by the barbarous and wilde Irish".[22]

The Duke of Medina-Sidonia has been unfairly censured for the most part for the disaster, and it is only fair to record both his courage and his administrative ability. Philip II was always chivalrous enough to say publicly that he did not blame the Duke. It is always convenient to find a scapegoat, and the poor man returned to Spain, only to be reviled and mocked by almost everybody, including the errand boys in the streets.

Meanwhile Howard, who had worked so diligently to ensure an English victory, felt no sense of vindictiveness in having over-come the enemy. Only a sublime thankfulness to God for having saved the nation from a terrible peril. "All the world", wrote the Lord Admiral, "never saw such a force as theirs was." While others celebrated the victory with triumphal processions, and bonfires, Howard continued to toil on behalf of the seamen. During the fighting the English had lost about a hundred men and not one ship, but the fleet was riddled with disease caused by the lamentable lack of knowledge of hygiene and by the filthy food and rotten beer. Nobody realized better than the Lord Admiral the debt England owed to the valiant efforts of the seamen, now dying in their thousands on their ships, or set ashore in the coastal towns to perish sometimes in the street. This was no time for ease and comfort.

He wrote to Lord Burghley on 10th August from Margate:

My Good Lord, sickness and mortality begins wonderfully to grow amongst us, and it is a pitiful sight to see, here at Margate, how the men, having no place to receive them into here, die in the streets. I am driven myself, of force to come a-land, to see them bestowed in some lodging, and the best I can get is barns and such out-houses; and the reliefe is small that I can provide for them here. It would grieve any man's heart to see them that have served so valiantly to die so miserably.

Two hundred seamen of the 500 on the Queen's ship the *Elizabeth Jonas*, who had performed such magnificent service, had died. He was compelled to send her to Chatham. One difficulty was that the seamen were very short of clothing, and possessed no money to buy it. Some had been a year at sea, while the most part had been eight months serving on ships. Howard urged that £1,000 or 2,000 marks' worth of hose, doublets, shirts and shoes should be sent. "Good my Lord," he added, "let mariners be prest and sent down as soon as may be and money to discharge those that be sick here." Hawkins was hurt, because he had received a critical letter from Lord Burghley. He wrote him: "I am sorry I do live so long to receive a sharp letter from your Lordship, considering how carefully I take care to do all for the best and ease charge."

The sea captains and mariners told Howard that sour beer was one of the main causes of infection. Howard had an interview with Mr. Darell, one of the suppliers of food for the fleet, who tried to excuse the poor quality of the beer by complaining of the scarcity of hops. The Lord Admiral, sorely perplexed, informed Walsingham that he knew no way to make the mariners contented with sour beer, "for nothing doth displease them more". He was also distressed about the plight of the lieutenants and corporals, who had served their country. These had not been paid. "God knoweth how they should be paid," he wrote Burghley on 27th August, "unless Her Majesty have some consideration for them." He thought that £500 and if he were to help them out of his own private means, it would suffice.

On 24th November the Queen took part in a service of national thanksgiving for deliverance from the perils recently experienced. In her magnificent state coach with its canopy a gilden crown, Elizabeth was driven up Fleet Street and Ludgate Hill to the west door of St. Paul's Cathedral. Although she seemed to the spectators calm and triumphant, she tried to conceal her grief for 'her Robin', the Earl of Leicester, who had died on 4th September at Cornbury in Oxfordshire. On New Year's Day* her favourite, Sir Christopher Hatton, gave the Queen of the Sea a wonderful necklace of golden scallop-shells, gemmed with pearls, diamonds and rubies.[23]

It is interesting to study the documents relating to the 397 Spanish prisoners who were firstly imprisoned in the Spanish Barn at Torre Abbey.[24] They were entrusted to the care of Sir John Gilbert of Compton Castle† and to that of George Cary of Cockington. Both these gentlemen were deputy-lieutenants of Devon. Cary had already proved himself a capable military

---

* 1589.
† Elder brother of Sir Humphrey Gilbert.

administrator, and had for some time during 1584-5 served as Commissioner-in-Charge of defensive works at Dover Harbour. Sir John Gilbert was Vice-Admiral of Devon, and had taken an important part in the defence of the county against the imminent Spanish invasion. He had been commended "for his great care and diligence used in Her Majesty's service in that County".[25]

It was now Cary's and Gilbert's duty to report the arrival of Captain Jacob Whiddon of the *Roebuck*, with the captured Spanish galleon, the *Rosario*. They wrote Sir Francis Walsingham, Secretary of State, on 26th July:

> Our humble duties to your honour remembered: whereas the *Roebuck* hath brought into Torbay one of the Spanish fleet, Jacob Whiddon, being Captain of the said *Roebuck*, appointed by Sir Francis Drake for the conducting of the said Spanish ship into some safe harbour. . . . We have taken out of the said ship all the shot and powder and sent the same to Her Highness' Navy. . . . We have also sent to the seas all the shipping and mariners in all our country, to be employed as My Lord Admiral shall appoint.

Cary and Gilbert wrote again to Walsingham, reporting that almost 400 Spanish soldiers and mariners had been brought safely guarded to the shore. They asked for instructions how these prisoners—"our vowed enemies"—should be treated. "The charge of keeping them is great," they informed him, "the perell greater, and the discontentment over country greatest of all that a nation so mitche misliking unto them should remayne among them." The feeling against the Spaniards was no doubt acute.

George Cary, who was extremely conscientious and may have possessed Catholic sympathies, wrote* to Walsingham, complaining that the allowance for the maintenance of the prisoners was insufficient, though supplemented from the writer's private resources. "People's charity unto them (coming with so wicked an intent) is so cold," he reported, "that without relief they must soon starve. Divers are already weak and some dead. The pilot of the ship is as perfect in our coasts as if he had been a native

* 29th August.

born." Some of the prisoners were soon taken to the town prison of Exeter, and others elsewhere. About 166 were put on board a captured Spanish ship, to save the expense of guarding them. George Cary was at loggerheads with Sir John Gilbert and seems to have hinted in no uncertain terms that his associate was deriving some personal profit from the government allowance for the prisoner's subsistence. Gilbert employed 160 Spanish prisoners in levelling the grounds of Compton Castle. After three months Cary learnt that the 211 prisoners were in some distress owing to lack of money to feed them. He proposed to relieve their misery by allowing to each of them 4d. per day—"out of my own purse", he told Walsingham. Fifteen pounds had already been spent to supply their urgent needs.

When the Spanish ship *St. Peter the Great*, loaded with drugs and medical stores for the fleet, had been wrecked in Hope Bay, Cary was ordered by the Privy Council to go immediately to Plymouth. He informed them:

> The shippe is not to be recovered; she lyeth on a rock and full of water to her upper deckes. They confesse that they were put into her at her coming out of Spayne 30 mariners, 100 soldiers, 50 appertaining to the hospital. . . . There was putt into her as mutche drugges and poticary stuff as came to 6,000 duckettes, of which I think there will come litell good of the same, being in the water almost.

Some of them were entrusted to the care of Sir William Courtenay, while the "potecary" (apothecary) and the surgeon joined Cary's household. Cary wrote the Privy Council: "I would humbly desyer, not for my profitt, but to make tryall what skyll is in them." So much for Cary's part in these troubled times. He was knighted in 1597 and became Sir George Cary of Cockington.

Many prominent West Country families took part in the defence of their country against the invasion of the Spanish Armada, including young John Rashleigh of Coombe, a Cornishman, whose family acquired much property in Fowey and its neighbourhood.

John Rashleigh had been brought up to be a sailor by his uncle John Rashleigh of Fowey. Although a plucky, adventurous youth, he was somewhat disorderly and had led a very rough life. John Rashleigh of Fowey was the grandson of Philip, the founder of the family's fortunes. His business as a merchant was so prosperous that in 1573 he was able to buy the lands of Menabilly near Fowey. He lived in a fine house in Fowey, now the Ship Inn, and much of the ancient carved panelling remains. It was John Rashleigh who about 1591* began the building of Menabilly —that mellow old home of the Rashleighs for four centuries. John owned a ship already mentioned named the *Francis of Foy*, which had sailed with Martin Frobisher on his expedition to discover the North-west Passage. In 1585 Rashleigh's vessel, the *Francis of Foy*, had sailed with Sir Francis Drake to the West Indies, when they captured the Spanish town of St. Domingo in Hispaniola (now Cuba and Haiti), Drake had watched the landing from the deck of the *Francis*.

In June 1588 young John Rashleigh of Coombe, now aged 25, was captain of the *Francis*, and hastened to join the fleet of Sir Francis Drake. Rashleigh also fitted up a pinnace named *Christopher*, named after one of his relations. Such nimble ships as the *Francis†* were very successful in their fight with the large Spanish galleons, and the stormy weather that summer helped the small craft. Five hundred pounds was paid by the Government towards the cost of her fitting out to fight the Armada.

After the fighting, young John Rashleigh, a quarrelsome seaman, seems to have had a sense of grievance against his uncle. Together with some of his crew he went to his house in Fowey, and threatened to throw him over the town quay, unless he was paid £20 due to his men. John Rashleigh senior refused to give him the money, and later brought a Star Chamber action against his nephew.[26]

The plaintiff alleged that John Rashleigh, the younger son of

---

* Menabilly was completed in 1624 by Jonathan Rashleigh. Now owned by Philip Rashleigh, a descendant of John Rashleigh.

† She was only 70 tons.

Robert Rashleigh deceased, was "a young man of most disorderly, envious desperate disposition, having taken deadly hatred to me as I was standing on a key [quay] of mine September 26, 1588". A great number of sailors and soldiers, being also disaffected had collected in a group. He accused young John Rashleigh of threatening him with oaths that he would throw him over the quay into 25 feet of water. It was alleged that on 14th August John Rashleigh with ten persons had entered people's houses at Lostwithiel, and thrown fireworks from the windows, thus causing damage and disturbance. Although he was found guilty of these offences, Rashleigh was later able to continue his life as captain of the *Francis of Foy*. The disputes between the Elizabethans in those stirring times makes the age very vivid.

As already mentioned, the Spanish menace did not cease after 1588. The Elizabethans were apprehensive during 1594 that they intended to send a more powerful armada against them. Spanish raiding parties attacked and burnt Mousehole, Newlyn and Penzance during 1595. There is an unpublished letter written by Sir Walter Ralegh on 14th April 1597 "to his loving friend John Rashleigh" of the town of Fowey.

> Whereas as you have at your own great charge made a place of defence in your house at Fowey and have furnished the same with ordnance and munition for the better repulsing of the enemy upon any attempt by them to be made by sea against the yarde and town which place hath been seen and very well allowed of by my deputy lieutenant. I therefore thought it requisite for Her Majesties service to require that you continue your care therein and not to suffer the same to be impaired or diminished and for the better effecting thereof I hereby assign and authorize you, your servants and families together with such twelve of your tenants ... to be always attendant to the said place of defence.*

It is sad to relate that the little *Francis of Foy* was one of the ships included in the joint unlucky expedition of Drake and Hawkins during 1595. She was captured by Peter Eustace the

---

* There is a tradition that the MSS. of Sir Walter Ralegh were at Menabilly—left there after he stayed there.

pirate and her crew tortured. This expedition consisted of twenty-seven ships. Drake commanded the *Defiance* and Hawkins the *Garland*, and the two navigators had absolutely equal authority. They hoped to capture two million ducats in San Juan de Puerto Rico. Whilst at sea bitter quarrels broke out between Drake and Hawkins. Captain John Troughton related: "There passed many unkind speeches and such as Sir John Hawkins never put off till death."[27] Hawkins became extremely angry when Drake told him that he had 300 men in excess of his proper numbers. Since the food on the ship would not suffice for all of them, he suggested that Hawkins should take over the surplus of seamen. Hawkins, always concerned for their welfare, complained bitterly. Under the strain of these disputes, and in bad health, Hawkins became less wary than usual, revealing the places whither they were bound in the hearing of the basest mariner. The great seaman died on 12th November 1595 in the cabin of the *Garland*, attended at the end by the faithful Troughton. His last message to the Queen, delivered by this sea captain, is but an example of how deeply the mariners reverenced her. Here is part of it:

> Sir John Hawkins, who upon his deathbed, willed me to use the best means I could to acquaint your Highness with his loyal service and good meaning towards your Majesty, even to his last breathing, and for as much as, through the perverse and cross dealings of some in that journey, who preferring their own fancy before his skill would never yield, but rather overrule him whereby he was so discouraged and as he himself then said, his heart ever broken, that he saw no other but danger of ruin of the whole voyage.

He had added a codicil to his will, leaving her Majesty £2,000 as some reparation for her losses.

The Hakluyt account relates that "Our Generall", Sir Francis Drake, also departed this life over two months later, "having been extremely sicke of a fluxe. . . . He died at 4 o'clock in the morning at sea. He used some speeches at or a little before death, rising and apparelling himselfe, but being brought to bed againe within one houre died."* His brother Thomas Drake, captain of the *Hope*, was appointed an executor of his will, and also Captain Jonas Bodenham. He left a widow, his second wife, Elizabeth Sydenham,† but no son. Though it is fitting that these illustrious men should die at sea, it is sad that their last days should be marred by quarrels and that the voyage itself should be a failure.

* 28th January 1596.

† After Drake's death she married Sir William Courtenay of Powderham. She was daughter and heiress of Sir George Sydenham of Combe Sydenham in Devon.

Notes

CHAPTER XII

1   George Sampson, *The Concise Cambridge History of Literature*, (reprinted 1942), p. 291.
2   John Knox Laughton ed., *State Papers relating to the Defeat of the Spanish Armada*, Vol. I.
3   Garrett Mattingley, *The Defeat of the Spanish Armada*, p. 198.
4   *Ibid.*
5   *Historia de Cadiz y sa provincia desde de los remotos tiempos Hasta 1814*
6   Lacey Baldwin Smith, *The Elizabethan Epic*, (1966).
    Also: *Calendar of State Papers, Venetian*, 1561–9. 356.
7   A. L. Rowse, *The Expansion of Elizabethan England*.
8   Camden, *History* (1675 edition), p. 407.
9   Lacey Baldwin Smith, *The Elizabethan Epic*.
10 See Sir Walter Ralegh, *Excellent Observations and Notes concerning the Royall Navy and sea-service*.
11 *Ibid.*
12 A. L. Rowse, *The Expansion of Elizabethan England*.
13 John Knox Laughton ed., *State Papers relating to the Defeat of the Spanish Armada*, Vol. I, p. 73.
14 John Knox Laughton ed., *State Papers relating to the Defeat of the Spanish Armada*, Vol. I.
15 Garrett Mattingley, *The Defeat of the Spanish Armada*, p. 228.
16 *Ibid.*
17 Laughton, Vol. II, p.357.
18 Garrett Mattingley ed., *The Defeat of the Spanish Armada*, (1959).
19 James A. Williamson, *The Age of Drake*, p. 324.
20 Richard Hakluyt, *Voyages* (Everyman Edition), Vol. II, p. 383.

21   Laughton, II, p. 366;
       also: A. L. Rowse, *The Expansion of Elizabethan England*.
22   Richard Hakluyt, *Voyages* (Everyman Edition), Vol. II, p. 399.
23   Elizabeth Jenkins, *Elizabeth the Great*.
24   C.S.P.O. Eliz., Vol. 213, Art. 420, 1581–90.
25   *Acts of the Privy Council*, 5th June 1578.
26   *Rashleighs of Combe*, Vol. I, 1519–1667.
27   James A. Williamson, *Hawkins of Plymouth*.

CHAPTER XIII

Essex and the Second Cadiz Expedition

Robert Devereux, second Earl of Essex,* favourite of Queen Elizabeth I and a nobleman of infinite charm and grace, was during his dazzling career a soldier rather than seaman by profession. Yet Robert Southey in his thoughtful lives of *English Seamen* devotes a whole chapter to this spoilt child of fortune, though he is, perhaps, more interested in discussing the enigmatic relations between the Queen and the proud young Earl than in writing about his life at sea. Essex was a Renaissance character, a man of generous impulses and many excellent qualities. His Quixotic bravery and his quickness to forgive an injury made him loved by his friends and even admired by his enemies. Marcus Gheeraerts the younger in his portrait successfully gives an impression of the man's romantic charm, and of his magnificence, with his brown hair and eyes, clad as he is in white. His air of regality made it appear that he had royal blood in his veins. The dangerous defects of character of this flamboyant Elizabethan were his jealousy of rivals; the fiery, passionate temper which he could rarely control; and an arrogance and rashness, which led to his undoing. Essex was his own worst enemy.

* Son of Walter Devereux, first Earl of Essex, and Lettice Knollys, a cousin of the Queen. Robert Dudley, Earl of Leicester, was his step-father.

After the failure of the Armada, it was proposed to send an expedition (1589) to Portugal to help Don Antonio, the Pretender to the crown of that kingdom. Essex—now twenty-two—was eager to join Sir John Norris and Sir Francis Drake, the commanders by land and sea on this voyage, not only because of his desire for glory, but because he was embarrassed by debts. Without the Queen's knowledge, Essex embarked at Falmouth in the *Swiftsure* for Corunna. With characteristic impatience Essex put to sea with an unfavourable wind, since he wished to avoid the importuning of messengers "that were daily sent for his return, and owing to other causes more secret to himself".[1]

One of Robert Devereux's finest qualities was his humanity. He was genuinely deeply concerned for the well-being of the soldiers under his command. In return they gave him their affection. On the march from Peniche to Lisbon, he ordered that his own baggage should be used to transport the sick and the wounded since other means of transport were extremely rare. This expedition certainly accomplished very little, though Essex with a gallant gesture was the first to land at Peniche, where a rough sea broke against that rocky coast. The Queen had been furious with her favourite for joining Norris and Drake, but soon forgave him. Elizabeth would say of him: "We shall have this young fellow knockt on the head, as foolish Sidney* was, by his own forwardness."[2] Sir Robert Cecil wrote jocularly enough to Essex, just about to embark for Cadiz: "The Queen says, because you are poor, she sends you five shillings, which Ned Dennis (her favourite jester) gave her and Mathias for playing on the three lutes."

At the time of the Cadiz expedition (1596) Essex was at the height of his meteoric career. One of the most powerful fleets ever to be assembled was secretly being prepared in the late spring. The element of surprise was absolutely essential to take the Spaniards unawares. Lord Howard of Effingham—he was now sixty—served as Lord High Admiral in the *Ark Royal*,

* She is referring to Sir Philip Sidney.

while the Earl of Essex was appointed Lord General of the Land Forces. Two more squadrons were commanded by Lord Thomas Howard—a competent seaman—and Sir Walter Ralegh, a rival of Essex. It fell to Ralegh to do much of the work in equipping the expedition and to carry out the disagreeable duty of impressing men to sail the ships. He cannot have relished the necessity of "dragging in the mire from ale-house to ale-house, in the sea-ports" (as he describes), trying to find seamen suitable for service.

The object of this mighty enterprise was to prevent Philip II preparing another Armada to invade England. It was intended to land an expeditionary force on the Spanish coast and to destroy their warships. Among the volunteers, eager to serve under Essex, were many gentlemen, such as Thomas Egerton* and Sir Edward Hoby. It is also interesting to record that John Donne, then a young man of twenty-four, was among the soldiers serving under Essex. That the intellect of this fiery genius was powerfully stimulated by his experiences at Cadiz is evident when we read his poem, "A Burnt Ship". The sea indeed inspired some of his finest work, conceived in a frenzy. The English fleet consisted of 110 or 120 ships, of which forty-seven were armed merchantmen. It included also a large number of pinnaces, fly-boats, transports and victuallers. According to a Spanish account,[3] there were 6,360 soldiers and 6,772 seamen taking part. The Dutch contingent included eighteen warships which were mainly small, nimble and heavily gunned.

Before the ships sailed, elaborate instructions were given to the captains. They were required to see that the decks were kept clean daily, and sometimes washed. To prevent sickness among the seamen, they were to distribute to them such good things as were to be had and that were needful for them. Special care was enjoined to serve God by using of common prayer twice every day except when urgent cause enforced the contrary. Directions were given that no man, soldier, or mariner, should argue about matters of

---

* Son of Sir Thomas Egerton, the distinguished Lord High Chancellor and Keeper of the Great Seal, later created Lord Ellesmere.

religion, and if he possessed any doubts, he should confer with ministers of the army. "For it is not fit", said the lords-general rather patronisingly, "that unlearned men should openly argue of so high and mystical matters and if any person shall forget himself and his duty herein, he shall upon knowledge thereof, receive due punishment to his shame, and after be banished the army." The watch was to be set every night with saying the Lord's Prayer and some of the psalms. No report or talk was to be raised in the fleet "whereby any officer or gentleman in it might be touched on reputation; nor any matter of importance spoken without naming the author, who should be surely punished as an evil number".[4] One man was executed for inciting a mutiny and another for desertion. A soldier in the Dutch regiment, who had murdered one of his comrades in a dispute about their drink, was sentenced by martial law to be bound to the murdered man, and hurled into the sea. Another man found guilty of theft was ducked from the yard-arm. He was then given a can of beer, a pound of bread, a pound of candles and told to shift for himself. Dr. Marbeck, who was Howard of Effingham's personal physician, relates in the Hakluyt account that a lieutenant having been found guilty of receiving bribes from some pressed men and substituting others in their place, "was, by sound of drum, publicly in all streets disgraced, or rather, after a sort, disgraded and cashiered from bearing any office at that time".[5]

Before the embarkation of the seamen and the soldiers, old Lord Burghley (two years before his death) published a manifesto, which he addressed to all Christian people, showing the great and urgent reasons why the Queen at that time sent forth so immense a fleet. It was printed in Latin, French, Italian, Dutch and Spanish; "to the intent that it might appear to the world that Her Majesty avowed only to defend herself and offend her enemies, and not to offend any other that should forebear to strengthen her enemies, but to use them with all lawful favour".

The Queen, too, composed a prayer, explaining to God her reasons for undertaking it.

The last of the *Revenge*, 31st August to 1st September 1591. A steel engraving by A. Willmore after O. W. Brierly

Sir Walter Ralegh *circa* 1554–1618. Miniature by Nicholas Hilliard

Most omnipotent maker and guide of all our world's mass, [she wrote] that only searchest and fathomest the bottom of all our hearts, conceits and in them seest the true originals of all our actions intended. Thou that by thy foresight doth truly discern how no malice of revenge, nor quittance of injury, nor desire of bloodshed, nor greediness of lucre, hath bred the resolution of our now set out army; but a heedful care and wary watch that no neglect of foes nor over-surety of harm might breed either danger to us, or glory to them. These being the grounds, Thou that diddest inspire the mind, we humbly beseech with bended knees prosper the work, and with the best forewinds guide the journey, speed the victory and make the return the advancement of thy fame and surety to the realm, with the least loss of English blood.

She had a fine feeling for words.

Just before the fleet sailed from Plymouth, there was the usual bitter quarrel of the Elizabethans concerning precedence. Sir Walter Ralegh and Sir Francis Vere—both rival commanders—accused each other of various offences, and it required all Lord Howard's tact, supported by Essex, to put an end to the dispute. It was a marvellous spectacle—that June morning—to see the mighty fleet leave Plymouth. It sailed in four squadrons. Howard and Essex commanded the first two, Lord Thomas Howard the third and Ralegh the fourth. A fifth squadron was composed of Dutch ships under their own admiral.

The Hakluyt account gives an interesting account of the ceremony known as hayling when the squadrons, separated as they were during the day "for the better procuring of sea-roome" all came together, with friendly salutations, "a ceremonie done solemnly and in verie good order, with sound of trumpets and noyse of cheerful voices". None of the seamen suspected whither the fleet was bound. "If there was ever any great designment in this our age and memory, discretely, faithfully and closely carried, I assure myself it was this." The Spaniards, who on other occasions obtained useful intelligence of all the English plans, were utterly taken unprepared by the secrecy of the Cadiz expedition.

16

The superstitious seamen were encouraged by a curious omen. On the arrival at Cadiz a very fair dove alighted upon the main-yard of the Lord Admiral's ship, the *Ark Royal*. There she sat quietly for the space of three or four hours, since nobody wished to disturb her. The narrator in Hakluyt also says that another very tame dove alighted on the *Ark Royal* when the fleet was about to embark from Cadiz, "and did so still keep us company, even till our arrival here in England". Perhaps such an omen only strengthened the sailors' belief that God supported England's cause.

Cadiz—'la Joyosa', as the Andalusians still call her—was a beautiful port, the richest in Western Europe and headquarters of the Spanish treasure-fleet. When the English fleet appeared so unexpectedly that Sunday morning in June in Cadiz harbour, the Spaniards were momentarily taken aback by the beauty of the spectacle: "*Una hermossisima vista*," they murmured. The commanders rapidly organized the retreat of their great galleons into the inner harbour. All over Cadiz the church bells chimed the alarm.

There was the customary clash of temperaments of the rival commanders. Essex and Ralegh warily watched each other, each suspicious that his opponent intended to steal the glory for himself. Essex had little experience of naval warfare. Ralegh found him trying to land fully armed soldiers from small boats on a choppy sea. Ralegh tactfully protested, because he knew that it was folly to land troops on a foreign shore before the enemy navy was defeated. Inexperienced as he might be as a naval commander, Ralegh knew all about the theories of naval warfare. Essex objected that Howard of Effingham favoured the course he was pursuing.

William Monson, the sea captain of Essex, advocated the attack of the Spanish ships and the possession of the harbour of Cadiz before they attempted to land. There now arose a fierce rivalry among the commanders, who should have the honour of first going in. As might be expected, Essex with a gallant gesture, claimed the right. He was, however, opposed by Lord Howard, who had been earnestly charged by the Queen, "not to let the earl expose himself except upon great necessity". Howard was also aware that if the tempestuous Essex failed in this object, it would cause the ruin of the whole action. The Earl ordered Monson to go on board the *Ark Royal*, and ascertain from the Lord Admiral who had been appointed. The honour was firstly given to Ralegh, which annoyed Lord Thomas Howard. He hastened to claim the right as vice-admiral to lead the van, and it was finally decided that Lord Thomas should go in first. Dr. Marbeck, Howard of Effingham's physician, wrote that this was done as an acknowledgement of Lord Thomas's superior seamanship.

A tremendous sea battle now began. For over three hours the English gunners pounded the Spanish vessels with their deadly gunfire. Ralegh was in the thick of the action in the *Warspite*, and provides us with a graphic description of when the *San Philip* and the *San Thomas* were set afire.

The spectacle was very lamentable on their side, [he wrote] for many drowned themselves; many, half burnt, leapt into the water; very many hanging by the ropes' ends by the ships' sides, under the water even to their lips; many swimming with grievous wounds, stricken under water, and put out of their pain; and withal so huge a fire and such tearing of the ordnance in the Great Philip and the rest, when the fire came to them, as if any man had a desire to see Hell itself, it was there most lively figured.[6]

Another sensitive spectator, fascinated, yet horrified at what he saw, was John Donne, a soldier in Essex's army, a poet still unknown. He wrote:

Out of a fired ship, which by no way
But drowning could be rescued from the flame,
Some men leap'd forth and ever as they came
Near the foes' ships, did by their shot decay;
So all were lost, which in the ship were found:
They in the sea being burnt, they in the burnt ship drown'd.[7]

The English loss was about one hundred in killed and wounded, though the Spaniards suffered much more severely. Two of their finest galleons the *St. Matthew* and *St. Andrew* were captured and others crippled. Towards the end of the naval action, Ralegh was grievously wounded on the deck of the *Warspite*.

When the signal for landing was given, Essex cried in a loud voice: "*Entramos! Entramos!*" and flung his hat into the sea. It was Essex who led the assault on the city, and he was much praised by his contemporaries for his bravery. Among those killed in the fighting was Sir John Wingfield, a very gallant soldier, who was laid to rest in Cadiz Cathedral. Monson had the pommel of his sword shot from his side, and afterwards declared that it had saved his life.

In the city of Cadiz all was confusion, and friars rushed through the streets trying to hearten the people. Three thousand Spaniards crowded into the Church of San Francisco, where they hastily made their confessions. Philip II, now ageing, received the news of the disaster at Toledo where he was recovering from a grave illness.[8] Even the Spanish King could not repress his admiration for the humanity with which Essex had treated the people. He commented: "*Tan hidalgo no ha vista entre herejés.*"* The Spanish historians, such as Alonso de Castro, corroborate the English accounts that Essex behaved with great humanity to the people of Cadiz. He gave orders that the lives of the priests and women should be spared. He instructed his subordinates to arrange for the evacuation of these people in his own barges. Alonso de Castro paints a terrible picture of the frightened citizens, struck dumb with misery, "*muertos antes de morir, cadeveres antes de espirar*".† Though the English behaved with such lack of cruelty, it was otherwise with the Dutch (Flemings), who indulged in pillaging and wanton brutality and destruction. The total financial loss, according to the Spanish historians, was 22 million ducats, while the English historians maintain that it was 20 million. The Duke of Medina-Sidonia, who was in charge of coastal defence, ordered that all the Spanish merchant ships should

* Such a nobleman has not been found among the heretics.
† Dead before dying, corpses before expiring.

be burnt, lest they fell into English hands. Thirty-six merchant ships were set on fire.

Howard, with faint irony, wrote to Medina-Sidonia, saying he thought that he might not be wholly unknown unto him. He requested in his letter, which had been translated into Latin, that fifty-one English prisoners* serving in the galleys should be exchanged for an equivalent number of Spanish prisoners. Some of these had been captured during Drake's last voyage, and others had been there for ten years. The Duke of Medina-Sidonia received the proposal most courteously, and immediately agreed to it. Howard was now on the *Ark Royal*, having been advised by his physician Dr. Marbeck to return to his ship because of a sudden indisposition. Certainly the most beneficial repercussion of the fight at Cadiz was the robbery at Ferrol of the valuable library of the Portuguese Bishop of Ossorius. He was a determined opponent of Queen Elizabeth, and had constantly attacked her in his letters concerning religious matters.[9] The library was transported to England, where it eventually became the foundation of the Bodleian Library, begun by Sir Thomas Bodley. Essex, too, had literary tastes, and was a patron of poets, while Ralegh wrote fine poetry.

Howard of Effingham, though he had quarrelled with Essex during the expedition, wrote of him: "I can assure you, there is not a braver man in the world than the Earl of Essex. . . . The chiefest for the sea service, besides the Earl were the Lord Thomas Howard, Sir Walter Ralegh and my son Southwell." Ralegh, too, was generous enough to write of his enemy: "The Earl hath behaved himself, I protest to you by the living God, both valiantly and advisedly in the highest degree without pride, without cruelty, and hath gotten great honour and much love of all." The bitter wrangling soon started again.

In July 1597 Essex and Ralegh again sailed in a naval expedition, and with the intention of destroying the Spanish Armada in Ferrol and Coruña. Essex went as General, while Lord Thomas

---

* Spanish accounts give the number as 51 and English accounts 31 or 39.

Howard and Ralegh both commanded a squadron. Though the fleet was a less powerful one than on the Cadiz expedition, it was composed of seventeen of the Queen's galleons, including two captured Spanish ships, and there were about 6,000 men. Twenty-two Dutch men-of-war formed a fourth squadron. The main objective was to destroy the Spanish fleet at Ferrol.[10] Once this had been achieved, it was proposed that Essex should sail for the Azores, where he might intercept the West Indian convoy and the carracks. Attracted by the presence of Essex, many volunteers assembled at Plymouth, making themselves ridiculous because of their gaudy clothes. They wore plumes in their hats, embroidered jackets, and gold jerkins. These gallants made a splendid display, but when a sudden storm arose at sea, none were more eager to desert. The ships were compelled to return to Plymouth. On 12th July they made another attempt to move out of the harbour, only to be driven back by violent storms. Samuel Purchas wrote: "The beams, knees, and staunching of Sir Walter's ship were shaken well nigh asunder, and on Saturday night they thought to yield themselves up to God, having no way to work that offered any hope, the men wasted with labour and watching, and the ship so open, her bulkhead rent, and her brick cock-room shaken to powder." There were the customary complaints of the victuallers' dishonesty. "The beer carried aboard the victual ships is found to be unsavoury by the great abuse of the victuallers and London brewers, as well for their careless brewing as for the unseasonable stinking casks."[11]

John Donne was also on board one of the ships, and his poem *The Storm*[12] reveals his personal experience and knowledge of a seaman's life. His realism is almost overpowering when he depicts the horror of "being coffined in their cabins when their only desire was to join their dead comrades". There is the imagery of the rigging snapping, like too high-stretched treble strings; of the tattered sails hanging like the clothing of a man being suspended from the gallows. One almost hears the howling of the gale in the swell of his poetry. "Lightning was all our light," he wrote:

> Then like two mighty kings, which dwelling far
> Asunder, meet against a third in war,
> The south and west winds joined, and as they blew,
> Waves like a rolling trench before them threw. . . .
> Lightning was all our light, and it rained more
> Then if the sun had drunk the sea before.
> Some coffined in their cabins lie equally
> Grieved that they are not dead and yet must die.

He was a sensitive observer of the heart-ache of the mariners.

> Pumping hath tir'd our men, and what's the gain?
> Seas into seas thrown, we suck in again;
> Hearing hath deaf'd our sailors; and if they
> Knew how to hear, there's none knows what to say.

Essex showed little aptitude as a naval commander. Instead of taking the advice of his sea captain, William Monson, he listened too readily to the hordes of flatterers around him. It would be surprising if Essex and Ralegh had managed to co-operate. Both were haunted by dreams of personal aggrandisement and glory and they regarded each other with suspicion. In fairness to the Earl, it must be stated that constant storms at sea made his task more difficult. The *St. Matthew*, one of the captured Spanish ships, was driven upon a rock, but, owing to the initiative of her Commander Sir George Carew, both seamen and ship were saved.

It was unfortunate that Ralegh got separated from the main fleet. He received false information from a pinnace that the Spanish *flota*, instead of being at Ferrol or Coruña, had left for Tercera (the Azores), to protect the Indian fleet. The pinnace passed the news to Essex, who immediately made for the Islands. At the same time he despatched some small boats to search for Ralegh with the instructions that he should make for Flores. On arrival there, Essex was highly incensed to find no sign of Sir Walter. Many of Ralegh's enemies now took the opportunity to insinuate that he had purposely separated himself from the main fleet, and that he had persuaded a number of small ships to follow him. Misunderstandings were eventually cleared away when Ralegh appeared on the scene. Essex with his impulsive temperament was always ready to acknowledge a fault, and the two men were again temporarily reconciled.

Essex ordered Ralegh, his vice-admiral, to meet him at Fayal in the Azores, but omitted to mention that he would not himself arrive for several days.[13] After waiting for three days, Ralegh decided to make a landing on the island. It is evident that Ralegh never regarded himself as being inferior in authority to Essex. Much has been written about Ralegh's foolhardy action in crawling forward, while Spanish bullets sputtered against his clothing. Both Ralegh and his cousin Sir Arthur Gorges wore gaily-coloured scarves, an obvious target for the enemy. His bravery, however, was highly esteemed by his contemporaries, and he was especially praised for his coolness in leading his men on the assault of the town of Villa Dorta.

Essex was naturally furious when he heard of his rival's successful exploit, and in the heat of passion vowed that he would court-martial Ralegh. Most of his subordinate officers urged him to do so. Eventually Lord Thomas Howard—the Queen called him "Good Thomas" in her letters to Essex—was obliged to mediate between the two men, and the Earl rather sulkily accepted Ralegh's apology. The eagerness of Essex to capture the Spanish *flota* caused him to make vital errors of judgement. With characteristic impatience he changed the position of his squadron so often, that the West Indian fleet, laden with silver and gold from the New World, was able to sail unmolested into the port of Angra on the island of Terceira through a place recently evacuated by the English fleet.

The Islands Expedition of 1597 accomplished very little. On his return to Court the Earl of Essex was coldly received by the old Queen. He had first aroused her jealousy after the Cadiz expedition because of his popularity with the people. Now she was becoming more and more disillusioned with her favourite. She told him: "When we look back at the beginning of this action which hath stirred so great expectation in the world and charged us so deeply, we cannot but be sorry to foresee already how near all our expectations and your great hopes, are to a fruitless conclusion."

Better for Essex if he had perished at Cadiz when his reputation was at its height. There lay before him the final bitter years, his disgrace and banishment from Court, when he was shunned by the Queen who had loaded him with favours. For an Elizabethan that was a terrible punishment. Last scene of all, a tragic episode in our history, the senseless, crazy act of treason, for which he was tried by his peers in Westminster Hall. When the Earl, dressed in a sober black cloak and hat, was executed in the Tower on 25th February 1601, there was Sir Walter Ralegh, captain of the guard, silently looking on. It was his duty to be there, but the people murmured around him, and Ralegh discreetly withdrew to the armoury of the White Tower. One wonders what mournful thoughts crowded Sir Walter's brain, for he could feel no sense of triumph that his enemy had fallen. He shed tears at his death, though he was one of the contrary faction.[14] From afar came the resounding crash of the executioner's axe, and his cry strangely unreal in the February air: "God save the Queen!"

Notes

CHAPTER XIII

1 Richard Hakluyt, *Voyages*, Vol. II, p.140.
2 Thomas Fuller, *The Worthies of England*.
3 Alonso de Castro, *Historia de Cadiz y Sa Provincia desde los remotos tiempos hasta* 1814.
4 Lediard, 314, 315. Robert Southey, *English Seamen*.
5 Hakluyt, *Voyages*.
6 Hadow's *Selections of Ralegh's Works*.
   J. H. Adamson and F. H. F. Folland, *The Shepherd of the Ocean*.
7 "A Burnt Ship".
8 Alonso de Castro, *Historia de Cadiz y Sa Provincia desde los remotos tiempos hasta* (1814), p. 402.
9 Evelyn Hardy, *Donne, a Spirit in Conflict*, p. 51.
10 A. L. Rowse, *The Expansion of Elizabethan England*.
11 Purchas, *His Pilgrimes*, Part II, book 10.
12 *Complete Poems of John Donne* (The Fuller Worthies Library).
13 Lacey Baldwin Smith, *The Elizabethan Epic*.
14 Sir Walter Ralegh's speech on the scaffold (1618).

CHAPTER XIV

The Privateers

The voyages and career of the greatest of the privateers, George Clifford, Earl of Cumberland, have already been described but there were many others, such as Captain William Parker, Sir Robert Dudley, Captain Christopher Newport, Michael Geare, John Chidley, Benjamin Wood and Sir James Lancaster, whose exploits deserve to be commemorated. The real difference between the privateering venture and the semi-official voyage is that whereas the former was financed and directed by private individuals, the latter was a national enterprise in which Queen Elizabeth's interest was the main element.[1]

William Parker of Plymouth, a friend of Sir Walter Ralegh's, was a brilliant seaman. Ralegh referred to him in 1596 as "sometime my servant". By 1587 he was already a captain, and during Drake's Cadiz expedition in 1587 Parker served in a ship named the *Richard of Plymouth*, which belonged to a merchant named Richard Hutchins. He possessed something of the dare-devil spirit of Sir Francis Drake. His voyage in the *Prudence*, a ship of 120 tons, together with Captain Richard Hern in a bark of 25 tons named the *Adventure*, and one hundred men is mentioned in Hakluyt.[2] This expedition sailed to Jamaica, and to the Cape of Honduras where Parker failed to capture the town of Truxillo for "it is invincible by nature, and standeth upon the top of a very steepe hill joyning close to the sea". Parker, however, succeeded in capturing Campeche in the Bay of Mexico. Here the Spaniards made a desperate resistance, and Captain Parker was wounded in his left breast by a bullet. The little *Adventure* was captured during this voyage, and Parker learnt from Spanish prisoners that Captain Hern and thirteen men had been captured and later executed. Arriving back in Plymouth they were in time to see the Earl of Essex setting forth with an imposing fleet for the Azores (1597). A year before, Parker had served as captain of the Queen's ship the *Rainbow* during the second Cadiz expedition. This gallant sea captain was also owner of several ships, including the *Prudence*, the *Penelope* and the *Pearl*.

Parker's most dramatic expedition was in November 1601, when he sailed from Plymouth with the *Prudence* and *Pearl* and other small ships containing altogether 208 men. Bound for the West Indies, he succeeded in capturing St. Vincent in the Cape Verde Islands, and also some Portuguese slave ships off Cape de la Vela. His most daring exploit was the capture of Porto Belo in the West Indies when he made its brave Spanish governor, Pedro Meléndez, his prisoner. Parker was renowned for his humanity. He himself relates that he did not insist on any ransom, because he had been so impressed by Meléndez's courage "in making resistance until he had tenne or eleven wounds upon him".[3] Parker very chivalrously instructed his chirugeon to dress and tend the Spaniard's wounds. Porto Belo was of great strategic importance being in the heart of the Spanish Empire. He made another voyage to Honduras and Campeche during the early reign of James I, and was denounced by the Spaniards as a pirate. He was later acquitted of all the accusations against him. Parker always retained close ties with his natal city of Plymouth where he was highly respected. In 1606 he became a founding member of the Virginia Company, and later served as Vice-Admiral of an East Indies expedition (1618) during which he died.

Robert Dudley, as already mentioned, inherited his interest in nautical discovery from his father, Robert Dudley Earl of

Leicester. He was a bastard son of Leicester by Lady Douglas Sheffield, a very beautiful woman.* She subsequently became the wife of the diplomat Sir Edward Stafford, a patron of Richard Hakluyt the younger. Robert Dudley may be far more truly described as a seaman than Robert Devereux, Earl of Essex. Even from the age of seventeen, the ardent young boy had been passionately interested in ships and the sea.[4] He early became acquainted with Thomas Cavendish, that renowned sea captain from Suffolk, who would tell Dudley stirring stories of his adventures in the Philippines, and in the Far East. Dudley married Margaret Cavendish, a cousin of the navigator's and the Queen's maid of honour. Sir William Dugdale recorded that he temporarily incurred Queen Elizabeth's displeasure "and was forbidden the Court for kissing Mistress Cavendish in the Presence, being his wife, as is said". It was fortunate for Dudley that he was forbidden by the Queen to join Thomas Cavendish and John Davis's last ill-fated voyage bound "for the South Seas, the Philippines and the coast of China". We can imagine him craving for a final look at the ships as they disappeared from Plymouth Harbour.

Dudley was anxious to own and build his own ships, and to gain experience he studied at Deptford under Matthew Baker, an experienced Elizabethan shipwright. He was ambitious enough to wish to make a voyage for the South Seas, but the Queen would not allow him to go. Instead, he prepared an expedition for the West Indies. As he himself relates; "His purpose was rather to see some practice and experience than any wonders or profit".

There is an account of this expedition, which left Southampton in November 1594, in Hakluyt.[5] Dudley's own ship was the *Bear*, which was 200 tons. The *Bear* was the family crest of the Earl of Leicester, who was now dead. Captain Monck commanded the *Bear's Whelp*, appropriately named because the young navigator felt the indignity of being the late favourite's bastard son. During the voyage experienced sea captains were impressed by the accuracy of Dudley's navigation. He himself relates in the Hakluyt

---

* Wife of Lord John Sheffield of Butterwick in Lincolnshire.

account: "Having ever since I could conceive of anything bene delighted with the discoveries of navigation, I fostered in myselfe that disposition till I was of more yeres and better ability to undertake such a matter." It was on 1st February 1595, that Dudley descried the island of Trinidad. He tells us: "We came to an anker under a point thereof called Cariapan, in a bay which was very full of pelicans, and I called it Pelicans Bay." He describes the Indians as "a fine shaped and a gentle people, al naked and painted red, their commanders wearing crownes of feathers". At least two other Englishmen, Jacob Whiddon and James Lancaster, had landed at Trinidad before Dudley. Sir Walter Ralegh was even now on his way to Trinidad, from whence he intended to explore the Orinoco river and to travel to Guiana.

Dudley's attitude towards the Spaniards was haughty and arrogant. He wrote from the *Bear*: "Let them know I so much disdain the Spaniards and his courtesies in respect of my dutiful service unto Her Majesty as I would they knew I neither trust them nor care for their force, be it never so great."[6]

Dudley's ambition was to be the first Englishman to ascend the Orinoco, but he was dissuaded by his lieutenant, Captain Thomas Jobson, from making the attempt. This brave man with a crew went instead, and after various adventures without guide or food in lagoons full of crocodiles, managed to return to Trinidad. On the way back to England Dudley's ship, the *Bear*, was engaged in a fierce battle with a Spanish man-of-war of over 300 tons. The *Bear* arrived at St. Ives towards the end of May 1595. During the Cadiz expedition, this valiant son of Leicester was Vice-Admiral in the *Nonpareil* to Lord Thomas Howard, and when the fleet returned triumphantly to Plymouth he was knighted by the Lords General. During a later expedition Sir Robert Dudley was unlucky enough to lose three of his favourite ships, the *Benjamin* wrecked off the Cape of Good Hope, while the *Bear's Whelp* was destroyed by fire, and the *Bear* also was never heard of again. It is related that seven survivors in a canoe made an adventurous journey across the Indian Ocean to Mauritius and that there was only one survivor, a Frenchman.

Whilst living in Tuscany in later life, Dudley wrote an important book on navigation, named the *Arcano del Mare*, "dedicated to the most serene Ferdinand II, Grand Duke of Tuscany".

Even such an important personality as the Lord Admiral, Charles Howard of Effingham, was an influential privateering promoter. He owned ships such as the *Charles*, the *Great Delight*, the *Lion's Whelp*, the *White Lion* and the *Cygnet*, used as his private men-of-war. Occasionally these vessels would accompany the Queen's ships during large expeditions. Lord Thomas Howard had a financial interest in the *Lion's Whelp*. In 1592 he organized a West Indies expedition under Benjamin Wood.[7]

Christopher Newport's career as a mariner was particularly associated with America.[8] Like William Parker, he served during Drake's Cadiz expedition. Towards the end of the first Elizabethan period (1592) he commanded an important privateering expedition to the West Indies, when he captured nineteen Spanish vessels and sacked three small towns in Hispaniola and one on the mainland of Honduras. This voyage is described in Hakluyt.[9] His ship was the *Golden Dragon*. A year later we find him off the Azores, helping Sir John Burgh in the capture of the carrack the *Madre de Dios*. As already mentioned, the prize was brought into Dartmouth. In September 1605 he presented King James I with "two young crocodiles and a wilde Bore", taken in the West Indies. With his curious tastes, that monarch must have been much pleased. A year later, he entered the service of the Virginia Company, and he made five voyages to that part of America. His distinction as a seaman is commemorated, for he gave his name to the town of Newport in Virginia.

His first expedition to Virginia consisting of three ships— the *Susan Constant*, the *Godspeed* and the *Discovery*—and about 120 settlers, left London on 20th December 1606. Sailing by way of the southern routes and the West Indies, the little fleet entered Chesapeake Bay towards the end of April 1607. It was during May that the site of Jamestown* was chosen as a settlement. Newport

---

* Named in honour of James I.

navigated the James river as far as the falls where now Richmond is.[10] George Percy, younger brother of the Earl of Northumberland,* a friend of Ralegh's in the Tower, wrote with a kind of pristine wonder about the beauties of nature in Virginia, "Of fair meadows and goodly tall trees, with such fresh waters running through the woods as I was almost ravished with the first sight thereof."[11] During his third voyage, Newport brought out one ship and some seventy settlers, including skilled craftsmen needed for the colony.

The most hazardous of his expeditions was the fourth. The Virginia Company had been reorganized during 1609, and Newport now served as vice-admiral. It was then that Sir George Somers and Sir Thomas Gates were shipwrecked in the Bermudas. According to Thomas Fuller, Somers was a "lamb on the land, so patient that few could anger him ... but a lion at sea, so passionate that few could please him".[12] The Bermudas were first named Somers Islands, to honour this Dorset seaman. Another earlier voyage of George Somers and a privateer named Captain Amias Preston† is mentioned in Hakluyt. Robert Davies, the narrator, mentions that during this enterprise to the West Indies in March 1595, some eighty seamen died of a fearful disease, known as flux of the belly.

One of Newport's officers, the intrepid Captain John Smith, richly enjoyed himself when the natives staged for his benefit a Virginian masque. Thirty young women came naked out of the woods, "only covered with a few leaves before and behind, their bodies painted". They pressed about the delighted seaman, exclaiming, "Love you not me? Love you not me?"

Newport continued to sail to Virginia. In 1611 he brought out Sir Thomas Dale and about 300 colonists in three vessels. Tradition relates that the enraged Sir Thomas pulled Newport's beard and threatened to hang him for giving too optimistic a report about the state of the colony. Newport married four times, and one of his sons, who settled in Virginia, acquired some land

---

* The Wizard Earl.
† Served with distinction during the Armada Campaign (1588).

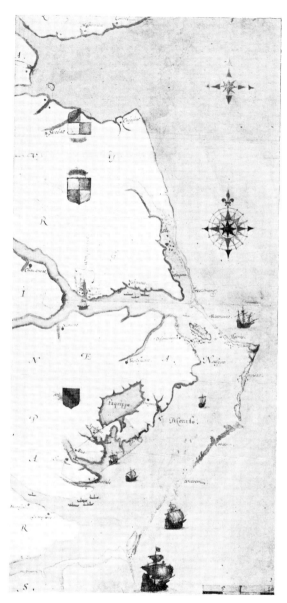

Map of Ralegh's Virginia. The east coast of North
America from Cape Lookout to Chesapeake Bay
and inland to approximately longitude 77° west.
Drawing by John White

(*right*) Ralegh Gilbert, colonizer in Maine, America. Painting by Cornelius Jansen

(*left*) Robert Devereux, 2nd Earl of Essex, painted by Marcus Gheeraerts shortly after Essex's return from Cadiz. The city can be seen burning in the background of the portrait

on his father's original investment of £400. He died during 1617 at Bantam.

If Christopher Newport's name will for ever be associated with the first permanent settlement on the American Continent, Ralegh Gilbert, the younger son of Sir Humphrey, is also remembered as an intrepid coloniser in Maine. On 10th April 1606 King James I permitted eight grantees, including Ralegh Gilbert, by letters patent the right to: "Make habitation, plantation, and to deduce a colony of sundry of our people into that part of America, commonly called Virginia." It was on 31st May 1607 that Ralegh Gilbert in the *Mary and John*, and George Popham, a kinsman of Lord Chief Justice Popham, in the *Gift of God*, accompanied by 120 settlers, sailed from Plymouth. They arrived on the coast of what is now Maine on 1st August. It was a hard winter for the settlers, for they remained at Sagadahoc* on the Kennek river, and the winters in Maine are very severe. On hearing of the death of his brother, Sir John Gilbert of Compton Castle, during 1608, Ralegh Gilbert† returned to England, where he became heir to the property. Unable to endure the rigours of another winter, many of the settlers accompanied Gilbert home. Others, including George Popham, had already died in America.

It is interesting to relate that the first white man to settle at Brunswick in Maine was Thomas Purchase,[13] who was a planter and fisherman from Devonshire. He went there in 1628 some years after the pilgrims had sailed in the *Mayflower* from Plymouth.

It cannot be pretended that a seaman's life aboard a privateer was to be envied. It was often a bitter struggle for survival, brutish and short. His usual food ration at the beginning of a voyage was bread or biscuit, oatmeal, salted beef or pork, cheese, and beer to drink. Before long the victuals would go bad and the beer sour. Small wonder if the crews were often tempted to rob other vessels whenever possible.

A classic example of the horrors of a privateer's life is the voyage of John Chidley, an enterprising mariner, who in August

---

* The colonists built a ship called *The Virginia of Sagadaho*
† Died 1634.

1589 sailed from Plymouth with three ships, the *Delight* (alias the *Robin*, 120 tons), the *Wildman* (300 tons) and the *White Lion* (340 tons) for the Magellan Straits, intending to go to the South Sea "and chiefly for the famous province of Aranco on the Coast of Chili". Chidley was twenty-four at this period and came from Devon. To finance this voyage with a partner, he was obliged to sell most of his country estate.[14] Chidley commanded the *Wildman*, while Benjamin Wood went as master. Polwhele was captain of the *White Lion* and Andrew Merrick commanded the *Robin*. There were about ninety-one seamen on all three ships. William Magoths of Bristol, one of the survivors, wrote the account of the expedition for Hakluyt. Sixteen of the ship's company "by God's visitation" died of various diseases off the coast of Brazil. After reaching the Straits of Magellan, they fed on salted penguins, which had to be eaten quickly or they went bad. Thus they struggled on: "after wee had spent 6 weeks in the Streight striving against the furie of the elements, and having at sundry times partly by casualtie, and partly by sicknes lost 38 of our best men". Some of the crew now became troublesome on the *Robin* and began to mutiny. Finally only six seamen survived to bring the *Robin* to the coast of Normany, where she was wrecked. Chidley and Polwhele both died on the other ships off the coast of Guinea. One of the survivors was Benjamin Wood, an experienced seaman.

Sometimes under the stress of failure, a privateer would turn to piracy. Such was Edward Glenham, a country gentleman from Suffolk, who sold his estates, so as to attempt the capture of St. George's Island in the Azores.[15]

Another wild, unscrupulous privateer was Sir Anthony Sherley, whose father lived on his country estates at Wiston in Sussex. His career is briefly described by Thomas Fuller.[16] The original purpose of Sherley's expedition in April 1596 was to sack Madeira and proceed to Saŏ Thome, but three of his ships and 500 soldiers were handed over to the Earl of Essex for the Cadiz expedition, and Sherley revised his plans. Instead, in his flag-ship the *Bevis* and five other vessels, he sailed for the Guinea coast, "where the rain did stink as it fell down from the heavens, and within six hours did turn into magots". In a small island named Fuego there was a shower of ashes "which fell so thicke into our ships . . . that you might write your name with your finger upon the upper decke".[17] When they arrived at Dominica in the West Indies, disease was so prevalent among the seamen "that men grew lothsome unto themselves, franticke and desperately raving". However, they were much refreshed by some hot baths on the island, and were treated very kindly by the Indians. Sherley at least did succeed in capturing Jamaica's settlement, La Villa de la Vega. Here Sherley's crews indulged in as much looting as possible. Sir Anthony eventually returned to Newfoundland, for his provisions were almost exhausted. Arriving back in England, he was in time to accompany Essex on the islands voyage. Sherley was typically Elizabethan in his ardent search for adventure, but he lacked the talent of the renowned seamen.

The piratical instinct was very strong in most of these privateers, and Michael Geare, who was part-owner of a privateer called the *Michael and John* during 1592, was typical of these. Although Geare was a hardened, unscrupulous seaman, not reluctant to engage in pillaging or smuggling operations, if it suited him, he was no worse than most of his contemporaries. He ended his career as Sir Michael Geare, a highly respected Elder Brother of Trinity House.

A sailor's life is a constant gamble, and many preferred to serve in a privateer, where their single share in a successful expedition might well amount to £4 or £5. Naturally there was the added attraction of pillage or embezzlement. Compared with the 10s. per month paid to seamen in the Queen's service, it certainly seemed more exciting.

One of the bravest of the privateers was James Lancaster, later knighted. Born in Basingstoke, probably in 1554, he became a merchant in Spain and Portugal. When he was 26 he took part in the fighting with Don Antonio, the Portuguese Pretender, against Philip II. Seven years later he sailed with Drake to Cadiz where he was captain of the *Susan*, a ship belonging to Paul

Bayning. His voyages during 1591 and 1594 are described in Hakluyt.[18] The first expedition was to the East Indies.

The part of the privateering merchants in attempting to penetrate the East India trade, culminating in the formation of the East India Company, is not really appreciated.[19] The purpose of this enterprise was to attack Portuguese shipping and to promote trade, if possible. Lancaster's 1591 voyage was a failure for various reasons. On the way to the Cape, many of the seamen were stricken with scurvy and died. Then, whilst attempting to double the Cape, one of the ships, the *Penelope*, was utterly wrecked. Some of the crews organized a mutiny, and, after going ashore on some islands near Porto Rico, failed to return to their ships. Edmund Barker, Lancaster's Lieutenant, related to Hakluyt that the ship's surgeon caught a feverish cold whilst on land searching for oxen and soon died. How thankful the survivors must have been to arrive at Rye in Sussex after a voyage lasting over three years.

In 1594 James Lancaster was appointed admiral of another enterprise, financed by some Aldermen of the City of London. It may be described as very successful, since Lancaster succeeded in capturing Recife, the port town of Pernambuco in Brazil. He proved himself a capable commander, and was fortunate enough to capture a rich East Indian carrack and various valuable commodities. Despite the constant Portuguese attempts to retake Recife, Lancaster managed to hold on to the town.

Lancaster seems to have held a very poor opinion of the Portuguese, and he certainly was intimately acquainted with them as a merchant in his younger days. Since they lay under Spain's domination, they were now his enemies. Yet Portugal throughout her history has ever enjoyed a long tradition of friendship with Britain, and it must not be forgotten that one of her greatest sons, Prince Henrique the Navigator, had an English princess as his mother.*

The hazards of a seaman's life incessantly plagued them. During this expedition, a careless gunner set a barrel of gunpowder on

---

* Philippa of Lancaster, daughter of John of Gaunt, who married John I of Portugal. Prince Henrique was born in 1394.

fire, which blew up the Admiral's cabin, killing three men and wounding twenty others in the process. As the narrator in Hakluyt tells us: "But the Almightie be praysed for ever, which deliverest us out of this and many other in this voyage. Our fire being well put out, and we taking in fresh men (God be praysed) we came to Blacke-wall in safety."

Notes

CHAPTER XIV

1 Kenneth R. Andrews, *Elizabethan Privateering 1585–1603*.
2 Richard Hakluyt, *Voyages* (Everyman Edition), Vol. III, p. 222.
3 Purchas, *His Pilgrimes*, IV, 1241.
4 Arthur Gould Lee, *The Son of Leicester* (1964).
5 Richard Hakluyt, *Voyages* (Everyman Edition), Vol. VII, p.164.
6 Arthur Gould Lee, *The Son of Leicester*.
7 K. R. Andrews, *English Privateering Voyages to the West Indies 1588–1595*. (Hakluyt Society).
8 *Dictionary of American Biography*, Vol. XIII.
9 Richard Hakluyt, *Voyages* (Everyman Edition), Vol. VII, p. 148.
10 A. L. Rowse, *The Elizabethans and America*, p. 66.
11 Purchas, *His Pilgrimes*, Vol. XVIII, 401.
12 *The Worthies of England*.
13 Isabel Whittier, "Brunswick on the Androsscogin" (published in the *Lewiston Journal Magazine*).
14 Kenneth R. Andrews, *Elizabethan Privateering 1585–1603*, p. 64.
15 K. R. Andrews, *Elizabethan Privateering 1585–1603*.
16 *The Worthies of England*.
17 Richard Hakluyt, *Voyages* (Everyman Edition), Vol. VII, p. 217.
18 Richard Hakluyt, *Voyages* (Everyman Edition), Vol. IV, p. 242 *et. seq.*; Vol. VIII, pp.26–44.
19 Kenneth R. Andrews, *Elizabethan Privateering 1585–1603*.

CHAPTER XV

Thomas Cavendish

It is true that Thomas Cavendish, one of the intrepid navigators, lacked the charm, grace and satirical wit of Sir Francis Drake, but he was a man of iron determination, ambitious to explore far distant countries, not so much for his own glory, nor out of lust of gold, but for the honour of his country. Lediard wrote: "Like Drake, he was a severe scourge to the Spaniards."[1] There was a hard streak of cruelty in his nature. It is recorded that Cavendish (or Candish as he is called by Hakluyt) sometimes tortured Spanish prisoners when he wished to acquire information, where Drake would have used more subtle methods. Among his unattractive qualities was a latent sulkiness, smacking of brooding suspicions. One senses that the seamen under his command feared rather than loved him, and that this hard, strange man was as capricious as the sea itself. Perhaps he thought of himself as one chosen by God to pour out the vials of His wrath upon those devils, the Spaniards. When he burnt houses and an ancient church in Mexico, where tradition says that St. Andrew once preached Christianity to the Aztecs, he may have seriously considered that he was only performing God's will.

Cavendish, who was born in 1556, had at least something in common with the younger explorer, Henry Hudson, for they were both betrayed and lured to their death by the treachery of their crews. As already mentioned, he was born at Frimley, in Suffolk, a peaceful place down by the Orwell, off the highroad to Felixstowe. His family was an old-established one in Suffolk. Like many another Elizabethan, Cavendish in his early life squandered most of his estate "in gallantry and following the Court", and no doubt in riotous living. Then there stole over him the strange restlessness, which haunted the consciousness of all the famous navigators. In 1585 we find him gaining experience in seamanship by serving as a volunteer in Sir Richard Grenville's expedition for establishing a colony in Virginia, and he retired with Grenville to England.

A year later, on 21st July 1586, Cavendish left Plymouth with the ships, the *Desire* of 120 tons, the *Content* of 60 tons and the *Hugh Gallant*, a bark of 40 tons. He intended to sail for the South Seas and from thence to circumnavigate the world. There is an interesting description of this expedition in Hakluyt, written by Master Francis Pretty, of Eye, in Suffolk.

By 1st August the navigators came in sight of Forteventura, one of the Canary isles, and four days later they arrived at Sierra Leone. Here "they spoiled a town of the Negroes" because a soldier named William Pickman had been killed by a poisoned arrow, which lodged in his thigh. He would not allow the surgeons to operate, so that "the poison wrought so that night, that he was marvellously swollen . . . and the next morning he died".[2] Cavendish named a harbour off the coast of America Port Desire, and there the mariners enjoyed the spectacle of "a great store of seals, huge and monstrous of shape, and for the fore part of their bodies cannot be compared to anything better than to a lion".[3] The seamen found young seal very tasty, and hardly to be distinguished from lamb or mutton. When they reached the South Seas, there was a great storm, and Francis Pretty, who was in the *Hugh Gallant*, relates that his ship, being separated from the others, nearly sank. For three days and nights nobody on board had any rest.

It was during this most successful expedition that Cavendish succeeded in capturing the great Spanish galleon, the *Santa Anna*, thought to be 700 tons. Cavendish had reached the west coast of Mexico when he was told by a prisoner that this treasure-ship laden with silks and other rich China goods, was on the way from Manilla, and expected to make for southern California. Cavendish lay in wait for this galleon for three weeks, and after discovering her made a surprise attack. There is an interesting description of the fight in Purchas.[4] "In the afternoon we got up into them, giving them the broadside with our great ordnance, and a volee of great shot . . . we now trimmed our sails, and fitted every man his furniture, and gave them a fresh incounter with our great ordnance and also with our small shot, raking them through and through, to the killing and maiming of many of the men." The Spanish captain was a very valiant man, and seems to have resisted stoutly for a time. "Our General (Cavendish) encouraging his men afresh with the whole noyse of trumpets, gave them the third incounter with our great ordnance." Only when the Spanish vessel was in danger of sinking, did their captain set out a flag of truce, suing for mercy.

One of the chief merchants on the *Santa Anna* together with the captain and the pilot came on board Cavendish's ship, falling down on their knees and offering to kiss his feet to show their gratitude if their lives were spared. Cavendish agreed to this, though the skilful Spanish pilot, Thomas de Ersola,* later proved treacherous. Purchas relates that the value of the goods on the *Santa Anna* amounted to 122,000 pesos of gold, besides rich silks, damasks, and other merchandise.

Master Francis Pretty wrote an interesting description of Manila in the Philippines, where they landed on 14th January 1588. "This island is a place much peopled with heathen people, and all woody through the whole land," he wrote. "Manila is well planted and inhabited with Spaniards to the number of 600 or 700 persons, which dwell in a town unwalled, which hath three or four small block-houses, part made of wood and part of stone."

During the night of 15th January a Portuguese named Nicholas

* From Acapulco.

Roderigo, who had been captured in the *Santa Anna*, secretly told Thomas Cavendish that the Spanish pilot, Thomas de Ersola, had locked a letter in his chest, which he intended to convey to the authorities in Manila.[5] In this document Thomas de Ersola treacherously revealed valuable information about Cavendish's ships, that their small fleet was at present at Capul, an island off Manila, that they had captured the King of Spain's ship the *Santa Anna* and that they had burnt many towns. When charged with duplicity, the Spanish pilot at first denied it, but the matter was proved against him. Cavendish ordered that he should be hung, and one cannot blame him for doing so.

Cavendish sailed through the narrow strait between Bali and Java, and after reaching a haven on the south coast was received in a friendly fashion by the Portuguese, who owned allegiance to Don Antonio. "Our General" was able to reassure these people that their king, known to his enemies as the Portuguese Pretender, was at present at Queen Elizabeth's Court. Through most of March and all April the seamen traversed the Indian Ocean between Java and the African coast. There were splendid opportunities during their lonely vigils for the seamen to observe "the heavens, the crosiers or south-pole, the other stars, the fowls, which are marks of fair weather, foul weather, approaching of lands and islands, the winds, the tempests, the rains and thunders, with the alteration of tides and currents".[6]

As already mentioned, Cavendish was the first Elizabethan to visit the island of St. Helena in the Atlantic. The account in Purchas only varies from the Hakluyt account on minor points. Purchas relates: "There is also upon this island great store of partridges, which are very tame, not making any great haste to flie away though one come very neere them, but only to runne away and get up into the steepe cliffs; we killed some of them with a fowling piece." Hakluyt, however, mentions that they differed very much from the English partridges, "both in bigness and also in colour". It must have been a sweet and pleasant place with its lemons, oranges and pomegranate trees. Both Hakluyt and Purchas describe the thousands of goats, called by the Spaniards *cabritos*, some of them "with a mane like a horse and a beard hanging down to the very ground".[7] The English mariners found that the Portuguese had established a permanent settlement on the island, and that it was a useful port of refreshment on the long homeward voyage.

This voyage of Cavendish's (1587–1588), so fruitful in results, was of considerable value to Hakluyt in providing scientific knowledge. It was much to Cavendish's credit that he was prepared to give Hakluyt the benefit of his experience. Thomas Fuller, the master of the *Desire*, also provided valuable technical information regarding the variations of the compass, latitudes, soundings, courses and distances.[8]

The last voyage of Thomas Cavendish in August 1591 was as disastrous as the earlier one had been successful. It is evident that under the strain of his privations the character of the navigator had deteriorated. Master Cavendish embarked at Plymouth as Admiral of the *Galleon*, while that intrepid seaman John Davis commanded the *Desire*. The expedition with all its miseries and horrors has been dramatically described for Hakluyt by John Jane, a Cornishman, who relates that he went on it for the sake of his friend, John Davis. It was proposed to sail for the South Seas and to China. There existed a tacit understanding between Cavendish and Davis that the latter should be allowed to part company with the main fleet at California, so as to search for the North-west Passage, a life-long obsession of the Devon navigator. Another narrator of this voyage was a young seaman named Anthony Knivet, and the Purchas account contains his terrible experiences,[9] so reminiscent of those suffered by Job Hortop and Miles Phillips in Mexico.

Besides the *Desire* and the *Galleon*, there was the *Roebuck*, commanded by Master Cook, and one of the pinnaces was owned by Adrian Gilbert. Knivet was among the wretched seamen cast ashore on the desolate island of San Sebastian five leagues from Santos in Brazil. He describes what happened:

The sicke men were set on shoare to shift for themselves ... my body was blacke ... I could not speake nor stirre ... the extreme heate of the sun pierced through my body, where by I came to myselfe, as a man awakened from sleepe; and I saw them that were set on shore with me lay dead and a-dying round about me: these men had eaten a kind of pease, that did grow by the sea-side which did poysen them. Thus I lived eight or nine days without any sight of any man, the stinke of some of the dead men . . . so noysome that I was fain to remove from that place.

Passing by a fair river, which flowed into the sea, Knivet was terrified by the approach of a beast

with greate scales on the backe with great ugly claws and a long tayle. This beast came towards me and I had not the power to shun it . . . I stood still amazed to see so monstrous a thing before me. Hereupon this beast opened his mouth and thrust out a long tongue like a Harping-Iron. . . . I commended myself to God, and thought there to have bin torne in pieces, but this beaste turned again, and went into the river and I followed to the rivers side.

In Brazil Knivet was nearly killed by a savage named Wayem-bath, who bore the Portuguese a great grudge. Accompanied by two concubines, the man approached the Englishman and, after dancing for a while, laid his hand on their necks, saying: "Dost thou see these women, by my valour I got their loves, and their desire I am sworne to fulfill, which is to kill thee as I have done many more." Fortunately Knivet's life was saved by an old man, who managed to dissuade the man from committing such a vile act.

Poor wretch! One can but feel sorry for him. He tells us that one day he went all alone a-fishing for pleasure's sake.[10] Musing there awhile he began to curse the time that ever he heard the name of the sea, "and grieved to thinke how fond [foolish] I was to forsake my naturall country where I wanted nothing".

It is evident that the relations between the seamen and 'Our General', Cavendish, were extremely poor during the voyage. Off Santos in Brazil, Knivet sat on a chest during a terrible storm when the ship reeled on one side, so that the chest went from starboard to larboard. "It was the will of God", he related, "that the chest never turned over, for if it had, I could not have escaped death the next day." The young sailors, known as men of top a yard, were so fatigued by the night's work that they angered Master Thomas Cavendish by refusing to come up on deck to do some necessary work. Instead they lay asleep below under the hatches. Seizing the end of a rope "as big as my arm" (according to Knivet), Cavendish struck a terror-stricken sailor, who had concealed himself behind Knivet. The latter was nearly cast into the sea, supposedly dead.

Cavendish later bitterly accused John Davis of deserting him during this expedition, but the navigator from Devon was too honourable by nature to play such a shabby trick. As already mentioned, John Jane described the sufferings of the seamen on Davis' ships. How they were forced to endure famine after "their dried penguins began to corrupt". They were then pestered by a species of worm of an inch long, "which would eat our flesh, and bite like mosquitos. Our men began to fall sick of such a monstrous disease, as I think the like was never heard of; for in their ankles it began to swell, from thence in two days it would be in their breasts, so that they could not draw their breath."[11]

Jane provides us with quite an intimate picture of Captain John Davis, a sincerely religious man. On one occasion when the latter had almost abandoned hope during a furious storm, Jane approached him with a glass of rosasolis, a cordial flavoured with sun-dew. This seemed to give him some comfort, and in his dire extremity Davis uttered a fervent prayer: "Oh, most glorious God, with whose power the mightiest things among men are matters of no moment, I most humbly beseech Thee, that the intolerable burden of my sins may, through the blood of Jesus Christ, be taken from me, and end our days with speed, or show us some merciful sign of Thy love and our preservation." Then a miraculous thing occurred. The storm abated and the sun suddenly appeared, so that Captain Davis and the master were able to steer for the Straits of Magellan. It was on 14th August 1592 that Davis descried the Falkland Islands, first discovered by this intrepid Elizabethan adventurer.

Eventually Davis and the survivors, "lost wanderers upon the sea", arrived back at Berehaven in Ireland, and within five days had managed to obtain a fishing-boat which landed them at Padstow, that quaint Cornish harbour.

As for Thomas Cavendish, he met a terrible death in the cruel and tormented sea, cursing the perfidy of the mutinous crew, who had abandoned him to his fate, and unjustly blaming Davis for the calamities which had pursued him. We have his last letter written to his friend and executor, Sir Tristan Gorges, a friend of Robert Devereux, Earl of Essex. It was to this doughty and respected Elizabethan that Drake had entrusted the care of the Spanish prisoner, Don Pedro de Valdes, during the Armada.[12]

On the threshold of death, Cavendish wrote Sir Tristan Gorges a long letter which begins:

Most Loving Friend,
   There is nothing in this world that makes a truer trial of friendship, than at death to show mindfulness of love and friendship, which now you shall make a perfect experience of: desiring you to hold my love as dear, dying poor, as if I had been most infinitely rich. . . .

   The *Roebuck* left me in the most desolate case that ever man was left in. What is become of her I cannot imagine. . . . and now to come to that villain that hath been the death of me, and the decay of this whole action, I mean Davis, whose only treachery, in running from me, hath been utter ruin of all. . . . But I, most unfortunate villain, was matched with the most abject minded and mutinous company that ever was carried out of England by any man living.

It is surely sad that Cavendish, one of the bravest of the navigators, should charge Davis with so grave an offence, though it is certainly untrue. The clash of temperaments between seamen of consummate ability—as they both were—only aggravated their strained relations. Once separated from his second-in-command on the vast ocean, Cavendish's brooding suspicions and resentment welled up in his mind, so that, tortured by ill-health and knowing he was doomed to die, he uttered the harsh words, which were a stain on his own character and better left unsaid.

Notes

CHAPTER XV

1   *Naval History*, Vol. I, p. 229.
2   E. J. Payne, *Voyages of Elizabethan Seamen*.
3   Select Narratives from Hakluyt.
4   Samuel Purchas, *His Pilgrimes Contayning a History of the World in Sea Voyages and Land Travels, Vol. I* (Maclehose edn.).
5   Purchas I. 65.
6   E. J. Payne, *Voyages of Elizabethan Seamen*.
    Select Narratives of the Principal Navigations of Hakluyt.
7   *Voyages of the Elizabethan Seamen to America*.
    Select Narratives from the Principal Navigations of Hakluyt.
8   James A. Williamson, *The Age of Drake*, p. 341.
9   Purchas I. XVI 151–177.
10 Purchas III.
11 E. J. Payne, *Voyages of Elizabethan Seamen*, p. 161.
12 A. L. Rowse, *The Elizabethans and America*.

CHAPTER XVI

Voyages of Henry Hudson

Henry Hudson, the Arctic explorer, with his insatiable scientific curiosity and his invincible courage, was essentially an Elizabethan in spirit, even if his four famous voyages occurred in 1607–1611, during the early reign of James I. Hudson's personality and his career reminds us of John Davis rather than Thomas Cavendish. Both were essentially seamen of sterling character, and both were obsessed by the Arctic. Hudson was almost certainly born before 1570, so that he would have been over 37 at the time of his first voyage (1607).

It is fairly well known that Hudson was the discoverer of Hudson's River, Hudson's Strait and Hudson's Bay, though it is perhaps more accurate to write that the navigator explored these territories extensively and was not their original discoverer. His early career is shrouded in mystery. It may well be that he was the grandson of Henry Hudson or Herdson, Alderman of London, who helped to found the Muscovy Company in 1555 and died during the same year.[1] The only solid fact is that he began as a northern explorer in the service of the Company of Merchant Adventurers, founded by that fine navigator Sebastian Cabot (1553) for the purpose of trading with India and China by a north-eastern route.[2] Somehow the explorations of this dauntless navigator inspire me more than those of most of his contemporaries.

A Dutch author named Adrian van der Donck tells us that Hudson made a prolonged stay in Holland during his early life, but this statement must be regarded with suspicion.

The Elizabethan navigators owed much to Sebastian Cabot, who has been underrated. It was Sebastian who invented the logbook, and he also made methodical experiments and observations regarding the needle. Hudson's service to future seamen was to add to the logbook a new feature, the study and observation of the dip of the magnetic needle.

Hudson's chief patron was Sir Dudley Digges,* a share-holder in the East India Company, who was greatly interested in the North-west Passage project. Hudson named an island near Hudson's Bay after his patron, and the cape opposite in honour of another of his friends, John Wolstenholme.† This Merchant Adventurer came of an ancient Derbyshire family, and was born in 1562. In December 1600 he was prominently associated with the incorporation of the East India Company, and, since he was much interested in the attempts to discover a North-west Passage, he helped to finance Hudson's voyages.

Hudson was obsessed with the idea of discovering a short northern route to China, though this proved mistaken. If he was not successful in solving this problem, he was determined, as he himself admitted, "to give reasons wherefore it would not be".

His voyage in 1607 had a very beneficial result, for it led to the establishment of the Arctic fisheries, begun by the English and Dutch. In such a way was a school of fearless and skilful seamen begun.[3] We are indebted to Samuel Purchas[4] for most of the information concerning Hudson's four expeditions and Purchas obtained accounts of the first three from Hakluyt, whilst he was permitted by Sir Dudley Digges, who had a financial interest in the last fatal voyage, to study the papers about it. Much of our knowledge of the 1607 expedition, for instance, is derived from the logbook partly written by Hudson, and also by John Playse,

* 1583–1639.
† Knighted in 1617.

18

a seaman. It is unlikely that an ordinary sailor such as Playse should possess any technical knowledge, so that the observation written on Saturday 30th May, "This day I found the needle to incline 79 degrees under the horizon", was almost certainly written by Master Henry Hudson. Purchas relates[5] that Hudson and his seamen attended Holy Communion at Saint Ethelburge in Bishops Gate Street before sailing.

On 23rd April 1607 he left London with a crew of twelve, including his son, John, who was only a boy. Their names are given: William Colines, mate; James Young, John Colman, John Cooke, James Benbery, James Skratton, John Playse, Thomas Baxter, Richard Day, James Knight and John Hudson. Hudson intended, if possible, to sail across the North Pole to China and Japan.

Towards the end of May, Hudson reached the Shetland Islands, and on 13th June the mariners were off Greenland (referred to by Hudson as Groneland). The writer tells us: "The chiefe cause that moved us thereunto, was our desire to see that part of Groneland which (for aught that we know) was to any Christian unknown." Hudson, however, erred in referring to the south of Greenland as an undiscovered island. John Davis during an earlier voyage had made the same mistake. After leaving the Greenland shores, Hudson made for Spitzbergen,* and here he again explored parts of the Greenland coast, naming some land Hold-with-hope.

Hudson failed in his main objective to find a route by the North Pole to China and Japan, but he made some very interesting observations relating to the varying colours of the sea near Spitzbergen. He noticed that the sea was blue where there was ice, and green where it was most open. He also was impressed by the large number of whales in the waters surrounding Greenland.[6] John Coleman and William Collins, two members of Hudson's crew, went ashore near Collins Cape (its exact locality is not known) and brought back to the ship whale bones and deer horns.

---

* Both the English and the Dutch made rival claims to Spitzbergen.

They noticed the foot-prints of rote-geese. One senses the constant danger from ice and fog, how near to death the seamen sometimes were. The simple narrative, so brief and factual, does not reveal the fortitude of the mariners. The writer tells us: "Before we cast about by means of the thick fogge, we were very neere ice, being calm, and the sea setting on to the ice which was very dangerous." Then their thankfulness to the Almighty for delivering them from mighty perils: "It pleased God at the very instant to give us a small gale, which was the meanes of our deliverance."

By 15th August Hudson had reached the Isles of Farre (Faroe Islands), and a month later the adventurers arrived home at Tilbury in the Thames.

Among those who sailed with Hudson on his second voyage in April 1608, was Robert Juet of Limehouse, who went as mate. He was to play a treacherous, despicable role in betraying his captain during the last voyage. It is probable, but by no means certain, that Juet was English by birth, though it has been suggested that the Dutch East India Company, when they appointed Hudson to the command of one of their ships, insisted that he should also employ Dutch sailors. Robert Juet wrote an account of Hudson's third voyage, and his knowledge of English is so fluent that it would seem unlikely that he was a foreigner. The Dutch are, however, very proficient linguists.

Henry Hudson himself wrote an account of the second voyage. The mariners sailed from St. Katherine's (later known as St. Katherine's Docks), "and fell downe to Blackewall". Hudson's object was to find a passage to the East Indies by the north-east. An important member of the crew was Philip Staffe, the carpenter, who became ill during the voyage and later on his recovery made a mast for the ship-boat. Sometimes the mariners heard the eerie sound of bears roaring on the ice. There is a curious description of a mermaid, first seen by two seamen, Thomas Hilles and Robert Rayner. "From the navill upward, her backe and breasts were like a womans, as they say that saw her; her body as big as one of us; her skin very white; and long haire hanging down behinde, of colour blacke: in her going down they saw her tayle, which was like the tayle of a porpoise, and speckled like a mackrell." Indeed, a curious phantom!

Hudson sailed along part of the coast of Nova Zembla, later known as the Goose Coast, first discovered by Sir Hugh Willoughby, who died in Lapland. Hudson describes Nova Zembla: "It is to a man's eye a pleasant land, much mayne high land with no snow on it, looking in some places greene, and deere feeding thereon; and the hills are partly covered with snow, and partly bare." Hudson made a heroic attempt to sail to the northeast beyond the Nova Zembla Group, but blocks of ice and the storms encountered here defeated his purpose. Near Nova Zembla Hudson explored Costin Shar, and discovered that it was a bay, not a strait.

Perhaps Froude when he tried to analyse "the great unrest" in the Elizabethan seamen, also thought of Hudson, that Herculean, solitary character, with his strange, obsessive kinship with the sea. No wife or mistress is more demanding. A dauntless explorer, such as Hudson, once he has accepted the challenge, knows no peace until the end. To battle against the elements when all seems hopeless, to hear the ominous movement of blocks of ice without faltering, very fearful to look on (as Hudson described it) requires an absolute mastery of self, not given to lesser men.

Hudson's third voyage, described by Robert Juet of Limehouse, took place in March 1609. It was at the expense of the Dutch East India Company. Hudson sailed from Amsterdam on the 25th, and the purpose of the expedition was once again the search of a north-eastern route. Near Nova Zembla, however, he encountered an unbroken mass of ice. It was during this voyage that the navigator explored Hudson's River, and Juet provides an interesting account. Hudson's real merit was his achievement in exploring the strait named after him, a work of such importance that it certainly justifies the immortality of his name. Unlike Hudson, Juet constantly refers to the North American Indians with suspicion and with malevolence. Here is an example:

> In the morning two great canoes came aboard full of men; the one
> with their bowes and arrows, and the other in shew of buying of

knives to betray us; but we perceived their intent. Wee tooke two
of them to have kept them, and put red coates on them, and would
not suffer the other to come neere us . . . The people of the countrey
came aboard us, making shew of love, and gave us Tobacco and
Indian wheat, and departed for that night, but we durst not trust
them.[7]

Juet relates that they possessed great tobacco pipes of yellow
copper, and that they used pots of earth to dress their food in.
One morning they came on board with indian corn, tobacco and
other commodities, "which wee bought for trifles". Hudson
certainly enjoyed amicable relations with the American Indians.
They brought him a great platter full of venison dressed by
themselves, and they requested Master Hudson to eat with them.
Among their presents were strings of beads made of shells.
These were used as a primitive kind of jewellery and as
money. Hudson invited two old men to dine with him, and two
young maidens, who behaved very modestly and discreetly, came
on board. Hudson gave one of the old men a knife, and in
exchange they gave him and other members of the crew a knife.
Hudson himself relates:

> I sailed to the shore in one of their canoes with an old man who
> was the chief of a tribe, consisting of forty men and seventeen
> women; these I saw there in a house well constructed of oak bark,
> and circular in shape, so that it had the appearance of being well
> built, with an arched roof. . . . On our coming into the house two
> mats were spread out to sit upon, and immediately some food was
> served in well made wooden bowls.

The navigators sailed down parts of the Hudson River, known
for its violent winds. The scenery here is beautiful and romantic,
especially in the highlands with its rocky cliffs towering above
the river banks. Beacon Hill, near Ploughkeepsie (Moulton) and
opposite New Windsor, is 1,685 feet high.[8] On one occasion they
anchored at Catskill Landing, three miles from Hudson, so as to
gather a good hoard of chestnuts. What a marvellous experience
it must have been for the great navigator to see the fine range of
the Kaatshenge or Catskill mountains, which are over 3,000 feet.

The highest ranges are nearly 4,000 feet. Hudson was not the first explorer to navigate the Hudson River. Giovanni Verrazano, the Italian navigator, in 1524 had sailed for a short distance up the Hudson,[9] but Hudson was the first to show its real importance.

Hudson's kindness and consideration for the American Indian seems to have been appreciated, for they invariably responded by giving him their friendship. His enlightened behaviour at least compares favourably with the suspicious, condescending attitude of his crew, including Juet. The latter, however, relates that by the river's side in a mountainous district, "we found very loving people, and very old men, where we were well used". Juet tells us that in order to determine whether the intentions of the Indians were treacherous, Hudson and his mate invited their chiefs to his cabin, where "he gave them so much wine and aqua vitae that they were all merrie; and one of them had his wife with him, which sate so modestly, as any of our countrey women would doe in a strange place". One of the Indians became very drunk.

The seamen returned from this expedition on 7th November 1609, when they landed at Dartmouth.

The tragic story of Hudson's fourth voyage, which began on 17th April 1610 is mainly based on the narrative of Abacuk Pricket, a servant of Sir Dudley Digges, the principal promoter of the expedition. Pricket was a member of Hudson's crew. Though the account is very interesting, it has been suspected that Pricket's reason for writing it was an attempt to justify the actions of the mutineers while simultaneously casting aspersions on Hudson's character. Hudson himself wrote a short journal about the expedition.[10] The sinister Robert Juet, who again acted as mate, was to intrigue against his commander almost from the beginning of the voyage. Among those who accompanied Hudson was a sailor named Colburne (Pricket refers to him as Colbert). Hudson seems to have resented Colburne, for he had been attached to Hudson's ship the *Discovery* as a kind of official adviser. After embarking at St. Katherine's Pool (St. Katherine's Dock) near the Tower, Hudson relates that at sea five days later he ordered Master Colburne "to be put into a pinke bound for London, with my letter to the Adventurers imparting the reason wherefore I so put him out of the ship, and so plyed forth". One companion of Hudson's was a young man named Henry Green, a lewd, treacherous fellow, who had been befriended by the navigator. He had stayed for a while in Hudson's house in London. Abacuk Pricket tells us that Green was born in Kent and, on account of his extravagant habits, had spent all that he had.[11] Hudson found him useful at sea because he could write well. It was unfortunate that he treated the young man so kindly, since Green, owing to his quarrelsome, intriguing nature, showed gross ingratitude for the benefits he had received. Whilst at sea, Green was not paid any wages.

Hudson relates in his journal that the mariners on the fourth day sighted Groneland (northern part of Greenland) "over the ice perfectly". Near Cape Elizabeth on the coast of Labrador, they found much ice.

As a commander of seamen, Hudson was certainly not a strict disciplinarian. It is manifest that dissension arose among the crew during this voyage, and that Hudson was obliged to displace Robert Juet as mate, and appoint Robert Bylot* in his stead.

Abacuk Pricket relates that the mariners killed a lot of fowls at Derefer (Dyve-fiord, a gulf on the north-west coast of the northern peninsula of Iceland). At Breyde Fiord (usually referred to as Brede Bay on English maps), a bay on the west coast of Iceland, the Englishmen enjoyed hot baths, "and the water was so hot that it would scald a fowl".

At one stage Hudson and his crew were in dreadful peril from solid blocks of ice, and even that stout-hearted explorer almost despaired. He summoned his crew and asked them whether they wished to continue, yea or nay; many cared not where they went, so long as they were out of the ice. One told the master that if he had an hundred pounds he would give four-score and ten to be at home. The carpenter, however, a brave man, favoured the

---

* Billet in the Pricket account. Known as an active northern navigator after Hudson's death. Scene of the mutiny is in Ungave Bay between the south-eastern shore and Akpatok island.

continuance of the voyage, whatever the cost. Near Akpatok island, the seamen sighted a solitary bear on a piece of ice, but after pursuing the animal in their boats he managed to elude them. Hudson named an island appropriately enough Iles of God's Mercy. Other capes commemorated King James I and Prince Henry,* and Queen Anne's Cape or Fore-land in honour of Anne of Denmark, James' consort.

Pricket accused Master Hudson of dealing unjustly with John Williams, "our gunner", who died during November. However, the circumstances are very obscure. Whilst in Iceland Henry Green and the ship's surgeon had a bitter dispute, and blows were struck. Hudson seems to have supported Green at this juncture, for after Pricket had told him of the incident, he merely bade him to leave the matter alone, "for the surgeon had a tongue that would wrong the best friend he had". No doubt the nerves of these men cooped up in their ships became frayed under the strain. When Master Hudson agreed to Green's request that he should be allowed to wear a grey cloth gown formerly owned by the gunner, John Williams, the others resented it. If Pricket's account can be relied on, Hudson used foul language when the carpenter refused to build a house on shore, because of the snow and frost. The master threatened to hang him, but the carpenter stoutly maintained that "he knew what belonged to his place better than himself, and that he was no house carpenter". However, the house was later constructed, but to no purpose. It is possible that under the strain of his privations Hudson became dour and morose.

It is evident that Henry Green later quarrelled with Hudson, and the latter taunted Green that none of his friends would trust him with twenty shillings. One of the grievances was that Green had no wages, though Pricket artfully insinuates that Master Hudson had promised him that his wages should be as good as any man in the ship. Pricket relates: "You shall see how the devil out of this so wrought with Green, that he did the Master what

* Prince of Wales 1594–1612.

mischiefs hee could in seeking to discredit him, and to thrust him out of the ship in the end." What rankled with the crew was the brooding suspicion that their master was hoarding food, aware that their provisions might not last out the expedition. Yet the mariners occasionally found diversion, especially when they killed over one hundred dozen partridges as white as milk.

The conspiracy against Master Hudson developed rapidly on Saturday 20th June 1611, when Wilson, the boatswain, and Henry Green stealthily came to Pricket's cabin at midnight. How dramatic the occasion. One senses the malign influence of Robert Juet, who bore Hudson many grudges. The object of the mutineers was apparently to confide in Pricket their intention to "turn the Master [Hudson] and all the sick men into the shallop", where they might shift for themselves. When considering Pricket's account of what happened, one must bear in mind that his principal purpose was to justify his own actions in the eyes of the authorities at home. It is evident that the mutineers were not prepared to make further sacrifices or to endure more hardships. They complained that they had not eaten anything for three days and that the food on the ship would not last a fortnight. Pricket begged his shipmates not to commit so foul an action as to mutiny against the master, and to force him and the sick men into the shallop. Were they not married men with children? Henry Green merely told him to hold his peace. He would rather be hanged at home than starved abroad. They now offered Pricket the chance to remain on the ship, if he were to agree to join the mutineers. Otherwise, he must take his chance in the shallop. "If there be no remedy," said Pricket, "the will of God be done." Green, quivering with rage, departed saying that he would cut his throat, if anybody attempted to dissuade him from the project. Wilson remained with Pricket, hoping to weaken his resolution.

In the narrative Robert Juet is referred to as "an ancient man", so it would seem that he was older than the others. Juet certainly was deeply involved in the mutiny, for he roundly declared that when he arrived home he would justify the deed. Meanwhile,

Pricket called to his shipmates in the darkness, begging them at least to wait till the morning. One can imagine the eerie atmosphere on the *Discovery* that terrible night, the furtive actions of the conspirators, the whispering, the blocks of ice dimly descried through the darkness, and the powerful surge of the sea. The mutineers bore John King, the carpenter, a special grudge, for they were jealous of Master Hudson's affection for this man. He had been appointed mate, instead of Robert Bylot (Billet). All that night Henry Green remained with Hudson, keeping him company.

When the master later came out of his cabin, Wilson the boatswain bound his arms behind him. Hudson, struggling no doubt to free himself, called to the carpenter, but to no avail. The master then summoned Pricket to speak with him, who came out of his cabin to the hatch-way. If the narrative can be credited, Pricket then begged the conspirators on his knees "for the love of God to remember themselves, to doe as they would be done unto". Hudson, perhaps not suspecting that Green was playing the part of Judas, exclaimed vehemently: "Juet will overthrow us all." "Nay," answered Pricket, "it is that villain Henry Green, and I spake it not softly."*

So, Henry Hudson and some of his men were thrown aboard into the shallop. Beside Hudson, there were John Hudson, a boy almost certainly his son; Arnold Ludlo; Philip Staffe; Sidrack Faner; Thomas Woodhouse or Wudhouse, a student of mathematics; Adam Moore; Henry King and Michael Bute. One of the bravest of Hudson's crew was Philip Staffe, described by Purchas as a skilful carpenter and lusty mariner. He was an Ipswich man, who from the beginning had tried to sustain "the drooping, darkened spirits" of his companions "with sparks from his own resolution".

One wonders whether Hudson, dying of lingering starvation with his companions, while the remorseless sea beat against their shallop, had any conception of the magnitude of his achieve-

* Green and Juet both perished miserably during the voyage home in their ship, being killed by Esquinos. Robert Bylot was in charge of the ship.

ments. Perhaps he merely thought that all his heroic efforts had been in vain. Yet Hudson, like most of the other illustrious seamen, had a vision of an English empire overseas, and his name will ever be venerated by our fellow-countrymen. He set himself an exacting standard. No man can be considered a failure, who achieved so much. Even today this intrepid explorer is revered by millions of people living on the banks of the Hudson river, where he once enjoyed friendly relations with the simple, savage Indians, who sensed the essential fineness of his character. Owing to his endeavours the fisheries of Spitzbergen were begun, and the members of the Hudson's Bay Company, long established with its vast fur trade, remember Henry Hudson with affection and gratitude. It was not until 1670 that Charles II granted a charter to Prince Rupert, his cousin, and seventeen other noblemen and gentlemen adventurers to trade into "Hudson's Bay".[13] The Americans, too, are deeply interested in the great seaman, who, during those momentous four years 1607 to 1611, explored nearly all the northern shores of Europe and Eastern America.

Notes

CHAPTER XVI

1   Sidney Lee ed., *Dictionary of National Biography*.
2   *Hudson the Navigator*, with an introduction by G. M. Asher.
3   *Ibid*.
4   Vol. III.
5   Purchas III, Chapter xiii, p. 567.
6   *Henry Hudson the Navigator*, with an introduction by G. M. Asher.
7   Purchas III.
8   *Henry Hudson the Navigator*.
9   *The Encyclopedia Britannica*, Eleventh Edition, Vol. XIII.
10   Purchas III, Chapter XVII, p. 596.
11   Purchas III.
12   Purchas III, p. 605.
13   *Encyclopedia Britannica*, Eleventh Edition, Vol. XIII.

CHAPTER XVII

Ralegh's Last Guiana Voyage

Even such is tyme, who takes in truste
Our youth, our joys, and all we have,
And pays us but with earth and dust;
Who in the dark and silent grave,
When we have wandered all our wayes
Shuts up the story of our days.
But from that earth, that grave, that dust,
The Lord shall raise me up, I truste.*

Thus did one of the last of the great Elizabethans, weary and disillusioned, look back at the vicissitudes of his life in the early hours of the morning of 29th October 1618, when he was about to be executed.

The tragic history of Sir Walter Ralegh's attempt to find a gold mine in Guiana is full of interest and drama. For almost thirteen years he had languished as James I's prisoner in the Tower, engrossed in his chemical experiments and writing his *History of the World*. Even whilst incarcerated his restless mind turned to his old love, and he dreamt of an English empire in Guiana. Ralegh has been mentioned too much as a man of action, but he was also a man of thought, a historian, a poet, and, above

* Verses found in Sir Walter Ralegh's Bible after his death. Harleian MSS. 4761 have a different version.

all, a patriot. As already mentioned, his fixation concerning Guiana had dominated Ralegh's mind for the last thirty years of his life. What he ardently desired was the complete destruction of Spanish power in South America and the establishment of an English empire in its place.[1]

Since Ralegh's first voyage to Guiana in 1595, several people had been there, including his faithful lieutenant Laurence Keymis, who had sailed during 1596 with two principal objects: to discover the exact whereabouts of Manoa and to obtain a supply of gold from the banks of the Caroni. The expedition of Laurence Keymis is recorded in Hakluyt.[2] Then in 1609 Robert Harcourt embarked on another expedition to Guiana, and in this venture he was fortunate enough to obtain the patronage of Henry, the young Prince of Wales. The Prince was deeply interested in colonization and had a warm admiration for Ralegh. He said of him: "Who but my father would keep such a bird in a cage." V. T. Harlow in his scholarly account and analytical interpretation in his book *Ralegh's Last Voyage* discusses Harcourt's expedition in detail. It consisted of three ships and ninety-seven men. When they reached the Wiapoca during May 1609, the Indians gave them a warm reception. Harcourt told the chiefs the reasons why he had undertaken the venture. "First," he relates, "I brought to their rememberance the exploits of Sir Walter Ralegh in their countrie." "Then," he continued, "I excused his not returning according to his promise, by reason of other employments of great importance imposed on him by the late Queene: showing them moreover, that when he culd not (for that cause) return himself hee sent Captain Keymis to visit them . . . to the end that reliefe and aid might bee prepared for them." He told them of the accession of James I, who had permitted them to settle in Guiana. Harcourt's object was "to make search in those countries for convenient places where such of our nation as shall hereafter come to defend them, may be fitly seated to dwell amongst them".[3]

In his work, *The Discoverie of the Large Rich and Bewtiful Empire of Guiana*, Ralegh wrote: "After the first or second yere I doubt not but to see in London a *contratación* house of more receipt for Guiana than there is nowe in Civil (Seville) for the West Indies."

Another adventurer who acquired an intimate knowledge of Guiana was Sir Thomas Rowe, the diplomat. He was a friend of James I's daughter Princess Elizabeth, known to her contemporaries as the Queen of Hearts.* In one of her delightful letters Elizabeth refers to him as "Honest Thom Roe", and ends it with the quaint postscript: "Your olde friend my monkey is in very good health heere and commands all my women with his teeth."[4] Roe later became ambassador to the Great Mogul, the Sublime Porte, and Gustavus Adolphus. Henry Wriothesley, Earl of Southampton, contributed £800 to Roe's expedition, while Sir Walter Ralegh subscribed £600. The expedition sailed from Dartmouth 24th February 1609. Roe's main achievement was to explore the River Amazon for a distance of 300 miles. "I have seene", he wrote, "more of this coast, rivers and inland from the Great River, of the Amazones under the line to Orenoque in 8 degrees, than any Englishman now alive."

By 1615 Sir Walter was now 63, old in that age, and his health had been weakened by his confinement in the Tower. He has been described by his biographer as "grey, lame and malaria-ridden".[5] The political situation, however, favoured his release. Sir Ralph Winwood, the anti-Spanish, puritanical Secretary of State, was his friend, while Anne of Denmark liked and admired Ralegh as much as her husband James I hated and mistrusted him. He was greatly admired by foreign sovereigns, such as her brother, Christian IV of Denmark, who had, during a visit to his brother-in-law's court in 1606 when he constantly indulged in drunken orgies, implored James that his prisoner might be freed so that he could enter his services as an admiral. James refused to entertain such an idea. Louis XIII of France's powerful minister, Cardinal Richelieu, referred to Ralegh as a great mariner. It is true that Sir Walter's friend, Henry, Prince of Wales, had died three years earlier, and by 1614 his perfidious enemy the Earl of

* Queen of Bohemia.

Northampton (formerly Lord Harry Howard) was also dead. The influence of Robert Carr, Earl of Somerset, the leader of the pro-Spanish party, was rapidly declining, and the courtiers all looked to the rising star, Sir George Villiers, James' new favourite, the tool of the opposing faction. Thus by a concatenation of circumstances he obtained his liberty.

In a newsletter Chamberlain wrote to Carleton 27th March 1616: "Sir Walter Ralegh was freed out of the Tower the last week, and goes up and down seeing sights and places built or bettered since his imprisonment."[6] During this year Ralegh made strenuous preparations for his voyage. He managed to raise as much as £30,000, partly by an appeal to his friends, using £8,000 from his own resources, which had been on loan after he had received it as compensation for the Sherborne estates. His devoted wife Bess contributed £2,500 by selling her estate in Surrey.[7]

In his autobiography* the celebrated shipwright Phineas Pett relates that on 27th March he bargained with Sir Walter to build him a ship of 500 tons. This was named the *Destiny*. It was constructed in His Majesty's yard at Woolwich, and Ralegh gave Pett £500 on account.

Meanwhile, the able Spanish Ambassador in London, Don Diego Sarmiento de Acuna, Count Gondomar, a diplomat of infinite charm and guile,† who had acquired a personal ascendancy over the mind of James I, was protesting vigorously during August, and attempting to prevent the expedition altogether. Gondomar knew how to flatter James. He told the King that he spoke Latin like a Master of Arts, though he himself only spoke it like a gentleman.[8] He now argued that the whole of Guiana belonged to his master Philip III (Philip II's son and successor), and he maintained as convincingly as possible that Ralegh had no intention of confining himself to the Orinoco, but wanted to turn pirate and either seize the Mexican fleet or plunder the towns of the Spanish Main. Besides, what was the use of feigning friend-

* Edited by W. G. Perrin.
† 1567–1626.

ship with Spain by sending Sir John Digby* to Madrid to negotiate a marriage settlement between Prince Charles, the new Prince of Wales, and the Infanta of Spain, if Ralegh at the same time was allowed by the King to prepare an armada against Spain? Ralegh never admitted the validity of Count Gondomar's argument. He wrote: "That Guiana be Spanish territory can never be acknowledged, for I myself took possession of it for the Queen of England [Elizabeth] by virtue of all the native chiefs of the country." He always denied Gondomar's accusation that he intended to turn pirate. His real purpose was to find a gold mine which existed near the banks of the Orinoco.

Ominously enough, James, after he had given Ralegh permission to sail on this voyage, insisted on various ignominious conditions, influenced no doubt by the constant protests of Gondomar. He refused a free pardon, and the customary words "trusty and well-beloved" were deleted from the commission.[9] Ralegh was required to give a solemn pledge not to set foot on Spanish territory, or "inflict the least injury in the world" upon a Spanish subject, almost intolerable conditions considering the circumstances.

Before embarking, Ralegh sought the advice of the Lord Keeper of the Great Seal, Sir Francis Bacon, now at the zenith of his career. The two brilliant men, with their eager, enquiring minds, walked together in Gray's Inn Walks, as Bacon relates. The latter advised Ralegh to go ahead with his venture, and not to wait for a formal pardon from the King. "Money is the knee-timber of your voyage," said Bacon and added: "Upon my life, you have a sufficient pardon for all that is past already, the King having under his Great Seal made you Admiral, and given you power of martial law." In uttering these sentiments Bacon was too sanguine, and he had studied James's shifty, evasive character. Suddenly, with an amused look in his hazel eyes, the Lord Keeper turned to Ralegh. "What will you do if after all this expenditure you miss the gold mine?" he asked. Ralegh answered impulsively: "We'll look after the Plate fleet to be sure!"

* Later Earl of Bristol.

19

"But then you will be pirates," said Bacon, in his ironical way, half mockingly. "Oh no!" replied his friend, "who ever heard of men being pirates for millions?"[10] Ralegh's folly was to talk too freely about the venture with people who were not always well disposed. The consequences were tragic, for he left England as a man still under sentence of death.* He was only to be pardoned, provided his venture succeeded.

In his own work,[11] Ralegh refers to the many abuses in the navy during the reign of James I. He wrote:

> The seamen goe with a great grudging to serve in his majesty's ships, as to be slaves in the galleys. So much doe they stand in feare of penurie and hunger ... and therefore the purveyors and victuallers are much to be condemned, as not a little faulty in that behalfe, who make no little profit of those polings, which is cause very lamentable, that such as sit at ease at home, should so raise a benefit out of their hunger and thirst, that serve their Prince and Country painfully abroad, whereof there hath a long time been a great complaining, but small reformation.

He was soon to acquire further experience about the low morale of some of the sea captains and seamen.

Ralegh's fleet consisted of seven warships, although the official list shown to the Spanish Ambassador only mentions six. There were also six pinnaces. 318 mariners sailed in these ships besides the captains and masters. There were also ninety gentlemen, a few land soldiers and servants. Ralegh served as general of the *Destiny*, commanded by his elder son, Wat. His captains were not all honourable men. Wollaston was half a pirate, while Bayley was a sly, despicable character. The *Convertine* was commanded by Laurence Keymis, a loyal, but ageing man, and Sir Warham St. Leger had the *John and Francis*.[12]

Before embarking Ralegh published his orders to the fleet at Plymouth on 3rd May 1617. He admonished the sailors not to indulge in swearing, or gamble at cards or dice. He showed his experience as a leader of men by inventing signals for apprising

---

* He had been condemned to death at his trial in 1603 at Winchester.

the fleet of the approach of the enemy. He warned the seamen to refrain from eating unknown fruits in the West Indies, and also unsalted meat. It was rash to swim in the alligator-infested rivers, and Ralegh told them not to do so. He charged the men not to take anything from the Indians by force. It cannot be pretended that the seamen's morale was high. At Gravesend there was a riot between sailors and the citizens, while the crews engaged in incessant disputes as they sailed down the Thames to assemble at Plymouth.

So once again after many years Ralegh was at sea, with his cabin laden with a trunk full of books. Unfortunately the weather was foul, and the fleet was soon forced to return to Falmouth. A member of the crew wrote: "Heere is no verretie of news but conteneuall quarrles and fyghting amongste our oune companye withe manye dangerous hurttes, but I thank God wee have loste never a man yett in all the flette."[13] Ralegh was glad to rid himself of such quarrelsome men, and he left some of them on shore at Falmouth. When Ralegh was able to sail, he was later forced by further storms to put in at Kinsale in the south of Ireland. In Ireland he was hospitably entertained in his old home of Lismore by Lord Boyle, the Earl of Cork. It was not until 19th August that he left Ireland, and his fleet made for Lancerota, an island in the Canaries, which was reached on 8th September. At Lancerota Captain John Bayley, who commanded the *Southampton* and who bore Ralegh a grudge, deserted him. After returning home he did his best to kindle prejudice against Sir Walter by falsely asserting that he had turned pirate. These malicious reports were denied by the master of a merchant ship named Reekes, who had been at Lancerota at the time and now returned to England. Actually, Ralegh had behaved with forbearance when a number of his men had, contrary to his instructions, wandered about the island. After two of them had been killed by the Spaniards, and another severely wounded, he refused to take any revenge. Even the Spanish Governor of Gomera in the Canaries, a courteous and honourable man, stated that Ralegh had behaved 'nobly' and justly during his stay there. Unfortunately

Bayley's stories were for a time credited at home. During October Gondomar derived great satisfaction when he learnt from Sir Thomas Lake,* that King James was very hostile to Sir Walter and would join with the King of Spain in ruining him. One cannot blame the Spanish Ambassador for pressing the case as strongly as possible against Ralegh. His first duty was naturally to his government. However, Bayley was later discredited and imprisoned in the Gatehouse at Westminster.

Once again Ralegh was at sea, watching delightedly the antics of the flying-fish and the white foam of the restless sea breaking against the *Destiny*. Unfortunately, however, together with some of his sea captains and many of his men, he soon became ill. He tells us in the private journal, which he kept:

> the last of October at night, rising out of bed, being in a great sweat, by reason of a sudden gust and much clamour in the ship before they could get down the sails, I took a violent cold which cast me into a burning fever ... for the first twenty days I never received any sustenance but now and then a stewed prune, but drank every hour day and night, and sweat so strongly as I changed my shirts thrice every day and thrice every night.

By mid-November he had descried the coast of Guiana, and the fleet sailed into the mouth of the River Caliana (Cayenne) on the South American mainland. His health was still very poor, for he wrote his wife:

> Sweet heart,
>   I can yet write unto you but with a weak hand, for I have suffered the most violent calenture, for fifteen days, that ever man did, and lived: but God that gave me a strong heart in all my adversities hath also now strengthened it in the hell-fire of heat.[14]

He told her that forty-two men had died and that there were many sick. He was grateful to a Countess at Gomera, who had given him a present of oranges, lemons, quinces and pomegranates, "without which I could not have lived". Ralegh's ill luck pursued him,

---

* A member of the pro-Spanish Party. Referred to as Alejandro in Gondomar's correspondence with Philip III. He received a pension from Spain.

for he had already lost his valued second-in-command, Captain Piggott, and Captain Hastings amongst others.

Ralegh at least had one blessing, the devotion of a remarkable wife, for Bess was constant in her attachment to him during all his adversities, even to the end. Among the wives of the Elizabethan adventurers, her character is outstanding, and one cannot think of one to compare with her, with the possible exception of Margaret, wife of George Clifford, Earl of Cumberland. Sir John Hawkins' first wife, Katherine Gonson, daughter of Benjamin Gonson of the Navy Board, was a solace to her husband when the carping critics accused him of corruption, and she has been described as godly and chaste.

What heartened Ralegh was the friendliness of the Indian chiefs in Guiana, who had not forgotten him. "Clad in jewels and parrot feathers,"[15] they came to welcome him, knowing that he was their protector, against the Spanish oppressors. He proudly wrote to his wife: "To tell you that I might be here King of the Indians were a vanity, but my name hath still lived among them. Here they feed me with fresh meat and all that the country yields; all offer to obey me."

His state of health was still so feeble, that he was in no condition to lead an expedition to find the gold mine. Since, however, he had faith in Laurence Keymis and considered that he was a man of good judgement, he instructed him to weigh anchor down the River Orinoco from Mount Aio.[16] Ralegh thought that this landmark was about three miles from the mine. He ordered Keymis to disembark his men twenty miles downstream from San Thomé. He was to order his troops to be stationed between San Thomé and the mine. Ralegh rather pathetically hoped that they would find a rich mine. He told Keymis that if the troops were attacked by the Spaniards whilst working the mine they were to be resisted. If the quality of the ore proved disappointing, Keymis was to produce a basket or two, to show at least that Ralegh had not lied when mentioning the existence of a gold mine.[17]

It is unnecessary to discuss the details of this disastrous affair, only to mention that Keymis for some obscure reason disregarded Ralegh's instructions. He sailed ten miles beyond Mount Aio, where he was five miles distant from San Thomé. Under cover of darkness he disembarked his men, who marched towards the town. Young Wat Ralegh, Sir Walter's elder son, a brave boy, was mortally wounded whilst leading some of his pikemen. "Come on, my hearts!" he cried, and as he fell dying, pierced by lance wounds, he managed to whisper, "Lord have mercy on me, and prosper your enterprise."

There are various Spanish accounts of the attack on San Thomé, written by the authorities to King Philip III. Here is one of them:

Sire, the city of San Thomé and the Island of Trinidad of the Province of Guiana and Dorado—represent that in the past month of January 1618, Walter Ralegh (Guatteral), an English pirate with ten ships and launches went up the River Orinoco to the said city of San Thomè, forty leagues from the sea, and at one league distance set on shore five hundred men, and the ships went up to its port. The Governor, Diego Palomeque, who with all diligence made preparations to defend it with the few soldiers he had, attacked him with very great valour, and as no other plan was available, he engaged him at eleven of the night by way of defending the city, seeing that he lacked men ... and was without artillery or regular troops: and there the two forces began slaying each other. The enemy then remained in occupation of the place for twenty-nine days, during which period they contrived to their side the peaceful Guiana Indians situated nearest the town, who straightway rose in rebellion in order to support the enemy.[18]

On hearing about the English attack on San Thomé, Gondomar at once went to the palace on 13th May 1618, and requested an audience. The King was otherwise engaged, but the ambassador was soon admitted. Gondomar now contented himself by shrieking "Pirates! Pirates! Pirates!" the best way to intimidate James. The Spaniard had an almost uncanny insight into James' character. Gondomar complained of Ralegh's activities, and demanded his punishment.[19]

Now the King confided in Gondomar that he would send Ralegh to be publicly executed in Spain, but an official inquiry with regard to his misdeeds must first be held in England.

How deeply Ralegh felt the loss of his elder son, is evident when we consider his letter to Bess written on 22nd March 1618.[20]

> I was loth to write because I know not how to comfort you. And God knows, I never knew what sorrow meant till now. All that I can say to you is, that you must obey the will and providence of God, and remember that the Queen's Majesty [Anne of Denmark] bore the loss of Prince Henry with a magnanimous heart. . . . Comfort your heart (dear Bess), I shall sorrow for us both.

Ralegh referred her to a letter he had written to Sir Ralph Winwood, but, unknown to Ralegh, the Secretary of State was already dead. He added a long postscript to his wife: "I protest before the majesty of God, that as Sir Francis Drake and Sir John Hawkins died heart-broken when they failed of their enterprise, I could willingly do the like, did I not contend against sorrow in hope to provide somewhat for you to comforte and relieve you." He told her that Keymis, having been very coldly received after the affair at San Thomé, had shut himself in his cabin and killed himself.

Ralegh's last voyage had been a failure, and his sea captains were in a mutinous mood. The tired old warrior had lost his decisiveness, and his mind wobbled painfully. Now he favoured a project for capturing Trinidad, now with a flicker of his superb courage he would lead them back up the Orinoco, or they would go to Virginia. It might have been better if Ralegh had considered his own safety and taken refuge at the French Court, where he had many admirers. Some of his sea captains urged him to sail for Newfoundland, where they secretly planned to seize an English ship at St. John's Harbour and indulge in piracy. The mutineers had gained such a hold that Ralegh had no choice but to comply with their demands. They were already on their way to New-foundland when Ralegh managed to persuade them to return to

England, but they insisted that they must be allowed to land at Killibeg, a haunt of pirates in Northern Ireland. They further stipulated that he must try and secure them a pardon for past and present offences. Was Ralegh tempted in his extreme adversity to turn pirate? We cannot be certain.

On 21st June 1618 the crippled ship, the *Destiny*, arrived at Plymouth. All Ralegh's sea captains had deserted him, with the exception of Captain King. Lady Ralegh was there to take care of her sick husband. It was reported that Sir Lewis Stukeley, Vice-Admiral of Devon, was on his way to Plymouth in order to arrest him. Meanwhile, one of Ralegh's captains, Roger North, had been received by the King towards the end of May, and given him his version of the voyage. In his opinion, Ralegh's story of a mine was pure invention, and he had intended to escape to France.

These confidences seemed only to confirm James' brooding suspicions, and increased his morbid distrust of the man. It is easy to condemn the King for his despicable actions against Ralegh, but we must try and understand his point of view. He felt that Ralegh had fooled him from the beginning, so as to enrich himself by piracy, and then turn traitor.[21]

On the 9th June a proclamation was made public, which declared the King's "utter mislike and detestation of the ... insolences and excesses" and straitly requiring all who had knowledge of the same to come forward and give their evidence, in order that exemplary punishment might be meted out to those found guilty of "so scandalous and enormous outrages". James' activities were no doubt influenced by the vehement protests of Gondomar, who urged him that Ralegh and some of his officers should be sent to Madrid, where they might be executed, although prisoners awaiting trial. In his apparent acquiescence with this iniquitous proposal James deserves the condemnation of posterity. One wonders how Elizabeth I would have dealt with Count Gondomar. She at least would have been a match for him. The matter was hotly debated by the Privy Council when Ralegh's supporters argued that to hand him over to King Philip III of

Spain was an insult to the Crown. It was unfortunate for Ralegh that Sir Ralph Winwood was now dead, for the new Secretary of State, Sir Robert Naunton, opposed him. The pro-Spanish party in the Council, now led by George Villiers, Marquess of Buckingham, triumphed. In his shameful surrender the King agreed that Raleigh should be given up, unless Philip were to make a special request that the execution should take place in England. Later, Spain's chief minister, the influential Duke of Lerma, on Philip's behalf, was condescending enough to agree that Ralegh's execution might take place in England.

Meanwhile, Ralegh had during the second week in July already begun his journey to London from Devonshire, attended only by his devoted Bess and the faithful Captain King. Near the country town of Ashburton he was met by Sir Lewis Stukeley, charged with his arrest, although this did not take place at once. Stukeley, however, was a corrupt man, and whilst in Plymouth made a profit for himself by selling the tobacco and stores of the *Destiny*. It was not until about 25th July that Stukeley, Ralegh, Bess, Captain King and a French physician named Manourie started again for London, having returned to Plymouth for a while. All this time Sir Lewis Stukeley pretended to be most solicitous for his comfort and feigned sincere friendship. Unfortunately Ralegh had never been able to curb his tongue. By nature indiscreet, he was unwise to say as they rode past Sherbourne castle, his old home: "All this was mine, and it was taken from me unjustly." Ralegh's indiscretion was duly reported to King James.

It is evident that the French quack Manourie was really a cunning rascal, whose task it was to spy on Ralegh and report his conversation to Stukeley. Ralegh was foolish enough to confide in the man that he wished to feign illness, so that he might gain time to contact his friends. With Manourie's aid, he produced on his body some sort of rash or spots giving the appearance of a fearful disease. One of Ralegh's objects was to obtain time, in order to write his *Apology for the Voyage to Guiana*. He had been apprised that King James was about to visit Salisbury during his summer progress, and he wished to bring his treatise to the King's attention. In this the great Englishman again tried to justify his actions by stating that Guiana was English territory and would never acknowledge that it was part of Spain.

It is not known whether James was given a copy of *The Apology*, but he gave orders that Ralegh must continue his journey to London. It was now that Ralegh must have abandoned hope that James would show him any clemency. He plotted to escape to France, with the aid of the loyal Captain King, who was to hire a ship at Gravesend. The project was betrayed to the Government.

Eventually he was formally arrested at Woolwich by Sir Lewis Stukeley, "Sir Judas" as he has been aptly named. Perhaps Ralegh was not completely taken by surprise, for he merely said in a mild, restrained voice: "Sir Lewis, these actions will not turn out to your credit." Sir Lewis Stukeley was later shunned by his fellow-men for his part in Ralegh's betrayal, and died on Lundy Island a raving lunatic.

We are not concerned with the legal devices, which secured Ralegh's execution. These have been fully discussed by his biographers. His noble death does not make him a saint, for men of genius usually have many faults of character, and Ralegh was no exception.

When he was about to leave the Tower for the Gatehouse at Westminster Palace, where he was to spend the last day and night before his execution, he was met by an old servant, Peter, who noticed that his master's hair was very untidy. Sir Walter had always been such a dandy. "May I comb it for you?" asked the man with tears in his eyes. "Let them kem* it that are to have it," replied Ralegh, humorously. Then he added: "Dost thou know, Peter, of any plaister that will set a man's head on again when it is off?"[22]

It would seem that Queen Anne of Denmark was not so frivolous as historians have depicted her, since she wrote to the

---

* Kem is a West Country idiom for comb.

new favourite George Villiers, Marquess* of Buckingham, pleading for Ralegh's life:

> My Kind Dog,
>
> If I have any power or credit with you, I pray you let me have a trial of it at this time, in dealing sincerely and earnestly with the King that Sir Walter Ralegh's life may not be called in question.[23]

He wrote to Bess on 4th October asking her to send him one of his paper books, *The Art of War by Sea.*

John Aubrey relates that Sir Walter "tooke a pipe of tobacco a little before he went to the scaffold, which some formall persons were scandalized at, but I think 'twas well and properly done, to settle his spirits".

When he was about to be executed, he felt the axe, saying to the Sheriff: "This is a sharp medicine, but it is a physician for all diseases." After laying his head on the block, Ralegh said: "So the heart be right, it is no matter which way the head lieth." Some had found fault that he faced westward, so he arose and laid his head on the block towards the east. His last words were: "What dost thou fear? Strike, man, strike!" When the executioner had raised the gory head and shown it to the stunned, groaning multitude of people, with the customary words: "This is the head of a traitor," a voice replied from the crowd, "We have not another such head to be cut off!"

Despite his faults of character, his sacrifice of the truth to serve a great purpose, his exasperating habits of prevarication and recourse to deceit when it served his purpose, there was nothing mean or petty about the man. He was a splendid Renaissance character. The greatness of Sir Walter Ralegh lies in his constant endeavours to inspire his fellow-countrymen with his own vision of a British Empire overseas in Virginia and Guiana.

---

* James I made Buckingham a Duke in May 1623, wanting him to receive all possible recognition from the Spanish Court.

Notes

CHAPTER XVII

1   V. T. Harlow, *Ralegh's Last Voyage*.
2   (Everyman Edition, 1932), Vol. VII, p. 35.
3   Purchas (Maclehose edition), Vol. XVI, p. 322.
4   The Letters of Elizabeth, Queen of Bohemia compiled by L. M. Baker.
5   Norman Lloyd Williams, *Sir Walter Ralegh*.
6   *Ibid.*
7   V. T. Harlow, *Ralegh's Last Voyage* (1932).
8   L. P. V. Arkrigg, *Jacobean Pageant*, p. 324.
9   V. T. Harlow, *Ralegh's Last Voyage* (1932).
10 Margaret Irwin, *That Great Lucifer*.
11 Excellent Observations and Notes concerning the Royall Navy and sea-service written by Sir Walter Ralegh, and by him dedicated to the Most Noble and Illustrious Prince Henry, Prince of Wales.
12 Norman Lloyd Williams, *Sir Walter Ralegh*.
13 V. T. Harlow, *Ralegh's Last Voyage*, p. 143.
14 *Remains of Sir Walter Ralegh, 1656–1657*. Reprinted Edwards II, p. 347.
15 Margaret Irwin, *That Great Lucifer*.
16 J. H. Adamson and H. F. Folland, *The Shepherd of the Ocean*.
17 *Ibid.*
18 Archivo General de Indias, Seville, Part I, c. 38.
19 *Diccionario de Historia de Espania*.
20 B.M. Sloane MSS. 3520, pp. 2–4.
21 V. T. Harlow, *Ralegh's Last Voyage* (1932).
22 J. H. Adamson and H. F. Folland, *The Shepherd of the Ocean*.
23 Norman Lloyd-Williams, *Sir Walter Ralegh*.

CHAPTER XVIII

Epilogue

The first Elizabethan mariners had a voracious appetite for knowledge, and to my mind one of their most remarkable achievements was their industry in making it available for the younger Richard Hakluyt. It was of enormous benefit, both for contemporary Elizabethans and for posterity. This naturally took many forms, the acquisition of technical knowledge concerning navigation by the great sea captains, curious information about the far-distant lands they visited, and fascinating material concerning the customs of the inhabitants. The part played by the famous sea captains must be emphasized. Philip Amadas and Arthur Barlow, who made an early voyage of discovery to Virginia in 1584, were particularly observant, so that their experiences were of inestimable value to others. So were those of countless mariners. Even the humble seamen, usually ill-educated men, felt primitive urges to acquire learning. Life at sea was often a lonely, awe-inspiring adventure for these simple men. It was the dedicated task of the Elizabethan mariners to arouse the national consciousness of the people of Britain, and to give them noble aims.

Shakespeare's lines put in the mouth of Lord Say in Part 2 of *Henry VI* are completely Elizabethan in spirit:

And seeing ignorance is the curse of God,
Knowledge the wing wherewith we fly to heaven.

The finest minds of that age had a compulsive urge to disseminate knowledge.

I have constantly stressed how deeply Shakespeare, Marlowe, Spenser, Philip Sidney, the young John Donne and other major and lesser poets and dramatists were influenced by the age of discovery. If the flagship of Sir George Somers had not been wrecked on the coast of Bermuda during a storm, one wonders whether Shakespeare's inspiration in *The Tempest* would be so vivid.

The real importance of these Elizabethan seamen, with all their virtues and faults, their valiant natures, and at times their maddening self-righteousness, was that they gave the people of Britain the first glimpses of the imperial path they were to follow. They were pioneers of Empire. The narrowness of the pattern of Elizabethan society when the Queen ascended the throne, was gradually transformed into something more spacious and exciting. To some extent this metamorphosis was due to the inspiration of the mariners and the encouragement of the statesmen and merchants, who made their voyages possible.

Almost all the great seamen possessed a vision of empire, particularly Humphrey Gilbert, Walter Ralegh, Francis Drake and Henry Hudson. They held strong beliefs on how native peoples should be treated, and their ideas were closely studied by those who came after them.

The part of Richard Hakluyt the younger has already been stressed. He possesses a secure and honoured place in our history, and our debt to him is immense. Up to his death in 1616, we find him inspiring the translation of works on the Far East and Africa, and industriously collecting the accounts of the navigators' voyages, so as to educate the people. Above all, his vast interest in American colonization remained constant. In 1603, the year of Queen Elizabeth's death, Hakluyt by his endeavours managed to persuade the Bristol merchants to send out the resourceful navigator Martin Pring to prospect in the northern latitudes first colonized by Sir Humphrey Gilbert, and it was necessary to obtain Ralegh's permission to do so.

That is, too, where the Elizabethan mariners made a fruitful contribution to the achievement and spirit of the age. For instance, Gilbert and Ralegh held advanced opinions regarding colonization, and they were to influence the empire-building in the future.

The adventurous, purposeful colonists of the early seventeenth century, men such as Captain John Smith in Virginia, were of a very different mettle to those seedy individuals who it was envisaged might first colonize Newfoundland in 1583. They owed much to the pioneering work of the mariners and the publicists in making the massive tasks of these emigrants seem worthwhile and possessive of a certain dignity. Men may fail at times, but by the force of their spirits they will triumph in the end. Such were the early colonists in Virginia, Maine and New England, driven to despair by the hardships they were forced to undergo. Yet they overcame their difficulties and prevailed at last.

As the First Elizabethan era receded, people during the seventeenth century looked back on it with nostalgia, thinking of it as a kind of golden age. Though the image was only partly true, elderly Elizabethans at least sensed that a country cannot be great, unless it is continually nourished by spiritual values. They were inclined to wax sentimental about the past (as men do today). They conveniently forgot the bitter struggles between the political factions during the last decade of Gloriana's reign, and that the poor starved after three disastrous consecutive harvests, 1594–97. The ageing Queen, too, was losing her magic.

It cannot be pretended that the early Stuart age was a beneficial one for mariners. Many of the abuses, which had existed under Elizabeth, continued into the reign of James I. Seamen were discouraged from entering the navy by the poor food, inadequate clothing and delay in the payment of wages.

Although the population of England and Wales consisted of about five million people, it is probable that there were not more than 20,000 professional seamen at the beginning of 1600. It was unfortunate that the Lord Admiral Charles Lord Howard of Effingham, now Earl of Nottingham, who had proved such a magnificent friend to the Elizabethan seamen, had grown too old and feeble to grapple with the corruption in the Admiralty. In 1618 he was compelled to resign.

Although Spain was gradually becoming weaker as a great power and was now decadent, the zenophobia of the English for that country remained strong, even after the peace. Yet an influential faction at Court supported Spain.

Today as we reflect upon the rapid and sad decline of our once glorious empire, many of us can at least take comfort in the thought that the Elizabethan spirit is still alive. The wonderful exploits of our Second Elizabethans, the lone voyages round the world of Sir Francis Chichester and of Sir Alec Rose animate and warm the cockles of our hearts, even as the people were aroused to enthusiasm by the circumnavigation of the globe by the fiery Sir Francis Drake in very different circumstances.

The illustrious First Elizabethan seamen were for the most part of a sturdy independence of character, and deeply religious. Not only their achievements, but their infinite faith in God was to have a profound influence on the spirit of their age. The lustre and the light are no more, but their glory abides for ever.

Bibliography

CONTEMPORARY AND SEVENTEENTH-CENTURY WORKS
The Observations of Sir Richard Hawkins (Edited from the text of 1622 by James A. Williamson, 1933).
Sir Harris Nicolas, *Memoirs of the Life and Times of Sir Christopher Hatton, Vice Chamberlain and Lord Chancellor to Queen Elizabeth*, C.S.P. Venetian (1603) and earlier editions.
'The English Voyages of the Sixteenth Century' in Hakluyt's *Principal Navigations* (Hakluyt Society).
John Taylor's poem, "A Discovery by Sea from London to Salisbury".
The Naval Tracts of Sir William Monson, edited by Oppenheim. Vols. I, II, III and IV.
Diary of Henry Machyn (Camden Society), edited by J. G. Nichols.
Hakluyt, *Voyages* (Everyman Edition).
Acts of the Privy Council. Vols. XII & XIII. 1570–1595. Record Office.
State Papers, Ireland 1586–1588.
Calendar of State Papers, Colonial Service, E. Indies. Record Office.
Fuller, *History of the Worthies of England*.
Samuel Purchas, *His Pilgrimes contayning a History of the World, in sea voyages and land travels*. Calendar of State Papers, Spanish. Published in 1625.
Bacon's Essays. Edited by W. Aldis Wright.
John Aubrey, *Brief Lives*. Edited by Oliver Lawson Dick.
Richard Hakluyt the younger's *Discourse on Western Planting*.
Roland Whyte's Letters to Sir Robert Sidney 1597–1598.
The Diary of Lady Anne Clifford (Countess of Dorset).
Sidney Papers. Vol. 2.
John Knox Laughton ed., *State Papers relating to the Defeat of the Spanish Armada*, Vol. 2.
Sir Walter Ralegh, *Excellent Observations and Notes concerning the Royall Navy and Sea-service*.

Agatha Latham ed., *The Poems of Sir Walter Ralegh*.
The Works of William Shakespeare (Oxford University Press).
Calendar of State Papers. Elizabeth. Vol. 213.
Thomas Lodge, *Rosalynde*.
William Camden *Annales* (1625).
H.C.A. High Court of Admiralty MSS (Record Office).
Add. MSS. British Museum.
Add. MSS. Caesar Papers 6994.
Archives of the Indies. Casa Lonja. Seville.
William Camden, *History*. Edited 1675.
William Strachey, *History of Virginia*.

MODERN WORKS
Ernie Bradford, *Drake* (Hodder and Stoughton, 1965).
James A. Williamson, *The Age of Drake* (A. and C. Black, 1938).
Christopher Lloyd, *The British Seaman* (Collins, 1968).
A. L. Rowse, *The Expansion of Elizabethan England* (Macmillan, 1955).
A. L. Rowse, *The England of Elizabeth* (Macmillan, 1951).
Shakespeare's England, Vols. I and II (Oxford University Press, 1932).
John Keast, *The Story of Fowey* (Townsend Parker, 1950).
James Anthony Froude, *English Seamen in the Sixteenth Century* (Long-
    mans, Green, 1901).
J. E. Neale, *The Age of Catherine de Medici and Essays in Elizabethan
    History* (Jonathan Cape, 1958).
Prof. Julian Corbett, *Drake and the Tudor Navy*, Vols. I and II.
Maritime History of Cornwall, Vol. I.
Maritime History of Devon.
James A. Williamson, *Piracy and Honest Trade*: An Elizabethan Con-
    trast (Blackwoods 1930).
A. L. Rowse, *Tudor Cornwall*.
A. L. Rowse, *Sir Richard Grenville of the Revenge* (Jonathan Cape, 1937).
John Izon, *Sir Thomas Stucley*, 1525–1578 (Andrew Melrose, 1956).
Conyers Reed, *Sir Francis Walsingham*.
Conyers Reed, *Mr. Secretary Walsingham and the Policy of Queen Elizabeth*,
    Vol II. (Jonathan Cape, 1955).
Katherine Garvin ed., *The Great Tudors* (Eyre and Spottiswoode, 1956).
Richard Deacon, *John Dee* (Frederick Muller, 1968).
John Buxton, *Sir Philip Sidney and the English Renaissance* (Macmillan,
    1954).
C. Henry Warner, *Sir Philip Sidney* (Thomas Nelson and Sons, 1936).
Eric St. John Brooks, *Sir Christopher Hatton*.
Sir Charles Petrie, *Philip II of Spain* (Eyre and Spottiswoode, 1936).

Henry Charles Lea, *A History of the Inquisition of Spain*, Vol. III.

History of the Inquisition, abridged from the elaborate work of Philip Lumborch.

Jean Plaidy, *The Spanish Inquisition*, 3 Vols., (Robert Hale 1959, 1960, 1961).

John Payne ed., *Voyages of Elizabethan Seamen*, 1st and 2nd series. (Oxford University Press, 1893).

Robert Southey, *English Seamen*. (1904 edition).

Lacey Baldwin Smith, *The English Epic*, (Jonathan Cape, 1966).

J. H. Adamson and H. F. Folland, *The Shepherd of the Ocean* (Bodley Head, 1969).

A. L. Rowse, *The Elizabethans and America*, (Macmillan, 1962).

A. P. V. Akrigg, *Jacobean Pageant* (Hamish Hamilton, 1962).

William Gilbert Gosling, *The Life of Sir Humphrey Gilbert*, England's First Empire Builder (1911).

Sir Clements R. Markham, *A Life of John Davis 1550–1605*.

David B. Quinn, *Voyages and Colonising Enterprises of Sir Humphrey Gilbert* (Hakluyt Society).

J. H. Parry, *The Spanish Seaborne Empire*.

Edgar Prestige, *The Portuguese Pioneers*.

G. P. Parks, *Richard Hakluyt and the English Voyages*.

David B. Quinn, *Raleigh and the British Empire*.

James H. Williamson, *George, Third Earl of Cumberland*.

Kenneth R. Andrews, *Elizabethan Privateering, 1585–1603* (Cambridge University Press, 1964).

Kenneth R. Andrews, *Elizabethan Privateering Voyages to the West Indies 1588–1595* (Hakluyt Society).

Arthur Gould Lee, *The Son of Leicester*, a biography of Sir Robert Dudley (Victor Gollancz, 1964).

Margaret Irwin, *That Great Lucifer*, a biography of Sir Walter Raleigh (Chatto and Windus, 1960).

Norman Lloyd Williams, *Sir Walter Ralegh* (Eyre and Spottiswoode, 1962).

Raymond Francis, *Looking for Elizabethan England*, (Macdonald, 1954).

George Sampson, *The Concise Cambridge History of English Literature* (Cambridge University Press, 1942).

Evelyn Hardy, *Donne, a Spirit in Conflict* (Constable, 1942).

Complete Poems of John Donne, The Fullers Worthy Library.

Zelia Nuttall, *New Light on Drake*.

Rashleighs of Coombe, Vol. I.

Elizabeth Jenkins, *Elizabeth the Great* (Victor Gollancz, 1956).

Alonso Castro, *Historia de Cadiz y sa Provincia desde los remotos tiempos*.

Garrett Mattingley, *The Defeat of the Spanish Armada*.

James A. Williamson, *Hawkins of Plymouth*.

Rachel Lloyd, *Dorset Elizabethans at Home or Abroad*.

John Bowle, *Henry VIII* (Allen and Unwin, 1964).

C. L'Estrange, *The Golden Chalice*.

N. Boteler, *Dialogues*.

James Orchard Halliwell ed., *The Private Diary of Dr. John Dee*, from the original MSS in the Ashmolean Museum, Oxford.

A. L. Rowse, *William Shakespeare* (Macmillan, 1963).

Professor E. C. R. Taylor, *The Original Writings and Correspondence of the Times of Richard Hakluyt*.

Irene Wright, *Further British Voyages to Spanish America* (Hakluyt Society).

V. T. Harlow, *Ralegh's Last Voyage*.

W. G. Perrin ed., *Autobiography of Phineas Pett*.

M. Oppenheim, *History of the Administration of the Royal Navy*.

Henry Hudson the Navigator. The original documents with an Introduction by G. M. Asher (Hakluyt Society).

E. M. Tenison, *Elizabethan England*. In 13 volumes 1933–61. (To subscribers only). County Record Office, Truro, Cornwall.

Index

The
Good
People

The
Good
People

Hannah Kent

PICADOR

First published 2016 in Picador by Pan Macmillan Australia Pty Limited, Sydney

First published in the UK 2017 by Picador
an imprint of Pan Macmillan
20 New Wharf Road, London N1 9RR
Associated companies throughout the world
www.panmacmillan.com

ISBN 978-1-4472-3335-0

1 3 5 7 9 8 6 4 2

A CIP catalogue record for this book is available from the British Library.

Typeset in Adobe Garamond Pro by Post Pre-Press Australia
Internal text design by Sandy Cull
Cartography by Pan Macmillan Australia
Printed and bound by CPI Group (UK) Ltd, Croydon, CR0 4YY

Visit **www.picador.com** to read more about all our books
and to buy them. You will also find features, author interviews and
news of any author events, and you can sign up for e-newsletters
so that you're always first to hear about our new releases.

For my sister, Briony.

There was an old woman and she lived in the woods,
weile weile waile.
There was an old woman and she lived in the woods
down by the river Saile.

She had a baby three months old,
weile weile waile.
She had a baby three months old
down by the river Saile.

She had a penknife, long and sharp,
weile weile waile.
She had a penknife long and sharp
down by the river Saile.

She stuck the penknife in the baby's heart,
weile weile waile.
She stuck the penknife in the baby's heart
down by the river Saile.

Three hard knocks came knocking on the door,
weile weile waile.
Three hard knocks came knocking on the door
down by the river Saile.

'Are you the woman that killed the child?'
weile weile waile.
'Are you the woman that killed the child
down by the river Saile?'

The rope was pulled and she got hung,
weile weile waile.
The rope was pulled and she got hung
down by the river Saile.

And that was the end of the woman in the woods,
weile weile waile.
And that was the end of the woman in the woods
down by the river Saile.

Traditional Irish Murder Ballad, c. 1600

When all is said and done, how do we not know but that our
own unreason may be better than another's truth?
for it has been warmed on our hearths and in our souls,
and is ready for the wild bees of truth to hive in it, and make
their sweet honey. Come into the world again,
wild bees, wild bees!

W.B. Yeats, *The Celtic Twilight*

PART ONE

Death is the Physician of the Poor
Liagh gach boicht bas

1825

CHAPTER
ONE

Coltsfoot

Nóra's first thought when they brought her the body was that it could not be her husband's. For one long moment she stared at the men bearing Martin's weight on their sweating shoulders, standing in the gasping cold, and believed that the body was nothing but a cruel imitation; a changeling, brutal in its likeness. Martin's mouth and eyes were open, but his head slumped on his chest and there was no quick in him. The blacksmith and the ploughman had brought her a lifeless stock. It could not be her husband. It was not him at all.

Martin had been digging ditches beside the fields that sloped the valley, Peter O'Connor said. He had seen him stop, place a hand on his chest like a man taking an oath, and fall to the gentle ground. He had not given a shout of pain. He had gone without farewell or fear.

Peter's chapped lips trembled, eyes red-rimmed in their sockets. 'I'm sorry for your trouble,' he whispered.

Nóra's legs collapsed beneath her then and in the fall to the dirt and straw of the yard, she felt her heart seize with terrible understanding.

John O'Donoghue, his thick forearms scar-speckled from iron-work, heaved Martin over his shoulder so that Peter was able to lift Nóra out of the mud. Both men were dark-eyed with grief and when Nóra opened her mouth to scream and found that she had choked on it, they bowed their heads as though they heard her anyway.

Peter wrested the chicken feed from Nóra's clenched fists and kicked the clucking hens from the doorstep. Placing her arm around his shoulders, he led her back inside the cabin to sit by the hearth where her grandchild, Micheál, was sleeping in the unfolded settle bed. The little boy, his cheeks flushed from the heat of the turf fire, stirred as they entered, and Nóra noticed Peter's eyes flicker to him in curiosity.

John followed them inside, his jaw clenched with the weight of Martin's body and his boots tracking mud over the packed clay floor. Grunting with the effort, he laid Martin on the bed in the small sleeping quarter off the main room. Dust from the disturbed straw mattress rose into the air. The blacksmith crossed himself with deliberate precision and, stooping under the lintel, murmured that his wife, Áine, would be there soon, and that the new priest had been fetched.

Nóra felt her throat close over. She rose to go to Martin's body in the bedroom, but Peter held her wrist.

'Let him be washed,' he said gently.

John cast a troubled look at the boy and left without saying another word, shutting the half-door behind him.

The dark rose.

'You saw him fall, did you? Saw him yourself?' Nóra's voice sounded strange and small. She gripped Peter's hand so tightly her fingers ached.

'I did,' he murmured, looking at Micheál. 'I saw him in the fields and raised my hand, and I saw him fall down.'

'There was a need for those ditches. He told me yesterday there was a need for them to be dug, so the rain . . .' Nóra felt her husband's death creep over her, until she began to shake with it. Peter draped a greatcoat over her shoulders, and she could tell from the familiar smell of burnt coltsfoot that it was Martin's own. They must have brought it back with his body.

'Someone else will have to finish those ditches,' she gasped, rubbing her cheek against the rough frieze.

'Don't be thinking of that now, Nóra.'

'And there will be the thatch, come spring. It needs thatching.'

'We'll all be taking care of that, don't you worry now.'

'And Micheál. The boy . . .' Alarm ran through her and she looked down at the child, his hair copper in the firelight. She was grateful that he slept. The boy's difference did not show so much when he was asleep. The keel of his limbs slackened, and there was no telling the dumb tongue in his head. Martin had always said Micheál looked most like their daughter when asleep. 'You can almost think him well,' he had said once. 'You can see how he will be when the sickness has passed. When we have him cured of it.'

'Is there someone I can fetch for you, Nóra?' Peter asked, his face splintered with concern.

'Micheál. I don't want him here.' Her voice was hoarse. 'Take Micheál to Peg O'Shea's.'

Peter looked uneasy. 'Would you not have him with you?'

'Take him away from here.'

'I don't like to leave you alone, Nóra. Not before Áine is with you.'

'I'll not have Micheál here to be gaped at.' Nóra reached down and grabbed the sleeping boy under his armpits, hauling him into the air in front of Peter. The boy frowned, eyes blinking, gummed with sleep.

'Take him. Take him to Peg's. Before a soul is here.'

Micheál began to squall and struggle as he hung from Nóra's grip. His legs tremored, rashed and dry-looking against the bone.

Peter grimaced. 'Your daughter's, isn't he? God rest her soul.'

'Take him, Peter. Please.'

He gave her a long, sorrowful look. 'Folk won't mind him at a time like this, Nóra. They'll be thinking of you.'

'They'll be gawping and gossiping over him, is what.'

Micheál's head slumped backwards and he began to cry, his hands drawing into fists.

'What ails him?'

'For the love of God, Peter, take him.' Her voice broke. 'Take him away!'

Peter nodded and lifted Micheál onto his lap. The boy was clothed in a girl's woollen dress, too long for him, and Peter awkwardly wrapped the worn cloth around the child's legs, taking care to cover his toes. ''Tis cold out,' he explained. 'Do you not have a shawl for him?'

Nóra, hands shaking, took off her own and gave it to Peter.

He stood up, bundling the bleating boy against his chest. 'I'm sorry, Nóra, so I am.'

The cabin door swung wide after him.

Nóra waited until the sound of Micheál's crying faded and she knew Peter had reached the lane. Then she rose from her low stool and walked into the bedroom, clutching Martin's coat around her shoulders.

'Sweet, sore-wounded Christ.'

Her husband lay on their marriage bed, his arms tucked close to his sides, grass and mud clinging to his calloused hands. His eyes were half closed. Their pearled whites glimmered in the light from the open door.

Martin's stillness in that quiet room sent sorrow pealing through her chest. Easing herself down onto the bed, Nóra touched her forehead against Martin's cheekbone and felt the cold of his stubbled skin.

Pulling his coat over the both of them, she closed her eyes and her lungs emptied of air. Pain descended with the weight of water and she felt that she was drowning. Her chest shuddered, and she was crying into her husband's collarbone, into his clothes reeking of the earth and cow shit and the soft sweet smell of the valley air and all the turf smoke it carried on an autumn evening. She cried like a pining dog, with the strained, strung whimper of abandonment.

Only that morning they had lain in bed together, both awake in the dark of early dawn, the warmth of Martin's hand resting on her stomach.

'I think it will rain today,' he had said, and Nóra had let him pull her close against the broad barrel of his ribs, had matched the rise and fall of her breathing with his own.

'There was a wind in the night.'

'It woke you?'

'The boy woke me. He was crying in fear of it.'

Martin had listened intently. 'There's no sound from him now.'

'Are you digging potatoes today?'

'Ditches.'

'And will you have a word with the new priest about Micheál on your way home?'

'I will.'

Nóra stretched herself out against her husband's dead body and thought of the nights they had slept in company together, the touch of his foot on hers in the unthinking custom of their marriage, and sobbed until she thought she would be sick.

It was only the thought that her cries might wake devils lying in wait for his soul that made her stop. She stuffed her mouth with the sleeve of Martin's coat and shook, silently.

How dare you leave me behind, she thought.

*

'Nóra?'

She had fallen asleep. Through the swelling of her eyes she saw the slender outline of the blacksmith's wife standing in the doorway.

'Áine,' Nóra croaked.

The woman entered, crossing herself at the sight of the body. 'May the Lord have mercy on his soul. I'm sorry for your trouble. Martin, he . . .' She paused and knelt by Nóra's side. 'He was a great man. A rare man.'

Nóra sat up on the bed and wiped her eyes on her apron, embarrassed.

'The sorrow is on you, Nóra. I can see it. And we'd do right to give him a proper wake. Would you be willing for me to wash and lay him out? Father Healy has been sent for. He's on his way.'

Áine put her hand on Nóra's knee and squeezed it. Her face, hanging from wide cheekbones, seemed spectral in the gloom. Nóra stared at her in horror.

'There now. Here are your beads. He's with God now, Nóra. Remember that.' She glanced around the room. 'Are you alone? Did you not have a child . . .'

Nóra closed her fingers over the rosary. 'I am alone.'

Áine washed Martin as tenderly as if he had been her own husband. At first Nóra watched, clutching the prayer beads so tightly that the wood baubled her skin into welts. She could not believe that it was her husband naked before them, his belly painful-white. It was shameful for another woman to see the pale secrets of his body. When she stood up and held her hand out for the cloth, Áine passed it to her without a word. She washed him then, and with every movement of her hand she farewelled the boned curve of his chest, the sweep of his limbs.

How well I know you, she thought, and when she felt her throat noose tighter, she swallowed hard and forced her eye to the neat cobwebbing of veins across his thighs, the familiar whorl of his hair. She did not understand how Martin's body could seem so small. In life he had been a bear of a man, had carried her on the night of their wedding as though she was nothing more than sunlight.

The dark fur of his chest slicked damp against his skin.

'I think he is clean now, Nóra,' Áine said.

'A little longer.' She ran her palm down his sternum as though waiting for it to lift in breath.

Áine eased the grey cloth from her fingers' grip.

The afternoon darkened and a bitter wind began to blow outside. Nóra sat beside Martin's body and let Áine stir the fire and fix the rushlights. Both of them jumped at a sudden knocking on the door, and Nóra's heart gave a scalding leap at the thought it might be Martin, returned to her by the evening.

'Blessings on this house.'

A young man entered the cabin, his clerical garb flapping in the doorway. The new priest, Nóra realised. He was dark-haired and ruddy-cheeked, with long limbs that seemed at odds with his soft, child's face and pouting mouth. Nóra noticed a conspicuous gap between his front teeth. Father Healy's hat dripped with rain, and when Peter and John followed him inside, their shoulders were wet through. She had not realised that the weather had changed.

'Good evening to you, Father.' Áine took the damp coat he held out to her and carefully arranged it over the rafter to dry by the heat of the fire.

The priest looked around the cabin before noticing Nóra sitting in the bedroom. He walked towards her, ducking under the low doorframe. His eyes were solemn. 'God be with you, Mrs Leahy.

I'm sorry for your trouble.' Taking her hand in his own, he pressed the flesh of her palm. 'It must be a great shock to you.'

Nóra nodded, her mouth dry.

'It happens to us all, but 'tis always sad when those we love go to God.' He released her hand and turned to Martin, placing two slender fingers against her husband's throat. The priest gave a slight nod. 'He has passed. I cannot give the last rites.'

'He had no warning of his death, Father.' It was Peter who spoke. 'Would you not give him the rites anyway? His soul may yet be in his body.'

Father Healy wiped his forehead on his sleeve and grimaced in apology. 'The sacraments are for the living and cannot avail the dead.'

Nóra gripped her rosary until her knuckles paled. 'Pray for him, will you, Father?'

The priest looked from the two men in the doorway to Nóra.

She lifted her chin. 'He was a good man, Father. Say the prayers over him.'

Father Healy sighed, nodded and reached into his bag, taking out a small, used candle and a glass bottle of oil. He lit the candle by the fire in the main room and placed the waxy stub awkwardly in Martin's hand, beginning the prayers and anointing the man's head with a firm touch.

Nóra sank down onto the hard floor beside the bed and let her fingers slide across the beads in blank habit. But the prayers felt empty and cold in her mouth and she soon stopped whispering and sat there, mute.

I am not ready to be alone, she thought.

Father Healy cleared his throat and stood up, brushing his knees of dirt and reaching for his coat and the coin offered by John.

'May God comfort you,' he said to Nóra, shaking the rain from his hat and setting it on his head. He took her hand again and she flinched at the feel of the bones in his fingers.

'May God protect you. Seek His love and forgiveness and keep your faith, Mrs Leahy. I will keep you in my prayers.'

'Thank you, Father.'

They watched the priest mount his donkey in the yard, squinting against the steady rain. He raised a hand to them in farewell, then whipped the animal's flank with a sally rod until the weather closed around him and the valley below absorbed his black, fleeing form.

By nightfall the cabin was filled with neighbours who had heard that Martin had died by the crossroads next to the blacksmith's, falling to the ground on the strike of hammer on anvil as though the ringing of iron had killed him. They gathered around the hearth, taking consolation from their pipes and murmuring condolences to Nóra. Outside, the rain blew against the thatch.

Confronted with a sudden crowd, Nóra concentrated on collecting preparations for the wake with Áine. There was no time to weep while they had *poitín*, clay pipes, tobacco and chairs to find. Nóra knew that death made people long to smoke and drink and eat, as though by tending to their lungs and stomachs they were assuring themselves of their own good health, of the certainty of their continued existence.

When she felt the weight of her grief threaten to press her to the floor, Nóra retreated to the cabin walls and pushed her palms against the cool limewash to steady herself. She took deep breaths and stared at the people in the room. Most of them were from the valley, tied to one another by blood and labour and a shared understanding of the traditions stamped into the soil by those who had come before them. They were quiet, close folk, those who lived on the shadowed side of Crohane, in the fertile crucible formed by the rising rock and hill of Foiladuane, Derreenacullig and Clonkeen. And they were familiar with death. In her small house Nóra could see that her neighbours were making room for sorrow in the way they knew to be best. They piled turf on the fire and built the flames high, filled the air with smoke, and told each other stories. There would be a time to cry, but it was not yet.

Thunder rolled outside, and the guests shivered and drew closer to the fire. As Nóra moved around the room, setting out drinking water, she heard the people whisper stories of divination. The men commented on the weather and the movements of jacksnipes and magpies, seeing in them signs of Martin's death. Much was made of his collapse at the crossroads where they buried suicides. Some spoke of the sudden change in the sky that afternoon, of the great blackening of clouds in the west and how they had surely heralded Martin's passing. Of the storm that was closing in upon them.

Unaware that Nóra was listening, Peter O'Connor was telling the men that, just before he had seen Martin clutch his heart, he had noticed four magpies sitting together in a field.

'There I was, walking the lane, and did those birds move? They did not. They let me pass within arm's reach of them and not once did they startle. "That's mighty strange," I thought to myself, and – I tell you, lads – a shiver went through me for it seemed they stood in conference. "Someone has died," I thought. Then sure, I make my way down the boreen until I reached the crossroads and, soon enough, there is Martin Leahy, lying with the sky in his eyes and the clouds darkening beyond the mountains.'

There was a slap of thunder and they jumped.

'So, 'twas you that found him then, lying there?' asked Nóra's nephew, Daniel, drawing on his pipe.

''Twas. And a sorrow 'twas to me too. I saw that great man topple like a tree. He had not yet the cold upon him, God rest his soul.'

Peter's voice softened to a hush. 'And that's not all of it. When John and I were bringing the body here, dragging him up the slope from the crossroads – and you know the heft of Martin, 'twas slow going – well, we stopped a while to catch our breath, and we looked down the valley, out towards the woods, and there we saw *lights*.'

There was a murmur of intrigue.

'That's right. Lights. Coming from where the *fairies* do be, down by the Piper's Grave,' Peter continued. 'Now, I might not have the full of my eyes, but I swear I saw a glowing by that whitethorn. You mark my words, there'll be another death in this family before long.' His voice dropped to a whisper. 'First the daughter passes, and now the husband. I tell you, death likes three in company. And if the Good People have a hand in it . . . well.'

Nóra's throat tightened and she turned away to seek out Áine. She found her taking chalk pipes and a lump of uncut tobacco from a straw *ciseán*.

'Do you hear that storming?' Áine whispered. She gestured to the basket. 'Your nephew Daniel's woman, the young wife, she's brought some preparations.'

Nóra picked up a small cloth parcel and untied its string with shaking fingers. Salt, damp from the rain. 'Where is she?'

'Praying over Martin.'

The bedroom was crowded, the air blue with the pipe smoke that the older men and women blew over her husband. Nóra noticed that they had turned Martin's body so that his head was at the foot of the bed, so as to avert further misfortune. His mouth had fallen open and his skin had already taken on the waxiness of the dead, his forehead greasy with the priest's oils. The candle stub, unlit, lolled amongst the bedclothes. A young woman knelt beside him, reciting Hail Mary with her eyes closed.

Nóra tapped her on the shoulder. 'Brigid.'

The girl looked up. 'Oh, Nóra,' she whispered, heaving herself to her feet. Her pregnant belly swelled, lifting the front of her skirts and apron so that her bare ankles were visible. 'I'm sorry for your trouble. Martin was a mighty man. How are you keeping?'

Nóra opened her mouth to speak but thought better of it.

'Himself and I brought what you might need.' She nodded to where Daniel sat smoking with Peter. 'I set a basket on the table.'

'I know, Áine showed me. 'Tis kind of you both. I'll pay you for it.'

'A bad year for you.'

Nóra took a breath. 'Do you know who might have the drink?'

'Seán has brought *poitín*.' Brigid pointed through to the main room where Seán Lynch, Daniel's uncle, was setting two clay jars of spirits on the floor. His wife, Kate, was with him, a woman with crowded teeth and a hunched, hounded look. She stood in the doorway, peering around the room in agitation. They had clearly just arrived; their clothes were dark with rain and the smell of cold was on them.

'Nóra, Brigid.' Kate nodded as the two women made their way back into the room. ''Tis a sad evening. Has the priest been? Do we need to hide the drink?'

'Been and gone.'

Seán's face was grim, his eyes and lips set in hard, leathered lines. He pushed tobacco into the bowl of his clay pipe with a calloused thumb. 'Sorry for your trouble,' he told Nóra.

'God save you kindly, Seán.'

'You've a visitor lurking out there,' he said, gesturing towards the door. Taking the offer of an ember from one of the men by the fire, he lit his pipe with the tongs and muttered, 'May God have mercy on the souls of the dead.' Smoke escaped from between his teeth. 'The herb hag. She's out by your dung heap, waiting.'

Nóra paused. 'Nance Roche?'

'Aye, the interfering biddy herself.' He spat on the floor.

'How did she know to come?'

Seán frowned. 'I wouldn't talk to her if she was the last woman alive.'

Kate watched him anxiously.

'Nance Roche? I thought she was the handy woman?' Brigid asked.

'I wonder what she wants,' Nóra muttered. ''Tis a long way for an old woman on a night of tipping rain. I wouldn't put my enemy's dog out tonight.'

'Looking for pipe smoke and drink, it is,' Kate remarked sourly, nostrils flaring. 'Don't go out to her, Nóra. Not that hag, that swindler *cailleach*.'

Night had fallen and the downpour had grown heavier. Nóra pushed out the wooden door of the cabin and peered into the yard, her head hunched under the low awning of thatch. Water poured off the straw ends. At first she couldn't see anything through the rain, only a thin rim of iron grey on the horizon where the dark had not yet suffocated the light. Then, out of the corner of her eye, she saw a small figure moving towards her from the gabled end of the house where the muck of the smallholding lay heaped against the stone wall. Nóra stepped down into the yard, shutting the door behind her to keep out the cold. The mud rose over her toes.

'Who's that there?' she called, her words drowned out by thunder. 'Is that you, Nance Roche?'

The visitor walked to the door and bent her head under the thatch, pulling the cloak from her head.

'So 'tis, Nóra Leahy.'

Lightning flared and Nóra saw the old woman before her,

drenched to the bone, her white hair slick against her skull. Nance blinked away the rain that slid down her forehead and sniffed. She was small, shrunken, with a face as wrinkled as a forgotten russet. Her eyes, fogged with age, looked up at Nóra from beneath heavy eyelids. 'I'm sorry for your trouble.'

'Thank you, Nance.'

"Tis the end of Martin's worry in this life.'

'So 'tis.'

'Your man is on the way of truth now.' Nance's lips parted, revealing the few stray teeth that remained in her gums. 'I've come to see if you will have me keen. Your Martin was a good man.'

Nóra looked at Nance dripping in front of her. Her clothes, heavy with water, hung off narrow shoulder blades, but for all her layers of sopping wool she had a certain presence. There was a sharp, bitter smell coming off her. Like bruised nettles, thought Nóra. Or rotting leaves. The smell of someone who lived close to the forest floor.

'How did you know to come?' asked Nóra.

'I saw that new priest on his ass, beating the dust out of the animal. Only the Devil or a dying man would drive a priest into a wet and dirty night.'

'Father Healy.'

'I had the knowledge then that it was your man, Martin. God rest his soul,' she added.

An icy thread ran the length of Nóra's spine. Thunder sounded.

'The knowledge?'

Nance nodded and reached for Nóra. Her fingers were cold and surprisingly smooth.

Healer's palms, thought Nóra. 'And so you've walked all the way in the wet and wind.'

'No one becomes a worse person for rain on her head. I would do a great deal more for your man.'

Nóra opened the door and flicked the mud off her feet. 'Well, come in so. Seeing as you're here.'

'I will.'

The conversation inside the crowded cabin halted as Nóra led Nance into the room. All eyes looked to the older woman, who stopped inside the doorway and gazed about her, chin raised.

'God save all here,' she said. Her voice was thin, husked with smoke and age.

The men nodded to her in respect. A few of the women looked Nance up and down, noting the thick clag of mud that clung to the hem of her skirt, her weathered face, her soaked shawl. Seán Lynch glared before turning his face to the fire.

John O'Donoghue rose, his blacksmith's bulk suddenly filling the room. 'And you, Nance Roche. God save you.' He moved forward to lead her to the fire, and the other men immediately made room by the hearth. Peter, pipe in mouth, fetched a creepie stool and placed it firmly down by the coals, and Áine brought water for her dirty feet. Daniel offered Nance a small nip of *poitín*, and when she shook her head, the young man mumbled, ''Tis not a drop big enough to fit a wren's bill,' and pressed it into her hand.

Those who had fallen silent resumed their talk once they saw Nance was welcome. Only Seán and Kate Lynch retreated to the shadows where they slouched, watching.

Nance extended her bare toes to the embers, sipping her spirits. Nóra sat beside her, dread unspooling in her stomach as she watched the steam rise from the old woman's shoulders. How had she known Martin had died?

The old woman took a deep breath and raised a hand towards the bedroom. 'He's in there?'

'He is,' Nóra answered, heart fluttering.

Nance cradled her cup. 'When was his hour?'

'John and Peter brought him to me when it was still light. Before evening.' Nóra looked at the ground. The close air of the cabin after the clean night outdoors was making her feel sick. There was too much pipe smoke. Too much noise. She wished she could go outside and lie on the soft slick of mud, breathe in the smell of rain and be alone. Let the lightning strike her.

Nóra felt Nance's hands close around her fingers. The tenderness in her touch was alarming. She fought the urge to push the woman away.

'Nóra Leahy. You listen to me,' Nance whispered. 'For all the death in the world, each woman's grief is her own. It takes a different shape with all of us. But the sad truth is that people will not want your grief a year after you bury your husband. 'Tis the way of it. They'll go back to thinking of themselves. They'll go back to their own lives. So let us mourn Martin now, while they will listen. While they have the patience for it.'

Nóra nodded. She felt like she would throw up.

'And, Nóra, tell me. What's all this muttering about him passing at the crossroads? Is that true?'

''Tis.' It was Brigid who had spoken. She was cutting tobacco at the table behind them. 'Peter O'Connor found him there. A dreadful sorrow.'

Nance turned her head, squinting. 'And who are you?'

'Brigid Lynch.'

'My nephew Daniel's wife,' Nóra explained.

Nance frowned. 'You are carrying. Young Brigid, you ought not to be in a corpse house.'

Brigid stopped cutting the plugs of tobacco and stared.

'You have a right to leave. Before you breathe the death in and infect your child with it.'

'Is that true?' Brigid dropped the knife on the table. 'I knew to stay out of the churchyard, but . . .'

'Churchyard, corpse house, grave mound.' Nance spat on the fire.

Brigid turned to Nóra. 'I don't want to leave Daniel,' she whispered. 'I don't like to go out when 'tis dark. And 'tis storming. I don't want to go alone.'

'No.' Nance shook her head. 'Don't you go alone. 'Tis an uneasy night.'

Brigid pressed both hands against the round of her stomach.

Nance waved at Áine, who was handing out filled pipes to the men. 'Áine O'Donoghue, will you take this girl to a neighbour's? Take her husband too, so he might come back with you. 'Tis no night for a soul to be alone on the road.'

'Take her to Peg O'Shea's,' Nóra muttered. 'She's closest.'

Áine looked between the women. 'What is it? What's wrong?'

''Tis for the good of the young one's child.' Nance reached out and placed her wrinkled hand on Brigid's belly. 'Make haste, girl. Put some salt in your pocket and leave. This storm is brewing.'

By midnight Nóra's cabin was oppressive with the smell of wet wool and the sourness of too many people in a crowded room. The eyelids of Martin Leahy were bright with two pennies, placed there by a neighbour, and there was a crusted saucer of salt balanced on his chest. A plate of tobacco and coltsfoot sat on the dead man's stomach. The air was unbearably close, smoke-rich, as the men nudged their lips with clay pipes, borrowing Nóra's knitting needles to tap out the ashes and wiping them on their trousers.

At the approach of midnight John O'Donoghue recited a rosary for the dead, and the company knelt and mumbled their responses. Then the men retreated to the walls of the cabin and watched the women keen the body by the poor light of the rush tapers, stinking of fat and burning too quickly from their brass pinch.

Nance Roche led the wailing against the muted cracking of thunder. Her forehead was grey with ashes, her hands blackened from where she had smeared cold cinders on the foreheads of the other women. Nóra Leahy felt each powdered cheek split with the hot, wet path of her tears. She knelt on the ground and looked up at the circle of familiar faces, furrowed in solemnity.

This is a nightmare, she thought.

Nance closed her eyes, let her mouth slip open, and began a low lament that vanquished the small conversation of the men like an airless room snuffs a flame. She crouched on the clay floor and rocked back and forth, her hair loosened and thin over her shoulders. She cried without pause, without words. Her keen was hollow, fear-filled. It reminded Nóra of the *bean sídhe*, of the silent, scrabbling death-yawns of drowning men

As Nance keened, the other women muttered prayers for the dead, asking God to accept Martin Leahy's departed soul. Nóra noticed Kate Lynch, brown hair dull in the gloom, next to her kneeling daughter, Sorcha, dimpled and whispering, and Éilís O'Hare, the schoolmaster's wife, crossing herself in a latticework of prayer, one eye open to Nance as she clawed the firelight. Her neighbours and their daughters. The glut of valley women, all wringing their hands. Nóra shut her eyes. None of them knew how she felt. None of them.

It was frightening, to be unbridled from language and led into anguish by the *bean feasa*. Nóra opened her mouth and did not recognise her own voice. She moaned and the sound of her grief scared her.

Many in the room were moved to tears by the *caoineadh* of the women. They bent their damp heads and praised Martin Leahy with tongues loosened by *poitín*, naming the qualities that recommended him to God and man. The fine father of a daughter, gone to God only months before. A decent husband. A man who had the gift for bone-setting, and whose wide hands could always calm horses in a hackle of panic.

Nance's moan dropped to a low ragged breathing. Sweeping up a sudden fistful of ash, she threw her body towards the yard door of the cabin, flinging the cinders towards it. Ashes to banish Those that would restrain a soul's flight into the other world. Ashes to sanctify the grieving of kith and kin and mark it as holy.

Amidst the prayers, Nance slowly dropped her head to her knees, wiped the ash from her face with her skirts, and rose from the floor. The keening had finished. She waited until the words and cries of those in the room subsided into respectful silence, and then, nodding at Nóra, retired to a dark corner. She knotted her white hair at the nape of her neck and accepted a clay pipe, and spent the rest of the night smoking thoughtfully, watching the womenfolk and mourners circle Nóra like birds above a new-shorn field.

The night ground down the hours. Many of the people, dulled and comforted by the heady fumes of burning coltsfoot, lay down to sleep on the floor, plumping beds out of heather and rushes and slurring prayers. Rain escaped down the chimney and fell hissing on the fire. A few kept their eyes open with stories and gossip, taking turns to bless the body and finding omens in the thunderstorm that thrashed the valley outside. Only Nóra saw the old woman rise from her corner, slip her hood back over her head and retreat into the darkness and the howling world.

CHAPTER
TWO

Furze

Nance Roche woke in the early morning, before the fog had eased off the mountains. She had slept in the clothes she had returned home in and their damp had spread to her bones. Pushing herself up from her bed of heather, Nance allowed her eyes to adjust to the low light and rubbed at the cold in her limbs. Her fire was out – only the faintest suggestion of warmth met her outstretched hand. She must have fallen asleep in front of its heat before she could preserve the embers.

Taking her shawl off a hook in the wall, she wrapped herself in the rough wool and familiar smell of hearth smoke, and stepped outside, snatching a water can as she left.

The storm had thrashed the valley with rain all night and the woods behind her stunted cabin dripped with water. The fog was thick, but from her place at the far end of the valley, where the fields and bouldered slopes met the uncleared wood-land, she could hear the roar of the river Flesk's swollen waters. A short distance away from her cabin was the Piper's Grave, where the fairies dwelt. She nodded respectfully towards the crooked whitethorn, standing ghostlike in the mist in its circle of stone, briars and overgrown grass.

Nance tightened the shawl around her, joints creaking as she walked to the sodden ditch left by a collapsed badger set. Squatting unsteadily over the edge, she pissed with her eyes shut, her fingers holding on to bracken stalks for balance. Her whole body ached. It often did after a night of keening. As soon as Nance left any corpse house, a great, pulsing headache would swell in her skull.

'Tis the borrowed grief, thought Nance. To stand in the doorway between life and death racks the body and bleeds the brain.

The slope down to the river was slippery with mud and Nance stepped carefully, wet autumn leaves slicked to the bare soles of her feet as she made her way through the brushwood. It would not do to fall. Only last winter she had slipped and hurt her back. It had been a painful week in front of the fire then, but the worst of it was that, injured, she had felt herself crease with isolation. She had thought she had grown used to a life alone, that the skittering presence of birds sufficed for company. But without visitors, without anything to do but rest in the darkness of the cabin, she had felt so violently lonely she had cried.

'If there is one thing that will sink sickness deeper into the body, 'tis loneliness.'

Mad Maggie had told her that. In the early days, when Nance was young. When her father was still alive.

'Mark my words, Nance. That man who came by just now? No wife. Few friends. No brothers or sisters. The only thing keeping him company is his gout, and 'tis the loneliness of him keeping it there.'

Maggie sitting in their cabin, pipe in mouth, plucking a chicken. Feathers in the air. The rain pelting outside. Feathers resting in her wild hair.

That fall was a warning, Nance thought. You are old. You have only yourself to rely upon. Since then she had minded her body with tenderness. Steady steps on grass slippery with weather. No more reckless journeys to cut heather on the mountains when the wind growled. An eye to the fire and its crush of embers. A careful hand with the knife.

The roar from the Flesk grew louder as Nance drew closer, until she could see the white foam of the current teeming at the top of the riverbank through the surrounding trunks of oak, alder and ash. The storm had stripped the trees of their remaining leaves, and the wood was black and tannic with moisture. Only the birch trees, moon-pale, shone in the wet.

Nance picked her way around the broken branches that littered the ground and the tangles of ivy and withered bracken sprawling over the bank. Folk did not often frequent this end of the valley. The women did not come for their water or washing this far upriver because of the Piper's Grave, the lurking fairy fort, and there was a feel of neglect and wildness from their absence. The stones had not been scuffed clean of their moss and the briars had not been cut back for fear of them snagging on laundry. Only Nance came to the water's edge here. Only Nance did not mind living so close to the woods that claimed this part of the river.

The storm had infuriated the current and Nance saw that the stones she usually trusted to take her weight had been dislodged by the high water. The bank crumbled underfoot. The river was not especially wide or deep here, but when in flood the current was strong, and Nance had seen it fatten with swollen-stomached foxes washed out of their holes by fast and violent rains. She did not want to drown.

Taking off her shawl and draping it on a low branch, Nance sank to her knees and crept as close to the river as possible. She lowered her can and the water surged into it, pulling at her arm.

Rubbing her skirts free of leaf litter and soil, Nance shuffled back up to her cabin, trying to clear the fog from her mind. Small wrens swooped the grass and brambles, darting in and out of the mist and its suggestion of light. Mushrooms scalloped out from rotting wood in the undergrowth. The smell of damp soil was everywhere. How Nance preferred to be outside, with the great, wide ceiling of sky and the ground full of life. Her squat cabin, half dug into the ground and slouched in front of the woods with walls of wattle and mud, thatched with potato stalks and heather, seemed ugly and squalid compared to the dripping canopy of trees. She paused and looked down the valley, away from the woods. The whitewashed cabins of the cottiers lay scattered across the curve of the cultivated fields, now stubbled and browning, potato patches with loose-stoned walls beside them. She could see smoke rising from their roofs through the thinning mist. On the bare mountain sides the cabins grew smaller, dug more deeply into the ground to sturdy them against the wind. Their limed walls seemed blue in the morning gloom. Nance cast a look up to where the Leahys' cabin lay on the slope of the hillside. It was the cabin closest to her, and yet even that house seemed far away.

No one lived within calling distance of Nance. Her own window-less cabin, once whitewashed like the others, had flaked and greened with moss and mould over the years, until it looked as though the woods had claimed it as their own.

At least the inside of her little home was as clean and tidy as she could make it, no matter the ceiling crusted with soot and the damp in the corner. The dirt floor was swept and unpocked, and heather and rushes tempered the mustiness of the hay where her goat stood tethered at one end of the room.

Nance stirred the fire into life and left the water pail to settle. The storm had muddied the river and she must be careful not to drink it too quickly.

Never had she felt so weary after keening. Her bones felt rimed with exhaustion. She needed to eat something, a mouthful to feel restored.

The death cry had come on strongly last night. With the ashes on her face, Nance had felt the world shiver apart and had abandoned herself to the wail that rose from her lungs. Dizziness had come upon her, and the room of dark-clothed men and women had spun until all she could see was the fire and, in the smoke, images. An oak tree burning in a forest. A river surrounded by wild iris, yolked with yellow. And then, finally, her mother, hair falling into wild eyes, beckoning her into the dark. She had felt she was mourning the world.

Sometimes, in the company of suffering, Nance felt things. Maggie had called it an inward seeing. The knowledge. Sometimes, as she guided babies from their mothers and into the world, she sensed what their lives would be like, and sometimes the things she sensed frightened her. She remembered delivering a child whose mother had cursed him in her pain and fear, and she had sensed a darkness fall on him. She had cleaned and swaddled the infant, then later, as the mother slept, crushed a worm in his palm for protection.

There were things you could do to answer visions, Nance knew.

She had been troubled by the storm last night. Walking down the mountain slope from the Leahys' cabin under a sky welted with lightning, she had felt movement. Had felt things shifting in the darkness. A summoning. A warning. She had stopped by the fairy fort and waited in the rain with a tug of expectation and portent in her chest, and while the wind blasted the whitethorn, the limestone in the *ráth* flashed purple. She had half expected to see the Devil himself step out of the woods beyond her cabin. Nance did not usually feel afraid to leave a corpse house alone. She knew how to guard her body and soul with ash and salt. But last night, as she waited by the Piper's Grave, she felt vulnerable to whatever unseen presence tremored in the black. It wasn't until she saw lightning strike the mountain high behind her cabin and set fire to the heather that she had understood that something was indeed abroad and had hurried home to her fire and to the company of her animals.

Nance looked over to where her goat stood amongst the nesting hens, impatient in her corner. A drain had been hollowed out of the dirt floor to separate the animal and her leavings from Nance's own quarter, while allowing her warmth to give heat to the room. Nance stepped over the rivulet of waste and water and placed a gentle hand on the goat's head, smoothing the hair on her cheek and combing her beard free of straw.

'You're a good girl, Mora. Faith, what a grand girl you are.' Nance pulled a stool out from the wall and set it beside the goat alongside an armful of beaten furze.

'Is it famished you are? What a great wind there was. Did you not hear it? Were you not afraid?' Nance crooned to the goat, slowly reaching for a tin pail. She leant her forehead on the animal's wiry coat and breathed in her warm odour of dried whin and manure. Mora was skittish and stamped, her hoofs dull against the packed earth and hay, but Nance hummed until she quieted and began to nibble at the dry furze. Nance took hold of her teats and milked, singing softly, her voice cracked from the keening the night before.

When the udder's stream failed, Nance wiped her hands on her skirt and picked up the tin. Stepping to the doorway, she tipped a little onto the threshold for the Good People, and drank the milk, sweet and warm and flecked with the dirt from her own hands, straight from the pail.

No one would come for her today, Nance knew. The valley folk would be swarming the house of the Leahys to pay their respects to the dead and, besides, people did not often come to her at a time like this. She reminded them too much of their own mortality.

The keener. The handy woman. Nance opened her mouth and people thought of the way things went wrong, the way one thing became another. They looked at her white hair and saw twilight. She was both the woman who brought babies to safe harbour in the world, and the siren that cut boats free of their anchors and sent them into the dark.

Nance knew that the only reason they had allowed her this damp cabin between mountain and wood and river for twenty-odd years was because she stood in for that which was not and could not be understood. She was the gatekeeper at the edge of the world. The final human hymn before all fell to wind and shadow and the strange creaking of stars. She was a pagan chorus. An older song.

People are always a little afraid of what they do not recognise, Nance thought.

Warmed and comforted by the goat's milk, Nance wiped her mouth on her sleeve and leant against her doorframe, gazing out to the valley. Above, the sky had unfurled to the grey of dirty fleece, but Nance knew the day would be clear. She would be free to sleep and rest, and perhaps walk the lanes and ditches in the quiet of the afternoon to gather the last of the flowering yarrow and ragwort, the last blackberries and sloes, before winter brittled the world. Whatever remaining rain lingered in the clouds would pass beyond the mountains before breaking.

In all things Nance bent her hours to the sky. She knew its infinite faces.

The wake went on for two days, during which the people of the valley walked the mud-slick path to Nóra's mountainside cabin, some with whiskey bottles held tightly in their hands, rosaries tucked into pockets, others hauling their own stools and rough *súgán* chairs. Rain returned to the valley on the second day. Water dripped off the men's peaked caps and felt hats. They came with cold embers in their pockets and hazel sticks, and sat on wads of bracken amidst the strewn rushes. The air of the corpse house was grey, and people coughed amongst the burning lights of fire and pipe. They knelt and prayed for Martin, touching his sheeted body. The women and children, unused to the draw of a pipe, coughed and blew smoke over the corpse, masking the rough, rising smell of death.

Nóra thought they would never leave. She was sick of their company, the crush of the rushes beneath their feet, the way they sat and spoke of Martin as though they had known him best above all others.

I am his wife, she wanted to spit at them. You did not know him as I knew him.

She could not bear the way the women moved about the walls like shadows, gathering in tight clusters of gossip then disbanding to come and talk of time and faith and God. She hated the way the men spoke endlessly of the whoring October rain, and raised their rough-shod drink in Martin's direction to slur, 'May the Lord have mercy on your soul, Leahy, and on the souls of all the faithful departed,' before returning to their chuckling conversation.

It was only when the rain broke that Nóra was able to leave the cabin to relieve herself behind the house, and to take in great lungfuls of fresh air. She rubbed her hands in the wet grass beside the dung pile and wiped her face, pausing to watch the children play with stones in the yard. Shin-streaked with dirt and bright-eyed with the excitement of an occasion, they piled stones into cairns and took turns to knock them over. Even the shy girls squatted on the ground in pairs to play Poor Snipeen, one holding palms together in prayer while the other stroked their fingers gently. 'Poor Puss,' they murmured, before striking out at the hands in violence. Their slaps and cries of delighted pain echoed through the valley.

Nóra watched them play, a hard lump in her throat. This is what Micheál would be doing if he were not ill, she thought, and she was overcome with a wave of grief so sudden she gasped.

It would be different if he were well, she thought. He would be a comfort to me.

There was a tug on her skirt and Nóra looked down to see a boy of no more than four smiling up at her, an egg in his hand.

'I found this,' he said, and placed it in her palm before scarpering off, bare feet kicking up mud. Nóra stared after him. Here is what a child ought to be, she thought, and pictured Martin holding Micheál before the fire, rubbing his legs to restore the life to them, the boy's eyes closing at the touch of his grandfather's hand.

Nóra blinked quickly to stop the tears from coming and looked out to the horizon.

A curtain of rain was slowly moving across the mountains on the far side of the valley, beyond the low land where the river ran, and the crouch of woods to the east. Other than a few ash trees around the white cabins scattered about the dale on untilled ground, and the tangle of oak and alder beyond Nance Roche's greening *bothán* in the distance, the valley was a broad expanse of fields ribboned with low stone walls and ditches, flanked with bog ground and rough hillside where little else but furze and heather grew amongst the slabs of rock.

Even under the low rainclouds, it was a sight that calmed Nóra. The valley was beautiful. The slow turning towards winter had left the stubble on the fields and the wild grasses bronzed, and the scutter of cloud left shadows brooding across the soil. It was its own world. Only the narrow road, wending through the flat of the valley floor, indicated the world beyond the mountains to the west: the big houses and copper mines, the cramped streets of Killarney bristling with slated buildings and beggars, or, to the east, the distant markets of Cork. Only the occasional merchant headed towards Macroom, his horses' sides laden with casks of butter, suggested that there were other valleys, other towns, where different folk led different lives.

There was a shout of laughter from the children, and Nóra was startled out of her reverie. She turned to see an old woman making her way over the uneven ground from the cabin closest on the hillside, leaning heavily on a blackthorn stick.

Peg O'Shea.

Her neighbour smiled at the children as she entered the yard, then caught Nóra's eye and shuffled towards her.

'Nóra. I'm so sorry for your trouble.' Her neighbour had the sunken cheeks of the very old, her lips curling inwards from loss of teeth. Her eyes, however, were wren-black and beady. Nóra felt them pass over her face, taking her measure.

'God and Mary to you, Peg. Thank you for taking Micheál.'

''Tis no trouble at all.'

'I didn't want him here. The house is full of people. I thought . . . I thought he might be frightened.'

Peg said nothing, pursing her lips.

'Martin and I, we thought 'twould be best if we kept him from crowds. Kept him quiet with us.'

'Aye, could be.'

'Who has an eye to him?'

'Oh, the house is full of my children and their weans. They give Micheál no mind. And 'tis not as though he'll be wandering off.' She leant closer. 'I didn't know 'twas so bad with him. All these months you've been caring for the boy . . .'

'Martin and I both. We managed between us. The one could mind him while the other worked.'

'How old is he, Nóra?'

'Four.'

'Four. And no more able to speak than a baby.'

Nóra looked down at the egg the little boy had given her, tracing a fingertip upon the shell. ''Tis the illness upon him.'

Peg was silent.

'He has the ability for it. I heard him speak before. When Johanna was alive.'

'Was he walking then too?'

Nóra felt ill. She shook her head, unable to answer, and Peg placed a hand on her shoulder. 'The sky has the appearance of rain. Let's inside to rest our bones. I'll pay my respects.'

The turf fire was at a high blaze inside the cabin, and the conversation amongst the visitors was loud. Laughter spilt from a corner.

'Mmm.' Peg's dark eyes flitted over the company in the room. 'Who brought the drink then?'

'Seán Lynch brought most of it,' Nóra replied.

Peg raised her eyebrows.

'I know. 'Twas not something I expected. Not a generous man.'

'The only thing that man is generous with is his fists.' She cast a sly look to where Kate sat amongst the women, picking at her teeth. 'Seán Lynch would skin a louse and send the hide and fat to market. I wonder what he's after.'

Nóra shrugged. 'We're kin. Don't you forget that my sister married his brother, God rest their souls.'

Peg sniffed. 'Faith, he's up to something. I'd keep an eye to him, Nóra. He'll be wanting something from you now Martin is gone. That one knows the price of everything and the value of nothing.'

They stared across the room to where Seán sat smoking by the fire.

'Believe me, Nóra. An old broom knows the dirty corners best.'

*

They carried the body of Martin to his grave the following afternoon under a colourless sky. The nephews and friends of the man shouldered the rough coffin, followed by other valley men, who would occasionally take turns at carrying the box. It was a long, familiar journey to the graveyard along the road, and the way was slow going. The rains had softened the path into mud and the men trod carefully, anxious not to lose their boots in the suck of it. The women walked behind, sending their cries up into the autumn air, studded with cold. They all knew the way to lead a body to soil.

Nóra gripped her shawl tightly over her head. She could not bear to look at the coffin bobbing beyond the heads in front, and instead cast her eyes to the birds spiralling above the balding branches. She felt strangely dry-eyed, and as she walked through the puddles, glossy with sky, she wondered if some small part of her had died too. The women around her seemed ridiculous in their lamentations, their wet skirts clinging to their legs. Nóra held her tongue still and let her grief sit in her like a stone.

The sight of a funeral drew people from the cabins that sat close upon the road. Children stared with their fingers in their mouths. Men letting their pigs graze on the lane joined the crowd to share a few paces with them, then stepped aside and waited solemnly for them to move on before slapping their pigs' sides with a switch.

Nóra kept her head tilted to the sky, letting the crowd push her onwards. Eagles circled above the hill heights.

The graveyard, slouched next to the little church and shadowed by an old yew tree, was overgrown, green with grass. The men stumbled over the tussocks and carefully set the coffin down beside the hole that had been dug in readiness. Father Healy was waiting for them, slack-jawed and slumped with the spine of a scholar. When his gaze sought out Nóra she pulled her shawl low over her forehead and cast her eyes to the ground.

The service was brief. The priest led the prayers in his halting voice, and Nóra felt the wet ground seep through her skirts as she knelt. She watched as her husband was lowered into the ground, watched as the gravediggers lay sods of grass over the lid of the coffin so that the earth might fall gently upon the wood.

When all was done and there were no more words to be said, and the hole had been filled with the rough black soil of the valley, the people placed their clay pipes upon the grave mound and left. As the crowd followed the curve of the hill down towards the valley, Nóra looked back at the churchyard. From a distance the pipe stems looked like nothing more than a smattering of slender bones, cleaned by birds.

The wind rose as Nóra walked the road after the funeral, at first in a crowd, and then, as people turned off towards their own cabins, in a smaller, silent number. By the time she was hobbling past the ash trees and up the muddy slope to her house, she was alone and the wind was peeling off the mountain crags into the valley, full of bite. A hard rain had started to sting and her knees felt the promise of another storm.

As Nóra approached the cabin she could hear screaming coming from inside. Micheál. The door was ajar, and as she entered she noticed that her house had been cleaned, all evidence of the wake removed. New rushes lay spread on the floor, a bright fire was burning and Peg O'Shea was seated next to it, cradling Micheál and laughing at Brigid, who was wincing at his pitching voice. 'You'd best be getting used to that,' Peg was saying, rocking the red-faced boy. Her smile faded as Nóra walked in.

'Martin is buried, then.'

Nóra sank down on the settle bed next to Brigid, relieved to have the house empty of people.

'And a crowd to bury him too. That's a blessing. Move up to the fire. You'll perish in the cold.'

Nóra held out her arms for Micheál and leant her cheek against his head. The weight of him in her arms, and the ragged, humid cries addressing her skin, made her feel careworn. Her bare toes ached with the cold.

Peg was watching her. 'They're a comfort, children.'

Nóra closed her eyes and pushed her face into the fragile scoop of his neck. His chest tightened beneath her hands as he screamed.

'Thank you for minding him.'

'Don't you say another word about it. I've been praying for you, Nóra. God knows 'tis been a bad and troubling year for ye.'

Nóra released her hold on Micheál, laying him out on her lap. Tears streamed down his face. She began to rub his limbs as she had seen Martin do, straightening his wrists back from where they bent inwards, fingers as stiff as pokers. At her touch Micheál ceased crying, and for a moment she thought he looked at her. His pupils, so dark against the blue of his eyes, seemed to fix on her own. Her heart leapt. Then his gaze slid from her face and he began to howl, his hands buckling back into crooks.

Nóra stopped rubbing him and stared. She was struck with the memory of Martin holding Micheál in his broad hands, spooning cream into his mouth.

How could you leave me alone with this child, she thought.

Peg reached across the hearth and gently smoothed Micheál's hair. 'Sure, he has Johanna's colour.'

Brigid glanced at Nóra.

'I know she was a great loss to you,' Peg continued. '*Is é do mhac do mhac go bpósann sé ach is í d'iníon go bhfaighidh tú bás*. Your son is your son until he marries, but your daughter is your daughter until you die. And now, to lose your man . . . Isn't God cruel, taking those we love most?'

'We all bear our cross,' Nóra murmured. She lifted Micheál higher onto her lap. 'What's troubling you then, little one?'

'Oh, Nóra, he's been squalling fit to wake the dead, the poor cratur. Full of noise and tears, and for what? All these days past too. How do you sleep with him crying so at all hours?'

Micheál screamed louder than before. Tears crawled down his flushed cheeks.

'Did you feed him?' Brigid asked, taking Nóra's cloak from the settle and draping it across the low beam by the fire.

'Did I feed him?' Peg gave Nóra a glinting look. 'I've had five of them myself, and sure, Brigid, 'tis a miracle they all lived to have their own, for I never once fed them but set them to the wind. I'll say, 'tis a good thing you know what you're doing, for the moon looks full with you.' She sucked her remaining teeth. 'Such company you send me, Nóra. This wean and *cailín*. Well, 'twas right to be keeping them away from the trouble.'

'I hope I've kept it out of danger.' Brigid put a protective hand over her stomach. 'Dan wouldn't have me in the house for the pig kill.'

'I knew a woman once,' said Peg. 'She was a doughty thing, had no time for old ways and full of pride. Well, didn't she set herself on catching the blood off the table when the time came for slaughter? And didn't her husband try to stop her? But for all the strong man he was, she had her way. And you can be sure, that child she was carrying came out with a face like raw liver and a mood to match.'

A dull murmur of thunder rolled overhead and Brigid grimaced. 'Is that so?'

'Oh, you wouldn't tempt the Devil. You wouldn't be messing with blood or bodies in your state.'

'It put the fear on me, what that old biddy said. The one with the white hair.'

'The *bean feasa*? Sure, Nance Roche has a peculiar way.'

'I haven't seen her before. I thought she was only a kind of handy woman.'

'Have you not? No, well, she keeps to herself. Until she feels the call on her. Or others go calling for her.'

'Or there's the promise of a warm cabin and a bite to eat,' Nóra added. 'I've never gone to her for the cure, and Martin only once or twice. And yet there she was at the wake. To keen.'

Peg gave Nóra a searching look. 'She has a way of knowing when she's needed.' Her voice was quiet.

'But why have I not heard anyone say she has the knowledge?' Brigid asked.

'Begod, whether you go to her or not, 'tis not something you talk about. People go to her for the things you wouldn't want a priest to know about, or your own mother to see. And well, sure, there's some folk think her name brings misfortune. She puts the fright on them.'

Brigid leant forward, curious. 'And why's that? What did she do?'

'A great crime to be sure.' Peg winked. 'She lives by the woods on her own. That's enough to set tongues going. There's plenty that go to her though. Aye, they do be saying she has the cure. Not like some of them who say they have the charms when all they have is a desire to part you with your whiskey.'

'I knew a Cahill, a cousin of my mam, he had the cure for the shingles.'

Nóra clucked her tongue and rocked Micheál. The exhausted child was finally falling into a whimpering sleep. 'Folk come all the way from Ballyvourney for the charms of Nance Roche. Eight hours hard walking for a man there and back, all for her to whisper something in his ear and look at his warts.'

Peg nodded. 'Musha, Nance of the Fairies, they call her. Nance *na bPúcaí*. There are plenty that will have nothing to do with her on account of it but more who go to her because they believe it so.'

'Do you believe it, Nóra?'

Nóra shook her head dismissively. 'I don't like to talk of it. The world is full of things I don't pretend to understand. They used to say she was going with the Good People, whether 'twas true or not.'

'Peg,' Brigid whispered, glancing to the door as if suddenly expecting it to fly open, 'is she in league with Them? What does the priest say?'

'Father O'Reilly always had a kind word for her when he still walked this earth. Some men of the Church might say she's no person of God, but those who have gone to her say she never performed any cure, only in the name of the Blessed Trinity. Oh, did you hear that now?'

Nóra flinched at the low growl of thunder. 'God be between us and harm.'

'Does she not have a man? Children?'

'No husband I ever heard of. Peg?'

The old woman smiled. 'Not unless she has a fairy man out by the *ráth*. Or that old goat of hers is really her husband, changed by the Good People.' She laughed, as if tickled by the idea.

Brigid was thoughtful. 'The way she came in, her hair all wet and the white lips of her. She looked like a ghost. She looked like someone'd been spending the night trying to drown her in a puddle. And the eyes of her – the fog in them. How can a woman with the cure be going about with eyes like that in her head?'

'You'd do well to keep on the right side of Nance Roche,' Nóra admitted.

Peg chuckled and wiped her gums with a corner of her apron. 'Brigid, all you need to know is that woman was born at the dead hour of night and so has a different way of seeing.'

'Has she always lived here?'

'Oh, long enough now to scare my children and my children's children. But not born here, no. I remember when she came. There were lots of people on the road in those times. Nance was just another poor wandering woman. The priest took pity on her, young as she was then, with no soul to help her. The men built her a *bothán*, just a wee room of mud by the wood. No potato garden to speak of, but she has chickens. And a goat. Oh, she's always put great store by goats. 'Tis all well for a woman to be living off sloes and hazelnuts and *praiseach* in the kinder months, but when she first came we were all expecting her to come knocking and begging for lumpers come winter. But didn't she keep to herself, and didn't she stay that winter, and the next and the next, until folk started saying that 'twas not a natural thing for a woman like her to be living fat off weeds and berries. Some thought she was stealing at night. Others thought she was in league with Himself.'

'The Devil?'

There was a loud clap of thunder. The women jumped.

'What a night to be telling of these things!' Nóra exclaimed.

'Sure, Nance was a queer one from the start.'

'Is it not time to eat? Are you hungry? Peg, will you be staying? 'Tis no night for walking.' For all her desire to be alone during Martin's wake, Nóra suddenly longed for company. The thought of spending the storming evening alone with Micheál made her stomach clutch in dread.

Peg looked around the empty cabin and, as if sensing Nóra's reluctance, nodded. 'I will, if 'tis no trouble to you.'

'Shall I take Micheál?' Brigid offered.

'I'll set him down.' Nóra laid the boy in a makeshift cradle of sally twigs and straw.

'He's a bit too big for that now, is he not?' Peg asked. 'His legs don't fit at all.'

Nóra ignored her. 'I'll go for the milk and then I'll get us a bite to eat.' Another roll of thunder sounded above the rain and the spitting turf fire. 'What a dirty night.'

Peg gave Brigid's belly a gentle pat. ''Tis a good thing you're here with your man's aunt and not out in the dark.' Her eyes narrowed. 'The thunder kills the unhatched birds in their eggs.'

'Peg O'Shea! Don't be frightening her with tall talk.' Nóra lifted a heavy pot of water onto the chain hanging from the hearth wall, squinting in the smoke.

'Go see to the beast, Nóra. She'll be in pieces from the storm.' Peg turned to Brigid. 'The lightning does be taking the profit from the milk. There'll be some fearful churning after tonight, you mark my words.'

Nóra shot Peg a stern look and pulled her wet cloak from its rafter and back over her head. She stepped out into the night with her pail, stumbling in the sudden wind, rain lashing against her face. She lurched towards the byre, eager to escape the downpour.

The cow blinked at her in the dark, eyes round in fear.

'There, Brownie. Easy with you.' Nóra ran her hands over the cow's flank, but when she reached for the stool and placed the pail on the ground, the beast started and pulled at her rope.

'No harm will come to you, girl,' Nóra crooned, but Brownie moaned. There's a fright in her, Nóra thought, and hauled an armful of hay into the bracket. The cow ignored it, panting, and as soon as Nóra took hold of her teats, the cow skittered sideways, leg kicking in its spancel. The pail clattered across the floor. Nóra got up, irritated.

Lightning flashed outside.

'Have it your way, would you,' Nóra muttered, and snatching the pail, she pulled the sodden cloak back over her head. She staggered back through the pelting darkness towards the cabin, pausing under the thatch to scrape the mud from her feet. As she wiped her heel on the step she heard Peg's voice, low with conspiracy, coming from inside.

'Wee Micheál. Would you look at him. He's an ill-thriven thing.'

Nóra froze.

'I heard Martin and Nóra had a cripple child with them. Is it true he hasn't taken a step yet?'

Brigid.

Nóra's heart began to hammer.

'I doubt he ever will! Four years old and the state of him! I knew Nóra was after caring for Johanna's boy, and that there was little keeping body and soul together when he came to them, but one like this? He hasn't the whole of his sense.'

Nóra felt her face flush, despite the chill. Hardly breathing, she pressed her eye to a gap in the wood. Brigid and Peg were staring at the boy.

'Has herself fetched the priest for him?'

'To heal him? I've always believed a priest has the power if he wants to use it. But Father Healy is a busy man. A man from the towns – he's most like spent his life in Tralee or Killarney. And I don't think he will be troubling himself with poor wicker-legged boys.'

Brigid was silent. 'I pray to God that mine is right.'

'Please God he will be. Keep yourself safe and warm. I suspect 'twas only when this one's mother sickened that he began to go soft in the head and his limbs moved to kippeens. I never heard a thing about a strange child while she was alive.'

Nóra's stomach dropped. Her own kin, sitting in her house, blacking her grandson. She pressed her face against the door, feeling her pulse jump in her throat.

'Did Nóra tell you that, so?'

Peg scoffed. 'What do you think? She won't have any talk about him. Why do you think she keeps him here like a clocking hen, and none of us knowing the state of him? Why do you think, with her husband just gone, she made Peter O'Connor bring him to me before there was a crowd in this place? 'Tis a rare soul who has set eyes on him, and for all us being kin, I'd not had a good look at the cratur until these past days. You can imagine the shock I had when I saw the boy.'

'She's shamed by him.'

'Well, something's not right. It must be a great burden. Her daughter dead – God have mercy on her – and now this ailing one to care for all alone.'

'She's doughty though. She'll get on.'

Nóra watched from behind the door as Peg leant back, running a tongue over her gums. 'She's got some spine, that woman. Nóra has always been a proud one. But I do be worried after her. Such a dark season of death and strangeness. Her daughter, and now Martin, and the child blighted with it all.'

'Peter O'Connor was saying he saw a light by the fairy *ráth* in the hour of Martin's passing. Said he thinks there's a third death coming.'

Peg crossed herself and threw another piece of turf on the fire. 'God protect us. Still, worse things have happened.'

Nóra hesitated. Rain dripped down her face, the damp of the cloak soaking into her clothes. She didn't care. She bit her lip, straining to hear what they were saying.

'Did Nance keen for Johanna?'

Peg sighed. 'She didn't, no. Nóra's girl married a Corkman some years back. She's buried there, somewhere out by Macroom. Nóra only heard Johanna had died when her son-in-law came to give her the child. Oh, 'twas a pity. Johanna's man appeared one night at dusk during the harvest just gone, Micheál strapped on a donkey. Told her that Johanna had wasted away and he a widower. Yes, a wasting sickness, the man said. One day she took to her bed with a pounding head and she never got up from it again. She faded day by day until she had gone completely. And he was in no place to care for the boy, and I know his people thought it only right that he be taken to Nóra and Martin. She never said a word like it, but there was a rumour that Micheál was half-starved when he came. A little bag of bones fit for a pauper's coffin.'

How dare she, thought Nóra. Gossiping about me on the day I bury my man. Spreading rumours about my daughter. Tears sprung to her eyes and she pulled away from the door.

'There's no shame in poverty.' Brigid's piping voice travelled over the sound of the wind. 'We all know the price of it.'

'There's no shame for some, but Nóra has always held her head high. Have you ever noticed that she doesn't talk of the dead? My own husband is long gone to God, and yet I talk of him as if he were still here. He remains with me in that way. But when Johanna died, 'twas as though Nóra struck her daughter's name from her tongue. I've no doubt she grieves, but any memories of her daughter she shares with the bottle alone.'

'Does she go the shebeen?'

'Sh. I don't know where Nóra gets her comfort, but if a woman can find peace in the drink, then who are we to grudge her for it.'

It was too much. Nóra hastily wiped her eyes and, jaw clenched, entered the kitchen, her cloak and face slick with rain. She shut the door against the storm and set the pail on the table under the window, packed with straw to keep the cold out.

The women were quiet. Nóra wondered if they guessed she had overheard them.

'Did she give much?' Peg eventually asked.

'She's spooked.' Nóra dragged her cloak off her shoulders and crouched by the fire to warm her hands, her eyes averted.

''Twas a time when we couldn't move for butter in this valley,' muttered Peg. 'Now every second cratur is blasted.'

Micheál murmured and, relieved for something to do, Nóra picked him up out of the cramped cradle. 'You great lad. Oh, the weight in him.'

Peg and Brigid exchanged looks.

'What were ye talking of?' Nóra asked.

'Our Brigid here was asking about Nance.'

'Is that so.'

''Tis. She can't hear enough.'

'Don't let me be interrupting you. Go on with your story, then.' Nóra thought she caught a glimpse of panic between the women.

'Well, now. As I was saying, folk back in the day thought it mighty strange for a woman to be living off thin air and dandelions. And they went to the priest about her. 'Twas not Father Healy, but the priest before him. Father O'Reilly, God have mercy on him. He would have none of their suspicion and gossip. "Leave the poor woman be," said he. Sure, Brigid, Father O'Reilly was a fierce man, a powerful man for those who had no voice or home for themselves. 'Twas he who urged the men to build her the cabin and sent them to her for the herbs and cures. He went to her himself. Terrible rheumatism.'

The water in the black pot trembled. Nóra, lips tight in anger, stared as the rain escaping down the chimney hole hit its iron sides.

'What happened next, then?' Brigid filled the silence.

Peg shifted in her seat, glancing at Nóra. 'Well, not long after Nance had got her cabin she began to get a name for herself. I was on the night-rambling one evening, down at Old Hanna's, and we got to be telling stories about the Good People. And Hanna starts telling us about a fairy bush, a *sceach gheal* that was very near cut down. It was your own Daniel's uncle, Seán Lynch, that was after doing it. Begod, he's some fool. Seán, he was a young man then, and he was up by the blacksmith's with the lads, boasting amongst themselves. Your man Seán was talking of cutting down the whitethorn and the lads were warning him against it. Somehow, word of his daring got back to Nance Roche. Surely you've seen where the tree stands, by the fairy *ráth*? She lives near it. And Nance went to Seán's cabin one night, frightened the life out of him and Kate by appearing in their doorway, and she tells him he'd best leave the whitethorn alone or They would be after him. "That is Their tree," says she. "Don't you be putting a hand to it, or I tell you, Seán Lynch, that you'll be suffering after it. Don't you be putting a hand to anything in violence." Well, didn't he laugh her off, calling her filthy names besides, and didn't he go to cut the *sceach gheal* that very day. Old Hanna said that she saw with her own eyes how Seán took a dirty great swing at the fairy whitethorn with his axe. No word of a lie, didn't Hanna see him miss the trunk completely. Didn't the axe swing through the air, missing the wood and land in his leg. He near cut himself in half. And that is why he has the limp.'

There was a soft gurgle from the floor and the women looked down to see Micheál staring at the rafters, a crooked smile on his face.

Nóra watched Peg lean forward and examine his face, her eyes thoughtful. 'He likes a story.'

'Go on, Peg,' Brigid urged. She was perched on the edge of the settle, the firelight full and flickering on her face.

'Well, that was the start of it. People saw in that axe swing proof Nance had the fairy knowledge, the *fios sigheog*. Folk started to go to her if they thought Them were abroad and at Their tricks. They thought perhaps she used to go with Them, which is how she got her way of understanding.'

'I never met a one who was taken by the Good People. I never met a one who was swept.' Brigid shuddered.

'I'll tell you something now, Brigid. This valley is full of old families. For all the folk on the roads, there's not often room for strangers that don't marry into the blood. Nance planted herself into this soil with herbs and death-cries and sure hands when a woman's time came. There was plenty that feared her after the whiterhorn, and there's plenty that fear her to this day, but there's more that need Nance. And as long as they need her, she'll be in that *bothán* by the woods. My man, when he was alive, woke one morning with his eye all swolled up and no seeing out of it. He took to Nance, and she said 'twas the fairies struck him in the eye. Said he must have seen them on the road, and 'twas not his right, so they brought the sight out of the eye that saw them. Said they spat in it when he was asleep. But she had the charm. She put the herb in his eye – *glanrosc*, I think it was – and cured the fairy spite out of it. Now, I don't know whether Nance was ever swept or not but there's no doubting that she has a gift. Whether that gift is God-given or a token from the Good People, well, that's not for us to know.'

'Will Nance be there when my time comes?'

'Sure, 'tis Nance for you.'

Nóra offered Micheál to Brigid, her voice cold. 'Hold him while I fix the tea.'

Brigid settled the boy awkwardly against the curve of her stomach. As if sensing Brigid's strangeness, Micheál stiffened, his arms shooting out from his sides. His mouth crumpled in discontent.

'He likes feathers,' Nóra said, easing potatoes into the steaming pot. 'Here.' She picked up a small downy feather that had escaped from the chicken roost and was blowing about the room in a draught. 'Martin always gave him a tickle.'

Brigid took the feather and stroked the boy's dimpled chin. He giggled, his chest in convulsions. Brigid started laughing with him. 'Will you look at that!'

''Tis a good sign,' said Peg, gesturing to the pair.

Nóra's smile emptied. 'A good sign of what?'

Peg picked up the iron tongs and idly poked the fire.

'Are you a deaf woman now? A good sign of what, Peg O'Shea?'

Peg sighed. 'A good sign that your Micheál might yet be well.'

Nóra pressed her lips together and continued tipping the last of the potatoes into the hot water. She flinched as it splashed her hand.

'We only mean well for the child,' Peg murmured.

'Do ye now?'

'Have you taken him to Nance, Nóra?' Brigid's voice was hesitant. 'I was thinking just now, it might be that he's fairy-struck.'

Silence filled the cabin.

Nóra suddenly dropped down on the floor. She brought her apron to her face and took a shuddering breath. She could smell the familiar scent of cow manure and wet grass.

'There now,' Peg whispered. ''Tis a hard day for you, Nóra Leahy. We had no right to talk of such things. God bless the child and see he grows up to be a great man. Like Martin.'

At the sound of her husband's name, Nóra groaned. Peg placed a hand on her shoulder and she shrugged it off.

'Forgive us. We only mean well. *Tig grian a n-diadh na fearthana.* Sunshine follows rain. Better times will be upon us soon, just wait and see.'

'Faith, God's help is nearer than the door,' Brigid piped.

The rafters creaked in the force of the wind. Micheál continued to laugh.

CHAPTER
THREE

Ragwort

S amhain Eve came upon the valley, announced by a wind that smelled of rotting oak leaves and the vinegar tang of windfall apples. Nóra heard the happy shrieks of children as they traced the field walls and their dressing of brambles, plucking the last bloody berries before night fetched the *púca* to poison them with his breath. They emerged from the ditches in the smoky peace of twilight like a band of murderers, their hands and mouths stained purple. Nóra watched them as they scrambled up the hills to their homes, some of the boys wearing dresses to deceive the fairies. It was a dangerous night to be caught outside. Tonight was a ghost night. The dead were close, and all the beings caught between Heaven and Hell would soon walk the cold loam.

They're coming, thought Nóra. From the graves and the dark and the wet. They're coming for the light of our fires.

The sky was fading. Nóra watched as two young boys were hustled indoors by their anxious mother. It was not the time to tempt the Devil or the fairies. People disappeared on Samhain Eve. Small children went missing. They were lured into ringforts and bogs and mountain sides with music and lights, and were never seen again by their parents.

Nóra remembered, as a very small girl, the fear and talk when a man from the valley did not return to his family's croft one Samhain Eve. They found him the next morning, naked and bleeding, curled into the soil and clutching yellow ragwort in his hands. He was abducted, her mother had told her. Taken to ride with the *sióga* until dawn broke out in feeble light and he was abandoned. Nóra had sat in the shadows, listening to the adults as they spoke in urgent whispers around her parents' fire. Wasn't he a poor soul to be found in such a way. His mother would die of the shame of it. A grown man, shivering and talking of the woods like a poor unfortunate.

'They took me,' he had muttered to the men of the valley when they helped him home, covering him with a coat and bearing his stagger on patient shoulders. 'They took me.'

The next evening the men and women had burnt all the ragwort from the fields to deprive the Good People of their sacred plant. Nóra could still remember the sight: tiny fires burning along the cant of the valley, winking in the darkness.

The brothers had reached their cabin and Nóra watched as their mother closed the door behind them. With a last, long look to the woods and the billhook moon rising over them, she made the sign of the cross and went indoors.

Her house seemed smaller, somehow, after the time outside. Nóra stood by the doorstep and looked at all she had left in the world. How it had changed in the month since Martin died. How empty it seemed. The crude hearth, the smoke of former fires blacking the wall behind it in a tapering shadow of soot. Her potato pot hanging from its chain and the wicker skib resting against the wall. The dash churn by the stopped-up window and the small table under it bearing two miserable pieces of delph and crocks for milk and cream. Even the remaining treasures from her dowry – the salt box on the wall, the butter print, the settle bed with its seat worn smooth from use – seemed dismal. Here was a widow's house. Martin's tobacco and pipe in the hearth's keeping hole were already covered with a film of ash. The low creepie stools were empty of company. The rushes on the floor had dried and powdered underfoot, their freshness long gone with no cause to replace them. There was little sign of life other than the fire's lazy burn, the murmuring of her chickens fluffed in their roost, and the twitching sleep of Micheál as he lay on a pile of heather in the corner of the cabin.

He is like Johanna, Nóra thought, examining her grandchild's face.

The boy looked unbearably smooth in sleep, bloodless and waxen. He had his father's furrow between chin and bottom lip that pushed his mouth out in a wet sulk, but his hair was Johanna's. Reddish and fine. Martin had loved it. Once or twice Nóra had entered the room to find her husband sitting with the boy, stroking his hair as he used to do with their daughter.

Nóra brushed the thin locks from Micheál's forehead, and for one moment, through the stinging blur, imagined that he was Johanna. If she squinted it was as though she was once again a young mother, her little girl sleeping before her. Copper-headed, sighing in sleep. Her only baby to draw breath and stick to life. An uncomplaining child with hair of down.

She remembered what Martin had said the night Johanna was born, swaying with a night empty of sleep and full of whiskey, jubilant and terrified and lightheaded. 'Wee dandelion,' he had said, stroking Johanna's feathery hair. 'Careful or the wind will come and blow you away and scatter you over the mountains.'

A proverb ran through her mind: Scattering is easier than gathering.

Nóra felt a sudden weight on her chest. Her little girl and her husband were gone. Scattered into the air and unreachable. Gone to God, gone to places where she, growing old and already too full of bones, too full of the weight of her years, ought to have gone first. She heard the breath in her throat rasping and snatched her hand away from Micheál.

Her daughter should still be alive. Should be as Nóra had found her when she and Martin had walked the full length of a day to Tadgh and Johanna's cabin in the moors, the first time Nóra had seen her daughter since the wedding. Johanna had seemed filled with happiness, waiting at the top of the lane against the flowering gorse and the sky, wide with light, her son in her arms. How she had smiled to see them. Proud to be a wife. Proud to be a mother.

'This is wee Micheál,' she had said, and Nóra had taken that little boy into her arms and blinked hard at the pricking of tears. How old had he been then? No more than two. But growing and well and soon tottering after the piglet that ran squealing about the damp floor of the cramped cabin.

'By my baptism, but he is the spit of you,' Martin had said.

Micheál had tugged on Johanna's skirt. 'Mammy?' And Nóra had noticed how her daughter swung her son onto her hip with practised ease, how she tickled him under the chin until he shrieked with laughter.

'The years go in a gallop,' Nóra murmured, and Johanna had smiled.

'More,' Micheál had demanded. 'More.'

Nóra sat down heavily on the stool and stared at the boy who now bore little resemblance to the grandchild she remembered. She stared at his mouth, ajar in sleep, the arms thrown up over his head, wrists strangely twisted. The legs that would not bear his weight.

What happened to you? she wondered.

The house was awful in its silence.

Since Martin died, Nóra had felt that she was merely passing time until he returned and, at the same time, was devastated by the knowledge that he would not. She still noticed the absence of sound. There was no whistle as Martin pulled on his boots, no laughter. Her nights had emptied of sleep. She endured their unfeeling hours by curling herself into the depression his body had made in the straw when he was alive, until she could almost imagine that he embraced her.

It was not supposed to be like this. Martin had seemed so well. A man who was ageing, sure, as she was, but a man who carried his winters on a strong back and who had two firm legs wired with the ropey muscle of a farmer. His had not been a sour body. Even as their hair had greyed, and she had seen Martin's face shaped by time and weather – mirroring her own, she imagined – he had seemed quick with life. She had expected him to outlive them all. She had envisioned her own death at his patient, watchful side. Had sometimes, in a gloomy mood, imagined him at her own funeral, throwing clay onto her coffin.

During the wake, the women had told her that the grief would subside. Nóra hated them for it. There was a void there, she understood now. How had she lived her whole life and not noticed it! A sea of loneliness that sang a siren song to the bereaved. What a gentle thing it would be to give into it and drown. What an easy keel into the abyss. How quiet it would be.

She had thought she'd never surpass the grief of that summer afternoon when Tadgh arrived, his eyes blank and his hair littered gold with the harvest chaff.

Johanna is dead, he had said. My wife is dead.

Johanna, dandelion child, gone like clocking seed on the wind and, as she felt the field of oats rise up about her, the scythe falling from her hand, there came the thought: This is it. The tide is come and I will let it take me.

Had it not been for Martin . . . He had found comfort in Micheál, that now-motherless foundling brought by Tadgh in a turf basket. He had urged her to care for the boy, to dribble milk into his piping, empty mouth. He had loved him. Found reason for happiness in him.

'He looks as though he is dying,' Nóra had said that night as they sat, drowned in grief. It was evening. The harvest sun had fallen and they had left the half-door open to allow the pinking dusk to spread throughout the room.

Martin had lifted the boy from the basket, holding him as though he were an injured bird. 'He is starved. Look at his legs.'

'Tadgh says he does not talk anymore. Has not spoken for six months or more.'

The griping boy calmed in the embrace of his grandfather. 'We will fetch the doctor for him, and we will make him well. Nóra? Do you hear me?'

'We cannot afford a doctor.'

She remembered Martin's wide hands, the kindness in the way he stroked the boy's hair. The dirt under the rough callouses of his skin. He had petted Micheál in the same way he soothed spooked horses, speaking with a calm tongue. Even that night, stabbed through with grief for their daughter, Martin had been calm.

'We will fetch the doctor, Nóra,' he had said. Only then had his voice broken. 'What we could not do for Johanna we will do for her son. For our grandson.'

Nóra stared at the empty stool that had held her husband that summer night.

Why could God not have taken Micheál? Why leave an ill-formed child in the place of a good man, a good woman?

I would throw this boy against a wall if it would bring me back Martin and my daughter, Nóra thought. The notion horrified her no sooner than it had crossed her mind. She glanced at the sleeping boy and crossed herself in shame.

No. It would not do. To sit slumped by the hearth, thinking dark thoughts, was no way to welcome the dead. This was no home for her daughter's spirit, or the returning soul of her man, God have mercy on them.

While Micheál slept, Nóra rose and filled the pot with water from her well bucket, dropping in as many potatoes as she could spare. With those set upon the fire to boil, she arranged stools around the hearth: Martin's place, closest to the flame, another for Johanna beside it. They might be gone, she thought, but with God's grace she could welcome them again for one night of the year.

When the lumpers had softened, Nóra drained them onto the skib and placed a noggin of salted water in the middle of their steaming flesh. She ate a few, slipping them out of their skins as quickly as she was able and dipping them into the water to cool and flavour the potato. Then she took Martin's pipe out of the nook in the hearth wall, wiped the dust out of the bowl and blew through the stem to clear it. She set it on his stool.

As she went about the room, snatching cobwebs from the low rafters and straightening the cross by the window, Nóra allowed herself to think again of when her daughter was little and when they were all together as a family. She remembered the first years, when Johanna was still soft-cheeked, playing with nuts gathered from wild trees: hazelnuts, acorns, chestnuts. She thought of the potato lamps they made, hollowed out by Martin and handed to Johanna to scrape out faces. Holes for eyes. Gaping mouths.

By the time Nóra finished the Samhain preparations, the usual evening sounds of lowing cattle and the cries and calls of men returning inside from work had long ceased, and all was still and silent except for the crackle of the fire and Micheál's quiet breathing. Nóra poured out piggins of buttermilk for Martin and Johanna, starting at the sudden screech of a barn owl outside. She placed the wooden cups beside the stools and knelt to say her evening prayers. Leaving the rushlights burning and her grandchild sleeping, Nóra went to bed with a small bottle of *poitín*, and sipped at it until she felt herself dissolve with the heat of the liquor. The high fire that had been burning all evening had dried the air in the house and, in the warmth of it, Nóra fell into a deep, exhausted sleep.

It was midnight when she heard the noise. A muffled thump, like a fist against a chest. Nóra sat up in bed, her head throbbing. It wasn't Micheál. The sound had come from outside. She had not imagined it, surely.

Looking out to the main room and the hearth, she could see her grandson's sleeping form. The turf burnt red. All was wine-dark.

Nóra heard the sound again. Someone was outside. Someone wanted to get in. There was a noise on the thatch, like a stone thrown against the house.

Her blood darted through her veins.

Was it Martin? Johanna? Nóra's tongue was dry with fear. She placed her feet on the ground and rose, glancing around the room, swaying. She was drunk.

There was another sound – a clinking, like a fingernail tapping on a tin bucket. She made her way into the main room of the cabin. There was no one there.

Another thump. Nóra let out a soft cry. She wished she hadn't been drinking.

Laughter sounded.

'Who's there?' Her voice sounded feeble.

Another muffled laugh. A man's laugh.

'Martin?' she whispered.

'Hallowe'en knock!' growled a low voice.

Nóra's breath caught in her throat.

'Hallowe'en knock! A penny a stock. If you don't let me in, I'll knock. Knock. Knock.' There was a sudden pounding against the mud wall of her cabin.

Nóra flung open the door. In the light of the high, slender moon she could see three men standing in front of her, their faces covered in masks of rough cloth. Holes had been cut out for their eyes and mouths, giving them an expression of menace. Nóra stepped backwards in fear as the young man in the middle skipped forward into the cabin, laughing.

'Hallowe'en knock!' He did a clumsy jig, rattling the long string of hazelnuts that hung around his neck. His fellows started giggling behind him, but their laughs faded as Nóra started to cry. The dancer stopped and pulled the mask from his face, and Nóra saw that it was John O'Shea, Peg's grandson.

'Widow Leahy. I'm –'

'Damn you all!' Blood drained from her face.

John glanced back at his companions. They stared, slack-mouthed.

'Get out, John,' Nóra hissed.

'We didn't mean to give you such a fright.'

Nóra gave a short, barking laugh. The other boys took their masks off and looked to John. Valley boys, all of them. Not her husband. Not her daughter. Just bold, masked boys.

'Taunting widows are you now, John?' She was shaking like an aspen.

John looked uncomfortable. ''Tis Samhain. We're after soul cakes.'

'And money,' his friend mumbled.

''Twas just for a laugh, is all.'

'And are ye laughing, lads?' Nóra raised her hand as if to slap them and the boys shrank back against the open door. 'Ye spalpeens. Stalking new-made widows in the dead of night! Waking good folk from their sleep with your unholy ways!'

'You won't say to *mamó*?' John twisted his mask in his hands.

'Oh, Peg'll be hearing of it. Away with ye!' Nóra picked up a stool and flung it at them as they ran out of the cabin into the night. She swung the door to, fastened the latch and leant her head against it. For one tender moment she had thought it was Martin and Johanna at her door. Stupidly, she realised that she had been anticipating their faces. The shock of the lads and their awful masks had shaken her, but it was the ruined expectation that had hurt the most.

I am a drunk old woman crying over ghosts that do not come, Nóra thought.

Micheál had woken. He wailed in his bed of heather, eyes round and dark. Nóra staggered over to where he lay and slumped to the ground. She stroked his head and tried to sing to him as Martin had done, but the tune was mournful and her voice broke on the words. Eventually she rose and fetched her husband's greatcoat from her bed. Wrapping it around her and breathing in his old scent of burnt coltsfoot, Nóra eased herself to the ground next to Micheál.

'God and Mary to you, Nance.'

Nance looked up from her knife to see a shawled figure in the doorway.

'Old Hanna?'

'And getting older with every passing day.'

'Come in and God welcome.' Nance helped her visitor to a stool by the fire. 'Is it for yourself you're come?'

The woman grunted as she sat down, shaking her head. ''Tis my sister. She has a fever.'

Nance passed Hanna a cup of fresh milk and nodded at it. 'Drink. Tell me, how long has she been sick, and does she eat?'

'She eats nothing, but takes a little water. The sweat pours from her and she shivers as though she is bitter cold. But we have the fire high, and 'tis warm as you like in with her.'

'I can give you the cure.'

'Praise be.' Hanna took a sip of the milk and pointed to the knife in Nance's hand. 'I've come and stopped you from your work.'

''Twas only thistles I was cutting. For my hens. Musha, curing fevers is my work.' Nance put the blade down and walked to the corner of the room, taking a little cloth bag from it. She untied the leather string of the bag and, using her fingertips, carefully sprinkled the herb from it into the neck of a brown glass bottle, muttering under her breath.

'What is that?' Hanna asked, when the bottle was filled and Nance had finished her charm.

'Meadowsweet.'

'Will it cure her?'

'Put the dried flowers drawing on the boil as soon as you get home to her. Give her three drinks off the top of it and she will be as well as she ever was.'

'Thank you, Nance.' Hanna was relieved.

'But don't be looking behind you until you've reached the lane. Don't be looking at the Piper's Grave or the whitethorn, or the bottle will empty.'

Hanna looked grave. 'Very well, so.'

'Finish that milk now, and God be on the road with you.'

The woman drained the cup and, wiping her mouth on the back of her hand, stood up and reached for the bottle.

'Remember what I said: don't look back.'

'Very well, Nance. And God bless you.'

Nance walked Hanna to the door, farewelling her with a wave. 'Close your fist around that bottle there.' She waited in the doorway and watched the woman walk from the woods towards the settled valley, her eyes down and her shawl pulled firmly about her head, as though to blinker herself against even a passing glance at the fairy *ráth* and the whitethorn, red haws glistening upon the branches, blood-bright.

It was not so often that women came to her for herbal cures. Most women in the valley knew enough to tend to the daily blights and bruises of living: wild honey for the inflamed and crusted eye, comfrey for pained bones, yarrow leaves pushed inside the nose to make it bleed and relieve the pounding head. Nance knew the people visited John O'Donoghue for brutal surgery, trusting his blacksmith's strength to pull the rotting teeth from their mouths or slip the dislocated shoulder back snug into its joint. They came to her only when their own poultices of gander dung and mustard or their teas of king fern failed to halt the infection or smother the cough. They came to her only when their panic had begun to fight the bridle, when their children continued to lie slack in their arms, or they knew that whatever illness plaguing them was more powerful than red dandelion or penny leaves or the salted tongue of a fox.

''Tis something else this time,' they would say, extending a twisted foot or breathing through a congested lung. ''Tis the evil eye,' they said. ''Tis the Good People.'

It was mainly the men who came for herbs. Those who worked in the fields and were less used to the sight of their own blood. Those who did not trust the doctor or could not afford his labelled tinctures. Men of the earth, they took comfort in seeing their sores stemmed by plants they had played with as boys, by a hand as wrinkled as the grandmothers they remembered by the fires of their childhoods.

But Nance knew that most of her patients did not come for herbs at all. Those with broken bodies came in the light of day in the company of family. Those who sought other advice, who found something deeply amiss, who could not lay a finger on the origin of their suffering, came in the shifting hours of dawn and twilight, when there was time for secrecy and they would not be missed. They came alone, wrapped against the cold, their faces ashen with anxiety. Nance knew that, for all her stoppered teas and mixtures of fat and ragwort, it was these visits that allowed her to remain in her cabin. They wanted her time. They wanted her voice, and her hands holding their own. They saw in her age and loneliness the proof of her cure.

What woman lives on her own with a goat and a low roof of drying herbs? What woman keeps company with the birds and the creatures that belonged to the dappled places? What woman finds contentment in such a solitary life, has no need of children or the comfort of a man? One who has been chosen to walk the boundaries. One who somehow has an understanding of the mysteries of the world and who sees in the clawing briars God's own handwriting.

Nance took a deep breath of the crisp autumn air and, nodding towards the fairy *ráth*, returned inside to her thistles.

Nóra set out to the Killarney fair early, a skiff over her arm to carry her shoes and save them from the mud of the road. The dark dawned to a white-knuckled day as she walked, the jackdaws shrieking at the November morning.

How odd to think that she would be returning with a stranger. Someone to live with and talk to, and who would share the heat of her fire. Someone who might help whittle the long winter days away until spring came with its comforts of birdsong and work.

It had been Peg O'Shea who had given her the idea to hire a maid. After Samhain Eve, Nóra's grief had sharpened into righteous anger and she had stormed into Peg's cabin.

'I've a mind to make a harness out of your boy, John,' Nóra had announced. 'Running around after dark, putting the fear into widows and children and disturbing my sleep. Here I am with no husband, himself fresh in the grave, and only myself and my nephews to work the ground, and now I have John and his spalpeens battering down the door in masks.'

Nóra winced as she walked along the road, remembering her words to Peg.

'He's gallows-bound with that larking. Do they want to be seeing me in my grave? Is that what they were after with their badness?'

'Ah, that's not it at all.' Peg had taken one of Nóra's hands and held it lightly in her own. 'I tell you, them boys scare more than widows. 'Tis a good thing they had their masks on or you would have been crying louder. Have you seen the face on our John? Like a flitch of bacon on the turn. You should see the girls running from the sight. Ah, Nóra. Come now. We're kin and all. I'll have a word with him.'

It was then that Peg had gently advised Nóra to find some kind of company. When she had pulled a face at Peg's suggestion that she move in with Daniel and Brigid, the older woman had encouraged her to look for someone at the November hiring fair.

'Get a girl, just to see you through winter,' she had said. ''Twould be a grand help to you, what with Micheál and all. 'Twill be hard looking after a wee cripple on your own. Was it that your man was in the fields and running errands, and you in the house with the boy? Well, what when you're off to sell your eggs and butter?'

'I can sell eggs and butter to those who come collecting for it.'

'And when you're in the fields in the summer? Doing the work of two to keep the thatch over your head?'

'I can't be thinking of summer yet.'

'Well then, Nóra, do you think it best to be sitting the dark hours through on your own? There are girls from up north, their families are starving. Would it not be a comfort to know you're taking one in? Would it not be a comfort to have an extra soul about the place this winter?'

There had been sense in what Peg had said. Later that day, sobbing to ruin on her bed while the child howled by the dying fire, Nóra understood that she was slipping. She was not like Martin. Her grandchild was no comfort to her; he was burdensome. She needed someone who might quiet the shrieking wean, who might help her resurface after she was hit with the waves of her grief. Someone who was not from the valley, who would not spread knowledge of Mícheál's withered legs amongst her neighbours, would not say he was astray in the head.

It was a ten-mile walk to Killarney through coarse, moory land, brindled in autumn, past small mud cabins huddled by the road-side, the sound of cocks and hens from within, waiting to be let out. Open, flat-boarded carts pulled by donkeys clattered past Nóra on the lane, and she shrank back against the briars and holly of the ditches to let them pass. The men nodded to her, reins in hand, while their sleepy-eyed, shawled wives, stared out across the morass to the mountains in the distance: Mangerton, Crohane, Torc, their familiar mass towering purple against the sky.

Nóra was glad to leave her own house, glad for the hours of walking to clear her head and breathe in the air. Since Martin had died, she had kept to her cabin, refusing to join the night-visiting for stories and song as she once had. Nóra didn't like to admit it, but she felt bitter towards the other women of the valley, found their sympathy cloying and insincere. Some had come to her door with food and offers of condolence and distraction, but Nóra, ashamed of Micheál, had refused to invite them inside to sit at the fire. Since then, in that cruelly imperceptible manner of grown women, the valley wives had slowly closed their company to her. There was nothing overt about their exclusion. They still greeted her when she met them at the well most mornings, but there was a way they had of turning in amongst themselves that made her feel unwanted. They did not trust her, Nóra knew. Those who stayed inside their cabins had something shameful to hide: bruises, poverty, sickness.

They must know about Micheál, Nóra thought. They must suspect something is not right with him.

She felt suffocated by the constant neediness of her grandchild. He made her uneasy. The night before she had tried to encourage him to walk, holding him up so that his feet brushed the ground. But he had thrown his red head back, exposing the pale length of his throat and the sharp ridges of his collarbone, and screamed as though she was pressing pins into his heels. Perhaps she ought to fetch the doctor again. There were plenty of doctors in Killarney, she knew, but accustomed as they were to the deep purses of tourists who came for the lakes, she doubted they would consider looking at Micheál for what she could afford. It was not as though the first doctor had been able to do anything for him. She would be taking food out of their mouths and for no good.

No. In the valley the sick were faced with the usual crossroads of priest, blacksmith or graveyard.

Or Nance, said a small voice in her head.

Killarney was alive with noise and smoke. New Street and High Street bristled with paupers and children begging halfpennies, and the buildings along the many filthy lanes were close and oppressive. Those who had come to sell their produce jostled for space beside the arbutus shops and cooperages and tanneries, carts wheeling close to jaunting cars, barrels and sacks. While most farmers had come to hire help for the winter term, there were people selling their autumn pigs and small, horned cows that lumbered slowly through the street, stirring it into mud. The unpaved roads were pocked, puddle-shined, and the air was clear. Men hauled creels of turf on their backs, cut from the black bogs beside the mountains in summer, and women sold potatoes, butter and salmon from the rivers. There was a crisp promise of winter in the air and a gravity to the fair's atmosphere. All must be sold, must be bought, must be piled and stacked and stored and buried, before the earth ground its teeth in frost and wind. Better-off farmers swung their sticks of blackthorn and bought themselves shoes, and young men, drink-taken, trailed their coats behind them, eyes and ashplants eager for fight. Women counted eggs from straw baskets, fingers loose around the creamy shells, and all along the lanes and in the dark corners, those advertising themselves as labourers waited silently.

They stood apart from the carts and produce, casting their eyes quickly at every man and woman walking past. There were more boys than girls, some as young as seven, shivering next to one another in attitudes of hope or reluctance. Each carried a small item to show that they were seeking work: a parcel of clothes or food, or a bundle of sticks. Nóra knew some of those parcels were empty. Mothers and fathers stood behind the smaller children, their eyes jumping from one farmer to another. They spoke with the hirers on behalf of their sons and daughters, and, although Nóra could not hear what they were saying, she could tell from the fixed smiles that they spoke of honest workers, hardy constitutions. The mothers folded their lips into narrow lines, their fingers tightly gripping their sons' shoulders. It would be a long time until they saw each other again.

Nóra noticed one grey-skinned woman standing beside a girl of twelve or thirteen. The girl was hunched over, coughing the sticky wheeze of the ill. Nóra watched as the mother, seeing a man approach, gently covered her daughter's mouth with her hand to muffle the sound and ease her upright. The sick did not get hired. No one wanted to bring badness into the home. No one wanted to pay for a stranger's coffin.

Nóra's eye was suddenly drawn to a tall, thin-faced girl standing apart from the other children, holding a parcel under one arm. She was leaning against a cart, frowning, watching a farmer inspect the teeth of a young redheaded man for hire. There was something appealing about the girl, in the thickness of the freckles on her face and the slight stoop of her back, as though she was reluctant to grow any taller. She was no beauty. Nóra felt a strange pull towards her.

'Good morning to you.'

The girl looked up and immediately pulled away from the cart, standing straight.

'What's your name?' Nóra asked.

'Mary Clifford.' The girl's voice was low, husked.

'Tell me, Mary Clifford, are you looking for work?'

'I am.'

'And where are you from? Where are your people?'

'Not far from Annamore. By the bog.'

'And how old are you?'

'I don't know, missus.'

'Fourteen by the looks of you.'

'Yes, missus. Fourteen, I'm sure. And fifteen next year, please God.'

Nóra nodded. She had thought that the girl might have been older, given her height, but fourteen was a better age. She would not be thinking of marriage yet.

'Have you brothers and sisters?'

'I have, missus. Eight of them.'

'You're the eldest, are you?'

'Eldest girl. That's my brother there.' She pointed across the lane to the redheaded boy. The farmer with him was now lifting his cap and inspecting his hair. They watched as the farmer ran rough hands across the boy's scalp, pushing his head this way and that, looking for lice. Her brother's cheeks were flushed with humiliation.

'And is your mother or father here?'

'My brother and I walked the road ourselves.' She paused. 'Mam and Da are at home with the young ones and the work.'

'Are you well? Has there been any sickness in your house?'

The girl blushed. 'I'm well, missus.' She opened her mouth to show Nóra her teeth, but Nóra shook her head, embarrassed.

'Can you milk and churn then, Mary?'

'I can. I've a good hand for it.' She held out her palms as though Nóra might be able to see evidence of ability in her swollen knuckles, the hard skin on the pads of her fingers.

'And you are used to minding children?'

'I've always helped Mam with the babies. There being eight of us, so.' The girl took a little step forward, as if afraid she was losing Nóra's interest. 'And I'm a fair spinner. And an early riser, too. I wake before the birds, my mam says, and I do her washing and card and I've a strong back. I can be beetling clothes all day.'

Nóra couldn't help but smile at the girl's solemn eagerness. 'Have you been hired before?'

'I have, missus. I was hired at a place north of here for a term this summer gone.'

'And did you like it?'

Mary paused, running her tongue over dry lips. ''Twas a hard place, missus.'

'You didn't care to stay on, then.'

She shook her head. 'I'm after a different farm.'

Nóra nodded, fighting a sudden headache. Martin had always hired what help they needed, and she was unused to so baldly interrogating a stranger. The men Martin had brought home had been quiet, hard workers who were uncomfortable indoors, holding their arms close to their sides as if afraid they would break something. They ate quickly, skinning a potato with their eyes already on the next. They mumbled the rosary, slept on the floor and woke before dawn; rough-nailed, yoke-backed men who smelt of hay and mayweed and rarely showed their teeth. Some came back every year, others did not. There had never been any need to hire a girl.

Nóra allowed herself a moment to study Mary's face and the girl looked back at her, clear-eyed, jaw clenched against the cold. Her clothes were thin and too small for her – her wrists extended well beyond the cuff of her blouse and the seams were tight around her arms and shoulders – but she seemed clean. Her hair was cut to her chin and combed, with no sign of lice. She seemed anxious to please, and Nóra thought of the eight other children at home in whatever damp *bothán* her parents had raised her in. She thought of Johanna, the whispers that rippled back to her about her daughter begging food off neighbours. This girl had the same hair as her. The same as Micheál. A light copper – like a hare, or pine needles drying out on the ground.

'Will you come for a term with me then, Mary? I have my daughter's child to care for. How much do you want for the six months?'

'Two pound,' Mary said quickly.

Nóra narrowed her eyes. 'You're too young for that money. One and half.'

Mary nodded and Nóra placed a shilling in her palm. The girl quickly tucked it into her parcel and cast her eyes to her brother, giving him a solemn nod. He had been abandoned by the farmer who had examined him and now stood alone amidst the crowd and the smoke. He watched them leave, and at the last moment raised a hand in farewell.

The journey back to Nóra's house was a quiet one. The sun emerged and the bright splatter left by cartwheels and footprints was clear on the road. The district's tramping to Killarney with hoof and flock had left the path churned. Mud glistened.

Nóra and Mary made slow work of the journey, but Nóra didn't mind. She was relieved to have the business of hiring done with. She walked close to the lane ditches, stooping now and then to pull starry clusters of chickweed for her hens. Mary, noticing, began to look too. She stepped carefully between the mud and rocks, avoiding the toothed leaves of nettles.

'Were you not afraid of coming such a long way in the dark?' Nóra asked.

'I had my brother,' Mary answered simply.

'You're a brave girl.'

She shrugged. 'There's so many of us. I didn't dare move for fear I'd miss a job. I would have stood there all day.'

They followed the road in silence then, through moor ground and small swathes of trees, already bare in the steady approach of winter; past the dark, lacquered shine of holly. The grass by the roadside was browned and long and beyond, in the distance, the mountains patched with heather and rock stood silent against the sky. Spirals of smoke from turf fires accompanied them as they walked.

It was late afternoon by the time the two women reached Nóra's cabin, and the sun had started to falter. They stood for a moment in the yard, panting after the trudge up the slope, and Nóra watched the girl assess her surroundings. Her eyes passed over the two-roomed thatched dwelling, the small byre beside it and the scattered hens. Nóra wondered whether Mary had expected something more, perhaps a larger home thatched with wheat straw rather than reeds. Perhaps the stumping mass of a pig in the yard or signs of a donkey rather than a quiet home with one tiny window stuffed with straw, the whitewashed walls greening with moss and a stony scoreground of potato.

'I have a cow. She keeps us in milk and dirt.' Nóra led Mary to the byre and they stepped into its warm darkness and its smell of flank and piss, the dark outline of the cow on the straw at their feet.

'You're to water, feed and milk her in the mornings and churn the butter. Once a week, you'll churn. I'll do the evening's milking.'

'What's her name?'

'Brownie, we . . . I call her.'

Nóra watched as Mary brought her chapped hands down to the cow's head and stroked her ears. Brownie slowly shifted her weight, her bony haunches rolling.

'Does she give much milk?'

'Enough,' replied Nóra. 'God keep her well.'

They stepped back into the soft light and walked the wet path to the house, the chickens running towards them over the yard. 'Decent hens,' Nóra said. 'Here, give them the chickweed. Sure, they're mad for it. They're not laying as much now, but I have my faithful few and they give their eggs right through the winter.' She shot Mary a stern look. 'You're not to take any. No eggs or butter. You'd be eating the rent. Do you eat much?'

'No more than I can help.'

'Hmm. Follow me now.'

Nóra pushed open the half-door and greeted Peg O'Shea, who was sitting by the fire with Micheál in her lap.

'Peg, this here is Mary.'

'God save you and welcome.' Peg gave Mary an appraising look. 'You'll be a Clancy girl, with the red hair of you.'

'Clifford. I'm Mary Clifford,' the girl said, eyes flicking to Micheál. Her mouth slipped open.

'Clifford, is it? Well, God bless you, Cliffords and Clancys alike. Is it far you've come?'

'She set out to the rabble fair in the dark of this morning,' Nóra said. 'Annamore. Twelve mile or more.'

'And the walk all this way too? Musha, you'll be dead on your feet.'

'She has two strong legs.'

'And two strong arms from the look of things. Take him, will you? This is Micheál. I expect Nóra's told you about him.' Peg gathered the boy up and motioned for Mary to come closer.

Mary stared. Micheál's nose was crusted and spittle had dried in the corner of his mouth. As Peg held him out to her, he began to groan like a man beaten.

She took a step back. 'What's wrong with him?'

There was silence, broken only by Micheál's guttural moaning.

Peg sighed and placed the boy back down on her lap. Casting a knowing look at Nóra, she scraped the dried saliva from the boy's face with a fingernail.

'What do you mean, "What's wrong with him?"' Nóra's voice was dangerous.

'What ails him? That noise he's making. Why is he carping like that? Can he not talk?'

'He's delicate, is all,' Peg said softly.

'Delicate,' Mary repeated. She edged backwards until her hands were resting on the doorframe. 'Is it catching?'

Nóra made an animal noise in the back of her throat. 'You're a bold girl to ask a question like that.'

'Nóra –'

'"Is it catching?" Do you hear her, Peg? The cheek of it.'

'No, I don't mean. Only, he does not seem . . .'

'Seem what?'

'Nóra. She has a right to ask.' Peg spat on a corner of her apron and scrubbed at Micheál's face.

'Only . . .' Mary pointed at his legs, exposed where the dress bunched up about his midriff. 'Can he even walk?' Her lip trembled.

'She's just a girl, Nóra,' Peg said quietly. 'Come here and see for yourself, Mary Clifford. He's not got a catching sickness. He won't harm you. He's just a child. Just a harmless child.'

Mary nodded, swallowing hard.

'Go on. Take a peep at him. He's a dear thing, really.'

Mary peered over Peg's shoulder at the boy. His eyes were half shut, gazing down the length of a snub nose, and his mouth was slack. Gurgled breathing came from his throat.

'Is he in pain?' Mary asked.

'He's not, no. He can laugh, and he can sit up a ways by himself, and he can move his arms sometimes to play with things.'

'How old is he?'

'Well, now,' said Peg. 'He'd be four years now, isn't that so, Nóra?'

'He likes feathers,' Nóra breathed. She sat down unsteadily on the creepie stool opposite Peg. 'He likes feathers.'

'Sure, four it is. And he likes feathers. And acorns. And knuckle bones.' Peg's voice held a forced liveliness. ''Tis just the legs of him.'

'He can't walk,' Nóra croaked. 'He used to be able to, but now he can't.'

Mary eyed the boy with apprehension, her lips pressed tightly together. 'Micheál? My name is Mary.' She glanced over to Nóra. 'Is he shy?'

'He can't talk to tell us.' Nóra was silent for a moment. 'I should have told you.'

Mary shook her head. Her hair had curled in the damp air of the walk back to the cabin and she looked young and frightened. Nóra felt sudden self-loathing. She is just a girl, she thought. She is just a child herself, and here I am shouting at her. A stranger.

'Well, now. You've come all this way and I've not even given you a drink. You must be thirsty.' Nóra stood and replenished the pot of water on the hearth from the well pail.

Peg gave Mary a little squeeze on the shoulder. 'Let's set him down there. On the heather. He won't go far.'

'I can take him.' Mary sat down next to Peg and lifted the boy onto her lap. 'He's all bones! He's light as a bird.'

The women watched her as she pulled the cloth of Micheál's dress down around his legs, then took off her own shawl and used it to swaddle his feet. 'There now. Now you're easy,' she murmured.

'Well. 'Tis a pleasure to have you amongst us, Mary Clifford. I wish you well and God bless. I'd best be on my way.' She gave Nóra a meaningful glance and shuffled out the door, leaving them alone.

Mary tucked Micheál's head against her collarbone, her arms awkwardly clasped around his body. 'He has a tremor in him,' she remarked.

Nóra poured out two piggins of buttermilk and began to prepare potatoes for their dinner. There was a tightening in her throat, as though a rope had been pulled against her neck, and she did not trust herself to speak. Several minutes passed before she heard Mary's quavering voice behind her.

'I'll do my best for you.'

'I'm sure you will.' Nóra choked on the words. 'I'm sure you will.'

Later that evening, once Mary and Nóra had finished their quiet meal and called the hens in for the night, they turned out the settle bed, placing a rough mattress of woven straw and a blanket down.

'You'll be warm here, by the fire,' Nóra said.

'Thank you, missus.'

'And you'll have Micheál to keep the heat in the bed.'

'Does he not use that cradle?' Mary pointed to the rough cot of woven sally twigs.

'He's grown too big for it. It cramps him. Now, mind you tuck him in well or he'll kick his bedclothes off in the night.'

Mary looked at Micheál, who was propped up against the wall, his head rolling on one shoulder.

'Tomorrow I'll show you a little of the valley, if 'tis fine. You'll need to know where the well is. And I'll show you the best place to wash clothes in the river. It might do you good to meet a few of the other girls about here.'

'Will Micheál come with us?'

Nóra gave her a sharp look.

'I mean, do you leave him here, or do you take him about with you? A boy like him, who hasn't the use of his legs . . .'

'I don't like to be taking him outside.'

'You leave him alone?'

'I won't have folk splashing water on drowned mice.' Nóra picked up the pail of dirty water they had washed their feet in. Easing the door open, she cried a warning to the fairies and threw it into the yard.

CHAPTER
FOUR

A s h

'Are you of the living or the dead?'

Peter O'Connor opened the door to Nance's cabin and ducked his head under the low frame, a bottle of *poitín* in his hand. 'Dead from dry-thirst.'

Nance beckoned him in. 'Sit down, will you. Grand to see you, Peter.'

''Twas a fine wake they gave Martin, and a fine *caoineadh* from you, Nance.' Peter lowered himself down by the fire and fussed with his pipe, taking Nance's crude pair of tongs and lifting an ember to light it. 'Lord have mercy on the souls of the dead,' he whispered. He sucked on the pipe until the tobacco flared and a coil of smoke rose.

'What brings you today, Peter? Is it the shoulder of you?'

Peter shook his head. 'The arm is alright.'

'Is it the eyes?' When the man didn't respond, Nance settled herself more comfortably on her stool and waited patiently.

'I keep having these dreams,' Peter said finally.

'Ah, dreams, is it?'

He clenched his jaw. 'I don't know what's bringing them on, Nance. Powerful dreams, they are.'

'And are they troubling you?'

Peter took a long draw on his pipe. 'Ever since I found Martin lying dead by the crossroads.'

'Full of trouble, are they?'

'Full of badness.' Peter looked up from the fire and Nance saw that his face was dark. 'I can't shake the feeling that something terrible is coming, Nance. I dream of dead animals. Their throats slit and them bleeding into the ground.' He cast a look at Nance's goat. 'Or I dream that I'm drowning. Or a hanged man. I wake choking.'

Nance waited for Peter to continue speaking, and when the man remained silent, his knees drawn up to his chest, Nance gestured to the bottle he had brought. 'Will we have a drink?' She pulled the cork out and passed the bottle to him.

He took a deep gulp, winced and wiped his mouth.

'Powerful *poitín*,' Nance muttered, taking a swig of her own. She sat back down by the fire. She was prepared to wait. Sometimes a listening ear was all that was needed. Just silence and time in a cabin where there was no chatter, or stories, or neighbours. Where there was nothing but a fire and a woman. A woman they didn't desire. A woman whose tongue didn't slip secrets to other wives. Just an old woman with an ear and a taste for the smoke and the drink. That was worth slipping out of their cabins for, worth the walk between the lazy beds and the mossed walls to visit her in the fading hours. Nance knew the power of silence.

The fire burnt. Peter smoked the bowl of tobacco down to ash and rapped it out against his knees. They passed the bottle of drink between them, until the damp night air seeped under the door, making Peter restless.

'Did I tell you about the four magpies I saw before our Martin passed, mercy on his soul?'

Nance leant forward. 'You did not, Peter.'

'Four of them. There's death coming, isn't there? I saw lights by your Piper's Grave. By the ringfort. And that night I had the first of these dreams.'

'I saw lightning strike the heather on the mountain,' Nance muttered.

'The night Martin died?'

'The very same. There's a strange wind blowing.'

'They're abroad. The Good People. Do you think that's why I've been dreaming the things I have, Nance?'

She reached out and patted his shoulder, and saw, briefly, his narrow cot against the wall in his cabin, the long hours spent smoking while the night pressed down. 'Weren't you born with a caul on your head, and isn't it truth that such a one has eyes for things that are beyond the knowing of most? Still, Peter, let you remember, a lot of fears are born of sitting too long alone in the dark.'

Peter picked his teeth with a dirty fingernail and gave a short laugh. 'Faith, what does it matter? I'd best be on my way.'

'Sure, Peter. Go on home.'

He helped Nance to her feet and waited as she used the tongs to pluck a coal from the fire, dipping it, hissing, in her water bucket to cool. She dried the dead ember on her skirt, spat on the ground and passed it to him. 'You'll see no *púca* tonight. God save you on the road.'

Peter put it into his pocket with a curt nod. 'Bless you, Nance Roche. You're a good living woman, no matter what the new priest says.'

Nance raised an eyebrow. 'The priest has been wasting words on me, has he?'

Peter chuckled. 'I didn't say? Oh, you should have heard him at Mass. He was trying to open our eyes to the new world, he said. 'Twas our duty to slough off the old ways that keep Irishmen at the bottom of the pile. 'Tis a new age for Ireland and for the Catholic Church. We're to be paying our pennies to the Catholic campaign, not to unholy keeners.'

'Slough off the old ways. He has a pretty mouth on him, then.'

'Not so pretty, Nance.' Peter shook his head. 'I'd give him a wide berth. Let him settle in. Learn how we do things around here.'

'I suppose he thinks I am one for those "old ways".'

Peter's face grew solemn. 'Heathen ways, Nance. He said he knows that people come to you and that we're not to anymore.' He paused. 'He said you're full of devilment and tricks to be keening for the money.'

'So. The new priest is against me.'

'Father Healy may be. But here I am, Nance. And by my soul, I see no devilment in your home.'

'The Lord protect you, Peter O'Connor.'

The man gave her a smile and set his hat on his head. 'We still have need of you. We still have need of the old ways and knowledge.' He paused, his smile fading. 'It reminds me, Nance. There's a boy, you know. Up with Nóra Leahy. A cripple boy. I thought you should know, in case the widow has need of you.'

'I saw no cripple when I was up there for the keening.'

'No. She had me take him away.'

'What ails him?'

'I couldn't tell you, Nance.' Peter looked out into the encroaching dark. 'But 'tis certain there's something terrible wrong.'

Nance spent the rest of the evening hunched close to her fireside, her tongue worrying the teeth in her gums. The night felt restless. She could hear the croak of frogs and a small scratching that might have been a burrowing rat, a jackdaw on the thatch.

In the unbusy hours, time lost traction. Often, as Nance sat quietly carding wool or waiting for her few potatoes to boil, she imagined that Maggie sat in the room with her. Marked, terrifying, calm-eyed Maggie, drying her herbs, skinning her rabbits. Maggie with her pipe clamped between her teeth, keeping her fingers busy. Showing Nance how to listen to the secret, knocking heartbeat of the world. Teaching her how to save others, if she could not save her mother.

How quickly the air thickened with ghosts.

'Some folk are born different, Nance. They are born on the outside of things, with a skin a little thinner, eyes a little keener to what goes unnoticed by most. Their hearts swallow more blood than ordinary hearts; the river runs differently for them.'

A memory of them sitting in her father's cabin, washing the road from their feet. Nance's heart thrilling in her chest at delivering her first baby into the world – the seventh son of a jarvey's wife. The first sight of the hair, the waxen slip of the child into her hands. How she had trembled at the sound of the infant's cry.

Maggie smiling at her, settling on the stool, lighting her pipe. 'I remember when you were born, Nance. Your mam was in some froth of pain. Colliding with nature, so she was. I came and all was chaos – your da was in a fit because you were showing a mighty reluctance to be dragged into the world. I loosened every lock. I unbarred the door and pushed the straw from the window. I untied the knots from my shawl and your mam's clothes, and told the men to set the cow free. They kicked her into the night. Only then, when everything was slack, did you slip amongst us like a fish from a loose net.'

'Did you know I was different then?'

Her aunt had smiled. Tapped the ash from her pipe. 'You came as children sometimes do, Nance. In the small, sliding hours of the night. Fists clenched. Already brawling with the world.'

There was silence.

'I don't want to have the difference upon me. I don't want to be alone like that.'

Maggie leant closer, eyes fierce. 'What is in the marrow is hard to take out of the bone. You'll learn that soon enough.'

Mary woke with a start, a weight of panic on her chest. Sitting up in a sweat, she gazed about her, taking in the rosy glow of the hearth and the unfamiliar walls of the cabin. A moment passed before she remembered where she was.

I am in the widow's house.

Mary looked at the sleeping child lying beside her, the thin buckle of his spine pressing against her leg.

I am in the widow's house, she thought. And this is the child I must care for.

She lay back down and tried to sleep, but the smells of the cabin were strange, and there was a gnawing at her chest. A desire to be back in Annamore, lying beside her brothers and sisters, the whole tangle of them in front of the fire on the sweet-smelling rushes, made her eyes fill with tears. Mary blinked them away, tucked her wrists under her chin and pushed her face against the makeshift pillow of rags.

Her stomach groaned. She had eaten too much. At least I will not go hungry here, she thought, for all the widow's warnings about eggs. There were worse places she could be. David had told her about the farm he had been hired to last autumn, a smallholding out on the peninsula where they spent the days cutting and carrying seaweed for the fields. Long days of standing in salt water, back bent to the cold, and the heavy trudge to the fields. The weed had soaked his clothes through the loose weave of the basket and turned his skin raw.

Pray to God you are hired to some place where they feed you well, he had said.

It wasn't the work David had minded. All the men and women of the place had taken their fair share of labour. But it was a poor thing to have your body trellised in salt, your feet bleeding from hidden rocks, and a belly full of sea air and little else.

Her brother had not told her these things in front of their mother. She would have worried herself sick with it, and it was hard enough to see her fretting over the children at home, with the coughs, and the potatoes too few in the ground and the bodies too many, and the rumour of evictions and the middlemen's crowbars that passed from cabin to cabin like a dark shadow. Her brother had waited until they were outside, looking for stray eggs in the tufts of grass.

Find yourself a place where they feed you, David had said. No matter the dirt. Sure, some families that do be hiring have nothing more than we. They lay down on rushes every night just the same as us. But find yourself a farmer who will see to it that you're fed.

They had fed her at the northern farm over the summer. Lumpers. Stirabout. But only after the family had eaten; she was left to drain the piggin of buttermilk and scrape the pot clean of meal.

Mary turned on her side. It could be worse, she comforted herself. One woman and a child, rattling around in a house with a cow and a bit of scoreground. But there was a strange feeling in the place, something she could not quite make out. Perhaps it was the loneliness of the woman. The widow, Nóra Leahy. Hollow-cheeked and hair greying about her temples. She looked as though she had been thrashed by womanhood; her ankles were swollen and her face threaded with deep lines. Mary had studied her at the fair, noticing the sun's trace on her skin, the expanse of furrows that suggested a life well lived.

David had warned her to take a good look at their faces. If a man has a red nose, he's a man in liquor and you'd best avoid his house because you can be sure all the money goes on the drink and not on those under his roof. The women with puckered mouths? Mary, gossip is sour. They'll be watching your every move. Best find a face where there's little shadow of a frown and their eyes are all crow's feet. They've either been staring into the sun all their lives, or they're a kind soul, and you can be sure that whether 'tis work in the field or smiling that gave them such a face, you'll be better off with them.

Nóra Leahy had crow's feet. She had seemed kind enough at Killarney, her clothes neat and her face open. But she had not told her that she was a widow, and she had lied about the boy.

What was it she had said?

I have my daughter's child to care for.

No word about a scragged boy with a loose, mute jaw. No suggestion of a house of illness, or death, or the need for secrecy.

Mary had never seen a child like Micheál before. Asleep he could almost be any skinny wretch, a little boy like any other, although stunted and pallid. But awake, there was no doubting that something was gravely wrong with him. His blue eyes seemed to slip unseeing over the world, passing over her as though she were not there at all. It was unnatural, the way he folded his wrists against his chest, the sloping angle of his mouth. He looked old, somehow. His skin was tight and dry, and there was a thinness to it, like the pages in a priest's holy book. He had nothing of the round-cheeked softness of the children Mary knew. When she had stepped through the door of the cabin and seen the old woman holding him on her lap, she had thought at first that it wasn't a child at all but some strange scarecrow. A baby's plaything, made from sticks and an old dress, like the effigy of St Brigid carried on the saint's holy day: shrivelled head, hard angles hidden by discarded cloth. And then, as she had drawn closer and seen that it, *he*, was alive, her heart had dropped in fear. Thin and flared with a disease like those that sucked the sap from a plant and shrivelled it to withered stalk. She had been sent to a home touched with sickness, and she would be tainted with it.

But no. He was not sick, they said. Only slow. Only struggling to grow as other children did.

A copperheaded, snub-nosed, wasting runt. A pattern of sally rods bound by skin and rash and groaning like a demon.

Mary brought a gentle hand to Micheál's forehead and pushed the hair back from it. He was drooling: a watery line of spittle ran from the corner of his mouth across his face. Mary smoothed it away with the back of her hand and wiped it on the blanket.

The widow must be ashamed of the boy. That is why Nóra had not told her.

What had her daughter done to deserve such a child?

If a woman could bestow a harelip on a baby by meeting a hare in the road, what ill thing was met with to turn a boy ragged and skew the bones in his skin? It must have been a grave sin, to thwart a child in the womb so.

But he had not been born this way, the widow had said.

Perhaps something had struck him down.

There was nothing for it, Mary decided. She could not go home. This farm, this valley – like a pock in the skin of the earth, sunk between the height of rocky mountains – was hers to know for the next half-year. She would have to bite down on her lip and work. She was earning real money for her family, and as long as she and David were out and gathering shillings, there would be no eviction. She could stand six months with a hard, contrary woman and a bone-racked boy. Then she'd be back on the rushes with her brothers and sisters, and her father's low voice saying the rosary, and they would all fall asleep by the warmth of their fire and not even the whistling wind would wake them.

Nóra woke with restless excitement. There was a stranger in the house. The girl, Mary. Throwing on her outer clothes, she dressed quickly and entered the main room.

The girl wasn't there.

The settle bed had been turned back in so that it resembled a bench once more, and the fire had been raked and was burning high. In the corner of the room, Nóra saw that Micheál had been placed in an empty basket and that the heavy iron tongs from the fire had been laid across it, inches from his unmoving head.

Mary was nowhere to be seen.

The chickens were no longer in their roost, and Nóra reached a hand in for the eggs. There were four, still warm. Placing them carefully in the egg basket, she heard the creak of the yard door and spun around. Mary stood there, bundled against the bright cold of the morning, a steaming pail of milk in one hand, covered with a cloth.

'Mary,' Nóra gasped.

'Good morning to you.' Mary lifted the milk onto the table and began to strain it through the cloth into a crock.

'I thought you had gone.'

'Just an early riser, missus. Like I said. And you asking me to milk mornings and . . .' Her voice tapered off. 'Have I done something wrong?'

Nóra laughed in her relief. 'Never mind it. 'Twas only because of last evening and, well . . .' She paused. 'Where is the spancel?'

'I couldn't find one.'

'You milked Brownie without it?'

'I did. She's a gentle dear.'

'The spancel is here. In that corner. I keep it inside so no butter stealer can use it against me.' Nóra pointed at the tongs resting over the basket. 'I've not seen that for some time.'

Mary reddened and picked them up, setting them back down by the fire. 'They're for the fairies, missus. So he isn't taken. 'Tis what we do in Annamore.'

'Well, I know what they're for and 'tis the same here. It has been a long time since I had to be worrying about the fairies taking my child.'

Mary pinked. 'Micheál . . . Well, the doty child wet himself in the night. I wanted to clean him but there's no water.'

'I'll show you the well.'

The morning was clean and damp and filled with a brightness that glanced off the wet moss on the field walls, turning them a vivid green. It was cold, but the early sunlight was soft and golden, and lit the haze of smoke that drifted from the cabins. Mist pooled in the bottom of the valley.

'The river is down there,' Nóra said, standing with Mary in the yard. They had left Micheál in the cabin, walled in the potato basket, safe from the fire. 'The Flesk, as we call it. You can go fetch water there if you like, but 'tis a long walk back with the pails and 'tis all uphill. Slippery too, in the rain. When the weather turns you'll go there to beetle the clothes. 'Tis a longer walk to the well, but 'tis steady and kinder on my knees. All the women go to the well for their water. 'Tis clearer.'

'Are there many that live in this valley?' Mary asked.

'Women? Just as many as the men, although there's a few unmarried farmers. See that house closest to us? That's where Peg O'Shea lives, the woman you met last night. She has a fine and full family. Five children and their children besides.' Nóra pointed down the valley, where the lane dipped around the mountain to the flatter plain, as they began to walk. 'And that place way down there – do you see the two buildings and the lime kiln a ways off? There, in the middle of the valley. That's the blacksmith's. John O'Donoghue and his wife Áine. 'Tis a great house for *cuaird*, for night-visiting. They've no children at all though they've been married ten years. People don't speak of it. My nephew's home is just beyond that, along the valley, though you can't see it for all the mist. Daniel Lynch is his name. His wife is expecting their first child. You might see him and his brother about the place. They'll help with the labour some. My husband died not long ago.'

'Sorry for your trouble, missus.'

There was the sound of laughter, and Nóra, suddenly fighting tears, was grateful to see two women come around the slope with water pails in hand, joining them on the lane.

'God bless you, Nóra Leahy,' said one of them, pulling her cloak off her face so she could better see. Curly wisps of fair hair escaped from her braid.

'And you too, Sorcha. Éilís. This here is Mary Clifford.'

The women looked at Mary with interest, their eyes narrowed. 'To the well, are ye?'

'We are.'

'Mary, Éilís is the wife of the schoolmaster here, William O'Hare. He takes the children for their lessons by the hedgerows. And Sorcha is the daughter of my brother-in-law's brother's wife.'

Mary looked confused.

'Don't worry, you'll meet them in time. There's no hiding. Everyone knows everyone here.'

'We're all tied together, whether we like it or no,' Éilís added, raising an eyebrow. She was a short bull of a woman with dark bags under her eyes.

'Did you hear about Father Healy, Nóra?'

'What about him?'

Sorcha puffed out her cheeks. 'He heard about your man Martin's wake. Didn't it fire him up?' She laughed. 'You should have heard him speak at Mass. Oh, he had the anger up.'

Nóra shook her head irritably. 'What are you saying?'

Sorcha leant in closer, swinging her water pail against her leg. 'He had the word against your keener, Nance Roche. Preached against her, like. Said she's not to be brought in for *caoineadh*. Said it is not in line with the Church.'

'And what sort of wake would it be without keening?' Nóra exclaimed. 'Did you ever hear of such a thing?'

'Oh, he was fit to be tied,' Éilís added. She was enjoying the scandal. 'He was spitting all over everyone. I had to wipe my face.'

'We've a new priest,' Nóra explained to Mary. 'Father Healy.'

Sorcha stooped to pick up a dandelion and put it in her mouth, chewing on the leaf. 'He doesn't stand for much. I wonder how he knew Nance was at your cabin? He'd already left. 'Twas pissing down that night.'

'Someone must have told him,' Éilís suggested darkly.

The well was cut into the slope of the valley where the mountain met the level ground, a rough hole, surrounded by bushes of furze and heather. An ash tree grew nearby, to mark the place and to make the water sweeter, and tattered ribbons flapped from its trunk and lower branches in the breeze. There were already a group of women talking by the well, pails of water by their feet. They looked up at the sound of Éilís and Sorcha's voices and greeted Nóra, eyes flashing quickly to Mary and glancing over her ill-fitting clothes. Some spat on the ground. 'God be between us and harm,' whispered another.

''Tis your red hair,' Nóra muttered to Mary.

'My red hair?'

'Do you not meet with the spitting in Annamore?'

'Never on my life.'

'Well, don't mind them.' She nodded to two of the women. 'This is Mary Clifford. She's come to work for me. I'm showing her the well. Mary, you've met Sorcha and Éilís. This here is Hanna and Biddy.'

The women murmured greetings, then turned back to the huddle, intent on their conversation. They were also talking of Father Healy.

'He thinks heathens are amongst us,' said one of those gathered.

'He didn't say that! He thinks the old ways are just a superstition. He won't give in to it.'

'A priest should believe it more than anyone,' Hanna remarked.

'Those were his words. He thinks the Devil's amongst us in more ways than one.'

As Nóra bent to draw the water she noticed that several women looked at her anxiously. A few patted her on the back as she pulled the bucket from the well, but few offered her little more than a greeting. When Nóra joined Mary with the filled pails, they began to walk the path back to the cabin without farewell.

'Are they your friends?' Mary asked.

'They're blood-tied to me, if that's what you're asking.'

'Why did they spit on the ground when they saw my hair?'

'They think you might have the evil eye.'

Mary shifted uncomfortably, but said nothing.

'Don't be vexed over it. 'Tis just the way of it here.'

'Sorcha seems a lively girl.'

'Sorcha? What that one knows at cow-time the whole countryside will be repeating before moonrise.'

'Is it true what she said about your priest giving out to the keener?'

Nóra snorted. 'I don't know what they be teaching them in the towns these days. What's the good of stripping us of our ways? They're as Christian as the both of us.'

'Has your man, the priest, seen to Micheál?'

'You're yet to learn a few things about the people around here. But you may as well learn now that a priest is not often in the homes of the people without a palm of money.'

A putrid smell met them as they opened the door to Nóra's cabin. Mary looked in the potato basket and saw that Micheál had shat himself. He sat upright in his own filth, hands sticky and eyes wide, as if surprised.

''Tis in his hair,' Mary exclaimed, pinching her nose with one hand.

'Take him outside and wash him then.'

Mary hauled the basket with the boy still inside out into the yard. The shit had already started to dry on his skin, and the dried ball of peck heath she scrubbed him with did little to loosen the dirt. Nóra brought out a scrap of grey soap made from fern ash and fat, and eventually Mary managed to clean the boy. The chill of the well water and the scraping of the heath on his skin made Micheál scream, and it was some time before Mary could soothe him. She paced the length of the yard, the chickens at her feet, bundling Micheál up in her shawl and singing to him. By the time he fell asleep, she was exhausted.

'Bring him here to me,' Nóra said, returning outside with her arms extended as soon as his cries had softened. She noticed the emptied pail. 'Did you not use the barrel water?'

'The what?'

'The rain water.' Nóra pointed to an old barrel standing by the byre. 'Go back to the well, would you, and get us more drinking water. If anyone asks you why you're back so soon, don't tell them the reason. Say you're a mighty one for cleaning. Don't mention Micheál.'

Mary lugged the water pail back to the well, trying to ignore the smell of shit that lingered on her clothes and hands. She hoped that the clearing beside the ash tree would be empty of people, but as she rounded the corner, she saw that Éilís O'Hare was still there, talking to another woman she had not seen before.

''Tis the maid again,' Éilís sang, noticing her at once and raising a hand. 'Kate, this is . . . What's your name again there, girl?'

'My name is Mary Clifford.'

'Mary Clifford. That's the one I was telling you about. The Widow Leahy has help in.' Éilís raised her eyebrows at the other woman, who stared at Mary with cold intensity.

'I'm Kate Lynch,' the woman said. 'Éilís here was saying that you're new to the valley. That you're a hired girl.'

'That's right,' Mary said. 'I'm from Annamore. Up north.'

'I know where Annamore is,' Kate said. 'Full of red-haired girls, is it?'

'Only some,' Mary said. She made to kneel down by the well to fetch her water, but Kate took a step in front of her.

'We know why you're here,' Kate said. 'I'm a relation of the widow's and Éilís here is my sister. My man is the brother of Nóra's dead sister's husband.'

'I'm sorry for your troubles,' Mary murmured.

'You're here because of the child, are you not? The widow's grand-child left after her daughter was swept.'

'Swept?'

Kate took hold of Mary's water pail. Her knuckles were red, swollen. 'That boy is no ordinary wean, is he?'

'I don't know what you mean.'

Éilís laughed. 'The widow keeps him safe in her cabin, but we know. We know.'

Kate leant down and looked Mary in the eye, still gripping her water pail. 'I'm going to tell you something now, girl, and you'd best be listening to me. Martin Leahy was a well man before the widow's daughter was taken, and before that child came to this valley. But no one drops down at a crossroads and dies in good health without some kind of interference. As soon as that changeling was delivered . . .' She stopped to spit on the ground. 'As soon as that blasted cratur came into Nóra's house, all manner of powerful trouble started, and now Martin is dead.'

'You're new to this valley, and I don't expect you to understand what is going on around you. Not yet,' Éilís said. 'But there's people here who are conspiring with Them, and it has caused a shadow to drop on us.'

'That child Nóra keeps away from the eyes of us? I ask you, do you think that's a natural boy?' Kate hissed between her teeth.

'He's a cripple,' Mary stuttered. She pulled at her water pail and Kate let it go with a grimace.

'A cripple, is he?'

'You've a lot to learn, Mary Clifford. The widow had no right bringing in a strange girl to care for that boy. Not after what he did to her daughter and husband.'

'Has she told you about her daughter?' Éilís asked.

'I know she died.'

Kate slowly shook her head. 'No, Mary Clifford. No. She did not die. She was swept. Taken. Carried away by the Good People. Oh, you're laughing at that, are you?'

Mary shook her head. The woman's breath was hot in her face.

'How well it is that you are not afraid,' Kate said. 'But you should be. If I were you, I would go on back home to Annamore.

No good will come of your work there, not in that house. Let you go on back to the widow and tell her that I know what that boy is, and that she ought to take remedies to banish him before someone does it for her.'

CHAPTER
FIVE

Alder

When Nóra heard the knock on her half-door she thought it was Peg. 'Come in,' she cried, not looking up from where she was dressing Micheál. She knotted the cloth about the boy's hips, then, not hearing any movement, looked up. At first she could not see the visitor – the sun outside cast their face into shadow. But as the door creaked open a man stepped inside, taking off a ragged felt hat, and her heart clutched in recognition.

Tadgh.

Nóra stood, her breath suddenly sharp. Her son-in-law had changed since she had last seen him, when he had arrived bearing his starving son on the donkey. Tadgh had always been small and wiry, but now he seemed shrunken. He had grown a beard, but it was patchy and thin. He seemed untended.

Grief has withered him, she thought.

'I heard Martin died,' Tadgh said. 'I'm sorry for your troubles.'

'Tadgh. 'Tis good to see you.'

'Is it?' he asked.

'How have you been keeping?' Nóra showed him to the settle bed and sank down on a stool. She felt weak.

Tadgh shrugged. 'Times are hard,' he said simply. 'How is the boy?'

'Grand, so he is.'

Tadgh nodded absently, gazing about the room. ''Tis a fine place you have. I saw the cow. He has milk, then.'

'Micheál? He does. There's enough for him.' Nóra pointed to where the boy, now cleaned, lay on a clump of heather.

Tadgh stood and regarded him from a height. 'He's unchanged then,' he said suddenly. 'There's still that queer look to him. Is it illness, do you think?'

Nóra swallowed hard. She said nothing.

'When he stopped walking Johanna thought he was ill. She thought he had caught something off her.'

'Faith, 'tis nothing that time won't heal, so I think,' said Nóra, trying to maintain a steady voice.

Tadgh scratched his head, the sound of his fingernails loud against his scalp. He looked troubled. 'He was such a bonny child. Such a fair little babby.'

'So he is still, for all the difference.'

'He is not,' Tadgh said decisively. He stared at Nóra. 'For two years he was well. Then . . . I thought it might be the hunger, you know. I thought 'twas our doing. The place was so awful cold, and there wasn't a lot we could give him. I gave him all I . . .' His voice broke. Nóra could see that he was fighting to speak without emotion. 'I thought I'd done it,' he whispered finally, glassy-eyed.

'Tadgh,' Nóra breathed. 'Tadgh.'

'I thought he might be better here. That's what they said. That it was just want of milk and things to eat.'

'I'm taking good care of him, Tadgh. I have a girl in with me now.'

'But he's the same, isn't he?' He squatted beside Micheál and extended a hand out over the boy, waving it in his face. Micheál took no notice of it. 'Do you think 'tis his mind, like?'

Nóra said nothing.

'Johanna didn't think 'twas the cold. Or the hunger.'

'She thought it was the bug.'

Tadgh nodded. 'At first. She thought it had gone into his legs like it had gone into her head. Stopped him from walking, like. Just as it stopped her from . . .' He bit his lip and lowered himself to the ground, sitting cross-legged next to Micheál. 'My little man. Your da is here.'

Micheál arched his back and shot a thin arm out in an aimless punch.

'Look at him fighting.'

'He does that of a time. He can move.'

Tadgh gave a sad smile. 'But he is not walking.'

'I try, sometimes. I set him up with his feet on the ground. Hold him, like, with the wee soles of him on the clay. But he can't seem to put the weight of him down.'

They both looked at Micheál. He was staring at something on the ceiling, and as they looked up to see what had captured his attention, he let out a pitching squeal of laughter.

Tadgh smiled. 'A laugh for your da. Maybe he'll be talking next time.'

''Tis awful good to see you, Tadgh. You seem changed.'

Tadgh looked down at his hands, as if considering the black crescents of dirt under his fingernails. 'I have been meaning to come.'

'You have been busy.'

'No. There is no work.'

'You have been grieving, then.'

'I have been afraid to come, Nóra. I have been afraid of what I would see. 'Twas not until I heard that Martin had passed, Lord keep him, that I knew I needed to visit you.'

'Tadgh? You're scaring me, the talk of you.'

'I wasn't going to say a word about it, Nóra.' He looked at her with the darkling, lowered stare of a hunted man.

'Johanna. 'Twas in the last days. She was in the bed, and the cloud was on her mind, and she was fighting it best she could, but the pain was awful on her and it made her say some things.' He frowned. 'She said some awful things, Nóra.'

'What did she say?'

'I don't want to tell you.'

'Tadgh, tell me. For God's sake, you're frightening me.'

'One time, she was lying abed, her eyes closed. For all of me I thought she was sleeping. And then I hear a queer muttering coming from her, and I says, "Are you awake, Johanna? Is it the pain?" And she shook her head, slight, like this . . .' He turned his head slowly from side to side, his eyes never leaving Nóra's. 'And I says, "What is it?" And she says, "Bring me Micheál." So I pick the lad up and put him on the bed next to her, and she opened her eyes a wee bit and took a look at him, and a queer expression crosses her face. Like she's never seen him before in her life. "That's not my child," she says. She's looking at me, shaking her head. "That's not my child."'

Nóra's mouth was dry. She swallowed thickly.

'"Sure, 'tis," says I. "He's your own son, so he is. Do you not know your own son?" And she tries to sit up and looks at him again. "That's not my boy," she says. "Bring me my boy." Sure, I didn't know what to do, so I keep telling her 'tis Micheál, and her strange way of talking was scaring me that much that I put him on her lap, and that was it. She started screaming. "That's not my son! Bring me Micheál!" And she's pushing Micheál off the bed, and were I not there to catch him he would have had a tumble.' Tadgh was breathing heavily. 'I didn't know what to do, so I took Micheál away, out of her sight. But all that night long she was like it. "My son has been stolen from me. My boy has been stolen." She was clawing at me to go and get the police, raise a watch, like. She wanted to put Micheál out the house. "Get rid of it!" she was saying. "Put it on the dung pile and bring me back our son!"

'That was it then. That was the last of it, before she fell asleep. 'Twas the last thing she said to me. In the days after, she was not herself. She was halfway to God.'

Nóra stared at Tadgh, feeling like she would choke.

'I didn't want to tell you, Nóra,' Tadgh said, pressing his fingers into his temples. 'But I see him now, Micheál . . .'

Nóra looked down at the little boy. He was jerking his head, as if stabbed by something unseen.

'I see him now and I wonder. I wonder at what she said. I see him and I know he's my son, but I don't recognise him at all.'

'I know why.'

They turned to see Mary in the open doorway, her apron wet and dripping, clutching the pail of water to her chest. Her face was chalk-white.

'He is a changeling,' she whimpered. 'And everyone knows it but you.'

The dark unpainted forge of the blacksmith's sat in the heart of the valley, by the crossroads that divided the community into quarters. On most days the patterned ringing of hammer on anvil could be heard in all directions, and the constant smoke from the forge proved an easy marker for those who required ironwork, or sought to have their teeth pulled. At night, once the day's labour had been done, people often gathered at the blacksmith's, the forge becoming a rambling house for the men and the small cabin beside it one for the women. It was a place of frequent company. On nights when the moon gave a clean, clear light to the valley, it was not uncommon for the young people to step outside and dance at the crossroads above the buried bones of suicides, the very place Martin Leahy had died.

Nance did not often come to the blacksmith's. There was little she owned that needed the attention of pumping bellows and sweaty-faced men – she preferred the quiet skill of the travelling tinkers. It was also a place where she felt her difference. It was often busy with farmers and labourers bringing workhorses to be shod or to be treated for spavins or farcy, and, despite her years in the valley, Nance had never become accustomed to the way conversation stopped in her presence. It was one thing to enter a wake house and have the company fall into respectful silence. It was another to move through a crowded yard in the prickled air of others' wary regard and to hear laughter at her back. They made her feel like nothing more than a strange old woman plucking herbs, her eyes clouded with age and the smoke of her own badly fired hearth. No matter that some of these men came to her with their carbuncles and congested lungs, or lay their wheezing children by her fire. In the broad light of day, amidst the noise of industry, their stares made her feel scorned and feeble.

'God bless your work, John O'Donoghue,' Nance said, standing in the doorway. She had lingered on the road until she saw that the yard of the smith's was clear of people, then clenched her teeth and made for the forge.

John paused, his hammer raised in the air. 'Nance Roche,' he said simply. A local boy, charged with pumping the bellows, gaped in Nance's direction.

'I was wondering if you would let me take some of that water there. Your iron water.'

John put down his hammer and wiped his sweating face with a greasy, blackened cloth. 'Iron water,' he repeated. He stared at Nance, breathing hard. 'How much do you need?'

Nance pulled her water pail out from under her cloak. 'As much as I might carry.'

John took the pail and lowered it into the bucket where he cooled the iron. 'I've filled it to half. Will that do you?'

'It will. It will. I thank you, John. Bless you.'

John nodded, then returned to the anvil. As he raised his hammer he motioned towards the cabin. 'Go see the little woman, Nance. She'll give you something to eat.'

The cabin of the O'Donoghues was built from the same mountain rock as the forge, but was thickly whitewashed, its thatch of heather and oats rising high over a cavernous ceiling. Both half-doors were open to admit the light, and Nance could hear a woman's voice singing inside.

'Bless you, woman of the house.'

Áine O'Donoghue was kneeling in front of the turf fire, scrubbing a shirt in a wide wooden tub. She looked up, squinting. 'Nance Roche?' Her face eased into a smile. 'Come in and welcome. 'Tis not often I see you here.' She rose to her feet, wiping her wet forearms on her apron. 'What's that you have?'

'Only a little forge water, Áine. Your man was good enough to give me some.'

'Did he now. I suppose I shouldn't be asking what you want that for?' Áine gave a wry smile and patted the stool beside her. 'Sit you down. Would you like something to eat?'

'Go on with your washing, Áine. I don't mean to stop you.'

'Sure, 'twould be a poor thing if I did.' Áine picked up a cold potato and gave it to Nance. 'How are you keeping?'

'I'm still alive, which is enough.'

'Are you prepared for the winter? Isn't it awful bitter out? And not even December.'

'Pure bitter. I see you and John are well.'

'Well enough.'

Nance gestured to the bucket of forge water at her feet. 'Protection. I thought Brigid Lynch might be in need of it. Her time is coming.' She peeled the potato and glanced at Áine. The woman was looking intently at the puckered skin on her fingers, leaning forward with her elbows on her knees.

'Why don't you come see me?' Nance heard herself asking.

Áine feigned surprise. 'See you, Nance?'

'I can help you.'

Áine blushed. 'And for what? The mouth sore is gone from me now. You gave me the cure and I thank you for it.'

'I don't mean the sore.' Nance took a bite of the cold potato and chewed it thoughtfully. 'It can't be easy, seeing the women of this place full of children and you having none yourself.'

Áine gave a strange, wan smile. Her voice was soft. 'Oh, that. Sure, it can't be helped, Nance.'

'There are ways, Áine. For every ill thing set upon this world, there is a cure.'

Áine shook her head. '*An rud nach féidir ní féidir é.* What can't be done, can't be done. I have made my peace with it.'

'You poor unfortunate.' Nance dropped the rest of the potato in her lap and took Áine's hands. The woman smiled at her, but as Nance continued to hold her fingers Áine's face tightened and her chin trembled.

'Have you truly made your peace with it? With your quiet house?'

'Don't,' she whispered.

'Áine.'

'Please, Nance. You're a good woman. Don't be upsetting . . . Please.'

Nance pulled Áine closer to her, until their foreheads were almost touching. 'Children are the curse of this country,' she whispered, gripping Áine's hands. 'Especially when you don't have any.'

Áine laughed, but pulled away to hastily wipe her eyes.

'Come and see me,' Nance whispered. 'You know where I am.'

Shuffling back to her cabin, the narrow handle of her water pail cutting into her hand, Nance thought about what had come over her. She didn't normally like to pry into others' business. Maggie had always taught her to stay away until she was summoned.

'The cure will always work best for those who seek it,' she had said. 'Those who look are those who find.'

But in that moment Nance had felt a quiet summoning to speak to Áine. There was a hesitation. A look of raw longing. That's how it was with most people. All that private pain kept out of sight, but sometimes, in the space of one breath, something opened and you could see the heart of things before the door was shut again. It was as good as a vision. A murmur of vulnerability. A tremor in the soil, before all was still.

How hidden the heart, Nance thought. How frightened we are of being known, and yet how desperately we long for it.

Father Healy was waiting for Nance outside her cabin, his stark figure cutting a black line against the rising alder. He stood still, watching her walk the path with his arms folded in front of him, and then, noticing the heavy pail she carried, stepped forward and took it from her.

'Thank you, Father.'

They walked in silence to the muddy ground before Nance's cabin, where he set the pail of forge water down and faced her.

"Tis Nance Roche they call you?'

"Tis.'

'I want time with you, then.'

'Time with me, is it, Father? What an honour.' Nance bent her aching fingers back. 'And how can I help you?'

'Help me?' He shook his head. 'I've come to tell you to help yourself, woman. I've come to tell you to stop your ways.'

'My ways, now. What ways would they be?' Nance put her hands on her hips and tried to catch her breath. Her chest felt dry and tight from lugging the water across the valley. All she wanted to do was return inside and rest.

'Word has travelled that you were keening at Martin Leahy's wake.'

Nance frowned. 'So I was. And what of it?'

'The synod forbids professional keeners wailing at wakes as an unchristian practice. It is a heathenish custom and abhorrent to God.'

'Abhorrent to God? I find it hard to believe, Father, that God does not understand sorrow. Sure, Christ died on a cross surrounded by his keeners.'

Father Healy gave a tight smile. "Tis not the same at all. I have been told that you make it your *trade* to cry at burials.'

'What is the harm in that?'

'Your sorrow is artificial, Nance. Rather than comfort those who are afflicted, you live upon their dead.'

Nance shook her head. 'I do not, Father. That's not it at all. I feel their sorrow. I give voice to the grief of others when they have not a voice for it themselves.'

'But they pay you for it.'

"Tis not money.'

'Food then. Drink. Payment in kind for immoderate, false sadness.' The man gave a sad laugh. 'Nance, listen to me now. You can't be taking money – or anything like it – for keening. The church won't stand for it, and neither will I.' He raised an eyebrow. 'When I heard about the keening I asked about you.'

'Is that so, Father?'

'People tell me that you drink. You take the pipe. You don't come to Mass.'

Nance laughed. 'If you're after visiting all them that don't go to Mass, you'll be out on that donkey of yours the whole week long.'

Father Healy pinked a little. 'Yes. I mean to correct the lack of religious feeling here.'

'But the people here do be having a spiritual temper, Father. Sure, we all have faith in the things of the invisible world. We're a most religious people. Come now, Father. Would you not care for a drink? Look, the sky is turning.'

The priest hesitated, and then followed Nance into her cabin, glancing around the dark room in uncertainty.

'Be so kind as to sit yourself down on that creepie there. Make yourself easy. I'll have the water on the boil now.'

Father Healy lowered himself down on the stool, his knees sticking out at angles. He gestured to the dried herbs hanging from the rafters. 'William O'Hare tells me that you act the charlatan.'

'The schoolmaster? What would he know? He's never visited me in his life.'

'Aye, him. He says you live by keening and quackery. That you lure the people of this parish with false promises of healing.'

'Some folk here . . . Well, we don't agree together.'

'So, 'tis not just the money-taking for the false bawling, but you act the *bean leighis* too?'

'Act?' Nance handed the priest a steaming cup. He regarded it with suspicion. 'Father. People come to me of their own accord and

I use the knowledge that has been given me to help them. They leave me gifts in thanks for it. I am no thief.'

'Well, now, see, this puts me in some state of confusion!' The priest ran a hand through his hair. 'For Seán Lynch tells me you prey on the trust of others and try to get something for nothing.'

Nance sucked her gums. 'I help them. I am a doctor to them.'

'Oh yes, so I have heard. Like the Dublin doctors, so you are. O'Hare said that you forced a gander's beak down his wife's throat when she came to you for thrush.'

'Ah, Éilís? 'Tis an old cure. Did it not heal her?'

'William did not say.'

'It healed her alright. Éilís O'Hare might be thinking she's above herself now, married to a Killarney man. But she's a liar if she says I never healed her. That woman would be in the ground if it weren't for me.'

'No one dies of thrush.'

'I healed her all the same.'

The priest peered at his tea and put it firmly on the ground. 'Can you not see that I am trying to help you?'

Nance smiled. 'I respect you, Father. Sure, you're a good and holy man with a heart for the people. But you should know that Father O'Reilly, God rest him, saw I had the gift. He sent folk to me. Drink your tea.'

'I won't, if 'tis all the same to you.' The priest looked up again at the herbs. 'I know the likes of you. I know the poor turn their hand to whatever living they can make. The vulnerable.' His voice dropped to a whisper. 'There's still a need in this parish for the . . .' He looked uncomfortable. '*Handy woman*. For the mothers. Give up the keening and the herbs and charms and all the pagan superstitions, and make an honest living by that.'

Nance sighed. 'Father, as little as the wren needs, it must

gather it. 'Tis by the cures and keening or my heart would break in hunger, but 'tis more than that. I have the *knowledge* given to me by the Good People and I must use it for the people here or 'twould leave me.'

There was a moment of silence. The jackdaws disturbed the trees outside.

''Tis not the fairies you're talking of. No, I won't have that.'

'Do you not believe in the Good People, Father?'

The priest rose to his feet. 'Nance Roche. I take no pleasure in being here. I take no pleasure in harsh words. But do you think of your stomach or your soul?'

'Ah, you're no believer. But I tell you, Father, 'twas the Good People that led me out of my misery on the roads and led me to this valley and to Father O'Reilly. 'Twas the Good People who saw me safe and not starving in Killarney when my family were gone and I alone with no man or money to my name. 'Twas Them that gave me the knowledge to cure folk and bring the fairy dart out of them and –'

''Tis pagan to say they exist at all.' The priest's face suddenly took on a look of pity, and Nance felt a wave of anger at the condescension in his expression.

'Well, God be praised. A priest who is against the curing of the sick. God knows 'tis hard I work for the bit I have, and 'tis poor I am and always have been, but never have I begged from any Christian in this valley, and haven't I always meant well? And haven't I cured the priest before you, and him always seeing the good in all?'

Father Healy shook his head. 'And to the bad he turned his eye. You know what they say, woman? The road to Hell is paved with good intentions.'

'And the road to Heaven is well signposted, Father . . .' Nance smiled. 'But badly lit at night.'

The priest snorted. 'I'll not have keening, and I'll not have women seeking to swindle the sick with talk of fairies. By all means, be a handy woman to those in need, but I'll not have this parish riddled with superstition by those who mean to profit by it.'

'Oh, you're a wonderful great man, taking our money and counting out sins in exchange, and not letting an honest woman have her bit in return for all the good she does.'

'I've tried to do right by you, Nance Roche. I came here to lead you to the better path. But if 'tis stubborn you are, I would see you leave this place.'

'The people would not let you drive me out. They need me. You will see that they need me.'

'Well, now. I don't think it will go well with you, Nance Roche, despite what you think.' The priest ducked his head under the cabin door and strode to his donkey, which was grazing beside the woods. Nance followed, watching as he mounted and gave it a hearty kick with his heels. He looked back at her as he rode towards the lane. 'Go on, Nance. Stop it with the keening and the fairy talk. You want a long spoon when supping with the Devil.'

PART TWO

A Mouth of Ivy, A Heart of Holly
Beul eidhin a's croidhe cuilinn

1825–1826

CHAPTER
SIX

Nettle

December arrived and bled the days of sunlight, while the nights grew bitter, wind-rattled. The water that pooled outside beneath the doorstep was tight with ice by morning and starlings lit upon the thatched roofs of the valley, circling the smoking chimney holes for warmth.

Micheál became restless in the cold. When the heat of the fire died away at night and the chill crawled into the room, he woke Mary with whimpers, arms jerking, fingernails sharp in her back like a kitten fighting a sack and a swift-flowing river.

Anxious to warm him, Mary wrapped him in their blanket, pressed his pointed chin to her shoulder and, sitting up, lumbered his shivering bones against her chest until he surrendered to fatigue. Sometimes she traced his eyebrows and the delicate skin of his eyelids with a gentle fingertip to encourage him to close his eyes, or opened the front of her clothes to place his cheek on the bare skin of her neck and reassure him with her warmth. She fell asleep with him upon her chest, slumped against the wooden corner of the settle, and would wake in the grey of morning with a stiff neck and her legs dead and unfeeling.

She had never felt so tired. Mary had thought that the winter days, with their lull in labour and their quiet, unfriendly weather, would be easeful after her term of working through harvest. Those days had been unceasing. She had fetched and flailed and stooped until she felt she would die, until she was spangled with chaff and her hands bled from handling flax. But the child exhausted her in a different way. He tortured her with constant, shrill needfulness. Sometimes it seemed that he screamed his throat raw and no amount of soothing would quiet him. She fed him and he ate like the starved, swallowing thick mouthfuls of potato mixed with milk, and yet he was as thin as winter air. He would not let her sleep the night through. Mary woke every morning with her body aching to rest, her limbs cramping from long hours of holding the boy close to her, her eyes as raw as if someone had tried to pluck them from their sockets. She would stumble in the half-light to uncover the embers from their blanket of ash and set water to boil, before lurching into the shocking blue of the yard, the air so cold it seized her lungs.

Her one moment of peace each morning was in the cramped, shit-stained byre, when she was able to lean her forehead against the dusty comfort of the cow and milk her, singing old songs to calm herself and the animal. Sometimes she cried from weariness, without caring. She pressed her face into the cow's belly and felt her eyes grow hot with tears, and as her fingers encouraged the teats, she let her song give way to sobs. The milk hardly came, no matter the sound from her.

Ever since the visit from the widow's son-in-law, Nóra had withdrawn into herself. Mary knew she had spoken out of turn, had let the fear of being cornered by the women at the well have the run of her mouth. As soon as she had spoken in the doorway she had flinched at her own accusation. She had thought she would be sent back to Annamore with empty pockets. But Nóra had simply looked at her with the preoccupied, inward stare of someone who is told there is a ghost in the room. The man, Tadgh, had reacted even more strangely. He had gazed at Mary with curiosity, then reached out and touched her hair, stroking the cropped ends between his fingers as though she was an angel and he could not decide whether to kiss or fight her. Then, just as quickly, he had recoiled. 'May the Good Lord protect you,' he had said to her before stepping out into the pale afternoon and stumbling down the lane, a hand over his mouth. He had not looked back and they had not seen him since.

Nóra, Mary noticed, had watched this without feeling. After Tadgh left, she had sat still and breathed deeply and steadily, as if asleep. Then she had beckoned Mary to the fire. 'Sit down.' When Mary had hesitated, Nóra's voice became edged with impatience. 'Sit down.'

As Mary sat on the creaking straw-seat, Nóra had fossicked in the nook of the hearth. Mary heard the squeak of a cork being pulled from a bottle, and when Nóra brought her forearm to the wall to hide her face, Mary had guessed she was drinking.

'People are calling Micheál a changeling, are they?' She turned and her eyes were bleary.

'They were speaking of him as changeling at the well.'

Nóra had begun to laugh in a wild panic, like a woman who finds a lost child and is split by anger and relief. Mary watched as Nóra bent over, shaking, tears spilling from her eyes. Micheál, attracted by the noise, had squealed, mouth wide. His shrieks brought her flesh out in goosebumps.

It was all too strange. The sight of Nóra laughing when there was nothing but dread, heavy and rolling in her stomach, made Mary's heart thud. She had been brought into a home where everything was on the point of collapse, where ill fortune and sorrow had eaten into the timber of this woman and she was breaking down in front of her.

Unsettled, Mary had wrapped her shawl about her head and had gone out to sit in the byre.

Mary had stayed beside the comforting warmth of the cow until the day faltered and she could hear the wind whistling through the stone wall. She wished that she could leave the widow to her mad laughter, and walk the rocky road back to Annamore that night. Were it not for the thought of her empty-bellied brothers and sisters, and the weariness pulling at the corners of her mother's mouth, she would have walked the whole night long to return home.

When she went back inside, Nóra had acted as though nothing had happened. She asked Mary to begin preparing their dinner and had sat with her knitting, fingers plying the needles furiously. Only once did she raise her head and address Mary, her face inscrutable. '*Briseann an dúchas trí chrúba an chait.* The true nature of the cat shows in the way it uses its claws.'

'Yes, missus,' Mary had replied. She had not known what the woman meant by the proverb, but it seemed ominous and had not comforted her.

Since then, neither of them had spoken of Tadgh's visit, nor the gossip at the well, nor what had happened after, although Mary thought that Nóra was not as attentive to Micheál as before. More and more it fell to her to bathe and feed him and to rise in the night to console him from the unseen terrors plaguing his soft, mysterious mind. Mary became used to the shadows that emerged in the ill-lit witching hours. She woke and tended the child like a mourner over a corpse.

One night, rasping awake at Micheál's scraping cry, Mary wriggled away from his grasping arms and buried her head under the rag-pillow, too tired to sit and warm him or rub the soles of his feet. She fell back into the blissful arm of sleep, until the smell of sour piss roused her and she woke to soaked hay, the boy wet-backed and freezing beside her, screaming like the murdered.

⚬

It had become cold in Nance's *bothán*. In the late autumn days she had spent many hours gathering what fuel for her fire she could find, cutting the prickled gorse from the mountain slopes and wild land with a black-handled knife and taking what dung had not already been gathered from the fields by the children. Some of the valley folk had brought her small baskets of turf in exchange for her cures, but she knew those few, precious scraws would not be enough to last her the winter. The cold would stalk her, threaten her, if she did not find some way to keep her fire alive through the months of biting wind. Always, the need to find ways to survive. No lingering children to take care of her. No parent living to help. Every year, this battle to keep on. Every year the fight to remain. It wearied her.

When did I become so old? Nance wondered as she huddled over her fire. My bones are becoming as fluted and hollow as the skeletons of birds.

How slippery time had become. When she was younger the days had seemed unceasing. The world had felt infinitely full of wonder.

Yet the more she aged, the more the mountains shrank against the sky. Even the river seemed colder than when she first arrived in the valley, those twenty years ago. Seasons came and went with staggering swiftness.

Nance remembered the woods of Mangerton when she was small. Walking through them with her cans of goat milk and *poitín* for the tourists, and the hard, clinking purse she brought back to the grateful hand of her father, she had felt that she was a child of the trees. The moss on the forest floor comforted her bare feet, and she had felt protected by the canopy of leaves, had felt the wind to be a voice that rushed through her hair for no other purpose than to speak to her alone. How well she had known God, then. How unknotted her soul. How easy to be.

Nance remembered walking the mountain, plucking snagged wool from the thorns of briars and gorse, waiting for ponies carrying tourists on their way to the Devil's Punch Bowl, only to be overwhelmed by the beauty of the sun lighting on the water of the lakes. Lough Leane golden, and the surrounding mountains bearing down in holy indigo. The shifting, unfurling clouds passing the sun like pilgrims past a saint. Nance remembered walking, only to be winded by the grace of the world.

'Why are you crying?' her father had asked her once, caulking his boat on the shore of the lough.

How old had she been? The summer before Maggie came with her herbs and visitors and mysterious ways of being. A child still. A bud unblossomed. A lifetime ago.

'Nance? Why are you crying?'

'Because everything is too beautiful.'

Her father had understood the profundity of her love. 'Nature is at her best in the morning and the evening. Sure, 'tis no bad thing to cry over. Most people go through their days without ever acknowledging her.'

Perhaps it was then that he began to teach her the language of the sky with his boatman's eye for weather. Before the slow disappearing of her mother, before Maggie came, when they were all together and they were whole and well.

'The world isn't ours,' he said once. 'It belongs to itself, and that is why it is beautiful.'

It was her father who had showed her the high mackerel clouds that brought rain and fish, and the deceitful emptiness of summer days which hid the sign of storms at night. The sky, he taught her, could be an ally, a messenger of warning. When it brought them the wheeling screams of seagulls, they knew not to stray too far from shore or cabin.

Sometimes, before the gentle-blooded tourists flocked to spend their money on the strawberry girls like Nance and boatmen like her father, and jarveys to the crumbling Muckross Abbey with its towering heart of yew, or when her mother had suffered through another terrible night, her father took her out onto the lakes and bid her look up.

'Can you see the clouds there, Nance?'

Nance remembered lifting her face to the sky, squinting against early sun.

'What do you make of them? Are they not like a goat's beard? A combed goat's beard?'

Even now, she could almost smell the clay and water.

'Do you see where the beard turns black, there?' He would haul an oar into the boat and raise his arm. 'That's where the wind'll be coming from today. Faith, a strong wind. And that black tip of his beard is full of rain. What do you think we're after doing with a beard such as that in the sky?'

'I think we should be going home.'

'That goat will bring us no good. No gentlemen and their ladies today. Let's get back to your mam.'

He had loved the lakes, her father. And the sea. Raised near Corca Dhuibhne, he had spoken of the ocean as some men speak of their mothers – with reverence and a great, choking love. 'When good weather is on its way, the sea will make a sweet and quiet sound. The sea will be settled and calm and you may trust in her. But gannets in the harbour in early morning and you know she's warning you to leave her alone. The cormorant on his rock shows you the wind and, depending on where he is facing to, where it is likely to come from.

'Most people don't see the world. But you've got the eye, I think, Nance. You've got the eye.'

There was a cough at the door and Nance started. The fire had gone out and there was a man standing on her threshold. She had not heard him approach.

'Who's there?' Nance croaked, bringing her palms to her cheeks. They were wet. Had she been crying?

"Tis Daniel Lynch, Nance.' He sounded nervous. 'I've come to see you about my wife, Brigid.'

Nance peered in the low light and saw the young man who had been smoking at the wake of Martin Leahy.

'Brought you a hen,' he said, nodding to the struggling chicken he held pinned under his arm. 'She's stopped laying, but I thought it might be good for your pot. I didn't know . . .'

'That's kind.' Nance beckoned him in with a trembling finger. 'Come in, son, come in and God welcome.'

Daniel ducked his head under the door and Nance noticed him take in the small cabin with its tethered goat, the drain of waste and the dead fire in front of her. He pulled the chicken out from under his arm and offered it to Nance, holding it by its legs. The bird flapped, sending the bunches of herbs swaying on their strings.

'Set her on the floor, there, good man. She can stretch her legs. Grand so.' Nance prodded at the fire and blew on the embers. 'Would you pass me some of that dried furze? Ah, I thank you. So, you've come about your young wife, your Brigid. The one with child. Is she in good health?' Nance nudged a stool towards Daniel and he sat down.

'She is. Only . . .' He let out a short laugh, embarrassed. 'I don't really know why I'm here. 'Tis nothing, only the little woman's taken to walking at night. In her sleep.' He watched the hen jump the drain and begin to scratch in the hay.

'Walking at night, is she? Not a thing for a woman in her state to be doing. Will you have a drink?' Nance reached for an empty piggin and poured out a liquid, tinctured yellow, from a pot near the fire.

Daniel regarded the cup with a frown. 'What's this, then?'

''Tis a cold tea. 'Twill calm you.'

'Oh, I don't have a need for calming,' Daniel said, but he took a tentative sip. 'It tastes like weeds.'

'Go on, Daniel. Tell me about your Brigid.'

'I don't like to make a fuss, only, begod, 'tis a strange thing she's doing and I have no wish for people to talk of it.'

'You say she's walking in her sleep.'

He nodded. 'A few evenings back I woke in the night and she wasn't to be seen. Her side of the bed was cold empty. My brother sleeps by the fire and we have the wee room to ourselves. Well, I woke up and thought to myself, "She's maybe after getting a sip of water," and so I waited. But a good time crept past and there was no sign of her. I went out and there's my brother, sound asleep, except the door is wide open and there's a fierce cold coming in. I look for Brigid's cloak and 'tis there, where she normally sets it on the rafter, but her shawl is missing. Well, I was frightened for her then. I didn't know if someone had taken her, or what. You hear stories . . .' His voice broke off and he took another sip of tea. 'I woke my brother and asked him had he seen her and he hadn't. So we set out to look for her and thank God for the bright moon! After a time we find her shawl lying on the ground and perhaps we walk on for another mile, and I see a flash of white, and . . .' Daniel frowned, pulling at his lip. 'Well, 'twas her. Lying down, asleep.'

'She was safe, then.'

'That's why I thought to come see you, Nance. She wasn't just lying any place. She was asleep in the *cillin*. Near the fairy *ráth*. Hardly a stone's throw from where we're sitting now.'

Nance felt the hair on the back of her neck stand up. The *cillín* was a small triangle of land next to the fairies' whitethorn. The grass grew long there, around a standing stone guarded by a ragged copse of holly trees. The thin slab of rock stood perpendicular to the soil like a tombstone, the vestige of an etched cross upon its surface. Surrounding it, like stars without pattern, were white stones marking where clusters of limbo-bones lay in the soil. Sometimes the people of the valley buried unwed mothers there, and sometimes those who had died in sin. But mostly the *cillín* was for children. Stillborns. It was not a place people visited unless they had an unchristened baby to bury.

'The *cillín*?'

Daniel rubbed at the stubble on his chin. 'You see now why I've come? She was lying there amongst the stones. Amongst all the poor dead, buried babies. I thought she was dead herself until I shook her awake. I've heard of folk that do be wandering in their sleep. But to a *cillín*?'

'Who knows of this?'

'Not a soul besides my brother, David, and myself. And I made him swear to keep it quiet. 'Tis the kind of thing to get tongues moving faster than a middleman to tithe day. Especially with all the goings-on in this place.'

'Tell me. What goings-on?'

Daniel grimaced. 'I don't know, Nance. There's just an uneasy feeling about the place. Cows are not giving the milk they once did.' He pointed at the chicken fussing in the straw. 'Hens have stopped laying. Folk are still talking of the way Martin Leahy died. A fit man in the full of his health, dying at a crossroads? People are saying 'tis unnatural. Some are getting on with nonsense about the evil eye. Saying he was blinked, like. Others keep talking about a *changeling* child. A changeling, like! We all know Nóra Leahy has a boy in with her. When her daughter died, the son-in-law came with a child in a basket. We saw him in the fields. But when no one saw the boy afterwards, we thought perhaps he was sick. Ailing, like. But Brigid has seen him. And she told me that there's something woeful wrong with him. Woeful wrong.'

Nance remembered the cripple Peter had spoken of. 'Not a sick child, then.'

'Sure, he's got no health about him, but it seems to be more than that. Brigid says the boy is a wee raw thing, all bones and no sense in his head. Not like any child she's seen before.'

'Have you seen him yourself?'

'Me? I've not seen him, no. But I'm thinking that perhaps . . . Perhaps if that boy has been touched by the Good People, then they're after touching others. Or maybe he has the evil eye and he blinked Martin Leahy, and now he's after blinking my wife.' Daniel pressed his thumbs to his temples. 'Holy Jesus, I don't know, Nance.'

Nance nodded. 'I think it best to keep this to yourself, Daniel. People here have enough troubles without finding cause for fear in things they do not understand.'

'Would explain it if the boy was changeling, though. The more I think of it, the more I wonder whether the Good People are abroad, and if they're after sweeping folk for themselves. Only, you hear the stories, about the women who are carrying. About them disappearing into ringforts.' He leant closer. 'I remember the stories. The old folk still tell them. The Good People have a need of women who are carrying, to take the human child for their own, and keep the woman to feed theirs . . .' He took a deep breath. 'Begod, I know there's plenty that laugh at those who believe every wind they meet with is a *sigh-gaoithe*. But I thought you might know, Nance. People say you go with Them. That they gave you knowledge and the eye to see Them.'

Nance dragged more furze onto the fire and the flames leapt up, casting wild light across their faces. 'How was your Brigid when she woke?'

'Her face was all white and washy when she saw where she was. She had no memory of walking out the cabin, nor down the lane.'

'And has she walked in her sleep before?'

'She hasn't. Well, not that she can remember, and not since she's been my wife.'

Nance cast him a sharp look. 'And is all well between ye? Are you great with each other? There's no reason for your wife to be wanting to go with the fairies, now?'

'Not on my life.'

'Naught to flee from, then. Well now, Daniel. Sure, 'tis a dangerous time for a woman when she's carrying. 'Tis a time of interference. Your wife is on a threshold and can be pulled back and forth. Either into the world we know, or the one that we don't. And 'tis true, what you say about the Good People. They are much given to taking young women. I've never known a woman to be swept into the fairy *ráth* by here, but 'tis not to say they won't or haven't.'

'They say 'twas the fate of Johanna Leahy by Macroom. That 'twas not to God she went, but to the fairy fort by there. That when she saw they'd changed her own son for fairy, she let them sweep her to be with her boy.'

Nance leant closer, her face growing flushed in the rising heat of the fire. 'The Good People are cunning when they are not merry. They do what pleases them because they serve neither God nor Devil, and no one can assure them of a place in Heaven or Hell. Not good enough to be saved, and not bad enough to be lost.'

'Are you saying that the Good People are abroad, then?'

'They have always been here. They are as old as the sea.'

Daniel had grown ashen. His blue eyes stared at hers in the firelight.

'Have you ever gone walking at the changing hours by the woods or in the lonesome places and felt Them watching you? Not so wicked as a man waiting to beat you, but not so gentle as a mother watching her children sleep.'

Daniel swallowed. 'I believe it. I do. I am not such a fool to say that there is no more to this world than what I can see with my own two eyes.'

Nance nodded approvingly. 'The Good People watch us with a kind of knowing that can undo a man. Make him want to turn heel. Sometimes they wish to reward him, and he finds he has fairy skill with the pipe, or that his sick cow is well again, and there's no accounting for it. But sometimes they punish those who speak ill against them. Sometimes they repay good with good. Bad with bad. Sometimes 'tis all unreason and no knowing why things are as they are, except to say 'tis the fairies behind it and they have their own intentions.'

'And so why are they after taking Brigid? What has she done to the Good People that they might like to steal her away?' He paused for a moment. 'Do you think 'tis something *I* have done?'

'Daniel, your Brigid is a dear one. There's no use in you believing she has some hand in this, or that she's astray. There's no fault on her. When They are here, watching us, they know the human of us and an envy comes upon them and there are some who will have of our kin, of our blood. I have seen them sweep a woman in front of my eyes.'

'Sweet Christ. 'Tis as folk are saying. There's some awful mischief about and 'tis the Good People behind it.' Daniel's face was pale. 'What must I do?'

'Is your Brigid changed at all? Does she eat? Is she injured in any way?'

'She eats. She was frightened to wake and see that she was sleeping in the *cillín* and her feet were bloodied from hard walking, but she is not changed.'

Nance leant back, satisfied. 'She was not abducted, then. She is still your wife.'

'Begod, what is happening in this valley, Nance? Moves my bones to powder. The priest said 'tis no reason for the cows and hens and Martin but the will of God, and all will be well, but he's a man from town.'

Nance spat on the ground. 'Perhaps someone has offended Them.'

'There is talk that one of Them is amongst us.'

'Aye, that boy your Brigid speaks of. With Nóra Leahy.'

Daniel looked at the floor. 'Or another,' he mumbled.

Nance gave Daniel a hard look. 'Do you know something? Has that Seán Lynch been swinging his axe at whitethorns again?'

'He has not. He'll have no talk of the Good People, and he spends his nights on ramble driving us all to tears with his talk of Father Healy and Daniel O'Connell. The priest has been in his ear about the Catholic Association. A penny a month and O'Connell will have us all emancipated, so says Seán. We all think he's on the drink and bouncing the boot off his wife again, but he has not been interfering with the fairy trees.'

'That one has trouble coming to him,' Nance said. 'Cheating the Devil in the dark, so he is.'

Daniel picked up his tea and drank it, avoiding her gaze. 'He has the hard word against you, Nance.'

'Oh. There's plenty that have the hard word against me. But I know what I know.' She lifted her hands in front of Daniel's face and he flinched, leaning away from the reach of her fingers. 'What do you see?'

He gaped at her.

'My thumbs. Do you see how they're turned?' She showed him her swollen knuckles, the crooked angle of her joints.

'I do.'

''Tis Their mark on me. 'Tis how you may know that whatever
Seán Lynch and Father Healy say about me, I have the knowledge
of Them and there is no lie in it. Whatever lies they tell about me,
there is no lie in this.' She fixed him with a kindly look. 'Do you
trust me?'

'Aye, Nance. I believe you.'

'Then let me tell you that all will be well if you do as I say. Your
wife must rest until her time comes. She is to get what sleep she can
and she's not to walk at all. Is she still up and about the house?'

'She is.'

'No more. You must do all the chores, Daniel. Churn the butter.
Feed her hens. Cook your praties. No fire must be taken out of the
house when she's in it. Not even the flare of your pipe. Not even a
spark. Do you understand?'

'I do.'

'Not a single flame nor ember, Daniel, or you'll be taking the luck
out of the house. You'd be breaking all that which serves to protect
her and keep her in the world. And give her these.' Nance shuffled
to the corner of her cabin and fetched a parcel of cloth tightly bound
with straw. She unknotted the ties and shook some dried berries into
Daniel's palm.

He peered at them nervously. 'What are these?'

'Bittersweet. They will urge her into a deeper sleep. So deep she
will not have the strength or wherewithal to rise at night. Let her take
them in the evening and I will hold the charm for her in my mind,
and I will think on protection for her.' She patted his arm. 'All will
be well, Daniel.'

'I thank you, Nance.'

'God bless you, and may you have a fine, long family. Come
back if she keeps at her walking. Wait . . .' Nance put a hand on
Daniel's arm. 'There is something else you may do. If 'tis the Good

People that are luring her out of doors, let you make a cross from birch twigs and nail it over your sleeping place. Birch will guard her.'

He hesitated by the door. 'You're a good woman, Nance. I know Father Healy preached against you, but I think he's a blind-hearted man.'

'Do you feel better, Daniel?'

'I do.'

Nance watched Daniel begin the slow walk home, holding the berries safe between his hands like a man in prayer. The sky soared with late-afternoon light, hemming the clouds with bright bloodiness. Just before he disappeared from view, Daniel turned around and stared at her, crossing himself.

The first snow arrived in the valley. Staggered winds blew white upon the fields until, from the height of Nóra's cabin, the stone walls dividing them looked like the whorls of a fingerprint. Men planted themselves by the fire, coughing up the season, and the women carded wool and kept company with their spinning wheels, as though compelled to wrap themselves and their families in more layers of homespun. It was a quiet, waiting time of year.

Nóra woke in the grey throat of morning and blinked in the feeble light. She longed to sleep. The nights were shattered with the boy's screaming, and it was all she could do to hang on to the balm of sleep's senselessness. How lonely waking in an empty bed had become.

Her head throbbed from the *poitín* bottle. Lying on her back, Nóra stared up into the thatch and listened for some sign that Mary was awake. Most mornings she waited until she heard the scuff of the girl's footsteps as she readied the fire and set water to boil, or her voice murmuring to the child as she bathed the piss from his legs. Then, Nóra would close her eyes and imagine that it was not Mary but Martin moving about the room, unlatching the door and letting the hens out to scrounge along the wall of the byre amidst the frost and dirty straw. She could picture him perfectly. His lips as he whistled the old songs, his nail pulling away the skins of his morning potatoes, and the careless way he threw them aside. She could hear his usual wry complaint that her hens were tearing into the thatch, and remembered the crinkle of his eyes when she, flustered, defended them. She allowed herself this lie, even when the disappointment on seeing not Martin but the long-limbed maid, puffy-eyed, by the fire was almost too painful to bear.

Nóra could hear nothing. Tying her shawl tightly around her, she went out and saw that the fire had been lit, although there was no sign of Mary. The settle was unfolded and Micheál lay in its corner. Not wanting to rouse his attention, Nóra crept slowly to the side of the bed before peering at him. The boy was listless, his hair sticking to his head with sweat. Nóra watched his mouth slowly undulate, his lips pert and softly wet. Who is he talking to? she wondered.

'Micheál.'

He ignored her, raising his eyebrows and grimacing at the wall.

'Micheál,' Nóra repeated. The boy's arms were stiff and turned inwards, like the broken wings of a bird pitched from the nest. She called his name for the third time and he finally fixed her with an unblinking stare. His lip curled and she could see the glisten of his teeth. For a moment he seemed to bare them at her.

Micheál had begun to scare her. Everything he did – his quick, unpredictable movements, his calls and shrieks at things she could not see – reminded her of Mary's words.

He is a changeling. And everyone knows it but you.

'What are you?' Nóra whispered.

Micheál looked up to the rafters and blinked. His chin was flaked with a tidemark of dried saliva. He was snot-nosed, his eyes fringed with pale lashes, slick with moisture. Nóra placed a firm hand on his forehead. She could see his jaw grind under his skin.

'Are you child or changeling?' Nóra whispered. She felt her throat jump with the pulse of her panicked heart.

Micheál closed his eyes and let out a pealing, wet shriek, bucking his spine against the straw bedding. Before Nóra could snatch her hand away, Micheál reached up and grabbed a fistful of her loose hair. She tried to uncurl his fingers but he jerked his arm backwards and the pain came, hot and searing.

'Micheál!'

Nóra winced and tried to twist herself free, but the boy's small, sticky fingers were knotted in her hair. He pulled harder. Tears sprang to her eyes.

'Let me go. Let me go, you bold cratur!' Hair ripped from her skin, and in the sudden glare of pain she lashed out and tried to slap Micheál across the face. The angle was awkward and she missed him, cuffing the top of his head instead. In her anger she released his fingers and, holding his jaw firmly with one hand, slapped him again with the other, hitting his cheek. Her palm stung.

'The badness in you!' she shouted, slapping him again. His face was pink, his mouth wide and bawling. Nóra wanted to stuff it shut. Wanted to push his soiled linen in his mouth to stop up his screams.

'You wicked thing,' she hissed, holding her smarting scalp.

'He can't help himself.'

Nóra turned and saw Mary standing by the door, the milk bucket resting on her hip.

'He was pulling the hair out of my skull!'

Mary closed the door against the white brilliance of snow. 'Are you alright?'

'I can't sleep for him! He screams all night.' Nóra could hear the hysteria in her voice.

The maid nodded. 'I think 'tis the cold. And he has a rash on his back. From the way he soils himself.'

Nóra sat by the fire, her hand against her throbbing skin. 'You could wash him, you know.'

'I do,' Mary protested, and her voice was so thin that Nóra felt ashamed.

'Well. How is Brownie milking?'

''Tis not a lot, missus. You said she's a good milker, but . . . I've been singing to her because I know they like the singing. But she's going to the dry.'

Nóra closed her eyes. 'The way we're going, we'll be short for rent.'

'Shall I churn today?'

'Is there enough?'

Mary lifted a corner of the cloth covering the crock of settled milk on the table. 'Sure, well. There might be just enough to churn. Just enough. Should I give Micheál the buttermilk? It might soothe him. I don't know whether 'tis the bitter cold or perhaps he's dreaming things that wake him so and lead him to screaming. I can't sleep for his screaming either.'

'Well, the road to Annamore is where you left it.'

'I don't mean that,' Mary said, anxious. 'Not that I want to go home, like. Only there seems to be a change coming over him and I don't know how to keep the peace in him. He's suffering, I think.'

'Have they been telling you this at the well?'

'They've not, no,' Mary protested. 'The women there have not been talking to me at all. I go and fetch the water and come back again, and I don't stop to gossip or talk about you or Micheál. I promise you.'

Nóra realised that the maid was near tears.

'One of the women sees me coming down the road and takes three steps backwards. On account of my red hair. Kate. Kate Lynch.'

'She's got an awful fear of the evil eye. Don't you mind her. She'll cross herself when meeting with anything in the road. Hare, weasel, magpie.'

'She spits on the ground and says, "The Cross of Christ between me and harm!"'

Nóra rolled her eyes. 'Kate'll be crossing herself at me soon, in fear of a widow's curse.'

Micheál took a shuddering breath and began to scream louder. 'Look at the legs of him,' Mary said, pointing. 'He's hardly kicking. Do you not think they look broken? Like he's no feeling in them at all.' She bent down to the crying boy and lifted his dress to show Nóra. 'Look.'

Micheál's legs were as thin as the winter-bare striplings outside. His skin clung to the bone, streaked with marks. Nóra felt sick at the sight.

Mary chewed her lip. 'He's being smoked up by some kind of sickness. I know he's not had the walking in them for some time, but now he has hardly the twitch in his toes.'

Nóra hastily pulled the cloth back over Micheál's thighs. 'I wonder, Mary,' she murmured. 'How much suffering can a person bear without something turning in them?'

The girl was silent.

Nóra combed her tangled hair with her fingers and stared at Micheál. When she slapped him she had felt on the brink of something dark, something she knew she would not be able to come back from. There was no knowing what she might have done had Mary not come inside at that moment, and it frightened her.

What has happened to me?

Nóra had always believed herself to be a good woman. A kind woman. But perhaps, she thought, we are good only when life makes it easy for us to be so. Maybe the heart hardens when good fortune is not there to soften it.

'Do you think we ought to send for the doctor?' Mary asked.

Nóra turned to her with weariness. 'The doctor, you say. Are there doctors on every lane up in Annamore? Do they come and tend you for nothing?' She nodded at the crock on the table. 'That's all the money I have there and precious little it is too. Do you think I have coins buried about the place? Do you think I am a rich woman? Cream and butter and eggs – that's what stitches body and soul together.' She began to plait her hair with quick roughness, tugging at the grey strands. 'I don't know how you all live up in Annamore, but down here, in this valley, we grease the landlord's palm with whitemeats. How do you think I keep the three of us out of the rain? Turf on the fire? And now the blessed cow is on the dry and you would have me fork out a fortune for a doctor to come and condemn my grandson! When next summer I'll have no man to go and work the fields and earn the keeping of the cabin, and 'twill be the crowbar and the lonely road for me!'

Mary was solemn. 'Have you not your nephews to work the ground for you?'

Nóra took a deep breath. 'Aye. Aye, I've nephews.'

'Perhaps it won't be as bad as you say.'

'Perhaps not.'

'And perhaps there is a doctor who will see to Micheál for nothing. Or maybe for a hen.' Mary's voice was soft. 'Your wee hens are good layers. You said so yourself. Would a doctor not come for a hen?'

Nóra shook her head. 'The hens are not laying as they did. And what do you think a hen is worth to a doctor who lives in town and eats eggs every morning like he laid them himself?' She sighed. ''Tis the priest we want. 'Tis the priest for folk like us.'

'Shall I fetch him then?'

Nóra stood and pulled the shawl over her head. 'No. Get on with your churning, Mary. If anyone is after summoning the priest for Micheál, it should be me.'

Nóra set out down the lane across the face of the valley slope. The air was cold and clean, and the snow on the ground stung her bare feet as she walked. There was no one else on the road. All was still, except for the circling of rooks above the empty fields.

The priest's house was a small whitewashed building set at the corner of the valley where the heather sprawled and the road bent around the mountain, leading the way to Glenflesk. After being admitted inside by a thickset housekeeper, Nóra waited in the parlour where the fireplace lay unlit, before the priest joined her. He had been at his breakfast. Nóra noticed egg yolk dribbling a fatty line down his clerical shirt.

'Widow Leahy. How are you getting on?'

'Thank you, Father, I'm well enough.'

'I'm sorry for your troubles. As they say, "'Tis a lonely washing that has no man's shirt in it."'

Nóra blinked back a prickling of irritation. 'Thank you, Father.'

'Now, how might I help you?'

'I'm sorry to be disturbing you. I know 'tis dreadful early and you a busy man.'

The priest smiled. 'Tell me why you've come.'

''Tis my grandson. I've come because his mother, my daughter, is dead and I was hoping you might be able to heal him.'

'Your grandson, is it? What sickness does he have?' Father Healy's face grew sombre. 'Is it the smallpox?'

"'Tis not the pox, or a sickness like that, no. 'Tis something worse. I don't know what.'

'Have you sent for the doctor?'

'I haven't the wherewithal. Not now.' Nóra could feel herself blushing and it embarrassed her. 'What means I have is spent on a live-in girl to help with him.'

'Begging pardon, Widow Leahy, but perhaps that is the problem.' Father Healy's tone was gentle. 'Getting a girl in when you could get the doctor and have him well again.'

'I don't think he can be made well again by a doctor,' Nóra said.

'Then why have you come for me?'

'He has a need for a priest's healing. He hasn't the full of his mind.'

'Ah. Is he soft-brained?' Father Healy asked.

'I don't know. He's hardly a child at all.'

'Hardly a child? What an odd thing to say. What are his symptoms?'

'He has not the use of his legs, Father. He won't say a word, although not two years ago he was talking like any other little boy. He is forever awake and screaming. He does not thrive.'

Father Healy gave her a look of pity. 'I see.'

'He was born well. That's why 'twould be a kindness for you to come and see him. Why I'm asking you to call, Father. I think . . . perhaps something has happened to him.'

'Such as?'

Nóra clenched her jaw to stop her chin from trembling. 'People are saying he is a changeling.'

Father Healy looked at her from under lowered brows, his face colouring. 'That is superstitious prattle, Widow. Don't be listening to talk like that. A woman like yourself – you've more sense than that.'

'Father,' Nóra added hastily, 'I know there's plenty folk who don't believe in a happening like that, but if you were to come and see the boy . . .'

There was silence. The priest looked apprehensive. 'If the boy is afflicted with a suffering of the usual kind, or if he is dying, I might attend to him. I would be glad to help. But if he is an idiot . . .'

'Would you not pray for him? Heal him?'

'Why do *you* not pray for him, Widow Leahy?'

'I do!'

Father Healy sighed. 'Ah, but you do not attend Mass. Ever since your husband died. I know 'tis a troubling time for you, but believe me when I tell you that it is at Mass where you will find your comfort.'

''Tis no easy thing to be widowed, Father.'

The priest's expression softened slightly. He glanced out the small window, clicking his tongue. 'Is the boy christened?'

'He is.'

'Has he had the Holy Eucharist?'

'No, Father, he is only four.'

'And no doctor has ever seen to him?'

'Once. This summer gone. Martin fetched a man from Killarney, but he did nothing. Just took our money.'

Father Healy nodded, as though he had expected as much. 'Widow Leahy, I think perhaps that it is your duty to care for this child and do the best you can.'

Nóra wiped her eyes. She felt lightheaded with frustration. 'Would you not come and see him and make the sign of the cross over him, Father? A priest such as yourself has the power to banish –'

'Don't be saying fairies, Widow. I'll have no talk of fairies.'

'But Father O'Reilly –'

'Acted the fairy doctor? Presumed to act the fantastic ecclesiastical? Father O'Reilly, may God bless his soul, had no right to engage in these vestiges of pagan rites. And not without leave in writing from the bishop of the diocese would I do the same.'

His face was earnest. 'Widow Leahy, 'tis my responsibility to raise the people of this valley to a morality that corresponds to the requirements of our faith. How can we insist on the rights of Catholics when the valleys are full of the smoke of heathen bonfires and the wailing of hags at wakes? Those who are after keeping us out of parliament need only point to the Catholics pouring beestings at the foot of whitethorns, dancing at cross-roads, whispering of fairies!'

Nóra stared as Father Healy pulled out a handkerchief to wipe the spittle that had gathered at the corner of his mouth. Her feet ached from the cold. 'Forgive me, Father, but your shirt is dirty with egg,' she said. Without waiting to see the priest's reaction, she stood and left the room.

Nóra turned off the lane by the parish house and walked a mile down a little-used path, her face hot with anger. The river could be heard in the distance and soon Nóra reached a ditch where a slow trickle of water had melted snow to mud. She sank to her knees beside a tumbled stone wall to which nettles clung in a thicket.

It was true, what she had said to the priest. Martin had gone for the doctor, though they could not afford it. Borrowing a horse down at the blacksmith's and rising in the mist of the following morning to ride into Killarney and fetch that man. How strange he had seemed, trotting beside Martin. The doctor had been tufted with white hair that clung to his balding scalp and covered the back of his hands like down, and his small wire spectacles had slipped down the greasy length of his nose with every jolt of his horse. When he had stepped into the cabin, he had glanced up at the ceiling as if he expected it to fall upon his head.

Nóra had been so nervous her teeth had chattered. 'God bless you, Doctor, and welcome, and thank you for coming, sir.'

The man had set his satchel upon the ground, nudging the fresh rushes with his foot.

'I'm sorry to hear you have a sickly child. Where is the patient?'

Martin had pointed to where Micheál lay, listless in his cot.

The doctor stooped over the bed and looked down at the boy. 'How old is he?'

'Three years old, sir. No, four.'

The doctor puffed his cheeks, his whiskers fluttering as he exhaled. 'Not yours?'

'Our daughter's child.'

'And where is she?'

'Passed, sir.'

The doctor had squatted awkwardly on the ground, the cloth of his trousers tight around his knees. The leather of his boots squeaked. He dragged his satchel towards him, opened the clasps and took out a long instrument. 'I'm going to listen to his heart,' he explained, glancing up.

The doctor had worked silently. He had pressed the silver stop of his instrument to Micheál's chest, before discarding it and bending down and placing the hairy whorl of his ear directly on the boy's white skin. Then he had tapped Micheál's chest, bouncing his finger-tips along the ridges of the boy's protruding bones as though the child was an instrument he had forgotten how to play.

'What is it, Doctor?'

The man had brought a finger to his lips and shushed her with a solemn eye. He pressed the fat pads of his fingers under the boy's jawbone, lifted his arms and examined the milky hollows of his armpits, prised his lips apart and studied his tongue, then fitted his hands around the back of the boy and, gently, as though he were handling glass, turned Micheál onto his stomach. He had clucked at the sight of the rash upon the boy's back, but said nothing, then ran his fingers down the ridges of the child's spine, turning his legs and arms this way and that.

'Is it the pox, Doctor?'

'Tell me, have you known this child from birth?'

Martin had answered. 'He is just come to us. He was born well. There was no sickness upon him then. We saw him once and he seemed a normal, healthy lad.'

'Did he ever speak?'

'He did. He was learning his words same as any other.'

'And does he ever speak now?'

Martin and Nóra glanced at each other.

'We know he is dreadful thin. Hungry, sir. Always hungry. We knew at once there was a wasting on him, and we thought 'twas the hunger. We think his mouth is so full of hunger he has no room for words.'

The doctor hauled himself to his feet, sighing, brushing his clothes down. 'He hasn't spoken a word since you took him in, then? Nor taken a step neither?'

Silence.

The man ran a hand over his shining scalp and glanced at Martin. 'I might have a word with you.'

'What you have to say you may tell to the both of us.'

The doctor took his spectacles off and polished their glass with a handkerchief. 'I don't have good news, I'm afraid. The child does not have the smallpox, nor is he consumptive. The rash on his back is no sign of disease; rather, I think it is caused by the wearing of his skin. On account of him being unable to sit up by himself.'

'But will he be well again? Will it pass? What have we to do for him?'

The doctor put his spectacles back on. 'Sometimes children do not thrive.' He returned his instruments to his leather case.

'But he was born well. We saw it ourselves. And so he may be well again.'

The doctor straightened, lips pursed. 'That might be, but *I* believe he will remain ill-thriven.'

'Do you not have something in your bag to give him? 'Tis not right that a healthy boy becomes this way.' Her tongue had dried on the words. 'Look. Look there. Hungry. Bawling. Not saying a thing. He was cold, he had not enough in his belly, and he is mouldered with it all, I know.'

'Nóra.' Martin's eyes had been soft.

'He was well. I saw him walk! There is surely something in your bag, some medicine. Would you not give him some medicine? All you've done is prod him like a piece of meat on the turn.'

'Nóra!' Martin had gripped her wrist.

'I think you should prepare yourself for the worst,' the doctor had said, frowning. 'It would be remiss of me to encourage hope when there is none. I'm sorry.'

'You cannot tell us what ails him?'

'He is cretinous.'

'I don't understand.'

'He is malformed.'

Nóra shook her head. 'Doctor, he has all his fingers and toes, I –'

'I'm sorry.' The doctor had pulled on his coat, spectacles slipping down his nose again as he shrugged the cloth over his shoulders. 'The boy is a cretin. There is nothing I can do.'

The day had turned querulous, the horizon blurred under far-off snowfall. Nóra felt a bone-deep longing for Martin, for his calm reassurance. Even when the doctor had departed, and Nóra had felt anger throb through her, Martin had drawn her into the warmth of his chest and murmured, 'For what cannot be cured, patience is best.'

For what cannot be cured, Nóra thought, leaning against the rough stones. I am burdened with a dying child who will not die.

She wished Micheál dead, then. She wished that he would fall asleep and never wake up, but be taken into Heaven by the angels or into the ringfort by the fairies, or wherever a mute soul went. Better that than to grow old in a body that could not accommodate the years. Better that than to suffer the bridle and bit of the world.

There was no use in denying the truth of it, she thought. 'Twould be a kind of grace if he died.

Nóra shuddered. She knew women sometimes did kill children. But the stories she heard were always of unwed mothers who gave birth in dirty private places, and who bore their anguish out in lapses of guilty violence. Sometimes they were caught. When the bloodstain was found, or the stones shifted from the river floor and the little sacked body rose to the water's surface to the shrieking surprise of those at their laundry. There was a woman who had drowned herself and her unborn child in Lough Leane and people said that a mist shrouded the water on the anniversary of their deaths every year since.

But I am no murderer, Nóra thought. I am a good woman. She wiped her swollen face with muddy fingers. I will not kill my own daughter's boy. I will save him. I will restore him.

A light snow began to fall, and a rook, feathers sweeping the still air, landed on the stones. 'I am alone,' Nóra said plainly.

The rook ignored her, wiped his grey beak on the wall. As Nóra watched him, marvelling at the bird's closeness, she felt a sudden weight to the air, a prickling at the nape of her neck.

Then she saw the nettles.

A memory came to her. Martin shouldering the door open one spring evening filthy with rain, his hand clutched to his chest. He had a dreadful cold in it, he said. As though there were no blood in it at all.

Nóra had examined the swollen fingers. 'Looks to be plenty of blood in there,' she'd said. 'Too much blood.'

But the hand had remained that way all night and the following day too, and the next evening Martin had said he would go to Nance Roche for a cure. 'Sure, hadn't she brought the worm out of Patrick's guts, and the lump out of John's arm, and no harm done?'

'She's an odd one,' Nóra had said, but Martin replied that anything was better than living the rest of his life with his hand a block of ice, and so he had gone.

Martin returned from Nance's the following morning with his hand swollen still, violent pink, but supple, moving.

'She's marvellous skill, that woman.' He was relieved, filled with wonderment. 'You'll never guess how she did it. Nettles,' he said. 'She returned the blood to it with nettles.' And he raised his hand to Nóra's cheek to show her how his warmth had been restored.

Now, wrapping the cloth of her dress around her hands to keep the leaves from stinging her fingers, Nóra tugged the nettles from the ground, heaping them in her apron. She knew that she must look like a madwoman, a hooded figure nettling in the snow. But her heart thrilled in her chest. She would cure him.

It will work, she thought. It worked for Martin and so it will work for Micheál.

'Sweet Mother of God, make this work.' The words folded under themselves and became a circle of prayer. 'I will warm the life back into him. It will work. Virgin Mother, I beseech thee.'

Nóra returned to the cabin, her apron filled with nettles, their toothed leaves dampened by snowmelt. Shutting the door behind her, she found Micheál on the ground and Mary in the middle of the room, lifting the heavy dash of the churn and whispering, 'Come butter, come butter, come butter, come.' She stopped as Nóra entered, panting from the exertion and rubbing her shoulders.

'What did the priest say?'

'He'll have none of it. So, I went nettling.'

'You went nettling? In the snow?' Mary frowned.

'I did, and what of it? Go on with that churning, then.'

As Mary resumed heaving the dash up and down, Nóra threw her cloak over the hearth beam, shook the nettles into a basket and knelt by Micheál. She dragged the boy gently towards her by his ankles, then lifted his dress to expose his legs. Wrapping her hand in a corner of her shawl, she picked up a nettle, and with her other hand lifted Micheál's bare foot. She tickled his toes with the plant, brushing the edge of the leaves against his skin.

The sound of the dash stopped. Nóra knew Mary was watching her, but she said nothing.

Micheál's foot sat in her palm, oddly heavy. There was not so much as a flinch from the boy. Nóra wondered how Nance might have laid the nettles upon Martin's ice-struck, immobile hand. She imagined her husband sitting in the dark of Nance's hovel, holding his palm out as she whispered words over it, rubbed the stinging into his skin.

Nóra lifted the plant up and brought it down on Micheál's lower leg, more firmly this time. A long stroke to drag the leaves from knee to ankle.

Micheál pointed his chin into the air in a weird expression of defiance and then, as the smart settled on his shin, his eyes closed and he wailed.

Mary cleared her throat. 'What are you doing?'

Nóra ignored her. She lifted the nettle again and brought it down on Micheál's crooked knees in a light slap, on his ankles and bare feet. His skin pinked under the stinging plant, welts rising.

He must feel it, she thought. If he cries, he must feel it.

Mary stood still, her grip tightening on the dash.

Nothing. His legs, blotched, did not move. Nóra felt desperation rising in her. It had worked for Martin. Her husband's hand was restored to him with nettles. Yes, it had hurt, he had said, but when the sting subsided he found that his flesh had been flooded with warmth. Martin, holding her face to prove that he was well again. The rough thickness of his thumb rubbing her cheek, soothing her. As good as new, he had said. It takes a lot more than that to bring me down.

Nóra thought she saw Micheál's toes curl and, heartened, brought the nettles down harder on his knees.

'Please stop that,' Mary whispered.

We will make him well again, Martin had assured her. We will care for him together, for Johanna. He will be a comfort to us. Our own grandchild.

The boy began to scream harder and Nóra paused to look at him. His face was scrunched. He seemed like an angry, bucking imp, red in hair and face. His eyes were crimped shut, tears streaming from them, and as he jerked he smacked his fists on the floor. Nóra winced as he struck the clay.

This is not my son, Johanna had said.

And at once Nóra, her heart fluttering at his screams, saw that the boy was not, could not be the child she had seen in her daughter's cabin. Her eyes began to water, and she saw plainly the puckish strangeness that people had been speaking of. All those months she had thought there was a shadow of Johanna about the boy, a familiarity that anchored him to her. Martin had seen it, had loved him for it. But now, Nóra knew that nothing of Johanna ran through this child's blood. It was like Tadgh said. She had not recognised him as her own because there was nothing of her family in the creature. He was a cuckoo in the nest.

There is nothing of them in him, Nóra thought. He is not Micheál. And she turned the boy over and brought another nettle down on his calves.

He wailed, his face against the rushes on the floor. Crumbs of mud spattered off the plants, dirtying his clothes and her apron.

'Stop!' Mary cried.

He is fairy, Nóra thought. He is not my grandson.

Mary rushed to the floor and attempted to rip the nettle out of her hand.

'Leave me,' Nóra said through clenched teeth. She yanked her hand out of the girl's grip.

'He doesn't like it,' Mary whimpered.

Nóra ignored her.

Without warning, the girl suddenly grabbed the basket holding the remainder of the nettles and tried to fling it across the room. Nóra snatched the woven edge in time, and hauled the basket back towards her, her mouth in a determined line. She refused to look the girl in the eye. Mary got to her feet and tugged at it, crying openly now, her mouth open and wailing, as pink as the boy's. They wrestled with the basket, each heaving it back and forth, jerking the other, until, finally, Nóra wrenched it out of Mary's grasp and sat it down beside her, stony-eyed.

''Tis a cruelty!' Mary sobbed.

The child was bawling so hard he had begun to choke. His head rocked from side to side.

Nóra continued to whip him with nettles.

Mary bent down and snatched the rest of the plants out of the basket with her bare hands, throwing them onto the fire. The embers blackened under the damp weight of the nettles. Then, before Nóra could say anything, Mary bolted for the door, flinging it wide and running into the snowy yard.

CHAPTER
SEVEN

Dock

'What is all this madness?'

Peg O'Shea stood in the doorway, gaping at Nóra and Micheál. Nóra was sitting on the floor, shoulders shaking, clenching her fists until her nails dug into the flesh of her palms. Micheál, half naked, was shrieking with pain. As he screamed, he lifted his head and let it fall on the floor in a repetitive, sickly knocking. His face was covered with dirt from the nettles.

Peg hobbled in and quickly picked him off the ground. 'Oh, come now. Oh, little one. Shush now.' She sank onto a stool next to where Nóra lay slumped. 'Nóra Leahy. What in God's holy name have you done to this boy?'

Nóra shrugged and wiped her running nose.

'That maid of yours, Mary, she comes running into my house in pieces, crying you're after whipping the boy with nettles. Are you turned in your mind? Does the boy not suffer enough already?' Peg watched Nóra closely then stamped her foot on the ground. 'Enough! Stop your crying and talk sense to me.'

'Father Healy,' Nóra gasped.

'What about himself?'

'He will not heal the boy. I asked him. He said he has surely turned idiot and there's nothing to be done. He said I'm not to be talking of the Good People, and that 'tis all superstition.' Nóra's chin trembled. 'Where is Mary to now?'

'I sent her to the Flesk for dock leaves. Pull the shirt of him down, Nóra. Here, I'll do it then. The wee lad is screaming like you've burnt him alive.'

Peg lay Micheál on her lap and bundled him in her shawl. 'You've a right to be telling me what is happening.'

'People are saying he is a changeling.' Nóra's face scrunched in despair.

Peg was silent. 'Well. There might be something in that. *Is ait an mac an saol.* Life is a strange son.'

'If you believe he is a changeling, then why do you touch him?' Nóra spluttered. 'Why do you care if I nettle him?'

'You are as cold as a holy trout, Nóra Leahy. Do you not know yourself that if the wee one is a changeling, your own good grandson suffers the ill you inflict on his stock? If the Good People have him, they will not take kindly to you treating one of their own like this.' Peg lifted Micheál's dress and examined his legs, turning them in her hands. 'You did a good job of it. What on earth were you hoping to do?'

Nóra hauled herself up onto the settle. 'I thought 'twould restore the quick to his legs. I thought the sting might give him cause to move.' She took a shuddering breath.

'That is some dreadful quackery if I ever heard it. Quite the herb woman, you are.' Peg clucked her tongue.

''Twas what Nance Roche did to Martin when he was alive and with me. Nettles brought the quick back to his hand.'

'Nance Roche has the knowledge. Some pride you have there,

Nóra, thinking you've the same skill as that one. 'Twould be better if you made a tea of the nettle and gave it to him, the doty child.' She pulled Micheál's head back against her skinny throat and held him tightly, murmuring into his ear. 'What have we to do with you, then? From what wild place have you come to us?'

'Peg, I know what they are saying of me,' Nóra said, her voice cracking. 'They say my own daughter was not called away by God, but by Them in the *ráth*. They say her own son is with her in the hill, and I am left with the fairy child. They say the misfortune in the valley is *his* fault and will be on my soul. They say . . .' Her voice broke. 'They say Martin died because of him being here. And I look at him, and I wonder, Peg.'

'Nóra Leahy. Hold your head up and not care a tinker's curse what anyone says to cheapen ye,' Peg replied. 'Night will come again, please God. You should be glad this one is a changeling, for then you bear no blame for him. There are ways to restore Micheál to you.'

'I know what they do to banish changelings,' Nóra spat. 'Put him on the dung heap in the night for the fairies to claim! Threaten him with fire. Would you have me put that one on a hot shovel and roast him? Would you have me smack him with a reddened poker and bring the eye out of him?'

Peg's face was serious. 'Enough. Enough with all your mad cures dreamt up out of despair, and enough of all this dark talk. You have a need to talk with one who knows of these things.' She looked Nóra in the eye. 'You have a need to speak with Nance.'

Mary ran down the grassy slope as fast as she could, briars snagging her skirt and the skin of her legs as she went. Her blood sang at the sudden pain of it, but she did not stop until she could see the riverbank beyond a tangle of fallen tree branches. The flowing water looked as dark as a nightmare. By the time she reached its edge, her shins were scraped bloody by brambles.

Taking jagged breaths, Mary kept her head down, searching for the long leaves of water dock amidst winter's ruin of dead grasses and the snap of withered bracken. She found a clump of dock growing on the side of the crumbling bank, and crawled towards the water on her belly to reach it without the soil giving way. Tugging at the leaves with an outstretched hand, she looked into the water and saw her own warped reflection staring back at her. She was shocked to see the fear on her face, and the urge to cry swelled again. She wiped her streaming eyes and nose on her sleeve.

Seeing Nóra whip the boy with nettles had unsettled something within her. There was an ugliness there that she had only seen a few times before in her life. Once she had seen a man sneer at a madwoman who had taken to wandering in her undershirt, contempt crowning his face in a dark halo. Another time she had seen a group of older girls crawl backwards, naked, through a briar on May morning. There was something about their pale bodies writhing against the grass, flinching at the prick of thorns, that had deeply disturbed her. At the time she had not known what it was they were doing, and had buttoned the secret sight of them deep down in her chest. It was only later that she heard of the powers of double-rooted briars, understood that the girls had been crawling through the Devil arch to curse someone. She had never seen those girls again. But the memory of them had clawed its way back to her mind at the sight of the muddy widow lashing the legs of the child.

It was not the beating. Mary had seen children younger than Micheál smacked into yesterday by their mothers in Annamore. She had felt the weight of a man's swinging arm at the northern farm.

It was the cruelty in the blows. The widow had looked demented. She had brought the nettles down on Micheál's skin like he was nothing more to her than a stubborn nag, or a carcass to be flensed. It turned the pulse of her heart.

The nettling had not looked like a cure. It had looked like punishment.

The slope was greasy with snow and mud and Mary found her feet sliding on her way back to the cabin. More than once she had to use her hands to scramble up the hillside, and she felt the smear of mud on her face when she wiped her swollen eyes. On the way to the river she had taken the path leading from the lane, but in her haste to return she had run towards the woods where the ground was most steep. The air burnt in her lungs. Suddenly, the soil beneath her left foot gave way, pain flared through her and she fell to the ground.

Mary let go of the dock leaves and gripped her ankle in both hands. She blinked back tears and sat there rocking in the mud, chest heaving.

I want to go home.

The thought ran through her like a thread, drawing tightly, until she felt puckered with longing.

I want to go home.

Clenching her teeth, Mary tried to stand. It was no use. The tendons in her ankle sprang with pain. Sitting in the mud she let the tears come. She hated the valley. She hated the brittle, unnatural child, and the damp loneliness that hung off the widow like a mist. She hated the broken nights and the smell of piss that clung to the cripple's clothes, and she hated the pity in the face of the old neighbour. She wanted her brothers and sisters. She wanted the feel of the younger ones' fingers combing her hair by the fire. She wanted the cheerful noise of the babies, and their red-cheeked faces, and their little hands on her shoulder, waking her in the morning. She wanted David and his solemn understanding.

'Tis too much, Mary thought. Why is the world so terrible and strange?

'I never saw anyone cry so bitterly.'

Mary flinched. An old woman stood behind her, wrapped in a tattered shawl, dragging a broken branch.

'Are you hurt?' The woman bent down, concerned. Mary, too surprised to move, stared back. The woman's skin was creased and her eyes were clouded, but there was softness in her voice. She reached out and placed her ancient hand on Mary's bent knee.

'You're hurt.' The woman answered her own question. 'Sit still for a moment now.' She fussed with the broken branch and Mary saw that she had been using it as a sled. It was piled with lumps of turf, dung and plants. The woman carefully took these off, placing them on the ground beside her, and snapped off the smaller twigs. She soon had a rough stick, which she gave to Mary.

'Try standing, girl. Take this.'

Mary hauled herself upright onto her good foot, and planted the stick firmly into the waterlogged ground.

'Now, put your other arm about my shoulders. I'm taking you to my home. I can do something for you there. See, that's my cabin.'

'What about your turf?' Mary sniffed. She could feel the thin ridge of the woman's shoulder blade against her arm.

The woman grimaced under her weight. 'Never you mind that. Can you hobble along, so?'

Mary leant heavily on the stick and held her sore foot aloft. 'I don't want to hurt you.'

'I'm as strong as an ox.' The woman smiled. 'That's it. This way.'

They stumbled back down the slope until they reached the dirty clearing beside the woods. A small mud cabin stood against a wall of alder trees, their bare branches knotted with the old nests of birds. There was no chimney, but Mary could see smoke listing from one end, where a gap in the thatch admitted it to the open air. A tethered goat grazing on the grass at the woods' edge looked up at their voices. It stared, gimlet-eyed, at Mary.

'You live here?'

'I do.'

'I thought this cabin was abandoned.' Mary could hear the river in the distance.

'I've lived here twenty years or more. Come in, girl. Come in and sit by the fire.'

Mary grasped the doorframe of the cabin and hopped inside. From the clearing the *bothán* had looked crude and damp, but the room was surprisingly warm. The floor was covered in cut green rushes, which gave off a clean, sweet smell, and a turf fire burnt upon a large hearthstone, away from the wall. There was no window to admit the light, but the fire's glowing heart prevented the darkness from gloom. Mary, glancing up, saw a vast number of St Brigid's crosses, blackened by years of smoke, fixed against the rafters around the low ceiling. In the corner of the room stood straw baskets, some filled with ratty, uncarded wool.

'Are you a *bean leighis*?' Mary asked, gesturing towards the drying herbs dangling from the rough-hewed crossbeams.

The woman was washing the mud off her feet and hands on the threshold. 'Have you not seen a one with the charms before?'

Mary shook her head, her mouth dry.

'Sit down on that stool there.' The woman shut the door and the room became darker, the firelight throwing long shadows against the walls. 'My name is Nance Roche,' she said. 'And you are the maid with Nóra Leahy.'

Mary paused. 'I am. I'm Mary Clifford.'

''Tis an unhappy house you're in.' Nance sat beside Mary. 'Nóra Leahy is an unhappy widow.'

'Aren't all widows unhappy?'

Nance laughed and Mary noticed her bare gums, the few teeth bunkered in them. 'Not every dead husband is mourned, *cailín*. Nor every wife.'

'What happened to your teeth?'

'Ah, there was time enough for me to lose them when I'd nothing for them to do. But here, let me take a look at you.'

Mary extended her bare foot in front of the fire, feeling the warmth of it against her sole. ''Tis my ankle.'

Nance examined the swelling without touching her. 'Musha, so 'tis. Will you let me give you the cure?'

Mary's eyes were wide in the dark. 'Will it hurt?'

'No more than it does now.'

Mary nodded.

Nance spat on her hands and lay them gently upon the ankle. 'Christ upon a cross. A horse's leg was dislocated. He joined blood to blood, flesh to flesh, bone to bone. As He healed that, may He cure this. Amen.'

Mary crossed herself in imitation of Nance, and as she did so she felt a slow rising of heat against her skin, as though she had drawn too close to a flame. But the pain faded, and she exhaled at its lessening. She tried to stand, but Nance shot out a finger in warning.

'Not yet. You'll need a poultice.' She stood and, as Mary watched in curiosity, filled a chipped earthenware bowl with plants from a basket covered with a damp cloth.

'What are those herbs there, then?' Mary asked.

'Oh, that's my secret.' Nance picked up an egg and cracked it sharply on the bowl's rim, straining the white through her crooked fingers. When the egg had separated, she slipped the remaining yolk into her mouth and swallowed it.

'Do I have to eat that?' Mary asked, pointing to the bowl.

''Tis for your skin and not your belly. Royal fern, watercress, nettles.'

'Nettles?' Mary couldn't keep the panic out of her voice.

'They'll not hurt you. I've soaked them and that takes much of the sting out.' Nance pestled the plants with a worn wooden beetle.

Mary closed her eyes and remembered the angry welts on Micheál's legs, the widow's wrapped hand bringing the nettles down on his skin. Her stomach clenched and she suddenly vomited, the splatter hissing on the fire.

'I'm sorry,' she gasped, and vomited again.

Mary felt hands smoothing the hair off her face, Nance's bony fingers rubbing her shoulder.

'There now,' she said. 'There now.'

A dipper of cool water was brought to Mary's lips.

'I'm sorry,' she stuttered. She spat out the acid bile and felt the sting of it in her nostrils.

'Ah, you poor thing. You've had a shock.'

''Tis not my ankle.' The touch of the old woman reminded Mary of her mother. Wiping her mouth with the back of her hand, she felt the residual sting of the nettles on her palm and sobbed.

Nance picked up Mary's hands and turned them over, studying the welts. Her brow furrowed. 'Is she hurting you?'

There was a long silence.

'Mary Clifford. Is it Nóra Leahy that did this to you?'

'Not me,' Mary finally blurted out. 'Him. Micheál. She's after hurting him.'

Nance nodded. 'The cripple boy.'

'You know about Micheál?'

Nance released the girl's hands and tucked her shawl firmly about her. 'I'm hearing a lot of talk about that child. A lot of rumour.'

'He's not natural,' Mary hacked. 'And she knows it. She hides him! She has me hide him because she's frightened of what people will say of him. But they already know, and they say he is a changeling and to blame for everything, and she is punishing him for it.' Mary felt the words tip out over her tongue. 'She whipped him with nettles. She drinks and she has a look in her eye that puts the fright on me. They're astray, the both of them. I'm scared of what is going to happen.'

Nance held her smarting hands tightly. 'There now,' she soothed. 'You've found me, now. You've found me.'

⚹

Micheál had finally stopped crying. Nóra offered to take him from Peg's tight clutch, but the older woman simply stared her down. 'Sit you there by the fire and breathe some sense back into your head.'

'I wish Martin were here,' Nóra gasped. She felt as though her soul was grinding itself into powder under the weight of her own unhappiness.

Peg's voice was stern. 'Of course you do. But Martin is with God, and you've a right to be getting on with life in the best way you can.'

'I wish Martin was here,' Nóra repeated. She could feel the blood beat in her face. 'And I wish that it was Micheál who was dead.'

Peg sucked her teeth.

'I would carry Micheál to the graveyard and bury him alive if my daughter would come to me!' She fell from her stool onto all fours. 'I would!' she screamed. 'I wish it were Johanna with me!'

'Enough!'

Nóra felt two rough fingers pinch her chin and pull her head upwards.

'Enough,' Peg hissed. Her grip was firm. 'Nóra Leahy, you think you are the only mother to lose a daughter? Five children I have buried in the *cillín*. Five.' Her voice was calm. ''Tis a great misfortune to lower two coffins in one year, but 'tis no reason to let your heart and mind go to the dogs and to be crying and crawling about the house like a man senseless with drink taken. And don't you be screaming of murder for the valley to hear. Don't you be threatening worse things to this child than what has already befallen him.'

Nóra pushed Peg's fingers away from her face. 'Who are you to tell me what shape my loss can take?'

'Nóra, I want to help you.'

There was the sound of voices in the yard outside. The women exchanged looks.

'Who is that?' Nóra hissed.

'Is it Mary with the dock leaf?'

''Tis not her voice.' Nóra got to her feet and fixed the bolt on the door, then waited by the wall, her ear craned to the gap in the doorframe.

There was a sharp knock.

'Who is it?' Nóra cried.

'Nóra Leahy, you'd best be opening to me. I've your Mary here, and a sorry state she's in too.'

Peg's eyes widened. 'Nance? In God's name, Nóra, let the woman in.'

Nóra wiped her eyes on her sleeve and undid the latch. Light flooded the cabin.

Nance stood before her, the old woman's eyes swimming in their clouded, bleeding blue. She was bundled against the cold, a straw basket over one arm. 'You're in a bad way,' she murmured. 'Secrecy does not agree with you.'

Nóra felt Nance take in her tear-stained face, the scratches on her wrist, fingernails bitten down to the painful quick. 'What are you doing here?'

'Your girl rolled her ankle by the river and I found her there. I've come to see her home safe, but I think . . .' Nance peered past Nóra to Peg and the boy at her chest. 'I think, Nóra Leahy, that you have further need of me.' She placed her free hand on Nóra's shoulder and, pushing her out of the way, stepped inside.

Mary followed, giving Nóra a wary glance as she limped over the doorstep.

'Are you badly hurt?' Nóra asked, pointing at the rough bandage.

The girl shook her head. Said nothing.

'So this is the nettled child. There now. Let me take a look at him, Peg O'Shea. This hidden boy.' Nance pulled the hood off her head, and took two dock leaves from her basket. Rolling the cloth away from Micheál's legs, she wrapped the leaves around his calves. 'You've marked him like a cat, Nóra Leahy.'

'I didn't mean to harm him. I only wanted to see him well.' She took a sharp breath. 'You did the same to Martin. He told me. You brought the life back to his hand.'

Peg passed Micheál into Nance's outstretched arms. The woman held him for a moment, gazing into his unspeaking face.

'Your Martin was not as this child is.'

Nóra saw the boy as Nance saw him then. A wild, crabbed child no heavier than the weight of snow upon a branch. A clutch of bones rippling with the movement of wind on water. Thistle-headed. Fierce-chinned. Small fingers clutching in front of him as though the air were filled with wonders and not the smoke of the fire and their own stale breath.

She watched as Nance ran a single fingertip over his forehead.

What had happened? What had her daughter done to lose her son? Had she not crossed his face with ashes? Not bit his fingernails until he was nine weeks old? Not sprinkled his mouth with salt, or barred his cradle with iron? All women knew how to protect their children from abduction. A hazel stick by the door. Milk spilt after stumbling.

Nance lay Micheál down on the rushes by their feet. 'He is very thin,' she said quietly.

'I'm not starving him, if that is what you are saying. He eats and eats.'

'Whist now. That is not what I'm saying.' Nance regarded her with a gentle eye. 'Mary tells me you were given this child when your daughter died, God have mercy on her soul. Did he come into this world a natural child, or has he been changed?'

'He was a fine boy at his birth, and in the two years after it. But when my daughter began to sicken, he became ill-favoured.' Nóra swallowed hard. 'They thought 'twas the cold and the hunger that did it. But my daughter thought her boy was gone from her. She did not see her own son in him. She asked . . .' Nóra took a deep breath. 'She asked that he be put outside in the last days of her life.'

Peg looked at her with curiosity. 'You never said a word of this to me, Nóra.'

''Twas no sin on her,' Nóra protested. 'She was a good mother.'

'Tell me.' Nance interrupted. 'Tell me how he is unnatural.'

'Do you not see it yourself? Look at him. Nothing of him is natural.'

There was a heavy silence. A gust of wind blew ice under the gap in the door.

'He screams at night,' Mary whispered. 'He will not rest, and he will not lie still in my arms. He kicks and bites me.'

'There is nothing of my family in that boy.'

'Sore-wounded Christ, Nóra.' Peg pressed her fingers to her temples. 'Faith, I don't know, Nance. He does not walk. He does not speak.'

'He tried to pull the hair out of my head!'

Nance studied the boy closely. 'Fetch me a thread, Nóra,' she said. 'I have a need to measure him.'

'Why?'

'It may well be that he is full of fairy, or that he has been overlooked.'

'By the evil eye?' Mary asked.

'Aye. That he has been blinked.'

Nóra reached for her knitting and pulled roughly at the wool. She bit a length off with her teeth and passed it to Nance, who pulled it tight between her fingers and held it to Micheál's toes and hips with a practised thumb, measuring each leg. The wind blew.

"Tis as I thought. He is not evenly grown,' said Nance, 'and sure, that can be a sign of strange things.'

'Sweet Christ. Not even the Killarney doctor saw that.'

'You're wanting a reason for his being changed, Nóra. You're wanting a reason for the unnatural in him.'

Nóra's face pinched in grief. 'I am afraid . . . I am afraid he is a changeling.'

The old woman straightened her back. 'Now, that he might be, or he might not. There are ways to see whether the Good People have merely blasted him and taken the growing and thriving out of his legs, or whether . . .' Nance lay a hand on the boy's ribcage. His hair had cotted about his temples and his face was flushed.

'Whether what? Nance?'

'Nóra, the Good People may have struck your grandson and left him a cripple, or it might be that they've taken him altogether and left this changeling in his place. This cratur here might be fairy-born.'

Nóra put her hand over her mouth, nodding tearfully. 'Mary, you saw it. You saw it the first time you stepped foot in here.'

Mary cast her eyes to the sputter of a rushlight.

'Johanna. She must have known. A mother always knows her own child.' Nóra took a shuddering breath. 'I knew it too. That first time I saw him. I knew because I expected to love him and . . . I thought something was wrong with me. That my heart . . .' She clutched at her shawl, piercing its weave with her fingers. 'But this – this would explain it. 'Tis the truth of it. There is no sin in my hard heart against him.'

Peg sucked her gums. She was sitting back, her face in disquiet. 'And how might we see if he is one of Them or merely suffering the fairy blast?'

'A change-child is ever eating, never growing. And silence in a child is a sign of the Good People's spite to us when They have been offended. It is by Their never talking that they might be known. His crying at all hours, that too is a sign of the changeling.'

'But Nance, surely a child's cries are no great sign of it belonging to Them. Were that the case, my own children were more fairy than human,' Peg said.

Nance gave her a sharp look. 'But your own children have had the use of their legs all their lives, Peg, and even I, in my little house, hear their prattle on the wind.'

''Tis the sound of his cry too,' Mary added. 'There is a strangeness to it.'

Nóra closed her eyes. 'Like the scream of a fox.'

Peg reached for the poker and stirred the fire, frowning. A constellation of sparks rose above them.

'There are ways in which we might ask the fairy to reveal its nature. To see if it is a changeling,' Nance said.

'I have heard of those ways,' Nóra said, a tremor in her voice. 'Heated shovels and burning coals.' She shook her head. 'I don't want to kill it.'

Nance sat back on her heels and gave her a long look. 'Nóra Leahy, we are not talking of murder. Only threatening the changeling to banish it. I would have your true grandchild restored to you.'

'My brother told me that those by the sea, they leave their change-lings below the high-water mark on the shore when the tide is out.' Mary's face was as pale as milk. 'When the child's crying can no longer be heard, they know the changeling has fled. 'Tis true,' she whispered, blanching at Peg's expression. 'He heard the story himself.'

'Many have lost their children to the fairies over the years,' Nance said. 'Their wives and mothers too. Nóra, you should know 'tis powerful difficult to recover one taken by the Good People. There are those who have chosen to care for the changeling instead, although they be contrary craturs.'

Mary nodded vehemently. ''Tis what I heard in Annamore.' Her voice dropped to a whisper. ''Tis a dreadful shame to lose a baby to the fairies, but 'tis best to care for the wee stock they leave behind and hope they bring the child back in time.'

'I would have Micheál restored to me,' Nóra said flatly. 'How can I love this one when I know the wished-for child is with Them? When I might yet see his face?'

'You would not live with his fairy likeness?'

A stillness passed through Nóra. She sat awkwardly, scrunching her clothes, hardly breathing. 'I have no family. My husband and daughter are passed, God have mercy on them. I have only my nephews, and this . . . cratur. This changeling, if that is what he is. Folk are talking about him. They are blaming him for Martin's death, and the omens they see, and the way the winter has dried up the hens and cows. And if what they say is true . . . I must do something,' Nóra whispered. 'I must try to have my grandson returned.'

Nance inclined her head to one side. 'There is a possibility, Nóra, if 'tis fairy interference here, that your daughter and her son are together under hill, in the *ráth*, dancing. They are fed and kept and happy together.' She waved her hand towards the door. ''Tis an easier life.'

Nóra shook her head. 'If I cannot have Johanna . . . If there is a chance I could have her true son, Martin's true grandson, instead of this . . . I will have her true son.'

The fire spat. Flames crept over the broken embers. Nance closed her eyes for a long moment, as if suddenly overcome with weariness, and lifted her palm from the boy's body. Nóra watched as he snatched at her retreating fingers, catching the back of Nance's hand with his nails. A tiny scratch opened on the old woman's papered skin.

'So it is, then, Nóra Leahy,' she murmured, glancing at the little bead of blood. 'Come to me at the turn of the year and we will begin. We will put the fairy out of him.'

CHAPTER
EIGHT

Yarrow

December moved slowly. The women sang to their cows against the heavy-clouded skies, their voices ringing out in vapour. They slipped their hands inside their clothes to warm their palms against their skin and take the shock out of their touch, and milked their beasts with fingers firm and pleading. They pressed their cheeks against the flanks and sang and milked, and prayed to God it was full of butter.

But the milk came meagre, and across the valley only a long churn would bring the butter against the dash. When at last it broke, the women, relieved, took a small ball of the fat and smeared it on the walls of their homes. They twisted the staff three times and placed it across the mouth of the churn, and some tied twigs of rowan on the dash. Others salted the wooden lids.

At night, under a gibbous moon, the women left their infants in the arms of older daughters and walked the frosted path to the cross-roads on *cuaird*. They lit around the fire of Áine's rambling cabin like moths, faces shining.

'Have you tried a horseshoe?' Áine was saying. 'Sure, himself can find you a shoe of one heating and if you tie it to the churn it will bring the butter.'

'Faith, just a nail would do it.'

'Or three sprigs of yarrow in the pail when you milk.'

'And don't be singing or drinking while you churn. Or starting something with your man. Butter will never come if you're combing and carding each other.'

The women nodded in agreement. There were six of them gathered, crowded around the heat of the hearth. They scuffed their bare feet on the cobbles.

'Did you see the ring around the moon tonight?' asked Biddy.

There was a murmur of assent.

'Sign of rain.'

'And all this fog. Fog on mountains, foul weather.'

''Tis no weather to be out in, that's for sure.'

'I've been seeing Nance Roche creeping about the fields these mornings, so I have.'

Several eyes glanced to where Kate Lynch sat huddled by the fire, her arms cosseted around her body.

'Not even daylight, and she's shuffling through the mist going from place to place, cow to cow. Cursing them. Putting the blink on them.'

Sorcha gave a nervous smile. 'Mam, I bet she was only bleeding them.'

'Aye, she'll be getting powerful hungry now Father Healy has preached against folk going to her for the cure or the keening. How else does she fit food to her mouth?'

'I often see her about,' said Hanna. 'She walks the long field by the road, gathering herbs at dawn or dusk for the cures. She has the knowledge of what herbs to gather, where and when, and how to keep the power in the plant. And what harm if she's also after taking the wool from the brambles, if there's any to be had? Sure, I wouldn't think anything of it.'

'Well, I mind her bleeding animals, Hanna, if that's the mischief she's up to, and the winter weakening the cows as it is.' Éilís sighed. 'Faith, there's no butter to be had in the milk. There's no profit at all in the churn. If that one is creeping about in the dark with her knife, plugging the necks of the beasts and boiling their blood with ill-gotten oats, well, I think that's something the priest should know about.'

'Aye, and the constable.'

'She'd steal the eye out of your head,' Kate hissed.

'She never did a thing against you, and here you are, heaping mud on her name.' It was Áine who had spoken. There was an awkward silence.

Hanna nodded to where Áine had risen to her feet, face flushed. 'She's right. 'Tis a disgrace. That woman gives out the knowledge, and you have cause to believe it, for didn't Nance cure my own sister of the fever not a few months back? My own sister, sick and sweating in her bed with a fever I thought would leave her dead and cold. And if it weren't for the cure that *bean feasa* gave me, 'twould be nothing for my sister but six feet in a graveyard.'

'Maybe 'tis that your sister would be well, charm or no.'

'You'd be a fool to think it. Nance gave me the cure in a bottle, and she told me not to be looking at the fairy *ráth* on my way home but to go straight back to my sister. Well, I did as she said, but – and God knows I tell no lie – as I walked passed that whitethorn, I felt the cure being pulled from my hands. I gripped it tight, and I kept my eyes to the ground, but the Good People were fighting me for it. 'Tis only that I didn't see them that I had the power to get home to my sister. I boiled the herb and gave her three drinks from the drawing of it, and she was out of bed and spinning by my side that very night.'

'You were always one for the stories.'

Hanna bristled. 'Have you no respect for the old amongst us, Éilís?'

'We're only having a laugh, like, Hanna,' Sorcha muttered.

Éilís's face twisted. 'I'm not laughing. The way I see it, Father Healy has a right to be calling her a pagan.'

Hanna sat up straight, indignant. 'Father O'Reilly credited her with the powers. He went to her himself. A priest. As did you, before you married that schoolmaster of yours. I remember when Patrick's cow was sickened, and she told him 'twas the blast and found the fairy dart about it too. The ice was dripping off the cow house though 'twas freezing outside. Such was the heat of the cure, so says Patrick.'

'My man says Father Healy will preach against her every Mass, if that's what it takes.'

'He'll learn to change his tune,' Hanna said darkly. 'There's good reason Father O'Reilly spoke for her. You'd best be listening to me, Éilís. Before Nance Roche lived here, she lived many places. She was no sooner in one place than in another, it used to be said, selling her besoms and dyes on the road, and giving out the cure for the afflictions of those she met.

'It happened that she passed through this valley, walking the long road to Macroom, and she stopped a while. She was sleeping under the furze, out in the open, poor woman. Bone-tired.

'Then who should go past her on the road but Father O'Reilly, and without even looking at him she said, "I know that you've a swelling in your hand, and I tell you, Father, I can give you the cure." Well, the priest asked her, "And what cure might that be?" And Nance said, "You walked past the fairy place and you took a stone from there, and 'tis the hand you took it with that has the swelling." Well, she was right about that, and Father O'Reilly couldn't say a word, he was so surprised. Nance said, "Now you've been shown that I have the knowledge and the healing and no harm in it." And Father O'Reilly, quick as a whip, said, "I see you've the knowledge, but you've given me no healing." And Nance said, "You're standing in it." And sure, the priest looked down and 'twas yarrow he was standing in. And he let her cure him with the yarrow, and all of us saw the swollen hand of the priest cured.

'That is why, until the day he died, Father O'Reilly never had the hard word against Nance, only praised her and gave her as much help as he was able, and assisted her in her living. That is why she has the *bothán* by the woods. He had it built for her, and she selected the site herself, for 'tis close to the Good People and those who gave her the knowledge. Close to the woods and the herbs that grow in them. Close to the boundary water. Sure, 'tis a place for a wise woman, and 'tis wisdom Nance Roche has.'

There was laughter from Éilís. 'Will you listen to that? Your tongue collects no rust, Hanna, with all the stories you tell.'

'That's the truth of it as it were told to me, and the one who told it was no liar!'

'I heard nothing about Father O'Reilly picking up a stone from the *ráth*, though my mam said he had the rheumatism,' mused Biddy.

'Sure, 'twas rheumatism and no fairy in it at all,' said Éilís. 'Nance is an old woman and she's soft in the head, and those who believe she has the cure are softer still.'

Hanna pursed her lips in anger.

'There's no doubting she's a strange one, Hanna,' Sorcha said sheepishly.

'Have you ever met one with the charms who had not the strangeness? It comes with the gift. You can't be expecting one who knows the things she does to be taking part in your almighty cackle every morning at the well. If you're looking for a friend without fault, you'll be looking for a friend forever.'

'Ah, but is that gift you speak of God-given, or is it from the Devil?'

''Tis nothing to do with the Devil at all, Éilís,' Hanna scoffed. ''Tis from her travelling with the fairies. 'Tis no Devil about it!'

'Father Healy says the fairies are for the pagans, and what is not for God is for the Devil.'

'Pssh, the Good People are for themselves alone. They belong to the water and soil and *ráth*. Devil! They're in the Piper's Grave with the whitethorn, not in Hell.'

'Don't you let the priest catch you saying that.'

There was silence. Hanna shook her head.

'Well, this has put you all in each other's hair combs,' Áine mused.

'Do you not see that Nance is after some badness? The priest would have her out. He has the word against her, and sure, she's living hand to mouth and the promise of a hungry year is upon her. Next thing the profit has been stolen from the milk?' Kate bit her lip. 'I saw her creeping about in the fog. God's truth, there are women who turn themselves into hares to suck milk from the cows at night.'

There were some raised eyebrows. Áine rolled her eyes.

'Faith, 'tis true with God as my witness. Once, there was a Corkman. He saw a hare drinking from his cow – suckling it, straight from the udder! – and he got his gun and shot it with a bullet made from sixpence. He followed the blood trail and sure, if he didn't find an old woman sitting by her fire, her leg bleeding.'

'Shame your Seán has such bad aim,' Hanna murmured. There was tittering.

'He sure never misses me!' Kate cried.

The women glanced at one another, their laughter snuffed.

'Kate, do you not . . . Yourself and Seán. Do you not agree together?'

Kate flushed red, her eyes fixed on the fire in front of them. She said nothing.

'Is that the truth of it? Is he after beating you again?' It was Hanna who spoke.

'Kate?'

Kate shrugged, her jaw clenched. 'To the Devil, all of you,' she muttered.

The smirk left Áine's face. She stood and gave Kate a pat on the shoulder. 'The cows will be in butter again. You'll see.'

'What's to be done?' Kate whispered to herself. She shook off Áine's hand. 'What's to be done?'

'It can't stay raining always. As soon as they calve, they will be back in butter.'

The women nestled closer around the fire, exchanging looks. Outside, the hungry wind keened.

The smooth whiteness of the fields melted to mud and dying grass, and the valley felt darker for it. It rained constantly, and the people stayed close to their smoking fires and the inconstant dripping from poor thatch. They muttered, 'A green Christmas leaves a full graveyard,' as they lit their candles and asked the Virgin to stave off winter sickness.

Nance spent the holy day inside her cabin, passing the quiet, rain-filled hours cutting besoms by the fire and dying the scrags of wool she had removed from thorns and brambles and carded into use. Seeing that change-child, that bony marvel nettle-welted in the cabin of Nóra Leahy, had plated her mind with disquiet. It had stirred embers of memory she had thought long dead. Things she had willed herself to forget.

Nance paused in her work to stretch her fingers and checked the simmering pot of stirabout on the fire. She had woken that morning to find turf and a bag of yellow meal lying in her doorway, protected from the rain by a square of oilcloth. There was no knowing who had left the sacks there, although Nance suspected the quiet generosity of Peter O'Connor and his habit of silent, unannounced kindness. Or the gifts might have been a gesture of gratitude from someone who had lately come to her with the winter lying in their lungs; one of those who continued to bring their complaints to her despite the priest's warning. The parade of sickness to her door had thinned since Father Healy had preached against her. No doubt her patients' concern for their souls was now greater than their anxiety over chapped hands or the fevers glittering through their children.

Her days had emptied. It reminded Nance of when she had first fled Killarney and gone to the quiet stretches of rock and moor in her grief. When she had climbed the dry stone walls and walked the fields and slept by the fires of strangers. Those hard years of grinding hunger after the death of her father and the disappearance of her mother and Maggie. Long years of wandering every road between Killorglin and Kenmare, smoking rabbits from their warrens and waiting with fast hands, poisoning rivers with spurge and collecting the rising bodies of dead fish under nightfall. Selling besoms, selling dyes of alder catkin, blackberry and birch. Bog myrtle for yellow. Dark green from briar root. Gathering galls for schoolmasters, some as poor as her, so they might make their ink. Nance of the Herbs, they called her, Nance of the Fairies, and she did as well as she could until her teeth began to fall out of her mouth, and she woke some mornings under hedges, bones aching, not knowing whether she could face another day of walking hungry, walking cold or sunburnt, walking thirsty.

It had been grief and fear that had driven her from Mangerton mountain, but it was hunger that called her back. There was always a living to be scraped off the Killarney tourists if you knew how.

Nance did not remember how she fell into begging, but she remembered the boredom of it. Ten years of crowding the inns, thrusting herself upon the coaches the minute they stopped, blocking shop doors if the shopkeeper was busy and unable to deliver a swift kick and threat.

'Oh, my lady, look at the poor who can't look at you. Heaven be your bed and give us something, blessings be with you on the road. Oh, help the poor cratur whose heart is broke in hunger. Charity, for the love of God.'

Nance shuddered. It was a good thing she had left that town again. It was a good thing she had heard the Good People summoning her to the valley and the priest who protected her, who saw the fairy in her skill, and who let her lay her hooked hands on his own troubled flesh.

She hoped never to go back to Killarney.

For all of Father O'Reilly's welcome, it had taken time before people walked the path to Nance's door. They had built her the *bothán* and left her there. Weeks had gone by without visitors, and she had thought she would go mad from the solitude after the noise and crowds of the town. Younger, then, she had scrambled up the bare shoulders of the mountains to find company in the clouds that brooded on the hilltops. There, in the presence of something ancient and immutable, she found her comfort. She could crouch on the wind-whipped grass and dig the stones from the ground and fling them down at the suspicious cottiers and their fear of any woman who was not tethered to man or hearth. There, upon the mountain, her difference – no matter its great weight, its sharp and restless ache upon her heart – was, in the face of such unyielding beauty, a small and passing shadow in a greater story.

Those days on the mountains had prevented her from turning mad with loneliness. She had climbed until her breath beat in her lungs, and she had watched the rain sweep across the valley below in its slow, grey veil, or the sun track its benevolence across the fields, and she had understood, finally, Maggie's words. Solitude, her difference, would make her free.

But those were younger years, and now Nance felt her age like a millstone around her neck. In the absence of company, without the distraction of boils and rheumatism and heavy coughs or stubborn, bleeding wounds, the past rose up around her like a tide of water, and there was no retreat to higher ground. There was no fleeing the slow flood of remembrance that came. She was an old woman condemned to sit by the fire, bones singing with weather.

Nance carded her stolen wool and her mind filled with her father and his smell of leather and river weed. The timber of his boat creaking, his stories of the Chieftan O'Donoghue rising out of the lakes on May morning. She tried to remember the weight of his hand on her shoulder.

But it was so long ago. And, as always, when she thought of her father, unbidden dark memories of her mother came also.

Nance could almost see that sallow face, looming over her like the moon in the midnight hours.

Mad Mary Roche.

She could almost hear her mother's voice again.

'They're here.'

Teeth bared. Hair uncombed over her face. Her mother waiting by the cabin door while she dressed. Quietly, so as not to disturb her father. Her mother leading her into the night.

Nance struggling to keep up with her mother's long stride. Walking out of the small yard beside their cabin, out past the potato bed, down the lane where the other cabins of the jarveys and lakemen and strawberry girls stood in slum, absorbed into the nightscape at the foot of Mangerton mountain.

Ten years old and pleading in fear, following her mother's dark back past the silver, slender trunks of birch and the sprawl of oak branches.

'Mam, where are we going?'

The water suddenly before them, balancing a fine cloud of mist. The lakes holding their dark mirror to the sky, holding the moon and the stars, until the startled flap of a duck in the reeds disturbed the water and the reflected night rippled. How the lakes had pulled the breath from her in their beauty. Staring at their silvered surface on that first night had felt like stumbling across a rare vision of holiness. It filled her mind with terror.

Her mother stopping. Turning. Face suddenly wide-eyed in fear, like a pig that sees the knife.

'They're here.'

'Who is here?'

'Can you not see Them?'

'I can't see at all.'

'You won't see Them there.' One cold hand against her chest. 'Here. You'll see Them here.'

That first night in the woods by the lake. Crying, curling herself into a nook of mossed limestone, watching her mother dart from tree to tree, muttering to herself, scratching patterns into the soil.

Her father, sitting by the fire when they returned at dawn, his head in his hands. Grabbing Nance, squeezing the breath out of her lungs. Stroking her dirty face as he put her to bed.

'Please, Mary.' Voices in the tremble of early morning. 'People will be making a fairy out of you.'

'I don't mean to do it.'

'I know.'

'I am not myself. I have been away.'

'You are here now.'

Heavy-lidded, watching him comb leaves out of her mother's hair with his calloused fingers.

'Am I? Am I here? Am I my own self?'

'You are my Mary Roche.'

'I don't know. I don't feel I am myself.'

'Mary . . .'

'Don't let Them take me again.'

'I won't. I won't.'

Was that when it all began? Was that when Nance first began to learn about the strange hinges of the world, the thresholds between what was known and all that lay beyond? That night, at ten years old, she had understood, finally, why people feared the darkness. It was an open door, and you could step through it and be changed. Be touched and altered.

Before then, Nance had loved the woods. In the daylight hours, waiting for tourists with cans of milk and *poitín*, the morning rain left the moss vivid underfoot, and the leaves cast their dappled shadow on the clay and stone and leaf. Birds rustled the berried briars. The sight of the forest floor carpeted with the beetled backs of acorns had rushed her with happiness. But afterwards, she understood that the woods changed at twilight; that they grew intolerant of strangers. The birds stopped cheeping and blinkered themselves against the dark, and the fox began to search for blood. The Good People claimed the darkling shadows for their own.

So many years gone and time stretching until she was thin with it all, and still Nance remembered that night in the woods, and the nights that came after. Shaken awake by a mother already half-swept, dragged to the woods where the branches creaked unseen and she choked with fear until piss ran down her leg.

*

She was older when her father began to fix the door at nights, winding rope about the latch. She had helped him. They thought it might stop her mother from leaving. Might stop her eyes from glinting wild, stop her trespass. But still, her mother was swept – on the wind, with the lights – and the strange woman left locked in their cabin, scratching at the walls and dirt floor until her nails broke and bled, was not Mary Roche. The woman They left in her place was a likeness who threw her food against the wall and would not eat, who did not recognise Nance, and who fought her father when he would see her safe in bed.

'I miss Mam,' Nance had whispered once, when the woman who was no longer her mother slept.

'I do too.' Her father's voice was soft.

'Why does she not know me?'

'Your mother is away.'

'She's there. She's sleeping.'

'She is not. Your mammy is away. With the Good People.' His voice had broken.

'Will she come back?'

Her father had shrugged. 'I don't know.'

'Who is the woman in there?'

'She is something left. A trick. They have hoped to trick us.'

'But she looks like Mam.'

The look on his face was one Nance had seen on the faces of other men many times in the years since. The shine of a man in desperation.

'Yes, she looks like Mam. But she is not her. She has been changed.'

What might have happened had her mother never gone with Them? If Nance had been free to marry the son of a jarvey, had lived amongst the people of her childhood all her life long? If Maggie had never been needed. If Maggie had never come in crisis and marked out the difference in her.

Her mother swept, Nance grown in her absence, and then a tall woman in the house, cheek marred by a long purple mark like the burn of a poker. Even in the streets of Killarney, spilling as they were with pockmarked children and men who hung a life's hard living off their cheekbones, the woman had seemed hard.

'This is your aunt, Nance. She brought you into this world.'

The woman had stood still, staring down at her. 'You've grown.'

'I'm not a child anymore.'

'Maggie's come to get your mam back from where she's been taken.'

Nance had looked over to the dark bundle lying in the corner of the cabin.

''Tis not your mam. Not there.' Maggie's voice was solemn. Deep.

'How will you get her back?'

Her aunt had slowly stepped forward and bent to her, until their faces were level. Nance had seen that, up close, the skin of the mark was tight, like scar tissue.

'You see that mark of mine, do you?'

Nance had nodded.

'You know about the Good People?'

Yes. Nance knew about the Good People. She had felt Them in the woods, by the lake, where her mother gave herself up to them. Where she, as a child, had curled into a nest of exposed roots and the moonlight made the world seem strange and the air was thick, occupied.

Her aunt smiled, and at once Nance's fear left her. She looked into the woman's grey eyes and saw that they were clear and kind, and without thinking she brought a finger up to touch the scar.

Dear, dark Maggie. From that first day when they cut bracken for her bed, Maggie began to show her the way in which the world was webbed; how nothing lived in isolation. God Himself signed the stalks of ferns. The world was in secret sympathy with itself. The flowers of charlock were yellow to signify their cure for jaundice. There was power in the places where the landscape met its own, in the meeting of waterways or the crucible of mountains. There was strength in all that was new: the beestings, the dew of the morning. It was from Maggie that Nance learnt the power in a black-handled knife, in the swarthy, puckering mix of hen dirt and urine, in the plant over the door, the garment worn next to the skin. It was Maggie who – in those years when they fought for her mother's return – had shown her not only which herbs and plants to cut, but when, and which to pull by hand and which to set a knife to, and which were made stronger by the moist footprints left by saints as they walked the evenings on their holy days, blessing the ground beneath them.

'There are worlds beyond our own that we must share this earth with,' Maggie told her. 'And there are times when they act on one another. Your mam bears no sin for being swept. Don't you be cross at her for being away.'

'Will you cure her?'

'I will do what I can with what I have, but to understand the Good People is to know that they will not be understood.'

The other families were all a little afraid of Maggie. Her father was too. Her aunt carried a presence, a stillness like that which precedes a storm, when the ants pour over the ground and the birds find shelter and stop singing to wait for the rain. No one dared speak out against her for fear she knew how to set curses.

'She's a queer one,' they said. 'That Mad Maggie. She who does be in it.'

'I never cursed anyone in my life,' Maggie told Nance once. 'But it never does any harm to let folk think you know how.' Her eyes had sharpened. 'People will not come to me if they don't respect me; if they don't fear me, just a little. Oh, there are curses to lay, you can be sure of it. But 'tis not worth the breath you spend. *Piseógs* are fires that flare in the face of those who set them. In time, a curse will always return.'

'Do you know the curses, Maggie? You have no hand in *piseógs*, do you?'

That glinting look. The slow stroke of the purple mark on her face.

'I never say either way to them that come.'

And the people did come to her. Despite her strange blemish, despite her pipe-smoking, and her manly hands, and her cold way of looking at you longer than was comfortable, they decided she had the charms and they came. During the long length of the year the door would be opened to faces waiting out in the cold; shawled, hopeful faces nodding at the sight of Maggie's broad back.

'Is the one with the knowledge in?' they'd ask, and it fell to Nance to meet them at the door and ask loud questions of their ailments, so that Maggie, greeting them under lowered brows, a pipe smouldering in her mouth, might know a little of what she was to treat and surprise them with foresight.

Her father did not remain at home when Maggie took her visitors. His wife was absent, and his home overrun. He spent long hours with his boat, and with the other boatmen, coming home to take up the *poitín* gifted to Maggie for her juniper, her sheep droppings boiled in new milk, her blistering rubbings of crowfoot, her worsted socks filled with hot salt.

'Mind you don't let Nance too close to them that come,' he'd say. 'Full of sickness as they are.'

'She's learning fast,' Maggie said. 'She has a hand for it. Isn't that true, Nance?'

'What's the smell in here?'

'Gladding root. Stinking iris,' Nance murmured.

Maggie pointed to the bottle. 'Let you don't take too much drink. That's powerful drink, and you on the water.'

'Aye, I know. I know. "Drink makes you shoot the landlord."'

'Worse than that, it makes you miss,' Maggie chided.

The sacred days past and Nance stayed close to her fire. She did not go to hear Mass, and no one came to see her with the priest's word so recently upon them. She wondered what he said of her.

Only the wren boys, faces hidden behind tapering masks of straw, ventured out into the dark fields close to her cabin on St Stephen's Day to beat their *bodhráns* of cured dog skin. She watched them march the muddy fields, bearing the wet-feathered body of the dead bird on a branch of holly. Their cry travelled on the winter wind: 'Up with the kettle, down with the pan, give us some money to bury the wren!'

The wren boys did not come near her cabin for alms or coin. They never had. Nance knew that most of the children feared her. She supposed she was now what Maggie had been to the children under Mangerton. A *cailleach* lurking in her cave of a cabin, able to whistle curses up from spit and hen shit.

In the early days, when Nance knew they believed in her power but did not know its kind, the valley people came to her for the working of badness against others. *Piseógs.* One hazy morning she had opened her door to a woman with her eye black and tooth loose in her gum, and words spilling out of her in fear. She had brought Nance money.

Kate Lynch. Younger then. Fear-filled. Raging.

'I want him dead,' she had said, shaking greasy curls out of her face and showing Nance the glint in her sweating palm.

'Will you sit down with me?' Nance had asked, and when Kate grabbed her hand and tipped the coin into it, she had let the money fall to the ground. 'Sit down,' she said, as the woman gave her a look of bewilderment and scrabbled for the rolling silver. 'Sit down and talk.'

'Why'd you drop it?' Kate demanded, on her knees. 'That's good egg money. I earned it myself. 'Tis honest, not stolen. I earned it with my own hens, and 'tis not his neither. I hide it from him.'

'I cannot take your money.'

The woman stared, her mouth a torn pocket in a pale face.

'I'll not be taking payment in coin. I'd lose the gift.'

Understanding had smoothed the furrows in Kate's brow. She counted the coins and, satisfied, slipped them into her pocket. 'You have the gift though.'

'I have the cure. And the knowledge.'

'The kind of knowledge that would see a bad man buried?'

Nance nodded at her bruise. 'Is that his badness I can see there?'

'You don't know the half of it.' Kate had bitten her lip, and then suddenly, before Nance could stop her, undressed, ripping at her outer clothes and lifting her shift to reveal a body pummelled into spoil beneath.

'Your husband?'

'I sure didn't fall.' She pulled her clothes back down, her face taut with determination. 'I want to be rid of him. You can do that. I know you can. They're saying you're in league with Them that does be in it, and that you have the power.' She lowered her voice. 'I want you to curse him.'

'Even if I wanted to, I don't know the ways.'

'I don't believe you. I know you're not from the valley, but I might show you a blessed well. Where you might walk against the sun. Where you might turn the stones against him.'

'An evil curse does no good to the one who lays it.'

'I would do it myself, but I don't have the skill. Look.' The woman had bent down and picked up the hem of her skirt, and with scrabbling fingers drawn out the slender flash of a needle. 'Every day I set it in my clothes to protect myself from him. Every night I wake and point the eye of it to his damned heart. To give him ill luck.' She waved the needle in Nance's face. 'But it does nothing. You have to help me.'

Nance had put her hands up, guided the needle away from her. 'Listen to me now. Whist now. Curses come home to roost. You do not want to be laying curses on your man, no matter how he rakes you.'

Kate shook her head. 'He's going to kill me. There's no sin in it if he's after killing me.'

'There are other things you might do. You might leave.'

Kate gave a sharp laugh. 'And bundle all my children on my back and take to the road and feed them on mushrooms and *praiseach*?'

'Long loneliness is better than bad company.'

'I want him dead. No, I want him to suffer. I want him to suffer as I have. I want his body to rot, and I want him to sicken, and I want him to wake each morning and spit blood as I have done.'

'I will give you mallow for the bruises.'

'You will not set a curse against him?'

'I will not.'

Kate sank onto the stool. 'Then you must tell me what *I* may do to curse him. Tell me how I might lay a *piseóg*.' Her face contorted. 'I have walked the well. I have turned those cursing stones at twilight. I point my needle at his chest and I pray to God that he be damned. But nothing. Nothing. He thrives. He bounces his fists off me.'

'I cannot tell you the ways.'

'But you know them. And there are other ways. I know there are. But no one will tell me.' Her voice cracked. 'Tell me how to lay a *piseóg* upon him, or do it yourself. Or I will turn the stones against you.'

CHAPTER
NINE

Selfheal

The eve of the new year returned the snow to the fields in whirling winds, the flakes sticking to the thatch and sweeping against the outer walls, hiding the mud spatter and the damp fingers of mould that stained the limewash.

Nóra kept glancing from her spinning to where Micheál lay sleeping in the settle bed, twitching like a dog.

'Is it time, do you think, Mary?'

The maid looked up from where she was slowly winding the wool and peered at the slant of light that fell in from the half-door that hung ajar. 'I think perhaps 'tis not yet twilight. 'Twas twilight she said to come.'

'I thought perhaps 'twas growing dark.'

'Not yet. Perhaps we might wait until the chickens return. Hens keep the hours.'

'Yes, I know that,' Nóra snapped. She wiped her waxy fingers on her apron. 'You pulled the herb? Where is it?'

Mary, hands busy, nodded to the bunch of mint lying in the corner of the room, the leaves a little wilted.

'’Tis straggly. Where did you fetch it?’

‘The well.’

‘Did anyone see you? Were the women there? Éilís? God forbid Kate Lynch saw. She’ll cry devilry.’

‘No one was there.’

‘I don’t see why Nance Roche didn’t cut the mint herself.’

Mary shrugged. ‘Perhaps there is no mint down by the woods. She’s an old woman. ’Tis a long way to go, just for some herbs.’

Nóra pulled a face. ‘Nothing stops that one, old or no.’ She hesitated. ‘Did she say there was a danger in pulling it?’

‘Not if we cut it in the name of the Trinity.’ Mary looked at Micheál as he stirred, his hand lifting in the air and then falling back behind his head. ‘I blessed the mint before I put the blade to it.’

Nóra pursed her lips. ‘I don’t understand it. Mint. Mint is good for fleas and moths. How is mint going to bring a child back from Them?’

‘I always tied it around the wrists of my brothers and sisters,’ Mary said.

‘And why was that?’

‘Keeps away the sickness.’

‘And did it work?’

Mary shook her head, her eyes fixed on the wool before her. ‘Two are with God.’

Nóra’s fierce expression softened, and she looked down at the spinning wheel. ‘I’m sorry for your troubles.’

‘’Twas the will of God, but He took a long time in taking them.’

‘They suffered?’

‘All day and all night they’d cough. They gave up their lives a little cough at a time. But now they are gone to the angels.’

There was a long silence. Nóra glanced at the girl and saw that she was clenching her teeth, her jaw working furiously under her skin.

‘But you have many other brothers and sisters.’

Mary sniffed. 'I do.'

'My daughter was the only child I had,' Nóra said. 'Her death was a great loss to me. I have lost my parents, and my sister, and my husband, but 'tis Johanna that . . .' She looked at Mary and, suddenly unable to speak, placed her fist on her chest.

The maid's face was unreadable. 'She was your daughter,' she said plainly.

'She was.'

'You loved her.'

'The first time I saw Johanna . . .' Nóra's voice was strangled. She wanted to say that with Johanna's birth she had felt a love so fierce it terrified. That the world had cleft and her daughter was the kernel at its core. 'Yes,' she said. 'I loved her.'

'As I loved my sisters.'

Nóra shook her head. ''Tis more than love. You will know it some day. To be a mother is to have your heart cut out and placed in your child.'

The wind groaned outside.

'Perhaps I will light the candle now. Just in case.' Nóra got up and closed the half-door, then stoppered the window with straw against the rising draught. The room fell into low light. The fire climbed. Dabbing at her eyes, Nóra lit a candle and set it on the table to guard the house from the coming night and its unseen swift of spirits. The flame whipped on its wick.

'Did you fetch water when you were at the well, or was it only the mint you took?'

'The mint,' Mary replied.

Nóra frowned. 'And what will you have us drink tomorrow when the new year is upon us?'

Mary looked confused. 'I will return to the well. As I do every morning.'

'You will not. I'll not have anyone sleeping under this roof going to the well to draw water on the first day of the new year. Don't you guard yourself up there in Annamore?'

'I fetch the water same as always.'

Nóra pushed the candle to one side and pulled out a small cloth bag filled with flour. 'I'll tell you how it is. There'll be no throwing of the ashes tomorrow. The feet water, you leave that be. From sun-up to sundown, you'll not be parting with anything of this house. And don't be sweeping the floor and all the luck from it either.'

Mary rose to her feet. 'What harm is there in well-going?'

Nóra pulled a face, added milk, water and soda to the flour, roughly mixing it with her hand. 'There's no good in drawing first water from a well on new year's day and that's all I know. Don't be questioning the old ways.' She cast an anxious look to the sleeping boy. 'Especially not now.'

The two women were silent as the new year bread baked. Nóra moved between the fire and loaf in its pot to the door, remarking on the slow descent of light outside, while Mary woke the boy and rugged him in the blanket for the journey to come. Nóra nipped the bread when it was cooked, breaking a corner to let the Devil out, and they ate it before the fire, Mary sopping the crust with milk and easing wet morsels into the child's maw with her fingers. He ate ravenously, chewing at her knuckles. His cries for more continued long after the bread was finished.

'Always hungry, never satisfied,' Nóra sniffed. 'Is that not what Nance was saying? The sign of the changeling?'

'There's a bonfire on the mountain,' Mary said, licking her thumb and sponging crumbs off her clothes. 'I saw some boys piling furze and heather and dead branches up there this morning. Do you think there'll be dancing?'

Nóra picked her teeth with a nail. 'You've a right to come with me to Nance. I don't pay you to go dancing.'

Mary glanced at the boy. 'Are the Good People abroad, do you think?'

''Tis as Nance said. Just as day is joined to night, so does the year have its seams.' She got up and opened the half-door, peering across the valley. 'And that is when They come. That is when They change their abode. Through the stitching of the year. Which way do you think this wind is blowing?'

The light was fading. Beyond the swathes of fast-falling snow, the glow of a fire could be seen on the hill. A dark plume rose from it, tracing the air with the heady smell of wood smoke.

Mary joined Nóra by the door, Micheál on her hip, his head resting on her shoulder. He was oddly quiet. 'I think 'tis coming from the west. Are we in for a storm?'

Nóra brushed her shoulders of snowmelt and shut the door fast again, sliding a wooden bolt against the wickerwork. 'They say there's portent in the direction of a new year's wind.'

'What does a wind from the west bring?'

'Please God, a better year than last.'

Nance sat in the dark of her cabin and, through her open door, watched the dying year surrender to snow. The night was falling holy, as though the glory of God was in the changing of the light. Sitting in her ragged shawls, she felt the silence ring in her ears as loudly as a monastic bell.

It would begin that night. The cures. The mysterious pleading. The unpicking of old magic.

Nance felt the sly pricking of dread.

The boy was not the first child she had seen who had the mark of the Good People. Back when she was new to the valley, after years of cold begging, long after Maggie and the woman who was not her mother had gone, a woman had come to her door, dragging a small, scrunched child behind her. The girl, five years old, had not smiled since the summer before, and while at first she had whispered to her brothers and sisters, she now refused to utter a word. Her mother had wrung her hands, picked at the chapped skin between her fingers.

'She does not answer to her name. She has no interest in playing. In going anywhere. In helping me about the house. And our house is full of strange strife over it.'

Nance had regarded the mute carefully. She was a tiny, folded bird of a child, knees grey with dust from the road. She sat watching them without expression, shoulders cowed.

'When did this begin? Did something happen to her?'

The woman shook her head. 'I blame myself. I left her to the care of her older sisters. I had to go haying . . . She is changed. Deep in my heart I feel that she is not my daughter. She will not respond to her name.'

The woman said that she had left the girl at the crossroads to recover her own daughter from the custody of the fairies. She did not have the heart, she said, to hold her over the fire, for she resembled her own child. The mother had tied her to the post but she had somehow escaped and wandered home. Put herself to bed in her daughter's place. The woman's husband was saying they must now beat the changeling and brand it on the forehead with the sign of the cross. He said they must anger the fairies and force Them to come collect Their own.

Nance had asked the woman to return to her seven times with the changeling. If the power in fire might not be used, they would use the Good People's own plants against Them.

Seven mornings of *lus mór*, the great herb. Nance had collected the foxglove at dawn, and given the changeling three drops of juice from the leaves on the tongue, three in the ear. When the fairy child's pulse dropped and she knew that the plant had gripped the blood, she and the mother had swung it in and out of the door with the words she had heard Maggie use, all those years ago.

'If you're a fairy, away with you.'

Seven days she plied the mute imp with foxglove. Seven days the heart of the changeling slowed. Seven days her skin broke in cold sweat.

'Does she suffer?' the mother asked.

'She resists her return to her own people.'

The day after the seventh treatment, the woman had returned alone, her face shining. 'She speaks! She speaks!'

Two fat roosters and a noggin of butter. But as soon as the mother had left, Nance curled up on the rushes of her floor and wept until she thought she would be sick. She could not tell if she was relieved, or terrified.

It was proof of her ability beyond the herbs. It was proof in her knowledge, proof that there was power in the soil, in the raving. All that Maggie had said was true. She was different. She straddled the river and its sorcered current. She left footprints on both banks.

Too late for her mother.

In the weeks after, her thumbs turned. Nance woke and saw the knotting of her knuckles, and saw that They had marked her. Gifted her, and ransomed her.

I have done it once, so I will be able to do it again, Nance thought.

She got up to close the door to preserve the warmth of her fire. She could see flames on the hilltops through the silent drifts, and shadows of dancing bodies flickering. She thought she could hear the beating of a drum.

A good night for ritual, she thought, and saw, then, two dark figures making their way down the path to her cabin.

'Nóra Leahy. Mary Clifford.'

The women were breathing hard, the maid gripping Micheál to her chest, slipping a little under his weight.

'Did anyone see you?'

'They are all atop the mountain.'

'Good. Come in from the cold. 'Tis turning bitter.' Nance led them into the cabin, pointing to a bucket of warmed water. 'Wash your feet there, so.'

Mary hesitated. 'I have Micheál – I mean, I have the . . . Where should I set him down?'

'Is he sleeping?'

Mary pulled away the blanket that swaddled the boy to her chest and shook her head. 'His eyes are open. He squalled to be taken outside, but I think the fresh air has settled him.'

Nance noticed that Nóra lingered by the doorway, shaking the ice from her cloak. 'Come in and bless you, Nóra. 'Tis right you are here. Sit down and take the cold off you.'

The widow pinched her lips and took a tentative step inside, glancing around the room. She started as a rustle came from the dark corner.

''Tis just Mora. My blessed goat. Did you bring the mint with you?'

Mary gently placed the child down by the fire and rummaged within the shawl crossed against her chest. She pulled out the mint and offered it to Nance.

''Tis nine sprigs you have?'

Mary nodded. 'They're a little wilted.'

'You need to chew them.'

Nóra looked confused. 'You're making her eat them?'

'Not eat. Chew. Chew the leaves into a pap. We will be needing the juice.' Nance opened her mouth and pointed to her dark gums. 'I'd do it myself, but . . .'

'Go on then, Mary.' Nóra was impatient.

The girl hesitated, studying the mint in her palm. 'I don't want to.'

''Tis only mint. Don't keep us waiting all night.'

Nance smiled. ''Tis nothing I'm asking you to do that I wouldn't be doing myself. Musha, 'tis only the mint you picked yourself.'

Mary reluctantly tugged the leaves from a stalk and slipped them into her mouth.

'Don't swallow the juice of them,' Nance warned. She fetched a wooden bowl and held it under Mary's chin. The girl, face stricken, spat the green pap into it and wiped her mouth with the back of her hand.

'All the leaves from the nine sprigs,' Nance said, nodding to the remaining stalks. She glanced sideways at the widow and saw that Nóra was staring at Mary, brow furrowed.

Mary crammed her mouth with the remaining mint and chewed it into a paste, her eyes averted. When she finally spat the wet mush into the bowl, her tongue and teeth were stained green.

Nance peered into the slaver, swirling it, then poured it into an old handkerchief to strain the liquid. Mary picked remnants of chewed mint from her lips.

'What is all this for, Nance?'

Nance gave the bowl to Nóra and shuffled to the corner of the room. She returned gripping a thimble.

'There is wisdom in beginning with small charms.' She motioned to the boy. 'Sit down on that stool there, Mary, and hold the child still for me. Aye, that's it. Now, hold his head.' She turned to Nóra. 'You don't want to hold him over the fire? Well, we've a right to be seeing if the cratur isn't struck with an illness of the plain kind.' She thrust the thimble in her face. 'Juice of mint in each ear, and we'll soon know if he's fairy or if the fairies have only made him deaf.'

Mary held Micheál across her lap and turned the fragile round of the boy's skull in her hands to expose the curl of his ear.

Nance dipped the hollow of bone into the bowl and spooned its fill into the boy's canal.

'And now the other?' Mary asked, grimacing as Micheál struggled under her grip, moaning. She turned her hands, exposing the other ear for Nance.

The air was fragrant with the herb. They watched as the liquid spilt into the boy's copper hair.

'What now?'

'Now you wait until morning to see if he has been cured, if he listens to your voices. Perhaps tries to speak. Or if he is unchanged.'

'Is that all?'

Nance shook her head. ''Tis a powerful dark night out there. The hours are more powerful for the changing in them.' She wiped a little of the mint from the rim of the boy's ear, then stooped and drew a cloth off a basket by the fire. 'Selfheal.'

Nóra peered inside. 'For sore throats?'

'And for the fairy blast. For the sudden stroke.' She knelt on the floor and, uncovering the boy's feet, kneaded the leaves of selfheal into his soles. Mary and Nóra's eyes bore into her as she smeared the herb into his skin. Nance thought she could feel the glower of Nóra's desperation, the tussle of her hope and her fear.

The child lay still, spumed with mint, blinking into sleep.

''Tis enough, now. Enough for tonight.'

Mary sniffed the bruised selfheal, nostrils flaring.

'When will we know if it has worked?' Nóra plucked the leaves from Mary's hands and cast them on the floor.

'By morning,' Nance murmured. 'You may wake and find your grandson, or you may not. There are other charms, other rituals . . .' Her voice dropped away. 'You will see. All will be well.'

'Do you believe so, Nance?'

'I do, Nóra. In time, all will be well.'

The fires on the hills smouldered orange as the women left, pockets charged with ashes to guard them from the night. Watching them fade into the grey fall of snow, Nance thought she could hear Maggie's voice. A whisper in the dark.

If you don't know the way, walk slowly.

She had chewed the mint herself that night. That first night of the many nights spent in trying to send the changeling woman away and force her mother back. Her father had gone on *cuaird*, and it was just Nance and Maggie, sitting on stools next to where the woman who was not Mary Roche lay. The cratur had not even stirred when they poured the herb into her ears.

'I don't think she will come back,' Nance had said miserably. They were sitting by the fire, staring at the embers, waiting for her father to return.

Maggie was pensive. 'I promised your father I'd do what I could for him.' She hesitated. 'But 'tis not often one who is swept is returned.'

'Why won't the Good People return her?'

''Tis hard to give up what is precious.'

'Maggie?'

'Yes, Nance.'

'How do you know all the things that you know?'

'Some folk are forced to the edges by their difference.' Maggie brought an unthinking hand up to her scar. 'But 'tis at the edges that they find their power.'

That night Nóra dreamt she was by the Flesk, washing Martin's clothes with the heat of the sun on her back. It was summer. The banks of the river were thick with grass and the wide high stretch of fern. She dreamt she held the wooden beetle in her hand, bringing it down again and again in a rocky pool to pound the dirt from the sopping laundry. As she thumped the beetle for the last time, a bloodstain erupted in the cloth. Curious, she beat at the clothes again, and the blood circled wider, creeping through the weave.

Dread searched her.

Nóra put down the beetle. Something moved under the shirt. Skin prickling, she ripped the wet clothes away.

It was Micheál, his skull stoved in. Drowning in the pinking water of her laundry.

Nóra woke in sweat. First light crept under the cabin door. Uneasy, she padded out to the settle bed where Mary lay snoring. The boy was beside her, a blanket over his head.

Nóra felt her heart stumble over its beats. She reached out and pulled the blanket from the child's face.

He was alive, blinking at her with gummed eyes.

Relieved, Nóra unwrapped the boy from his swaddling and examined his stained feet, the green crust in his ears.

'Are you Johanna's son?' Nóra asked. 'Are you Micheál Kelliher?'

The boy lifted his hands and clawed at her hair, and in mouth-thick gibber he made his answer.

CHAPTER TEN

Hogweed

'**Nóra Leahy sent me.** She says to tell you that the cratur is unchanged and still spitting and screaming and the cretin he was when we came to you.'

Nance looked up from where she sat in her doorway, skinning a hare. Her hands ran bloody. 'Is that so, Mary Clifford?'

''Tis. There was no cure to be had in the leaves. In the herbs.' The girl hesitated, standing with arms folded and her shawl tightly gathered around her head. 'But in case you're thinking 'twas me that sent the charm out of the mint . . . I promise. I pulled it in the name of the Trinity. And the dew was on it. I did all as you said.'

Nance wiped her hands on her skirt and held the hare out to Mary. 'Take this for me now.'

Mary took it. Nance noticed the girl examine the raw stretch and sinew of the skinned animal.

'Don't you have a fear of eating this?'

'Why is that?' Nance picked up the swimming bowl of guts beside her.

'All the magic that does be in it.'

Nance motioned for Mary to follow her inside the cabin and

shut the door. 'I don't have a fear of eating anything that makes a mouthful. Hares, rabbits, eels.'

Mary pulled a face. 'My brother says an eel can travel the county in a day. Says it takes its tail in its mouth and rolls like a hoop.' She shuddered. 'I don't like anything as cunning as that.'

'I like them well enough if I can catch them.'

Mary sat down by the fire and pointed to the hare skin laid out on the floor. 'Will you be selling that? I've seen boys with caps of hare. The ears still on.'

Nance took the skinned hare from Mary and set it in the empty crock. 'I sell what I can. Dyes mostly, but also skins and besoms. Peck soap.'

'I like the black there,' Mary said, pointing to a loose ball of wool in a basket.

'Alder catkin. Or the roots of spurge. I make them from crottle lichen, bogwater. Sell them. Even heather can wring out a dye. Oh, there's colour to be had from even the humblest of what grows in God's soil.'

'You know a lot.'

'I've lived a long time.'

Mary regarded Nance in the gloomy light. ''Tis not the years in a person that gives them knowledge, is it? 'Tis Them that belong to the wilds. They say you speak with Them. You know where the fairies do be, and you speak with Them, and that is how you know these things.' She lifted her chin to the dried plants hanging from the ceiling. 'Is that true? That you learnt it from the fairies and that is why you will return the widow's grandson to her? Because you know Their ways and tricks.'

Nance washed her hands, greasy from handling the hare innards. There was more than youthful curiosity in Mary's voice. There was suspicion there. A sharp-shouldered wariness.

There was a sudden thump of boots outside and Mary stood up quickly, knocking her head against a bunch of St John's wort and sending dried flowers scattering to the ground.

'Here! Here!' It was a man's voice. 'She's here. There's smoke, there's a fire lit. Come on with you, David.'

There was a scuffle outside and three heavy knocks on the cabin wall. Silt fell from the ceiling. 'Nance Roche!'

'Open the door for me, Mary.'

The girl got up and pulled the wicker door ajar.

'May God and Mary and Patrick bless you, Nance Roche, for you must come with me.' It was Daniel Lynch, his face shiny with sweat, chest falling heavy in laboured breathing. He entered and another man, a stoop-shouldered youth that looked much like him, followed, clearly embarrassed by their intrusion.

'Daniel. God save you. What's wrong?'

'We have need of you. The little woman is in the straw. Brigid. My wife.'

'What hour did it begin?' Nance asked.

'Dawn. Her face is all chalk and the pain is on her. I told her I'd come for you.'

Nance turned to Mary, who was gawking at Daniel, slack-jawed. 'Mary, run home to Nóra. Tell her to bring women with her to the Lynches' cabin. Brigid's cousins, her aunts, if she has any other kin. Ask them to bring what clean cloth they have. Milk, butter. Bless yourself as you set out, and bless them before they step inside the Lynches' cabin. I will be there, waiting for them.'

The girl nodded furiously, then pelted out of the door, long legs running, shawl slipping off her head. The brothers watched her flee up the path, mud flicking from her bare feet.

Nance asked them to wait outside while she filled her basket with what she might need. She pulled handfuls of dried herbs from the ceiling and wrapped them in rags. Dried ox-eye daisies and water-cress. Yarrow. She gathered a hazel stick, black threads, and the pail of forge water she had kept covered with a cloth.

'I'm ready,' she said, handing the heavy pail to Daniel. 'Take me to your wife.'

When Nance walked in the Lynches' cabin she knew immediately that all was not well. Brigid lay on a heap of broom and heather by the fire, and the blanket she had placed under her was soaked with blood. Nance turned back outside and held up her hands to stop the brothers from following her inside.

'You did well in fetching me. Now, go on and don't be hovering about this door like horseflies. I'll have you told when there is news to tell.' She spat on the ground. 'God be with you.'

Brigid's eyes were screwed shut with pain. At the sound of the door closing she threw her head back. 'Daniel?'

'God bless you, child, 'tis Nance. Your man's gone and fetched me for you.' She knelt on the floor beside the woman and pushed a folded blanket under her back.

Fear rose off the girl in waves. She is a spooked mare, Nance thought.

'I'm frightened,' Brigid choked. 'Is it supposed to feel like this? It doesn't feel right.'

'I'll see you safe.' Nance bent over the girl and began to whisper a prayer in her right ear.

Nóra arrived at the Lynches' cabin with Éilís O'Hare, Kate and Sorcha. She hadn't wanted to ask the women to come at all, so bitter did she feel towards them and their constant spluttering of gossip, but they were the only women bound to Brigid through her marriage, and if blood could not be fetched to mind her, it was right that a kind of kin be in the room. She had sent Mary to Peg with Micheál.

Nóra opened the door and found the room full of smoke and smell. Brigid was moaning in protest as Nance insisted that her hips face the fire. The heat inside the cabin was insufferable. Brigid's face rolled with sweat, and the old woman's hair was damp against her skin.

The women stopped in the doorway, staring as Nance urged Brigid to lay still and not kneel as she was trying. The young woman's thighs were slippery with blood.

'Sorcha, come in and help your cousin settle. I need her to face the fire, so.' With her help, Nance picked up Brigid's feet and hauled her closer to the hearth, blazing it with dried furze until the darkness peeled back to the corners of the room.

Brigid's pupils were dark and wide and unseeing. Éilís stood by the wall gripping a jug of water, her jaw set, tense. Kate hovered beside her daughter, taking a long red ribbon from the neck of her crossed shawl and holding it out in her left hand.

'What are you doing with that ribbon there, Kate?' Éilís asked. 'What's that for?'

Kate didn't answer, but began to knot and unknot it over Brigid's heaving form.

'What are you doing?'

'To ease the birth,' Kate muttered. Nance cast her a long look but said nothing.

'Nance, how are you getting on?' Nóra asked.

'There is watercress in that basket. Pound it to a poultice, will you. And you two can make yourselves useful. Take the black thread in there and tie it where I tell you.'

Éilís and Sorcha glanced at each other.

'Quickly! You need to arrest the flow of blood. Tie that thread there on her wrists.'

The two women heard the urgency in her voice and bent closer.

'Bite it if you must, and tie it on each ankle, each finger. Each toe. Tightly, mind.'

There was a light tapping on the door, and Mary's face peered inside, eyes growing wide at the sight of the blood on the ground.

'Nance.' Nóra gestured at the girl with the pestle.

'Send her away. For pig dung. Try the blacksmith's.'

'You heard her,' Nóra said.

Mary disappeared outside and the women continued their slow work on Brigid. She lay still, teeth bared. Nóra passed Nance the poultice and knelt behind Brigid so that she might rest her head on her lap.

Nance's lips pressed tightly together in concentration as she lifted the girl's damp dress, exposing the swell of her belly. She smeared the pounded watercress on Brigid's thighs, skin and pubic hair.

Blood rippled out of her. All the women saw it.

An hour dripped by. Mary returned from the blacksmith's, her hands dirty with pig dung. Áine was with her, gripping a rosary and woven cross.

Nance looked up at the sound of their entrance. 'Áine,' she cried. 'Bless you, but I can't be letting you stay.' She stood, her apron as bloody as a butcher's, and took Áine by the shoulders.

'I want to help,' Áine protested.

Nance whispered an apology and walked Áine outside, shutting the door firmly behind them.

'Why can't Áine come in?' Mary whispered to Nóra. 'What has she done?'

Nóra clucked her tongue and continued to sponge Brigid's temples with forge water.

'She only wanted to pray over her.'

'Everyone knows Áine's barren,' Kate spat. 'She might cast the evil eye over the child.'

'She would not! She's a good woman.'

'Whether she's good or not has nothing to do with it. Most of them with the evil eye have no knowledge of when they cast it.' Kate licked her lips. 'You could be casting it for all we know. The redheaded girls do be with the evil eye. Unlucky.'

Nóra had just opened her mouth to protest when Nance returned inside with a small clay jug. A stink of ammonia filled the room.

'What is that?' Mary gaped.

'The water of the husband,' murmured Nóra.

Using a heather besom, Nance began to dash the urine around the room and on Brigid's face, stomach and lower body, flicking the last of it on the small wicker cradle in the corner.

'An old and holy blessing,' Nance muttered.

The women said nothing.

Throughout the day they tended to Brigid under Nance's direction. They mixed the pig dung with forge water and pasted it over her abdomen with their bare hands. They took turns knotting and untying Kate's ribbon ceaselessly over her until their arms ached and the ribbon grew stained with the grease of their fingers. They watched Brigid's toes and fingers seize and swell with trapped blood under their ties of thread, and dribbled ox-eye daisy boiled on new milk into her open mouth.

It was only as the day eased back into darkness that the child came.

It was dead, its lips dark.

Brigid, weak as water, tumbled into unconsciousness.

Daniel was ushered into the cabin and shown the tiny body of his son. The women stood around him, faces grey with exhaustion, too tired to grieve. He looked down at his unconscious wife and brought a hand over his mouth as if afraid of what might come out of it. Mary stepped aside and watched as he walked back out into the cold blue of the evening to fight his grief out with the sky.

Nance told Sorcha to wrap the baby and cover its face.

'Is Brigid dead?' Kate asked.

'Not yet.' Nance took a small piece of paper from her basket, unfolded it and shook something into an earthenware bowl. 'Fetch a light,' she muttered.

Mary raked over the smoking fire to uncover the belly of embers and carefully pincered a live coal with the tongs.

'Set it here.' Nance held out the bowl, and Mary saw it was full of hogweed seed and dried horse dung. She placed the ember in the bowl and smoke uncurled from the mix. 'Let her breathe of it,' Nance said.

Mary crouched beside Brigid and placed the smoking hogweed beneath her nose.

'Does she stir?'

'I can't be sure she's breathing.' Smoke covered the woman's face like a veil.

'Pull her chin down for me, girl.' Taking the bowl from Mary, Nance blew the smoke into Brigid's open mouth.

Nothing happened.

'Shall we say a prayer?' Mary asked.

Brigid's nostrils flared and she began to cough.

'Praise be,' Nance said, wiping her hand across her forehead. It left a trail of blood. 'She's life in her yet.'

The evening was a strange, silent one. Brigid woke and wailed for her child and for her husband, and clamped her mouth against

Nance's insistent hand offering her berries of bittersweet. She fell asleep only when exhaustion overtook her. Then the women rolled her body to remove the bloody heather and replace it with fresh straw. Nance shoved the afterbirth on the fire, where it hissed and gave off a meaty smell.

'Where is her man?'

'Outside,' Mary said. She peered out the door. 'He's on his knees in the field.'

Nance was sitting on a stool, her head in her hands. 'He must be fetched.'

Nóra's face was white. 'Let him grieve, Nance. Let him sit in the soil.'

'No. The young have weak spirits. They are hard put to defend themselves against the devils that hover all places.'

'Give him a moment alone.'

'Mary Clifford,' Nance said. 'Go and bring Daniel back in. He has a right to protect the soul of that child.'

Sorcha looked down at the little bundle in her lap. 'I . . . I blessed him. I crossed his forehead with the forge water. Is that not a christening? Is that not enough to get him to Heaven?'

Kate sniffed. ''Twas dead afore it came out.'

'Still,' Sorcha protested. 'A blessing is a blessing.'

'Go get Daniel, Mary,' Nance repeated. She pushed herself to her feet and staggered over to the chicken roost against the wall of the Lynches' cabin. Peering at the line of blinking hens, Nance reached in and grabbed one, pinning it underneath her elbow to prevent the bird from flapping. It struggled against her grip. 'Fetch Daniel,' she said.

Mary ran out into the field, her ankle jarring on the uneven ground. Mud splashed up her dress.

Brigid's husband was kneeling amongst the lazy beds, his head on his knees. Áine, Peter, Seán, John and his brother, David, stood around him, keeping him company in silence. Above them the clouds had vanished and the sky was bright with emerging stars.

'Leave him be, girl,' Seán said.

'Nance says she needs him.'

'He's done all he can.'

'She's worried about the devils.'

Áine's brow creased. 'What now?'

Mary bit at her nails. They tasted of dung.

Peter nodded. 'Nance is right. That child is not gone to God. Brigid is ill protected. There is evil that would seek to enter your house, Daniel.'

Seán spat on the ground. 'Peter. Don't be talking of this now.'

Daniel looked up and Mary flinched at the sight of his red-rimmed eyes, the raw look of his mouth. 'She wants me?'

Mary nodded. 'She's taken one of your chickens and asked me to fetch you.'

Seán groaned and placed a hand on Daniel's shoulder. 'She's done enough, nephew, don't you think?'

Daniel shrugged him off angrily.

'Go on, Daniel,' Peter urged. He turned to Seán. 'Let the man do something for his child.'

Nance met Mary and Daniel by the open door and passed the hen over the threshold. 'You know what I need from you,' she said, placing a knife in his hand. 'I'm sorry for your trouble. Kill it.'

Daniel didn't look at her, but accepted the chicken and, in one swift movement, cut its head off. He gave it to Nance and she threw it on the fire, where it smouldered. The women inside brought their hands to their faces as the smell of burning feathers filled the air.

Nance took the dead bird, which jerked wildly in death throes. Holding it firmly by the feet, she turned the hen upside down and dripped its blood on the floor of the cabin by the entrance. She returned it to Daniel, wiping her hands on her skirt. 'Circle the cabin with blood. Protect your wife.'

Mary stepped inside and sat next to Nóra, who was watching over Brigid, her eyes swimming. 'Missus. What was that for?'

'For the wee babby's soul,' Sorcha answered, crossing herself. 'Protection.'

Éilís stood up suddenly. 'If spilt blood can waylay the Devil, then sure this place is holy, for Brigid's blood is burning with the straw on the fire and the air is full of it!' She spat on the ground and stormed out the open door without looking back.

Mary noticed that one of the Lynches' farm dogs had appeared outside. It stood on the threshold of the cabin, crouched close to the ground, sniffing the chicken blood.

Before Mary could say anything, Nóra rose and kicked it from the door.

Nance returned home from the birth reeking of blood and shaking with exhaustion. No food had passed her lips since that morning and, walking the narrow path home in the starred night, she felt overcome with dizziness. The night was cold but clear, and the full moon cast pure over mist that lingered on the ground, unmoved by any wind. The air seemed impossibly damp and sweet after the heat and smoke of the cabin.

Suddenly Nance stumbled sideways to the stone wall that bordered the lane, falling against thorny briars and dropping her basket of soiled linen and the remains of her herbs.

How she wished the child had been born alive.

She had delivered a generation of children in the valley, it seemed. She saw them every day: small, shrill children who buried their snotty faces into their mothers' skirts, scraped their knees on the walls, and grew strong scarpering along the fields. But amongst the children she delivered who stuck to life like burrs were others who came too still, too small, knotted with cord. There were those who did not catch to the fabric of the world. It happened. She knew it happened.

So why did the death of Brigid Lynch's child fill her with such dread? She had done all that was needed. She had done all that Maggie had taught her to do.

The besom of broom and the piss of the husband.

The heat of the fire set to the slope of the hips.

The thread, when the blood came, and the pig muck on the abdomen, and the forge water and watercress, and even Kate's relentless unknotting of the blessed ribbon.

Nance remembered then. She had not brought her cloth. The white swaddling cloth that she had dragged through the dew of every St Brigid's morning to be blessed by the saint, to be wrapped around the mother if the labour was long.

Would that have saved the child?

Nance slowly picked up her basket and pushed herself from the wall. The brambles snagged her clothes. It no longer mattered. She had done everything in her power, but the child was not meant for the world.

The woods and her small cabin before them looked cold and empty in the deep blue of the night. Her goat, a ghost in the distance, stood looking at her, waiting to be led indoors.

She reached the cabin and threw her arms around the animal, comforted by the round heat and smell of her.

'Truth, you are a patient girl,' she murmured, nuzzling her face into Mora's wiry coat. She led her indoors and tethered her to the hook in the wall, then lit the fire. She drank some milk, scattered groundsel and a little yellow meal to her chickens, some already roosting, and lay down wearily on her bed.

But sleep did not come. Nance lay on the heather, cradled by her own exhaustion, her mind uneasy. Again, she had the sense that something terrible was happening. That in some irreparable way the world was changing, that it spun away from her, and that in the whirl of change she was being flung to some forsaken corner.

The fire cracked as the turf sods slowly disintegrated into ash.

What would her father say to her now, if he were alive? He who understood the strange winds that blew, who understood the anatomy of storms.

'The cod swims in deeper waters,' she remembered him murmuring, pulling her head to his shoulder. 'There's a mighty peace in the deep, and that is all the cod is after. The untroubled deep. But a storm will toss the water about like a devil. Fish, weed, sand, stones, even the old bones and bits of wrecked ships, 'tis all tossed feathers when the storm hits. Fish that like the deep are thrown into the shallows, and fish that have a need of the shallows are pushed into the deep.'

His hands stroking her hair. The smell of boiling potatoes as they waited for their dinner.

'Begod, I tell no lie. But what does the cod do when he senses a storm in the water? He swallows stones. Faith, 'tis true or I'm not your da. Your cod will fill himself with stones to stay out of the mighty swell of the sea. He will sink himself. All fish are afraid of thunder, but only some know how to keep themselves out of the way of it.'

Nance closed her eyes and her heart clenched in pining for her father.

The dead are close, she thought. The dead are close.

*

Sometime before dawn Nance heard a noise outside. Rising to her feet, she took a dead ember from the fire for protection against the fairies and peered into the uncertain night. The sound came from the Piper's Grave. Nance set out in the direction of the *ráth*.

The moon had listed to the horizon, but its light still cast a varnish over the valley and Nance could see a man standing next to the great slab of stone in the *cillín*, his hand resting on its slender edge. He was praying, it seemed. His head was lowered.

Daniel.

Nance stole closer and watched him from beyond the low wall that marked the sacred space from the surrounding fields. A small box lay by his feet.

Nance wondered whether Daniel had made the coffin himself, nailing together what poor, unhallowed wood he could cobble from his home, or whether a neighbour had, in generosity, made one to accommodate the unbaptised child.

She watched as Daniel wandered the *cillín*, his eyes to the ground, then having decided on a place and retrieved a spade, began to dig a grave. The soil was cold and hard, and for many long minutes all Nance could hear was the rasp of the spade's iron edge against the untended ground. Nance watched as Daniel fetched the tiny coffin and placed it gently into the earth on his knees. He stayed there for some time before wearily rising to his feet and filling the grave in with clay.

It was only when he walked to the wall to lift a large white stone to mark the unconsecrated grave that he saw Nance. He stopped and stared at her in the moonlight, holding the rock in both hands as though he could not trust his eyes. Then slowly, without a word of greeting, he turned, placed the stone on the disturbed soil and walked away, his arms holding the spade across his shoulders like a man crucified.

Nance stood there in the unfolding dark until the crow of a cockerel broke the stillness of the valley. Casting one long look to where the stillborn lay in the silent, eternal soil, she crossed herself and returned to her cabin.

CHAPTER
ELEVEN

Foxglove

Brigid's terrible labour and the dead child were all the women seemed to talk about in the days after the birth. Mary noticed that they came to the well in greater numbers than was usual, standing in dark clothes like the jackdaws that clustered in the fields. Some wore expressions of sympathetic sorrow, mothers who had lost their own children and who understood the woman's loss, but some seemed, to Mary's ears, more interested in finding fault with what Brigid had or had not done to secure the life in her child.

'David said she did not visit John O'Donoghue to blow the bellows.'

'Sure, I've done that six times and 'tis six fine children I now have in this world.'

''Tis a powerful way to promise safe delivery, the bellows.'

'She was at the wake of Martin Leahy. I saw her. She knelt by his dead body. Do you think there's something in that?'

'Ah, but she was not there when the body was coffined.'

'No,' said one woman with an air of conspiracy. 'But where *was* she? Was she not with Peg O'Shea, who, I hear, was minding Nóra Leahy's grandson?'

There was a murmur of incredulity.

'I would not be easy in my mind to stay in the same room as that cratur.'

'Now, tell me. Do you know what illness is upon him? I knew Nóra was brought the child when her daughter died, but I've never seen her with him. I've not seen the child at all.'

'She hides him.'

'Because he is a changeling! He's no child at all!'

'Begod, I've heard he will not walk in company, but dances and sings when alone.'

'And how would you know that, if no one's with him to spy all that dancing?'

There was laughter, then someone nudged the woman who had spoken and gestured to Mary.

'You're the maid of Nóra Leahy, are you not?'

'Mary Clifford is her name.'

Mary looked up from her well buckets and saw a kind-faced woman sizing her up.

'Is it true, *cailín*? What they say about that boy? Is he a changeling?'

Mary swallowed hard. The women were all looking at her. 'Nance Roche will have him restored.'

The woman chewed the inside of her cheek thoughtfully. 'You know, I saw a changeling child before.'

'Hanna!'

There were some surprised chuckles. The woman spun around. ''Tis no thing to laugh at. Terrible sorrow for the mother. How would you feel if your own son was stolen and you were left with a bawling withered root sickening in your own child's cradle?' The laughter subsided and she clucked her tongue. 'Good, well. Nance knows what she's doing.'

There was a cry, and Mary saw Kate Lynch storming through the group, her empty water pail banging against her leg. She was scowling. 'You should be asking yourselves what hand Nance had in Brigid's trouble!'

'What are you saying, Kate?'

One of the women, her throat flushed with excitement, raised her voice. 'I always knew she was a baby-dropper.'

'What do you mean by that?'

The woman's voice fell to a whisper and the others shuffled into a tighter circle. ''Tis the word for them. After what they do.' She glanced at the women, her eyes narrowed. 'I heard 'tis why she came here, all those years ago – to escape those who would see her hang.'

'Faith, I've always thought she came here running from something.'

'She's a baby-dropper. She knows all the ways.'

'And what ways might they be?' asked Hanna, staring at the others with distaste.

The woman rolled her eyes, lips moist with scandal. 'Truth, they call them baby-droppers as they know how to let the baby, when it comes, drop straight into a pail of water.' She stopped to see if the women knew her meaning. 'Sure, if the baby drowns in that pail before it takes a breath, then no judge could say it was done intentional.' She shuddered. 'Or, soon as the baby is born, she wraps the cord around its neck. Quick, like. Strangles it with its own cord and says it came that way, the poor misfortunate.'

'Are you saying that Brigid Lynch asked Nance to kill her own child?'

The woman blushed. 'I'm not. I'm saying you don't ask a fox to mind the hens.'

Mary had heard enough. She stood up and, thrusting her chin down, made to force her way through the group.

''Twas the herbs she gave her.'

Mary paused.

It was Kate Lynch who had spoken. She stood there with her arms held out from her body, her shawl pulled down past her eyes, face shadowed.

'Daniel told Seán he went to see Nance a few weeks ago. Brigid was wandering in her sleep. He found her in the *cillín*.'

There was a gasp. Several women crossed themselves.

''Tis not the half of it! He asked Nance for a cure for the sleep-walking and Daniel told Seán she gave him berries of *bittersweet*.'

'And what is the harm in bittersweet?'

''Tis nightshade!' Kate threw her pail on the road and it rattled over the stones. ''Tis poison. Nance Roche is corrupting her own cures. Don't you see it? You're blind, the lot of ye. She's summoning illnesses so she might put food in her mouth.'

'What do you think it was, then?' Mary was sitting on the floor with Micheál while Nóra strained potatoes for their morning meal.

''Tis just the way of it with some children.'

'Do you not think 'twas Nance's herbs that did it?'

'Herbs?'

'The bittersweet. Kate Lynch said Daniel went to Nance for a cure to stop Brigid from walking the fields in her sleep, and now they're saying 'twas the berries Nance gave him that killed the child in her.'

Nóra frowned. 'We were there. You saw with your own eyes Nance Roche doing all she could to bring that child forth whole and living.'

Mary sighed and absently brushed the hair from Micheál's forehead. 'Do you not think there's some danger in us taking Micheál to her for the cure?'

Nóra glanced sideways at the boy. ''Tis not Micheál.'

'Still, 'tis not likely to hurt him, the herbs, do you think? If 'twas the bittersweet that killed the wee baby . . .'

Nóra slapped the skib of potatoes on the pot. ''Twas only a mush of mint, and it did nothing at all! No good. No bad.' She drew back away from the cloud of steam.

'Not the mint,' Mary mumbled. 'But whatever she'll be using next. Sure, Nance'll be using a mighty herb next. Might be a danger in that.' Micheál gurgled beneath her, and she smiled, gently batting at his swinging fists.

'What would you have me do, then? Raise that fairy as my own? Have him crying like a *bean sídhe* every night with no stopping him? Your eyes look like two burnt holes in a blanket, and mine feel the same.' Nóra picked up a hot potato and dropped it back on the wicker, sucking her fingers.

Mary's smile fell. 'I just worry for him, is all.'

'There's no point worrying about that cratur. Look.' She pointed to the boy, her lips pincered. 'See? It smiles.'

Mary gave the child a tickle on his chest and he squirmed in pleasure.

'It has you wrapped around its wee finger.'

'Why do you call him *it?*'

Nóra pretended she hadn't heard.

'When he's not after crying or screaming or sleeping he almost looks like a real boy, don't you think?' Mary tapped him on the chin and Micheál shrieked in laughter.

Nóra watched them, frowning. The maid looked younger when she smiled. Mary's face was so often solemn, so often puffy and red-eyed with weariness, that Nóra had forgotten how young she was. How far away from home she was. With the cold sunlight from the open half-door lighting on the red of Mary's hair, and the girl's laughter softening her face, Nóra was reminded of Johanna.

'You must miss your family,' she said suddenly.

Mary looked up, her face twisting. 'My family?'

'Well?'

'I do.' The girl looked back at Micheál and ran her hands through his hair. 'I miss them mightily. All the little ones. 'Twas me that looked after them and I worry for them with me gone and my mam with no time on her hands to be giving them.'

'You think of them, from time to time.'

Mary hid her face, and Nóra saw that she was pinching the skin on the back of her hand.

She's trying not to cry, she thought, and a little of the hardness she had felt towards the girl at the sight of her playing with the boy crumbled away. Without saying a word Nóra rose and walked into her bedroom. Lifting the mattress from the bedstead she felt around the rough boards until she found a parcel. She unwrapped it, her heart beating rapidly.

It was as she had left it. A clipping of her daughter's hair. Rust-red. Bound together with string with the curl of childhood still at its ends.

A comb with only a few of the teeth missing, a stray hair still caught in the bone.

An arbutus carving from Killarney, their initials carefully marked amidst a tangle of carved roses. The mirror it had held had long broken and fallen out, but the wood remained. A wedding present from Martin.

Nóra brought the lock of Johanna's hair to her nose, searching for the smell of her child, but it had faded. All was straw bedding and dust. She put it back in the cloth with the carving, casting a gentle thumb over Martin's initials, and returned the parcel to its hiding place.

The comb she picked up and took with her back to the fireside. Before she could change her mind she handed it to Mary. 'Here.'

The girl frowned, not understanding.

Nóra picked up the maid's hand and pressed the comb into it. ''Twas my daughter's. She had the same hair as you. Pretty.'

Mary held the comb lightly in her hand and ran her thumb over the fine teeth of bone.

''Tis a gift.'

'I've never had a comb before.'

'Well, now you do.'

'Thank you, missus.' Mary smiled, and Nóra brought a hand to her chest at the sudden aching she felt there.

'Your daughter must have been beautiful.'

Nóra pressed her fingers to her ribs, but the ache deepened. 'Well, its own child is bright to the carrion crow.' Her voice shook. 'You'll be a mother one day, Mary Clifford. You'll know.'

Mary shook her head. 'I won't be married.'

'You don't want children of your own, then?'

'There's enough children in this world for me to look after.'

'Ah, but they'll grow up. Your brothers and sisters will grow and then you'll be lonesome for your own.' Nóra picked up a cooled potato and passed it to Mary. 'Feed it, then. Go on.' She began to peel a lumper for herself, watching the way the maid fed the mewling boy. Rather than break off small pieces for the child, Mary took bites of potato flesh, then spat the chewed mush in her hand to slip into Micheál's mouth.

She caught Nóra's glance. 'So he doesn't choke,' she muttered.

'You dote on it.' Nóra bit into her potato and chewed, watching.

'That mint. It has done nothing for it. I've been thinking. We'll be taking it back to Nance's tonight.'

Mary blanched. 'Do you not want to wait to make sure that the selfheal –'

'Tonight. There's no fixing in the boy. There's none of my grandson returned. How can you sit there feeding the fairy, knowing it has not even enough blood in it to earn its place in Heaven? Knowing that Johanna's poor Micheál is out with the fairies when he ought to be in here with me?'

'He has to be fed, still.'

Nóra shook her head and swallowed. 'I can't be waiting for the selfheal.' She shivered, stood and fetched the bottle of *poitín* from the keeping-hole in the hearth wall. She could feel Mary's eyes on her.

'Now, you're not to be thinking 'tis mine. The drink was Martin's and 'twas only for the men who came for a night of company.' Nóra grimaced as she pulled the cork. 'But I've a need to calm . . . I've a need for . . .' She took a tentative sip, closing her eyes, and a vision of her daughter's hair in its cloth shivered through her. She coughed on the fumes of the drink and offered the bottle to Mary.

The maid shook her head, picking up the comb.

Nóra sat, clutching the bottle. 'We will take the changeling back tonight, Mary. I can't be waiting like this. Hearing it scream, waiting for it to change. I can't be waiting.' She took another sip. 'Ever since Nance pronounced it fairy, I can't help but think on what Johanna's son will be like. Her true son. He will have grown. I can almost see him . . .' Nóra lifted the bottle to her lips and took a deeper draught. 'I dream about him, Mary. I see her boy. A right natural little lad, laughing. I hear him. His voice speaking to me. Just as when I first saw him in his mother's arms. And I hold him and I tell him of his mother. How good she was, how . . . how beautiful. Oh, she was a beautiful child, Mary. Every night I combed her hair with that you've got now. Combed it till it shone. She loved that. I dream of combing her hair, Mary. I dream of the both of them, Johanna and Micheál, and them both alive and with me, and . . .' She shut her eyes and her voice grew bitter. 'But then that one starts up with its screaming.'

Mary was silent. She brought a hand to her mouth and spat a gob of chewed potato into it.

Nóra waved the *poitín* in the boy's direction as Mary fed him, his body jerking. 'That one has no love for me. It knows nothing like that. All it is . . .' She pushed the cork back into the neck of the bottle. 'It's all need and no thanks for it.'

Mary wiped her hands on her skirt and eased the child up onto her chest, tucking his head against the side of her chin.

'But Johanna's true son . . .' Nóra took a deep breath. 'Even in my dreams he is a consolation. He is a gift. Something left for me.' She looked across at the maid and saw both Mary and the boy watching her. The changeling was quiet, his eyes sloping over her face.

'Do you know, Mary, in my dreams he looks like Martin.'

Mary glanced at the *poitín* bottle in Nóra's hands and began to brush the fairy's hair. He blinked at the light pull of Johanna's comb.

Nóra shuddered.

'Tonight,' she said, tugging the cork and taking another swift sip. 'We'll take it at dusk.'

They returned to Nance's cabin that evening, the boy bundled in rags, pale legs dangling against Mary's thin hip. The sky was crowded with clouds threatening rain, but as they reached the end of the valley the horizon broke clear, letting in a late sun. Light fell on the puddles in the fields until they seemed like pools of gold amidst the mud. Mary glanced at Nóra and saw that she had seen the sudden seams of light on the ground too. A good omen. They smiled, and Mary thought the widow seemed calmer for the drink. She had seen Nóra tuck the bottle safely into her shawl before they left.

Nance was sitting on a stool in her doorway, smoking the evening hours. She waited until Mary and Nóra stepped into her yard before rising and greeting them. 'God and Mary to you.'

'You knew we'd be coming.' Nóra's words were slurred.

'Your Mary Clifford there told me that there was no change in him. I thought you'd be here one of these nights.'

'There's no change in him at all.' Nóra reached out to take Micheál from Mary's arms, but her grip was weak and she stumbled, nearly dropping the boy. Mary quickly grabbed the child and hoisted him back onto her hip. He began to squeal.

Nóra righted herself, blushing. 'There, see.' She pointed to the way his legs fell useless, toes pointed inwards. 'Do you see, Nance? No kick at all.'

'Mmm.' Nance narrowed her eyes at Nóra, then took a drag on her pipe and blew smoke over the boy's face. He needled the air with his cries. 'Best come in then.' As they stepped into the cabin, Nance caught Mary's arm. 'Has that one liquor taken?'

Mary nodded and Nance ran a tongue over her gums. 'Right so. Well, put him down.' She pointed to her bed of heather in the corner. 'Nóra Leahy, I'll not be lying to you. The cure of mint and selfheal was a small thing but it proved the child changeling as we suspected. Now, to banish the fairy calls for stronger stems.'

Nóra sat down on the stool by the fire and looked at Nance expectantly. Her face was flushed, her hair dishevelled from the walk outside. 'What is it you'll be trying next?'

Nance waited until Mary had settled the boy on her bed. '*Lus mór*. The great herb.' She showed the women some green leaves, slightly crumpled.

'Foxglove,' Mary whispered, her eyes flashing to Nóra. ''Tis poison.'

'Fairy blasts calls for fairy plants,' Nance chided. 'And no plant is a poison to the one who knows how to use it.'

Mary's heart began to pound in fear, as though the current of her blood had changed direction. 'You'll not be giving it to him for the eating, will you? Just for the soles of his feet like before?'

Nance regarded Mary with a smoky eye. 'You have a right to trust me.'

Nóra nodded absently in agreement.

Mary bit her lip. She felt sick. The cabin air was hot and stuffy, and she could smell the goat waste lying in the drain. She closed her eyes and felt sweat break out on her upper lip. In his dark corner, Micheál was bleating like a lamb separated from its mother. A strained wavering cry sounding over and over.

''Tis a bath we'll be giving him tonight,' said Nance, and she placed the foxglove leaves in a large pot of water. Nóra rose to help her lift the black crock directly on the embers of her fire.

'We'll wait until 'tis warm enough for the water to take on the power of the *lus mór*,' Nance said, settled back on her stool.

'There's no need to have the boy on the bed when I might hold him,' Mary said. Without waiting for the women to respond, she rose and stumbled to the child. His eyes darted over her face as she approached. Mary picked him up, her eyes averted from his lolling head, the quiver of his face.

'She's forever holding it,' Nóra muttered to Nance.

'It keeps him from crying,' Mary said.

'Well, there's truth in that,' murmured Nance. 'Not a sound from him now.'

Nóra frowned. 'But sure, aren't you holding it the whole night long, and it screaming like you're about to cut the throat of it?'

Mary tucked Micheál close against her chest, and arranged his legs so that they fell neatly over her knees. 'I think it does calm him some. To be held.'

Nóra blinked slowly, staring. 'It screams and screams.'

Nance was thoughtful. ''Tis no harm in the girl holding the changeling, Nóra. Sure, 'tis right that she be kind to it for the sake of your Micheál with Them.' She picked up a piece of knotted rag and soaked it in goat's milk, handing it to Mary. 'Here, give the cratur this to suck on.'

They waited for the water to take hold of the plant. Nóra sat staring at the leaves floating in the crock, her hands trembling. When Nance handed Nóra a small cup of *poitín* the widow drained it in silence.

When the water had warmed, Nance and Nóra hauled the pot off the embers and Nance motioned to Mary. 'Take the wee dress off him now. We'll put him in the bath.'

Mary's mouth was dry as she lay Micheál on the floor and began to unwrap the clothes from his body. She could feel the women's eyes on her, feel the fragile neck of the boy cradled in her hand as she lifted his skull off the floor to slip the cloth over it. As she took the last of the rags off him, his white body purled in gooseflesh.

'The water won't burn him, will it?' she asked.

Nance shook her head, reaching for the boy. Together they eased his dangling legs into the crock. 'Down into it now. That's it, girl. Hold his arms. Don't be getting the water on your skin. Dip him in so.'

The boy's eyes widened at the heat of the water, then fixed on the shadows moving against the wall.

'He's too big,' Mary gasped, breathing hard. 'I don't think he'll fit.'

'Sure, the fairy's all bones. We'll get him in there.'

Water lapped over the side of the pot as they folded the boy's arms across his chest and slipped him into the crock. His knees bent high about his neck.

'Let go of him now.'

Mary hesitated. 'If I let go of his head he'll knock it on the side of the pot.'

Nóra's voice came out in a husk. 'Do as Nance said, Mary.'

Mary took away her hand and the boy's head dropped to the side, his ear close to the water. The women stepped back and watched him.

'The fairy in him is suspicious,' Nance muttered, and Mary saw the truth of it as soon as the words were spoken. Micheál's head lolled back above the water, his chin pointed to the soot-stained rafters. A shudder went through him like wind rippling over water and he yelped, tongue stretched.

'That's the fox cry of him,' Nóra whispered.

Mary felt her stomach cramp and she could not tell if it was from fear or excitement. The darkness seemed to hum around them.

'Now we must give him the juice of it.' Nance leant forward and reached for the boy's chin. At her touch his jaw snapped shut, hinges of muscle suddenly tense. Glancing back at Nóra and Mary, Nance tried to slip her finger between his lips and behind his teeth, but the boy jerked his head, struggling.

'Mary. Open his mouth for me, would you?'

''Tis as though it knows,' Nóra marvelled. 'It knows we're after banishing it.'

'Mary?'

Mary knelt by the crock and reached for Micheál's mouth. He groaned as she touched him, his arms wresting and splashing the water from the pot. She recoiled, waiting until the boy had stilled and she wasn't in danger of the liquid spilling on her. Then she reached for him again and gently inserted the tips of her fingers between his lips. Micheál looked at her from the corner of his eye, his head slumped towards his shoulder. The pink gleam of his

THE GOOD PEOPLE

inner lip sat beneath her fingers. She could feel the hard press of his teeth.

'Will this hurt him?' she asked.

'Not at all,' Nance reassured her. 'Remember, girl, we're only after sending him back to his kind.'

Mary felt for the gap in the ridge of teeth and, quickly pushing her fingers into the wet of Micheál's mouth, pressed down on his molars. His jaw dropped open. Nance pinned one crooked finger on his tongue and squeezed the juice of foxglove leaf down his throat.

'There. 'Tis done.'

Mary pulled her fingers from the boy's mouth as though she had been burnt. When she glanced down at them she could see the vague imprint of his teeth on her knuckles.

'What do we do now?' Nóra asked. Mary turned and saw that the widow was swaying behind them, grey hair sticking to her forehead in sweat.

'We wait,' Nance said.

Micheál sat scrunched in the crock, moaning, disturbing the water like a fish in a pail. Mary thought that perhaps the warm bath comforted him, had lifted the chill from his marrow and soothed the flaking rash on his back. His eyes were glazed and his cheeks flushed red, and she thought that, for the first time since she had seen the child, he was peaceful. She exhaled in relief.

Then, slowly, so that at first it was almost imperceptible, a shaking rose in him.

'So it begins,' Nance murmured.

The shaking grew stronger. He tremored like the crushed catkin of birch, like the fluttered seed of an ash tree, and within minutes the convulsions grew so violent that he seemed to be shivering out of his skin.

Panic flared in Mary's chest. 'Nance?'

'The herb is doing its work.'

Water splashed from the pot as the convulsions turned to thrashing. Micheál's head swung forward, his chin suddenly tight against his throat. Water swallowed his face.

'He'll drown,' Mary whispered. She reached for Nance's shoulder, but the woman gently pushed her back.

'Nóra. Lift him. Help me lift him.'

Nóra, looking bewildered, drunk, did as Nance said. Together the older women lifted the convulsing boy, wet-skinned and dripping, from the bath of boiled leaves. He shook in their grip like a rabid dog, his mouth rent open in a terrifying gape, arms rod-straight and trembling, and his head shaking from side to side as though in terror of what was being done to him.

'Mary! Open the door for us.'

She held her breath in horror, unable to move.

'Open the door!'

A strange noise began to come from the boy. A shrill gasping, as though there weren't enough air in the world and he was struggling to breathe.

'Open the door! Mary!'

Mary, fear sparking through her, did as she was told. She ran to the door and pushed the wicker open to the night, then shrank back against the wall. Outside the night sky was gripped with stars.

Nance's face was solemn, intent. She looked at Nóra with her clouded eyes, trying to catch her attention. 'Help me swing him,' she said. Nóra nodded, jaw clenched in concentration. Holding the shaking boy firmly about the ribs and shoulders they staggered to the doorway.

'I'll say what must be said, and you'll help me swing him. Don't let go, only swing him out the door. Back and forth with him.'

Nóra nodded, mute.

'Mary! Get the shovel from the corner of the room. There. Quickly now!'

Mary, a plummeting in her bowels, did as she was told.

'Set it under his legs. Under him, as though he were sitting on it. Nóra, hold tight of him. Now we'll swing him.' Nance closed her eyes and took a deep breath. 'If you're a fairy, away with you!'

Following Nance's direction, Nóra swung the boy out towards the darkness. Her fingers gripped the sinewy knot of his shaking shoulder.

'If you're a fairy, away with you!'

Mary grasped the shovel tightly, holding it under Micheál's swinging legs, stretches of bone heaving out towards the woods, the flare of his rash dull in the firelight.

'If you're a fairy, away with you!'

They swung him towards the night and its harbour of sprites; the crouching, waiting cunning of the unseen world. Mary held the shovel and they swung him like a body from a scaffold as he shook under their hands. And when they lowered him to the ground, she cast the shovel aside and picked him up and wrapped her shawl against his clammy, trembling nakedness, his skin now pricked with cold, and as she held him to the warmth of her chest by the fire, she felt the pulse of his unnatural heart slow, until it seemed to pattern out into a beat she no longer recognised.

CHAPTER
TWELVE

Germander speedwell

One week after she had delivered Brigid of her still, unbreathing son, Nance returned to the Lynches' cabin with her arms full of germander speedwell. She had dreamt of Brigid every night since the birth. Had felt the painful pull of her breasts, full of unsuckled milk, and had woken, wild, turning to the woods to hunt down milkwort, speedwell and watercress, and all the green that might calm the summoning on the girl's body.

When first light spilled in haze over the mountain summits she walked into the valley and knocked on the Lynches' door.

Daniel answered, his face gored with lack of sleep.

'What do you want?' he asked.

Nance heard the gravel in his voice and simply showed him what she carried in her basket.

'What's that for then?'

'To ease her pain, so it is.'

'She needs more than herbs,' Daniel said, leaning against the doorframe with crossed arms. When Nance peered past him into the room, he blocked her view. 'I think you've done enough here, Nance.'

'Let me see to your wife, Daniel.'

'She's not been churched yet.'

'I know. Let me see her. I can help her.'

'More bittersweet, is it?' Daniel's mouth twisted and he leant forward and stared Nance hard in the eye. 'I told you,' he spat. 'I told you she went walking to the *cillín*, and you did *nothing*. And now our baby lies buried there.'

Nance held his eye firm. 'It happens, so it does, Daniel. No one bears the fault for it. We did all we could for it, I promise. 'Tis just the way of the world. 'Tis just the will of God.'

Daniel ran a hand over his unshaven chin, his blue eyes hard. 'Who is to say that those berries didn't kill my son?'

'The bittersweet was to help her sleep and nothing more.'

'So you say.'

Nance straightened her back. 'Daniel, I've lived long years upon this earth. I've delivered more children than I can count. Do you think I'd turn murderer upon babes in my late hour?'

He laughed, his breath vapour in the half-light. 'Yes, well. Can you blame a man?'

'Will you let me tend to her?'

'Like I say, Nance, she's not been churched. You're the one always talking about spirits. Are you not afraid she'll poison you with her unclean breath? The sin of the birth is on her.'

'I have no mind of churching. That's the priest's business. That's the Church, so it is. I'm here as her handy woman.'

'Aye, her handy woman. Some handy woman.' He nodded to the lane. 'Off with ye.'

'Will I leave the herbs with you then?'

'Off with ye!' His voice rang out in the early morning. A flock of starlings lifted out of a nearby ash tree.

Nance eyed him, then placed the basket of herbs on the ground.

'Use them as a poultice,' she said, but before the words were out of her mouth, Daniel stepped forward and kicked the basket clear off the ground. He was breathing hard, his anger two pink spots in his cheeks.

Nance froze, her heart suddenly crossways. She looked to the ground, stared at her toes, their yellow nails.

The air was charged. Neither of them moved.

There was a slight creaking by the cabin and both Nance and Daniel turned at the sound. The door was pushed out, and Brigid stood there in the gap, her head resting on the doorframe. She was pale, her dark hair undone and tangled about her head. She cast a long look at Daniel, and Nance thought that something passed between them. Then, without saying a word, she retreated back into the house, closing the door behind her.

'I can help her,' Nance said.

Daniel stood with his head bowed, and then tramped across the yard to where the basket had rolled to a stop. Nance watched as he stooped and picked her herbs out of the mud in clumsy handfuls and threw them back into the basket. He wiped his hands on his trousers and offered her the creel. 'Go on home, Nance.'

'Would you not give her the herbs yourself?'

'Please, Nance. Go on home.'

'All you need do is wash them and press them into a poultice.'

'Please. Nance. Go on home!'

Nance silently accepted the soiled herbs, her tongue dry. Without meeting Daniel's eye, she turned and walked back to the lane.

A change had come over the boy, although it was not as Nóra had hoped. Every morning, while it was still dark and the cock had not yet crowed, she woke, bleary-eyed, and fumbled her way out from the bedroom to stand over the sleeping maid and the changeling beside her. Nóra hovered above the settle bed, draped in Martin's greatcoat, trying to make out the child's features. Each morning he seemed to be neither asleep nor awake, but in a strange, slit-eyed daze. At times he moved, but there was little of the vigorous jerking of before. Instead he seemed to list between loose-limbed stillness and an eerie trembling, like the tremor of an aspen tree. She examined his mouth, wondering if it lay slack as any normal child's would in sleep, or whether it was the slung yawn of the fairy. Sometimes she saw the boy's tongue slip out over his lips, and her heart would pound in anticipation of hearing him speak, of the return of language.

Nóra stood like this over the settle bed one morning, thinking that perhaps the foxglove had worked, that the breathing coming from the boy was the beginning of words, when Mary gasped awake. She shrank from the sight of Nóra hunched over, staring.

'You frightened me.'

Nóra hunkered down over the child on her knees, inclined her ear towards his mouth. 'I thought I heard the shape of a word.'

Mary sat up, her hair mussed from sleep. 'You heard him talking?'

'Not talking. But a sound. A breathing. As though he were about to whisper something to me.'

They listened for a moment, but Micheál's lips were sluggish, unmoving.

'He was sick again in the night.'

'Sick?'

The maid gestured to a pail beside the bed, a cloth swimming in the dirty water. 'Retching up over himself. All over with the sick of him, the piss of him.' She drew closer, her forehead crinkled in concern. 'He trembles.'

Nóra stood up, fingers pulling at her bottom lip. 'Surely that is a good sign.'

Mary picked up one of Micheál's limp hands, considering it. 'He is not as he was before.'

'The *lus mór* is working in it.'

Mary stroked the little hand. 'He is as my sisters were before they died. All loose. No sound coming from him at all.'

Nóra acted as though she had not heard. ''Tis cold, Mary. Get up and unrake the fire, would you?'

The girl placed the boy's hand back under the blanket. 'You don't think he'll die, do you?'

'God willing, the fairy will die if that's what it takes for Micheál's return.' Nóra opened the door and peered out into the fog of the morning.

Mary stilled. 'You want him to die? The fairy?' She joined Nóra at the door. 'Missus, sure, is there not sin in that? The foxglove poisoning him like that?'

''Tis no sin if 'tis the fairy banished. 'Tis no matter. No sin in seeking to rid the fairy and save Micheál.' She turned and gripped Mary about the shoulder. ''Tis a good thing, what we're doing for it. Can you not see that the scream is gone from it? The kicking and punching and all the fighting in it? If we can banish the fairy and fix it to leave, the Good People will have Their own back, and I will have mine. The foxglove will work and God be praised for it. Now, would you not light the fire? The cold is on me.'

The girl obeyed, retreating to the hearth where she began to fuss amongst the coals.

Nóra turned to the view of the misty valley. Through the gloom she could see the shifting of cows already turned out of byres, hear the clank of empty milk pails and the voices of women. The brief glimmer of new-lit fires as doors were opened and closed. And down by the river, the dark mass of evergreens and the hatched outline of bare branches. Nóra thought she could see the whitethorn of the Piper's Grave and, as she stared, a flitting light in the murk around it. Like a candle flame quivering, held by someone moving in and out of the darkness. Like a rushlight lit and blown out into smoke, and lit and blown out again by the breath of someone unseen.

A shiver went down Nóra's back. She thought of what Peter O'Connor had said the night of Martin's wake.

I saw a glowing by that whitethorn. You mark my words, there'll be another death in this family before long.

Then, just as suddenly as the lights had appeared, they vanished.

'Missus?'

Mary was watching her, the iron poker in her hand, the flames quickening in the hearth.

'What?'

'The cold is coming in, and you said you were feeling it, so.'

Shaken, Nóra shut the half-door and returned to her place by the fire. Wrapping Martin's greatcoat firmly about her, she felt a hard bump in her side and, sliding her hand into the coat's pocket, pulled out an irregular jag of charcoal. It sat in her palm, light and crumbling.

Mary placed a scraw on the fire. When Nóra remained silent, she glanced up.

'What's that?'

''Twas in Martin's coat.'

Mary peered at it more closely. 'Ashes?'

Nóra shook her head. 'A dead ember.'

'Protection.'

'Protection against the *púca*.'

'Did Nance give it to you, then?'

'She did not, no. 'Twas here, in Martin's coat.'

The girl nodded absently and tucked the blanket in more firmly around the boy's shoulders. 'His hair is growing long.'

Nóra stared at the ember in her hand. Martin had never mentioned it, had never gone to Nance for anything other than the cold swelling in his hand. It was to the blacksmith's for the teeth that troubled him, the broken rib all those years back when he fell from a horse. Never Nance.

'And his nails too,' Mary was saying. 'Missus?'

Nóra turned the ember in her fingers. Had he gone in secret? Had he gone for something to protect the boy? Or had he gone for protection against him?

'Missus?'

'What?' Nóra snapped, shoving the ember back into the coat pocket.

'Micheál's nails. They're too long. He might scratch himself with them.'

''Tis not Micheál!' Nóra reached for her shawl and began to wrap it around her head.

'The . . . boy. I meant –'

'I'll milk the cow this morning.'

'Shall I cut his nails?'

'Do what you like with it.'

Nóra slammed the door behind her and paused in the yard, letting the damp of the morning cool the burning of her cheeks. She gripped the handle of the milk pail until it pinched hard against her skin, swung it against her leg until she could feel the lip bruising her thigh.

Nóra looked down towards the Piper's Grave where the white-thorn was emerging in the gathering light. She would have burnt it down, stuffed their clothes full of ashes had they been able to help against the fairies and their slow malevolence.

Let it tremble, she thought. Let the foxglove shake the fairy out of my house, and give me back my daughter's son. Please, God, rid the fairy.

'Nance Roche, are you in there?'

It was a man's voice, coloured with impatience. Nance paused and put the eel she was skinning back in its bucket of river water.

'Are you of the living or the dead?' she asked.

'Mercy woman, 'tis not one of your patients come to be tricked. 'Tis Father Healy. I've come to speak with you.'

Nance rose and went to the door. The priest was standing outside with his feet apart, his coat flapping in the wind.

'Father. What a pleasure.'

'And how are you keeping, Nance?'

'Still alive.'

'You didn't hear the Mass on the holy days?'

Nance smiled. 'Ara, 'tis a long way for an old woman.'

'But you got your meal and turf?'

Nance paused, wiping her bloody hands on her apron. 'That was you, was it?'

'Did you think 'twas a gift for the quackery?' Father Healy peered past her. 'Are you alone in there?'

'Not if you count the company of goats.'

'I don't.'

'Come in to the warm, so. Let me make you welcome in thanks for the meal. Sure, 'twas kind of you to be thinking of an old woman like me, alone on the day of our Lord.'

The priest shook his head. 'No, thank you, I'll not be coming in.'

'Have it your way then, Father.'

'I will.'

Nance waited for the priest to speak. The eel blood had started to dry to a rusty stain on her skin. 'Well now, Father. Say what you've come to say. Constant company wears out its welcome.'

He crossed his arms tightly over his chest. 'You should know, Nance, 'tis with a heavy heart I come to you today.' He shifted his weight. ''Tis a serious matter I've come about.'

'Best say it and be done with the saying of it, then, Father.'

Father Healy swallowed. 'I've had good word that it was by your hand that Brigid Lynch lost her baby. There is an accusation against you. Some folk came to me saying you sought to poison Brigid Lynch.'

Nance looked at the priest. 'That is quite an accusation.'

'Did you or did you not give her berries of bittersweet?'

'Bittersweet is no poison. Not when taken as it should.'

'I'm told 'tis nightshade.'

'Her man came to me looking for a cure. She was walking in her sleep and he was afraid for her. I am no murderer, Father. The herbs I pull are taken with prayer. In the name of the Lord.'

Father Healy shook his head. 'Well, I can tell you now, Nance Roche, that herb-pulling like that . . . 'Tis an abuse of God's holy ordinance. I can't stand for it. There's people here in this parish who have had enough of you bringing misfortune down on them with your pagan, unmeaning practices.'

'Say what you will about my practices, Father, but they are full of meaning.'

'They've had enough of your bawling.'

'Aye, you're against the keening, so you said.'

Father Healy fixed her with a grim look. 'No, Nance. No. This has gone beyond keening. This is about nostrums and *piseógs*.'

Nance's body ached and she fought a sudden desire to lie down on the grass and turn her face up to the sky. *Piseógs* and curses.

That was what it was about. *Piseógs* and the dark things people did to one another when their hearts blacked with anger and the edges of their souls curled in bitterness. *Piseógs.* Muttered supplication to the Devil before the sun rises on a feast day. Curses wrought out of the wellbeing of another. The shifting, secret trade of vengeance and ill intent.

'Aye. *Piseógs.* And 'tis not just Brigid Lynch I've come about. Seán Lynch found a wreath of mountain ash on his gate,' Father Healy continued.

'Did he now?'

'And he is saying 'tis a *piseóg.*'

'Now, Father, I know a few things about this world we're in, and a wreath of ash is no *piseóg.* A good, clean fire, a hurley and a fence – that is what the quicken tree is for. 'Tis not useful for any kind of *piseóg.*'

Father Healy's eyes lit up. 'Oh, you know what is good for a *piseóg,* do you, Nance?'

'I have no part in *piseógs.* I don't lay curses. I have no hand in that.'

'Then would you tell me, Nance, why there are plenty coming to me now saying 'tis your custom? They're saying 'tis how you survive here, Nance. Taking people's money for wickedness. Stealing the butter profit from the milk. Cursing churns. Setting neighbour against neighbour and cursing those that would not let you steal from them.'

'Is it stealing the butter, I am?' Nance gestured to her *bothán.* 'Rolling in riches, am I?'

'Nance, whether 'tis people thinking you're stealing with curses, or whether you're stealing by plugging the necks of beasts . . .' He paused as if to note her reaction. 'I can't be standing for thievery. I'll be fetching the police for that. Sure, the constable will take you in if that is what you're after doing.'

Nance lifted her stained hands to the priest. ''Tis eels that fill my belly, not stolen butter.'

'Look at you, red-handed as the Devil.'

'You know as well as I that no one is bothered by a bit of eel catching.'

'Nance, go on and catch as many eels as you like. You're right, 'tis no bother to anyone who knows. But don't be stealing the blood out of beasts, and don't be putting the fear on the valley with your *piseógs*!'

Nance laughed in exasperation.

''Tis not a thing to be laughing at!' The priest took a step towards her. 'Nance, I tell you, my patience is mighty thin with you. If keening is unholy, then laying mountain ash and giving herbs to women in a delicate state to earn your place here is devilry.'

'Father –'

'Nance! I warned you to be a handy woman to those who need and no more.' His face softened. 'If bittersweet be a cure, and the death of Brigid Lynch's baby the work of God, then no more about it. But . . .' He pointed a finger of warning at her chest. 'Don't be laying curses.'

Nance threw her hands up in the air. 'Father, I have no hand in *piseógs*! I have no hand in curses.'

'Just a hand in with *Them that does be in it*. I know 'tis your mouth that's been spreading the word about fairies.' Father Healy turned his palms upwards in ecclesiastic habit. 'Nóra Leahy came to me begging magic, gabbling superstition. Saying the poor boy she has in her care is the talk of the valley, that he's fairy. That wouldn't be your worm in her ear, would it, Nance? Sure, folk will pay handsome when they're desperate. No harm in claiming cures when they bring food and turf to the door.'

Nance felt anger rise in her. 'That boy is not natural.'

'And you are doctor to the unnatural?'

'I am.'

'And you plan to cure him.'

'I plan to banish the fairy and bring Nóra Leahy back her grandson.'

Father Healy gave her a look of weary frustration. ''Twould be a kindness for you to tell Nóra Leahy that she has a right to care for the cretin, and to expect nothing more.'

'There's no kindness in helplessness, Father.'

'But there is in false hope?' The priest sighed and looked out to the valley. 'People are suffering, Nance.'

'Yes, Father.'

'They're worried about the butter. About being forced on the road. About having no money to pay the rent with. About neighbours turning on them, wishing them ill. Wishing sickness and death on them.'

'Yes, Father.'

He looked back at her, his brow furrowed. 'If I find out that you do have a hand in it, I'll not be as kind as I have been, Nance. I will see you out on the road. I will see you out of the valley.'

CHAPTER
THIRTEEN

Devil's-bit scabious

S t Brigid's Eve came to the valley and with it the assurance of spring. Winter-weary, the eve of the holy day lured people out of their stuffy cabins down to where the field rushes grew and tremored in the wind.

Mary thought she could almost feel the swelling of the earth beneath her feet as she escaped the confines of the widow's cabin and ran down the mountainside to the grassy stretch of moor. It was cold, but the sun was bright, and she felt that the waterlogged fields carried the promise of growth. Even in the gloom of dipped soil, where old snow lay patterned with the midnight flight of rabbits, early daffodils had emerged. She watched the robins, blood-smocked against the sky, and imagined they were leading her to the rushes, that they were pleased to know that warmth would return to the light.

It was a relief to be in the open air. A relief to leave Nóra and her constant crouching over the boy, watching him like a cat staring at a dying bird. A relief to leave the sight of the child fitting and moaning like the Devil was inside him, fighting for purchase. The very air of the cabin seemed leaden to Mary. She suffocated in the weight of the widow's expectation.

As Mary walked towards the clumps of rushes, she took deep breaths to clear the dust from her lungs, to take in the smells of the trembling fields. Wet grass, cow shit, turf smoke and clay. Golden discs of coltsfoot and the raggy flowers of groundsel clustered against the dun and green. The day was fresh, slapped with cold, and Mary's eyes watered in the light.

She had left the child in Nóra's care, so eager had she been for a minute to herself outside without the twitching weight of the boy against her hip. She had suggested to Nóra that she take Micheál into the yard. Wrap him against the cold and let the sun fall on his pallid skin, while she went for the rushes and made the St Brigid's cross for the house. But the widow, eyes red-rimmed, had said that she would be keeping it out of sight, and for Mary to hurry and not dawdle but come straight back to the cabin.

Mary's brothers had always made the St Brigid's crosses at home. They would walk miles of bog to find the best rushes, pluck out the tangled grasses and wipe them clean of mud, before returning to sit and twist the plants while Mary and the younger children watched.

'See, 'tis important to pull them, not cut them with a knife. That's how you keep the holy in the reed. Sure, you fashion the cross with the sun.'

Mary pictured David sitting in the yard, the green rods over his knees, tongue inching from his mouth in concentration as he folded the rushes around each other.

'What happens if you make the cross against the sun?'

David had frowned. 'What would you be doing that for now? That's some contrariness there, Mary. Faith, 'tis with the sun you do be making it, to keep the power in the charm.

They would watch his quick fingers work the tapered stems until they could see the green pattern take shape. A four-legged cross made in the name of the saint, to bless and hang above the door in protection against evil, fire and hunger. It would keep them safe even as the shine of the green rush dried to straw, and the smoke from the fire blacked it with soot.

Mary wanted a cross to hang in the widow's house. She wanted to know that she was guarded anew by a nailed blessing. The sight of the boy under the power of the foxglove filled her with a horror so deep and unsettling that she felt calcified with it. There was something evil in his fitting, she knew. Something that made her stomach drop every morning on waking, knowing that she would have to hold the child while his body shook with the supernatural.

Nóra was hunched over her knitting when Mary returned, her hand gripping the bunch of bright rushes. But the boy was no longer in his place by the fire. Mary stood in the doorway, her eyes flitting around the cabin.

She has done something to him, she thought suddenly. She has set him on the mountain, or buried him, or left him at the crossroads. Her stomach knotted with dread.

'Where's Micheál?' she asked.

The widow sniffed and inclined her head to the corner of the room. Mary saw then that the boy lay on the heather Nóra kept for kindling, on his back, unmoving. Her relief, on rushing to him and finding him alive, finding his little bracket of bones still lifting and falling in breath, was overwhelming.

She wedged the rushes under her arm and used her free hands to lift him onto her hip.

'I'm taking him out for the air,' she said to Nóra, snatching at the blanket hanging over the settle bed. 'I'll watch him while I make the cross.'

Nóra's eyes followed her as she left. 'You see anyone coming, you bring it right back inside.'

With the sunlight on his face and the breeze stirring his hair, Micheál seemed to rouse from the limp half-sleep he had lain in since the bath of foxglove. Mary settled him down on the blanket by her feet and, as she perched on a stool and began to weave the rushes, she noticed that his eyes widened, their blue reflecting the sky above him.

''Tis a fair day to be out in,' she murmured, and he blinked, as though he heard her and agreed. She paused to watch him, smiling at the tiny flare of his nostrils, the pink slip of his tongue. He wants to taste the air, she thought.

For all the years' growing in him, Micheál seemed newborn lying in the daylight. The foxglove had left him pale, as though his skin had never seen the sky. Lying in the light, the sun caught the fragile cartilage of his ears and Mary saw how they grew pink, how they blushed transparent. She noticed the fine blond hairs on the side of his face.

''Tis St Brigid's Day tomorrow,' she said. 'Spring is here.' And she set the rushes down by her feet and walked to where a dandelion grew, its fluffy head of seed nodding in the breeze.

'See?' Mary held the downy globe on its stalk above the boy and he looked up at it, his mouth opening. She blew at the clock of seeds and they scattered on the air. Micheál shrieked, his hands suddenly aloft, clutching at the sailing down.

'There was no cure in that foxglove.'

Mary turned. Nóra stood in the doorway, staring at them.

'Look at it! As it was before. All the trembling is all gone out of it. The struggle is all gone.'

'He does seems better.'

'Better!' Nóra ran a hand over her face. 'It screamed in the night again.'

'I know.'

''Tis not better if 'tis back to screaming. 'Tis not better if the changeling has fought the foxglove and won! 'Tis not better if the fitting and the sickening is all out of it, after we've spent the time with Nance, after the way we thought 'twas working.'

'But surely, missus, 'tis better to have a child with air in his lungs than shaking as he was.' Mary's lip trembled. 'It put the fear on me, to see him like that.'

'The fear on you? Girl, you should be afraid to see the fairy strong. You should be afraid to have one of Them amongst us.' She blinked rapidly. 'There's no knowing but that one, himself, there, blinked my man and my daughter. And there you are, playing with it. Doting on it. Cutting its hair and biting its nails and feeding it as though 'twas your own.'

'He likes the dandelion clocks,' Mary whispered.

'As well it might, fairy-child.' Nóra made to go back inside but paused, turning again. Her eyes were full of tears. 'I thought 'twas working,' she whispered, and she gave Mary a look of such wretched sadness that the girl fought a compulsion to go to her, to lay her palms against the widow's cheeks and stroke her face, and comfort her as she sometimes comforted her mother.

But just as quickly as the impulse arrived, it faded, and Mary remained kneeling beside Micheál. She said nothing, and after some silence Nóra turned back into the cabin, her head hung like the dead Christ.

Mary woke early on St Brigid's Day to the muted sound of rain falling outside. Gently rolling the boy and checking that his rags were not soiled, she rose and peered at the hearth. At home she and her brothers and sisters had always fought each other for the first peek at the smothered fire, to look for the mark of St Brigid's passing.

'There 'tis,' the little ones would cry, and they would see a soft crescent in the powdered ash that was surely the print of the saint's holy heel. 'She has come and blessed us.'

Mary sat on her haunches in the widow's cabin and examined the raked hearth. Nothing. The soot was as she had left it.

Homesick, Mary walked to the yard door, unlatched the upper half and pushed it out. She leant on the fixed lower barrier, breathing in the smell of rain. A rough day, she thought. A pelting day. Drops stammered in the puddles of the yard.

There was a soft clattering behind her and Mary turned, expecting to see Micheál – woken, fractious, wild.

The St Brigid's cross. It had fallen from where she had fastened it above the door.

Mary stared at the woven legs of reeds. It was not right. She had fixed the cross tightly, anxious to have its protection, its familiar eye to watch over her at night, to keep the fire from the thatch, to be assured of healing should she need it. To keep the fairies from the house.

Fear dried her mouth. She pressed herself flat against the door and called for Nóra. Nothing. She called again.

There was a low creaking from the next room and the widow emerged, her face soft with sleep. She held her head in her hands.

'What is it? What's the matter? You'll let the rain in. Look, 'tis coming down.'

Mary pointed to the lintel.

'What?'

'St Brigid's cross. Gone.'

Nóra bent and picked up the cross from where it had skittered across the floor.

'I fastened it, so I did,' Mary swallowed. 'What do you think the meaning is in it falling? I never heard of a cross falling. The protection . . .'

Nóra turned the rushes in her fingers, then brushed the dirt from the cross with her shawl and handed it back to Mary. 'Put it up. It means nothing. 'Twas the wind. The charm is still in it.'

Mary accepted the cross silently. For all the widow's dismissive words, she knew from the queer look on Nóra's face that she shared Mary's hollow nagging that all was not right. There was no wind. None at all.

Something had moved the cross. Something had cast it to the floor.

Nóra stood over the sleeping boy, her face grey. 'Did it shake last night? Was it sick and vomiting?'

'No, missus.'

'Is it after soiling itself?'

'Not as he was. None of the running and watering out of him. And no fever.'

A pained expression came over Nóra's face and her eyes glazed. 'We will never be rid of it with herbs.'

Mary blanched at Nóra's expression.

'I've been thinking, Mary. Fairies do not like fire. Or iron.' Nóra's eyes glanced to the smoored hearth. 'In the stories they threaten them with it. Tell them to leave or you'll bring the eye out of them with a reddened poker. Hold them over a shovel.'

'We held him over a shovel,' Mary whispered.

'We hold it over a *hot* shovel.'

'No.'

Nóra looked at Mary in surprise and some of the strangeness went out of her manner.

'No, I don't think we should be doing that.'

'We wouldn't burn it. Just threaten it.' Nóra bit at the skin around her nails.

'I think there's sin in that, missus. I don't want to.'

'It won't leave if we keep giving it herbs, Mary. Micheál will never come back if 'tis just foxglove and mint.'

'Please, missus. Don't be burning it up.'

Nóra ripped the skin from her nail, glanced down and smudged the blood. 'Just the threat would do,' she muttered to herself. 'Iron and fire. That is what it surely takes.'

'Nance. How are you getting on?'

'Musha, a good day and a bad day, thanks be to God. I was wondering when you might visit me.' Nance nodded at the straw-seated stool beside the fire and Áine sat down, smoothing her skirts in front of her.

'I think I am caught on the chest.'

'Your chest, Áine?'

'I feel a rattle.' The woman brought a slender hand up to her throat and blushed. 'I think 'tis the cold.'

'A bad chest, is it? And how long have you been caught?'

Áine glanced around the cabin. 'Oh, a while now. Since the new year. We threw the door open to let the old year out and the new one in, and I think a sickness was in its company.' She attempted a laugh. 'Now there's a catch on me. I cough, sometimes.'

'How is the damp with you?'

'The damp?'

'How have you and your man John stood the cold and the wet? Is the floor of your home dry?'

Áine absently pulled at a loose thread in her shawl. 'The storms last year disturbed the thatch. And the blackbirds pick it apart. A little rain comes in. We'll thatch again this year.'

'And have you enough to eat?'

'God provides plenty, though the butter's not coming thick at all. The profit is not in the milk.'

'Faith,' Nance said. 'There's no profit to be found in the whole valley, as I hear it. But I'm pleased to hear you've enough to eat. You deserve it all and more. Will you let me feel for the rattle?'

Áine nodded and Nance placed her hand flat against the woman's chest. She closed her eyes and searched for the clag on her lungs. She could sense nothing. Áine's breath seemed normal, although her heart was beating rapidly.

'Can you feel it?'

'Hush now. Close your eyes for me, Áine. Take a deep breath.'

Nance felt her hand grow warm against the woman's clothes. She felt Áine's desire for a child. She felt how she wanted it more than anything. How when Áine bled, bent double by the pain of it, the woman imagined her body was breaking faith with her, punishing her for its emptiness.

Nance saw Áine forcing herself to rise from bed and set the water to boil on the fire for John's breakfast. She saw her sweeping the cabin floor while her body knotted and unknotted itself in aimless ferocity. She saw how Áine hated the visitors who came on night-rambling, the men with greasy fiddles in hand, saw how she hated the way the women took up the precious warmth of the fire, how the men threw pieces of potato to the corner of the room for the fairies that she, cramped, falling out of herself, would have to kneel and sweep up when they left.

Nance saw Áine creeping to the ditch behind the house to replace her rags, marvelling at the violence of her womanhood. The bloody reminder of her unmothering.

There was a cough. Nance opened her eyes. Áine was looking at her, frightened.

'What?' she asked, her voice trembling.

Nance removed her hand and pulled her stool closer. 'You're a good woman, Áine. Faith, God knows we all have our troubles to bear. And God knows there are enough people in this world who turn their anger onto those around them. But some, I think, turn their anger against themselves. I think perhaps your body is sickening because you are sad.'

'Faith, I'm not, Nance.'

'The mind is a powerful thing, Áine. A mighty thing.'

'Sure, what reason have I to be sad?'

Nance waited. Silence settled.

Áine pulled at the tassled ends of her shawl. 'I know what you're thinking, Nance.'

''Tis about a child.'

The woman hesitated, then nodded, miserable. ''Twas shameful for me. The night Brigid's baby died. 'Twas shame in being taken out of there like I was no help at all. Like I was no woman at all.'

Nance said nothing.

'Sure, I know what they say about us,' Áine whispered. '"A stick of yew in a bundle of kindling."'

'You want a child. There is no shame in that.'

'There is shame in a wife not being able to give her man what he wants.' Áine looked up, pained. 'John is a good man, but his family think ill of me. They suspect me because I am barren. They blame poor crops on me. They say the potatoes are in sympathy with me. The cow . . .' She clenched her jaw and shook her head. 'All the women here in this valley, they come to my house on *cuaird*, and . . . sometimes they bring their weans and the children dig holes in my floor and chase my chickens. They make me feel my childlessness. Nance, I think they mock me. One of the women! Her daughter refused to take food from my hand because the girl thought I had been away with Them and that was the reason for my having no children!' Áine choked back a strange laugh. ''Tis not though, is it? 'Tis not the Good People who have had a hand in my . . .' She brought her hands to her stomach.

'Would it frighten you to think so?'

''Twould give reason to it. But I never did anything against Them. I've a mighty respect for the Good People.' She hesitated. 'Kate Lynch told me of a woman whose own man struck her with a band of elm to fix a child in her.'

Nance gave a wan smile. 'Áine, are you asking after a beating of elm?'

'I don't know.'

''Tis right for you to visit me. Don't be blaming yourself. There is a natural sympathy in this world. For every ill thing that can come upon us, there's a remedy to lift it. All cures are within our reach.' Nance stood and offered Áine her hand. 'Here, follow me.'

The two women walked out of the *bothán* and into the cool calm of the evening. Everything was still except for a fog slipping down into the valley from the mountains.

''Tis a queer place here,' Áine whispered. 'I forget what silence is, married to a blacksmith.'

'Sure, 'tis quiet. Even the birds are silent in the mist.'

As they drew closer to the woods, Áine fell back. 'Perhaps I'll wait for you at the cabin, Nance. Perhaps I'll come another time. John might be wondering where I'm to.'

'I'll let no harm come to you.'

'How can you see the way? There's such a fog.'

'All the better. No one will see us.'

They walked into the trees. The ground was soft with leaf litter and the oak and alder, appearing out of the mist as they walked, sent a slow dripping from the branches above. Áine lifted her face, letting the drops dash onto her forehead, the water trickling down her nose and chin.

'It has been a long time since I wandered in this way.'

'Sure, a woman with a husband shares her marriage with the hearth.'

'Did you never get married yourself, Nance?'

Nance smiled. 'Ah, 'twas never a one would have me. I spent all my time as a girl in the mountains. I went courting with the sun.'

'I used to go walking up the mountains as a girl. To the west.'

'Did you now?'

'The wind up there always smelt sweeter.'

'Sure, I know it.' Nance crouched down and began to rummage amongst a tangle of ferns and ivy. 'Do you know what plant this is?'

'*Dearna Mhuire.*'

Nance plucked the soft, pleated leaves of lady's mantle, setting them on the ground beside her. When she had a neat pile she crossed herself, and Áine helped her to her feet.

'What are they for?'

'You'll see now.'

Back inside the warmth of the *bothán*, Nance quickened the fire with dried furze and set her crock, filled with river water, on the flames.

'Could you know this plant in the wild? Pick it safely?'

Áine nodded. 'I picked lady's mantle for my mother.'

'When the air grows warmer, the leaves will have a dew on them, and the best way to fix a child in you would be to mix that dew with water and bathe in it. Until then, we can hope for the same with an infusion.' She passed the leaves to Áine. 'Now. Boil these in a little clean water and drink of it for twenty mornings.'

'What is that pot there for, then?'

'Tansy.' Nance plucked several withered leaves off a dried plant hanging from the rafter and crumbled them into the water. 'If you cannot go far from the house for the *dearna Mhuire*, tansy leaves brewed as a tea will also help you.'

The boiling water became aromatic and Nance poured off the steaming liquid, handing a piggin to Áine.

She hesitated. 'There's no word of truth in what they're saying, is there, Nance?'

'What's that? What are they saying?'

'The bittersweet berries. Brigid.'

Nance felt her heart drop, but she kept her face calm. 'What do you believe, Áine?'

The blacksmith's wife looked at the cup in her hands, and then, as if deciding, took a long draught. ''Tis bitter.'

Nance was relieved. 'So is life. Make it to your taste, but take care not to use too much. Drink it for seven days. Today will be the first of your seven.'

Áine held her nose and drained the piggin.

'Will you remember, Áine?'

'I will.'

'Distilled lady's mantle for twenty days and a tea of tansy leaf for seven. And there is something else you must do.'

Áine paused. 'What is that?'

'When you turn your cow out to grass, let her eat the flowers of the field and then catch her water. 'Tis all-flowers water. All the good of the herbs she has eaten will be in it, and if you bathe in it you will have their cure.'

'Thank you, Nance.'

'And I will hold the charm for you in my mind, Áine O'Donoghue. Know you that. Boil the herbs on a hot turf fire, and all the while I will be holding the charm for you, and we will see you with a child before this year is out.' Nance gripped her hand. 'And then you may tell them that there was no harm in that bittersweet.'

*

Long after Áine had left, Nance sat brooding in front of her fire. For the first time since she had moved to the valley, she felt a threat against her, a summons to prove her ability. When she was younger it had been enough for people to know that she was the niece of Mad Maggie, that she had been taught the cure, shown the ways of the Good People. Then, when she was on the road, they saw the fact of her ability in her loneliness, in the absence of a husband, her crooked hands, her habit of smoking, of drinking like a man. They placed their faith in her because she was different from them.

But now Nance sensed doubt. Suspicion.

I must get this child back, Nance thought. If I can restore Micheál to Nóra, then they will see that there is no word of a lie in my dealings with Them. If I give Áine O'Donoghue a child, and return Micheál Kelliher to his grandmother, they will all return to me.

Nance shivered, thinking of the foxglove treatment. She had not had another visit from Nóra Leahy, and she guessed that this meant the changeling was still in the house. It had not worked to return her mother either, although they had tried. Maggie had made Nance sit on Mary Roche's chest to pin her arms to her side, and they had poured the foxglove down her throat while she spluttered and cursed them, while she spat it back in Nance's face. It had taken a long struggle before the fairy woman had swallowed the liquid, but when she did the change had been unsettling. The heart of the change-ling had slowed to an erratic pumping. She had grown listless, then foamed at the mouth with her eyes wide and rolled, had vomited throughout the night. But the *lus mór* made her docile. Made her quiet when she had been screaming. Made her placid and waxen when she had been red-faced and scratching.

Her da had not liked to see the change, for all he was desperate for his wife to return. He had taken Maggie's gifts of *poitín* and gone on rambling, and had not returned some nights at all.

'Your da only needs a bit of time to himself,' Maggie had said. ''Tis no easy thing to see your wife swept and the violence needed to bring her back.'

Nance, older then, had struggled to remember her mother as she had been before the Good People took her. She had grown used to the fairy woman left in her place.

'What will you do if there's no restoring Mam through *lus mór*?'

'There are other ways.'

Nance was silent for a moment. 'Maggie? I want to ask you something.'

'What is it?'

'How did you get that mark on your face? You never told me.'

'I don't like to be talking of it.'

'I heard a man saying you got it after your mam was hit in the face with a blackberry. When she was carrying, like.'

Maggie rolled her eyes, began to fuss with her pipe. ''Twas not that at all.'

'Were you born with it?'

Plumes of blue smoke in the evening air. The whirring of a summer night.

'I was swept. Once. Just like your mam. They brought me back to myself with a poker reddened in the fire.'

'They burnt you?'

'I was away. The fire brought me round to myself.'

'You never said.'

''Twas when I was away that I got the knowledge.'

'Maggie, you never said. All these years you've been living here with us and you never told me you were swept.'

Her aunt shrugged and absently touched the mark on her face.

'Does Da know?'

Her aunt nodded.

'We should do that to Mam.'

Maggie drew on her pipe and let out a shuddering breath. 'Never on my life.'

'But it worked!'

'Nance, we'll not be putting the fairy out of her with fire.'

Silence between them then. Corncrakes rasping their pattern outside.

'Did it hurt?'

But Maggie never answered. There was a knock on the door, and there stood the boatmen of the lough, holding the body of her father aloft. Drowned, they said. Under before they could fish him out. Terrible accident. Terrible misfortune for the family. For Nance. Her mam gone soft in the head, and how would she and her aunt keep up with rent? How to stop the crowbars breaking down the door and pulling the thatch apart? They would do what they could but they had families of their own. Terrible misfortune. God be with them.

In her cabin Nance closed her eyes and rested her head on her knees. All this time past, the years lived through, but the sight of Maggie kneeling over her da and the howling between them that night, a cry taken up by the fairy woman in the bed, her mother's shadow, all ringing in her ears as though she were in that room again with her father's lungs filled with water. That sound, the mourning of three women all touched by the fairies, all unmoored.

There was no one Maggie turned away afterwards, no matter the sickness upon them or the badness they were after. Her aunt never said, but Nance knew. When the ones with the glower on them came, asking for the tides of luck to be turned, Maggie began to send Nance on errands.

'Let them in.' Maggie's voice would rise from the gloom of the cabin. 'It may be that I can help them after all. And won't you go and pick the Devil's-bit? 'Tis all a-flower and I have need of it.'

Her aunt must have known that it could not last. That whatever wickedness was being worked for their praties and scraws, the canker would return upon them in time.

Piseógs are fires that flare in the face of those who set them.

Three months later and Nance had come home to a dead hearth, no fairy woman in the bed, no Maggie by her side. The cabin cold and empty. She had kindled the fire and waited for their return. Wound the hours with worry.

It was only when she noticed that Maggie's things were missing – her pipe, her stores of herbs and ointments, the *poitín* – that she knew she had gone. Nance had sat on the rushes and cried herself to sleep.

Returned to the fairies, they said later. And taken Mary Roche with her. Both of them as mad as the other, gone back to the Good People and no sight of them since. And that poor Nance, all alone and a young woman too. Not two coins to rub together and no kin neither. She'll be on the roads with nothing but herbs to her name.

Nance's stomach creased in hunger. All the years past, but this was how it would be for her again if they did not come for cures, if she did not banish the changeling. Hunger and hollow and cramping. She would be back to waiting in ditches and shadows to calm animals that had been turned out to pasture. Nicking their veins to tap their blood, plugging the wounds with fat and the blessed untoothed leaves of devil's-bit scabious. Picking turf from where it had tumbled off piles, only coming close to those houses where the families were still asleep, where the smoke was not yet rising. Retreating to the rough footing of hills when the stir of morning began and the milking girls emerged puffy-eyed, and the men began the long walk to cut turf or tend their animals and crops.

Nance remembered that life on the road. Gathering blackberries and *fraocháin*, and untangling stray wool from thorny thickets of furze, and cutting watercress and coltsfoot, three-cornered garlic and bogbean. Nights spent sleeping beneath the flowering black-thorn, the pale blossoms against the dark branches like faces in the night. Turning her knife to Mary's fern for bedding. She had cut the bracken and found the initials of God whorled within the inner working of the stem.

Maggie had taught her how to survive in the face of misfortune. Before she had vanished, she had told Nance how a hungry woman might gather a little blood to boil with grain. How she might best beg milk off a farmer's wife. How to trap and skin an eel, or catch a hare, or take a little turf where it would not be missed. How to scrape a scythe through a cow pat and summon the goodness of the butter to yourself, muttering, 'All for me. All for me. All for me.'

But she had never taught her how to sleep on the road when there was nothing left, and you had only yourself. Nance had learnt that alone.

CHAPTER
FOURTEEN

Hart's tongue

'God's blessing on this place.'

Mary and Nóra looked out the open door of the cabin and saw Peg O'Shea making her way towards them, leaning on her blackthorn stick.

'Ah, the devils are into your thatch.' She paused and raised her crook at the birds that were wheeling about Nóra's roof. 'Stolen straw makes cosy nests.'

'Are you well, Peg?'

'I am. I've come to see how you're all getting on. My, Nóra, you look a grievance.'

Nóra stepped forward to help Peg into the house. ''Tis the changeling. Oh, Peg. 'Tis back to bawling and shrieking the whole night through. Not natural, the lungs on it. Begod, Peg, I don't get a wink, nor the maid either. We're beside ourselves with lack of sleep.'

Peg eased herself down by the fire and looked at the child lying in Mary's lap, arms juddering, mouth querulous. 'The poor lad. An empty vessel makes most noise.'

Nóra sat down beside her. 'Do you see any change in it? I thought I could, but . . .'

'Nance is curing him?'

Nóra nodded. 'Just concoctions of herbs so far.' She lowered her voice. 'You should have seen it a week ago, Peg. Like something going through. A shaking.'

Peg frowned. 'A shaking? Nance was shaking the fairy out of him? Shaking him back and forth, was she?'

'Not a shaking like that,' said Nóra. ''Twas a herb she gave it and a shaking rose up in the body, like. Froth in the mouth and all.'

They watched Mary as she spat on a corner of her apron and wiped the boy's chin.

'I never heard of such a thing.'

''Twas *lus mór*,' said Mary.

Peg looked apprehensive. 'Foxglove? Oh, that's some powerful plant.'

''Twas awful,' Mary said, her eyes not leaving Micheál. 'There was a bath of it, and then we set the juice of it on his tongue, and he was fitting like a mad dog with it all. Like he was dying.'

'Good God. The poor wretch.' Peg looked at the child, concerned. There was a damp, pinched look about his face.

'Only, the shaking and trembling's gone out of him now,' added Mary. 'He's not so sick with it, God be praised.'

'It hasn't worked,' Nóra said abruptly. She gripped Peg's shoulder. 'Peg, 'twas as though we came close to having the fairy gone out of it, and then . . . nothing. I'm in pieces over it.'

'Oh, Nóra,' Peg murmured. ''Tis no easy thing. As Nance was telling ye, sometimes 'tis better to care for the changeling in your grandson's place if you can't be getting rid of it.'

Nóra shook her head vehemently. 'I'll be getting rid of it. I could never forgive myself if I did not try to find my grandson, Peg. For

Martin's sake. For my daughter's. I'm going to get Micheál back. I'm after other ways.'

'And what ways might they be?' Peg asked, her tone careful. 'You're not after nettling him again, are you, Nóra Leahy? I tell you, 'tis best you follow the advice of Nance, although . . .' She stopped and sucked her teeth. 'There's a lot of talk about that one going round.'

'About Nance?'

'Surely you've heard. There's talk she's got some darkness working against Father Healy and those that would have her out. Seán Lynch. Kate Lynch. Éilís and her man. Aye, that woman has the word against her. And Brigid, all that talk of the berries spread by Kate. And now Seán has been fighting over her.'

'What's that now?'

'Well, I say fighting over her, though there's more to it than that. Seán Lynch was making trouble at the blacksmith's today. The son-in-law told me. There was some quarrel over a horse between Seán and Peter O'Connor, and Nance was mentioned.'

Mary picked the boy up and moved him to the unfolded settle bed.

'Seán's fault?' asked Nóra. 'Had he drink taken?'

'As like as not. The daughter's man was up with me now, and he says there was some scuffle in O'Donoghue's yard.'

'What happened?'

Peg raised an eyebrow. 'Seán had taken his share of Peter's horse to make up the team. That's how it began.'

Nóra grimaced. 'Martin always said Seán was a stingy sort when it came to horses. Keep his too long and he'll be calling you lazy. Bring his mare back sharp and he's in a fit and saying she's been worked like a devil. He takes care of his own, does Seán.'

'And by his own you mean he takes care of himself,' Peg snorted. 'As I heard it, Seán was feeding Peter's horse hay with the seed slapped out of it, and his own the better oats. So when Peter saw Seán at the smith's he asked him to give the horse the same feed as his own, and Seán . . . well. Gave him a look that would wither grass and told him he did as he saw fit, and there was no strength in the horse at all, and did he want to be robbing a neighbour with no money coming in? And Peter said the dry was on the whole valley and 'twas not his fault. And then . . .' Peg paused, licking her lips. 'Then your boy was mentioned.'

Nóra blanched. 'The changeling? What was said, Peg?'

'Seán said Kate's turned over in her mind about the changeling in Nóra Leahy's house, and he knows there's some malice being worked on the place by Nance. He said that's the true cause of the dry. Said Kate thinks the boy is one of Them summoned by Nance to blink us all in anger at Father Healy. Oh, and Seán was spitting and fitting over it, the lad was telling me. Spitting on the ground like he was putting out a fire. Says he's after finding what looks to be *piseógs* on his land. Says someone's working to curse him. The horses were getting nervous with his racket, and Peter put out an arm to calm them, like, to keep them from the panic, but Seán thought he was after him and grabbed Peter's shirt. Brought him eye to eye. "I know you walk to her den of an afternoon," says he. "I know you're awful great with that *cailleach*." Then he said . . .' Peg took a deep breath, shaking her head in disgust. 'He said, "Sure, 'tis a sad state of affairs when a man who can't get a wife will go after the Devil for his."

'Well. You know Peter, quiet as a church mouse on a holy day, would soon as fight a man as a priest. You wouldn't believe it. Didn't the red come down over him, and didn't he grab Seán's own collar and say he had no right to be calling a poor honest woman such a thing when he's a devil himself.'

'A man's mouth often broke his nose.'

'But Peter O'Connor! Nóra, have you ever heard such a thing? Peter O'Connor giving Seán a hearing! He said to him: "You're a devil. Pissing on Nance and starving every man's horse but your own!" Then Peter started on about Kate. "And we all know you're beating the dust out of your woman again. Wonderful hard man to go after them that can't be fighting back." He was saying, "You're some man, Seán Lynch! Some hard man!"'

'And then what happened?'

'Seán knocked the feathers out of Peter. Punched him everywhere except the roof of his mouth and the soles of his feet, as I heard it. Brought him down into the mud and stomped the face of him so that, once the men had dragged Seán off – swinging all the while – the bellows boy was out in the yard, picking teeth like flowers.'

'Sweet Jesus. How is the face on Peter?'

'John and Áine took him in and patched him up as best they could, but if the man was a bachelor before, they say he'll be an ugly one his whole life long now, more's the pity. Mouth like a broken window. Nose broke. They'll be chalking his jacket for a laugh this shrove, you mark my words.'

'He's right,' Nóra said, rubbing her chin in thought. 'Seán Lynch is a devil.'

'My bet is that Peter will be straight for Nance's tonight. He'll have need of her.'

Nóra hesitated. 'I wanted to go and talk to Nance myself this day. About another cure for the changeling. How we might banish it for good.'

Peg gave the boy a long look. 'If it can wait until tomorrow, I'd not go, Nóra. Let Peter have his word with Nance. If Seán or one of them see you and the child together with Peter and the *bean feasa*, that'll get the tongues wagging faster than the tail of a butcher's dog. I don't like to be talking ill of others, but sure, there's trouble coming, and you don't want Kate Lynch or Seán up here and asking to see the changeling, or saying you're against them. You've no man now, Nóra. If you don't have your reputation, what will protect you?'

Nance walked the river's length, dragging a broken branch behind her. It was a rare day of February sunlight, and she could see that spring had sent its first flush through the world. Despite the cold, she could smell the change in season.

The trees would soon be tipping with green. In a month or two bluebells would rise to make hallow the forest floor. Bare branches were brimming with life, and there was a haze over the fields. Alder buds swelled, and the men had begun to prepare the ground for crops. Soon there would be movement in the soil, pollen in the water.

Nance staked out the waking earth and pulled the tender shoots of herbs before the dew dried. They were gifted to her. She knew the smell of their sap like a mother knows her children. She could have found them in the dark.

As she walked Nance thought of the changeling, remembering the long purple mark on Maggie's face. Would it be enough to wave the hot iron close to the skin? Would it be enough to tell the fairy child what they planned to do if he did not leave for good? Maggie had told her the other ways they might try to force the return of her abducted mother if the foxglove did not work. St John's wort. Measured doses of henbane. Boundary water.

But never the blistering poker. 'Not on my life,' Maggie had said. Even though it had brought her back from the fairies. Nance closed her eyes and pictured the scar tissue, the puckered skin tight against the cheek. She imagined the iron against it, the hiss and steam and the sticking burn at the touch of the red poker and shuddered.

A strange noise interrupted Nance's thoughts. A hard, ragged breathing repeating itself on the breeze. Putting down her makeshift sled she crept between the trees until she could see the smoke of her cabin. There was a figure making its way down the path. A man, coughing, almost running to her door. His arms were wrapped about his ribs as he jumped over exposed roots and fallen branches.

Peter O'Connor.

Nance stepped out from behind the alder and oak and into the clearing. Sensing movement, Peter turned and slowed to a walk.

'Nance,' he called throatily.

'What is it, Peter? What has happened to you?'

The man retched loudly, dropped to his knees and threw up. Hunched over on all fours, he vomited again, then wiped a long strand of saliva from his mouth and sat back on his heels.

Nance placed a gentle hand on his back. 'There now,' she said. 'Take it easy. Take a breath, now, Peter. Take a breath.'

Peter looked up at her, wiping his lips. One eye was purpled, swollen, the lashes squeezed between the puffed, bruised lids. His nostrils were crusted with blood, and he wore an expression of such abject anger that Nance crossed herself.

'Peter. Come inside.'

He nodded, unable to speak. She helped him rise and directed him towards her cabin. After glancing around to see if anyone was about, she shut the door and tied it fast with straw rope.

Peter stood, his head and arms hanging from his body like a man condemned.

'Sit down.' Nance tugged his arm and pointed to her pile of heather. 'Better yet, lie down. Let me get us a drink.' She fetched a bottle.

Peter's hand trembled as he pulled out the stopper and brought the lip to his mouth.

'And another. Now, when you can, tell me what has happened.'

'Seán Lynch,' Peter spat. He rummaged in his coat and pulled out his pipe and tobacco. Nance waited as he stuffed the bowl with a shaking thumb and kindled the dry leaf. 'He turned on me. He had the lend of a horse. Treated her ill. And when I went to have words with him about it, he nodded his fist at me.' He sucked deeply on his pipe, wincing as the stem brushed against his split lip. 'Sure, Seán is no easy man to get along with, but you should have seen him. He was in one. He would have killed me.'

'Is there no other grievance he has against you?'

Peter blew out a heavy lungful of smoke, shrugging. 'I mentioned his woman, Kate. That fired him up some.'

'They're not great with one another.'

He shook his head. 'She looks like a kicked dog these days.'

'He'll get what's coming to him.'

'Will he?' Peter squinted at Nance through the smoke. 'I'm worried for you, Nance. Seán is after telling Father Healy that you're against God. 'Tis a hard start to the year, Nance. Tomas O'Connor had a cow down and for no good reason. Found her dead and swollen by the river, and no knowing how she wandered there. Took five of us to haul the body out the water, and she in calf too. Daniel Lynch's woman. Brigid. The wee mite dead. I've no mind for hen talk, but didn't Old Hanna find all her chickens dead and laid out without their heads. Some say foxes, but to just take the head? The bleedin' women are in pieces over their churns. I was on rambling to O'Donoghue's, and there's a pack of them there, fussing John for nails and ironwork and charms to bring the profit back to the milk. There's a woman up the mountain, says she cracked one of her eggs the other day. 'Twas no yolk to be had in it. 'Twas filled with blood! Some say 'tis our Good Neighbours at mischief. Some say 'tis the Leahy boy.' He offered Nance the draw of his pipe. 'Some say 'tis you.'

Nance was silent. She accepted Peter's pipe, wiped the blood from the stem and let her mouth fill with the rough smoke.

'You have no hand in *piseógs*, do you, Nance? Seán's saying he's after finding the suggestion of *piseógs* on his land. Stones turned strangely. Flints pointing at the crop ground.'

'To lay a curse is to set it on your own head.'

Peter nodded. 'Faith, I knew you were a Christian woman. You've always been kind to me.'

'Would you tell them when you hear it, Peter? Tell them I have no hand in that badness.'

'Not even for Seán Lynch?' He cast her a sideways look.

'Seán Lynch has been against me for years. If I had it in for him, he'd have been pissing bees and coughing crickets long before now.'

Peter smiled and Nance saw that he was missing several teeth. He took another long draw. 'Do you think 'tis the Leahy changeling?'

'You tell them I will have that boy restored. I will have the fairy out and the boy returned.'

'Has he the evil eye, do you think? Only, it makes sense, Nance. The cratur comes to the valley and 'tis only grief we've known since. And a strange kind, too. Eggs of blood and men passing at cross-roads, and rumours of hares sucking the cows dry of milk.' He cast Nance a dark look. 'The dreams I told you about, Nance. I keep having them.'

'You dream you drown.'

'Aye. I'm all under water and there's hands holding me there. Holding me fast. There's a burning in my lungs and I have a yearning to breathe, but though I'm looking up and I can see the sun beyond the surface, and the trees, there is a face there too.'

'Who is murdering you?'

Peter shook his head. 'I can't make him out. But Nance . . .' He sat up on the heather, dropping his voice to a whisper. 'After today, I'm thinking it might be Seán.'

''Tis a dark thing to think of a man.'

Peter was insistent. 'I couldn't account for his belting me the way he did. Like he wanted to kill me, so I said. And then, I was sitting there with John and Áine, as battered as a *sliotar*, and I think of it. He knows I think well of you, Nance. Even mentioned it. And if he's thinking you're behind the badness in this place, the powerful mischief going on, well.' He leant back, raising his hand to his swollen eye. 'He might have a notion that I've a hand in it too.'

Nance sighed. 'Peter, bless you, no one thinks you've a hand in *piseógs*. No one gives in to that.'

'They might think you've taught me.'

Nance thought of Kate all those years ago. The flashing needle in her hem. Her talk of turning stones, of walking against the sun. 'If someone has it in for another, the *piseógs* come natural. God forgive them, they always think of something.'

Peter gave her a careful look, then tapped out the dead ash in his pipe. He was about to refill it when he paused, glancing at the door. 'Did you hear that?'

Nance listened. The sound came again and they looked at each other, eyes widening. Somewhere in the valley, a woman was screaming.

It seemed that everyone in the fields had heard. As Peter and Nance made their way from her cabin to the lane they saw men running from their work, throwing their tools down and dropping their reins. Women emerged from the cabins by the Macroom road, blinking in the sunlight, children gawping by their aprons.

'What's that?'

'Did you hear it?'

'Good God, do you think someone's after being killed?'

'Where's it coming from?'

A group of people gathered in the lane, fear on their faces. ''Tis not an eviction, surely,' they said. ''Tis not yet rent day.' Then one of the men pointed at the O'Donoghues' bellows boy, running full pelt up the road to where they stood. His face was wild, his dirty hair sticking to his forehead in sweat.

'Help!' he cried. He stumbled on a rock and went flying on the road, then picked himself up and continued to run, arms wheeling in panic, knees grazed. 'Help!'

'Tell us! What is it?' The men ran to meet him, grabbing his arm and the boy let out a yelp. ''Tis Áine O'Donoghue,' he shouted. 'She's caught herself on fire.'

There was a crowd of people in the blacksmith's yard by the time Peter and Nance arrived, their faces anxious and intent. They stared at Nance from lowered brows as Peter dragged her across the dirt and pebbles into the open door of the O'Donoghues' cabin.

'I've Nance Roche here! The doctress! I've brought her,' Peter cried, spitting blood and pulling Nance through the doorway. For a moment Nance could see nothing in the dark room. Then she saw two figures on the ground. Áine was writhing on the floor as her husband tried to calm her and hold her down.

There was an awful smell of burnt flesh. The bottom of Áine's dress was black and burnt, the cindered cloth sticking to her legs. Nance could see her skin through the weave, already blistered and gruesome in moist, pink shine. It looked as though she had been flayed across the shins. Áine's eyes were shut and her mouth was wide and issuing a hellish scream.

'God have mercy on her,' Nance whispered. There was the smell of vomit, and Nance saw that John was being sick on the ground. The sight of the retching blacksmith holding his wife's blistered ankles jolted her from horrified silence, and she found herself telling Peter to find some butter and *poitín*, and to get John a sip of water.

Nance dropped to her knees. 'Áine,' she said calmly. 'Áine, 'tis Nance. You are going to be alright. I'm here to help you.'

The woman kept thrashing on the ground. Nance caught hold of her arms. 'Áine, be still. Be still.'

There was a sudden silence and Áine stopped struggling and fell limp.

'Is she dead?' John gasped.

'Not dead,' Nance answered. ''Tis too much for her to bear. 'Tis a faint. John. John, listen to me. I need you to go outside and tell everyone there to leave. Tell them to go and pray for her. And then I need you to go and fetch me ivy leaves.'

John got up at once and left, lurching sideways across the yard in the disorientation of his horror.

The bellows boy was standing rigid against the wall. 'We heard her shouting. John and I. We were out in the forge and we heard a screaming. We thought she was being murdered and all. We came in and she was all aflame. John got the blanket from the bed and beat her with it until the fire was out.'

'He did well to think so quickly.'

Peter was silent for a moment. 'Look at the legs of her. Nance, will she die of it?'

Nance sat back on her heels. 'I'll tell you if there's need to send for the priest and the sacrament. But now we have to take her to the river. Can you carry her, do you think?'

Peter and the bellows boy lifted Áine from the floor and carried her out of the room. John had sent some of the people on their way, but many remained, watching with hands over mouths, as the men stumbled down the slope to where the river lay.

Peter and the boy held the unconscious woman in the flowing water by the neck and feet. The water was freezing and the men shivered, their jaws locked with cold, their clothes wet to the waist. John had his eyes closed and was praying on the bank, muttering to himself. Peter held Áine with gritted determination, gently lowering her legs into the water in an even, steady rhythm. Ashes lifted from the woman's dress and were swept away by the current, greasing the surface of the river.

Nance crouched on the bank, watching the men with a keen eye. 'You will not die,' she announced to Áine. 'You will not die.' She held the hem of her skirt to her waist and filled it with hart's tongue fern and ivy leaves, plucking them with John from where they grew at the feet of the oak and alder, ash and holly.

The crowd had not dispersed. Many of the valley people were still stubbornly standing in the blacksmith's yard when they returned from the river, dripping and shaking with the cold. The onlookers crossed themselves at the sight of Áine's burns, but none ventured inside the cabin with them. The hearth had grown cold, and the room was filled with smoke and the smell of burnt hair.

Peter and John placed Áine on the bed in the far corner of the room, and as they settled her on the blanket she murmured, the lid of one eye rising unsteadily before falling shut. Nance ordered Peter to return to the river for more water and asked John to build up the fire. It was only when the turf had been kindled and the flames threw an uneasy glow about the room that they saw the gifts and tokens lying on the cabin's table. Noggins of butter and a basket of turf and kindling. Someone had placed a small salted nugget of bacon next to some eggs. Yellow flowers for protection: sprays of gorse and a cross woven of reeds. And on the edge of the table, a small, clean folded cloth of dowry linen.

That night was as long as the howl of a dog. Nance sat hunched over Áine for the full, slow swing of the moon, dribbling water into her mouth as the ivy and hart's tongue boiled on the fire. She urged Peter to give John as much *poitín* as would send him into sleep on the rushes, and kept the hearth alive, getting up only to refill the piggin of well water, feed the flames with turf and, once, to scrub the blood and ashes off the stone. The woman had left a shadow of her own scorching on the flag.

Shortly before dawn Nance drained the ivy and fern leaves and pummelled their paste into softened butter. She stepped out into the brittle chill and let the rising fingers of sunlight touch the poultice. Then she returned inside and dressed Áine's raw skin, painting the woman's wounds with the herbed fat under prayer and a blessing of her own tongue, soothing her with a stream of words that carried in them no other meaning than a calm urgency to stay alive. She closed her eyes and thought of her da and Maggie, and Father O'Reilly, and all those who had seen in her hands a higher healing, who believed she carried a light. And she thought on her light, her knowledge and her cure, and felt her hands grow hot with it, until all suddenly spasmed, and there were rough fingers gripping her wrists and the sound of the clay vessel breaking on the floor, and when she opened her eyes it was Father Healy and Seán Lynch taking her outside, pulling her so hard that her muscles tightened with the pain of their grip, and her toes scraped against the cobbles, and there was the fresh morning air and mud, and she lay in it and there was Father Healy, pale-faced, mouth saying something to John, who argued in desperation, and above her the birds circled and the sun was rising bloody, rising red in night's slaughter.

CHAPTER
FIFTEEN

Oak

'You'd think nobody ever died, there were so many there!'

'Hearing the Mass!'

Peg nodded, glancing down to the wicker basket where the boy was concealed beside her. She and Nóra were sitting out in the yard knitting, taking in the rare sun of a thin-clouded day while Mary washed the child's soiled rags, steam rising from her barrel.

''Tis the fear,' Peg said. ''Tis a nervous time, what with the animals in foal and calf, and the potatoes about to be put into ground. Folk are vexed. They want reassurance that all will be well. They're praying for the strange happenings to stop. There are them that might not believe in such things but for what has been happening.'

'Áine.'

Peg crossed herself. 'God be with her. Yes, Áine, but also your Martin. Brigid. There's queer things happening up the mountains if you believe half of what goes round. And they're after finding patterns in it all. They're after finding reason for it.'

The boy emitted a loud shriek from his basket and the women exchanged glances.

''Tis back as it was,' murmured Nóra, nodding at the child. 'Pounding its head against the floor, pounding its fists. The *lus mór* took all the cross ways out of it, but now it's after screeching for milk again, and scratching the maid.' Nóra reached down and pushed the boy's extended arm back into the basket. 'Will she live, do you think?'

'Áine?'

'Aye.'

'I pray to God 'tis so. There's a Killarney doctor with her. The priest brought him himself. He's hard against Nance now, and her that had the knowledge to take Áine to the river.'

''Twas swift thinking.'

'Aye, and I say 'tis what saved her. But Father Healy will have none of it. Tossing her out into the yard like that! Now, I understand he has no time for a woman like Nance, that he does be thinking she's a wonder maker. But, sure, 'tis a sad day when a priest is pushing a woman into the mud, with a grand age on her too.'

''Tis shameful.'

'Throwing after her all the herbs brought in good faith.' Peg sniffed. 'John O'Donoghue asked him to let Nance treat the woman, but there's no arguing with a priest. Sure, Father Healy will have Nance out of this valley. He's already after turning minds against her. Nóra . . .' She stopped knitting and sat the needles on her lap. 'There are those that used to go to Nance for the cure and now they won't even look in her direction. A man came the other day asking for her. Said his mother told him of a woman who could take the jaundice out of his child. But would you know, the man he asked was Daniel Lynch, and your own Dan wouldn't be telling him where she lives. Told him to go on home and that no one with the charms was hereabouts.'

'Dan's gone with the shock of the child, may God protect him.'

'And Brigid too, I'm sure. 'Tis a sad thing for her to be waiting for the churching and no one to be talking with but her man, when what she surely needs is company.'

'Faith, I can't imagine Dan speaking out against anybody.'

'It may be he's after believing Father Healy. The man is preaching against Nance at the altar. At the Mass he was saying she's nothing more than a quackered hag, turned to the rot and meddling in lives to bring food to her mouth.'

'Sure, Kate Lynch was telling all about the bittersweet Nance gave to Brigid.' Nóra nodded at Mary. 'The girl heard it herself at the well. Talk of poisoning. I don't believe a word of it.'

Peg nodded. 'I don't believe it either. But Nóra, that's what folk are saying of Áine.' She reached out and placed her hand on Nóra's knee. 'Someone saw her go to Nance's. Alone, like. They found tansy and lady's mantle in the house.'

Nóra shook her head. 'Sure, Nance was healing Áine with herbs afore Father Healy threw her out. The night she was burnt. They were just for the healing.'

Peg dropped her voice. 'But that's not all they're saying. Nóra, how do you think Áine caught fire?'

'Her dress caught light. From the hearth.' Nóra brushed Peg's hand away and resumed knitting. 'How many women do you know with a smouldered apron? Begod, Peg, pity on her, but when a woman spends her hours by a fire, she's bound to be burnt. Áine was unlucky to have it so bad, and God love her and heal her from it.'

Peg took a deep breath. 'Nóra, I'm with you. I have no hard word against Nance. I believe she has the knowledge. But folk are saying 'twas no ordinary fire Áine was building that burnt her. They found the piss of a cow in the crock.'

'In the crock?'

'On the fire. The doctor found it and told the priest, and Father Healy asked John what Áine was doing, boiling potatoes in the water of a beast. John, bless his soul, told him then. 'Twas a cure told by Nance. All-flowers water.'

From across the yard Mary lifted her head and stared, open-mouthed.

'Áine went to Nance to fix a child in her, so says John, and Nance gave her the herbs. The tansy. The lady's mantle. She also told her to bathe in all-flowers water. 'Twas when Áine was fixing a bath of it that she caught alight. That's what the high fire was for. 'Twas when she was following Nance's charm.'

Nóra looked out past the yard across the valley. There was a softness on the hill, rendering the distance into golden haze. She could hear the ringing of tools on the air. ''Twas an accident, sure. No one is to blame.'

'I know that, but Father Healy is saying the sin is on Nance. Muttering *piseógs* and the like. And Nóra, those that have a reluctance to trace it back to Nance's hand are finding reason elsewhere.'

Nóra noticed Peg's eyes flicker to the basket, and felt her stomach drop. 'They're saying 'tis the changeling?'

'They're scared, Nóra. There's a fear in them.' Peg sucked her teeth in thought. 'I don't tell you this to put the fright on you. But I thought you should know what's being said in case anyone comes to pay you a visit, like.'

'I'm going to Nance today, Peg. She will return my grandchild to me. She will bring back Micheál and they will not be able to lay blame at my door.'

'I pray 'tis so, Nóra. Sweet, sore-wounded Christ. But be careful of folk. I wouldn't let them see you go to her. I don't know what they'll think, but I can tell you, it won't be good.' Peg shuddered. 'Not now.

Anyone who still has a desire to go to Nance will be waiting for all this to blow over.'

'Nothing is working,' said Nóra. She stood before Nance's door, reluctantly holding the changeling on her hip. 'You said you could banish it, Nance. Why won't the Good People give me my grandson back? What have I done?' She was near weeping. She could feel the bones of the changeling's chest against her side, feel his bleating breath.

'It takes time,' Nance replied. She was standing within the dark mouth of her cabin, her white hair mussed, arms held out from her sides like a man preparing to fight. 'There's no forcing the sea.'

Nóra shook her head. 'You talk to Them. They gave you the knowledge. Why don't you ask Them where Micheál is? Ask Them to return him to me. Tell them to take back *this*.' She thrust the boy out in front of her, her hands gripping the rounded staves of his ribcage. His toes buttoned inwards, bare to the cold.

'I am working the cure for you,' Nance said, eyeing Nóra warily.

'You do nothing! All you've done is stuff it with herbs that make it shit and tremble. It was leaking with your herbs. The lips of it have split for all the water that passed through it.' Nóra heaved the changeling back upon the ridge of her hip and lowered her voice to a hiss. 'Please, Nance. What you've done with the herbs and the foxglove, 'tis not enough. All it's been doing is crying the louder and dirtying itself. It was all quiet and shaking, but now 'tis just as it was before. I asked you to make Them take back their own, not have it grow weak and sick, and then strong and well again. Sure, if it was a burden before, the changeling's a weight on me now.'

Nance closed her eyes, swaying a little on her feet. She did not reply.

There was a long silence.

'You're filthy with drink,' Nóra finally spat.

Nance opened her eyes. 'I'm not.'

'Look at the state of you.'

Nance sighed and took an unsteady step forward, lurching for the doorframe. She gripped the wood and pulled herself out over the doorstep. 'Nóra.'

'What? Look at you.'

'Sit down with me.'

'Here? I'm not sitting in the mud.'

'Sit with me there. On that log by there.'

Nóra reluctantly followed the stumbling woman to the rotting tree trunk that lay fleeced with moss on the border of the woods.

Nance eased herself down onto it. She took a deep breath and patted the space beside her. 'Sit you down, Nóra Leahy. Put the fairy on the ground. By there, on the grass. Under the oak.'

Nóra hesitated, lip curled, but her arms ached from carrying the changeling. Placing the child on a clump of new grass, she grudgingly sat beside Nance.

The old woman peered up at the oak's bare branches. '*When the ash comes out before the oak, you'll have a summer of dust and smoke.*'

'What?'

Nance sniffed. 'An old rhyme. Sure, the trees do be knowing what will come, long before it passes.'

Nóra grunted.

'Do you see that there?' Nance asked, pointing out beyond her cabin.

'The Piper's Grave.'

'That's it. The oak. The rowan. The whitethorn. That's where They be.'

''Tis no news to me, Nance Roche. We all know where the Good People make their home.'

'I've seen Them. I've heard Them.' Nance blinked slowly, letting her arm drop to her side. 'My mother was a great favourite of Theirs. They would come for her. On the fairy wind. They gave her a steed of ragwort and she went with them to the beautiful places. My aunt too. Faith, that's where they went. And they left me, but they left me with the knowledge.'

Nóra looked at the old woman. Her eyes were half shut and her hands scratched at the moss on the trunk. She looked deranged.

Nance suddenly opened her eyes and frowned. 'I know what you're thinking, Nóra Leahy. You think that the years have wormed into my mind and made tunnels of my sense. You think I am riddled with age.' She leant into Nóra's face, her breath hot. 'You are wrong.'

There was silence. Both women looked to the woods.

'I thought it might be enough to hear one such as yourself pronounce him fairy,' Nóra said eventually. 'Ever since my daughter passed, I've been thinking how it was that the boy was wasting. The thought that it might have been Johanna and Tadgh, the hunger . . .' Her voice cracked. 'I thought they might have caused it to their own son. Maybe they were neglecting him. Maybe my own girl was no mother at all to him. I was after asking, did I not teach her how to protect a child? When Martin died I was thinking to myself that there must have been something I did to bring all the bad luck upon myself. That the boy was not on Johanna's soul but on mine.'

''Tis no sin on you, Nóra.'

'But I felt somehow that 'twas. And people were talking! I was so ashamed of him. A cripple like that. When Peter and John brought Martin to me, my own man's body on their shoulders, the only thing I could think of was to get the boy out the house. The shame to have folk inside and peering at his crooked legs and wondering why 'twas so.

Thinking on what sin brought the sense out of him when I saw him well and thriving not two years ago. Thinking ill of me. Blaming me.'

'Nóra, listen now. That boy is not Johanna's son. 'Tis not your grandson. 'Tis fairy. You know that! The look of him, the wasting on him. I tell you now that the cratur is nothing more than an old, withered fairy, changed for Micheál. And why did they take away your daughter's boy?' Nance placed her hand over Nóra's. 'Because he was the dearest lad they could find.'

Nóra smiled, eyes watering. 'I saw Micheál once, before he was changed. He was beautiful. A bud.' She looked down at the changeling. 'Not like this false child.'

'We will return him to the Good People, Nóra. I knew a woman who was swept and returned.'

'You did?'

'I knew two women swept. One was not returned, but the other . . .' Nance frowned. 'They brought her back to herself through a reddened poker. They lay the hot iron in her face and that was enough to banish the fairy forever and for her to be restored.'

Nóra paused, thoughtful. 'Fire returned her?'

''Twas my own aunt, and 'tis how I know it to be true,' Nance said. 'I saw the mark of it on her face with my own eyes. The scar. Like a brand.'

'And it worked?'

Nance rubbed her eyes, swaying on the log. 'Aye. It worked.'

Nóra sat up sharply. 'Then we must try a reddened poker.'

'No.' Nance's voice was firm. 'No, we mustn't be doing that.'

'But it worked, so you say yourself!'

'My aunt told me she'd never have it done to another. "Never on my life," so said she, and I've a mind to heed her.' Nance paused.

Nóra's mouth twisted. 'It needn't be a scalding or a branding. It might be enough to threaten the cratur with the flames. To frighten the fairy back to its own kind.' She pointed to the spade which lay against the outer wall of Nance's *bothán*, next to the waste heap. 'To sit the cratur on that and make as if to shovel it into the fire.'

''Twould not be enough to threaten it.'

Nóra's lip trembled. 'Then we burn it. Just a wee burn. On the face.'

Nance stared at her. 'We'll not be doing that.'

'I want it gone.'

There was silence.

'Nóra, think of Áine. Did you not hear the screaming of her? The skin was clean burnt off her legs. To the bone. Blistered.' Nance folded her mouth into a grim line. 'Not through fire . . . I know you want to be rid of the cratur, but we can't be burning him.'

'Áine's no fairy.'

'I can't be going against the word of my aunt.'

'You say we cannot burn it, but what else would you have me do? Tell me! You are the one with the knowledge!'

Nance grew very still. Nóra saw that her eyes were closed again. Her sparse, pale lashes flat against her cheek. She is old, Nóra realised. There was a weariness that clung to her. A vulnerability. Nóra noticed the slow rise and fall of her chest, the tiny rounds of her shoulders. The woman wore so many layers that Nóra had never thought of Nance as frail before. But sitting this close to her, in daylight, she saw that the *bean feasa* was thin. She was weak.

Nance's eyes opened, muted, fog-soaked. 'There is another way. We can take the changeling to where the fairies do be and banish it there.'

'The Piper's Grave?'

Nance shook her head. 'Where the water greets itself. A place of power. Boundary water.'

'The river.'

'You, me and the girl. Three women at the place where three running rivers meet, for three mornings in a row. We will all of us fast. We take the changeling before sunrise to the Flesk. Three times before sunrise for three mornings, and when you return home on the last morning, the changeling will be gone. And perhaps you will find Micheál restored to you. Maybe it is that the Good People will have returned him to you. The fairy will be gone.'

'We'll be going to the water?'

'Boundary water. We'll duck the fairy in water with the power in it. A mighty power.'

Nóra stared at Nance, gaping. Then, as if deciding, she pressed her lips together and nodded hurriedly. 'When will we begin?'

Nance hesitated. ''Tis only now March; the water will be cold,' she muttered, as if to herself. 'The water will be cold and the current will be strong.' She looked at Nóra, her expression unreadable. ''Twould be better if it were closer to the approach of May Day. That is when the Good People will be changing abode. They will be restless. They will turn their eyes to us.'

'May Day? But that is a good while away.'

''Tis only that it will be cold.'

'But the days are warmer than they were. Sure, they say it will be a fine month. Nance, I can't be waiting until May Day.'

Nance paused, before nodding. 'Tomorrow morning, then. Before sunrise, in a state of hunger. Don't be eating a thing from sundown, nor let the girl take any. Not Mary, not yourself and don't be letting the change-child near water nor a bite of food. And I will be fasting too.' Nance looked down the slope to where the river ran. 'Meet me here. I will be waiting.'

It had rained during the night and the ground was soft and forgiving, relenting under Mary's bare feet. It was dark, and she walked awkwardly along the overgrown path, unable to push away the ferns and low branches with the boy in her arms. She carried him on her hipbone, his unmoving legs shifting loose against her thighs as she walked, eyes fixed on the dark blur of Nóra in front of her. Nance was leading them to the river, the white of her uncovered hair bobbing in the gloom like an apparition.

Mary felt light-bodied and hollowed with hunger. Her arms ached. 'Is it much further?' she whispered. Neither of the women answered. Her stomach dipped in trepidation.

The widow had returned from Nance's the evening before in a state of high excitement. She had burst through the cabin door and pushed the child roughly into Mary's arms, breathing hard, eyes shining. 'Tomorrow,' she had gasped. 'We're to be taking him to the water, to the river. Boundary water, says Nance. There's more power in that than the herbs. Boundaries where the fairies do be. They can't cross running water, she says. They gather there, but can't be crossing.'

Micheál had started crying. Mary laid a gentle hand on his soft hair and guided his head to her shoulder.

Nóra had paced the cabin floor. 'You're not to eat anything,' she said, pointing at Mary. 'And don't be feeding it. Fasting, there's a need for fasting.'

'What are we going to do by the river?'

The widow had sat down by the fire and then almost immediately rose to her feet again. She went to the open door and peered down the valley. 'We'll bathe it. In the river where the three waters meet.'

Mary had stroked Micheál's hair, felt his hot breath and tears against her neck. ''Twill be freezing.'

Nóra had seemed not to hear. She took a deep breath of the evening air and closed the door, latching it tight. 'Three mornings. Three women.'

'Are we to fast for three days?'

'Don't you eat a thing. Not a crumb.'

'We'll be starving for it.'

'I think, Mary, that I will soon have my daughter's child with me. And you –' she had pointed a long finger at the child in Mary's arms '– you will be gone.'

There was no morning breeze and the trees were still. The woods held their breath in the hours before daybreak, and there was a hush of waiting, the ringing silence of unsinging birds. Mary felt the air grow damp as they approached the river, in the darker shadows cast by elm trees. Then, suddenly, she heard the burble of water and the canopy opened up, revealing a paling sky. The moon and a few lingering stars glowered above them.

'Through here,' Nance said. She stopped to make sure that Mary and Nóra were still following her before continuing. The women pushed past long grass and the sound of the water changed, became softer. Here was deep-running water, Mary thought. Nance had told them there was a pool of the three boundaries, where the Flesk met its sisters and the water threaded in dark trinity. The ferns and undergrowth thinned and Mary paused to cast her eyes down at the river. The early-morning sky was held in its trembling skin.

'This is the place,' Nance whispered. She turned to Mary and reached for the boy. 'Give him to me now. You'll be going first. You'll be bathing him.'

Mary's stomach lurched. She looked at Nóra. The woman was staring at the water, her face drawn.

Nance beckoned her. 'Quickly now. We need to bathe him before the sun comes up.'

'Sure, won't the water be too cold for him?'

''Twill be quick enough. You can wrap him again after you've dipped him.'

Mary handed Micheál to Nance. He was waspish, groaning.

'That's it, that's a good girl.'

'Are the Good People here?' Nóra whispered. Her shoulders were tense, her neck arched like an unbroken horse, eyes darting the length of the swift-moving river.

Nance nodded. 'Oh, you'll know when They're here. You'll know when They've come to retrieve their own.' She pointed at the unflowering iris that grew low to the river's edge. 'Yellow flaggers in bloom are a sure sign that a changeling has been banished into the water. You'll see. He'll be turning into yellow flaggers the third morning, when he's back with his own kind.' She turned to Mary. 'You'll need to take your shawl off now.'

Mary's arms were weak from carrying the boy such a long way, and they shook as she unwrapped her shawl from her shoulders. She thought, briefly, of her family in Annamore, what they would say if they could see her now, about to bathe in the darkness of a March morning with a stricken child. *Piseógs*, they would call it. Mary folded her shawl and placed it on a mossed stone. She started to tremble.

'Do I have to be the one to do it?'

Nance was firm. 'We'll all have a turn with the bathing. One morning each.'

'It won't harm him?'

''Tis a fairy,' Nóra whispered. 'Mary, get in the water. Come on now with you, before the sun rises.'

Gripping a low-hanging branch for balance, Mary stepped down the bank to the water's edge, using the exposed roots of trees as steps.

'Not yet,' Nance called. She beckoned Mary back. 'You've to take off your outer things.'

Mary stood there in the gloom, her knuckles white around the branch and its green fur of moss. Her teeth chattered uncontrollably. 'Can I not go in with my clothes?'

'You need to be bare.'

Mary thought she would cry. 'I don't want to,' she whispered, but she climbed back up the bank and took off her skirt and blouse until she stood naked in the pre-dawn light, hunched in modesty and shivering. Mary watched as Nance undressed Micheál from his wrappings, then carefully leant out to take him. She gripped him fast to her ribs, his bare skin clammy against her own, and inched her way carefully down to the river.

How she wished she was back home. She thought of the girls she had seen that May morning, crawling naked through the briars.

God forgive me, she thought.

The river was deep cold, black with tannin. Its touch brought a peal of shock from her lips, and she looked up and saw both women staring at her. Nóra's fingers gripped the cloth of her apron. 'It won't take long,' Mary heard her say, as if to herself. 'It won't take long.'

Gasping in the shock of the bitter water, Mary could see the white of her skin mirrored on the surface. She held the child aloft, his legs dangling. 'What do I do?' She had to raise her voice over the rush of the current. It pushed against her hips, and she inched her toes into the mud of the riverbed to steady herself.

'Put him in the water three times,' Nance called. 'Put his head under. His whole body.'

Mary looked at the boy's face. His eyes canted in his head, sloping sideways as one arm fought the air.

He is full of fairy, she thought, and she lowered him into the river.

CHAPTER
SIXTEEN

Yellow iris

D awn broke as Nóra and Mary trudged their way back up the slope to the cabin after their trip to the river. Mary's skin under her clothes felt numb with cold, and she worried that Micheál, too, was freezing. The boy was quiet in her grip, his face scrunched into her neck, his breathing slow.

'He's frightful chilled,' Mary muttered.

Nóra looked back at her, panting as she took long strides up the path. 'Quickly now. We don't want anyone to be seeing us. Wondering what we're after doing away from home at this early hour.'

'He's not moving at all. He's caught the cold.'

'We'll be inside soon enough.' She waved Mary on, clearly frustrated at her slow pace. 'Quickly!'

Inside the cabin, Nóra grabbed the pail and went to milk the cow, leaving Mary to tend to the fire. The girl's stomach groaned as she fed twigs to the crackling flames. Three days of fasting, she thought. She already felt lightheaded.

Micheál lay on the settle bed, eyes slipping back and forth. Once the fire was high, Mary picked up the shawl she had draped over his body and held it to the hearth to warm the wool. Before she placed it over him, she peeked at his skin and saw that the boy's flesh was blue with cold. Without thinking, she picked up one of his hands and placed his icy fingers in her mouth to warm them.

He tasted of the river.

After the cow had been milked and the fire stoked to a rustling pile of embers, Nóra suggested to Mary that they return to their beds for a few hours' sleep. Mary, stomach rumbling and her eyes aching from the early morning, agreed. She folded her blanket over and tucked Micheál in with her shawl, where, finally warm, he surrendered to sleep. Mary lay down next to him and studied his face. She had never seen his features in such detail. It was usually dark when she lay beside him, and in Micheál's waking hours she was too busy dribbling water into his mouth, or feeding him, or scrubbing the caked mess from his skinny buttocks, or soothing his rash with tallow to stop and look at him carefully. But now, as the early-morning sunlight cut through the cracks in the door, she saw how his nose was lightly freckled, the crust in his nostrils flaking. His mouth had slipped open, and she could see that a lower tooth in the centre of his mouth was at a strange angle. Reaching gently, so as not to wake him, she placed her fingertip on its tiny, ridged edge. The tooth wobbled, and then, as she added more pressure, came away from his gum and fell onto the mattress.

Micheál stirred, eyelids creasing, but did not wake.

Mary picked up the tooth and held it up to the light. A pearl, she thought. A little pearl. She ran her finger over the rough hollow, briefly filled with wonderment that a fairy child could have something so ordinary, so like a human tooth.

Rising, Mary went to the door, pushed open the top half and – as she had done so many times with her own brothers and sisters – threw the first-fallen tooth over her right shoulder into the dirt of the yard.

That will help keep you safe, she thought, and she returned to the settle bed and fell into a deep and dreamless sleep.

'Mary, wake up. Wake up now.'

A rough hand was shaking her shoulder. Mary blearily opened her eyes and saw Nóra's face – pale, alarmed – above her.

'Mary!'

Suddenly afraid, she sat upright and looked for the boy. He lay sleeping beside her, his arms thrown above his head. She breathed out in relief. 'What time is it?'

'We've slept the day through. 'Tis well past noon.' Nóra was wearing her husband's greatcoat, its broad shoulders making her body seem small, fragile. Wisps of grey hair fell over her face. 'Mary, they've found a *piseóg*.'

'A *piseóg*?' She felt her stomach turn.

'I was outside passing my water, and I saw Peg coming over the way. She told me. She's after telling everyone on the mountain. There's a crowd going there to see it. 'Tis a nest of something. A charm. Something bad.'

Fear flapped in Mary's chest. 'Something bad?'

Nóra nodded, picking up the shawl from where it lay over the boy and throwing it at her. 'Up with you. I want you to go and see it and tell me what it is.'

Mary rubbed her eyes and began to wind the shawl about her head. 'Who set it?'

'They don't know. 'Tis what everyone wants to find out.'

'Where?'

'At the Lynches',' Nóra whispered. 'Kate and Seán Lynch.' She helped the girl to her feet. 'Go and find out what it is.'

*

Mary found her way to the Lynches' farm by following the crowd of people walking the fields. There was a sense of nervous excitement amongst them, of anxious gossip.

'He was at the scoreground when he saw it. Says he doesn't think 'tis the first set upon his land.'

'Musha, I heard him talking of others at the smith's.'

'Stones turned up on their edges, branches and plants tied to his gate.'

'Ah, but this is a right old dark *piseóg*. 'Tis a nest of straw and a bloody mess inside it. Rotting. None of your stones and plants. This is some new darkness. Meant to be found, too, by the looks of it.'

'Seán's saying 'twas left by Nance Roche.'

'The priest has been sent for. 'Tis that bad, that troubling.'

'Oh, I don't like any of it.'

They neared the smallholding, and Mary squeezed through the crowd to get a closer look at the *piseóg*. It lay on the ground behind the Lynches' whitewashed cabin, partly obscured by a dung pile. It was a small thing, a nest, but clearly made by a human hand. There was none of the twigging wrought by beak, but careful, deliberate weaving. In the nest's hollow was a dark mass of bloody matter in a state of decay. The smell of it seethed in Mary's nostrils.

The crowd stood around in horror, crossing themselves and whispering out of the corner of their mouths.

'There's no saying that's an accident.'

'Sure, there's malice in this. Terrible malice.'

'What do you think 'tis there? The rot in it?'

'Would it be a bit of meat, do you think?'

A male voice suddenly rang out amongst the murmuring. 'The priest is here! Father Healy is here!' There was a rush of movement as the people parted to let the priest through.

He has come in a hurry, thought Mary. His clothes were spattered with mud.

'Here 'tis, Father.' Crabbed hands pointed at the ground where the *piseóg* lay.

The priest stared at it for a moment, fingers pinching his nose. 'Who did this?'

There was silence.

'Who here has lost the run of his senses?' Father Healy glared at the crowd, his blue eyes sliding over excited, fearful faces.

'Father, there's none of us knows who set it.'

'Sure, we've just come to see it.'

'What will you do, Father?'

The priest's eyes watered at the stench. 'Bring me a spade.'

One of the labourers sent his son to fetch a tool, and as he waited the priest took out a small clear bottle of holy water, carefully drawing its cork. With an air of great ceremony, he poured a little on the *piseóg*.

'A drop more, would you, Father?' piped a voice. There were chuckles from the crowd.

Father Healy clenched his jaw but did as asked, and splashed the nest and the ground around it liberally. When the spade was brought, Father Healy snatched it from the boy and, with an expression of impatience, slid it under the *piseóg*, lifting it into the air. The crowd took several steps back as it teetered on the metal edge.

'Where is your nearest ditch, man?' he asked. Seán, face dark with outrage, pointed to a corner of his field. The priest immediately set off towards it, the crowd of people following behind. Mary walked with them, the blood hissing through her veins.

The ditch was wet-bottomed, filled with nettles. Father Healy carefully lowered the *piseóg* down on the drier part of the ditch wall, then wiped the spade on the grass.

'What now, Father?'

'Will you bless the spade, Father?'

'Should ye have not used a stick instead? Will the *piseóg* not poison the work of the spade?'

Father Healy rubbed his eyes, then took out his holy water and flicked a palmful on the blade, murmuring a prayer under his breath.

'Burn it, Father.'

'The spade?' The priest looked momentarily confused.

'The *piseóg*. Will ye not burn the *piseóg*?' A man stepped forward, cheerfully offering his smoking pipe.

Father Healy, suddenly understanding, shook his head. 'The ground is too wet. Seán, will you fetch some dry fuel? Hay, furze. Whatever will burn. And a light.'

For some time there was a buzz of excited activity as the crowd followed Seán back to his cabin, helping themselves to his stores of kindling, furze and animal feed. Seán himself said nothing, although he seemed to smoulder with anger. Mary kept her distance from him, although at one point he caught her eye and held it, giving her a look of such disgust and hostility that she quickly averted her gaze and turned her attention to gathering sticks. Kate, she noticed, stood apart from the crowd, her shawl wrapped closely about her face. She seemed dazed, one eye purpled. At the sight of Mary she flinched, then took three careful steps backwards, spitting on the ground and crossing herself.

They burnt the *piseóg* in the cold, blue arm of twilight, under a pile of wood, turf, dried furze and straw. The fire blazed in the buckled air, the flames carrying a heart of violet. A sign of the perishing wickedness of the thing, Mary thought. It gave her a strange feeling, watching the bloody nest burn, while the priest climbed back on his donkey and the people remained, standing sentry around the fire.

Her mind crawled with uneasy thoughts. Who had plaited that nest of straw? What kind of devilment was abroad?

The smell of rot stayed with her long after the fire had died and the people walked back to their cabins, numb with the evening's chill. For all the priest's holy water she could still smell the moulding bloodiness of the *piseóg* on her hair long after she returned to Nóra's cabin.

⤴

Men gathered outside Nance Roche's hut that night, full of liquor, brandishing ashplants.

Nance heard them arrive. Their footsteps were loud as they crashed through the undergrowth, slashing at the bracken. Peering out of a gap in her wicker door, she saw Seán Lynch swaying at the head of the pack, stopping to unbutton his trousers. A few men cheered as he started to piss, aiming the dull splatter towards her hut.

There was the sound of something smashing. One of the men had thrown a *poitín* jug at the trunk of the oak tree.

'You're a black bitch!' Seán suddenly spat, a thick line of spittle flinging out of his mouth. The men grew silent at the fury in his voice. Through the chink in the door Nance could see five of them standing not ten yards away, their faces shining with sweat and drink.

Seán Lynch lurched to one side, waving his stick unsteadily in the air. 'You're a black bitch, Nance Roche, and may the Devil take you with him!'

There was silence. Nance held her breath. Her heart thudded like a man buried alive.

The men stood there for a long while, each of them staring at her hut. She knew it was dark, knew they could not make out the glisten of her eye in the gap of the woven door, but it seemed that each man looked directly at her. Five faces full of vim and cursing. Five walls of anger.

After what seemed like an hour's siege, the men finally turned and walked unsteadily back to the lane, talking amongst themselves.

When they had disappeared into the darkness and Nance could no longer hear anything but the sound of the wind moving through the woods and the light rush of the river, she sank back down against the wall, breathing hard, terrified. Her body trembled uncontrollably.

Men had broken into her cabin two days after she'd arrived home to find Maggie and the fairy woman gone. She found the room overturned, the delph smashed on the floor, the ashes of the fire kicked over as though someone had searched for something buried in the powder of the dead hearth.

It was dark when the men returned, boots knocking against the doorframe, fists on the whitewash.

'Where is she?'

Nance, scrambling to her feet, trying to open the back door to escape, finding it jammed against the clay.

'None of that, *cailín*. Where is she?'

'Who?'

'Where's the mad one? Your woman who sets the curses?'

'The cures?'

One of the men had spat, had glared at her for that. 'Mad Maggie of Mangerton.'

'She has no hand in *piseógs*.'

He had laughed. 'No hand in it, does she?'

Nance thought of what Maggie had taught her in the days before. Ways to gather the luck due to others and harvest it for yourself. Ways to strike a man barren. The things you might do with a dead man's hand should there be need for it.

'She's not here.'

'Not hiding out in yonder ditch?'

Nance shook her head. 'She's gone.' Tears then at the fear of the men standing in her dead father's cabin, the disappearance of the only kin she had left in the world.

The men had pointed their fingers in her face. 'If your mad whore of an aunt comes back, you tell her she'll get what's coming to her. Tell I know 'twas her that blasted my cows. Tell her I'll slit her throat same way I had to slit theirs.'

Now, slumped in her tiny *bothán*, Nance's hands were shaking just as they had shaken all night after the men had finally left her alone.

Virgin Mother save me, Nance thought. I am an ash tree in the face of a storm. Despite the woods, I alone court the lightning.

When Nóra woke the second morning, her stomach prickling in anticipation, Mary was already dressed and waiting by the lit fire with the changeling on her lap, hands firmly crossed over his stomach. The boy's head twitched on her shoulder. He was pining like a dog.

'Look at you, up and ready. You could have woken me. We could be halfway there.'

Mary gave Nóra an imploring look.

'What's the matter with you, then?'

'I don't want to go.'

'And why is that?' Nóra asked irritably. Her guts swooped in a thrill of excitement. She wanted to be by the river already. She wanted her turn at sinking the fairy child in the water. Wanted to feel its reluctance to leave.

'I'm scared,' said Mary.

'Scared of what? What fear is there in bathing in the river? You took your turn with it yesterday morning. You can watch this time.'

''Tis too cold for him. You saw how he was shivering and shaking, and how he turned blue with it. I'm afraid for him. And this morning he was yawping for his milk, missus. He's hungry!'

'So am I. So are you.'

'But with nothing in his belly I'm scared he won't stand the cold and he'll catch his death.'

'Mary, that's no child sitting on you there. And there's no saving Micheál unless we do as Nance says and put it in the water.'

The girl seemed on the brink of tears. 'I have an ill feeling about it,' she stammered.

Nóra took a sip of water from the dipper and splashed a little on her face. 'Enough, Mary.'

'I do. I have an ill feeling. I think of what the priest would say if he knew.'

'The priest had his chance to help me.'

'But missus, do you not think there's sin in it? I told you about the *piseóg* yesterday. This feels like we're having a hand in that same bad business. Getting up before dawn and baring ourselves in wild places. I don't want to be sinning. I don't want to be hurting the child.'

'You're only afraid because you saw the *piseóg* yesterday and it has turned your head.'

'They're saying 'twas Nance that set it!'

'That's a lie.'

'They're saying she wishes ill on the valley because Father Healy preached against her at Mass.'

'Gossip and hen talk!'

'But perhaps we can't be trusting her, missus. Perhaps she –'

'Mary!' Nóra rubbed her face with her apron and tied it around her waist. 'Would you have my daughter's son returned to me?'

The girl was silent. She pulled the boy closer to her.

'There is no sin in this,' Nóra said. 'There is no sin in returning to the Good People what was always theirs.'

Mary stared at the clay beneath Nóra's feet. 'Can I bring the blanket to warm him afterwards?'

''Tis yours to carry if you do.'

They walked to Nance's cabin under a clear black sky, the faint suggestion of pink to the east. Nóra noticed that Mary swayed on her feet as she carried the wrapped changeling. She must be hungry, she thought. The previous day's fasting had left Nóra feeling euphoric. Walking in the darkness, she felt as though her senses were sharper than usual. The cold air slipped into her lungs and left her nostrils ringing with the usual scents of earth, mud and smoke, but also the nearing damp of the river and the musty undergrowth of the forest. She felt thrillingly awake.

Nance was sitting up by her fire when they arrived. She started in surprise when they opened the door, and Nóra was dispirited to see that the old woman seemed distracted. Large bags hung under her eyes and her white hair, usually carefully knotted at the neck, was loose and tangled over her shoulders.

'Nance?'

'Is it time?' she asked, and when neither answered, she slowly rose to her feet. 'Let's to the boundaries, then.'

The silence, once they entered the woods, was oppressive. Nóra could hear nothing but the soft padding and rustle of their footsteps and the strain of Mary's breath as she wearied under the changeling's weight. The shadows under the trees seemed horribly still.

A sudden, shrill screeching carried along the valley, and all three women jumped at the sound.

A duck, thought Nóra. Just a fox killing a duck. But it left a prickling at the back of her neck.

'Did you hear the dreadful business at the Lynches'? The *piseóg*?' she whispered, trying to make her voice as steady as possible.

In the darkness Nance was silent.

'A *piseóg*,' Nóra repeated. 'The priest was sent for. He sprinkled the holy water upon it, and 'twas burnt, after. So said Mary.'

Mary's voice rang out in front of her. ''Twas a nest and some blood.'

'Sure, the girl told me it smelt like the Devil. 'Twas the way Seán found it. He smelt it out.'

'Trouble's coming,' Nance muttered. She seemed preoccupied. It wasn't until they had reached the same place in the river that she spoke again.

'Nóra, 'tis your turn.'

Nóra did not know whether the cramping in her guts was from excitement or fear. 'What have I to do, Nance?'

'The rite is the same as before. Do as the girl. Undress and take the wee fairy into the water with you. Be sure to place him all the way under three times. Every hair on his head under the surface. Let all parts of him under the power of the boundary. Let you don't slip. That river looks mighty high this morning.'

Nóra nodded, her mouth dry. She took off her clothes with shaking fingers.

'Perhaps I should do it again,' Mary said. She had crouched down on a tree root and was holding the boy close to her chest. He groaned at the sound of the water, his head thumping against her shoulder.

Nóra held out her arms for him. 'Enough of that, you know 'tis my turn. 'Tis how it must be. Give it to me, Mary.'

The maid hesitated. 'Will you be careful with him?'

'There's no harm intended,' Nance reassured her. 'We're only after sending the fairy child back to his own kind.'

'He was so cold yesterday. 'Tis terrible cold for him. And him being so little, so thin.'

'Give him to Nóra, Mary.'

'Quickly!' Nóra stepped over and took the child from Mary's arms. Letting the blanket drop from his shoulders she lay him on the ground and pulled the dress over his head.

'You've set him on a briar,' Mary protested. Nóra pretended she hadn't heard. She picked him up again and the boy suddenly grew angry, squawking, his fists swinging. Nóra felt his head smack against her collarbone.

'Into the river with you now, Nóra. That's it. Hold that branch there as Mary did yesterday. Don't slip now.'

The changeling, when Nóra first held him under the fast-flowing water, opened his mouth in surprise. But it was no more than a baptism, a rush of river into the mouth, and Nóra lifted him into the air before plunging him down again.

'In the name of God, are you or are you not Micheál Kelliher, son of my daughter?'

She had the sense that the changeling fixed her eye as the water flooded over his face for the third time, bubbles streaming from his mouth. She lifted him, dripping, and the sun broke across the surface. She had not noticed it grow light. Nóra clutched the fairy child against her bare chest and held him there until he burbled the river down her breasts and his lungs grew less ragged. She stood, shivering in the dappled water, and felt that it was true, in one day's time she would have her daughter's son restored to her, full-limbed and speaking. Standing in the river, she felt the promise of it in the current's quiet insistence and in the skylarks above, suddenly praising the sky with flight.

There was a dark knot of women at the well later that morning, cloaks drawn over their heads despite the clear March weather. Their voices were hot with conspiracy.

Mary glanced at them from where she stooped to let down her bucket and saw several pairs of eyes flick her way, some of them looking boldly. All at once the huddle of women moved towards her. Mary jerked upright, lifting her chin and staggering from sudden dizziness.

'You're a friend to Nance Roche, are you not, Mary Clifford?' It was Éilís O'Hare who spoke, a slant of accusation in her voice.

'We were talking here amongst ourselves, thinking on who might have set that *piseóg* on Seán's land.'

'Well, it wasn't me that did it, if that's what you're thinking.'

Éilís gave a high laugh. 'Isn't she a proud girl, thinking we were accusing her. Piss on nettles this morning, did you?'

The women laughed. Mary felt her spine run cold.

'Whoever did it was up and about while 'twas dark. Not even the dog was barking, so says Seán.'

'Might not have been so recent as that,' said another woman. 'Whoever set the *piseóg* might have put it down fresh, let it rot in time.'

'Kate did say she's been seeing Nance stealing about the fields in the blue of the morning when no one was about.'

'Sure, but my man is an early riser and he says he would swear on his mother's grave he saw an old woman accompanied by the Good People walking the lane in the dark. Near the Piper's Grave, out where 'tis wild. And his eyes are keen.'

'Keen enough to be seeing fairies now, is he?'

'Faith, many men see things through the bottom of a *poitín* bottle.'

There was laughter.

'It wasn't drink! He hasn't tasted a drop in his life.'

'Is he after thinking 'twas Nance and her spirits?'

'Ah well, they say she does be speaking with Them.'

'Begod, 'tis true. She *conspires* with Them. She's been asking them for the knowledge to steal butter and dry hens and burn up black-smith's wives.'

'Terrible business.'

'I wonder what the blood was,' said one woman, eyes flicking nervously to Mary.

The women glanced at each other.

'Could be from an animal,' suggested one. 'Could be a hare, killed and bled.'

Mary looked at the ground. She thought she was going to be sick.

Éilís spoke again. 'If you see Nance, Mary, best tell her to watch who she's after setting curses on. There's none here who will be tolerating badness like that. Setting the fire against Áine. Bloodiness on Seán's farm.'

'Tell her to take to the road.'

'She has the cure,' Mary said feebly.

'Sure, I went to her for the cure in days past, didn't I?' Éilís smirked. 'And didn't she near poke my eye out with a gander beak. She's soft in the mind.'

'Is it soft in the mind or hard in the heart, Éilís?'

Mary saw that Hanna had wandered over, her forehead creased. 'You'd best get your story straight.'

'Only a fool would go to a herb hag such as she.'

'And are you still a fool, Éilís? Or did you leave that off when you married that great man of yours?'

Éilís scowled, but walked away, leaving Mary shaking.

Hanna reached over and placed a hand on her shoulder. 'Don't you mind her,' she said. 'You're after taking that Leahy boy to Nance, are you not?'

Mary nodded.

'You tell Nance Old Hanna knows that *piseóg* was none of her making.' She dropped her voice. 'Any woman could tell you what was in that nest. Sure, there's plenty blood amongst women, and God himself knows that business is beyond Nance these days. My own self too! No, 'twas a hand closer to home, so I think.'

Mary stared at her, horror-filled.

'Aye,' Hanna said, nodding to where Kate Lynch was drawing her water. 'Kicks her about the house. You mark my words, young Mary Clifford. She'll kill him one day. If anyone is soft in the mind, 'tis her. His fists have knocked it so.'

Nance stood in the dark, smoking coltsfoot and watching the lane. For three days she had eaten nothing and in her hunger she felt altered, alert. The flare of her pipe was painful bright, her ears pricked to every rustle, every suggestion of movement in the dark. Hunger had hollowed her until she felt like a *bodhrán*. Tight-skinned, every impression on her body amplified. She thrummed.

Nance heard it then. Cutting through on the still near-dawn, the fox cry of the changeling. She shuddered, sucked on her pipe. Several long minutes passed until Nóra and Mary reached her, following the tiny light of the burning leaf to where she stood in the doorway of her cabin. The widow was walking strangely, her hands curled into fists, her legs wooden. As she got closer Nance saw that the woman's jaw was chattering, although there was no frost on the ground. She seemed agitated.

'God's blessings on you both.'

'Faith but 'tis dark this morning.' Nóra's voice was high, saddled with expectation.

''Tis the last morning. 'Tis always darkest on the last morning.'

'Were it not for that slip of a moon, we'd be lost.'

'But you're here. And Mary, were you afraid to lose the way?'

The girl said nothing, only the white of her apron showing in the gloom. Nance reached for her shoulder and felt her flinch.

'There now. There's nothing to be afraid of. I'll be protecting you and 'twill be light soon.'

Mary sniffed, and the changeling cried out again, spooking them all.

Nance held her arms out. 'He knows we will return him to where he came from. Give him to me, Mary. I'll carry him down to the water.'

'He's too heavy.'

'I'm strong.'

'I want to take him. Let me hold him.'

Nance saw Nóra cuff the girl on the shoulder. 'Give it to Nance.' The widow turned and addressed her. 'You'd best be having words with the girl. She's been whimpering and carrying on all the night through.'

'Mary? Let me take the fairy.'

'He knows,' the girl whispered, as she reluctantly handed the boy over.

'What?'

'He knows where we're going,' she said, her voice plaintive. 'As soon as he saw we were on our way to your cabin he started up with the screaming.'

'Sure, the wee changeling doesn't want to be going back under hill! He has had you to care for him. But 'tis time to be changing him back for the widow's grandson.'

'What will happen to him?'

'He'll return to his own kind.'

'And it won't hurt him?'

'Musha, not at all,' Nance replied, but an image of Maggie crossed her mind. The long scar.

The journey to the river seemed impossibly long with the changeling tight against her chest. The child, alarmed by Nance's strange hands, cried into the wrinkled skin of her throat as they walked, the dew-strung grass slapping against their skirts. She felt his piss seep through his linen, a spreading warmth against her hand.

The widow whispered excitedly to Nance as they walked.

'I had a dream last night. 'Twas no ordinary dream. Do you remember Peter O'Connor talking of lights at the Piper's Grave the night Martin died? I dreamt I was out walking the fields in the near dawn – 'twas a kind of blue as this – and as I neared the fairy place, I saw three lights under the whitethorn. At first I was afraid to see them, but my legs would not stop their walking, and sure, as they brought me closer, I saw the thorn in bloom and the petals were on the wind, and in the raining and fluttering of all that blossom, I saw that the lights were no lights at all, but Johanna and Martin and Micheál.' Her voice caught on their names. 'The three of them, Nance, standing under the tree. Waiting for me. And there was music playing of a kind you've never heard before.'

'Fairy music?'

'Like something the angels might play. Singing, too. And I could see the Good People dancing behind them. Such dancing.' There was fervency in the widow's voice. 'What do you think it means, Nance? Sure, 'tis a good omen. Do you not think 'tis a good omen?'

'We will find out soon, Nóra Leahy. So, we will find out.'

The valley grew lighter until it became clear enough to see the river, darkly brown and fringed with the green unfurl of bracken, tipping over the stones in high current. Nance, breathing hard, handed Micheál to Mary and undressed, pulling her many layers of felt and wool over her head and folding them on the ground.

Her breasts were moon-pale in the early light; the cold air tightened her skin.

''Tis the last time then,' Nance said. She looked at Nóra and saw the widow standing stiffly upright, her arms tightly folded around her chest, eyes wide. Her whole body was trembling.

'Mary, wait until I am in the river, then pass the boy to me.'

Mary stared at her, face white, saying nothing. She was on the brink of tears.

The cold of the river ripped the breath from her lungs. Nance waded in slowly, wheezing, stumbling as the mud of the bank gave way under her weight, gasping as the waterline rushed over the slack skin of her thighs and belly. God Almighty, it was fierce cold. The current was strong. Her hips ached. She felt the river against her legs, the way it stirred the small stones dislodged by her feet and turned them silently over.

'Pass him to me now, then, Mary.' Her teeth chattered and Nance wondered what would happen if she fell in the water. She felt old. Suddenly fragile.

The girl didn't move. She crouched down on the bank and curled the boy further into her chest.

Nóra took a step towards her. 'Mary, would you hand it to Nance!'

The girl pushed her face against the top of the boy's head, averting her eyes. He let out a low groan.

'Give him to me.'

''Tis a sin to be doing this to him,' she whispered.

Nóra reached for the boy, who shrieked louder, but Mary held on tightly, her arms locked about his chest. She began to cry. Furious, Nóra plucked at her fingers, prying them from the child's ribcage. 'You're a bold girl to be doing this. Shame on you.' She slapped Mary across the face and the girl cried out, releasing him. Nóra slung the wailing boy over her shoulder, placed a hand over his screams, and stepped directly into the water fully clothed. She waded towards Nance, bracing herself against the press of the river, and offered her the crying child.

'Please!' Mary shouted from the bank. 'Please! 'Tis a sin! 'Tis a sin to be doing this to him!'

Nance, shaking uncontrollably from the cold water, took the changeling and made the sign of the cross over his chest, the skin clinging to the bone. She looked at Nóra standing in the river, her back to Mary. The widow nodded and Nance plunged the screaming child under the water.

Mary collapsed onto the edge of the mossy bank, tears running down her face. ''Tis too cold for him!' she cried. Her hands scrabbled at the dirt and she began to choke on her tears. ''Tis a sin!'

'Whist, Mary,' Nóra muttered, nodding to Nance as she hauled him up.

'In the name of God, if you are a fairy, away with you!'

'Please, Nóra! Please don't be doing this to him!'

Nance thrust him into the river again, then lifted him clear of its surface, copper hair slick on his forehead, water gurgling from his mouth and eyes. Then finally, before he took a breath to cry again, she tightened her hands about his ribcage and pushed him into the rushing current for the third time. She glanced at Nóra and knew the woman could see the white thrashing of him under the foaming skin of the river, the flash of his hair like the quickening of a fish. Nóra met her eyes and nodded again and placed her hands on Micheál's chest as Mary wept. Nance locked her arms and looked to the willow, long-fingered with catkins, and the slip of watercress nuzzling the bank. She felt her hands grow painful numb in the racing water, and felt the nick of the boy's nails on her skin as he flailed, and she looked to the budding iris, their leaves clasped around their yellow flowers like hands folded in prayer, felt the wind in her hair as it suddenly embraced the trees and sent leaves and seed spinning onto the water's surface, now broken by the child as he raised his hand and clasped at the air above him. Nance closed her eyes and felt his struggles subside and she knew then, without looking at the fight gone out of him, at the eyes glassy, that the river had taken the fairy as one of its own; that the river had taken its due.

PART THREE

When the Hag is in Danger, She Must Run
Annair is cruadh dón chailligh caithfidh sí rith

1826

CHAPTER
SEVENTEEN

Bramble

Mary ran as though the Devil was after her. Splashing through the puddles lying glossy in the fields, over the lane and up the slope, with the flint of the hill studding her feet, pain striking through her heels and dawn light flooding the valley. She ran, her eyes blurred with tears, and her lungs hot and tight, cramps tearing through her side. She ran. She ran with terror pulling at her blood.

It wasn't until Mary saw the shape of Peg's cabin on the mountainside that she knew where she should go. Her instinct had been only to flee, to leave the horror at the river and the sight of Micheál's pale head lolling against the sag of Nance's body.

They had killed him.

Oh God in Heaven, they had murdered him and she had seen it, had let it happen.

The stillness of that little body as he was lifted from the water, ribs pressing against the skin of his torso, the drops slipping from his feet, falling back into the river. The triumphant, happy crying of Nóra, her skirt puffed about her, air trapped under the weave, as she had turned and, exalted, pointed to a blooming flagger. The head hanging at an angle, throat exposed to the sky above. And the birds: the birds suddenly filling the trees so that Mary's shrieking was drowned out by their dawn chorus. All the birds, screaming at the light.

Mary ran until, tripping on a hidden stone, she fell, her hands immediately rising bloody from the scrape along the ground. She sat in the flint and soil and howled, bog-soaked, terrified.

It took an hour before Peg O'Shea could calm Mary and understand what it was she was saying.

The sound of the girl's screaming had woken the house, and her son-in-law had run out to see what had happened. He had returned, carrying Nóra's maid in his arms. She was in muddy hysterics, unable to talk, her breathing fast and rapid and her body shaking so hard that Peg had made her daughter swaddle the girl in a blanket and hold her fast.

'Mary, what has happened to you? Tell us what has happened.'

The girl wailed, her nose streaming, mouth open.

'Dear one, you're safe now. You're with friends. Tell us, Mary, what has happened to you?'

'I want to go home.' Her voice was notched with fear. 'I want to go home.'

'And so you will. But tell us first, Mary. Please, it vexes us to see you so.'

'They will hang me.'

Peg's family glanced at each other.

'Hang you?' asked Peg.

'She done him in,' the maid sobbed. 'He's dead.'

'Who?'

'Micheál!'

'Breathe easy, Mary. There you are, take a breath and talk to me now. Are you saying Micheál is dead?'

The girl fought her arms out of the blanket and grabbed at her hair, pulling it over her face. She rocked back and forth on the floor of Peg's cabin. 'Mam,' she whispered. 'I want Mam.'

'What did you see, Mary?'

'I want to go home,' the girl wept. 'I don't want to die. They'll hang me for it. They'll hang me for it.'

'Don't be thinking of hanging. Shhh. Tell me, Mary, what did you see? What has happened?'

Mary took a shuddering breath. ''Twas Nance,' she stammered. 'She drowned him and now he's dead.'

Peg found Nóra sitting alone by her hearth, gazing into the dead ashes. The widow was sitting very still, the greatcoat bulging around her, hands folded around a *poitín* bottle in her lap.

'Nóra? 'Tis Peg come to see you.'

The widow turned, her face blank. Peg saw that she had been crying: her eyes were red-rimmed and her nose wet.

'He's not here . . .' She gave a little shake, then quickly uncorked the bottle and drank, spluttering, wiping her mouth.

'Nóra. In God's name, what has happened?'

'I've looked for him, but . . .' She squeezed her eyes shut and shuddered. 'I came straight back, so I did. I ran here, Peg. I ran. I thought he might be frightened to be here alone.'

'Are you talking about the boy, Nóra?'

'He's not here,' she said in disbelief. 'I came back because I thought . . .'

Peg eased herself down onto a stool. 'You're soaked through. Your clothes are wet and dirtied.'

Nóra looked down, as if surprised to see her damp skirts covered in leaf litter and soil. Bramble thorns clung to her apron. 'I was in the river.'

'What were you doing in the river?'

'And then I came here. To see if Johanna's –'

'Nóra. Mary says that the change-child is dead. She's beside herself and saying that he was drowned in the river. Is that true?'

Nóra's expression darkened. 'Have you seen him?' She clutched at Peg's shoulders, bringing her face close. 'Mary. What did she say?'

'Nóra, you're frightening me.'

The widow's breath was sour with whiskey. 'Tell me what she said. Tell me what she said!'

Peg gently pushed Nóra away from her. 'Mary Clifford tells me that Micheál is dead. She is saying he is drowned.'

Nóra was silent, jaw clenched. 'No, Peg. Not Micheál.'

'She's saying she saw Nance drown the boy. Nóra, is that what happened? Did Nance drown the wee stricken child?'

''Twas fairy,' Nóra bleated.

'And did Nance drown the fairy?'

'Mary ran. We turned and saw her running away.'

'We? 'Twas you and Nance?'

'I thought Micheál would be here,' Nóra said. 'I thought he would be returned to me.'

Peg took a deep breath. 'Nóra. Is the wee cretin drowned?'

There was a knock and both women jumped. Father Healy stood in the open doorway, Peg's son-in-law standing behind him. The priest's face was grave, pouched with concern.

'Nóra Leahy? What have you done?'

Nóra shook her head, unable to speak.

'Your servant maid has just told me she witnessed the drowning of your grandson this morning.'

'No.'

'Nóra, is this the same lad you came to tell me about? The cripple boy? Have you gone and drowned him?'

'He was fairy.'

The priest stood over her, aghast. 'God forgive you. Where's the boy? What have you done with him?'

'He is not here.'

'Nóra, have you gone and murdered that child? Tell me the truth now, or . . . I tell you, God will condemn you for what you have done.'

Nóra pressed her lips together and remained silent.

The priest had turned white. 'Good God! Is she out of her mind?'

'She's had a shock,' Peg muttered. 'She's not herself.'

Father Healy put a hand over his mouth. 'You listen to me now. I've sent a man to the barracks. He is coming back with policemen. Do you understand me? Widow Leahy, listen to me. There are men coming to take an information from you. A sworn information. Do you hear me? Widow Leahy?' His eyes dropped to the *poitín* in her lap. 'Don't be telling me she's drunk. I'd not be taking any more of that, now.' He nodded to Peg, who eased the bottle out of Nóra's fingers.

'I . . .'

The priest bent down to Nóra. 'What's that? What are you saying?'

'I . . . I don't want to be leaving this place.'

'They'll be sending a constable to speak with you. And it might be that they will take you with them.'

'I won't be going. I can't be going.'

'Nóra, 'twill only be for a small while,' Peg cajoled. 'I'll look after your cow. Your hens.'

Nóra shook her head. 'No, I'll need to be staying. It might be that Micheál will be coming. If he's not come today, perhaps he'll be returned tomorrow. I'll need to be waiting for him.'

Father Healy's voice rose in exasperation. 'If your servant maid is saying he is dead, he'll not be coming back. Do you know where your grandson is? His body?'

'Micheál is with the Good People, but now he will be coming back. Now he will be returned to me. Nance said 'twill be so.'

The priest said nothing. He walked towards the open door, then paused and looked back at Nóra with a mixture of disgust and pity. 'If I were you, Nóra Leahy, I'd be praying.' He gestured to Peg. 'Make sure she doesn't leave this place until the constable arrives.'

By the time Nance had returned to her cabin, she was shivering helplessly with cold. The river water had flooded her to the bone and she ached with it. The hunger she had felt so keenly over the past days had faded to nausea, and now that it was done, she wanted nothing more than sleep. Crawling to her bed of heather, Nance covered herself with her blanket and shut her eyes.

She dreamt then. She dreamt she was young and walking down the high street of Killarney, the mud of the road hardened by the heat of an early summer.

Suddenly, she was surrounded. Young women. Faces browned from their work outside. Baskets of fish on their backs, oozing scales. They called her name, mouths wide on the shape of it.

'Nance!'

'Nance, stop walking! We've a mind to talk to you.'

Her feet stopped. The ground warm on her soles.

The women crowded her.

'We thought we saw you May Eve. Up in the fields.'

'Aye, you were so. Walking alone, and in disguise.'

'I didn't do a thing like it.'

'But you were seen, Nance Roche.'

'Aye.'

'Aye, you were seen scrabbling through a briar.'

'I never.'

'But you were seen so. And the person who said he seen you swore it God's own truth.'

'Who says it?'

'He said you undressed and crawled through the bramble, and after he heard you saying some queer things too.'

'Tell me who said these lies.'

'I don't dare, Nance. You might curse him.'

'I never did such a thing.'

''Tis an awful sin, sure, Nance.'

'Is it true you've been away with the Good People?'

''Tis not. Never in my life.'

'We all know your mam's been swept.'

'Aye, and your aunt is Mad Maggie. She's in with Them. She's a grand one for curse work now.'

'They're all mad. Her mam too. 'Tis madness in the blood.'

'Aye, that's why your da drowned himself.'

''Twas an accident.'

'You're a liar, Nance. The madness turned him to it.'

'Or were it the fairies?'

'You'll be on the road soon. That's what happens to those who lay curses. Who do be in it.'

'Sure, there won't be any living for you in the cabin with your da gone.'

Anger swept through her until she felt that surely she was on fire. The women stood around her, and yet there she was, standing in the street, burning.

'You're mighty cruel,' she whispered.

And when they laughed, Nance dreamt she reached out and

touched each of them on the heart with her finger, burning like a wick. 'I curse you,' she said, and they screamed. 'May the grass grow high at your door, may you die without a priest in a town with no clergy, and may the crows have your carcass! *Imeacht gan teacht ort!* May you leave and never return!'

And they screamed. They screamed and they screamed, until the noise woke her and she sat up, panting.

Her cabin was gloomy with the low light of an overcast afternoon. She could hear footsteps and low conversation outside. There was the smell of crushed grass.

'Tis the Good People, Nance thought. They are coming to take me away.

For one long moment she could do nothing but stare at the smoking hearth and the streaks of soot on the whitewash, the rushes on the floor.

They are coming for me, she thought. As They came for Mam. As They came for Maggie.

'Nance Roche. Open the door.'

'Are you of the living or the dead?'

'Open the door.'

There was no time left to protect herself. No time to guard her life and soul with herbs or charms. Only the dead embers of her fire.

When the constable and his men shouldered in the wicker door, they found Nance on her hands and knees, stuffing her pockets with soot.

The arrival of two policemen from the Killarney barracks stirred the valley into speculation. People gathered on the road and watched the men on horseback as they rode to the small chapel, and then, with the priest in their company, along the slope, past the blacksmith's, past the well and its huddle of gaping women, to the foot of the hill beneath the cabins of Leahy and O'Shea. The crowd followed behind, staring as the police handed their reins to the priest and made their way up the pass on foot. One went into the O'Sheas' cabin, the other into Nóra Leahy's.

When they emerged several minutes later, holding the bewildered widow and her sobbing maid between them, an excited whispering broke out. They watched the men lead the women away up the road, back towards the chapel, before rushing up the hill to speak with the O'Sheas and learn of what had happened. Had the maid been caught stealing? Had the widow some hand in the death of her husband? When they spotted the police returning for Nance, they wondered whether all three had been in league with the fairies, blinking the valley and thinning the butter in the churns, killing animals for devilment. Setting *piseógs* against the priest.

It did not take long. By sunfall the valley was humming. An accusation had been brought against Nóra Leahy, Mary Clifford and Nance Roche. The fairy cretin Nóra had hidden from sight had been drowned in the river, and they were calling it murder.

CHAPTER
EIGHTEEN

Whitethorn

The police inspector was sweating, his neck pink against the dark green tunic of his uniform.

''Tis important you tell the truth to me now. Did you employ this woman –' he glanced down at a piece of paper in front of him '– *Anne Roche*, to kill your grandson?'

'Nance,' Nóra murmured.

The policeman looked down at the paper again. 'I have Anne.'

'She goes as Nance. Nance Roche.'

He looked up at her from under bushed eyebrows. His nostrils flared. ''Tis a simple question. Did you pay this woman money to have her kill your grandson, Micheál Kelliher?'

Nóra stared at the man's Adam's apple, bobbing above his tight collar. She brought a trembling hand to her own throat. 'I didn't pay her a thing.'

'Was it a favour then? Did you ask her to kill Micheál?'

Nóra shook her head. 'I did not. 'Twas nothing like that. She was going to cure it. To banish the fairy.'

The constable raised an eyebrow. 'The fairy?'

Nóra looked around the barracks room. It smelt of sweat and boot polish and bacon fat. Her stomach groaned. They had given her only one bowl of watery porridge each day since they'd brought her here from the valley. Four nights of hard sleeping on a damp straw mattress, locked in a room of stone. Four bowls of gruel delivered in silence. None of the men who brought her the food had answered her questions. No one would tell her if a small boy had been found in the valley. He would be looking for her, she'd told the officers who handed her the bowls. He has red hair. He is four years old.

'I need an answer from you, Mrs Leahy. Was that *fairy* you said?'

Nóra watched a fly drop from the chimney. It hovered over the dead grate, then smacked itself against the small, dirty window.

'Mrs Leahy?'

Nóra jumped.

'Your servant maid, Mary Clifford, is saying that this Anne Roche wanted to put your grandson in the river, on account of his being a cretin. Not her words. She called him "rickety".' He leant closer, his voice lowered. 'Sure, no easy thing to have a child like that in the home. Was it a kind of mercy you were after, Mrs Leahy?'

When Nóra didn't respond, he sat back and rolled a cigarette, licking the paper and eyeing her. 'I have a dog, you know. Every year that bitch has a litter. Eight pups, every year. I sell what I can, but sometimes, you know, Mrs Leahy, there's a runt.' He pushed back his chair with a squeak and fished in his pocket for some matches. 'Nobody wants a runt.'

Nóra watched as he lit the smoke, waved the match in the air until it expired.

He pointed the cigarette at her. 'So what do I do every year with the runts I can't sell? Do you know, Mrs Leahy?'

'I don't.'

He took a drag and blew the smoke into the air above him, his eyes still fixed on Nóra. 'I drown them. I take them down to the river, and I drown the wee things before they know any different. But Mrs Leahy . . .' He took another puff on his smoke, the dry paper catching on his lip. 'Mrs Leahy, a pup is no child.' He shook his head, his eyes never leaving hers. 'I don't care if that boy was no more than a runt to you. If you drowned him intentional you'll hang for it, so you will.'

Nóra closed her eyes and saw again the wan flicker of the changeling under the tan of river water. The dappled sprawl of first light on the bank. The branches filled with the witness of birds.

''Twas no boy.'

'How old was the child, Mrs Leahy?'

'It . . . He was four years old.'

'"It" you say again.' He wrote something down on the paper. 'And for how long was he in your care?'

'Ever since my daughter passed, God rest her soul.'

Nóra wished she could understand what the policeman was writing down. She wondered how a pattern of such slender markings could come from a hand so rough-fingered and calloused.

'And how long was that, Mrs Leahy?'

Nóra paused, eyelids fluttering. 'Since last harvest. August last.'

'Can you describe the state of Micheál?'

'The state?'

'His health, Mrs Leahy.'

'Can I please have some water?'

'Just answer the question.'

'It . . . He couldn't walk. Couldn't talk. Astray . . .'

'Pardon? You'll need to speak up.'

'Astray in his mind.'

The constable gave her a hard look, then slowly ground out his cigarette. He picked up the piece of paper. 'Mary Clifford has given us a sworn information. She –'

'Where is Mary? Where's Nance?'

The constable ran a hand around his collar, tugging at the starched cloth. 'For the present, the same charges have been brought against the three of you, Mrs Leahy. Arrested for wilful murder. It has been found that . . .' He hesitated and picked up another document from the table, examining the cursive. 'You have all been charged on the verdict of the coroner. "We find that the deceased, Michael Kelliher, came by his death in consequence of drowning in the river Flesk, on Monday, the sixth of March, 1826, by Anne Roche, and that Honora Leahy, the child's grandmother, and Mary Clifford were accessory to the same."'

Nóra sat up in confusion, aware of the sudden weighted knocking of her heart. 'Micheál? Did they find him? Did he come to the cabin?'

'Given the grave nature of these charges, Mrs Leahy, the case will be forwarded to the Summer Assizes in Tralee. You will be taken to Ballymullen gaol and tried with judge and jury. And unless the charges are dropped against them, so Mary and Anne will stand trial too.'

'Did you find Micheál?'

'Do you understand me now? Mrs Leahy?'

'Did you find my grandson? I was asking –'

'Your grandson's body was found at a location very near the residence of Anne Roche. The "Piper's Grave", as it is known locally.'

'The Piper's Grave?'

Nóra pictured the whitethorn in the deep blue of new morning, the dance of light about its branches.

'When Anne was confronted by the constabulary she led them to where she had left Micheál's body.'

'Micheál? Please, can I see him?'

The policeman gave her a long look. 'The three of you drowned Mícheál Kelliher, Mrs Leahy, and 'twas Anne Roche that hid his body.' He glanced at the paper again. 'A shallow grave at that. Barely a grave at all. No more than ten inches deep.'

Nóra began to breathe rapidly, pressing her temples. 'I do not think 'twas Mícheál.'

'Your grandson. Buried like a dog.'

'No. I do not think 'twas Mícheál.'

She began to sob. A wail that filled the room.

'Mrs Leahy?'

'I do not think 'twas Mícheál!'

'Come now.'

''Twas a fairy!' Nóra put her elbows on the table and cried into her hands.

'Mrs Leahy, 'tis important that you gain control of yourself and tell me what happened. Did Anne Roche tell you that your grandson, Mícheál Kelliher, was a fairy?'

Nóra nodded, her face still hidden in her hands.

'And you are remorseful, for you understand that this was not the case?'

She wiped her nose on her sleeve and looked down at the shiny smear. ''Twas not Mícheál they found then,' she whispered. 'That child was not my grandson.'

'Surely you would know your own grandson.'

She shook her head. 'No. He was changed. I saw him, and when he was brought to me, he was changed.'

'And this Anne told you that the change in him was because he was now a fairy?'

'She said that Mícheál had surely been taken by the fairies. The cripple was one of Them. She told me she would have my grandson returned to me.'

The constable regarded Nóra carefully. Rolled another cigarette.

'Mrs Leahy. You, a woman of otherwise good repute, believed this woman when she told you your paralytic grandson was an other-worldly sprite?'

'Paralytic?'

'Had not the use of his legs.'

Nóra used her shawl to wipe her eyes. 'What? What is the word again?'

'Paralytic. 'Tis a medical term, used to describe children such as yours who have not the use of their legs, or arms, or anything at all. 'Tis a known affliction, Mrs Leahy. A disease of immobility. And 'tis what the coroner and his peers are saying Micheál suffered from.'

'No. 'Twas not a suffering. 'Twas not him at all.'

'Yes, it was, Mrs Leahy.' The man suddenly leant forward. 'All this talk of fairies. Sure, people will tell themselves anything to avert their eyes from the truth of a matter.'

'He will be waiting for me.' Nóra began to weep again. 'He'll be waiting for me, and no one there to welcome him home. Oh God in Heaven!'

'Mrs Leahy, did you tell yourself what you wanted to believe? Or was it some other understanding you were working towards? Give an old poor woman a chicken. Some fuel. And in return she'll deliver you of a runt, all the while gabbling about the fairies.'

'You're wrong.' Nóra drew her hands into fists. 'Micheál will be there, returned. And after all I've done, all to have him back with me. And you're keeping me here! 'Twas all I wanted, to have him back with me.'

The constable narrowed his eyes and took a long drag, watching her. The paper flared between his lips. 'Sure it was, Mrs Leahy. Sure it was.'

Nance looked up from where she sat on the cart rattling on the road through Killarney. Every rock and rut knocked through her bones, until she felt that her remaining teeth would shudder from their gums. She was unused to travelling so quickly. Unused to the rapid pull of a horse, its ears upright to the urging of the dark-coated man sitting in front, dirty collar about his ears.

She had lost track of time.

The widow was sitting across from her, pinned against the corner of the cart and the broad shoulder of a policeman. Nance could not tell if Nóra was awake – a shawl covered her face, and her head hung forward. When they had brought them out from the barracks and set them on the cart, the widow – pale, feeble-looking – had leant across and whispered to Nance. 'They will not believe me,' she'd breathed. But not a word since.

Nance looked past the bulk of the constable beside her and stared out into the streets of Killarney. The inns and lodgings, the fine line of the high street and the close, filthy lanes and yards that ran off it. Smoky, sunny Killarney with poxy children spitting in the alleys and men carrying baskets of scraw and sod. After five nights in her tiny barracks cell there was suddenly too much noise, too many dirty faces staring at them, noses wrinkling. She had fled this place twice. This unkind town. Mad Maggie, Mad Nance: one and the same. Father gone to the water, mother to the fairies, there's no knowing which way this one'll turn, but 'tis clear she goes with Them. She goes with Them that does be in it. She is of the Good People.

Nance shut her eyes tightly and braced herself against the jolt of the lane. When she opened them again the muck of the town had faded and they were on the old mail coach road to Tralee, between the mountains of rock and grass, a blessed distance from the towering horizon of trees, the lakes and hiving swarm of Killarney. Men were in the fields, seeding the eyes of cups, while other potato plants were stalking up and out of the earth. The world had finally flowered. Ditches starry in dog violet and gorse, sow thistle, dandelion and cuckoo flower creeping into the fields. The lone fairy whitethorns left to themselves amidst the cultivated ground, blossoming into thick curds of white. Her heart soared to see the bee-blown, petal-filled trees.

It will be May Eve in time, Nance thought. And she thought of how, in the valley, the people would soon pluck the yellow flowers for the goodness they drew from the sun, pulling primrose and marsh marigold and buttercups, rubbing them on the cows' udders to bless the butter in them, placing them on doorways and doorsteps, those thresholds where the unknown world could bleed into the known, flowers to seal the cracks from where luck could be leached, on that night of *Bealtaine* bonfire.

Twenty miles from Killarney to Tralee. Thirty from the valley. Even when she was younger and used to hard walking, a road like this would have taken her sun-up to sundown to tramp.

The light faded. The afternoon became quiet and the crickets began to chirp against the far-off call of a cuckoo singing down the dusk. Nóra had begun to weep quietly. The cart rattled the irons about their wrists.

Here is God, Nance thought. I see him still.

Mary was sitting on the floor of the narrow Killarney barracks room with her head resting against the corner of stone, her fingers pinching the skin of her arm. Ever since the policeman had taken her from Peg O'Shea's cabin, a trembling had set up in her hands, and she had fallen into the habit of nipping her flesh to quell the shaking.

Her head ached. She had wept for the first two nights, sobbing into her hands, still dirty with the mud from the river, until her eyes swelled and she was dazed with exhaustion. The policeman who had questioned her had seemed uncomfortable at her distress. He had handed her his handkerchief, waited patiently until she could answer his questions.

But now Mary felt dry, tearless. She glanced down at the cloth, balled in her lap, and brought it to her face. It still smelt of shop soap, tobacco smoke.

The afternoon had darkened. There was a small square window high in the cell, and throughout the day Mary had focused on the sunlight falling across the wall, transfixed by its slow shifting. She closed her eyes. She could hear men speaking to one another outside in the barracks yard, and then the echo of footsteps walking down the long corridor beyond her cell.

There was a sudden clanking as the door was unlocked and opened, and Mary, expecting to see a constable, was surprised by the sight of a familiar face.

Father Healy waited until the door had been closed and locked behind him before speaking to her.

'Good afternoon, Mary Clifford.'

'Father.'

The priest looked around for somewhere to sit, then, seeing only the bare stone floor, stepped over to Mary and squatted on his haunches.

'This is a sorry business.'

'Yes, Father.'

He paused. 'I have been told that you swore an information.'

Mary nodded, tucking her knees up to her chest. She was aware of the grime on her feet, the muddy hem of her skirt.

'I have some good news for you. The Crown counsel would like you to be their chief witness.'

Mary felt her mouth dry in panic. 'Their chief witness?'

'Do you understand what that means?'

'No, Father.'

'It means that they are willing to drop the charge of wilful murder against you, if you turn witness. If you tell the court and the jury and the judge what you saw. What you did.'

'I did not mean for him to die, Father.' She glanced down at the handkerchief in her hands, the tiny bruises on the inner flesh of her wrist.

'Mary, look at me.' Father Healy's face was sombre. 'They are going to free you. All you will need to do is make your oath, and tell the court what you told the policemen. What you swore in your information. Answer their questions as best you can.'

Mary blinked at him.

'If you turn witness, they will not charge you. Do you understand? You will be able to return home to your mother and father.'

'I will not hang?'

'You will not hang.'

'And Nóra? Nance? Will they hang?'

'They are gone to Ballymullen today.' Father Healy shifted his weight, pulling at the cloth of his trousers. 'You understand that Micheál Kelliher was not a fairy child, don't you, Mary? He was a little boy suffering from cretinism. He was not taken by the fairies, but by the ignorance of his own grandmother and an old woman. He was not banished. He was *murdered*. You understand this, don't you?'

Mary clenched her teeth against the tears that suddenly threatened. She nodded.

Father Healy continued, his voice low. 'God has protected you, Mary. But let you find a lesson in the fall of Nóra Leahy and Nance Roche. Pray for their souls, and for the soul of Micheál Kelliher.'

'Can I go to Annamore?'

Father Healy rose, wincing. 'That's where you're from, is it?' He rubbed at a cramp in his leg. 'Not until the trial is over. You'll be coming with me to Tralee. The Crown counsel, the lawyers, will want to speak with you there. Do you have anywhere to stay in that town? Any kin?'

Mary shook her head.

The priest paused. 'Let me see if I can't arrange something for you. A place where you can work for your keep for the next few months, until the trial is over. Then you'll be on your own, do you understand?'

'Thank you, Father.'

He turned and knocked sharply on the door, and the sound of boots could be heard. As the key was turned in the lock, Father Healy glanced back. 'Give thanks to God for this, Mary. It is by His mercy alone that you are saved. I'll return for you tomorrow.' And then he was gone.

Mary looked down at her soiled hands, her heart pounding. I am free, she thought, and she waited for relief to sweep through her.

But it did not come. She sat, pinching her skin between her fingers.

Nipping the bread to let the Devil out, she thought.

They arrived in Tralee at dusk. Nance shrank into her seat at the sight of the town and its streets of business, at the fine houses along the promenade. Mail coaches, upright with gentlemen, clattered in the road amongst crowds of servants, tradespeople and the usual dregs of beggars. The widow briefly listed her head to gaze at the town, until they neared the limestone gates to Ballymullen gaol, when she glanced at Nance, terrified.

'We will never leave this place,' she whispered, eyes wide.

'No talking,' one of the policemen interrupted.

Nance became frightened then. They passed through the gates and immediately the air felt heavier, dank. Under the weight of the shadows thrown by the high walls, her body began to tremble.

Stone-silled, iron-grilled. The gaol was dark, and the constables moved them from the gate and into its passageways by lamplight. Nance's throat filled with bile and she thought back to her cabin and Mora, who would surely be waiting for her, udder heavy with milk.

The gaolers took Nóra and weighed her first, then after some discussion with the policemen they hauled the widow off into the dark corridor. Nóra looked back over her shoulder, her lips parting in terror before the shadows fell over her face, and Nance felt hands take her firmly about the arms and direct her to the scales.

'Anne Roche. Unknown age. Four feet eleven inches. Ninety-eight pounds. White hair. Blue eyes. Identifying marks include: tender eyes; enlarged joint, left and right thumbs; front teeth; cut mark on forehead. Catholic. Pauper. Charged with wilful murder.'

The women in the cell with Nance were mute and dirty. They lay on straw piled over the flagged floor, eyes large in the dark. One, her skin pocked like mountain soil, muttered to herself. Every now and then she shook her head, as if in disbelief at her imprisonment.

That night Nance woke to a piercing shriek, and when the guard came to see what the fuss was about, holding a lamp aloft, Nance saw that the mutterer had thrown herself at the wall, splitting her head on the rock. The guard took her away. When they had left and the cell was once more snuffed of light, a voice spoke from the corner of the room.

'I'm glad that one is away.'

There was a pause, then another voice replied. 'She's turned in the head.'

'Wantonly scalding with hot water,' said the first woman. 'That's what she's here for. Tried to boil her child like a pratie.'

'What did they pinch you for then?'

There was another pause. 'Begging. And yourself?'

'Borrowed some turf.'

'Drink.'

'And you, old biddy? Public nuisance was it?' There was a snide chortle at this.

Nance said nothing, her heart beating fast. She closed her eyes against the darkness and her ears against the faceless voices and imagined the river. The flowing river, in the height of summer. She thought of the green light cast by moss, and the berries on their brambles swelling with their sweetness, and the eggs in the hidden places breaking with tapping beaks. She thought of the life that thrust itself onwards outside the prison, and when she could see it there, see the unconquerable world, she finally fell into sleep.

Grey light slid down the wall like a stain. Nóra had been unable to rest in the close air of the cell with the suggestion of bodies around her, their coughing and weeping, and the scuttering sounds she could not place that filled her with terror. It was a relief to have respite from the pitch-black she had wept into all night. Rubbing her eyes, she saw that there were seven other women in the tiny cell with her, most of them asleep. Nance was not amongst them.

One girl, dark hair streaked with early grey, slept next to Nóra, her head resting on the wall. Another was sprawled by her feet, snoring. Both were thin, their feet black.

Only one other woman was awake. Mouse-haired, she sat with her legs tucked up beneath her, eyeing Nóra carefully. After catching

Nóra's glance she slid forward, crawling across the floor until she was beside her. Nóra sat up hurriedly.

'Mary Foley,' the woman said. 'Sleep well?'

Nóra drew the canvas dress she had been given about her. It was damp.

'I know what you're here for. You murdered a child.'

Nóra could smell the tang of the woman's breath.

'You'd best be after the priest. They're after hanging women that do be murdering now.' The woman tilted her head, examining Nóra with a cool eye. 'Johanna Lovett. They dropped her out the front of the gaol not a month ago for the murder of her man.' She winked. 'Like a fish on a line, she was. Bouncin' like a feckin' fish on a line.'

Nóra stared at her.

'I'm in and out of here more often than a sailor up a whore,' she said. 'I know everything.'

'I didn't murder him.'

Mary smiled. 'And I don't take the drink. But sure, the Devil manages to pour it down my throat anyway.' She sat back on her heels. 'Baby-dropper, are you?'

Nóra shook her head.

'How did he die then?'

''Twas no child at all.'

Mary Foley raised her eyebrows.

''Twas a changeling.'

Mary grinned. 'You're a mad one. Still, better to be mad than bad. That one there? Making an almighty racket?' She pointed to the snoring girl. 'Mary Walsh. Tried to conceal the birth of her baby. She'll be getting three months or so, unless they also decide to charge her with deserting her child. Then she'll be getting more. That's the badness in it.'

Nóra stared at the young girl and thought of Brigid Lynch, the blood rippling between her legs. The longed-for child in the *cillín*.

The changeling buried in the Piper's Grave. Ten inches of soil over that little body.

'Yer one there with the burn mark on her face? Moynihan. Attempted self-murder.' Mary sniffed, wiped her nose with the back of her hand. 'Tried to drown herself. Kept bobbing up like a cork so they fished her out.'

Nóra looked at the freckled girl Mary was pointing to, curled asleep in the corner, her hands tucked under her chin.

'Surprising, the amount of them here after a ducking. 'Tis stones you want, if you're after drowning yourself. 'Twould not be the way I'd go. Unless 'twas drowning in a bottle.' The woman nodded to herself. 'Sure. Only those who are born to hang are not afraid of the water.'

CHAPTER
NINETEEN

Mint

Mary's blouse was pinching under her armpits and she could feel sweat seeping through her collar. The Tralee courthouse was the finest, largest building she had ever stepped inside, but it teemed with people and Mary thought she might faint from the heat, from the stale air and the fear that lingered in the court from all those who had stood behind the spiked stand, protesting or accusing badness in the world. The violence in it. Beatings and burglary and theft and rape.

Mary searched the crowd for Father Healy. He had brought her to the courthouse from the home of the merchant family she had been placed with these past three months, but in the crush of the crowd she had lost sight of his face.

I have grown, Mary thought, running her fingers along the tight seams. 'Twill be the first thing I do when I return home. I will unpick these clothes and I will make room for myself.

She would have liked to burn them. Burn the skirt and the shift and the shawl and everything she had gone to the widow's with. Put them on the fire and burn them into nothing, and dress in new cloth that Micheál had never touched. Despite the hard scrubbing she had given her clothes on arriving in Tralee, she could still smell the boy on her. The piss and sourness of him. Smell the nights awake, the wet mouth of him screaming into her chest. The peck soap. The mint. The dark mud of the riverbank.

Mary cast a look at the men who had been sworn in as jury. Over twenty of them. A shoal of gentlemen, black clothes and beards trimmed, sitting placidly amongst the swarming, jostling horde of those who had come to hear the verdicts pronounced over the prisoners led to dock. It had taken Father Healy and Mary a long time to reach the front of the crowd. People collected in dense masses around the lawyers, pulling at their sleeves, asking for justice. Court reporters stood nearby, eagle-eyed, some of them sucking at pencils. Mary took a deep breath. Her hands were damp with nerves.

One of the jurymen caught her eye and gave her a kindly smile. Mary looked away, towards the chair where the judge sat. The Honourable Baron Pennefather. He looked tired.

At the end of this rope of words was Annamore. That was what she had to remember. She had to answer the questions and tell them of her fear, of the strange and sorry things they did to the boy. How frightened she was of all the fairy talk, how she did not understand what it was they were doing. That she was fearful of God and prayed that He would forgive her.

God forgive her. For saying nothing, for doing nothing, for not splashing through the river to slap the widow and take up the boy and carry him home to her brothers and sisters. They would have made a pet of him, she thought. They would not have minded that he screamed from hunger when they, too, were always crying from it. In a cabin of too many, one more would not have made a difference.

Mary started. A hush had fallen, although an undercurrent of babbling continued amongst the people still squeezing themselves into the room. There was a straining of necks and she saw that they were bringing Nance and Nóra into the room, their wrists in irons.

The women's months in gaol had changed them, had thinned them. Nance looked ancient. Dressed in the garb of the prison, she seemed to have shrunk ever smaller. Her white hair had taken on a yellow sheen in its unwashed state, and her shoulders were hunched. Nance's eyes, as fogged as ever, looked around her in confusion and fear. She seemed alarmed to see such a vast crowd of people.

Nóra, behind her, was weeping. Mary was struck by the difference in her appearance. Gone was the righteousness, the stubborn chin. Now Nóra's complexion was sallow and drawn, and she seemed to have aged several years. Her forehead was deeply lined. Despite the heat in the courtroom, she shivered uncontrollably.

Perhaps they will decide to hang them here, Mary thought, and fear creased through her stomach. It might have been her, standing there.

She wanted to leave the room. How could she speak in front of all these people? All these men in their fine clothes, and the judge come all the way from Dublin. She was only a girl from a bog. A girl of the rushes and the turf ground, where the soil oozed black and it was only ever grass and dust and clay underfoot, never the cobbles, never the lacquer of wood.

The counsel gave Mary a careful look. Smoothed his hair from his forehead, glossy with perspiration. She could feel her legs turn to water beneath her.

'Let the record state that in the case of wilful murder against Honora Leahy and Anne Roche the first witness called is Mary Clifford of Annamore.'

Mary stepped up to the witness box. They passed her the Bible and she kissed it, her fingers gripping the leather tightly.

'Mary Clifford, can you please identify the prisoners?'

Mary looked out at the sea of staring faces and saw, finally, the long forehead of the priest. He held her eye. Gave her a nod.

''Tis Nance Roche. And Nóra Leahy, who I served as maid to.'

'Mary, in your own words, please tell the court how you came to work for Mrs Leahy.'

''Twas Mrs Leahy who came for me when I was standing at the hiring fair last November in Killarney. She offered me work and said she had a grandson, and offered me money to help her care for him and help her with the washing and cooking and the milking. So I went with her.'

'Did she give any indication that the child was a cripple?'

Mary hesitated. 'Do you mean, did she say he was crippled?'

The lawyer gave her a tight smile. 'Yes. That is the question.'

Mary glanced at Nóra. She was staring, her mouth ajar. 'She did not, sir.'

'Can you please describe the state of Micheál Kelliher when you saw him?'

'He was in the cabin with a neighbour, and I was frightened to see him. I had never seen a child like it. "What ails him?" I asked, and Mrs Leahy said, "He is delicate, is all."'

'Can you please describe what she meant by "delicate"?'

Mary took a deep breath. Her hands were shaking. 'He was making a strange sound, and though old enough to be talking, he could not say a word. Mrs Leahy said, "There's no walking in him either." "Is it a catching sickness?" I asked, and she says, "No, he is delicate. There is no catching in it."'

'Did Mrs Leahy at any time describe the boy as anything other than her grandson?'

Mary looked again at Nóra. She was red-eyed.

'She said, "He is my daughter's boy."'

'In your sworn information you said that, although she had

introduced the child to you as her grandson, in time Honora Leahy believed that the child was not her grandson at all, but was –' the prosecutor paused, turning to face the jury '– a *changeling*. Is this correct?'

''Tis. She thought he was a changeling. There were others who also believed it.'

'Can you tell the court what you mean by "changeling"?'

Mary felt the eyes of the jury on her. She stood, faltering, suddenly aware of her hammering heartbeat.

'I mean a fairy.'

There was laughter in the crowd, and Mary was winded with shame. She could feel herself redden, feel the pricking of sweat under her arms. This was how they saw her, a stupid girl jumping at shadows, demented with fear. She remembered the mortification she had felt when the constable had asked her to sign the sworn information, and she had scratched a clumsy cross on the paper, fumbling the pen in her hand.

'When did Mrs Leahy begin to refer to her grandson, Micheál Kelliher, as a *fairy*?'

'She believed he was a changeling when Nance Roche pronounced him so.'

'And when was this?'

'In the new year. Or 'twas December. 'Twas the new year that we took the boy to Nance's for the first cure.'

Mary saw, with a horrible jolt of recognition, several men from the valley amongst the mass of faces. Daniel and Seán Lynch were there, stony-eyed.

'Mary, can you tell us why you went to Anne Roche?'

'She came to us.' Mary hesitated. ''Twas before Christmas. I was out milking and I came in and saw Mrs Leahy slapping Micheál. "The badness in you," she was saying. She was beating him.'

There was a murmur amongst the onlookers.

'She was beating him?'

'His hand had caught in her hair and it had pained her. "He can't help it," says I, and Mrs Leahy said she was going to get the priest for him. But when the widow returned 'twas not with the priest but with an apron of nettles. Then she got down on her hands and knees over the boy and stung him with the nettles. "That is hurting him," I said, but she did not listen to me. So I took the nettles and put them on the fire and I ran to Peg O'Shea for help.'

'Did Honora Leahy ever explain why she was "nettling" Mícheál Kelliher? Do you think she meant to hurt him?'

Mary hesitated. The laughter had stopped, and there was now a silent tension in the room. 'I don't know.'

'Please speak up.'

'I don't know.'

'How did this incident lead to the involvement of Anne Roche?'

Mary licked her lips. Father Healy had not taken his eyes off her. 'Peg told me to go to the river and fetch dock for the boy, and so I went, but 'twas on my return that I hurt my ankle. I could not walk. There was a woman come up to me – 'twas Nance Roche. She took me to her cabin for the ankle cure, and 'twas there I told her what Mrs Leahy had done. "I have a right to be talking to that woman," she said, and then we returned to the cabin together and she saw Mícheál.'

'What did Anne Roche say to Honora Leahy when she saw the boy?'

'"This cratur here might be fairy-born," says she.'

'And how did Mrs Leahy seem when Anne said this?'

'I thought she was relieved to hear it, sir.'

'Tell us, Mary, why do you think Honora Leahy, an established member of her community, a woman of good repute with a late husband of excellent standing, chose to listen to the opinion of Anne Roche – a woman who, as the court will hear, was impoverished, unmarried and, by all accounts sworn, an outsider with little to no financial, commercial or familial influence?'

Mary gaped at the lawyer, not understanding. She could feel sweat beading on her lip.

The counsel cleared his throat. 'Mary, please tell us why you think Mrs Leahy listened to someone like Anne.'

Mary looked over at Nance. She had been slumped against the dock, frowning. At the mention of her name, however, she straightened her back and gave Mary a wary look.

'Because she is a woman who goes with Them.'

'Them?'

'The Good People. The fairies.' Mary waited for more laughter, but none came. 'She has the knowledge of Them and their herbs. She told the widow that she could put the fairy out of him.'

Out of the corner of her eye, Mary noticed movement. A reporter stood, quickly writing something down.

'Mary, referring now to the information provided in your sworn testimony regarding the treatment of Micheál, can you please tell the court how these women attempted to "put the fairy out of him", and your own involvement, if any?'

Mary blanched. 'I only did what was asked of me. I did not want to lose my wages.'

The prosecutor smiled. 'That is understood. You are not on trial here.'

'They – we – tried to put the fairy out of him with herbs at first. There was mint put in his ears, and another herb rubbed on his feet.'

'Do you know the herb? Was it "lusmore"?'

'Lus mór was given in the next cure. When the mint did not work I was sent back to Nance by Mrs Leahy. "There is no change in the boy," I said, and so we were told to return and that is when they – we gave Micheál the foxglove.'

'And when was this?'

'January, sir.'

The prosecutor turned to the judge. 'Let the court note that foxglove, *Digitalis purpurea*, is poisonous.' He faced Mary. 'Do you believe that the prisoners knew, in giving Micheál Kelliher foxglove, that they were giving him a substance capable of causing death or illness?'

There was a stifled cry. Nóra had brought her hands to her face.

'I knew 'twas poisonous and I said so. But Nance said, "'Tis a powerful plant," and I knew that *lus mór* belongs to . . .' Mary stopped herself. 'They say *lus mór* belongs to the fairies and so I thought there would be a cure in it. But now I know 'tis only superstition.'

'Please describe how the foxglove was administered to Micheál Kelliher.'

"Twas a bath of it. And the juice set on his tongue. And when he started up with a trembling, and his mouth was foaming, we were told to set him on a spade and make as if to shovel him out the door, saying, "Away with you!"'

There was another stirring amongst the crowd. The court reporter was writing furiously. Mary wiped her sweating palms against her skirt.

'In your information, Mary, you stated that the foxglove *did* have an ill effect on the child in the days after its application. You said that you were frightened for his life.'

She saw the boy again then, in the weak light of the cabin's dying fire. Saw him shudder ceaselessly against her, his head listless on the mattress. Remembered the feel of his tongue against her finger as she hooked the vomit from his mouth and made sure he would not choke.

'In the days afterwards I was scared he would die, so much water was coming from him, and he was unable to keep his food down.' She blinked away a sudden urge to cry. 'All the time he was shaking, sir. I thought he would die.'

'It must have been terrible to see. Was Mrs Leahy as upset as you?'

Nóra was weeping openly.

She is scared, Mary thought.

'Mrs Leahy was happy, sir. She thought she would have her true grandson returned to her. "'Tis no sin if 'tis fairy," she said. But when he did not die from it, she went to Nance herself and they decided to take Micheál to the river.'

'This was another "cure"?'

'Yes, sir. I was to take the boy the next morning down to Nance's with Mrs Leahy and together we would go to the river and put him in the boundary water. 'Tis the place where three streams meet. Nance said the power in the water would banish the fairy. "'Twill be cold," says I, but 'twas decided and, although I was afraid, I did as told. And I hope God forgives me for it.'

'What happened next?'

'We bathed him in the river for three mornings running.' Mary paused. Sweat trickled down her back. 'And . . . on the last morning Nance and Mrs Leahy kept him under the water for longer than usual.'

'And is that when Micheál Kelliher died?'

'Yes, sir.'

'What did you do when you saw the prisoners drowning the child?'

Nance was leaning forward in the dock, her mouth moving, muttering something under her breath.

'I was not sure then if the child was drowned. I thought only that the water was cold. I did not want him to catch cold. And then I saw that he was not moving, and I thought, "They have killed him," and 'twas then that I took fright.'

'Did you say anything to the prisoners when you realised that the child had, in fact, drowned?'

Mary paused. Her pulse jumped in her throat. 'I think so, sir.'

'You swore to it in your information.'

The boy lifted from the river. The water running from him, his skin pearled with it, the dripping from his fingers glittering in the light.

'What did you say, Mary?'

'I said, "How can you hope ever to see God after this?"'

A murmur immediately rose from the crowd.

'And did the prisoners reply to your question?'

Mary nodded. 'Nance said, "The sin is not on me."'

'Was anything else said?'

'I don't know, sir.'

'You don't know?'

'That was when the fear took me. I turned and ran to Peg O'Shea's and I told her that the boy was killed. I was frightened for myself.'

'Mary, before the defence examines you, could you please tell me what it was like to care for Micheál Kelliher? Do you believe he was burdensome to his grandmother?'

'He could not help it.'

'But was he a burden to your mistress? Was he a difficult and unloving child?'

The nights of wailing. The great, rasping screams. His head smacking against the clay, against her fingers as she tried to calm him, unplug his nose, ease his breathing.

'Yes,' Mary whispered. 'Yes, he was a burden.'

'Did Honora Leahy wish to be rid of him?'

'She wished for the fairy to be gone. She wanted her grandson back, sir. A boy who would not scream and trouble her.'

The courtroom became noisy with conversation as soon as the counsel returned to his chair. Mary, relieved to have the gaze of the crowd off her, wiped the sweat from her neck with her sleeve. She looked at Father Healy, and he gave her a small nod of reassurance.

After one noisy minute, the defence lawyer rose. He introduced himself as Mr Walshe over the din, and waited several moments until the chatter subsided.

When there was absolute silence, he spoke. His voice was clipped, his words carrying across the room.

'Mary Clifford, do you believe that Honora Leahy and Anne Roche took Micheál to the Flesk because they intended to drown and kill him?'

Mary hesitated. 'Did I know he was to be killed?'

'Do you believe that the prisoners intended to drown the child from the time they decided to bathe him in the river?'

'I don't understand, sir.'

Mr Walshe gave her a cool look. 'Do you believe that murder was their thinking all along?'

Mary's heart flipped in her chest. 'I don't know.'

'You don't know if Mrs Leahy and Nance Roche intended to kill the boy?'

'I think they meant to be rid of the changeling.'

'Mary, forgive my insistence, but if they meant to be rid of the "changeling", as you call him, and you knew that would mean the boy would be drowned, why did you let them bathe him at all? Why not alert the neighbour you speak of, as you did when you saw Mrs Leahy "nettling" Micheál? Why not send word to the priest?'

'I did not think they meant to kill Micheál.' Mary could hear the uncertainty in her own voice. Her hands had begun to shake again, and she gripped her skirt.

'Then why take a small, helpless boy and bathe him in the river?'

Mary looked over at the dock. Both Nance and Nóra were staring at her, their hair lank and loose. Nóra was trembling, as though suffering from a fever.

Mary took a deep breath, the cloth pulling tight against her ribcage and the wild beating of her heart. ''Twas done with the intent to cure it, sir. To put the fairy out of it.'

Mr Walshe smiled. 'Thank you, Mary.'

CHAPTER
TWENTY

Elder

Nóra thought that she would never be warm again. She could see the glisten of sweat on the foreheads of the lawyers despite the early hour, could see people in the vast, shuffling crowd fan their faces and mop their brows with handkerchiefs, and yet she shivered as though she were standing in the snow against a high wind.

She wondered, not for the first time, if she was turning mad. Time no longer seemed to tread past in measured steps, but flung forward and back. The trial had bled from the previous day of the assizes into the next, but as Nóra stood, tense with the pressing threat of a full and painful bladder, she could not remember who had testified. As soon as one witness stepped forward to be examined, she looked and saw another in their place.

It was only Mary Clifford's testimony that she remembered in detail. She stood in the dock, shaking, and saw again the girl tilting from one foot to another under the pinch of questioning. Her gaze, when it met Nóra's, had seemed firm. For a brief moment Nóra could have sworn that it was her own redheaded daughter kissing the book, swearing an information against her.

My mother, who killed my son.

They are going to hang me, Nóra suddenly thought, and she gripped the fetters about her wrists. Beneath the droning of the Crown counsel, she thought she could hear the rattle of her teeth.

Nóra tried to focus on the new witness gesticulating to the court. She recognised him as the policeman who had arrested her in the cabin. He had shaved for the trial, she noticed, and she pictured him standing at a slip of mirror that morning, strop and razor in hand, while she had lain in her cell, picking at the skin of her feet. Nauseous. Sick with anxiety. Did he have a wife to boil the water for his shave? Had his breakfast been cooked for him? Nóra pictured the policeman carefully scraping the blade along his neck, until she felt a tightening around her own throat and, sickened, stared at the floor.

'And tell me,' the counsel was saying to the constable, 'what was the state of Anne Roche when you arrested her?'

'I went inside the house and saw the prisoner on her hands and knees. She was taking the ash from the hearth. I thought she was a woman out of her mind, and I said: "Anne Roche, do you know why I am here?" and she did not answer me. I told her I had a warrant for her arrest, and asked her if she knew where the body of Micheál Kelliher was, for she was accused of drowning him that morning. She answered me, "The Good People took Micheál and left a fairy in his place," and 'twas only when I asked her where the body of the *fairy* was that she took me to the deceased.'

'And where was the grave?'

'The grave was in an abandoned area known locally as the "Piper's Grave". It had not been dug deep, sir. The body was partly visible through the soil.'

'Did the prisoner seem distressed?'

The constable cleared his throat. 'She seemed surprised to hear that Mrs Leahy had been arrested also, and asked if there had not been a little boy with her. When asked which child she meant, Anne Roche replied, "Micheál Kelliher."'

'She said this despite having brought you to the grave and body of the deceased?'

'That is correct, sir.'

'Was there anything otherwise remarkable about the prisoners' appearance or attitude at the time you arrested them?'

'The clothes of Mrs Leahy were wet through. Sodden. We surmised that she had been in the river at some point that morning. There was the smell of river mud about her.'

'Were the clothes of Anne Roche also sodden?'

'No, sir. And I thought that was curious given both Mary Clifford and Mrs Leahy told me she had also been in the river, until the prisoner explained that she had bathed the child – the *changeling*, as she called him – in an undressed state.'

Nóra's body ached. Every night in the gaol she had pictured her empty cabin in the valley, imagining the creak of the door and Micheál entering the room, looking for her. She wondered what he would be wearing. What the fairies might have clothed him in. Perhaps he would be bare, and she imagined her grandson crawling under Martin's greatcoat, curling up on the cold straw mattress, or by the dead ashes of her fire, and waiting for her to return. Imagined the small round of his face peering out the window, imagined him standing in the yard as the wind tousled his hair, looking along the broad flank of the valley for the sight of his grandmother walking the lane.

He will be frightened, she thought. It may be that he has returned and is frightened. He is only a little boy.

What would happen if she were hanged? Would he stay in her

cabin until the grass grew long at her door? Would he leave and wander, lost, until he grew as thin as the one they had put in the water?

'Honora Leahy?'

Nóra started and lifted her face, biting down on her knuckle. The courtroom was staring at her.

The policeman who had been talking was no longer there. Instead, the lawyers and the judge were looking at her expectantly.

'Honora Leahy?'

She looked at Mr Walshe, who was urgently gesturing for her to move to the end of the dock.

'Yes?'

'Would you kiss the book and give your oath?'

Nóra did as they asked. She took the Bible into her trembling hands and felt the weight of its pages.

'Honora Leahy, can you please describe the state of Micheál Kelliher when you first took him into your care?'

Nóra gazed around the courtroom, her eyes landing on the faces of the jurymen. They were looking at her with interest, their foreheads wrinkled.

'Mrs Leahy, do you need me to repeat the question? How did you come to care for Micheál?'

Nóra turned to the lawyer. Someone in the crowd coughed. ''Twas me and my man both. My daughter, Johanna, had passed and 'twas her husband that brought him. He was all bones and we were worried for him. He looked starved. He was not walking, but I thought then maybe it was only a weakness.'

'And was this the first time you had seen your grandson?'

'I saw Micheál a time before. Two years ago. But he was a well boy then. He was talking and he had the use of his legs. I saw that he was well with my own eyes.'

'Mrs Leahy, your husband died shortly after Micheál was brought to you, is that not true?'

'He died in October.'

'It was surely a great misfortune for you to find yourself a widow and the sole support of a cripple boy?'

Martin, his eyes pennied, stomach offering up the plate of dried herbs, pinched and pushed into clay pipes and the smoke blown over his greying skin. Martin, smelling of the sky, of the valley, dropping to the earth with a hand over his chest while lights flared under the whitethorn.

'Mrs Leahy?' It was the judge who had spoken. 'Can you please answer the questions when addressed?'

The prosecutor frowned. 'Would you say it was difficult to be widowed and the sole support of a cripple?'

Nóra licked her lips. ''Twas a great sorrow to me.'

'Mary Clifford said that the boy was a burden to you without the assistance of your husband. Is that true?'

'Yes, he was a burden. That is why I hired her. For the extra pair of hands.'

'Mrs Leahy, Mary Clifford also said that, while she was in your service, you stopped referring to your grandson as Micheál, but called him a "fairy". She also said you referred to the child as "it". Can you please tell the court why you stopped referring to Micheál Kelliher as your grandson?'

Nóra hesitated. 'I had met my grandson before. There was no likeness between the one I had met and the one delivered to me. At first, I thought that he was only ill, and I tried to cure him, but the cures did not work and 'twas because the boy was a changeling.'

'Where did you believe your true grandson to be, if he were not with you under your care?'

'Swept. In the fairy fort. With the music and the dancing and the lights.'

There was a ripple of hushed conversation through the crowd.

Nóra closed her eyes. Under hill. Under whitethorn. On the fairy wind with a weed to carry you, to bring you to the boundary places, the threshold between this world and the other. Swept away from all anger, all suffering. Not good enough for Heaven and not bad enough for Hell. All places. In the air, in the soil, in the water.

'Mrs Leahy?'

Nóra felt lightheaded. She opened her eyes and suddenly recognised her nephew, Daniel, standing still and pale behind a sea of heads. She stared at him, her heart lifting, but he lowered his gaze.

'Mrs Leahy, having a cripple child in the home can be a terrible shame. A sorrowful burden. Your own servant maid has said that Micheál was forever crying, unable to feed or bathe himself, unable to speak or – indeed – love. He kept you from sleeping. And you, recently widowed and no doubt still in the grip of grief.' The man's tone changed. 'You were surely frustrated by Micheál's cretinism, Mrs Leahy. Angry, perhaps. So angry you saw nothing wrong in whipping a helpless boy with nettles you had *deliberately* and with intention picked for the purpose of applying to his skin.'

Nóra shook her head. ''Twas to restore the moving to his legs.'

'So you say. But to no avail, Mrs Leahy. And so, as Mary Clifford has said, you turned to the services of Anne Roche. Had you ever consulted Anne for her "cures" before this time?'

'Had I gone for the cure?'

'That is what I am asking, yes.'

'I had not, no.'

'And why was that?'

'I had no reason. My husband . . .'

She remembered the dead ember hidden in the pocket of Martin's greatcoat. Embers carried for protection. Where had it come from? From what hearth, what fire?

A glowing coal carried three times sunwise around the house for luck. An ember thrown into the potato field on St John's Eve. A coal drawn thrice over a nest in which birds are ready to hatch. A live coal placed in feet water to preserve a man during an absence from the home.

An ember to save against the trespass of evil spirits.

'Can you please repeat that, Mrs Leahy? The court cannot understand you.'

'My husband had gone to Nance. Once. For a hand.'

'A hand?'

''Twas ice. Ice cold and no moving in it. And she healed him.'

'So you knew who she was and were familiar with her position in the community as a quack doctress?'

'I knew she had the knowledge.' Nóra felt Nance looking at her then, and a sudden flare of uncertainty rose up in her. ''Twas her who said it was fairy, and 'twas her who offered to banish it!'

The prosecutor was thoughtful for a moment. 'It must have been a great relief to you, Mrs Leahy. A helpless, onerous child filling you with shame and grief and trouble, and lo – a woman who tells you he was no child at all, but a fairy. How relieved you must have felt to discover that you bore no duty towards him! How easy to have your own disgust and horror sanctioned with the knowledge that *it was not your grandson!*'

Nóra stared at the lawyer as he threw his hands up in the air, gesturing to the jury. They looked uncomfortable. She shook her head, unable to speak. They could not understand. They had not seen the great change in the child. There had been no human in the boy, in the bones brimming with fairy, the sour-skinned squall of him. If only she could return to her cabin and find her daughter's boy, show them the child returned to her.

'Will you tell the court, Mrs Leahy, if you agreed to pay Anne Roche for this great alleviation of guilt and trouble?'

'She does not take money.'

'Please speak up!'

'Nance does not take money. Eggs, chickens . . .'

'She takes payment in kind, is this what you are saying, Mrs Leahy? Was this the arrangement made between the two of you? That she would pronounce your crippled grandson a *fairy*, then work to *put the fairy out of it* through application of nostrums, herbal poison and, finally, *drowning*, and in kind you would supply her with the food and fuel she needed to survive?'

'I don't . . .'

'You must answer yes or no, Mrs Leahy.'

'I don't know. No.'

All Nóra could think of as she stood there, hearing the counsel repeat his questions, was that her body was failing her. She trembled uncontrollably, her bare feet curling in cramp on the floor as she attempted to keep up with his questions. Had she been glad to see the foxglove taking its effect on the child? Had she been saddened when it had not killed him? Had she been in the river the morning Micheál was drowned, and if Nance was in a state of undress, why had she been fully clothed? Why did she insist on referring to the child as a fairy when, as she had heard, Micheál's body had been found? Had she panicked and fled when she realised he had drowned, or had the drowning been her intention all along?

He was saying she had killed him. There was a pricking between her legs and, horrified, Nóra felt warm drops of urine roll down her thighs. She brought her hands to her face and began to weep in shame.

A hushed silence then. When Nóra opened her eyes she saw Mr Walshe rising out of his seat, his lips pursed in thought.

'Is it true that you wished the best for the boy in your care, Mrs Leahy?'

Nóra's tongue felt sluggish. She opened her mouth but no sound came out.

Mr Walshe repeated his question, as though he was speaking to an invalid. 'Mrs Leahy, is it not true that you nurtured the boy when he came into your care? That you sought assistance from a doctor?'

Nóra nodded. 'Yes. In September.'

'And what treatment did the doctor prescribe for your grandson?'

'Nothing. He said there was nothing to be done.'

'That must have caused you great distress, Mrs Leahy.'

'It did.'

'Mary Clifford, the Crown's witness, said that you sought assistance from your priest, Father Healy, also?'

'I did.'

'And what assistance did he offer you?'

'He said there was nothing to be done.'

'Mrs Leahy, am I correct in saying, then, that when the most careful nurture failed to restore the boy to health and strength, when neither doctor nor priest were able to avail you with medicine or help, you sought to find a cure via the only other means available to you? Through the local *doctress*, Anne Roche?'

Nóra's voice came out in a whisper. 'Yes.'

'And when Miss Roche told you that she believed she would be able to *restore* your grandchild to you, in full health and with all the capabilities and mobility you saw in him when you visited your daughter two years ago, you had *hope*?'

'I did.'

'And who could blame you for that, Mrs Leahy? Was it *hope* that led you to believe that the crippled boy we now understand to be Micheál Kelliher was *fairy*? Was it *hope* and a *longing* to preserve the life of your grandchild that led you to assist Anne Roche in her "cures"?'

'I . . . I don't understand.'

The lawyer hesitated, wiped his forehead. 'Mrs Leahy, did you hope to preserve the life of Micheál Kelliher?'

Nóra's head swam. She gripped the irons about her wrist. The fairies do not like iron, she thought. Fire, iron and salt. Cold embers and tongs over the cradle, and new milk spilt on Maytime earth.

'Mrs Leahy?' It was the judge, leaning forward, his blue eyes rheumy, voice deep and concerned. 'Mrs Leahy, the court is asking you if you have any further statement to make.'

Nóra brought a trembling hand up to her face. The iron was cool against her flushed cheeks. 'No, sir. None other than that I only wanted my grandson with me. None other than that.'

Nance listened as the man they called Coroner presented himself as a witness, his clipped red moustache uttering words she did not understand.

'Our inquest found that Micheál Kelliher came by his death following asphyxia, caused by inhalation of fluid and consequent obstruction of the air passages. Signs presented were consistent with drowning. The lungs were waterlogged, and there was evidence of river weed in the hair of the deceased.'

There was no mention of the yellow flaggers on the bank, the unfurling gold against the green and all the suggestion its blossom held. They did not mention the power in the boundary water, in the strange light that flooded the earth before the sun rose, in the actions of hungered hands.

'In your professional estimation, sir,' asked the counsel, 'how long would the deceased have been held under the water for drowning and death to occur?'

The coroner was thoughtful. 'Given that it seems the deceased was paralytic, either fully or in part, it may have taken less time than what may be deemed usual. I would venture to propose three minutes.'

'That is three minutes of sustained submersion?'

'That is correct, sir.'

'Are there any other findings you feel compelled to include in your statement today?'

The man sniffed, twitching his moustache. 'There were marks which indicate the possibility of struggle.'

'And by marks do you mean bruises?'

'Yes, sir. About the chest and neck. Inconclusive, but they did raise suspicions that the child was forcibly held under water.'

The counsel placed the tips of his fingers together, his eyes darting towards the jury. 'Mr McGillycuddy, in your professional opinion, do you believe that the findings of the coronial inquest indicate that the deceased was murdered with intent? That his was a violent death?'

The man looked at Nance and lifted his chin. He gave a brief, curt nod. 'I do, sir.'

Nance was ready when the court finally called for her statement. She had been waiting for the opportunity to tell her story, to reveal to the room the kernelled truth within the mass of stories and sworn informations and cross-examinations. She stood as Maggie would have done, straight-backed, eyes narrowed, and when they handed her the book to kiss, she did so with sincerity. They would not be able to fault her. She would show them the truth of her knowledge, her cure.

'Miss Roche, please tell the court how you make your living.'

'I give out the cure.'

'Speak up, please, the court cannot hear you.'

Nance took a deep breath and attempted to raise her voice. But the room was hot, and the air seemed to catch on her lungs, and when she spoke again there was a groaning from the crowd.

'Your worship, will you allow the prisoner to make her statement from the witness stand so that she may be heard?'

'I will.'

An officer of the court led Nance to the box where she had seen the various speakers give out against her. After a day and a half listing in the dock against the courtroom wall, it felt strange to now be standing at a different place in the room, so much closer to the dark-suited men sitting with their shined shoes catching the gleam from the glass windows. Before they had appeared shadowy, but now Nance could make out their features: their dry lips and greying eyebrows, the lines surrounding their eyes. Some, she saw, were surely her age, and she wondered if, as a girl, she had seen them and their gentle-blooded parents on excursion to Mangerton. Had her hands picked the strawberries that their mothers had bought and pressed into their pink mouths?

'Anne Roche, can you please tell the court how you make your living?'

'I help people with the knowledge that I have been given, and they give me gifts in return.'

The counsel glanced at the jurors, and Nance caught the suggestion of a smirk on his lips. 'And can you please explain what this "knowledge" is?'

'I have the knowledge to heal all manner of ills and sickness, both those of an ordinary kind and those wrought by the Good People.'

'Can you please describe the difference between the two?'

'There are those which are of a common kind, but there are some ills which are the mark of the Good People, and they call for a different cure.'

The counsel studied her for a moment. 'But, Miss Roche, what is the difference between the two?'

Nance paused, confused. She had already explained to him that she divined the mark of the Good People amongst the sick, that she administered to the ordinary bruise, the extraordinary swelling. 'It might be that a man has built his house on a fairy path, and it is that which brings the sickness to him, or it might be something else entirely.'

'So what you are saying is that people come to you with sickness, and it is only then that you *diagnose* whether their sickness was caused by *the Good People*, or otherwise?'

'That is the truth of it.'

'And how did you learn these things?'

''Twas taught to me by my own aunt when I was a girl and growing.'

'And where did your aunt learn these nostrums and mysteries?'

'When she was away with the Good People.'

The lawyer raised his eyebrows. 'And by Good People, you mean to say the fairies?'

'Yes, the Good People.'

'Forgive me for my *ignorance* –' there was a smattering of laughter from the crowd '– but why do you call the fairies *Good People*? It is my understanding that they are not people at all.'

'It is out of respect that I call them the Good People, for they do not like to be thinking of themselves as bad craturs. They have a desire to get into Heaven, same as you, sure, Counsel.'

'Miss Roche, I am acquainted with the fireside stories, but I must say that I do not give them credence. How do you know the fairies to be true?'

'Because they took my mother and my aunt. I know there is no word of a lie in Them, for didn't they lead me out of Killarney when I was poor and had no living at all, and didn't they show me the way to the valley where I have been living for these past twenty years?'

'You have seen them? How did they "show you the way"?'

'Oh, I have heard Them talking, and 'tis truth I see Them as lights coming to me and leading me, and there have been times I heard Them dancing or fighting.'

'They fight?'

'The Good People are fond of fighting and hurling and dancing and singing. And 'tis true that they sometimes cause mischief, and that is why the people come to me: because I have the knowledge of the ways in which to undo the damage they cause. I have the knowledge and the cure if the fairies do be striking you or taking the profit out of your animals or crops, or the power out of your legs.'

A rising murmur lifted from the crowd, and Nance could see several onlookers whisper to each other from behind their hands. They were listening to her. Relieved to finally be heard, she began to talk of the ways the Good People pressed up against the known world. She spoke of the power in saliva, in urine, in dung, in water from the holy wells, or that which held the leavings of iron. Of holed and hollowed stones, of soot and salt.

'The Good People have a mighty fear of fire and iron, and sure, 'tis the threat of these which will serve to banish Them, so they have no power against a reddened poker. And though they lay their claim to fairy plants and trees – elder, foxglove – if certain plants can be got without their interference, the power in them can be turned against those who lay claim to them. Sure, elder has a mighty mischief and *crostáil*, and the Good People ride its branches, but sure, I can wring the bad temper out of it. And there are a great many things aside, cures given to me by the Good People, which I may not say, for if the secret goes out of a cure, there will be no power in it at all.'

When she had finished, Nance took a deep breath and examined the jury. The men were looking at her with an expression she could not place. There was none of the lawyer's acid curl of the lip, none of the scowling or wariness she had experienced before. No anger, no fear. She realised, then, that they regarded her with the same expression of those she had begged from: pity, shadowed with disdain. Her stomach sank.

The lawyer was smiling to himself.

'Miss Roche, do you accept payment for your . . . services?'

'I don't be taking money, for I'd surely lose the knowledge and cure.'

'But it is true that you will accept gifts of fuel and food? Goods.'

'Sure, that is true.'

'Did you drown Micheál Kelliher in the Flesk on Monday, the sixth of March, in exchange for goods?'

Nance frowned. 'I'm not after drowning Micheál Kelliher, no.'

'Both Mary Clifford and Mrs Leahy have stated that you ordered them to bathe Micheál Kelliher in that pool of the river Flesk, where the boundaries of three rivers meet. They say they had so bathed him for three mornings running, and on the last morning you kept the child longer under the water than usual.'

''Twas to banish it. The fairy.'

'Not it, Miss Roche. Himself. Micheál Kelliher.'

''Twas no natural boy.'

'He was a paralytic, we hear. Could neither stand nor walk nor speak.'

''Twas the fairy of it.'

'He was your patient?'

'He was.'

'But you are not a doctor. You are ignorant of medical knowledge. Your training is only in *nostrums*. Old folk cures. Is that not so?'

Nance felt a kick of anger in her chest. Over and over they circled with their questions. Did she not make herself clear? 'I have the knowledge. Of the charms and the cures. Of the herbs.'

'Mrs Leahy has said you led her to believe that you were capable of curing the boy, Miss Roche. If you have the *knowledge*, then why is Micheál Kelliher dead? Why could you not cure him?'

Nance thought of Maggie, smoking by the warmth of the fire at night while the corncrakes filled the air outside with their long, scraping cries.

What is in the marrow is hard to take out of the bone.

''Tis not Micheál Kelliher who is dead,' she said finally.

'Do you truly believe that, Miss Roche?'

Nance brought her gaze level to that of the counsel. 'That child died a long time ago.'

There were exclamations from those listening in the court. Nance noticed the jurors shift in their chairs and exchange knowing looks.

'Is there any other statement you would like to make to the court?'

Nance hesitated. 'I have told you my truth.'

'That is all then, thank you.'

Nance was fetched down from the witness box and returned to her place in the dock next to Nóra. While the counsel made his closing remarks, Nance ran the pads of her fingers over her crooked thumbs, swollen sore in the heat of the courtroom. They throbbed, and she tucked them into her palms, balling her hands into fists.

There was a whimper beside her, and Nance saw that Nóra was shaking, staring as Mr Walshe raised a hand in an attempt to settle the crowd. An atmosphere of nervous excitement was issuing throughout the courtroom. She heard the judge wearily call for order, and one of the jurors sent a man to open the outer door of the court. There was a collective murmur of relief as fresh air fanned through the room.

Nance saw that, for all the defence lawyer's outward ease, Mr Walshe's face was shining with sweat, his shirt visibly damp beneath his suit. He regarded the sober-faced jury.

'Gentlemen, this case, although unusual and repugnant in the extreme, is not one of wilful murder. The Crown's chief witness, Mary Clifford, who was present at the time the accident occurred, who witnessed *firsthand* Micheál Kelliher's treatment not only at the Flesk on the morning of Monday, the sixth of March, but also in the months prior to his death, stood before you and – under oath – admitted that she did not believe the prisoners had deliberately drowned the child. Given her testimony, Anne Roche and Honora Leahy cannot be rightly convicted of wilful murder.

'Gentlemen, Micheál Kelliher lost his life through superstition. It is true that the circumstances surrounding his treatment at the hands of the accused are extraordinary. It is true that the gross delusion these women operated under is horrifying. The scale of their ignorance is appalling. But it cannot be discounted as incidental. The accused acted on the belief that the deceased child, Micheál Kelliher, was a fairy spirit. A *changeling*, in the words of the Crown's witness. Anne Roche selected a particular site of the river Flesk believed to be fairy-inhabited waters, and bathed him there with the assistance of Honora Leahy three mornings consecutively, contending that the falsely believed changeling would return to his supernatural realm.'

Nance remembered the wildness with which Nóra had hauled herself up the bank when they had lifted the banished changeling from the water.

'I will go to see if he is returned!' The widow's grey hair unfastening down her back as she grasped at tree roots and moss to drag herself from the river. 'I will see if he is there!' Lurching wildly through the ferns and bracken, branches swinging in her wake.

Burying the body of the changeling in the Piper's Grave, pimpled with cold.

'Neither of the accused can write, gentlemen. Anne Roche, particularly, is unlettered and ignorant of the modern world, and her statement that "the child died a long time ago" is evidence of her benighted belief that the boy she was curing was *fairy*. Again, let me remind you that even Mary Clifford, who was witness to the act, has stated under oath that the child was bathed not with intent to kill, but to *put the fairy out of it*. Given this testimony, and the pitiful intellectual and moral ignorance and the advanced age of the accused, I recommend to you an acquittal of this charge.'

Nance stared as the lawyer returned to his seat, fear rising in her throat. I have no ignorance upon me, she wanted to tell him. Don't be telling them that would have me hang that there is no knowledge about me.

Baron Pennefather cleared his throat. He waited until there was absolute silence before addressing the jury.

'Gentlemen. Let me impress upon you that while a charge of murder may be commuted to manslaughter where life was taken away under the influence of sudden passion, this cannot apply to the defence's argument that the life of Micheál Kelliher was taken as a result of superstitious belief.'

'We will hang,' Nóra whispered. 'They do not believe. They think it superstition.' Her voice shook, her tongue catching on the words. Nance's heart thudded in dread.

The judge took a moment to examine the waiting faces in the room. 'It is clear that the ignorant actions of the prisoners demonstrate their belonging to a caste derived from hereditary or progressive immorality. Yet, it is not a mark of wickedness we find in this case, but rather the overwhelming suggestion and likelihood of low intellectual power in combination with strongly developed passions of the lower nature.'

Nance began to breathe rapidly. What is he saying? she wondered. What is he saying about me?

'In short, while this is a case of suspicion, and requires to be thoroughly examined into, I encourage you to recognise the superstitious motives that are clearly, albeit disturbingly, evident. And I ask you to consider the problems of women of advanced age in prison, unfit for transportation, who demand much attention through infirmity. Thank you, gentlemen.'

Nance watched as the jurors rose together like a flock of grey-hooded crows and exited the room to decide their verdict. The noise in the courtroom was suddenly overwhelming.

I don't understand, thought Nance. I don't understand.

Looking down she saw that she still held her hands in fists.

The jury were gone less than half an hour before the clerk and officer of the court began to settle the crowd. Nance felt her heartbeat rise in apprehension as Justice Baron Pennefather entered the room and resumed his position in the chair, pressing his hands together as stragglers forced their way inside, fighting for a clear view of the prisoners.

Next to her, Nóra leant against the dock, her body slowly sinking towards the floor. Nance reached out to grasp her about the arm and Nóra's eyes flashed open.

'Don't touch me,' she hissed, before fear splayed through her expression and she clutched at Nance's retreating hands. 'I don't want to die,' she murmured. She lifted her fetters and attempted to cross herself. 'I don't want to hang. I don't want to hang.'

Nance felt the widow begin to shake again.

'Sore-wounded Christ. Oh, sore-wounded Christ, I don't want to hang. Oh, please, Lord.'

Nance began to rock on her feet, fear filling her stomach. She bit on her tongue until she could taste the iron of her blood.

'Sore-wounded Christ, Martin! Oh!'

'Quiet now.' An officer nudged Nóra and she gasped, suddenly gripping onto the wooden spikes in front of them to hold herself upright.

The atmosphere in the court was like that in the face of an approaching storm. An uneasy hush. A gathering tension in the air as the jurors were admitted back into the court and, faces solemn, returned to their chairs.

'I don't want to hang,' Nóra continued muttering next to Nance. 'I don't want to hang.'

The judge's voice carried across the room. 'Have you found your verdict?'

A white-haired man stood, hands carefully brushing down his trousers. 'We have, Your Worship.'

'What say you?'

Nance closed her eyes. Imagined the river, the peaceful unknotting of water.

She could feel Nóra shaking violently next to her.

'We agree with Your Worship that this is a case of suspicion, however, in the charge of wilful murder against Anne Roche and Honora Leahy, we find insufficient evidence for conviction. Our verdict is not guilty.'

There was a pause, and then the courtroom erupted in excited and furious reaction.

Nance sank to the floor, her legs collapsing in relief. Shutting her eyes, the clamour in the hot air around her sounded like nothing more than a sudden downpour of rain. Summer rain breaking over the pine needles hot-scented in the woods, crisping leaves browning in the oak, the alder, the torrential blessing of heavy cloud over the forest, and the sweet gurgle of water towards the river.

Nance only opened her eyes again when they hauled her to her feet to unlock the fetters. Blinking against the light, she was vaguely aware of Nóra, bent over, howling with relief, and beyond her, in the shifting, tidal crowd, Mary, staring at them with tears streaming down her pale cheeks.

'Mary!' Nance croaked. There was a heavy tug and the irons came off her wrists and in the sudden feel of lightness and freedom, she raised both palms to the sobbing girl. 'Mary!'

The girl spat on the ground. 'I curse you,' she mouthed. Then she turned and disappeared into the seething crowd.

Heather

Mary stood in the crowded market street of Tralee, her eyes scanning the flocks of people that milled in the road. The day was hot, and she sweated in the new shift she had bought with the widow's shilling. She had wrapped the clothes still filled with Micheál's smell in a neat bundle and held this conspicuously at her hip, standing straight as a poker, her eyes meeting every casual and curious gaze that reached her. Let them see that she was for hire.

Pigs lay humped in the road, their squealing piglets in makeshift pens staked with pegs and string. Sheep, new-shorn, huddled under the eyes of boys and their fathers, capped, smoking, laughing at the women chasing a terrified chicken that had flown the straw coop.

Mary had asked Father Healy the road to Annamore after the trial. Had started walking the way, exultant, her heart thrilling in anticipation. She imagined the shouts of surprise as she rounded the corner, the little thumping feet hitting the dust as her brothers and sisters ran to her, wrapped their arms about her legs and waist and dragged her away to show her new-hatched chickens, scooping up the puffing, cheeping yellow. Her mam, lined and sombre as usual, but relieved to see her safe. Happy to have her home to work. And how she would work. She would tend the lazy beds until the stalks came thick and fast, and she would shake the soil from the clutch of lumpers, as yellow as butter, and no one would be hungry. They would boil them briefly, to eat them 'with the bones still in', as her da would say. And she would hold the little ones afterwards, or set them to sleep against the belly of the snoring pig in the corner, and all would be well.

She would forget Micheál. She would forget the strange boy bleating from the cold, who had curled into her neck for the warmth her body held there.

Mary had been thinking these thoughts, imagining her life back home, when she had stopped to drink from a well at the side of the road. A beggar woman was sleeping there, face heavily pocked. At first Mary thought she was alone, but at the splashing of the water something stirred under the woman's dirty cloak, and a small, naked child emerged. A little girl, her blonde hair greyed with dirt, holding her hand out to Mary in patient expectation. Mary stared at her, water still dripping down her chin, and then slowly unwrapped the food the priest had given her for the journey. Dried fish. A heel of stale, buttered bread.

The little girl took them from her hand, then crawled back under her mother's cloak to eat, the material quivering.

Mary had turned around then. The road back to Tralee seemed longer than the one she had taken from it, but a man and his wife heading into market on an open cart offered her a ride, and Mary took it, setting her bare feet on the spokes of the wheel and climbing up to the boards. She had set her eyes on the horizon, watching as the distance to Annamore lengthened with every step of the mule.

She would stand in the streets of Tralee all day if she had to. She would stand there until someone came and asked her, would she like to work a farm in summer, could she thresh and carry turf, and was she strong, and did she know how to churn?

I will take the first offer I get, Mary thought. There was no use in taking the measure of a face to gauge whether a place of work would be a safe one. It did not matter if the nose was red with drink taken, or if the eyes were webbed with the lines of laughter. There was no telling the shape of a heart from the face of the one who carried it.

The sun beat down on her. She was thirsty. Lifting the bundle up to her forehead to shield her eyes, she caught the scent of the fairy child in the old linen. Sour milk and stale potato. Hearth smoke and the cold night. All the witching hours awake with the changeling, all the wrapping of blankets and the fighting of his limbs, the sharp feel of his nails between her teeth as she carefully bit their lengths so he would not scratch himself in his dancing, in his fitting, in his strange reaching for the world around him. The hot feel of his tongue against her fingers as she fed him, the eyes sliding over her face and the feathers on his skin, the laughs dissolving into the air, and the screaming that pealed from him.

It knocked the breathing out of her.

Uncaring that people stared, Mary hid her face in the dirty bundle and wept.

After the trial, Nóra travelled back to the valley with Daniel. She had found her nephew waiting outside the courthouse, smoking in the sunshine and speaking with Father Healy. Both men had looked up as she approached, squinting in the glare of daylight.

'They freed you then,' Daniel had murmured, turning his pipe in his hands.

The expression on the priest's face had been one of ill-hidden aversion.

'You have much to thank God for,' he had remarked. 'You should have listened to me. I warned you, Nóra. I warned you that nothing good would happen for talk of fairies.' His face had pinked. 'Nance Roche did not stop with her nostrums, with her *piseógs*, with her heathen practices, and the Church will not stand for it, verdict or no. I can't be tolerating superstitious belief upheld over true faith. Nóra, blind yourself no longer to the sin of pagan delusion.'

Nóra had stared at the priest, unable to say a word. It wasn't until Daniel had placed a heavy hand on her shoulder and guided her away that she fully understood the meaning of the priest's words.

'He will excommunicate her,' she had whispered to Daniel.

Her nephew had sighed and gestured down the road. 'I'll take you home, Nóra.'

They travelled to Killarney by mail cart, neither of them speaking. The other passengers stared at her, and Nóra realised that her clothes, returned after the trial, were still covered in river mud. She covered her head and face with her shawl, despite the heat. Nóra was glad Daniel did not want to talk. There was a weight in her mouth, upon her tongue. She did not quite know what had happened. All she knew was that she must return home, must see if Micheál was returned.

When the cart stopped in Killarney, she and Daniel walked to the outskirts of the town, then stopped at the door of a cabin, asking for food and a night's lodging. They were hungry themselves, the woman of the house said. July was a mean month, a hungry month. God provide them with a fine crop and soon, or they would all be on the roads. Still, they were good people, she would feed them what she could and let them make beds out of straw and find a corner where they might sleep under cover, away from the night sky crawling with moonlight. Nóra fell asleep with straw scratching her cheek and woke before dawn. She washed her face in dew, and when Daniel woke, they walked the pale lane in the early-morning light as the robins swooped and the chitterling, waking animals rustled. As the day warmed and filled with people going about their business, carrying *sleánta* and creels, Nóra let her mind return to the child that would surely be waiting for her, saw her daughter's face echoed in his features, saw Johanna when she was young and all seemed light and full of possibility, until she barely saw the road in front of them.

It was only as they returned to the valley and its crib of mountains, clad with heather purpling in the twilight, that Daniel spoke to her.

'You'll be staying with us, then.'

They had crested a hill, and Nóra was breathing hard. She stopped and stared at Daniel. 'I'll be staying in my cabin.'

Daniel kept his eyes firmly on the road before them, maintaining an even stride. 'There was no rent paid on it.'

'I've been late with the rent before.' Panic rose in her chest. She ran to catch up with him. 'Sure, 'tis no uncommon thing, to be late with the rent.'

'You'll be in with me and the little woman, Nóra.'

'But Micheál will be waiting for me at my cabin.'

There was an uncomfortable silence. Daniel lit his pipe and clamped the stem between his teeth.

'And what about my belongings?' Nóra protested.

'You can fetch them. But there's a need to be selling the bed.'

Nóra cried then, wiping her face with dirty hands, until they rounded a corner and saw John O'Shea, face already browned with the summer, the shadow of a moustache lighting golden.

'Widow Leahy?' He was standing in the lane, his hands full of rocks he had been pelting at a bird's nest. 'They didn't hang you then.'

Daniel squinted against the setting sun. 'She can't stay to talk, John. Let her pass.'

'Do you know there's a rhyme about you?'

Nóra sniffed. 'A rhyme?'

The boy put his hands in his pockets and began to sing. '*Nóra Leahy, what have you done? You drowned your daughter's only son! The lad could neither speak nor stand. Did fairies take him, hand in hand? Or did you take him to the water, the only son of your only daughter?*'

Nóra stared at him, a sick feeling spreading through her chest. 'God forgive you.'

John's grin faded.

''Tis only a rhyme,' Daniel interjected. 'There's been worse said. John, go and tell Peg that the Widow Leahy's returned.'

The boy nodded and began to run down the lane.

Daniel turned to Nóra. 'Don't mind him. Go on with you to your old place and start collecting what you need. I'll fetch Brigid. She can help you carry your things. You'll be spending the night with us. She'll make you comfortable. I won't be in tonight. There's business to attend to.' He nodded to her, his face grim, then continued down the lane after John at a quickened pace.

When both men were mere specks in the distance Nóra sank to her knees in the dust of the road. The words of the boy ran through her head and she vomited, bile stringing in the summer wind.

The grass was high around her cabin. Nóra, gasping for air, pulled the door to and stood on the step. The room was musty. Dirt had blown in and the straw blocking the window was gone. Old rushes were eddied in the leavings of the wind.

'God bless all here,' Nóra cried, stomach heaving. She looked around the room, desperate for some sign of the boy, but all was still. The room was as she had left it, the hearth dead, the settle bed unfolded.

Nóra took a tentative step inside. 'Micheál?'

Nothing.

'Micheál? Dear one?'

Nóra shut the door behind her. Then a sudden noise sent her spirits soaring. She rushed into the bedroom, unable to breathe, hope mounting in her chest. She had been right! Micheál was here! He was under the greatcoat on her bed, here was the form of him, here he was sleeping.

But there was nothing under the coat except an unfolded blanket. Nóra clasped it, breathing quickly. There was a quiet murmur of a hen by her feet, and as her eyes adjusted to the dim light, Nóra saw that the chicken was broody, had settled on a nest scratched from old rushes and straw pulled from the mattress.

A slow uneasiness dripped through her.

Please God, she prayed, pulling back the blankets on her bed, growing frantic, more desperate. Please God, please Martin, please let him be here. 'Micheál!'

Nothing. No sound but the cluck of the disturbed hen.

Unsure of what she should do, Nóra pulled on Martin's greatcoat and staggered out into the main room, sinking onto a stool. Silence rang in her ears.

He wasn't there. He had not been returned.

She had been so certain she would find him, perhaps sitting by the fire, eyes looking up to her as she entered. Martin's face, Johanna's colour. She rubbed her cheek against the rough frieze, taking long breaths of her husband's remaining scent. Reaching into the pocket, she took out the dead ember and turned the char in her hands.

He was not there. She had been so sure.

Outside the birds sang down the sun.

*

'God and Mary to you.'

Nóra turned, her eyes swollen. Peg stood at the threshold of the cabin, leaning on her blackthorn, looking on in silence.

'He isn't here.'

The old woman offered her hand to Nóra. 'You've returned to us, God be praised.' She waited as Nóra wiped her face. 'What trouble,' she murmured. 'What sorrow. Come on with you, now. Sitting in the dark like this, and no fire lit. Well. At least the night is warm. I'll sit with you for a bit now, shall I?'

She eased herself down next to Nóra, and together they sat by the ashes in the orange light of the sunset.

Peg pointed to the table and Nóra saw that cream was rising in a clean crock.

''Twas the son's woman. She couldn't bear to hear the beast bawling. Your butter is with me. For the safe keeping.' Peg sucked her teeth. ''Tis back in the milk.'

Nóra nodded wearily. 'That's a blessing.'

'There's need of blessings in this valley.'

There was a sudden chorus of crickets. The women sat in silence, listening to the chirring.

'They buried him in the *cillín*,' Peg said finally. 'Father Healy said 'twas best.'

Nóra blinked, staring at the dead fire.

Peg leant closer. 'What in God's holy name happened to the cratur?'

'I was after being rid of the fairy, Peg,' Nóra murmured.

'When I saw you that morning, Nóra, you were soaked to the bone.' She placed a hand on her knee and lowered her voice. 'Did you give him a wee push?'

Nóra didn't know what to say. She gently nudged Peg's hand away before standing and rummaging for the bottle she'd left in the hearth nook. 'Where is it, Peg?'

'I'm not accusing you. 'Tis only, if you did, 'twould be –'

'Where is it?'

'Where is what?'

'The *poitín*.'

Peg sighed. 'Gone, Nóra. There was someone here . . .' She threw up her hands. 'I sent the boys down when I saw what they were about, but they took what they felt was theirs.'

'Seán Lynch.'

Peg shook her head. ''Twas Kate. 'Twas a fear on everyone after the *piseóg*. After Áine. Kate was here and looking all about your churn. She was thinking 'twas the boy that blinked the milk and brought the baby out of Brigid. She was looking for signs of cursing. Says she found a flint by the dash. She said Seán had laid claim to your goods, that you were sure to hang, and she was to take some things while he was up in Tralee.'

'What did she take, Peg?'

'Some things of Martin's. The *poitín*. The pipe. The coin you had. Clothes. What butter was here before, and some other food. The salt.'

Nóra looked up and saw that the wooden box was gone. ''Twas from my wedding.'

'She would have taken the cow only there were some of us told her to wait until we had news of the verdict.'

'I might have been hanged, Peg.'

'I know.'

Nóra felt like she would choke. She pulled at the loose skin of her throat, pressing her chin against her knuckles, and began to weep. Peg extended a hand to her and Nóra took it with the grip of the drowning, squeezing her fingers until the old woman grimaced in pain. Still, she let Nóra sink her nails into her skin.

'He isn't here,' she sobbed.

'I know,' Peg said softly. 'I know.'

It was some time before Nóra could speak again. She sat with her face streaming, chin slippery.

Peg crossed herself. 'Thank God in his infinite mercy you are saved.'

Nóra wiped her eyes. 'They thought us mad. The fairy talk. They didn't give in to it, but the girl said 'twas not done with the intent to kill and so they could not be calling it murder.'

'After the arrest Father Healy read to us from the *Chute's Western Herald*. It said you were of good character, Nóra. There's none here who can say you are anything other.'

'There's a rhyme about me that says otherwise.'

'You're a good woman, Nóra Leahy.'

'I wanted to be rid of the fairy.'

'He was a burden to you.'

'He was not Johanna's son. There was none of my blood in him.'

Peg brushed the hair out of Nóra's eyes. ''Tis a queer thing. For all the badness that has been in this place, folk are saying that with the changeling out of the valley there is peace again. That surely the boy was blinking the hens and the cows, for now the profit is back. Women who thought they might not have enough to keep shadow stitched to heel are calling for the egg man, purses filling again. Those who thought they might be on the road paid their rents after all.'

'Daniel says this place is lost to me.'

Peg clucked her tongue. ''Tis a shame, but sure, you'd be rattling around on your own.'

'Did they find who lay the *piseóg*?'

'They say 'twas surely Nance, but fortunate that 'twas found so soon and set to rights by the priest. There was no time for the curse to be sinking in the soil. Kate was spouting at the well, saying sure 'twas Nance, for don't curses come home to roost, and 'tis what happens to folk who wish others ill. Their wickedness catches up with them and they find themselves in Tralee with a nice rope collar.'

'Kate Lynch!' Nóra spat, growing tearful. 'Coming in here and taking what belongs to me after Seán's bidding. I'll be going over there and taking it all back. The salt box!'

'Nóra . . .'

'She believed it more than anyone. She believed it more than anyone! How dare she talk about rope collars. We're kin, after all.'

Peg tenderly wiped the tears from Nóra's face. 'Kate's gone.'

'What?'

'Kate Lynch. Seán returned from Tralee this morning to an empty cabin. She left some days ago, we think. Taken all she took from you, and all the egg and butter money. Seán says 'twas a small fortune gone missing from under the bed.'

Nóra gaped at her.

'Oh, he's in a fit over it. Went straight out today searching for her, saying she might have been taken.' Peg gave a small smile. 'Says the tinkers have been on the roads, might have stolen her. Oh, and there's the usual talk of the fairies at the biddy well. Some are saying she's been swept, others are telling Seán to go to the Piper's Grave on Sunday night and she'll be riding out on a white horse.'

'Kate's gone?'

Peg nodded. 'Aye. I'd bet my good leg and my bad that the poor woman won't be coming back.'

Nóra was thoughtful. 'And Áine?'

'She lives. I heard Brigid Lynch has been going in to care for her.'

'Thanks be to the Virgin.'

There was silence.

'Peg, I thought for a moment . . . When I came back, I thought I heard him in the bedroom.'

'Nóra . . .'

'I thought 'twas him. Peg, when I was up in Tralee, I kept dreaming of him. Dreaming I'd return and he'd be here, waiting. That perhaps there was some delay on him that morning in the river, that it would take time before he was restored to me.' She began to cry again. 'Peg, the fear was on me that I'd be hanged and he'd be here waiting for me!'

'Oh, Nóra.'

'Waiting for his grandmother, but she'd be lying in the pit at Ballymullen!'

'There, now. You're not to be hanged. You're back where you belong.'

'But he's not here!' Nóra shook her head. 'Oh, I can't stay in the valley.'

'Nóra, there's no place else for you to go.'

'Look!' She swept her arm around the empty cabin. 'This is all the home I had, and 'tis gone to me. I am all alone. All alone, and no choice but to go in with Daniel and Brigid when I was the woman of my own house.' She wiped her eyes. 'Martin is dead. Micheál . . . He's not here.' She clutched at her heart. 'I don't know . . . I don't know what has happened.'

Peg took up her hand and stroked it. 'Ara, you've got me, have you not? And 'tis a blessing to have your nephews, God protect them. You'll keep company with Brigid, and sure, 'tis no bad thing to be in a full house.'

'Full house or no, I am alone,' Nóra whispered.

'Come now, woman. Count your blessings! You're not alone – you have plenty kin in this world left to talk to and share the heat of a fire with. God knows it has been a terrible winter for you, and a terrible hardship it must have been sitting in gaol thinking you'd be gone to God. Nóra, there's none that envy you for that. But you've come home to hens in the roost and cream in the pot that you might be taking with you. And would you look next to you, Nóra, for don't you have old Peg too?'

Nóra squeezed Peg's hand. 'Do you think . . . Micheál, it might be that he'll come home to me. One day . . .'

Peg pursed her lips.

'He will. For that was no human child. Was it, Peg?'

'No,' murmured Peg eventually. She rubbed Nóra's hand. 'No, Nóra.'

'And it may be that he'll come back.'

Peg gave her a long look. 'But if it happens that he stays away under hill, with the Good People and the lights and the dancing . . . Well, 'tis worth knowing that there is always worse misfortune to be had.'

There was a sound at the door and Nóra looked over to see Brigid staring in at them, a large basket in her hands.

'God and Mary to you, Nóra Leahy.' Brigid blinked at her, unsmiling. She was pallid from her time indoors, and Nóra thought she seemed frail.

'Why, Brigid! 'Tis good to see you up and out,' said Peg, a note of forced cheerfulness in her voice. 'I've not seen you since your churching.'

'A lot has happened since I saw you last.' Brigid stepped over the threshold and stood by the dead fire, looking down at Nóra. Her face was blank. 'Daniel said they very nearly hanged you.'

Nóra nodded, her mouth dry.

Brigid's expression hardened. 'Dan said Nance deserved to hang. For what she did to Áine. For the *piseóg*. For the bittersweet.'

Nóra stared at her, unable to speak. It was Peg who answered.

'Brigid, come now. Let's have none of that. I'll tell you something. Nance was always a strange one amongst us, but 'tis no rhyme nor reason behind her murdering babies and catching women on fire, no matter the preaching Father Healy has against her. Áine's skirts caught as women's skirts sometimes do, and 'tis no use in blaming another for the fire's liking of a low apron. And did Nance not do her best to be with you in your time of need?'

Brigid paled, still looking down at Nóra. 'She did it, didn't she?'

'Did what?'

'She drowned that boy.'

Peg glanced between them, her beady eyes alert.

''Twas fairy,' Nóra croaked.

Brigid chewed her lip. 'Did you see her? After the trial?'

'No. I lost her in the crowd.'

'Do you know if she was thinking of returning to the valley?'

''Tis where she lives. She'll be wanting to get back to her cabin. 'Twas all I could think about on the road. Getting home.'

Brigid shook her head. 'She'll have no home here. Not now. Get what you need, Nóra. I can't be waiting all night. 'Tis near dark.'

Peg held out a hand. 'Brigid? What are you saying, child?'

''Tis her fault, after all. Come on, Nóra. You can't be staying here.'

'Brigid. What is happening?'

'Dan said I wasn't to tell. Nóra . . .'

'What?'

Brigid bit her lip. She was breathing quickly, gripping her basket so hard that her knuckles were white.

Peg was reaching for her blackthorn stick. 'Let's go, Nóra. To Nance's.' She shuffled towards the door, looking sickened.

Nóra started rising to her feet.

'There's nothing to be done,' Brigid burst out. ''Tis decided.' She shot a finger out to Nóra in warning. ''Twas decided when you were away. And you are lucky that 'twas not decided against you!'

Nóra's stomach swooped in fear. Slowly, her hands trembling, she took Brigid's proffered basket and silently began to collect her belongings.

Nance stood by the woods, gazing at where her *bothán* had stood. Four days' slow walking on the road from Tralee, the long shuffle home on feet stippled with pain, and the cabin was gone.

They had burnt her out. All was ash.

She sank down in the long grass at the edge of the clearing, in the shadows where she would not be seen from the lane, and, exhausted, she slept. She curled into the sweet-smelling summer ground and let her fatigue overwhelm her, until the evening breeze began to blow. She sat up to a sky washed in red cloud.

They must have been careful about it, she thought, sitting up against a tree and looking out over the scorched ground. Had they heaped the roof with dried fuel? Maybe they had quickened the flames with *poitín*. The fire had been high – the uppermost leaves of the nearby trees were black, and half the trunk of the oak was burnt. She stood and walked to the tree and ran her hands carefully over the sooted bark. Charcoal crumbled away, leaving her fingers dirtied. Without thinking why, she brought her palm to her face and blessed herself with the ashes.

Nothing was left. Nance stepped over the crumbling lengths of cindered beams that lay on the ruined ground, poking amongst them for any belongings that might have survived. She found what remained of her gathered wool, once carefully combed and carded, and now a hairy clot upon the ground. The smell of smoke was thick. There were no herbs left. Her stools, the turf, even the clay pots of fat had been burnt to nothing.

It was only when she found the small iron clasp of her goat's lead that she felt the surge of grief, gutting her as swiftly as the swoop of a knife. She closed her eyes and folded her hands tightly about the flaking metal, and imagined Mora, the door shut against her, the fire rising about her. Crying, she began to dig in the ashes for bones, but the light was fading and she could not tell what might be the handle of her tin pail, and what might be the slender remains of her faithful goat.

The night fell starry. The moon rose thin-lipped. Nance sat down in the dead embers of her home, and dug with her hands until she felt the residual warmth of the fire in the soil. She lay in it and blanketed herself with ashes.

Nance gasped awake the next morning at the sound of footsteps. Hauling herself up out of the weight of soot, she looked wildly around her. It was not yet dawn, but the sky had paled to the blue of a robin's egg.

'Nance?'

She spun around. A man stood at the edge of the fire's dark stain, peering intently at her.

Peter O'Connor.

'I thought you were dead,' he said, covering his mouth. He stepped over and helped Nance to her feet. She noticed he was trembling.

'Peter. God bless you.'

He was staring at her, sucking his bottom lip. 'Praise God they freed you,' he stammered.

Nance placed her hand on his forearm, and he gripped it, overcome.

'I thought you were gone from me,' he choked out. 'There was so much talk of the trial. They were saying you'd be hanged or sent away. And you only trying to help.' He raised her fingers to his face and pressed them against his stubbled cheek, chin quivering. 'I was afraid for you.'

'They could not touch me.'

'I was afraid for you, Nance.' He turned away, wiping his eyes. When he turned around again, he was calmer.

'They have burnt me out,' Nance said.

'When the verdict was heard, 'twas decided.'

'Seán Lynch.'

'He came back and found his wife gone and his money with her, and he came here the night before last. He had an anger in him.'

'Kate Lynch is gone?'

'Swept. He was in a state, Nance. He thought you had a hand in it. I couldn't stop them.'

'I know.'

'I tried.' Peter placed a hand over his eyes. 'He had a party of hard men behind him. I'm sorry for it.'

''Tis not your fault.' She took him by the shoulder and he leant into her touch.

'You never did a thing against me. Against anyone.'

They sat in the ashes then, until rain appeared on the hilltops in the distance, and the lowing of animals filled the air.

'You can't stay here,' he said.

'No.'

'Come with me.'

He took her to his cabin, tucked on the raw face of the mountain-side, helping her up the steep slope. As they approached he began to explain what had happened.

'They did it at night. All of the men except John O'Donoghue. He wouldn't have a part in it.'

'Daniel Lynch?'

Peter frowned. 'All but John and myself. But when I saw the pack of them going off after sundown, I followed.' He looked at Nance, disgusted, then motioned her inside the cabin.

Nance stood for a while in the darkness, then gasped.

Her goat stood in the corner of the room, tethered to a battered dresser, piles of droppings at her feet. The exhaustion and relief Nance had been suppressing since the trial suddenly overwhelmed her, and she staggered towards Mora, falling over and throwing her arms around the animal and her familiar warmth, her smell of hay and milk. She rubbed her face in Mora's coat, her eyes suddenly wet.

'My dear one. Oh, my dear one.'

'They were going to slit her throat.'

Nance stroked Mora while Peter stood aside, watching.

'I thought she was dead,' Nance murmured, finally releasing the goat and gingerly drying her eyes with her dirtied shawl. 'You took her.'

'I would not let them kill her like that. Now, Nance. Would you not lie down and close your eyes for a small minute? You must be dead tired from the road. 'Tis a long way you've come.'

Nance slept in the quiet cool of Peter's cabin that day. From time to time she woke and saw him sitting in the doorway, squinting out across the rain-soaked valley, or walking softly about indoors, setting the room to rights. At dusk he woke her and handed her a piggin of warm goat's milk, a cold potato. He watched her as she ate. 'You're looking mighty thin on it, Nance.'

''Twas little feasting to be had in Ballymullen.'

'I was meaning to tell you. You're welcome here, Nance. With me. 'Tis not much, what I have, but there's no kin of mine left in the valley and . . .' He flushed. 'What I'm trying to say is that I could marry you. There's nothing they could do then. Against you.'

'I'm an old woman, Peter.'

'You've always been kind to me, Nance.'

She smiled. 'An old woman without a man is the next thing to a ghost. No one needs her, folk are afraid of her, but mostly she isn't seen.'

'Will you think it over? I'm an able man.'

'I will, Peter. Thank you, I will.'

They said little else that evening. Peter sat by the hearth while Nance rested on the heather, and occasionally they looked at one another and smiled. When night had finally wrapped itself around the cabin, Peter said the rosary, and they washed their feet and lay down to rest by the smoored fire.

Nance rose before dawn. Peter was still asleep, snoring softly where he lay by the raked hearth, sprawled, arms above his head. He looked older in sleep, Nance thought.

Quietly, so as not to wake him, she unraked the embers on the hearthstone and selected a fat lump of charcoal. She let it cool as she milked Mora, and when she had the pail filled, she placed the drink and the dead ember on the dresser and blessed them both.

Then she untied the goat and silently left Peter's cabin.

Her bones ached. Nance set out towards the lane, the goat's rope loose in her hand, limping from the soreness in her hip.

When did I become so old? she wondered.

The air was sweet and damp. A morning mist rolled down off the mountains and their purple skins. Hares moved lightly through the heather, white tails scuttling through the dark tangle of brambles before the rowan trees, blossom-white, the clover. The lane was empty before her, and there was no movement in the waiting valley, no wind. Only the birds above her and, in the slow unpeeling of darkness, a divinity of sky.

AUTHOR'S NOTE

This novel is a work of fiction, although it takes as its inspiration a true event of infanticide. In 1826, an 'old woman of very advanced age' known as Anne/Nance Roche was indicted for the wilful murder of Michael Kelliher/Leahy (newspaper accounts list different names) at the summer Tralee Assizes in Co. Kerry. Michael had been drowned in the river Flesk on Monday, 12 June 1826, and had reportedly been unable to stand, walk or speak.

At her trial, Nance Roche claimed that she had been attempting to cure the boy, not kill him. The boy had been brought to the river in an attempt to 'put the fairy' out of him. Nance was acquitted on these grounds.

There have been several recorded cases of death and injury suffered as a consequence of people attempting to banish changelings and recover those believed to be lost to them. The most famous of these cases is that of twenty-five-year-old Bridget Cleary, who was tortured, then burnt to death by her husband and relatives in 1895, in Co. Tipperary. Angela Bourke's *The Burning of Bridget Cleary* (1999) is an outstanding account of this case, and I recommend it to anyone curious to discover more about how and why such tragedies have occurred in Ireland and abroad. *The Good People: New Fairylore Essays*, edited by Peter Narváez (1991), also provides modern-day considerations of the medical afflictions possibly suffered by those considered to be changelings.

Irish fairy lore was (and remains) a deeply complex, ambiguous system of folk belief – there is little that is twee or childish about it. As Bourke mentions in her preface to *Burning*, 'A large part of this book is concerned with considering fairy belief as the products of rational minds, operating in circumstances that are outside the experience of most people in modern, literate societies.' In writing this work of fiction I have sought to portray fairy and folk belief as part of the fabric of everyday rural nineteenth-century Irish life, rather than as anomalous.

In creating the fictional character of Nance, I drew heavily on the stories and accounts mentioned in Gearóid Ó Crualaoich's *The Book of the Cailleach: Stories of the Wise-Woman Healer* (2003), and the fairy stories of Lady Augusta Gregory, Thomas Crofton Croker, and Eddie Lenihan and Carolyn Eve Green's *Meeting the Other Crowd: The Fairy Stories of Hidden Ireland* (2004). Nance's use of and reference to herbal medicine was informed by Patrick Logan's *Making the Cure: A Look at Irish Folk Medicine* (1972), Niall Mac Coitir's books *Irish Trees: Myths, Legends and Folklore* (2003) and *Irish Wild Plants: Myths, Legends and Folklore* (2006), as well as the work of John Windele, James Mooney and W.R. Wilde on superstitions and popular practices relating to medicine and midwifery, much of which was published in the mid-nineteenth century.

My depictions of Irish rural life in the pre-famine days of the nineteenth century were informed by many sources, including but not limited to the work of Kevin Danaher (Caoimhin Ó Danachair), E. Estyn Evans' *Irish Folk Ways* (1957) and the scholarship and publications of Claudia Kinmoth, Jonathan Bell and Mervyn Watson, Patricia O'Hare, Anne O'Connor and – the 'bible' (as I so often heard it called) – Seán Ó Súilleabháin's extraordinary *A Handbook of Irish Folklore* (1942).

ACKNOWLEDGEMENTS

While researching this book I was blessed to have the opportunity to meet and speak with many erudite historians, curators and academics who generously gave up their time to answer my sometimes strange (and often ignorant) questions about Irish folklife. Thank you to the National Folklore Collection at University College Dublin for its vast specialist library on folklore and ethnology, and to Bairbre Ní Fhloinn for her assistance, suggestions and time. Thank you to Clodagh Doyle, curator at the Folklife Division of the National Museum of Ireland, for the tour and for offering me access to the division's research library. Immense gratitude to Stiofán Ó Cadhla from the Department of Folklore and Ethnology at University College Cork for his correspondence and for providing me with much invaluable research material. Thank you to Sarah O'Farrell and Helen O'Carroll from Kerry County Museum in Tralee for their assistance and kindness, and for allowing me to borrow the 'treasure chest' of information from the Poor Inquiry. Thank you to Patricia O'Hare from Muckross House Library for generously giving me a private tour of the grounds and permitting me access to the library records.

Any inconsistencies or fallibility found in my depiction of Irish folklore, folklife and fairy belief in this novel are my own, and should bear no reflection on those who so kindly sought to inform and support my work.

Thanks must also go to Seán O Donoghue from Salmon Leap Farm in Co. Kerry for showing me the old *cillín* on his property next to the original 'Piper's Grave', and for allowing me to wander over his farm to see the Flesk. Thank you to Michael Leane for giving me a tour of the river, and for telling me of times past. Thank you to Chris and James Keane, and to James's mother, Mary, for their hospitality and for so patiently letting me step on everyone's toes at the *ceilidh*.

Thank you to the staff of Flinders University and my colleagues at *Kill Your Darlings* for their ongoing support. Thank you to the friends who shared their various stories and ideas with me, and who may recognise, in this novel, traces of past conversations.

I am indebted to the support and passion of my publishers, editors and early readers. Heartfelt thanks to the marvellous Alex Craig, Judy Clain, Paul Baggaley, Sophie Jonathan, Mathilda Imlah, Gillian Fitzgerald-Kelly, Natalie McCourt, Cate Paterson, Geordie Williamson and Ali Lavau. Thank you to my incredible agents: Pippa Masson at Curtis Brown Australia; Gordon Wise, Kate Cooper and colleagues at Curtis Brown UK; Dan Lazar at Writers House; and Jerry Kalajian at the Intellectual Property Group. It is an honour to work with you all.

Finally, love and gratitude to dearest Heidi, and to Pam, Alan and my sister, Briony, to whom this novel is dedicated.